Confronting Security and Privacy Challenges in Digital Marketing

Paulo Botelho Pires
Centre for Organizational and Social Studies, Polytechnic of Porto, Portugal

José Duarte Santos
Accounting and Business School, Polytechnic of Porto, Portugal

Inês Veiga Pereira
Accounting and Business School, Polytechnic of Porto, Portugal

Ana Isabel Torres
University of Aveiro, Portugal

IGI Global
PUBLISHER of TIMELY KNOWLEDGE

A volume in the Advances in Marketing, Customer Relationship Management, and E-Services (AMCRMES) Book Series

Published in the United States of America by
IGI Global
Business Science Reference (an imprint of IGI Global)
701 E. Chocolate Avenue
Hershey PA, USA 17033
Tel: 717-533-8845
Fax: 717-533-8661
E-mail: cust@igi-global.com
Web site: http://www.igi-global.com

Library of Congress Cataloging-in-Publication Data

Names: Pires, Paulo, 1967- editor. | Santos, José Duarte, 1966- editor. | Pereira, Inês Veiga, 1977- editor. | Torres, Ana Isabel, 1965- editor.
Title: Confronting security and privacy challenges in digital marketing / edited by: Paulo Botelho Pires, José Duarte Santos, Inês Veiga Pereira, and Ana Isabel Torres.
Description: Hershey, PA : Business Science Reference, [2023] | Includes bibliographical references and index. | Summary: "Confronting Security and Privacy Challenges in Digital Marketing identifies the most relevant issues in the current context of digital marketing and explores the implications, opportunities, and challenges of leveraging marketing strategies with digital innovations. This book explores the impact that these disruptive innovations are having on digital marketing, pointing out guidelines for organizations to leverage their strategy on the opportunities created by them. Covering topics such as blockchain technology, artificial intelligence, and virtual reality, this book is ideal for academicians, marketing professionals, researchers, and more"-- Provided by publisher.
Identifiers: LCCN 2023011153 (print) | LCCN 2023011154 (ebook) | ISBN 9781668489581 (hardcover) | ISBN 9781668489598 (paperback) | ISBN 9781668489604 (ebook)
Subjects: LCSH: Internet marketing. | Marketing--Technological aspects.
Classification: LCC HF5415.1265 .C657 2023 (print) | LCC HF5415.1265 (ebook) | DDC 658.8--dc23/eng/20230324
LC record available at https://lccn.loc.gov/2023011153
LC ebook record available at https://lccn.loc.gov/2023011154

This book is published in the IGI Global book series Advances in Marketing, Customer Relationship Management, and E-Services (AMCRMES) (ISSN: 2327-5502; eISSN: 2327-5529)

British Cataloguing in Publication Data
A Cataloguing in Publication record for this book is available from the British Library.
All work contributed to this book is new, previously-unpublished material. The views expressed in this book are those of the authors, but not necessarily of the publisher.
For electronic access to this publication, please contact: eresources@igi-global.com.

Advances in Marketing, Customer Relationship Management, and E-Services (AMCRMES) Book Series

Eldon Y. Li
National Chengchi University, Taiwan & California Polytechnic State University, USA

ISSN:2327-5502
EISSN:2327-5529

Mission

Business processes, services, and communications are important factors in the management of good customer relationship, which is the foundation of any well organized business. Technology continues to play a vital role in the organization and automation of business processes for marketing, sales, and customer service. These features aid in the attraction of new clients and maintaining existing relationships.

The Advances in Marketing, Customer Relationship Management, and E-Services (AMCRMES) Book Series

addresses success factors for customer relationship management, marketing, and electronic services and its performance outcomes. This collection of reference source covers aspects of consumer behavior and marketing business strategies aiming towards researchers, scholars, and practitioners in the fields of marketing management.

Coverage

- Cases on Electronic Services
- Web Mining and Marketing
- Legal Considerations in E-Marketing
- Online Community Management and Behavior
- E-Service Innovation
- CRM in financial services
- Relationship Marketing
- Cases on CRM Implementation
- B2B marketing
- Mobile Services

IGI Global is currently accepting manuscripts for publication within this series. To submit a proposal for a volume in this series, please contact our Acquisition Editors at Acquisitions@igi-global.com or visit: http://www.igi-global.com/publish/.

The Advances in Marketing, Customer Relationship Management, and E-Services (AMCRMES) Book Series (ISSN 2327-5502) is published by IGI Global, 701 E. Chocolate Avenue, Hershey, PA 17033-1240, USA, www.igi-global.com. This series is composed of titles available for purchase individually; each title is edited to be contextually exclusive from any other title within the series. For pricing and ordering information please visit http://www.igi-global.com/book-series/advances-marketing-customer-relationship-management/37150. Postmaster: Send all address changes to above address.

Titles in this Series

For a list of additional titles in this series, please visit: http://www.igi-global.com/book-series/advances-marketing-customer-relationship-management/37150

Handbook of Research on Achieving Sustainable Development Goals With Sustainable Marketing
Iza Gigauri (St. Andrew the First-Called Georgian University, Georgia) Maria Palazzo (Universitas Mercatorum, Italy) and Maria Antonella Ferri (Universitas Mercatorum, Italy)
Business Science Reference • © 2023 • 455pp • H/C (ISBN: 9781668486818) • US $305.00

Global Developments in Nation Branding and Promotion Theoretical and Practical Approaches
Andreas Masouras (Neapolis University, Cyprus) Sofia Daskou (Neapolis University, Cyprus) Victoria Pistikou (Democritus University of Thrace, Greece) Dimitrios Dimitriou (Democritus University of Thrace, Greece) and Tim Friesner (University of Winchester, UK)
Information Science Reference • © 2023 • 320pp • H/C (ISBN: 9781668459027) • US $240.00

Origin and Branding in International Market Entry Processes
Carlos Francisco e Silva (Universidade Europeia, Portugal)
Business Science Reference • © 2023 • 320pp • H/C (ISBN: 9781668466131) • US $250.00

Global Applications of the Internet of Things in Digital Marketing
Arshi Naim (King Kalid University, Saudi Arabia) and V. Ajantha Devi (AP3 Solutions, India)
Business Science Reference • © 2023 • 410pp • H/C (ISBN: 9781668481660) • US $250.00

Applications of Neuromarketing in the Metaverse
Monika Gupta (Chitkara Business School, Chitkara University, India) Kumar Shalender (Chitkara University, India) Babita Singla (Chitkara Business School, Chitkara University, India) and Nripendra Singh (PennWest University, Clarion, USA)
Business Science Reference • © 2023 • 338pp • H/C (ISBN: 9781668481509) • US $255.00

Influencer Marketing Applications Within the Metaverse
Rohit Bansal (Department of Management Studies, Vaish College of Engineering, Rohtak, India) Sikandar Ali Qalati (School of Business, Liaocheng University, Shandong, China) and Aziza Chakir (Faculty of Law, Economics and Social Sciences, Hassan II University, Casablanca, Morocco)
Business Science Reference • © 2023 • 334pp • H/C (ISBN: 9781668488980) • US $250.00

IGI Global
PUBLISHER of TIMELY KNOWLEDGE

701 East Chocolate Avenue, Hershey, PA 17033, USA
Tel: 717-533-8845 x100 • Fax: 717-533-8661
E-Mail: cust@igi-global.com • www.igi-global.com

Table of Contents

Detailed Table of Contents

Artificial intelligence, blockchain, IoT, and virtual reality are technologies that are driving significant changes in marketing. At the same time, these technologies are introducing new issues and challenges, most notably issues related to privacy and security. To know and understand these effects, a review of the bibliography on these different themes was carried out, having consulted the referential databases. The results of the literature review showed that artificial intelligence is having an impact on the transversality of marketing activities. The number of publications, the benefits, and the impact on marketing are well recognized. As for blockchain, IoT, virtual reality, privacy, and security, the results are different. While the potential of the technologies and the challenges they introduce are recognized, the number of publications is somewhat small, and their application is limited to a restricted number of marketing activities.

Marketing information systems, scale, scope, and functionalities have grown due to the substantial rise of new technologies such as the internet, mobile devices, and social media. This chapter aims to analyse the impact of implementing a marketing information system to manage marketing business processes in a multinational organization. Interviews were carried out with organizations using the same marketing information system. The interview structure and its questions were based on the information system's evaluation model, which is extensively used in this area of research. The results obtained were relevant not only from a benefits analysis perspective, but also from a system quality perspective, information quality and service quality matter.

Recent advances in artificial intelligence have had a growing impact, and the marketing discipline is no exception. This study carries out an analysis of the impact of artificial intelligence, presenting first its different techniques and then the impact of these techniques on marketing areas and activities. A systematic study or literature review was used. The following marketing areas and activities have been identified: product recommendation, brand and trademarks management, purchase decision forecast, price, advertising management, chatbots, distribution and retail, engagement, and planning process. Findings show that artificial intelligence is having a widespread impact across marketing areas and activities, and they also show that this impact is disrupting marketing areas and activities, as well as causing gradual changes.

This chapter examines the drivers for the adoption of artificial intelligence (AI) in digital marketing and the challenges that organizations face while implementing AI-based marketing strategies. The chapter begins with an overview of the potential applications connected with using AI in digital marketing, including automation. It then explores the key drivers for the adoption of AI in digital marketing. This chapter also provides a framework for greater adoption of AI in digital marketing. The framework has many well-known components relative to other known AI frameworks but is focused upon digital marketing. The chapter discusses the challenges that organizations face when implementing AI-based marketing strategies. The chapter also explores the potential risks associated with using AI in digital marketing, including algorithmic bias and the risk of over-reliance on AI. Overall, this chapter provides insights into the drivers and challenges of using AI in digital marketing and offers recommendations for organizations looking to implement AI-based marketing strategies.

The usage of consumers' personal data is considered by companies as capable of creating immense value in terms of business. The rise of using social networks to access users' shared information, gathering, processing, and using it, has become a normal proceeding by companies. This data represents value to entities that use them to reduce research costs to develop new products, as well as transaction costs while increasing their marketing incomes. The objective of this study is to determine what feelings are related to sharing personal data online. The research questionnaire for this study was developed through a literature review, later shared on social networks, with 103 valid answers having been collected. Data analysis was performed using IBM SPSS Statistics and Excel programs. The results obtained allow us to understand what perceptions the population has regarding data sharing, suggesting that the individual

perception of the transmissibility of personal data online is starting to be an area of interest for society since there is a greater awareness of the dangers online.

The objective of this study is to investigate the level of understanding that internet users have regarding data privacy, security, and protection. The study aims to determine the extent to which individuals are conscious of the potential hazards of sharing personal information online and the steps they take to secure their data. The research also examines the role of technology companies and government agencies in educating internet users about data privacy and security. The study was conducted in Bhopal using stratified random sampling, and data were collected from employees and students of an educational institution in Bhopal. The findings of this study will give an understanding of the current awareness of internet users and aid in future efforts to enhance data privacy and security for all users.

The ubiquity and demand of sharing content by social networks (SN) led marketers to deal with challenges regarding the perception of privacy and intimacy and to consider dichotomies between preferences and real behaviours. Research is still needed to address how SN impact legitimacy. Also, there is a need to study how the de-definition of privacy and intimacy boundaries has affected the behaviours of SN users. The authors look at the issue from a theoretical point of view, considering authors from different fields of knowledge to break down the challenges for marketers regarding users' perception of privacy and intimacy on SN. The redefinition of privacy and intimacy boundaries has impacted the behaviours of SN users. It so has the effect of privacy and intimacy on the organisational legitimacy of brands advertising on SN. They suggest several techniques to alleviate privacy and intimacy concerns based on the theoretical implications. Ignoring these concerns can cause problems for brands and institutions and lead to a loss of trust and brand reputation, which translates into lower profits.

Digital marketing presents both challenges and opportunities when it comes to security. As more and more customer data is collected and stored digitally, the potential for sensitive information to fall into the wrong hands increases. Digital marketing also offers opportunities for improved security. Implementing two-factor authentication and using unique and complex passwords can also minimize the risk of unauthorized access to accounts and personal information. Overall, the key to maintaining security in digital marketing is to be proactive and stay informed about the latest threats and vulnerabilities. This includes staying up to date on best practices for data protection and regularly monitoring and testing your systems for security weaknesses. Based on this research gap, a systematic review of the bibliometric literature was performed, and data were synthesized from 80 documents identified through Scopus indexing. This research aims to assess the challenges and opportunities.

Researchers recently became interested in mixed reality (MR) because of the availability of hardware that integrates the advantages of two worlds. As an immersive and innovative technological solution for consumers and brands, research has provided insights into the implementation of MR. This technology is promising to transform business models and consumer behavior. Studies have revealed how MR boosts consumer engagement and purchase intentions. In this chapter, the diverse concepts and techniques of recent technological breakthroughs are reviewed. This includes the differences between augmented reality (AR), virtual reality (VR), and MR. Also, MR will be explored to understand the fusion of reality and virtuality, challenges, and limitations in emerging trends. Thus, providing insights from the perspective of digital marketing that results in better interaction with consumers due to the immersive and interactive experiences it offers.

The developments in technology have presented many opportunities as well as threats to businesses in interacting with their customers. Mixed reality (MR) technology is one of those disruptive technological developments that many organizations have taken advantage of in order to enhance interaction with consumers. Consumers are not always eager to interact with organizations through the internet due to security and privacy concerns associated with the use of the internet. On the other hand, mixed reality technologies combine the physical and digital worlds allowing better interaction with consumers. Mixed reality technology allows effective consumer interaction, improved consumer experiences and enhanced engagement. There are however challenges associated with the use of mixed reality technologies which include costs, privacy, and security issues; hence, the adoption of these technologies in developed countries is minimal. It can be recommended that there is a need for companies to invest in infrastructure that promotes the full implementation of mixed reality technologies.

Measuring immersive marketing experiences in the metaverse is a new area of study and it includes a wide range of algorithms to make better assessments and predictions. Any algorithm or metrics to measure the effectiveness of metaverse marketing will require a large amount of data, and then comes the challenge of data security and privacy. This study primarily aims at providing a framework for measuring the effectiveness of metaverse marketing considering the key drivers of virtual-commerce experiences and the metrics like engagement rates, conversion rates, customer acquisition costs, and the privacy and security-related changes in metaverse data analytics.

This chapter analyses the role and potential applications that blockchain as a technology can bring to C2C e-commerce business models. The main goal is to present a systematic analysis of potential applications of blockchain in C2C e-commerce, presenting the expected benefits and the main challenges. As a proof-of-concept, the chapter will specifically address the aspect of developing a C2C market based on blockchain, addressing the specifics of the business model, implementation aspects, and interest of potential customers. The authors propose a design of a C2C platform based on blockchain, that enables efficient and secure C2C transactions without intermediaries. The authors also present the results of a preliminary readiness study, based on the UTAUT2 model of assessing technological readiness. The results point out the importance of the effect of social influence on behavioral intention. The results aim to help business and technical developers shape their blockchain-based e-commerce business models.

Preface

Disruptive innovations are posing a threat to marketing, and particularly its digital marketing component. These breakthroughs are generating novel, uncommon, and unconventional opportunities, and it is expected that new paradigms, models, and even realities will arise. These breakthroughs have been quickly adopted by other fields of knowledge, which have quickly adjusted and used them as a catalyst to develop these new paradigms, models, and realities. In stark contrast, marketing has been somewhat contemptuous of these growing new contexts, some of which are already impossible to escape, and has failed to recognize their potential. Blockchain, artificial intelligence, and virtual reality are a few of these disruptive breakthroughs. But even if these situations can't be avoided, several issues are starting to surface that need to be resolved, particularly those pertaining to privacy, security, and anonymity.

This book helps to clarify the effect that these disruptive breakthroughs are having on digital marketing by outlining best practices for businesses to use their strategy to take advantage of the opportunities they provide. It covers a few issues that are essential to an organization's performance and imparts knowledge to those who will work in the field of digital marketing. Its focus on developing themes that result from disruptive innovations gives it a significant influence. As a result, it contributes with new and distinctive knowledge that is highly valued by individuals who want to stay informed about the significant changes happening in digital marketing.

The chapters are organized thematically, starting with the general implications of the technology, information systems, and the associated challenges and opportunities. These are followed by a series of chapters focusing on artificial intelligence, machine learning, and artificial neural networks. Issues relating to privacy, security, protection, and anonymity are then addressed. Virtual reality in its various dimensions and blockchain are the last two groups.

Chapter 1: Significant developments in marketing are being driven by technology like artificial intelligence, blockchain, IoT, and virtual reality. At the same time, these technologies are creating new problems and difficulties, most notably problems with security and privacy. After consulting the reference databases, a survey of the literature on these many themes was conducted in order to identify and comprehend these effects. The findings of the literature review demonstrated that artificial intelligence is influencing how broadly marketing operations are used. The quantity of publications, their advantages, and their effects on marketing are all well known. The outcomes differ when it comes to blockchain, IoT, virtual reality, privacy, and security. Although the technologies' potential and the difficulties they pose are acknowledged, there aren't many publications about them, and they are only used in a tiny number of marketing activities.

Chapter 2: The size, scope, and functionality of marketing information systems have expanded because of the rapid development of new technologies including the internet, mobile technology, and social media. To handle marketing business processes in a global corporation, this article analyzes the effects of installing a marketing information system. Interviews with businesses utilizing the same marketing information system were conducted. The information system evaluation model, which is widely used in this field of study, served as the foundation for the interview's framework and topics. The outcomes were applicable not just in terms of benefits analysis but also in terms of system quality, information quality, and service quality.

Chapter 3: This chapter's goal is to look at how new technologies like AI, NLP, VR, and AR are changing the landscape of digital marketing. In the areas of enhancing consumer experience, virtual retail, and personalization, it emphasizes how disruptive these technologies are. The chapter focuses on the innovative options that modern technologies present for organizations to interact with customers and improve marketing plans. But it also acknowledges the serious security and privacy issues brought on by these developments, notably in relation to data mining, customer data use, and virtual environments. The chapter also analyzes how voice search technologies, influencer marketing, and social media platforms are influencing the direction of digital marketing. To stay competitive and handle the shifting interface between AI, privacy, and customer experience, the authors advise firms to prioritize data privacy and security when adopting developing technology.

Chapter 4: The world has changed significantly because of artificial intelligence (AI). The fundamental concerns regarding privacy and security in AI must be acknowledged by both the corporations using it and the people who are vulnerable to its flaws, notwithstanding the advantages of its application. This book chapter examines recent research on AI, trustworthiness, and privacy and security principles to better understand the impact of these concepts on AI. It also employs bibliometric tools to comprehend and recognize current trends in the subject. Finally, the authors discuss the results of the bibliometric analysis, which offer insight into the various implications for managers and contributions to future research and policy, highlighting the challenges that AI and machine learning face.

Chapter 5: The field of marketing is no exception as a result of recent advancements in artificial intelligence. This study analyzes the effects of artificial intelligence by first outlining its many strategies, then examining how these techniques affect various marketing-related sectors and activities. A thorough investigation or literature review was employed. Product suggestion, brand and trademark management, purchase decision forecasting, price, advertising management, chatbots, distribution and retail, engagement, and planning process have all been highlighted as marketing sectors and activities. According to research, artificial intelligence is having a significant impact on a wide range of marketing-related fields and activities. This impact is disrupting these fields and activities as well as bringing about subtle modifications.

Chapter 6: This chapter looks at the factors influencing the use of artificial intelligence (AI) in digital marketing as well as the difficulties that businesses have when putting AI-based marketing strategies into practice. A review of the potential uses for using AI in digital marketing, including automation, opens the chapter. The main factors influencing the adoption of AI in digital marketing are then explored. A foundation for a wider deployment of AI in digital marketing is also provided in this chapter. Although the framework is focused on digital marketing, it features more well-known components compared to other well-known AI frameworks. The chapter covers the difficulties that businesses encounter when putting AI-based marketing techniques into practice. The chapter also looks at some of the possible drawbacks of employing AI in digital marketing, such as algorithmic bias and the dangers of over-relying on AI. Overall, this chapter includes guidelines for businesses wishing to implement AI-based marketing strategies and insights into the motivations for and difficulties associated with employing AI in digital marketing.

Chapter 7: Companies believe that using consumers' personal data for corporate purposes has enormous potential. It has become common practice for businesses to gather, process, and exploit user-shared information from social networks to access it. For organizations, this data has value since they may utilize it to lower the costs of product development research as well as transaction costs while raising their marketing revenues. The goal of this study is to identify the emotions people have when sharing personal information online. The findings help us understand how the general public views data sharing, and they indicate that as people become more aware of the risks associated with the internet, society is beginning to take an interest in how people perceive how easily their personal information can be shared online.

Chapter 8: The goal of this study is to find out how much knowledge internet users have about data privacy, security, and protection. The purpose of the study is to ascertain how much people are aware of the risks associated with disclosing personal information online and what precautions they take to protect their data. The study also looks at the role that technology firms and governmental organizations play in educating internet users about data security and privacy. The results of this survey will help in future attempts to improve data privacy and security for all users by providing a knowledge of the existing awareness of internet users.

Chapter 9: Marketers had to deal with issues relating to the perception of privacy and intimacy as well as analyze dichotomies between preferences and actual behavior as a result of social networks' (SN) widespread use and demand for content sharing. Investigation is still required to understand how SN affect validity. Additionally, research is required to determine how the definition of intimacy and privacy boundaries has changed how SN users behave. We approach the problem from a theoretical perspective, taking into account authors from several fields of study to deconstruct the difficulties for marketers related users' perceptions of privacy and intimacy on SN. The behaviors of SN users have been impacted by the redefining of intimacy and privacy limits. Thus, privacy and intimacy have an impact on the organizational legitimacy of firms that advertise on SN. We recommend a number of methods to allay privacy and intimacy worries in light of the theoretical consequences. Ignoring these issues may result in issues for institutions and companies as well as a decline in trust and brand reputation, which has a negative impact on earnings.

Chapter 10: When it comes to security, digital marketing offers both potential and concerns. Sensitive data could potentially end up in the wrong hands as more and more customer data is gathered and kept online. Additionally, digital marketing presents chances for increased security. Using two-factor authentication and creating strong passwords that are both unique and complicated helps reduce the danger of illegal access to accounts and personal data. Overall, being proactive and being up to date on the most recent dangers and vulnerabilities is vital to ensuring security in digital marketing. This entails frequently monitoring and testing your systems for security flaws as well as keeping up with the latest best practices for data protection. Based on this knowledge gap, a thorough examination of the bibliometric literature was conducted, and data from 80 papers discovered by Scopus indexing were synthesized. The purpose of this study is to evaluate the opportunities and challenges.

Chapter 11: Recent hardware developments that combine the benefits of two worlds have piqued researchers' interest in Mixed Reality (MR). Research has revealed information regarding the application of MR as a new and immersive technology solution for consumers and brands. This technology has the potential to alter consumer behavior and corporate strategies. According to studies, MR increases consumer engagement and purchasing inclinations. This chapter reviews the many theories and methods behind cutting-edge technological innovations. This covers the variations among augmented reality (AR), virtual reality (VR), and mixed reality (MR). Additionally, MR will be examined to comprehend the blending of reality and virtuality, its difficulties, and its limitations in regard to emerging trends. Consequently, by offering immersive and interactive experiences, digital marketing can help marketers communicate with customers more effectively.

Chapter 12: Technology advancements have given organizations numerous opportunities as well as threats in how they interact with their clients. One of those disruptive technical advancements is mixed reality (MR), which many businesses have embraced in order to improve customer contact. Due to the security and privacy risks involved with internet use, customers aren't always ready to communicate with businesses online. Contrarily, mixed reality technologies merge the real and virtual worlds to improve customer engagement. Technology that uses mixed reality enables efficient consumer interaction, better customer experiences, and higher levels of engagement. Costs, privacy concerns, and security issues are only a few of the difficulties that come with using Mixed Reality technologies; as a result, these technologies have not been widely adopted in industrialized nations. In order to fully adopt Mixed Reality technology, it is advised that businesses invest in the necessary infrastructure.

Chapter 13: A recent field of research, measuring immersive marketing experiences in the metaverse uses a variety of algorithms to provide more accurate evaluations and forecasts. A lot of data will be needed for any algorithm or metrics to determine how effective metaverse marketing is, which presents the problem of data security and privacy. This study's primary goal is to provide a framework for evaluating the success of metaverse marketing, considering the major influences on virtual-commerce experiences, as well as metrics like engagement rates, conversion rates, customer acquisition costs, and changes in metaverse data analytics related to privacy and security.

Chapter 14: This chapter examines how blockchain technology might benefit various e-commerce company models and examines its potential uses. The major objective is to give a methodical review of potential blockchain applications in B2B, B2C, and C2C forms of e-commerce, outlining the anticipated advantages and key difficulties. The chapter will specifically cover the issue of creating a C2C market using blockchain technology as a proof-of-concept, addressing the particulars of the business model, implementation issues, and interest of potential customers. We provide a proposal for a blockchain-based C2C infrastructure that enables swift and secure C2C trades without middlemen. On the basis of the UTAUT2 model for evaluating technical readiness, we also provide the findings of a preliminary readiness study. The findings highlight the significance of how social influence affects behavioral intention. The findings are intended to assist technical and commercial developers in creating blockchain-based e-commerce business models.

Chapter 15: An old idea called consumerism is getting a lot of attention in contemporary writing. In an increasingly commercialized society, power disparities between businesses and consumers gave rise to the consumerism movement. Its main goals are to advance consumer rights, market openness, and consumer choice. Market equalization, or well-balanced marketplaces where market inequities are eliminated, is the goal of consumerism. This creates a more functional market environment for both businesses and consumers. Blockchain is a revolutionary technology that was primarily created to modernize financial system transactions, but it has potential uses in many different fields. Blockchain is a decentralized network that uses cryptographic protocols to create a public, unchangeable, and permanent ledger that serves as a database. This chapter, which is framed by consumerism literature, examines potential blockchain applications by concentrating on core consumerism claims, such as marketing ethics, the security of online transactions, and supply chain traceability and transparency.

Paulo Botelho Pires
CEOS.PP, Portugal

José Duarte Santos
CEOS.PP, ISCAP, Polytechnic of Porto, Portugal

Inês Veiga Pereira
CEOS.PP, ISCAP, Polytechnic of Porto, Portugal

Ana Isabel Torres
ISCA, University of Aveiro, Portugal

Chapter 1
Digital Marketing Perspectives: Challenges and Opportunities Raised by Technology

Paulo Botelho Pires
https://orcid.org/0000-0003-3786-6783
CEOS.PP, Polytechnic of Porto, Portugal

José Duarte Santos
https://orcid.org/0000-0001-5815-4983
CEOS.PP, Polytechnic of Porto, Portugal & ISCAP, Portugal

ABSTRACT

Artificial intelligence, blockchain, IoT, and virtual reality are technologies that are driving significant changes in marketing. At the same time, these technologies are introducing new issues and challenges, most notably issues related to privacy and security. To know and understand these effects, a review of the bibliography on these different themes was carried out, having consulted the referential databases. The results of the literature review showed that artificial intelligence is having an impact on the transversality of marketing activities. The number of publications, the benefits, and the impact on marketing are well recognized. As for blockchain, IoT, virtual reality, privacy, and security, the results are different. While the potential of the technologies and the challenges they introduce are recognized, the number of publications is somewhat small, and their application is limited to a restricted number of marketing activities.

INTRODUCTION

The discipline of digital marketing is always changing due to new technological advancements. Understanding the significance of these technologies is becoming more and more important as more organizations turn to online platforms. This chapter will examine how new technologies are affecting digital marketing and how the sector is evolving.

Significant improvements in digital marketing have resulted from the development of new technologies. Artificial intelligence (AI) is one such technology that has enabled organizations to simplify their

DOI: 10.4018/978-1-6684-8958-1.ch001

marketing initiatives while making them more efficient and effective. Virtual and augmented reality (VR/AR) is another technological innovation that has influenced digital marketing. The way businesses communicate with their clients has been changed by these technologies. Blockchain is one technology that has significantly changed the game. Blockchain technology has the potential to transform digital marketing by making online transactions transparent and secure. It provides a tamper-proof record of transactions and interactions between brands and consumers. The term "Internet of Things" (IoT) describes a network of interconnected gadgets, including wearables and smart home devices, that may gather information on customer behavior and preferences. It is also a technology that has an impact on the marketing discipline, as the customer experience may be enhanced overall, and marketing initiatives can be developed more personalized using this data.

While technology creates opportunities, it is also true that it creates a number of remarkable challenges.

Recent trends have led to a proliferation of studies that focus on the following challenges. The first major challenge is associated with privacy. Digital marketers collect and use large amounts of data about consumers, which can raise privacy issues. Consumers are increasingly aware of their data privacy rights, and regulations such as the General Data Protection Regulation (GDPR) in Europe and the California Consumer Privacy Act (CCPA) in the US, which are designed to protect consumers' personal information.

Related to the privacy challenge is anonymity, which is the second challenge faced by marketers. Digital marketing uses various techniques, such as targeted advertising and personalized recommendations, that make consumers feel like they are being followed and targeted, eroding their sense of anonymity online. Marketers need to strike a balance between providing personalized experiences and respecting consumers' anonymity. Also related to the previous two is the third challenge, which is transparency. As digital marketing becomes more data-driven and automated, it is increasingly difficult for consumers to understand how their data is being used and by whom. Marketers need to be transparent about their data collection and use practices to build trust with consumers. The last and fourth major challenge, and a new area for marketing, is security. Digital marketing involves the collection and storage of sensitive consumer data, such as payment information and personal information, which can make businesses vulnerable to cyberattacks. Marketers need to ensure they have robust security measures in place to protect against data breaches and need to ensure compliance with all relevant laws and regulations, which may vary by country and region.

We are witnessing important developments in the Internet of Things, Artificial Intelligence, Virtual Reality, and Blockchain, as highlighted by Kumar et al. (2021). It is anticipated that the adoption of these cutting-edge technologies will have an effect on consumers and enterprises. However, they are dynamically changing technologies whose potential has not yet been fully realized and whose full exploitation, as well as their respective roles in marketing, has not yet been fully understood. This research will focus on the opportunities – artificial intelligence, blockchain, virtual reality, and the internet of things – and the challenges – privacy, anonymity, transparency, and security – facing digital marketing. To achieve this aim, the research will be exploratory and will focus on the compilation and analysis of existing literature.

ARTIFICIAL INTELLIGENCE

Main Techniques and Models

IA is a wide-ranging disciplinary area that includes a broad set of models or techniques that stem from principles, insights, or orientations from various domains. The main techniques or models are (Haleem et al., 2022; Kopalle et al., 2022): Machine learning (ML), Artificial Neural Networks (ANNs) and Deep Learning, Natural Language Processing (NLP), Decision trees, Support Vector Machines (SVMs), Bayesian networks, Reinforcement learning, and Evolutionary algorithms. A description of these models and techniques follows.

ML is a subset of AI that enables machines to learn from data without being explicitly programmed and uses algorithms to identify patterns in data and make predictions or decisions based on those patterns (Cohen & Feigenbaum, 2014). ANNs and Deep Learning are a type of machine learning model that is modeled after the structure of the human brain and they consist of interconnected nodes that process information and can be used for tasks such as image recognition, speech recognition, and natural language processing (Frankish & Ramsey, 2014). NLP includes analyzing and processing natural language data, such as text and speech, to derive useful insights. It allows computers to comprehend and interpret human language (Goyal et al., 2018). Decision trees are a type of model used in machine learning and data mining and they use a tree-like structure to represent decisions and their possible consequences (Barr et al., 1981). SVMs are a type of model used for classification and regression analysis and work by finding the best hyperplane that separates data points into different classes (Marwala, 2018). Using a directed acyclic graph and probability distributions, Bayesian networks are a sort of probabilistic graphical model used for probabilistic inference and decision-making (Marwala, 2018). A system that learns to maximize a reward signal by acting in an environment is said to be engaging in reinforcement learning, a sort of machine learning model that gains knowledge via interactions with the environment (Marwala, 2018). A population of potential solutions is used in evolutionary algorithms, a class of optimization algorithms that draws inspiration from biological evolution. These candidate solutions change over time as a result of selection, mutation, and reproduction (Chambers, 2019).

AI Definition

After describing the different areas of IA, a description of its impact on marketing follows. According to Manis and Madhavaram (2023), technology has the power to enable any marketing capacity and in fact, it influences the majority, if not all, areas of marketing practice, and contemporary marketers significantly rely on it to execute their marketing strategies. The authors contribute with a definition of IA: AI is the study of how an information system learns over time by effectively completing one or more tasks (such as the acquisition, integration, analysis, or interpretation of information). Haleem et al. (2022) stated that AI will eventually play a significant role in all global corporate organizations. A new intelligent machine that thinks, reacts, and completes tasks in a manner akin to people has been constructed utilizing AI and the data provided. AI is a discipline in computer science that trains computers to understand and mimic human behavior and communication and refers to techniques that enable machines to perform mental operations that require human intelligence, involving thinking, learning, and engaging with the environment. Another definition is proposed by De Bruyn et al. (2020): "AI is intelligence demonstrated by machines". But the authors also mention that the term "intelligence" can be defined in more than

70 different ways, according to surveys of psychologists, sociologists, biologists, neuroscientists, and philosophers, and therefore is not surprising that the term "artificial intelligence," despite being widely used, continues to be poorly defined and a vague concept. Nevertheless, AI is considered the most recent disruptive technology that has the most potential to change marketing, and professionals from all over the world are looking for the best AI marketing solutions (Verma et al., 2021).

A very accurate and impressive definition of IA is provided by Kumar et al. (2021), saying: AI is the intelligence that powers data-based analytics and enables automated decision-making; it functions in the fields of continuous learning and automation; AI can be widely construed as a technology that can mimic human behavior and perform tasks in a way that is thought to be intelligent and AI's capacity to update and expand its knowledge base and capabilities allows it to continuously learn from its mistakes and get smarter.

Benefits or Hype

For van Esch and Stewart Black (2021), the breadth and depth of AI applications in marketing are significant, potentially even staggering. Suleiman et al. (2021) advise digital marketing companies to incorporate artificial intelligence capabilities in their activities because it ensures efficacy, enhances productivity, and considerably decreases the expense of executing activities. According to Wang and Wang (2002), in general, artificial intelligence development has a significant impact on digital marketing.

However, some authors oppose the value of IA, expressing their reluctance to accept the benefits it provides. Liu-Thompkins et al. (2022) claim that the value of marketing interactions facilitated by AI is far less clear, and this has led to concerns regarding the short- to medium-term potential of AI in marketing, even though the potential gain from AI is clear. According to the authors, consumers are much less enthused about AI-enabled interactions than businesses are, and they frequently choose genuine relationships with human employees over AI bots.

Integrating AI and Marketing

Manis and Madhavaram (2023) point out the advantages of applying AI increasing the enabling of marketing capabilities due: performs more operations in an interconnected manner, utilizing data from a wider range of sources improving market orientation and marketing planning capacity, specific marketing capabilities like online personalization and customer relationship management will be more successfully enabled by the use of information from a smaller range of sources, gathers more aspect-relevant data from more of the capability's relevant information sources, discovers a deeper level of aspect-relevant data in one or more of the relevant information sources for a marketing capacity and conducts more mutually reinforcing types of studies on relevant data. Haleem et al. (2022) highlight the applications and advantages of artificial intelligence (AI) that are significant for marketing: digital marketing; reduction of human mistakes; connect business processes; analyze massive amounts of market data; deliver valuable information; enable convenient customer support; better marketing automation tool; ease workload; speeds up data processing; make customer centered choices; examine data about customers; improve stock control; customize shopping processes; digital advertising; better customer experience; assisting marketers; increased customer satisfaction and revenue; development of a predictive model; learning about customer preferences; make better decisions; target audience; deliver the right message in time; assist businesses. The benefits of AI are mentioned specifically in B2B by Hossain et al. (2022), where the authors claim that export-oriented manufacturing companies appear to be using B2B marketing analytics and AI to recognize, seize, and reconfigure the market, giving them a continued competitive advantage.

Manis and Madhavaram (2023) highlight the areas of research for the technological components of marketing capabilities: marketing strategy, in general; brand equity strategy; market orientation strategy; market segmentation strategy; Relationship Marketing (RM) strategy. But for Haleem et al. (2022), pricing, strategy and planning, product, promotion, place management, targeting and positioning, scenarios, and thinking models for product design and end-user requirements have all been mentioned as key marketing activities for AI applications. The work of Mikalef et al. (2021) cite the following activities as likely to benefit from the application of IA: customer needs identification; identifying target markets; quality monitoring; process adaptation; resource orchestration; new business models; reconfiguration of capabilities. Another perspective is given by Verma et al. (2021), suggesting the activities of autonomous customer experience management, enhancement of customer experience, data processing through AI and ML algorithms, CRM, smart retail stores, and e-commerce. The authors also refer the use of AI in strategy and planning, product management, pricing management, place management and promotion management.

A different framework is indicated by Mustak et al. (2021). The authors highlight ten themes that have emerged and require evaluation, these being understanding consumer sentiments, industrial opportunities of AI, analyzing customer satisfaction, electronic word-of-mouth – based insights, improving market performance, brand management, measuring and enhancing customer loyalty and trust, novel services, improve customer relationships, and strategic marketing. For Petrescu et al. (2022), IA must be applied from the perspective of the combination of three theories: Dominant Logic Service (SDL), Knowledge Theory, Transaction Cost Economics (TCE): K+SDL as a marketing knowledge and innovation enhancer; TCE + SDL as a collection of innovative actors and agents; SDL as a collection of information technology and tools within the resource environment; SDL+ TCE+K as a communication and exchange facilitator. Mariani et al. (2021) identified eight clusters of research: computer science (memory and computational logic, neural network, machine learning, and linguistic analytics); psychological sciences (decision-making and cognitive processes); And themes related to technology acceptance/adoption and applications to marketing and consumer research (technology acceptance and adoption, big data and robots, social media and text mining and social media content analysis). The authors have identified the main theories and models that are often integrated: game theory, theory of mind, theory of planned behavior, computational theories, BRT (Behavioral Reasoning Theory), decision theories, evolutionary theory, flow theory, fuzzy theories, graph theory, institutional theory, ART (Adaptive resonance theory), cognitive dissonance theory, CCT (Consumer Culture Theory), and UTAUT (including its predecessor, the TAM). They also identified emerging theories: anthropomorphism, CLT (Construal Level Theory, ANT (Actor-Network Theory), and RBT (Resource-Based Theory).

For Stone et al. (2020), an AI deployment in marketing should be evaluated on the dimensions:

1. Deployment of AI in marketing strategy (Overall strategy – target markets, marketing mix for each, objectives, KPIs and goals; business model of customer management; overall branding and proposition; developing new revenue streams; ecosystem management, partnering, outsourcing and value chain redefinition; competitive strategy – who are main competitors, targeting for winning and defense; resource management).

2. Deployment of AI in the marketing mix (branding; product; proposition; price; advertising; direct marketing; personal selling; public relations; dales promotion; content; customer management (acquisition, retention, development, customer service and customer experience; distribution).
3. Deployment of AI in marketing management (people; marketing analysis; market research; market targeting; Data and systems; marketing resource management; content management; managing marketing people; marketing operating model; marketing finance).

A drastic and ambitious perspective is stipulated by Campbell et al. (2020). They support that IA has the potential to be applied in nine stages, corresponding to the full formulation and implementation of the strategic process:

1. Examining the current circumstance involves comprehending macroenvironmental elements that may have an impact on the firm, its stakeholders, and its marketing.
2. Understanding markets and customers: entails learning about microenvironmental elements that have a direct impact on the business, such as market-share trends, product/category demand, and customer attributes such as needs, wants, behaviors, attitudes, and brand loyalty.
3. Developing an understanding of consumer segments and assisting with targeting and positioning decisions are all aspects of segmenting, targeting, and positioning.
4. Developing longer-term goals and related short-term targets to support larger strategies entails planning direction, objectives, and marketing assistance.
5. Creating the range of products, a company sells is a component of developing product strategy.
6. Creating a pricing strategy focuses on figuring out pricing techniques to increase sales.
7. Developing a channel and logistics plan involves making decisions about distribution, logistics, and product stocking.
8. Focusing on providing clients with the proper promotion at the right moment, marketing communication and impact plan development.
9. Choosing performance metrics, monitoring them, and finally implementing any necessary corrective actions are all steps in the planning metrics and implementation control process.

Although several authors state categorically that IA can be applied to strategy and the decision-making process, such is not the position of Stone et al. (2020). The authors declare that since the boundary of AI application to decision-making is shifting from operational to strategic in many management disciplines, there is a limited study into using AI in strategic marketing decision-making. It is important to concentrate on using AI to make strategic marketing decisions due to the competitive nature of such judgments and the insights gained from applying AI to defense and related fields (Stone et al., 2020). For van Esch and Stewart Black (2021), it is essential to evaluate the integration of IA into marketing in three dimensions:

1. Ethical questions.
2. Application questions.
3. Strategic questions.

Another relevant work with an extensive and detailed classification is proposed by Ljepava (2022). They state that IA has the potential to be applied in five major areas, each with a subset of activities:

1. Analysis analytics for sentiment analysis; machine learning to discover insights from large datasets and improve efficiencies of the existing processes; predictive analytics; automated image analysis; choice modeling; determining consumer preferences based on the conjoint analysis model).
2. Strategy (creative analytics; decision support systems and expert systems; predicting outcomes in emerging marketing environments; forecasting; pricing decisions).
3. Tactics (campaign automation; creative optimization, product development; advanced targeting and attribution; programmatic sampling retargeting; programmatic media buying; marketing analytics; sales promotion; purchase prediction; recommendation systems; dynamic pricing; personalization – advertising and search; customer acquisition; user engagement in social media; add targeting; email targeting).
4. Customer relations (CRM; churn management; automated implementation of CRM; chatbots).
5. Value proposition (reinforcing customer journey; evaluating brand image).

Following the same line of thought are Ngai and Wu (2022). They claim that IA intervenes in the following marketing activities: product recommendation; brands and trademarks management; purchase decision prediction; price; promotion (advertising management, demand prediction, chatbots); place; people (churn prediction, targeting customer prediction, engagement, facial recognition); process (marketing segmentation, planning process); physical evidence (content marketing). Vlačić et al. (2021) found five major theoretical dimensions employed by studies in AI and marketing which are behavioral theories, CRM, KBV, network theory, and technology-related theoretical foundations. In addition, they identified several research themes, namely, the application of AI in marketing, technological advancement, ethics, marketing channels, marketing strategy, performance, and STP. Boddu et al. (2022) identified marketing activities and technologies with the potential for AI incorporation: chatbots; advertising enhancement; email marketing; marketing increasingly focused on customer behavior; lead generation; automated content creation; image recognition. But Moradi and Dass (2022), indicated only two themes which are customer identification and personalization. Furthermore, Paul et al. (2022) claim that throughout the consumer life cycle, digital marketing uses a variety of artificial intelligence approaches, including voice search, predictive analysis, and ad targeting. As asserted by Vinaykarthik and Mohana (2022), apps with extensive features only have a chance to keep their customer and attract new consumers for the web application. Modern web applications require much more than just content distribution and displaying products on the web pages, and a personalized user experience is a translative application of artificial intelligence (AI) in marketing in the age of AI everywhere.

Klaus and Zaichkowsky (2020) argue that IA has had an impact on consumer behavior and in particular on the decision-making process. By choosing bots as their service of choice, consumers outsource their decision-making to algorithms, giving little thought to conventional consumer decision-making models and brand emphases, according to the authors, who argue that AI has elevated convenience for consumers to a new level. They said this is particularly true for judgments with low involvement, while high-involvement decisions are almost ready to be handed off to AI. A shift in the service marketing strategy is required in the realm of AI due to the change in consumer behavior. The authors state that the search and decision-making for many buying scenarios are now handled by the bot, the new service platform. Lee and Trim (2022) support the idea that marketers need to be aware of the many methods for employing AI/ML in terms of the information they make available to relevant groups of consumers to increase their efficacy and avoid falling victim to digital myopia. They said that it might be seen as applying AI/ML to enhance the consumer journey.

Lee and Trim (2022) also suggest a division based on the stages of consumer behavior. They advise that IA be applied in the following marketing activities:

1. Utilizing data mining to discover and acquire consumers.
2. Creating (possible) client groups based on data analysis and initial clustering.
3. The ability to send customized and/or customized messages based on the outcome of merging numerous data sets and analyzing the market and consumer intelligence to define client groups.
4. Initial client retention approach involving the development of a reliable and simple payment system. Initial client retention approach involving the development of a reliable and simple payment system.
5. Based on a follow-up survey of the customer's purchasing experience, third-party service delivery, social listening, and customer churn observation, customer retention, and loyalty are measured.

Wang and Wang (2022) claim, that, overall, it was discovered that the impact of AI on consumer purchasing behavior includes making suggestions for all retail purchases, improving user experience, increasing the efficiency and effectiveness of content, assisting in the correlation of pricing and sales trends, identifying user database segments at the stage of churning, ensuring better customer engagement, gaining a deeper understanding of marketing, sales, and operation trends, and a better understanding of consumer behavior overall. The authors also stated that there are advantages to adopting AI for digital marketing and consumer purchasing patterns. A greater understanding of client perception, increased availability of marketing decisions, improved marketing procedures, and time savings are all made possible by artificial intelligence (AI). Additionally, AI offers better information analysis and efficient handling of marketing operations, as well as sales and marketing tactics that significantly enhance company performance. It also minimizes error rates, tracks user sessions, and demonstrates the efficacy of digital advertising.

Moving on to the topics of influencers, it is relevant to add the following facts and study. Sands et al. (2022) demonstrated the parallels and divergences between how customers perceive artificial intelligence (AI) and human influences., and they discovered no distinctions in terms of personalization or intention to follow. This shows that consumers are as willing to follow an influencer who uses artificial intelligence or a human being, and they view the level of personalization offered by both influencer types as comparable. Furthermore, despite often being viewed as having a lesser level of source trust, AI influencers are more likely to encourage word-of-mouth intents. According to the authors, an AI influencer may occasionally be just as powerful as a human influencer.

A more incisive and classic prescription is authored by Ma and Sun (2020), which points to trends in the application of AI in marketing: interactive and media-rich; personalization and targeting; real-time optimization and automation; customer-journey focus; Marketing mix; customer engagement; search; recommendation; attribution. Another input sytems from Kumar (2021) when he says that to remain competitive and generate a high return on investment, digital marketing strategies need to be regularly improved according to AI-ML methodologies, and numerous AI-based tools can improve digital marketing. They include audience identification, content creation and customization services, Chabot's customer support, email marketing, predictive analysis and marketing, AI recommendations for engaging the targeted customers, and they also include professional website construction with AI assistance. Paul et al. (2022) synthesized some essential guidelines for digital marketing areas using artificial intelligence: one must be more concerned with the right use of data collecting and data analysis methodologies since the data needed to enable artificial intelligence and machine learning in digital marketing is insufficient; one must prioritize customer interactions and promotional activities if we wish to apply artificial intelligence approaches in the sphere of digital marketing; to carry out efficient operations in the field of digital marketing, it is suggested to use Neuro-Linguistic Programming (NLP), Natural Language Understanding (NLU), artificial intelligence-enabled chatbots, customer service chatbots, personal assistant chatbots, and NLP-powered Search Engine Optimization (SEO) techniques; user experience building (UX) and user interface (UI) should be adjusted with the aid of AI for smart product recommendations and in-the-moment information customization.

In a different scope, still concerning the marketing area, but on the human resources (HR) side, van Esch et al. (2019) acknowledged that due to the introduction of AI recruiting technology to various HR functions and hiring decisions, certain HR practitioners may no longer be required or able to execute their existing jobs. Additionally, because there will be less human engagement, this may have an impact on how HR professionals use and collaborate with AI recruiting technology as well as how candidates respond to organizations. The authors raise the pertinent concern about the emergence of ethical, legal, privacy, moral, and defamation issues for potential candidates arising from promoting the integration of IA into human resource management. Volkmar et al. (2022) introduced a new concern by stating that organizations should be aware that managers frequently have a lower tolerance for AI/ML failure than for human error, and that this lower tolerance is not just applicable to activities that are objective and numerical. Even though AI and ML aim to improve operational excellence and efficiency from an internal perspective, they should improve the customer experience from an external perspective. Businesses must be aware that operational efficiency and improved customer experience can lead to tensions and delicate tradeoffs.

A significant contribution to the study of the integration of IA and marketing, and the potential implications of such integration, is authored by Mariani et al. (2021). The authors found it surprising that crucial subjects did not appear to receive the study focus they believe they should. First, among the most significant issues that have not received the attention they merit in their three fields of research, AI-related ethics, fairness, and privacy are perhaps the most pressing. The extraordinary power of AI poses significant ethical questions in addition to privacy-related ones and among these is how consumer outcomes may be prejudiced and unfair due to the utilization of customer data in AI systems for automated decision-making. AI on a more profound level may give rise to worries about loss of autonomy, dignity, social isolation, dehumanization, and other things (Mariani et al., 2021).

BLOCKCHAIN

Blockchain Definition

The underlying technology, nowadays regarded as Blockchain (BC), was proposed in 2008 under the pseudonym Satoshi Nakamoto, who introduced the first application of BC, and whose true identity has not yet been revealed. BC has multiple definitions: as a name for a data structure, an algorithm, a suite of technologies, and as an umbrella term for purely distributed peer-to-peer systems with a common application, which results in issues related to the conceptual foundation of BCT in research (Stallone et al., 2021). The name blockchain is a blend of two words: "block" which refers to batched transactions, and "chain," which refers to blocks that are cryptographically connected (Kumar et al., 2021). Following Silva and Moro (2021) description, a shared distributed ledger of cryptographically hashed blocks is known as a blockchain and these blocks contain published transactions or information that has been cryptographically signed by the sender; the network nodes, or a group of them, come to a consensus and make a decision, validating the blocks, and as additional blocks are added, the chain of blocks lengthens, making it more challenging to modify previous blocks; the publishing nodes copy newly published blocks. These features make any attempt to alter a ledger of published blocks difficult to conceal, in addition to the cryptographic techniques (Silva & Moro, 2021). The same is supported by Kumar et al. (2021), stating that BC is a fundamental technology that uses an electronic distributed ledger to build an immutable database and secure data movement. The authors also highlight that by accelerating and protecting the procedures and data records that underlie interactions and transactions, BC delivers process economies. Since there is no one point of vulnerability thanks to the decentralization of records, there are fewer chances of hacking and data breaches. There is a permanent, verifiable, and traceable trail of transactions going back to the first record in a blockchain ledger since past data cannot be wiped or destroyed, despite new blocks of information being added to an existing ledger. As a distributed peer-to-peer system made up of an unknown number of unreliable and untrustworthy peers, BC should be viewed as a cryptographic, append-only decentralized ledger in which interlinked timestamped blocks of data are kept. Immutability, transparency, programmability, decentralization, consensus, and distributed trust were the traits that stood out as being the most significant as a result of various reviews and exploratory study (Stallone et al., 2021).

Blockchain Benefits

Transparency and immutability can aid in preventing fraud in marketplaces, which are prone to it due to the continuously expanding large-scale transactions that lure people, hackers, and business owners to perpetrate fraud. The two capabilities listed above are supported by BC. By using BC, it is possible to address issues with scalability, user privacy, and fraud (Far et al., 2022; Far et al., 2023). Consumer commitment, loyalty, product acceptance, and positive long-term connections with businesses and brands are all based on consumer trust. The explicit protection of consumer data, production openness, labor conditions, and social responsibility are all factors that contribute to trust-building. Consumer trust can be supported through BC's trust-free distributed network of nodes and tamper resistance features (Silva & Moro, 2021).

According to Peres et al. (2022), BC has several benefits:

1. The main advantage is the ability to record transaction data from various sources into a distributed database allows businesses to document a large number of actions and transactions that take place on the distribution chain across outlets and through various communication channels in real time.
2. A second major advantage of BC is the peer-to-peer network structure, which allows for direct communication between network participants and provides higher levels of security so that users can conduct transactions without the additional layers of security offered by third parties like banks or social media platforms.
3. The capability of confirming the transaction's origin since the data contained in a block cannot be changed by anyone, and each blockchain transaction has a clear owner, resulting in a high level of verification might make it possible to keep an eye on crucial marketing procedures.

4. With blockchain, usage rights and data disclosure are highly flexible because information can be constructed with pseudonymity, hashes, encryptions, and smart contracts so that only those with the proper access can access it.
5. Blockchain has the power to completely change how intangible asset valuation is done. Important company assets such as brand equity and customer equity are challenging to quantify and manage. They are also difficult to trade, manage their disclosure, and manage their licensing. The blockchain's ability to tokenize allows for the quantification of a variety of intangible assets.

For Marthews and Tucker (2022), BC, from an economic standpoint, a BC technology deployment has two key features as a technological solution:

1. A set of shared data, which in the instance of the cryptocurrency use case has been extensively established, they are entries in a digital ledger that create an unalterable audit trail of all unspent balances and previous transactions in the digital asset.
2. To ensure that such shared data can be updated and maintained in a way that it always reflects the truth, an incentive system (also known as "consensus rules") has been developed.

Integrating Blockchain and Marketing

Reviewing the statements of Stallone et al. (2021), the interest of BC in marketing is mostly attributable to the expectations that improving sincerity, consideration, accountability, and transparency in trustworthy relationships in society and business. The authors also contended that although most of the research was conceptual in nature, academic sources revealed their potential effects on marketing. In the same direction is the opinion of Peres et al. (2022), who refers to marketing research and practice are still hesitant about the use of blockchain technology and have yet to properly comprehend and embrace it, even though BC has a wide range of potential uses. The same holds for Treiblmaier and Petrozhitskaya (2023) when they declare that BC technology is expected to revolutionize marketing in significant ways. The majority of envisioned application cases are currently in an early stage, with an undetermined influence on the industry and a still-evolving theoretical foundation in academic research. Due to its strong foundations of distribution, decentralization, encryption, immutability, and tokenization, blockchain technology is the rage right now (Jain et al., 2021). Its application is expanding across several economic areas. Due to the abundance of data available, there are issues with big data, privacy, ransomware attacks, marketing fraud, and spam. Stallone et al. (2021) show the state of integration, using a systematic analysis of the academic literature on the use of BC in business painting a dismal image for marketing academics. Blockchain applications for marketing were not included in any of the surveyed papers, according to a first study, while a second review failed to even notice their complete absence.

A different position is held by Marthews and Tucker (2022), who argue that BC technology has gained popularity, raising the possibility that it could have important marketing uses. But although BC is an incredible technology with numerous uses, the authors contend that its usefulness in many conventional marketing applications may be constrained since BC, when utilized carelessly for marketing objectives, may by its very nature result in major privacy damages. Nevertheless, Silva and Moro (2021) emphasize the disparate multidisciplinary of BC research on consumer trust and point to studies that suggest important components of consumer trust, such as traceability and privacy, are getting only sporadic attention from academics.

One of the areas with the greatest potential for the application of BC is the creative industry. Malik et al. (2022) point out that NFTs (nonfungible tokens) and smart contracts built on the BC offer creative industries fascinating new prospects. Usually, to share and monetize their works, creators in the creative industries frequently had to rely on strong distributors. NFT and smart contracts bring content creators and customers considerably closer together. NFTs detect distinctive works of art and keep ownership records on the blockchain. When certain criteria are satisfied, smart contracts, which are maintained as programs on a blockchain, automatically carry out the terms of an agreement. The guidelines for the purchase, use, and licensing of NFTs can be codified using them. Alternative distribution channels for material have been made possible by blockchain, NFTs, and smart contracts, which do not entirely rely on conventional distributors like publishers and distributors.

Along the same lines are the ideas proposed by Chohan and Paschen (2023). The authors describe that NFTs are a blockchain-based record of ownership, primarily for digital media and NFTs have the potential to drastically alter marketing operations. Therefore, marketing managers who want to use NFTs must be aware of the ramifications of marketing. They also refer that although marketers have no control over how blockchain transactions operate, they may make purchases easy and familiar for customers by pushing NFTs in well-known campaigns. Chohan and Paschen (2023) emphasize the trust construct when they said that consumers weigh risk and trust when deciding whether to buy anything, supporting the previous assertions of Silva and Moro (2021). Stallone et al. (2021) go further, holding that BC can be used for more than only recording details of transactions between nodes positioned inside of connected time-stamped data blocks. The authors highlight the particularities of Smart Contracts, which enable agreements between parties, which are automatically enforced, and establish a new paradigm with practically endless applications, moving the BC from a second generation to a third generation. This generation also includes smart contracts and a set of applications that go beyond cryptocurrency transactions. Also, Peres et al. (2022) refer to the combination of NFTs and smart contracts. By combining NFTs and smart contracts, users can build intricate contractual arrangements for the licensing, distributing, and protection of NFTs as well as for the payment of content providers based on the consumption of that content. Due to BC technologies, these contracts will be tamper-proof, transparent, and auditable in real-time, and arbitration procedures will be streamlined and expedited as needed.

Stallone et al. (2021) give us a general overview of the use of BC in marketing, indicating the areas and activities: e-commerce, online social networks, advertising, data markets, supply chain management, digital marketing fraud prevention, loyalty programs, improvement brand positioning, and corporate brand image, increasing brand storytelling capabilities, authenticate brand communication. The authors propose this integration in five major classes: advertising, content, social, e-commerce, and data.

According to Peres et al. (2022), marketing can undergo BC applications in a very broad scope, encompassing strategy, and the marketing mix. In the marketing mix component, the authors mention the next applications: Distributed new product design; Maintaining product provenance; Transactions between buyers and sellers in the absence of a centralized authority and creating and verifying authenticity. As for the marketing strategy component, the applications are: targeting and stakeholder mix; direct-to-consumer marketing; competitive structure, and power balance. Returning to the marketing mix, the authors also mention that BC can be applied to the remaining elements, namely, price, place (retailing, online commerce), promotion (advertising, consumer interactions, and social networks), and marketing intangible assets (brand equity, customer equity). Also, Jain et al. (2021) propose a comprehensive classification, consisting of five streams:

1. Blockchain and Electronic Commerce.
2. Blockchain and Marketing.
3. Blockchain and Data.
4. Blockchain and Data Analytics.
5. Blockchain-Privacy and Security.

In another domain, Treiblmaier and Petrozhitskaya (2023) have identified five potential advantages of blockchain-based programs over traditional loyalty programs pertaining to usage, accrual, relevance, expiration, and transferability. The authors state that a technology that will change customer loyalty programs" is blockchain, specifically. Lastly, for Marthews and Tucker (2022) the best uses of blockchain in marketing are in situations where keeping records of unchangeable, entirely digital data is suitable right immediately, like keeping track of digital ad purchases, and where there are no significant real-world repercussions that can be foreseen from existing privacy laws, business regulation, or law enforcement analysis of those transactions years from now.

IOT

IoT Definition

IoT operates in the functional specification, providing users with comfort and ease of use through the application of sensors (Kumar et al., 2021). The IoT is built on a network of sensors that collect data about each item and may be uniquely identified and IoT devices can link with one another to create a wireless sensor network and are capable of sensing, computing, and communicating wirelessly across short distances (Kumar et al., 2021). IoT devices can recognize, and capture events occurring in the real world and transmit them to computer systems and data centers for real-time analysis and interpretation. While the sensing and analyses take place behind the scenes of the IoT networks, hidden from the user, warnings based on this analysis are automatically given to the device user. These alerts may include simple graphics and pertinent information. IoT device-to-device and device-to-IoT device communication are extremely efficient and straightforward. As a result, IoT devices may seamlessly integrate into consumers' lives, automate mundane tasks, and improve functionality by requiring less human involvement (Mondal et al., 2022).

IoT Benefits

Jindal et al. (2022) claimed that the deployment of IoT improves a variety of business services, including customer care, online shopping, and market digitalization, which has a significant impact on the total market expansion. Examples of Internet of Things (IoT) products and services that generate enormous amounts of data by integrating and analyzing people include mobile devices, online commerce, social networking sites, digital communications, navigation systems, and equipment. In other words, big data is just a method of recognizing that customers are now producers of both structured and unstructured behavioral data (Jindal et al., 2022). IoT is now increasingly more accessible and widespread, prompting businesses to implement IoT solutions to enhance the experiences of their consumers. This is because modern life is becoming more instantly connected and because technological disruption is happening at a quicker rate. IoT opens up the potential for businesses to become more effective and responsive to market changes by enabling physical items to connect and exchange data through the Internet (Lo & Campos, 2018).

Jindal et al. (2022) also support the claim that the adoption of IoT presents a big potential to repair client relationships: the move toward multichannel, multidimensional, and multilingual interactions will increase user involvement, consequently raising consumer engagement and information accessibility. It is impossible to emphasize the importance of digital marketing in the provision of services given the versatility of IoT devices and machine learning, from remote monitoring of the modern environment to mechanical automation (Mondal et al., 2022). Consumers frequently provide marketers with data that is used to improve services and offer a tailored customer experience but the use, storage, and processing of data have been a major problem (Sachdev, 2020).

According to Jindal et al. (2022), organizations must regard the IoT as a commercial opportunity, not just a technological one, because it has the potential to create better learning environments and change infrastructure, operations, and commodities as part of a revival plan. Weng (2021) informed that academics and businesses have paid close attention to the new advances in the IoT, which not only provides enterprises with cutting-edge tools for operations but also has an impact on how well those operations perform. Finally, Dwesar and Kashyap (2022) present a set of precise benefits, stating that the combination of AI and IoT can improve operational efficiency and assist businesses in developing new goods and services: enhancing and improving existing consumer products; enabling predictive maintenance; helping to lower risk; improving operational and production performance; cuts down on unplanned downtime.

Integrating IoT and Marketing

Mondal et al. (2022) suggest that IoT can be applied to marketing in the following solutions:

1. Targeting by location (digital marketing allows facilities to focus on a particular population, such as age, gender, region, and much more).
2. Improved search engine transparency.
3. Increased customer visits (with digital marketing, managers have access to a variety of professional tools and technologies that can help you boost their strategy for maximum effectiveness and generate high-quality prospects for the business).
4. Decisions based on information (digital marketing makes it simple to make an educated and informative choice).

Lo and Campos (2018) corroborate that IoT can be applied in activities associated with customer behaviors and in the development of specific strategies. They also contend that the usage of innovative IoT solutions positively affects the process of developing long and successful relationships through relationship marketing actions.

Tariq et al. (2020) give a more detailed and incisive description, revealing that physical home devices are now a source of huge data and information due to technological advancements, and this wealth of knowledge about these devices can help companies find new ways to enhance their current products or create entirely new ones. Additionally, the authors also state that the huge amount of data is an opportunity for organizations to introduce new customer-oriented services. In short, IoT and marketing can be integrated into marketing outcomes (new product development, product support, customer relationship management) and analysis of customer-driven data. Najafi et al. (2022) go one step further by stating that IoT will advance marketing to a new level by ensuring that there is no aspect of life, no product or service, and no non-marketable solution. Also, Dwesar and Kashyap (2022) describe a broad scope, summarizing current applications of IoT in consumer products and marketing: smart speakers, personal assistants, and smart homes; home appliances with IoT capabilities; IoT in automobiles; IoT-driven customer service; smart medical devices and healthcare.

VIRTUAL REALITY

Definition

Although the term virtual reality is being used, it is necessary to clarify that other designations, associated with similar paradigms, should also be observed, namely augmented reality and mixed reality. Virtual Reality (VR) is an artificial environment experienced through computer-generated sensory stimuli like sights and sounds (An et al., 2021). Pose tracking and 3D near-eye displays are used in this simulation to provide the viewer with an immersive sense of the virtual world. Designers construct it to transport users to 3D environments where they can freely move and interact to complete specified activities and achieve goals. It can be used for entertainment, education, and business purposes. VR is the use of computer technology to simulate the experience of a three-dimensional, interactive world where things have a sense of spatial presence (Huang & Liu, 2021). Augmented Reality (AR) is a technology that overlays digital information or objects on top of the real world, enhancing the user's perception of reality and it uses computer vision, machine learning, and other technologies to recognize real-world objects and then adds digital content to them in real-time (Scholz & Smith, 2016). Unlike virtual reality, which creates a completely immersive and simulated environment, augmented reality blends the digital and real-world environments, allowing users to interact with both, and can be experienced through a smartphone or tablet app, or specialized AR headsets (Rauschnabel, 2021). Mixed Reality is a technology that combines elements of both VR and augmented reality AR to create a completely new experience. It is also known as hybrid reality, as it blends the digital and real-world environments in a way that allows users to interact with both.

How to match consumers' demands for material, knowledge, and customized solutions in real-time during their purchasing experience is a challenge that marketers are currently confronting (Parise et al., 2016). Future digital consumption patterns will be altered by virtual technologies since they can give users a multisensory experience as opposed to the single-sensory stimulation of the current online world and virtual technologies offer a better potential to influence consumer decisions than the current digital environment because human senses play a significant part in consumption choices (Laukkanen et al., 2022).

Integrating VR and AR and Marketing

The academic literature on VR and AR is, if anything, sparse, not to say almost non-existent for the potential that the technology offers. Del Vecchio et al. (2023) state the term *phygital* refers to the use of technology to link the digital and physical worlds to give users a distinctive interactive experience. The authors identified five main clusters, related to the adoption of *phygital* technologies:

1. Marketing and consumers behaviors.
2. Cultural heritage, Tourism, and urban development.
3. Education and learning.
4. Social issues and politics.
5. Technical and legal issues.

Huang and Liu (2021) assert that humanizing the digital experience through anthropomorphism, self-representation, and intimacy is crucial for promising disruptive technology to break through the limitations of contactless service journeys and fulfill online consumers keen to have a humanizing experience. In their new concept, Silva and Bonetti (2021) envision interactions between customers and virtual people. They explain that consumer connection with digital people may alter how businesses engage with customers in terms of communication and sales channels, which may have repercussions for the future of several academic subjects and their practice. The authors also assert that the relationship between humans and technology must be as realistic as feasible and that having humanized characteristics is essential to making the digital human socially acceptable. Parise et al. (2016) bring up a new possibility, stating the digital assistant and the remote expert are the two main technology-based approaches that businesses will use to meet consumers' urgent demands. Another approach is referred to by Scholz and Smith (2016), where the authors sustain that creative marketers can use augmented reality to design immersive brand experiences, produce more interactive advertising, and give customers new ways to interact with products and environments. They also mention that by incorporating branded content into consumers' social and physical contexts, augmented reality gives marketers a dynamic approach to engage with customers and incorporate branded content into their discussions. Engagement can be divided into user-brand engagement, user-user engagement, and user-bystander engagement.

Furthermore, according to Rauschnabel (2021), there is broad consensus that once AR establishes itself as a dominating medium, it will have a significant impact on both management and marketing. The authors, in Rauschnabel et al. (2022), also introduce the concept of augmented reality marketing, which they define as "a novel, strategic, and potentially disruptive subdiscipline in marketing". Finally, it is worth mentioning the contribution of Laukkanen et al. (2022), who write that the usage of virtual technology may be utilized to encourage customers to engage in sustainable consumption.

PRIVACY AND ANONYMITY

For several reasons, consumers are wary of privacy in digital marketing. First, marketing requires the gathering and utilization of sensitive personal data, including browsing history, location, and online behavior. Customers are concerned that this information might be utilized improperly or sold to unaffiliated third parties. Second, customers are alarmed by the tactics used in digital marketing that lack transparency. They frequently feel that they do not fully understand how businesses gather, store, and use their data. This lack of openness has the potential to reduce customer and corporate trust, which can harm brand loyalty and reputation. Third, consumers are concerned that hackers may hack into or steal their personal information. Consumers are understandably concerned about the protection of their personal information due to the rising frequency of data breaches and cyberattacks. The prevalence of digital marketing, which can give the impression that you are being watched and tracked constantly, is the last issue that worries consumers. This may cause emotions of privacy invasion and a lack of control over personal data. The previous words are corroborated by Hill and Zubielqui (2022) when they confirm that security and privacy infringements, online fraud, identity theft, and online scams have increased consumers' privacy fears recently.

For many years, the issue of privacy and anonymity has been surprisingly neglected by governments and consumers. Only recently have government initiatives emerged to regulate data management, specifically, the GDPR which stands for General Data Protection Regulation and is an EU regulation for data protection and privacy for EU residents, and the CCPA which stands for California Consumer Privacy Act. Malgieri (2021) acknowledges that GDPR is a robust conformity framework that can improve to recognize legitimate marketing from illegal ones and brings transparency through four legal tests: fairness test, lawfulness test, significant effect test, and the high-risk test. To the author, enhancing crucial openness and avoiding the exploitation of particular vulnerabilities are two strategies that marketers can use to respect and capitalize on consumers' privacy expectations. He also states that at the junction of four crucial criteria is the marketing practice of privacy-intrusive manipulation: personalization, secrecy, advanced analytics, and vulnerability exploitation. But Pope and Lowen (2009) find out that the privacy-protecting behaviors differed significantly between countries and that consumers' level of worry and propensity to engage in privacy-protecting practices are influenced by demographic factors.

But technology does not necessarily imply a decrease in privacy or less protection of consumer data, says Hakkarainen and Colicev (2023). Smart contracts, cryptocurrencies, play-to-earn games, and non-fungible tokens are four blockchain-enabled innovations that have gained traction recently and have ramifications for the marketing industry since they affect customers and businesses. The fundamental ideas behind blockchain technology and improved digital connectivity suggest that consumers can take more control over their data and privacy rights, be more in charge of their decisions, and be more connected online. Pope and Lowen (2009) recommendations for marketers to respond to customer concerns and behaviors are to provide greater transparency and use privacy seals. The authors also refer that due to disparities in governmental and cultural practices, international businesses confront even larger difficulties when it comes to privacy-related concerns and associated consumer behaviors. An interesting contribution comes from Bleier et al. (2020), who point out that digitization makes it easier for companies to build their innovation and marketing efforts around consumers' personal data and such practices can trigger privacy concerns. Another relevant point indicated by the authors is associated with the size of the companies, mentioning that small entrepreneurial companies are often at a particular disadvantage compared to large incumbent firms. At the same time, there are several strategies companies can use to mitigate privacy concerns, and in some circumstances, privacy concerns may also exert positive effects on data-driven marketing by stimulating privacy innovation and providing a source of competitive advantage.

Personalization, a much sought-after goal by marketing managers, is considered one of the biggest concerns regarding privacy and data protection (Lee et al., 2022). Real-time personalization is one of the most recent developments in data-driven marketing that has rendered customers more vulnerable (Cloarec, 2022). Lee et al. (2022) stated that the use of personalization is common in contemporary social media marketing techniques, but social networking service users could consider personalized material to be obtrusive. In social media personalization campaigns, these two elements could have an impact on consumers' purchase intentions. They revealed that personalization positively affected but intrusiveness negatively affected the purchase intention. When consumers perceive an intrusive context due to personalization their reactions are peculiar. As a result, some customers purposefully invent information in an effort to restore the balance of power, posing a severe threat to the digital economy (Cloarec, 2022).

In addition, the author claimed that information is obtained through privacy restrictions, and that information is fabricated as a coping method, with vulnerability standing in for the threat appraisal process and self-efficacy for the coping appraisal mechanism. Sáez-Ortuño et al. (2023) found that some user profiles are more inclined to make mistakes and others to forge data intentionally. They also discovered that the primary drivers behind purposefully disseminating false information are amusement-related, such as playing practical jokes, and a lack of confidence in the company's data protection and security safeguards. Consumers' levels of trust and feelings of control over their information are directly correlated with the steps they are likely to take to protect their identity and personal information (Pope & Lowen, 2009). Privacy is also an emerging issue for multisided platforms, which are subject to digital privacy risks (e.g. data breaches and unauthorized access to data) (Chen et al., 2022). According to Liu-Thompkins et al. (2022), there are circumstances in which artificial empathy may be undesired. It is crucial to consider all of the unforeseen or unanticipated effects of artificial empathy, particularly the considerable implications for customer privacy.

Another area that requires privacy policies, protection, and regulation is social media in general, and social networks in particular. As mentioned by Jacobson et al. (2020), social media has made a plethora of data readily available and accessible, which marketers are using for digital marketing and strategic insight. However, there are no industry standards for the use of social media in marketing, and it is unclear how comfortable customers are with marketers using their social network data. According to the authors, consumers' perceptions of the risks and advantages of using social media relate to how comfortable they are with marketers using their publicly available social media data. The same is supported by Pope and Lowen (2009), when they say regrettably, consumers' levels of trust and feelings of control over their information are directly correlated with the measures they are likely to take to protect their identity and personal information. As personal information becomes more widely available, marketing uses have risen to the top of business practices. Nevertheless, in many businesses, data sharing is a strategically significant marketing activity and companies are increasingly attempting to increase the value of their customer data by augmenting it with customer-level data from other businesses. The disclosure of a company's customer-level data to another under this arrangement exposes it to privacy issues, which could result in significant losses in brand value, customer trust, and competitive advantage and it could also result in legal repercussions for breaking legislation (Jacobson et al., 2020).

Martin and Murphy (2016) summarize the reasons for companies to pay attention to this concern:

1. Businesses that genuinely emphasize data privacy will succeed well, benefiting from a favorable market reaction, customer loyalty, and engagement advantages.
2. Businesses that engage their clients in the conversation about information privacy will perform better.
3. Businesses that adopt privacy-promoting procedures will perform better as long as their data privacy practices are consistent throughout all divisions of the company.
4. Businesses who concentrate on what they do well in terms of data protection will succeed well.
5. Consumers seem to respond better when one emphasizes one's own advantages over others' potentially flawed methods.
6. Long-term commitment to data privacy measures will benefit businesses in terms of performance as well as lax governmental supervision.
7. Finally, consumers will have greater trust in businesses that adopt privacy principles as strategic pillars. The main mechanism for effective performance is trust.

As described by Pope and Lowen (2009), companies can relieve consumers' worries about the security of their personal information by providing greater openness of information, altering how privacy policies are conveyed, getting privacy policies certified, and providing opt-in programs. It is crucial that businesses clearly explain to customers what advantages they will gain in exchange for providing personal information when they request that information from them. Lastly, Jacobson et al. (2020), it is crucial to resist the urge to use any available data for profit without first considering the risks that could be involved because doing so could raise serious privacy issues with far-reaching effects.

SECURITY

Protecting digital assets and information from illegal access, use, disclosure, disruption, alteration, or destruction is the practice of security in the digital marketing field. In the context of digital marketing, security entails safeguarding the systems, networks, and tools used to gather, process, store, and transmit customer, employee, partner, and other stakeholder data (Xu et al., 2022). Data privacy, data protection, network security, device security, application security, and adherence to regulatory and industry standards are just a few of the many facets of digital marketing security. To guarantee that any security breaches or interruptions are handled effectively and efficiently, it also involves risk management, incident response, and disaster recovery planning (Alshurideh et al., 2023).

Pham et al. (2019) reports that sensitive information losses continue to be a very serious worry on a worldwide scale, and the hazards to an organization's sensitive information are continually evolving. The authors also acknowledge that the security of information and related computer resources is frequently ensured by organizations via a variety of procedures, however in recent years, cyber-incidents have increased in frequency, organization, expense, and overall hazard. Mathur (2018) holds the same concept, adding that although cybersecurity is crucial for any organization, businesses often lack a thorough knowledge of the effects of perceived cybersecurity risks and how marketers may prevent their unfavorable effects. The author also points out that customers' views of cybersecurity risk and marketing potential have grown as a result of businesses' recent inability to stop significant data breaches. According to Suleiman et al. (2021), more security measures should be incorporated into digital initiatives to help customers assuage their fears about insecurities like fraud and hackers. Pham et al. (2019) present another perspective, saying that although employees are aware of the significance of safe cybersecurity practices, there is a significant gap between their attitudes and behaviors. To date, most studies on security compliance have concentrated on identifying initiating factors of the expected behavior and have not given enough attention to understanding organizational factors enabling it. This is a different view, which brings internal factors rather than external ones to the forefront of the situation.

The most interesting study from the perspective of digital marketing prescribes that applying the 7P mix to evaluate a cybersecurity program provides the systematic recording of users' security compliance and IT system approval (Pham et al., 2019). Also important is the statement of Mathur (2018), informing that with the use of social media marketing, businesses can lessen the negative effects of cybersecurity risk on their falling brand value and reputation. He also points out that to carry out marketing activities effectively, marketers have only recently realized the importance of addressing customer cybersecurity concerns. Cybersecurity risk jeopardizes the carefully and rigorously cultivated customer relationships by marketers. Eventually, he said that perceived cybersecurity risk sinks reputation, but reputation enables it to reduce risk.

CONCLUSION

The most obvious finding to emerge from this review is that the integration of AI in marketing, and in particular in digital marketing, has been the subject of in-depth research and publication by the academic community when compared to the other topics addressed, namely blockchain, IoT, virtual reality (in its different aspects), as well as the problematic aspects arising from the application of the technology which is privacy and anonymity, and security. The disparity in the number of academic publications found on IA is vastly greater than the totality of all the other topics covered in this chapter. The conclusions regarding IA are uncompromising and it is possible to say that the generality of marketing activities can be targeted by its integration with benefits. Even unstructured and semi-structured activities such as marketing strategy and marketing mix have possibilities to integrate IA. Consequently, AI has almost total pervasiveness in marketing and digital marketing.

As for Blockchain, the literature also refers to an extended set of benefits arising from its application in marketing and digital marketing. Nevertheless, the number of applications is much smaller, and the hypothesis of transversality in its use is not put forward. If AI guaranteed an increase in efficiency, effectiveness, and reduction of resources, the Blockchain's main merits are increased security, transparency, and consequently, impact on trust. But its application in a marketing context is very limited.

The situation for IoT is very similar to that for Blockchain. The number of academic publications on the topic is small, indicating a very small number of IoT applications in marketing. This is a paradox, because IoT is probably one of the technologies with the most potential to provide data about products and consumers to companies, and large companies today value this data very highly. We are, therefore, facing a context in which marketing managers have not yet realized the full potential of the technology.

Moving forward to virtual reality, we find a similar situation to blockchain and IoT. The number of academic publications is small, the benefits are recognized, and the number of applications of virtual reality and its similar is limited to a few activities. The possibility of virtual reality being applied across the board in marketing is not feasible.

It should be noted, however, that if, on the one hand, the set of technologies referred to provides relevant advantages and benefits, on the other hand, they raise new challenges and problems, or exacerbate others. The ones that stand out most are precisely the issues of privacy, anonymity, transparency, intrusion, and security. Privacy, anonymity, transparency, and intrusiveness were analyzed under the heading privacy in one section, while security was isolated in its own section. With the emergence of the GPDR and the CCPA, inevitably the issue of privacy and data protection has become a mandatory topic in any marketing strategy. However, it was found that from an academic point of view, these issues have been the subject of little research. But if privacy assumes a small role, the issue of security is characterized by a significant absence of interest from the academic community and a lack of concern from marketers. Finally, and by way of conclusion, the literature reviewed suggests that the technologies described will continue to impact marketing and pose new challenges.

REFERENCES

Alshurideh, M., Kurdi, B. H. A., Masa'deh, R., Alzoubi, H. M., & Salloum, S. (2023). *The Effect of Information Technology on Business and Marketing Intelligence Systems*. Springer International Publishing. doi:10.1007/978-3-031-12382-5

An, S., Choi, Y., & Lee, C.-K. (2021). Virtual travel experience and destination marketing: Effects of sense and information quality on flow and visit intention. *Journal of Destination Marketing & Management*, *19*, 19. doi:10.1016/j.jdmm.2020.100492

Barr, A., Feigenbaum, E. A., & Cohen, P. R. (1981). *The Handbook of Artificial Intelligence*. HeurisTech Press.

Bleier, A., Goldfarb, A., & Tucker, C. (2020). Consumer privacy and the future of data-based innovation and marketing. *International Journal of Research in Marketing*, *37*(3), 466–480. doi:10.1016/j.ijresmar.2020.03.006

Boddu, R. S. K., Santoki, A. A., Khurana, S., Koli, P., Rai, R., & Agrawal, A. (2022). An analysis to understand the role of machine learning, robotics and artificial intelligence in digital marketing. *Materials Today: Proceedings*, *56*, 2288–2292. doi:10.1016/j.matpr.2021.11.637

Campbell, C., Sands, S., Ferraro, C., Tsao, H.-Y., & Mavrommatis, A. (2020). From data to action: How marketers can leverage AI. *Business Horizons*, *63*(2), 227–243. doi:10.1016/j.bushor.2019.12.002

Chambers, L. D. (2019). *The Practical Handbook of Genetic Algorithms: New Frontiers* (Vol. II). CRC Press.

Chen, S., Tamilmani, K., Tran, K. T., Waseem, D., & Weerakkody, V. (2022). How privacy practices affect customer commitment in the sharing economy: A study of Airbnb through an institutional perspective. *Industrial Marketing Management*, *107*, 161–175. doi:10.1016/j.indmarman.2022.08.020

Chohan, R., & Paschen, J. (2023). NFT marketing: How marketers can use nonfungible tokens in their campaigns. *Business Horizons*, *66*(1), 43–50. doi:10.1016/j.bushor.2021.12.004

Cloarec, J. (2022). Privacy controls as an information source to reduce data poisoning in artificial intelligence-powered personalization. *Journal of Business Research*, *152*, 144–153. doi:10.1016/j.jbusres.2022.07.045

Cohen, P. R., & Feigenbaum, E. A. (2014). *The Handbook of Artificial Intelligence* (Vol. 3). Elsevier Science.

De Bruyn, A., Viswanathan, V., Beh, Y. S., Brock, J. K.-U., & von Wangenheim, F. (2020). Artificial Intelligence and Marketing: Pitfalls and Opportunities. *Journal of Interactive Marketing*, *51*, 91–105. doi:10.1016/j.intmar.2020.04.007

Del Vecchio, P., Secundo, G., & Garzoni, A. (2023). Phygital technologies and environments for breakthrough innovation in customers' and citizens' journey. A critical literature review and future agenda. *Technological Forecasting and Social Change*, *189*, 189. doi:10.1016/j.techfore.2023.122342

Dwesar, R., & Kashyap, R. (2022). IOT in Marketing: Current Applications and Future Opportunities. In S. N. Mohanty, J. M. Chatterjee, & S. Satpathy (Eds.), *Internet of Things and Its Applications* (pp. 539–553). Springer. doi:10.1007/978-3-030-77528-5_29

Far, S. B., Rad, A. I., & Asaar, M. R. (2022). ACR-MLM: A privacy-preserving framework for anonymous and confidential rewarding in blockchain-based multi-level marketing. *Data Science and Management*, *5*(4), 219–231. doi:10.1016/j.dsm.2022.09.003

Far, S. B., Asaar, M. R., & Haghbin, A. (2023). A privacy-preserving framework for blockchain-based multi-level marketing. *Computers & Industrial Engineering*, *177*, 177. doi:10.1016/j.cie.2023.109095

Frankish, K., & Ramsey, W. M. (2014). *The Cambridge Handbook of Artificial Intelligence*. Cambridge University Press. doi:10.1017/CBO9781139046855

Goyal, P., Pandey, S., & Jain, K. (2018). *Deep Learning for Natural Language Processing: Creating Neural Networks with Python*. Apress. doi:10.1007/978-1-4842-3685-7

Hakkarainen, T., & Colicev, A. (2023). Blockchain-enabled advances (BEAs): Implications for consumers and brands. *Journal of Business Research*, *160*, 160. doi:10.1016/j.jbusres.2023.113763

Haleem, A., Javaid, M., Asim Qadri, M., Pratap Singh, R., & Suman, R. (2022). Artificial intelligence (AI) applications for marketing: A literature-based study. *International Journal of Intelligent Networks*, *3*, 119–132. doi:10.1016/j.ijin.2022.08.005

Hill, S. R., & Zubielqui, G. C. d. (2022). Managing Privacy in B2B Marketing: A Systematic Literature Review. *Journal of Computer Information Systems*, 1–18.

Hossain, M. A., Agnihotri, R., Rushan, M. R. I., Rahman, M. S., & Sumi, S. F. (2022). Marketing analytics capability, artificial intelligence adoption, and firms' competitive advantage: Evidence from the manufacturing industry. *Industrial Marketing Management*, *106*, 240–255. doi:10.1016/j.indmarman.2022.08.017

Huang, T.-L., & Liu, B. S. C. (2021). Augmented reality is human-like: How the humanizing experience inspires destination brand love. *Technological Forecasting and Social Change*, *170*, 170. doi:10.1016/j.techfore.2021.120853

Jacobson, J., Gruzd, A., & Hernández-García, Á. (2020). Social media marketing: Who is watching the watchers? *Journal of Retailing and Consumer Services*, *53*, 53. doi:10.1016/j.jretconser.2019.03.001

Jain, D., Dash, M. K., Kumar, A., & Luthra, S. (2021). How is Blockchain used in marketing: A review and research agenda. *International Journal of Information Management Data Insights*, *1*(2), 100044. doi:10.1016/j.jjimei.2021.100044

Jindal, T., Sheoliha, N., Kishore, K., Uike, D., Khurana, S., & Verma, D. (2022, April). A Conceptual Analysis on the Impact of Internet of Things (IOT) Towards on Digital Marketing Transformation. In *2022 2nd International Conference on Advance Computing and Innovative Technologies in Engineering (ICACITE)* (pp. 1943-1947). IEEE.

Klaus, P., & Zaichkowsky, J. (2020). AI voice bots: A services marketing research agenda. *Journal of Services Marketing*, *34*(3), 389–398. doi:10.1108/JSM-01-2019-0043

Kopalle, P. K., Gangwar, M., Kaplan, A., Ramachandran, D., Reinartz, W., & Rindfleisch, A. (2022). Examining artificial intelligence (AI) technologies in marketing via a global lens: Current trends and future research opportunities. *International Journal of Research in Marketing*, *39*(2), 522–540. doi:10.1016/j.ijresmar.2021.11.002

Kumar, A. B. R. (2021). AI-Based Digital Marketing Strategies - A Review. In S. Smys, V. E. Balas, K. A. Kamel and P. Lafata (Eds), *Inventive Computation and Information Technologies: Proceedings of ICICIT 2020* (pp. 957-969). Springer.

Kumar, V., Ramachandran, D., & Kumar, B. (2021). Influence of new-age technologies on marketing: A research agenda. *Journal of Business Research, 125*, 864–877. doi:10.1016/j.jbusres.2020.01.007

Laukkanen, T., Xi, N., Hallikainen, H., Ruusunen, N., & Hamari, J. (2022). Virtual technologies in supporting sustainable consumption: From a single-sensory stimulus to a multi-sensory experience. *International Journal of Information Management, 63*, 102455. doi:10.1016/j.ijinfomgt.2021.102455

Lee, J., Kim, C., & Lee, K. C. (2022). Exploring the personalization-intrusiveness-intention framework to evaluate the effects of personalization in social media. *International Journal of Information Management, 66*, 66. doi:10.1016/j.ijinfomgt.2022.102532

Lee, Y.-I., & Trim, P. R. J. (2022). Enhancing Marketing Provision through Increased Online Safety That Imbues Consumer Confidence: Coupling AI and ML with the AIDA Model. *Big Data and Cognitive Computing, 6*(3), 78. doi:10.3390/bdcc6030078

Liu-Thompkins, Y., Okazaki, S., & Li, H. (2022). Artificial empathy in marketing interactions: Bridging the human-AI gap in affective and social customer experience. *Journal of the Academy of Marketing Science, 50*(6), 1198–1218. doi:10.100711747-022-00892-5

Ljepava, N. (2022). AI-Enabled Marketing Solutions in Marketing Decision Making: AI Application in Different Stages of Marketing Process. *TEM Journal, 11*(3), 1308–1315. doi:10.18421/TEM113-40

Lo, F.-Y., & Campos, N. (2018). Blending Internet-of-Things (IoT) solutions into relationship marketing strategies. *Technological Forecasting and Social Change, 137*, 10–18. doi:10.1016/j.techfore.2018.09.029

Ma, L., & Sun, B. (2020). Machine learning and AI in marketing – Connecting computing power to human insights. *International Journal of Research in Marketing, 37*(3), 481–504. doi:10.1016/j.ijresmar.2020.04.005

Malgieri, G. (2021). In/acceptable marketing and consumers' privacy expectations: Four tests from EU data protection law. *Journal of Consumer Marketing, 40*(2), 209–223. doi:10.1108/JCM-03-2021-4571

Malik, N., Wei, Y. M., Appel, G., & Luo, L. (2022). Blockchain technology for creative industries: Current state and research opportunities. *International Journal of Research in Marketing*.

Manis, K. T., & Madhavaram, S. (2023). AI-Enabled marketing capabilities and the hierarchy of capabilities: Conceptualization, proposition development, and research avenues. *Journal of Business Research, 157*, 113485. doi:10.1016/j.jbusres.2022.113485

Mariani, M. M., Perez-Vega, R., & Wirtz, J. (2021). AI in marketing, consumer research and psychology: A systematic literature review and research agenda. *Psychology and Marketing, 39*(4), 755–776. doi:10.1002/mar.21619

Marthews, A., & Tucker, C. (2022). What blockchain can and can't do: Applications to marketing and privacy. *International Journal of Research in Marketing, 40*(1), 49–53. doi:10.1016/j.ijresmar.2022.09.001

Martin, K. D., & Murphy, P. E. (2016). The role of data privacy in marketing. *Journal of the Academy of Marketing Science*, *45*(2), 135–155. doi:10.100711747-016-0495-4

Marwala, T. (2018). Handbook Of Machine Learning - Volume 1: Foundation Of Artificial Intelligence. World Scientific Publishing Company.

Mathur, M. (2018). Where is the Security Blanket? Developing Social Media Marketing Capability as a Shield from Perceived Cybersecurity Risk. *Journal of Promotion Management*, *25*(2), 200–224. doi:10.1080/10496491.2018.1443310

Mikalef, P., Conboy, K., & Krogstie, J. (2021). Artificial intelligence as an enabler of B2B marketing: A dynamic capabilities micro-foundations approach. *Industrial Marketing Management*, *98*, 80–92. doi:10.1016/j.indmarman.2021.08.003

Mondal, T., Mugaloremutt Jayadeva, S., Pani, R., Subramanian, M., P, A., & Sumana, B. (2022). E marketing strategy in health care using IoT and Machine Learning. *Materials Today: Proceedings*, *56*, 2087–2091. doi:10.1016/j.matpr.2021.11.417

Moradi, M., & Dass, M. (2022). Applications of artificial intelligence in B2B marketing: Challenges and future directions. *Industrial Marketing Management*, *107*, 300–314. doi:10.1016/j.indmarman.2022.10.016

Mustak, M., Salminen, J., Plé, L., & Wirtz, J. (2021). Artificial intelligence in marketing: Topic modeling, scientometric analysis, and research agenda. *Journal of Business Research*, *124*, 389–404. doi:10.1016/j.jbusres.2020.10.044

Najafi, S. E., Nozari, H., & Edalatpanah, S. A. (2022). Investigating the Key Parameters Affecting Sustainable IoT-Based Marketing. In J. L. Verdegay, J. Brito, & C. Cruz (Eds.), *Computational Intelligence Methodologies Applied to Sustainable Development Goals* (pp. 51–61). Springer. doi:10.1007/978-3-030-97344-5_4

Ngai, E. W. T., & Wu, Y. (2022). Machine learning in marketing: A literature review, conceptual framework, and research agenda. *Journal of Business Research*, *145*, 35–48. doi:10.1016/j.jbusres.2022.02.049

Parise, S., Guinan, P. J., & Kafka, R. (2016). Solving the crisis of immediacy: How digital technology can transform the customer experience. *Business Horizons*, *59*(4), 411–420. doi:10.1016/j.bushor.2016.03.004

Paul, S. P., Aggarwal, S., & Jha, S. (2022, October). A survey on the use of artificial intelligence (AI)-enabled techniques in digital marketing. In AIP Conference Proceedings (Vol. 2555, No. 1, p. 050003). AIP Publishing LLC.

Peres, R., Schreier, M., Schweidel, D. A., & Sorescu, A. (2022). Blockchain meets marketing: Opportunities, threats, and avenues for future research. *International Journal of Research in Marketing*, *40*(1), 1–11. doi:10.1016/j.ijresmar.2022.08.001

Petrescu, M., Krishen, A. S., Kachen, S., & Gironda, J. T. (2022). AI-based innovation in B2B marketing: An interdisciplinary framework incorporating academic and practitioner perspectives. *Industrial Marketing Management*, *103*, 61–72. doi:10.1016/j.indmarman.2022.03.001

Pham, H. C., Brennan, L., Parker, L., Phan-Le, N. T., Ulhaq, I., Nkhoma, M. Z., & Nhat Nguyen, M. (2019). Enhancing cyber security behavior: An internal social marketing approach. *Information and Computer Security*, *28*(2), 133–159. doi:10.1108/ICS-01-2019-0023

Pope, J. A., & Lowen, A. M. (2009). Marketing implications of privacy concerns in the US and Canada. *Direct Marketing (Bradford)*, *3*(4), 301–326. doi:10.1108/17505930911000883

Rauschnabel, P. A. (2021). Augmented reality is eating the real-world! The substitution of physical products by holograms. *International Journal of Information Management*, *57*, 57. doi:10.1016/j.ijinfomgt.2020.102279

Rauschnabel, P. A., Babin, B. J., tom Dieck, M. C., Krey, N., & Jung, T. (2022). What is augmented reality marketing? Its definition, complexity, and future. *Journal of Business Research*, *142*, 1140–1150. doi:10.1016/j.jbusres.2021.12.084

Sachdev, R. (2020, April 20-23). Towards Security and Privacy for Edge AI in IoT/IoE based Digital Marketing Environments. *2020 Fifth International Conference on Fog and Mobile Edge Computing (FMEC)*.

Sáez-Ortuño, L., Forgas-Coll, S., Huertas-Garcia, R., & Sánchez-García, J. (2023). Online cheaters: Profiles and motivations of internet users who falsify their data online. *Journal of Innovation & Knowledge*, *8*(2).

Sands, S., Campbell, C. L., Plangger, K., & Ferraro, C. (2022). Unreal influence: Leveraging AI in influencer marketing. *European Journal of Marketing*, *56*(6), 1721–1747. doi:10.1108/EJM-12-2019-0949

Scholz, J., & Smith, A. N. (2016). Augmented reality: Designing immersive experiences that maximize consumer engagement. *Business Horizons*, *59*(2), 149–161. doi:10.1016/j.bushor.2015.10.003

Silva, C. F. d., & Moro, S. (2021). Blockchain technology as an enabler of consumer trust: A text mining literature analysis. *Telematics and Informatics*, *60*, 102430.

Silva, E. S., & Bonetti, F. (2021). Digital humans in fashion: Will consumers interact? *Journal of Retailing and Consumer Services*, *60*, 60. doi:10.1016/j.jretconser.2020.102430

Stallone, V., Wetzels, M., & Klaas, M. (2021). Applications of Blockchain Technology in marketing—A systematic review of marketing technology companies. *Blockchain: Research and Applications, 2*(3).

Stone, M., Aravopoulou, E., Ekinci, Y., Evans, G., Hobbs, M., Labib, A., Laughlin, P., Machtynger, J., & Machtynger, L. (2020). Artificial intelligence (AI) in strategic marketing decision-making: A research agenda. *The Bottom Line (New York, N.Y.)*, *33*(2), 183–200. doi:10.1108/BL-03-2020-0022

Suleiman, D. A., Awan, T. M., & Javed, M. (2021). Enhancing digital marketing performance through usage intention of AI-powered websites. *IAES International Journal of Artificial Intelligence, 10*(4).

Tariq, B., Taimoor, S., Najam, H., Law, R., Hassan, W., & Han, H. (2020). Generating Marketing Outcomes through Internet of Things (IoT) Technologies. *Sustainability (Basel)*, *12*(22), 9670. doi:10.3390u12229670

Treiblmaier, H., & Petrozhitskaya, E. (2023). Is it time for marketing to reappraise B2C relationship management? The emergence of a new loyalty paradigm through blockchain technology. *Journal of Business Research*, *159*, 159. doi:10.1016/j.jbusres.2023.113725 van Esch, P., Black, J. S., & Ferolie, J. (2019). Marketing AI recruitment: The next phase in job application and selection. *Computers in Human Behavior, 90*, 215–222. doi:10.1016/j.chb.2018.09.009

van Esch, P., & Stewart Black, J. (2021). Artificial Intelligence (AI): Revolutionizing Digital Marketing. *Australasian Marketing Journal, 29*(3), 199–203. doi:10.1177/18393349211037684

Verma, S., Sharma, R., Deb, S., & Maitra, D. (2021). Artificial intelligence in marketing: Systematic review and future research direction. *International Journal of Information Management Data Insights, 1*(1), 100002. doi:10.1016/j.jjimei.2020.100002

Vinaykarthik, B. C. (2022, October). Design of Artificial Intelligence (AI) based User Experience Websites for E-commerce Application and Future of Digital Marketing. In *2022 3rd International Conference on Smart Electronics and Communication (ICOSEC)* (pp. 1023-1029). IEEE.

Vlačić, B., Corbo, L., Costa e Silva, S., & Dabić, M. (2021). The evolving role of artificial intelligence in marketing: A review and research agenda. *Journal of Business Research, 128*, 187–203. doi:10.1016/j.jbusres.2021.01.055

Volkmar, G., Fischer, P. M., & Reinecke, S. (2022). Artificial Intelligence and Machine Learning: Exploring drivers, barriers, and future developments in marketing management. *Journal of Business Research, 149*, 599–614. doi:10.1016/j.jbusres.2022.04.007

Wang, Y., & Wang, H. (2022). Reinventing the Wheel of Marketing: Assessing the Impact of Artificial Intelligence (AI) on Digital Marketing and Consumer Buying Behavior. In J. C. Hung, J.-W. Chang, Y. P., W.-C. Wu (Eds.), *Innovative Computing: Proceedings of the 4th International Conference on Innovative Computing (IC 2021)* (pp. 827-834). Springer.

Weng, W. W.-H. (2021). Effect of Internet of Things on Marketing Intelligence and Business Strategy: An Organizational Capability Perspective. *International Journal of Electronic Commerce Studies, 12*(2), 209. doi:10.7903/ijecs.1906

Xu, Z., Alrabaee, S., Loyola-González, O., Zhang, X., Cahyani, N. D. W., & Rahman, N. H. A. (2022). *Cyber Security Intelligence and Analytics: The 4th International Conference on Cyber Security Intelligence and Analytics (CSIA 2022)* (vol. 1). Springer International Publishing.

KEY TERMS AND DEFINITIONS

Artificial Intelligence: AI is a type of computer technology that enables machines to simulate human intelligence and behavior.

IoT: Stands for the "Internet of Things". It refers to the network of physical devices, vehicles, appliances, and other items that are embedded with sensors, software, and connectivity, enabling them to exchange data and interact with each other over the internet.

Ledger: Is a record-keeping system that tracks financial transactions. It is a book or a computerized database that contains all the financial information of a business, such as sales, purchases, payments, and receipts.

Machine Learning: ML is a type of artificial intelligence (AI) that involves the use of algorithms and statistical models to enable machines to learn and improve from experience without being explicitly programmed.

NFT: Stands for Non-Fungible Token. An NFT is a unique digital asset that is stored on a blockchain and represents ownership of a specific piece of digital content, such as an image, video, or music file. Unlike cryptocurrencies, which are fungible and interchangeable, each NFT is unique and cannot be replicated or exchanged for another NFT.

Phygital: Refers to the merging of physical and digital experiences. It combines the words "physical" and "digital" to describe experiences that blur the line between the two.

SEO: Search Engine Optimization. It is the practice of improving the quality and quantity of traffic to a website from search engines through organic search results.

Smart Contracts: Are self-executing contracts that are coded and stored on a blockchain. They are essentially computer programs that automatically execute the terms of a contract when certain conditions are met.

Wearables: Also known as wearable technology, refers to electronic devices that are worn on the body, typically as accessories or clothing. These devices are designed to collect data about the wearer's behavior, health, fitness, and other parameters, and communicate that data to other devices or applications.

Chapter 2
Marketing Business Processes in a Multinational Organization:
A Case Study of an Information System Implementation

Nuno Valente
Instituto Universitário de Lisboa (ISCTE-IUL), Portugal

Bráulio Alturas
https://orcid.org/0000-0003-0142-3737
Instituto Universitário de Lisboa (ISCTE-IUL), ISTAR-Iscte, Portugal

ABSTRACT

Marketing information systems, scale, scope, and functionalities have grown due to the substantial rise of new technologies such as the internet, mobile devices, and social media. This chapter aims to analyse the impact of implementing a marketing information system to manage marketing business processes in a multinational organization. Interviews were carried out with organizations using the same marketing information system. The interview structure and its questions were based on the information system's evaluation model, which is extensively used in this area of research. The results obtained were relevant not only from a benefits analysis perspective, but also from a system quality perspective, information quality and service quality matter.

INTRODUCTION

Marketing Cloud Platform (MCP) is a cloud-based tool used to manage marketing business processes, with new features being launched on a quarterly basis. This platform aims to provide a real time deeper understanding of customers, through key performance indicators (KPI) and marketing campaign measures. MCP helps businesses getting to know their customers and interact with them, by sending personalized and relevant marketing communications.

DOI: 10.4018/978-1-6684-8958-1.ch002

Deciding on a marketing information system implementation is a high investment for an organization from a resource, time and money perspective. However, there are many reasons and motivations for a marketing information system implementation, such as getting to better know and understand their consumer database, capturing consumer interactions with the organizations brand, increase sales and brand awareness, and improving relationships with customers, amongst others.

Specially in these days where business is changing faster than ever, it is essential to have an information system able to follow the required innovation within marketing processes. Based on the interest on those areas, decision was taken to analyse the impact of implementing a marketing platform on a multinational organization, especially considering the marketing department and their users.

However, in digital marketing there must be a balance between obtaining information from customers, in order to better serve them, and guaranteeing the security and privacy of their data (Figueiredo et al., 2021). Companies need to mitigate potential issues related to data security and privacy, balancing their desire for innovation and advantage with consumers' expectations and ethical norms (Sestino et al., 2020).

From an academic and research community point of view, it is an added value to add more knowledge on the recognized benefits of using a marketing platform to manage marketing business process and being able to understand what users consider to be the key functionalities and benefits to support them running their daily activities.

The research question of this study is: What are the benefits of implementing a marketing information system to manage business processes?

Based on this matter, the main goals were defined for this research, based on Gorla et al. (2010) model to measure the impact of information systems in organizations. As far as we were able to find, there are no studies in which this model has been applied to marketing information systems.

BACKGROUND

From Traditional Marketing to Digital Marketing

As mentioned by Yasmin, et al. (2015) "digital marketing is one type of marketing being broadly used to reach consumers using digital channels" or to promote services and products. Digital marketing is broader than internet marketing, including channels that do not require internet, such as mobile phones (SMS and MMS), social media marketing, display advertising, search engine marketing and many other forms of digital media.

Saura et al. (2017) suggested that digital marketing is not only used as a transactional tool, but also it transformed marketing practice and theory demand. All types of companies had to adjust their business practices according to the development of technologies and come up with new management and communication approaches. Digital marketing integrates strategies on the web related to specific processes, seeking clear goals using different tools, platforms and social media. The relevance of digital marketing for organizations consists in adjusting the current ways in which consumer's gather and access information, as well as purchase choices, on top of the existing channels.

According to Todor (2016), in most cases, traditional marketing is reaching a local audience even though it is not limited to one. There are many aspects of traditional marketing, and examples might include tangible items such as newspapers or magazines, print ads and business cards. It can also include posters, commercials on TV and radio, billboards and brochures. Traditional marketing is anything except digital means to advertise a product.

As Yasminet al., (2015) indicated "traditional marketing is the most recognizable form of marketing". It is a non-digital way to promote the product or services of an organization. On the other hand, digital marketing is the marketing of products or services, that utilizes digital channels to reach consumers.

Leeflang, et al. (2014) have found that, with regards to digital channels, home pages, e-mail and social media were the most commonly used. Social media and mobile applications represent the biggest indicator of growth for companies. Digital marketing capabilities (DMCs) contribute positively to performance. Firms with greater entrepreneurial orientation leverage DMCs more effectively and have better performance. Small firms with strong digital capabilities perform as well as medium-sized firms (Wang, 2020).

Acceptance of internet marketing, as suggested by Pomirleanu, et al. (2013), is visible from the academic community as there is an increasing number of published journals and studies around this subject, including in journals dedicated to marketing, which demonstrates how this trend brings new opportunities to position researchers on this area.

According to Pavlou and Stewart (2000) the internet makes some things simpler and cheaper with regards to communication with consumers, as it helps consumers communicate with each other, and assists in selling products and services to them, using other media and distribution channels. In fact, that digital marketing when used wisely, makes marketing more effective and marketing objectives are met with less cost and with focus on intended market segments only (Kapoor & Kapoor, 2021).

E-Mail Marketing Communications

As Merisavo and Raulas (2004) have stated, e-mail is a tool that contributes to improving brand loyalty and supporting marketers to communicate regularly with their customers, at a relatively low cost compared with printed mail.

E-mail supports targeted and personalized marketing communications and has become a marketing communication medium to share updates about services and products, product promotions, direct consumers to a brand's website, and other initiatives.

To carry out such marketing initiatives, professionals use newsletters, reward programs, e-mail promotions and communication building.

According to Chittenden and Rettie (2003), e-mail is "the fastest-growing communication technology in recent history, growing from two million e-mail accounts in 1985 to 891.1 million e-mail accounts at 2001". Considering this fast-growing channel of marketing communication, professionals have begun to understand how much cheaper, quicker, and easier this online toll could be, and its potential.

They acknowledge that e-mail can provide them the possibility of establishing a two-way communication channel that allows for a relationship with the costumer and for further interactions.

The same author mentioned that a report by Forrester Research in August 2001, showed that almost 90 per cent of US e-mail marketing was directed at existing customers. As part of this research, fifty US marketing professionals were interviewed, and asked "Do you use e-mail to accomplish the following marketing goals? How effective is it?". The results of this study demonstrated that the focus of e-mail initiatives is customer retention.

According to Salehi et al. (2012) internet marketing is more economical and quicker than non-internet marketing and is considered a way to target consumers directly, with the possibility of advertising locally or internationally. E-mail marketing is seen as a form of direct marketing which uses electronic means to deliver commercial messages to an audience and has the ability to trigger an immediate impact.

Chittenden and Rettie (2003) believe that consumers and customers treat their e-mail inboxes as a personal domain. Since organizations require permission to send messages and contact customers and consumers, they have the capacity to enrich consumers and customers profiles and the ability to build a profitable relationship with them.

This author also did a clickthrough analysis study in 30 campaigns and their response rates, which suggested that the length of an e-mail has a significant effect, meaning that lower responding e-mails had a bigger length and more scrolls, and a bigger number of images has a lower effect on the response rate.

As suggested by Merisavo and Raulas (2004), keeping a regular contact with customers supports marketing professionals in determining and enhancing customer loyalty. Direct mail can be used to cross and up-sell and lead customers to be more active and purchase more, as the more customers buy or respond to marketing e-mails, the more accurate is the perception of customer's loyalty.

Fariborzi and Zahedifard (2012) suggested a few disadvantages in e-mail marketing, such as undelivered e-mail, since e-mail service providers put a lot of filters to avoid spam, it is difficult to assure those e-mails are delivered). The authors suggested that it is expensive to deliver a sophisticated e-mail that will stay in the consumers mind, as it requires resources to think about the e-mail design and create it. Finally, the authors considered it can be overloading for consumers to get a high number of e-mails in their inbox from different organizations, and they might struggle to separate which are relevant or nonrelevant to them.

Marketing Performance and Key Performance Indicators

Marketing professionals are continuously under pressure to show their contribution to their organization's performance. O'Sullivan and Abela (2007) have found that to respond to this pressure, marketing professionals are investing in developing performance measurement abilities.

According to Saura et al. (2017) with regards to digital marketing, key performance indicators play an important role in formulating marketing strategies. As digital marketing metrics are evolving, it might be challenging to calculate the return of investment of a campaign in digital marketing. Organizations need to use all available information to analyze whether the budget spent on digital marketing initiatives is generating more business in return.

As stated by Gronholdt and Martensen (2006), there is a value chain which links marketing actions to the financial performance of the company. This value chain provides a wider view to create a better understanding of the profit generated by marketing activities. This study also concluded that many moderating factors could impact moving from one stage to the other in a value chain, such as quality of marketing programs, market conditions, competitiveness, customer characteristics, etc.

Gronholdt and Martensen (2006) systematized the most valuable marketing performance measures based on an extensive literature review. However, keeping in mind that organization and market conditions changes quite quickly, these measures might need to be revisited in the future and will most likely change over time. A unique set of performance measures that could be applied to all companies regardless of their industry and market conditions hardly exists.

Monitoring performance, as stated by Ambler et al. (2004), is a tool to support planned marketing activities, to achieve the desired results. Metrics choice is a very important process which provides the ability for marketing managers to improve performance by changing the marketing key variables.

According to Saura et al. (2017) each individual company can make use of different key performance indicators in digital marketing according to its business needs. This literature review is consensual in terms of identifying useful key performance indicators with the following parameters: they should be measurable, achievable (the objective set in the KPI must be credible) and available for a time period (KPIS must be available for a reasonable time period).

To Milichovsky and Simberova (2015) the right choice of performance indicators is part of the company's strategic process. However, this selection process is difficult due to the complexity of certain measurable areas. For the purposes of measuring marketing effectiveness, it is necessary to focus on customers and their potential behavior trend. Due to this, it is very important to choose the right measurement, corresponding to their current market situation, to support potential expansion.

As markets become more and more competitive, Gounaris et al. (2007) have demonstrated that companies largely rely on their ability to better understand their markets, and therefore being able to run effective marketing information systems becomes essential. An effective system can improve information Marketing business processes in a multinational organization processing in a timelier manner, as this supports management decision making and provides a clearer picture of customers' needs to the marketing professionals.

Permission-Based E-Mail Marketing

Tezinde et al. (2002) defined permission marketing as a promotional e-mail to recipients who consented to receive commercial messages from the sender, typically by signing up at the organization's website. This is based on the consumers' explicit consent to receive marketing and commercial messages, and provided with the possibility of declining to receive e-mails at any time.

To effectively engage with a community of customers, brands must ask for permission. Permission marketing, introduced by Godin (1999), revolves around this idea of asking for customers' consent prior to delivering marketing messages. However, when asking for permission, brands must act as friends with sincere desires to help, not hunters with bait (Kotler et al., 2017).

Marinova et al. (2002) added that permission marketing improves the relationship with customers who have given the marketing professional the go-ahead to send them information about a product, a service, special offer or sale. This approach decreases the mailing volume, but also enhances the percentage of success and becomes a potentially more effective use of information technology. Consumers who allow their names to be added on e-mail lists can foresee receiving commercial and marketing messages, which from the company perspective can be personalized, so they can be more relevant to the customer's needs.

The adoption of permission-based email marketing enables establishing strong relationships between companies and their target audiences, developing emotional, conative, and cognitive responses to the distributed messages. Therefore, salespersons should ensure compliance with legal requirements in email marketing and develop effective strategies of reducing spam emails to avoid negative impressions and increase response rates (Rosário, 2021).

According to Merisavo and Raulas (2004) while the increasing number of unsolicited ("junk") mail threatens consumers' acceptance of e-mail marketing, consumers who have given permission to be contacted may appreciate receiving brand information from the marketing professional whom they want to hear from. Permission allows consumers to make the choice on whether they wish to be subjected to communications or not. The principal of targeting those who voluntarily provided contact permission increases the chance of consumers paying more attention to the message. But even with permission, the consumer does not open all e-mails. Mouro and Alturas (2016) concluded that the factor that most influences the opening of an e-mail are promotions and campaigns.

Marinova et al. (2002) indicated that permission marketing involves a long-term process that requires the organization to plan a strategy by investing time, information, and resources. The outcome of this approach can potentially result in having an active and interactive relationship between the organization and the consumer. Marketers can plan marketing campaigns considering the volume of e-mail permissions, which allows them to gain a better understanding of their consumer's data base and have a better idea of who may give them permission in the long run.

Godin (1999) emphasized the importance of opt-in e-mail, mentioning that getting consumer's permission to receive tailored and customized e-mail communications improved segmentation and targeting precision.

However, Chittenden and Rettie (2003) noticed that in case customers and consumers receive e-mails they do not want and unsubscribe, this has a big cost on the list owner, as the organization can no longer communicate with them. The organization will face reduced ability to market to these customers and consumers and less capacity to advertise useful product information or new product marketing.

Krafft et al. (2017) have conducted a study in marketing permissions and privacy matters, which suggested that due to high registration effort, privacy matters can stop users from providing e-mail permission. Those concerns with privacy and bureaucratic processes can negatively influence the consumers when it comes to providing consent on e-mail permission to receive marketing content.

Digital Marketing Content

Koiso-Kantilla (2004) suggested that the concept of digital content marketing, as being delivered to consumers or customers in a digital form, has a strong contribution to the commercial landscape. As cited by Opreana and Vinerean (2015), content marketing can be used as a tool to create added value in distributing relevant and consistent content, and to be able to attract and keep a consumer audience and transform it into a profitable relationship between consumer and company. There are currently a series of digital content forms, such as slideshow presentations, e-books, blogs, vlogs, images, text, infographics, and many other forms delivered using electronic means.

Rowley (2008) highlighted the relevance of information in marketing messages, both with regards to image design and call to action, and the need to use interactive content within e-marketing communication. According to Kalyanam and McIntyre (2002), e-marketing focuses on relational exchanges in digital and interactive environments. Additionally, marketing communication distributed through digital channels has brought new approaches with regards to content display such as: banner ads, portal and search engines, trackable URL's, hyperlinks, e-mails, e-mail newsletter etc.

Baltes (2015) concluded that content marketing is a key tool, especially when it comes to the development of digital marketing and broadly speaking, of marketing itself. To be able to have a successful digital marketing strategy, quality content is a key factor, and organizations need to conduct deeper research in order to design and build content marketing that meets the consumer's interest. The target goal of content marketing is to educate audiences, inform them, and be able to build a privileged relationship with them. To be able to build a powerful brand and be relevant for consumers, organizations must win their trust and admiration, and must aim to be able to determine brand loyalty. Retaining loyal customers and changing inactive ones to be active are major challenges that service organizations currently face (

Chittenden and Rettie (2003) also concluded that e-mail content can be related to the unsubscribe rate, if there are any key elements which contribute to the consumers and customers unsubscribe rate. If this is the case, it could be analyzed by looking at the e-mail content design. These authors conducted a study which analyzed 30 live marketing campaigns and sorted them in a descending manner according to the unsubscribe percentage. In this analysis, the length of the e-mail (number of scrolls) seems to affect the percentage of people who unsubscribed.

Marketing Information Systems

As a result of digital transformation, the role of marketing for consumers and businesses has rapidly evolved (Hair et al., 2018). Digital transformation, alongside data analytics and mobile devices, have empowered consumers and businesses to make quick decisions at the speed of a search or click.

According to Wang (2008) web-based destination marketing systems have been used as a marketing tool by organizations. This is defined as a system which uses computer and communication technologies, using the internet to fulfil the system functioning. He also suggested that in today's competitive market having a web presence is not enough, and that successful web marketing requires an understanding of the key factors supporting its management and implementation.

As cited by Layton (2007), a marketing information system is a network of individuals, groups and/or entities linked directly or indirectly though sequential or shared participation in economic exchange that creates a set of products, both tangible and intangible, provided in response to a customer demand (Layton, 2007). The output of marketing systems is a set of products, tangible and intangible based on several attributes such as location, price, and quality.

Another author suggested that a marketing system is a group of complete facilities and procedures that are carried out to provide the administration with accurate information related to marketing environment, opportunities, strategies, and marketing plans (Alafeef, 2015).

McLeod Jr. and Rogers (2015) believe that marketing information systems can support organization's managers in to planning, organizing, staff and control. Additionally, marketing information systems support marketing decisions, taking into consideration the so-called marketing mix: product, pricing, distribution, and promotion. Also marketing information systems are important when utilized by contemporary business ventures seeking to internationalize their operations (Limański et al., 2018).

Nedeva (2004) investigated and reviewed a set of marketing information systems, using different review criteria upon two major dimensions: functional purpose and information technology purpose. In terms of functional criteria, the conclusions demonstrated that using information integration within the different data sources, can contribute to bring more satisfaction to management, in terms of decision making. The internet and web-based work have a big influence on the information readiness to help marketing professionals making decisions (Alshurideh, 2019).

With regards to information technology, platform independence has been demonstrated to be very important to provide the ability to adapt marketing systems, and to have the capacity to receive data from different sources. Security of information has been revealed to be a very important asset, especially with regards to accessing the internet when there is a big number of users operating in the marketing system. The management and marketing literature especially, have almost exclusively viewed technology as a mean to the end of meeting user requirements. Marketers see technology as a means by which needs and wants are met (DesAutels et al., 2014).

The conceptual design of comprehensive marketing information systems that support a company in decision making gives competitive advantages (Torres et al., 2017). According to Ismail (2011), marketing information system design is important, as their quality has been demonstrated to impact the effectiveness of decision making. The function of marketing information systems is to provide decision makers with timely and trustworthy data to facilitate the implementation of the necessary measures and decisions. The following are four elementary pillars: Data base, marketing intelligence, marketing research and marketing information analytics, which are relevant with regards to designing a marketing information system.

EVALUATION MODEL

Model of Organizational Impact of Systems

The impact of technologies is often indirectly influenced by human, organizational and environmental factors, so it is difficult and complex to measure the success of Information Systems (IS).

According to Gorla et al., (2010) and cited by Martins and Alturas (2016), the model used to assess the organizational impact (Figure 1) comes from the Quality of the system, which represents the processing quality of the system itself, the Quality of the information concerning the quality of the results of the information produced by the system, and the Quality of the service, which is defined as the degree of discrepancy between the consumer's expectation of the service and their perception of the service's performance (Martins & Alturas, 2016). A study with data gathered from China automotive companies' customers, demonstrated that costumers' perceived information quality, system quality and service quality positively caused the user satisfaction in the cloud-based marketing system (Liu & Wang, 2022).

Figure 1. Model of organizational impact of systems proposed by Gorla et al. (2010)

Model Constructs

Organizational impact at an organizational level can be classified into two categories: organizational impacts which are internal to the organization and organizational impacts which are external to the organization (Gorla et al., 2010).

Organizational impact consists of five indicators, two of which are related to internal impact (product cost control and internal organizational efficiency) and three to external impact (supplier switching/research costs, product and service improvements, and market information support). Product cost control concerns cost reduction, new product design and product marketing. Internal organizational efficiency reflects efficiency in the decision-making process, internal communication/coordination, strategic planning and profit margin. Supplier switching/search costs reflect the ease with which it is possible to find alternative suppliers and products/services, and the profitability of suppliers in bargaining power. Product and service improvements are responsible for improving the quality and availability of products/services to the customer. Market information support has been defined as the information provided to the company in relation to customer needs, market trends and new markets (Gorla et al., 2010).

According to Gorla et al., (2010), the quality of the system "represents the quality of the information system processing itself, which includes software and data components, and it is a measure of the extent to which the system is technically sound". The attributes for system quality are grouped into two categories: system resources from the architect's perspective (called system flexibility) and system resources from the end user's perspective (called system sophistication).

The flexibility category of the system considers two factors: the system must be designed with necessary and useful resources, that is, without unnecessary resources, and modifications to the software which can be easily made by the architect.

The sophisticated category of the system denotes a user-friendly system (which is easy to use, intuitive), well documented, with fast response times and modern technology that allows ease of use.

Gorla et al (2010) have stated that the quality of information "refers to the quality of outputs the information system produces, which can be in the form of reports or online screens". This can be defined in four dimensions: accuracy, integrity, consistency, and format:

- Accuracy is the agreement with an attribute about an entity in the real world, a value stored in another database, or the result of an arithmetic calculation.
- Integrity must be defined with respect to a given application and relates to the presence of all relevant information relating to the application in question.
- Consistency refers to the absence of conflict between two datasets, and timeliness refers to using the most current information possible.
- The format is related to the presentation layer of the information to the user.

The four dimensions are brought together and divided into two categories for the quality of the information: the content of the information and the format of the information. The content of the information measures the relevance of the information presented to the user in the reports, and its accuracy and integrity. The information format measures the style in which the information is presented to the user and if it is presented in an easy-to-understand format.

Gorla et al. (2010) have defined service quality as "the degree of discrepancy between customers' normative expectations for service and their perceptions of service performance". This characteristic is measured by four indicators: reliability, responsiveness, safety, and empathy:

- Reliability measures the extent of the supplier's effort to improve the information services provided to users.
- Responsiveness includes parameters that measure the extent to which the provider is willing to assist users and provide a rapid service.
- Security is the supplier's ability to build a relationship of trust with users.
- Empathy measures the personal attention and concern provided by the supplier.

The importance of quality of information and quality of service provided are often related. In a study published in 2021, it was shown that these constructs have an organizational impact, through the benefits obtained and the impact on the end user (Alvim & Alturas, 2021).

It should be noted that the three constructs of the model are related to security and privacy. The quality of the system must guarantee data security and privacy. The quality of the information also means that the information is secure, and that no information is kept that violates the privacy of customers. Finally, quality of service implies a secure service with respect for everyone's privacy.

METHODOLOGY

This study was conducted using a qualitive exploratory approach, and data collection was based on semi-structured interviews. Thematic analysis was carried out, since as suggested by Braun and Clarke (2006), this promotes interaction between participants allowing them to share their ideas, beliefs and thoughts (Braun & Clarke, 2006). This approach allows for open-ended questions within the interview, providing the flexibility and the ability to gain powerful insights from the participants, capturing feelings, impressions and understandings. Thematic analysis reports to experiences, picturing the reality of the participants. In order to connect and guide the semi-structured interviews with the MCP benefits analysis, a model was chosen, as suggested by Gorla et al., (2010) in order to measure impact on information systems in organizations. This model aims to evaluate a system considering the following main pillars: system quality, service quality and information quality. The interview structure followed these three focus areas and each of these individual areas or constructs (system quality, service quality and information quality) had a set of relevant questions. A total of 12 questions were part of the interview process (Table 1).

To be able to measure the importance and recognized benefits by the users of the Marketing Cloud Platform, the interviews were carried out, lasting approximately 20 minutes, over the phone. These users have a relevant role in the marketing department of their organization. Interviews were recorded and transcript. To carry out text analysis, the Leximancer online platform was used to find relationships between words (Leximancer, 2021). Leximancer built the relationship between words stated by the users through the interview process; those relationships supported the analysis of recognized benefits, as well as an overview on system quality, service quality and information quality. In this context, the following Research Goals (RG) were elaborated:

- RG1 - Analyze main limits of previous situation before going for MCP.
- RG2 - Analyze service quality within MPC:
    - Analyze the impact of MCP on interactions with the end customers.
    - Analyze what are the main features in MCP as recognized by the users in their daily tasks.
- RG3 - Analyze information quality within MCP: how the available measures and data in MCP support taking marketing related decisions.
- RG4 - Analyze system quality within MCP: Analyse how flexible the platform is in adapting to new business needs.
- RG5 - Analyze benefits recognized by the users when using MCP.

Table 1 shows the link between each interview section, which corresponds to a model construct, and the research goals.

Table 1. Interview questions.

Section 1 - Marketing Cloud Platform Implementation Motivation (RG1)
Q1: What is the name of your function in the organization?
Q2: In terms of managing marketing business processes, what were the main limits of the previous situation before implementing Marketing Cloud platform?
Q3: Why did the organization decide to go for Marketing Cloud Platform to manage marketing business processes?
Q4: How does the implemented solution cover the limits of previous situation?
Section 2 - Service Quality (RG2)
Q5: Has the platform contributed to the increase of interactions of consumers with your brand? If so, what measures are more significant to capture those?
Q6: Has the solution contributed to increase consumer's brand awareness? If so, how?
Q7: Considering the implemented marketing tool, what features do you consider key to support your daily activities?
Q8: Is there any other benefit of using Marketing Cloud Platform you would like to mention?
Section 3 - Information Quality (RG3)
Q9: Has the integrated data coming from different sources contributed to enrich consumer profile information? If so, how?
Q10: How has the available data and measures in the marketing tool supported decision taking in marketing initiatives?
Section 4 - System Quality (RG4)
Q11: How flexible the tool is in adapting to new business needs? Please specify.
Q12: Are you confident in terms of information security management of the marketing tool? Please specify.

The targeted sampling of this study was the users who use MCP on their daily business tasks. They use the same Platform to manage marketing business processes and interact with their end customers. That said, three users were available to provide their input and participate on the interviews, two persons had strategic positions with regards to Marketing business in their organization and one user worked as the bridge between Marketing and E-commerce business processes.

The interviewed participants were contacted via LinkedIn, it was explained the relevance of the study and the importance of their input. The interview questions were shared in advance with the participants, to make them more aware of the topics to be discussed.

FINDINGS AND DISCUSSION

After uploading the answers, using Leximancer, the text was analyzed, and a list of concepts was built based on words and their relationship to each other. That information was shown in a Conceptual Map. In this graphical representation it was visible the name of main concepts taken from the interview replies text which are represented by words connected to circles (Leximancer, 2021). Themes were shown in the Conceptual map as colored circles grouping cluster of concepts. The circle colors are heat-map based, meaning that hot colors (orange, red) represent the most relevant themes.

Below there is a list of analysis and comparisons that were carried out using Leximancer to find relationships between words.

RG1. Analyze limits of previous marketing business processes situation before implementing MCP.

The conceptual map was presented showing the analysis of previous situations before implementing MCP. The connection between concepts like "Time", "Understand", "Marketing" and "Communication" themes was visible. Based on the reply's analysis, the Global Marketing Manager mentioned that before implementation MCP a lot of marketing processes were manual and the lack of automation in running the business processes was very time consuming.

Other relevant concepts were visible in the Conceptual map such as "understand", "know", "database". The users mentioned in the replies not being able to communicate with the customer, promote products or relevant information of the brand. Global Commerce Solution Directors said they could not understand the database, which makes it more complicated to get to know the customer and their interests, in order to perform targeted and personalized marketing communications.

RG2.1. Analyze the impact of MCP on interactions with customers.

In the conceptual map, the "marketing" theme was connected to the following concepts: "clicks", "information" and "campaign". Within the analysis of the replies, the Global Commerce Director and Marketing and Loyalty Director, said the interaction with customers had increased. They captured e-mail campaign measures such as number of clicks, clickthrough to measure interactions with customers and customer's interest on certain topics. These measures provide insights in understanding what content is more appealing to customers, considering the amount of interaction with the e-mail. The Global Marketing Manager noticed that there has been an increase in e-mail open rates and click throughs since they started using MCP.

"Subscription" and "market" concepts were visible in the Conceptual Map, since users noticed that there has been an increase in subscriptions and customers registering in the company's website, triggered by specific marketing campaigns. They capture subscription rates in order to compare the number of new subscriptions against the traffic the website that has been generated from specific marketing campaigns.

The Global Commerce Director and Marketing and Loyalty Director believed the interactions with customers through marketing campaigns contributed to an increase in brand awareness, as they were sending marketing communications not only focused on products, but also sharing more information about the brand and the company itself.

RG2.2 Analyze user's perception of MCP features to support daily tasks.

The conceptual map shows a perception of MCP features with relationship to marketing, suggesting that there is a relationship between the two.

The concepts of "Campaign" and "Segmentation" are connected to the "Marketing" theme, having most of the terms been generated by text analysis. When looking at the users replies, the Global Marketing Manager mentioned that campaign building is a key feature to bring a lot more relevant content to the customers. On top of this, it was mentioned that automation in campaign run contributed to a quicker pace in sharing content with customers.

It was possible to see a connection between the "Database", "Communication" and "Audience" concepts. The Marketing and Loyalty Director highlighted that understanding the database was an obvious feature they perceived, which allows them to know more about the customer and get a better insight about their profile. They were segmenting customers in MCP and using analytical reports to better understand the marketing campaign's audience.

The Global Commerce Director said that MCP helped to speak to customers with regards to general communication of the organization and brand promotion.

RG3. Analyze the importance of MCP in taking business decisions.

In the Conceptual Map when looking at the "marketing" theme, there was a visible connection between a few concepts such as "Rates", "Clickthrough", "Reporting", "Information" and "E-mails". The Global Commerce Director mentioned that the number of clicks and the number of opened e-mails are relevant information in the decision-making process. Having insight on the number of clicks on certain products in a marketing e-mail, helps the user understand what products were more relevant to the customer and in making decisions regarding future marketing campaigns. They analyzed e-mail open rates and clickthrough interactions as well as A/B Testing, to understand which content was more interesting to the end customers. Within A/B testing, a few e-mail design variants are sent to a testing customer audience. The e-mail variant with the most interactions (for example number of clicks) is considered the winning e-mail and is then sent to the remaining customers' data base. The Global Marketing Manager has stated that as the organization grows with the use of MCP, they aim to have a constant review of marketing campaigns analytical reports.

He also stated that they are now able to track e-mail failures Analyzing this data has created an opportunity to turn something negative into an opportunity. This is something that could not be done before the implementation of MCP. Additionally, with MCP they had the chance to conduct data cleansing on their customer's database, which allows for a clearer picture on their active customer's audience.

RG4. Analyze how flexible MCP is in adjusting to new business needs.

In the Conceptual Map (Figure 2) we can see a few concepts highlighted such as "needs", "requests", "Flexibility", "Requirements" and "Opportunities", connected to marketing. The Global Commerce Director and the Marketing and Loyalty Director considered MCP to be a flexible platform, easily adjusted to business needs. They are expecting the business to grow fast, with technology supporting this growth They expect the technology (MCP) to be able to follow that fast-growing pace, not only in terms of volume, but also in terms of offering innovative solutions for marketing business processes management. They mentioned that they would like to continue to benefit from new functionalities and evolutions, since as described before, MCP is a cloud-based platform launching new marketing features on a quarterly basis.

The Global Marketing Manager believes that MCP fits the organization's needs and facilitates different kinds of campaign building. As there are people in the organization and its subsidiaries working in different ways, following different processes, in the future they planned to expand MCP to those subsidiaries, so that the platform is be able to run different kinds of campaigns.

Figure 2. Conceptual map with analysis of MCP flexibility in adapting to new business needs

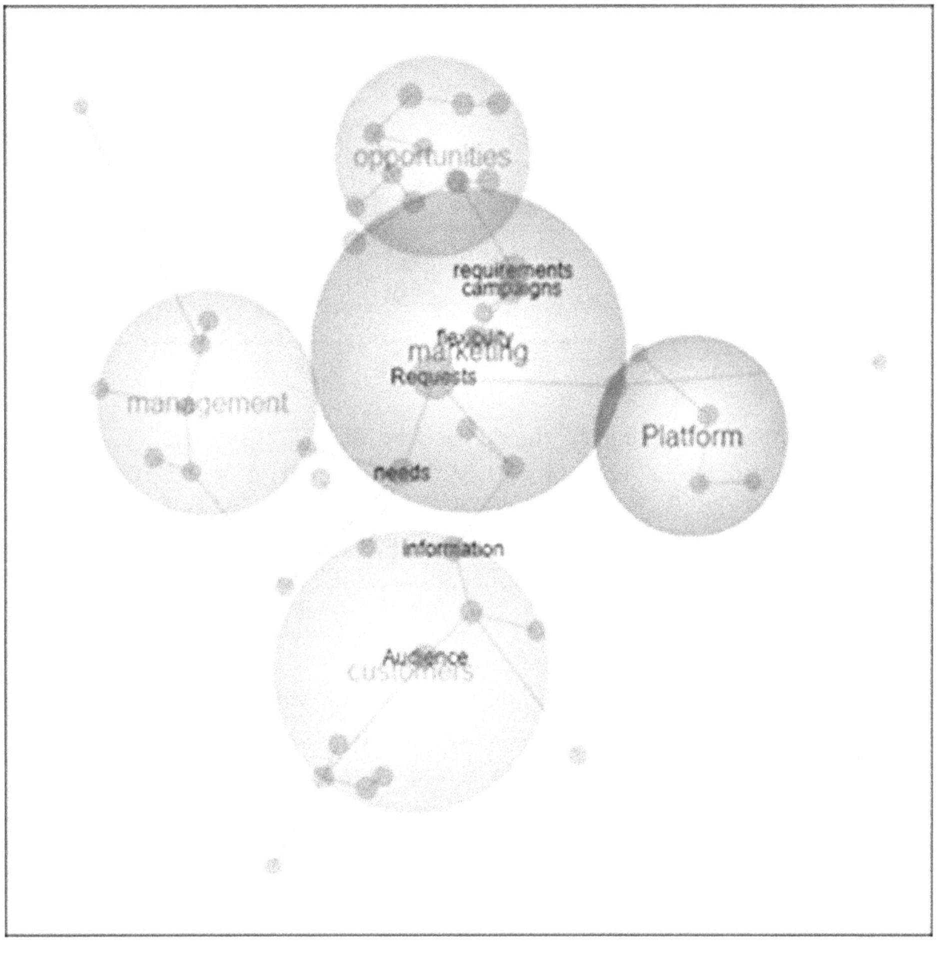

RG5. Analysis of benefits recognized by the users when using MCP.

There was a synopsis analysis taken from Leximancer (Figure 3) which shows the relevance of "benefit". The synopsis analysis output was split into two main areas: themes and hits. Themes (themes column) are ranked by their relevance, as represented in the circles (conceptual Map). Hits are visible in the hit's column; this represents the number of text blocks associated with a theme (Leximancer, 2021).

Figure 3. Synopsis analysis of MCP recognized benefits

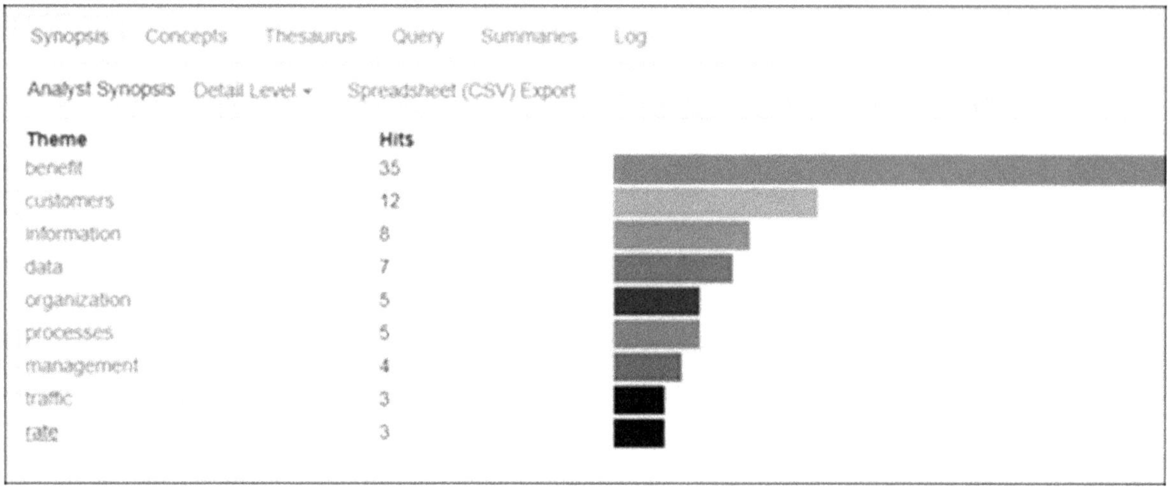

As displayed on Figure 3, the "benefit" theme has a hit of 35, "customers" has a hit of 12, "information" 8, "data" 7, "organization" and "processes" 5, "management" 4, "traffic" and "rate" 3. This information aligns with the Conceptual Map shown in Figure 4, where we can see that the "benefit" theme was represented with a red color, demonstrating it is very relevant (hot color) for the analysis. The relationship between those themes is explained in the section below, alongside an interpretation of the Conceptual Map.

As visible in Figure 4, the "Benefit" theme is connected to the concepts of "target", "communication", "automation" and "campaigns". The "Benefit" theme circle was represented with a hot color (red). Users stated in the interview replies that a key benefit was the campaign automation when promoting a product or sharing information on the brand. In Figure 4, we see a connection between the "benefit", "processes", "management" and "organization" themes. If we look deeper at the "benefit" theme, we see a connection with the "automation" concept. As previously described, the automation of a campaign could be recognized as a process improvement, leading to a less time consuming and less manual campaign building process.

Figure 4. Analysis of benefits recognized by the users when using MCP

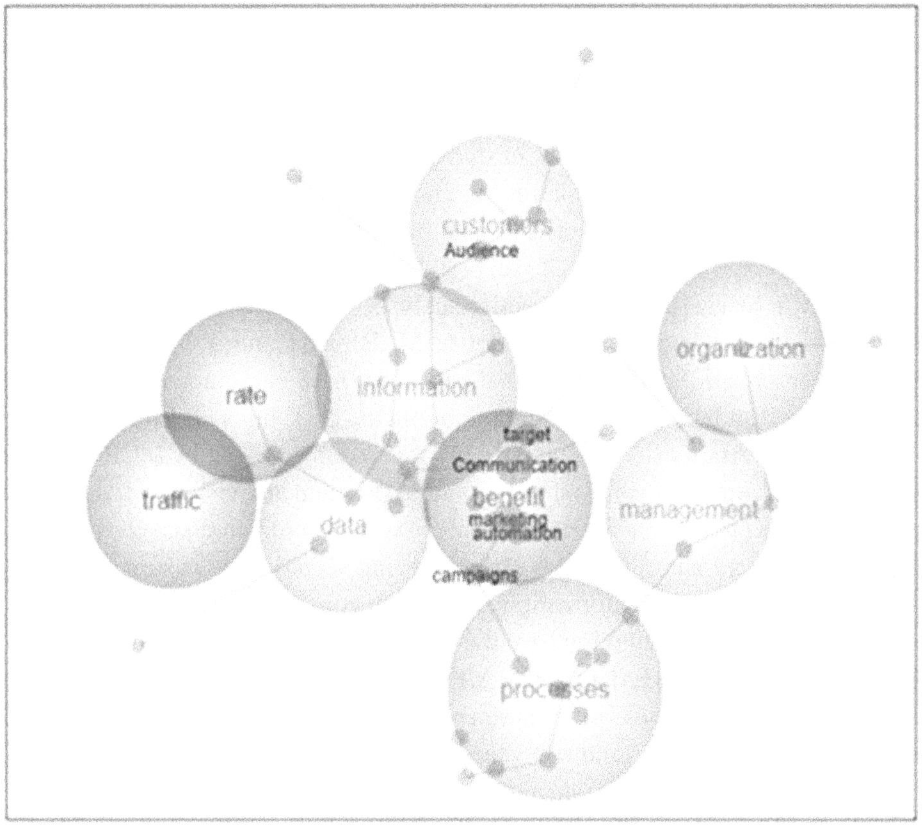

Looking at the link between the "target" concept and the "benefit" theme from the user's perspective, segmentation and customers targeting was described to be very helpful in MCP, in finding out what customers want to be included in certain marketing initiatives. They highlighted that communication with end customers has been improved, being able to send personalized marketing communication, tailored to the customers interests, based on previous interactions. Connection between other themes was also visible such as "Data", "Information" and "Customers". It has been mentioned that an important benefit to achieve was to get to better know the data base, to understand their customer audience, their interests, and their navigation behavior in the brand website.

Finally, we have themes, such as "rate" and "traffic", visible in the conceptual map. Users said that there was an increase of traffic on the brand's website triggered by certain marketing campaigns. They noticed that e-mail opening rates have increased since they started using MCP. Marketing e-mail content could contribute to this increase, as they believed to be sending personalized content according to the available customer information, such as number of clicks in certain items in e-mails, interests, and website navigation behavior.

Although we are not aware of other studies on the organizational impact of MCP, the results found are in line with the results of other studies on the organizational impact of other information systems (Alvim & Alturas, 2021; Costa et al., 2016; Martins & Alturas, 2016).

CONCLUSIONS AND IMPLICATIONS

Although there is an increasing demand for information systems which can provide information in real time to organizations and improve processes automation, it was noticed that in some organizations achieving that could be a work in progress.

From the perspective of the organizations in study, before using MCP, a lot of marketing processes were very manual and time consuming. Getting to know their customers was challenging, which had an impact on communication, as they wanted to send relevant and tailored marketing communications to their customers.

With regards to MCP service quality perspective analysis, there were two focus areas: impact of MCP on interactions with customers and user's perception on MCP main features. There was a set of marketing e-mail campaigns measures in MCP showing that customers have continuously increased interactions, as demonstrated through an increase in the number of clicks, URL links clickthrough and e-mail open rates. It was noticed that certain marketing campaigns advertisements sent by MCP were increasing the traffic on the brand's website. The achieved product advertisement and visibility triggered by MCP was relevant, as it was pointing to the website page where customers could purchase the product. In addition to this, as the marketing communications have been flowing according to customers interests, with regards to product information, brand information and organization updates, the MCP users believed that tailored communication contributed to improve the brand's awareness next to customers.

When looking at key features recognized by MPC users, marketing campaign building was recognized as a main feature, which helps bring more content to the customers, not only from a relevancy perspective, but also from a higher volume perspective. Campaign building in MCP was considered a highly automated process and efficient from a time perspective. Segmentation capabilities in MCP were highlighted by the users as a key feature in getting the right marketing content to be sent to the right audience. Individual customer profile insights in MPC, was also shown to be relevant in terms of getting to know more, not only from an audience perspective, but from an individual customer viewpoint too.

Regarding information quality analysis in MCP in support of marketing business decisions, users believed that the available e-mail campaign marketing measures were relevant to support decisions regarding marketing initiatives. Having the information of a set of e-mail campaigns measures in MCP, helped the users to understand what products were more relevant and interesting to customers and decide on what content should be included in future marketing initiatives. Additionally, the available marketing analytical reports in MCP provide the possibility to track marketing e-mail failures, which provides the chance to get a better understanding of their customer database and a clearer picture of their active customers.

In terms of system quality and focusing on the flexibility of MCP to adapt to new business needs, the users believed that MCP fits organization's needs, as it works as a campaign building app with the flexibility to adapt to new and different campaign types. This flexibility is a key feature, as it is planned to expand MCP to other subsidiaries in the organization. Having users doing the marketing business processes in different ways, MCP is expected to fit everyone's needs in the organization.

Summing up, MCP users stated it was beneficial to communicate better with the customers, to address the right content to the right audience and to be able to send personalized and tailored marketing communications to customers. Marketing segmentation and the possibility to target the right audience for a certain product advertisement, was also recognized as being a key benefit.

The possibility to drill down from a customer audience to a specific individual customer profile was considered relevant to get further insight about a specific individual customer if needed. As it has been mentioned, a key benefit was to get to know the customers better and understand their interests. The available marketing campaign measures were considered very important to evaluate what product advertising content was relevant for a certain audience and help decide what product related content should be included in future marketing initiatives. Finally, from a data security perspective, users commented they have no reasons to not trust MCP so far and consider it to be a robust platform from a data security perspective.

A limitation of this study was related to the few numbers of organizations who were part of this research using the same MCP. Therefore, having the chance to interview more organizations who use the same MCP could contribute to a deeper understanding of benefits of MCP in managing marketing business processes.

The analysis of KPI readiness in MCP to make marketing business decisions was based on e-mail marketing campaigns measures and interactions that customers engage in when navigating in the brand's website triggered by certain marketing campaigns Eventually other marketing KPIs could be useful to get a wider view on this matter.

In future research it could be beneficial to interview more organizations and have organizations from different business industries. Therefore, other analysis and comparisons could be done, such as for example finding out for business industry "X" what are the main benefits of using MCP, in comparison to business industry "Y".

Also, the item flexibility may include the analyses of the relevance of the treatment of Big Data and its effects on Organizational Impact, namely on market information support. It should also be thought how the use of Artificial Intelligence to interact with the consumer, collect and treat data could affect the System Quality and Organization Impact. Technologies such as AI, Big Data, CyberSecurity, Ethics and its potential impact on the implementation and use of marketing information systems, should be considered in future studies.

Other aspect that could be valuable is to interview people with different profiles, such as: marketeer, marketing director, system administrator/developer, social media manager and creative content manager. Those different stakeholders with different connections to the marketing business could have a different view and give more diverse inputs on MCP key functionalities, analysis and overall benefits. In future research, it would be interesting to have wider marketing KPI's, in order to be able to conduct a deeper analysis on the information's readiness to support marketing business decisions.

REFERENCES

Alafeef, M. A. M. I. (2015). The impact of marketing information system to increase the marketing efficiency of stores in KSA (case study-Al-baha and Beljarshy city). *British Journal of Marketing Studies*, *3*(5), 22–33.

Alshurideh, D. M. (2019). Do electronic loyalty programs still drive customer choice and repeat purchase behaviour? *International Journal of Electronic Customer Relationship Management*, *12*(1), 40–57. doi:10.1504/IJECRM.2019.098980

Alvim, D., & Alturas, B. (2021). Impact on organisations of changes in information systems: The case of two Lisbon universities. *International Journal of Information and Operations Management Education*, *7*(2), 137. doi:10.1504/IJIOME.2021.119105

Ambler, T., Kokkinaki, F., & Puntoni, S. (2004). Assessing Marketing Performance: Reasons for Metrics Selection. *Journal of Marketing Management*, *20*(3–4), 475–498. doi:10.1362/0267257041323080506

Baltes, L. P. (2015). Content marketing - the fundamental tool of digital marketing. *Bulletin of the Transilvania University of Brasov. Series V, Economic Sciences*, *8*(2), 111–118.

Braun, V., & Clarke, V. (2006). Using thematic analysis in psychology Virginia. *Qualitative Research in Psychology*, *2*(3), 77–101. doi:10.1191/1478088706qp063oa

Chittenden, L., & Rettie, R. (2003). An evaluation of e-mail marketing and factors affecting response. *Journal of Targeting. Measuring and Analysis for Marketing*, *11*(3), 203–217. doi:10.1057/palgrave.jt.5740078

Costa, C. J., Ferreira, E., Bento, F., & Aparicio, M. (2016). Enterprise resource planning adoption and satisfaction determinants. *Computers in Human Behavior*, *63*, 659–671. doi:10.1016/j.chb.2016.05.090

DesAutels, P., Salehi-Sangari, E., Berthon, P., Rabinovich, T., & Pitt, L. (2014). It is emergent: Five propositions on the relationship between creative consumers and technology. *International Journal of Technology Marketing*, *9*(1), 72–85. doi:10.1504/IJTMKT.2014.058084

Fariborzi, E., & Zahedifard, M. (2012). E-mail Marketing: Advantages, Disadvantages and Improving Techniques. *International Journal of E-Education, e-Business, e-. Management Learning*, *2*(3), 232–236. doi:10.7763/IJEEEE.2012.V2.116

Figueiredo, F., Gonçalves, M. J. A., & Teixeira, S. (2021). Information technology adoption on digital marketing: A literature review. *Informatics (MDPI)*, *8*(4), 74. doi:10.3390/informatics8040074

Godin, S. (1999). *Permission Marketing: Turning Strangers into Friends, and Friends into Customers*. Simon and Schuster.

Gorla, N., Somers, T. M., & Wong, B. (2010). Organizational impact of system quality, information quality, and service quality. *The Journal of Strategic Information Systems*, *19*(3), 207–228. doi:10.1016/j.jsis.2010.05.001

Gounaris, S. P., Panigyrakis, G. G., & Chatzipanagiotou, K. C. (2007). Measuring the effectiveness of marketing information systems: An empirically validated instrument. *Marketing Intelligence & Planning*, *25*(6), 612–631. doi:10.1108/02634500710819978

Grønholdt, L., & Martensen, A. (2006). Key Marketing Performance Measures. *The Marketing Review*, *6*(3), 243–252. doi:10.1362/146934706778605287

Hair, J. F. Jr, Harrison, D. E., & Risher, J. J. (2018). Marketing research in the 21st century: Opportunities and challenges. *Revista Brasileira de Marketing*, *17*(5), 666–699. doi:10.5585/bjm.v17i5.4173

Ismail, S. T. (2011). The Role of Marketing Information System on Decision Making: An Applied study on Royal Jordanian Air Lines (RJA). *International Journal of Business and Social Science*, *2*(3), 175–185.

Kalyanam, K., & McIntyre, S. (2002). The e-marketing mix: A contribution of the e-tailing wars. *Journal of the Academy of Marketing Science*, *30*(4), 487–499. doi:10.1177/009207002236924

Kapoor, R., & Kapoor, K. (2021). The transition from traditional to digital marketing: A study of the evolution of e-marketing in the Indian hotel industry. *Worldwide Hospitality and Tourism Themes*, *13*(2), 199–213. doi:10.1108/WHATT-10-2020-0124

Koiso-Kanttila, N. (2004). Digital Content Marketing: A Literature Synthesis. *Journal of Marketing Management*, *20*(1–2), 45–65. doi:10.1362/026725704773041122

Kotler, P., Kartajaya, H., & Setiawan, I. (2017). *Marketing 4.0: Moving from Traditional to Digital*. John Wiley & Sons.

Krafft, M., Arden, C. M., & Verhoef, P. C. (2017). Permission Marketing and Privacy Concerns — Why Do Customers (Not) Grant Permissions? *Journal of Interactive Marketing*, *39*(1), 39–54. doi:10.1016/j.intmar.2017.03.001

Layton, R. A. (2007). Marketing systems - A core macromarketing concept. *Journal of Macromarketing*, *27*(3), 227–242. doi:10.1177/0276146707302836

Leeflang, P. S. H., Verhoef, P. C., Dahlström, P., & Freundt, T. (2014). Challenges and solutions for marketing in a digital era. *European Management Journal*, *32*(1), 1–12. doi:10.1016/j.emj.2013.12.001

Leximancer. (2021). *Leximancer User Guide: Vol. Release 4*. Leximancer Pty Ltd.

Limański, A., Popławska, Ż., & Drabik, I. (2018). Marketing information system and risk reduction in managing a company on foreign markets. *Ekonomia i Prawo*, *17*(1), 43. doi:10.12775/EiP.2018.004

Liu, Y., & Wang, T. (2022). Quality factors and performance outcome of cloud-based marketing system. *Kybernetes*, *51*(1), 485–503. doi:10.1108/K-11-2020-0778

Marinova, A., Murphy, J., & Massey, B. L. (2002). Permission E-mail marketing as a means of targeted promotion. *The Cornell Hotel and Restaurant Administration Quarterly*, *43*(1), 61–69. doi:10.1177/0010880402431006

Martins, A. R., & Alturas, B. (2016). Impacto organizacional da implementação de um módulo ERP em PME portuguesas [Organizational impact of implementing an ERP module in Portuguese SME*]. 11th Iberian Conference on Information Systems and Technologies*, 33–38. 10.1109/CISTI.2016.7521542

McLeod, R. Jr, & Rogers, J. C. (1985). Marketing Information Systems: Their Current Status in Fortune 1000 Companies. *Journal of Management Information Systems*, *1*(4), 57–75. doi:10.1080/07421222.1985.11517715

Merisavo, M., & Raulas, M. (2004). The impact of e-mail marketing on brand loyalty. *Journal of Product and Brand Management*, *13*(7), 498–505. doi:10.1108/10610420410568435

Milichovsky, F., & Simberova, I. (2015). Marketing effectiveness: Metrics for effective strategic marketing. *The Engineering Economist*, *26*(2), 211–219. doi:10.5755/j01.ee.26.2.3826

Mouro, C., & Alturas, B. (2016). Fatores que influenciam o consumidor a aceitar publicidade via e-mail [Factors influencing the consumer to accept advertising by e-mail]. *11th Iberian Conference on Information Systems and Technologies*, 27–32. 10.1109/CISTI.2016.7521365

Nedeva, V. I. (2004). Concept of an Integrated. *Trakia Journal of Sciences*, *2*(4), 17–21.

O'Sullivan, D., & Abela, A. (2007). Marketing performance measurement ability and firm performance. *Journal of Marketing*, *71*(2), 79–93. doi:10.1509/jmkg.71.2.079

Opreana, A., & Vinerean, S. (2015). A New Development in Online Marketing Introducing Digital Inbound Marketing. *Expert Journal of Marketing*, *3*(1), 29–34.

Pavlou, P. A., & Stewart, D. W. (2000). Measuring the Effects and Effectiveness of Interactive Advertising : A Research Agenda. *Journal of Interactive Advertising*, *1*(1), 62–78. doi:10.1080/15252019.2000.10722044

Pomirleanu, N., Schibrowsky, J., Peltier, J., & Nill, A. (2013). A review of internet marketing research over the past 20 years and future research direction. *Journal of Research in Interactive Marketing*, *7*(3), 166–181. doi:10.1108/JRIM-01-2013-0006

Rosário, A. T. (2021). E-Mail Marketing: Research and Challenges. *International Journal of Online Marketing*, *11*(4), 63–83. doi:10.4018/IJOM.2021100104

Rowley, J. (2008). Understanding digital content marketing. *Journal of Marketing Management*, *24*(5–6), 517–540. doi:10.1362/026725708X325977

Salehi, M., Mirzaei, H., Aghaei, M., & Abyari, M. (2012). Dissimilarity of E-marketing VS traditional marketing. *International Journal of Business and Social Science*, *2*(1), 510–515.

Saura, J. R., Palos-Sánchez, P., & Suárez, L. M. C. (2017). Understanding the digital marketing environment with kpis and web analytics. *Future Internet*, *9*(4), 1–13. doi:10.3390/fi9040076

Sestino, A., Prete, M. I., Piper, L., & Guido, G. (2020). Internet of Things and Big Data as enablers for business digitalization strategies. *Technovation*, *98*, 102173. doi:10.1016/j.technovation.2020.102173

Tezinde, T., Smith, B., & Murphy, J. (2002). Getting permission: Exploring factors affecting permission marketing. *Journal of Interactive Marketing*, *16*(4), 28–36. doi:10.1002/dir.10041

Todor, R. D. (2016). Blending traditional and digital marketing. *Bulletin of the Transilvania University of Brasov*, *9*(1), 51–56.

Torres, M. R., González, A. A., & Mendívil, B. C. (2017). Conceptual Model of Organizational Management as A Reference in The Development of An Integral Marketing Information System. *3c. Tic*, *6*(4), 54–69. doi:10.17993/3ctic.2017.58.54-69

Wang, F. (2020). Digital marketing capabilities in international firms: A relational perspective. *International Marketing Review*, *37*(3), 559–577. doi:10.1108/IMR-04-2018-0128

Wang, Y. (2008). Web-based Destination Marketing for Management and Implementation. *International Journal of Tourism Research*, *10*(1), 55–70. doi:10.1002/jtr.633

Yasmin, A., Tasneem, S., & Fatema, K. (2015). Effectiveness of Digital Marketing in the Challenging Age: An Empirical Study. *The International Journal of Management Science and Business Administration*, *1*(5), 69–80. doi:10.18775/ijmsba.1849-5664-5419.2014.15.1006

ADDITIONAL READING

Kingsnorth, S. (2022). *Digital Marketing Strategy: An Integrated Approach to Online Marketing* (3rd ed.). Kogan Page.

Laudon, K. C., & Laudon, J. P. (2021). *Managing Information Systems: Managing the Digital Firm* (17th ed.). Pearson.

KEY TERMS AND DEFINITIONS

Digital Marketing: Digital Marketing is any and all marketing that rely on electronic devices, and in extension, the internet. It's the group of activities that a company (or individual) performs online to attract new business opportunities, create relationships, and develop a brand identity.

E-Mail Marketing: E-mail marketing is a powerful marketing channel, a form of direct marketing as well as digital marketing, that uses email to promote your business's products or services. It can help make your customers aware of your latest items or offers by integrating it into your marketing automation efforts.

Information System: Any system that manipulates data and generates information, using or not using information technologies, can be generically considered as an information system.

Marketing Business Process: Marketing business process is the series of steps businesses follow to promote their products or services to potential customers. It involves identifying the target audience, creating a marketing strategy, implementing the plan, and capturing customer value. Essentially, it's the process of making people aware of what a business offers and convincing them to buy it.

Chapter 3
Exploring the Intersection of Digital Marketing and Retail:
Challenges and Opportunities in AI, Privacy, and Customer Experience

James Hutson
https://orcid.org/0000-0002-0578-6052
Lindenwood University, USA

Naresh Kshetri
https://orcid.org/0000-0002-3282-7331
Lindenwood University, USA

Kyle Coble
Lindenwood University, USA

Andrew Smith
Lindenwood University, USA

ABSTRACT

The objective of this chapter is to examine the impact of emerging technologies, such as AI, NLP, VR, and AR, on the digital marketing landscape. It highlights the transformative nature of these technologies in the realms of personalization, virtual retail, and customer experience enhancement. The chapter emphasizes that these technologies offer novel opportunities for businesses to engage with consumers and optimize marketing strategies. However, it also recognizes the significant security and privacy challenges arising from these advancements, particularly with regards to data mining, customer data usage, and virtual environments. Additionally, the chapter discusses the growing influence of social media platforms, influencer marketing, and voice search technology in shaping the future of digital marketing. The authors conclude by recommending that businesses prioritize data privacy and security while embracing emerging technologies to remain competitive and navigate the evolving intersection of AI, privacy, and customer experience.

DOI: 10.4018/978-1-6684-8958-1.ch003

INTRODUCTION

The digital marketing world is evolving rapidly with the emergence of innovative technologies, such as the metaverse, immersive tech, and blockchain (Rizvanović et al., 2023). These technologies are changing how businesses interact with customers, by providing personalized and immersive experiences that blend the online and in-store shopping experiences (Valaskova et al., 2022). Augmented reality (AR) and virtual reality (VR) have enabled brands to create engaging virtual experiences that enrich product visualization and increase customer loyalty (Quiroz-Guitierrez, 2022). Spatial computing, telepresence, and holographs are expected to expand digital marketing capabilities in the future (Huynh-The et al., 2023). The metaverse, a shared virtual space populated by digital representations of users, is still in development but presents many opportunities for digital marketing. As the platform evolves into a scalable and interoperable virtual space (Ball, 2022), businesses will be able to create unique customer experiences and establish deeper connections with their audience.

The interoperable virtual platform promises to go beyond current restrictions in centralized banking and provide more flexible e-commerce exchanges. Blockchain technology offers a prospect of decentralization that can address the limitations imposed by centralized digital economies (Kshetri, 2021a). This technology enables a trustworthy and user-centric digital environment (Hollensen et al., 2022) and can empower users to interact seamlessly in the digital marketing landscape (Berg et al., 2019). The foundation of contemporary digital currency market was established by blockchain technology, initially introduced with the advent of Bitcoin cryptocurrency, by enabling the creation of a shared economy (Gadekallu et al., 2022). Blockchain serves as a ledger that records committed transactions, facilitating digital asset tracking and security within financial networks. This allows for secure sharing in an insecure commercial environment without requiring a centralized authority (Yang et al., 2022).

The decentralized and transparent nature of blockchain technology, along with its consensus mechanism, proof of work, make it an excellent match for e-commerce platforms and the emerging metaverse (Avital et al., 2016; Rückeshäuser, 2017; Weber et al., 2016). By eliminating the need for intermediaries like central banks and counterparties, blockchain offers accountability and security in uncertain digital financial ecosystems (Alt & Puschmann, 2016; Nakamoto, 2008). However, the potential benefits of blockchain come with challenges as cryptocurrencies can bypass existing legislation on money laundering and facilitate illegal activities (Fanusie & Robinson, 2018; Foley et al., 2018; Möser et al., 2013). Consequently, there are calls for further regulation of distributed ledger technology in finance (Auer & Claessens, 2018; Carstens, 2018; Landau & Genais, 2018). In addition to blockchain, the emergence of immersive technologies also poses significant social, professional, and economic transformations that are likely to shape the future global economy and how information and currency are exchanged (Hutson et al., 2023). As a result, businesses need to adapt to the evolving digital landscape and its three dimensions of commerce, where physical stores, websites, and metaverse retail are essential to stay competitive (Ramadan, 2023).

Nowadays, having a website is essential for professionals and businesses as it provides a platform for customers to browse and purchase goods and services, and it also helps establish credibility and legitimacy (Ramadan, 2023). Furthermore, customers now expect high-quality product representations when shopping online. The value of a website domain, like that of a physical store, is measured by the goods and services it offers. To enhance customer experiences, companies are turning to the new virtual space provided by the emerging metaverse to create immersive, interactive, and three-dimensional products that provide a unique retail experience (Yoo et al., 2023). In addition, immersive technologies such as

AR and VR are becoming more accessible to the public due to advancements in hardware, software, and distribution channels. Consequently, top e-commerce brands are incorporating these technologies to boost engagement, memory recall, sales performance, and dwell times (Thykier, 2022). To meet the increasing demand for immersive and personalized shopping experiences, retailers are using AR technology to offer captivating virtual product visualization that replicates in-store experiences, thus strengthening customer loyalty and increasing conversion rates (Butt et al., 2023; Shah, 2023). As the metaverse continues to grow and become interoperable, retailers must leverage the potential of immersive technologies while preparing for the future integration of spatial computing, telepresence, and holographs in digital marketing and e-commerce (Huynh-The et al., 2023).

Therefore, the chapter objectives are to explore the current state of digital marketing and its transformation by emerging technologies, particularly in the areas of personalization, virtual retail, and customer experience enhancement. The chapter will also delve into the significant security and privacy challenges related to data mining, customer data usage, and virtual environments. Finally, the chapter will examine the growing influence of social media platforms, influencer marketing, and voice search technology in shaping the future of digital marketing. By the end of this chapter, readers will gain a comprehensive understanding of the impact of emerging technologies on digital marketing and how businesses can navigate this evolving landscape to remain competitive and prioritize data privacy and security.

DISRUPTIVE INNOVATIONS IN DIGITAL MARKETING

At its core, digital marketing has become an integral aspect of marketing proper, with the boundary between this subcategory and the traditional field becoming increasingly blurred. The convergence is evident across various marketing dimensions, including market research (Du et al., 2021), consumer behavior (Palla et al, 2023), product development and differentiation (Catapano et al., 2022), sales (Mullins & Agnihotri, 2022), and advertising (Bruce et al., 2017). The multifaceted nature of the field of digital marketing enables marketers to achieve traditional marketing objectives more efficiently. For instance, in the realm of market research, there is less need for costly and time-consuming consumer observation studies when digital observation methods can provide answers to most research questions quickly and cost-effectively (Dodds et al., 2023). Moreover, the growth of digital marketing has led to the development of specialized subfields, such as social media marketing, email marketing, and search marketing, all of which have found their place within the broader marketing literature (Desai & Vidyapeeth, 2019). The expansion has led to a more seamless integration between consumers and marketers, allowing for more personalized and engaging marketing experiences.

However, this increased integration raises concerns about consumer privacy (Quach et al., 2023). As digital marketing becomes more pervasive and sophisticated, balancing the benefits of personalized marketing with the need to protect consumer privacy will be a critical challenge for marketers and researchers in the field (Strycharz et al., 2019). Moreover, acknowledging the ever-changing nature of the field in terms of facets, methods, and technologies provides a clearer vision for the future of digital marketing. For instance, through exploring different facets the field, a thorough comprehension of how it's transforming conventional marketing methods and what lies ahead for marketers, researchers, and consumers can be achieved.

Business Processes and Customer Persuasion

In addition to the various marketing dimensions discussed, digital marketing has also revolutionized the way businesses interact with customers. With the growth of social media and other digital platforms, businesses now have unprecedented access to potential customers and can engage with them directly in ways that were previously impossible (Kimble & Milolidakis, 2015). Through targeted advertising, businesses can reach specific customer segments with personalized messages, increasing the likelihood of conversion and customer retention. Additionally, businesses can use email marketing to reach customers directly in their inbox, offering promotions, new product information, and other incentives to make a purchase.

However, it is important to note that as digital marketing becomes more sophisticated, there is a risk of alienating customers with overly aggressive or intrusive tactics (Puntoni et al., 2021). Contacting and persuading customers requires a delicate balance between being informative and engaging, while also respecting their privacy and preferences. This is particularly important when it comes to personalized marketing, as customers may feel uncomfortable with the collection and use of their personal data. Thus, businesses must take a customer-centric approach, placing their needs and preferences at the center of their marketing strategies (Sheth et al., 2020). By doing so, businesses can build trust with their customers, foster more meaningful relationships, and ultimately achieve greater success in their marketing efforts.

Understanding Consumer Behavior in the Age of Big Data

As data mining continues to raise concerns regarding privacy and ethics, there is a growing interest in sentiment analysis which uses AI and NLP to analyze social media content to gauge public opinion and emotions towards brands, individuals, and events (Balakhonskaya et al., 2022). In fact, sentiment analysis in digital marketing has become an indispensable tool for researchers focusing on consumer research. As the field of digital marketing thrives, sentiment analysis has experienced substantial growth, particularly in its application to social media platforms for understanding brand sentiment among users (Saura et al., 2019). Traditional research methods may struggle to cope with the vast amount of data generated on social media; however, both lexicon-based and machine-learning techniques have been successfully employed to handle this challenge. Combining these approaches has proven especially effective in identifying positive sentiment in consumer interactions (Dhaoui et al., 2017).

Understanding sentiment is crucial for evaluating engagement with digital marketing content. Studies have shown that positive sentiment, even when associated with false statements, leads to increased targeted consumer engagement (Silva et al., 2023). This finding underscores the vital role that sentiment analysis plays in identifying consumer responses to marketing efforts. In the context of digital marketing, sentiment analysis offers valuable insights into consumer opinions and emotions, enabling marketers to tailor their strategies to resonate with their target audience. By leveraging sentiment analysis, digital marketers can identify trends, monitor brand reputation, and adjust their campaigns based on the feedback received from consumers. Therefore, more informed decision-making, enhancing marketing effectiveness and increasing overall consumer satisfaction through using the strategy (Nandwani & Verma, 2021).

The Intersection of Social Media and XR in Digital Marketing

As the potential of extended realities (XR) in digital marketing is explored, it is crucial to recognize the evolution of social media that has paved the way. The journey began with text-based platforms such as Twitter, Friendster, and MySpace, which eventually gave way to the cultural phenomenon of Facebook in the late 2000s (Solis, 2010). Subsequently, image-based social media platforms like Flickr, Tumblr, and Pinterest emerged, with Instagram capturing the market's imagination. Facebook's strategic acquisition of Instagram in 2012 proved highly successful (Frier, 2021). Meanwhile, video-based social media experienced a rocky start with platforms like Vine, Periscope, and Meerkat. However, TikTok (formerly Musically) managed to dominate the space (McRoberts, 2020). Instagram, known for adopting popular features from other platforms, integrated augmented reality (AR) from Snapchat and launched Reels as a competitor (Moriuchi, 2021).

By the early 2020s, virtual reality (VR) began to emerge as a potential fourth modality and arena for digital marketing. Meta, the parent company of Facebook and Instagram, sought to stay ahead of the curve by investing heavily in a VR platform based on their 2014 acquisition of Oculus. Despite operating at a loss, Meta's Reality Labs remains committed to developing the infrastructure needed to support the anticipated influx of users seeking immersive experiences, entertainment, and digital goods (Kraus et al., 2022). The metaverse and other XR-based platforms offer intriguing opportunities for digital marketers by creating a more immersive and interactive consumer environment, allowing users to connect with digital assets in ways that were previously unattainable (Luangrath et al., 2022). The development of XR technologies in social media and other more immersive platforms draws parallels with earlier open-world experiences like *World of Warcraft* and *Second Life*, which have been operational since the mid-2000s (Ball, 2022).

The Future of Electronic Commerce: Trends and Predictions

Regardless of modality with which digital marketers seek to influence consumer behavior, the exchange of currency is always critical. Therefore, the development of payment rails in these new emerging digital realms is paramount. Communication technologies have led to the creation of various new payment rails, significantly reducing the use of cash for transactions. As Ball (2022) mentions, the share of US transactions using cash dropped from 40% in 2010 to nearly 20% in 2021. Presently, the most common payment rails in the US include CHIPS (Clearing House Interbank Payment System), Fedwire (formerly the Federal Reserve Wire Network), ACH (Automated Clearing House), credit cards, and peer-to-peer payment applications such as PayPal and Venmo (Hutson et al., 2023).

Despite the growth of virtual worlds like those built by Meta, one might expect advancements in payment rails to be more flexible and innovative. In 2021, consumers spent over $50 billion on digital-only video games, and the virtual world's GDP has quintupled since 2005. However, the payment rails in the virtual economy tend to be more restrictive due to the forced bundling of services, such as PlayStation's wallet, Apple Pay, and in-app payment services. Consoles like Xbox and PlayStation enable consumers to download game versions exclusively for use on their respective hardware (Heitner, 2016).

In 2003, Valve introduced Steam as a PC alternative to the console economy. As many multiplayer online games were transitioning to a "games-as-service" model, Valve managed game updates and installations internally through a "game launcher" that indexed and centrally managed game installer files. This approach also controlled users' rights to games, allowing automatic downloads when desired

(Hart, 2017). The economic model still ensured 30% ongoing revenues for Valve, similar to console game platforms. The 30% payment rails also govern Apple and Google with their app stores, further constraining virtual world platforms. The development of payment rails is a crucial factor in shaping the exchange of currency within the digital realm. Although advancements have been made in this area, there remain limitations and restrictions imposed by existing platforms and services. As digital marketing continues to evolve, it is essential for marketers and businesses to adapt to these changes and explore new and innovative solutions for seamless transactions in the virtual economy.

RISE OF METAVERSE RETAIL

The rise of so-called metaverse retail has been a significant development in the world of commerce, with the term "metaverse" applied to retail for almost two decades. Bourlakis and Papagiannidis (2009) examined the emergence of metaverse retailing after the introduction of the first smartphones, dividing the evolution into three distinct phases: traditional, electronic, and metaverse. The study emphasized the need for retailers to adopt new strategies to operate in these three different, yet interconnected, spaces. Key promotional aspects and challenges faced by traditional (brick-and-mortar) retailers, e-retailers (using the internet), and metaverse retailers were highlighted. The researchers analyzed the "metaverse phenomenon" of *Second Life*, also noting *World of Warcraft, EverQuest, Eve Online*, and *Star Wars Galaxies* as the starting point for the 'third dimension of commerce.' Most metaverses initially began as games, specifically massively multiplayer online role-playing games (MMORPGs), and rapidly evolved into alternate worlds that extended players' virtual and electronic spaces (Arnold IV, 2012).

The growing number of consumers spending substantial amounts of time in these virtual environments led to the development of new social and business environments within larger spaces. As economic and social exchanges took place between players in these games and metaverses, there was an increasing crossover between physical businesses in the real world and e-businesses in the virtual realm. These advancements have resulted in a multifaceted, multispace economic environment that has become increasingly complex. To navigate the intertwined nature of this new business environment, which encompasses electronic, virtual, and physical spaces, it is essential to map out and understand the economic, social, and policy implications (Hackl, 2020). To succeed in this evolving landscape, Bourlakis and Papagiannidis (2009) recommend a holistic promotional strategy that operates across all three arenas, enabling businesses to effectively engage with their customers and adapt to the rapidly changing face of commerce in the metaverse.

The precursor to the modern metaverse, such as *Second Life*, provides valuable insights into the evolution of virtual commerce and the possibilities that lie ahead. Launched in 2003, *Second Life* enabled users to monetize their efforts within the virtual world. Users retained copyright for the content they created on the platform, which allowed them to generate revenue from their creations. Before the advent of NFTs and blockchain technology, Linden Lab's *Second Life* provided content creators with a system to safeguard their works using three options: allowing or blocking the ability to copy, modify, or transfer their creations or purchases (Rospigliosi, 2022). This system also tracked items and their creators, functioning similarly to current technologies that create unique and identifiable digital items.

Transactions in *Second Life* were based on the Linden Dollar, which could be exchanged in-world for goods and services or converted into real-world currency to benefit creators. Since a business license is not required to operate as an entrepreneur on the virtual platform, it is difficult to determine the exact number of traders and their success. However, the Positive Linden Dollar Flow (PMLF) is used to estimate that there are over 66 million "business owners" on the platform. Recognizing the potential of reaching customers through this medium, several real-world businesses began operating within *Second Life* (Strobel & Hawkins, 2022). Examples of these firms span various markets and industries, including ABN AMRO, Adidas, American Apparel, Dell, Harvard Law School, IBM, Microsoft, Pontiac, Reuters, Sony Ericsson, the Swedish Government, Toyota, and more. While most of these companies primarily used Second Life for marketing purposes, some have expressed intentions to conduct actual trade within the platform. Despite the early adoption of virtual commerce by these businesses, mainstream acceptance of this mode of trade has yet to be fully realized (Fernandes & Chatterjee, 2022). As the metaverse continues to evolve and expand, businesses must adapt and explore the potential of virtual commerce to stay competitive and engage with their customers in these immersive environments.

The primary distinction between traditional or e-retailing and metaverse retailing lies in the level of customer interaction and engagement with the brands encountered. In conventional two-dimensional marketing and advertising, print, images, videos, and music may be used to convey an idea of the product being sold. However, in a virtual space like the metaverse, customers expect to interact with the products in a three-dimensional simulation. The practice aligns with what Harris et al (2001) anticipated with the rise of "retail theater". Papagiannidis and Bourlakis (2010) argue that some retailers in Second Life designed experiences allowing potential customers to interact with products to drive sales. Other retailers aim to foster a sense of community or belonging among their consumer bases. Although this approach provides even greater access and the opportunity to tailor marketing to specific customers, Haig (2001) cautioned, and Bourlakis and Papagiannidis (2009) echoed, that businesses should be mindful of the effects of overwhelming potential customers. For instance, in busy metaverse locations, automated systems may deliver messages or notecards with product or service information. While users can mute bots or automated agents, doing so repeatedly may lead to frustration (Ahn et al., 2022).

On the other hand, if experiences are thoughtfully designed, the augmented 3D information provided can positively impact sales and the retail shopping experience. Virtual retail offers the potential to merge augmented reality (AR) and virtual reality (VR) to create a seamless shopping experience. Customers can view and review virtual objects and digital information within a virtual space. The advantages are apparent: instead of viewing products on a flat screen, billboard, or piece of paper, products can be virtually transported into the real environment, or clothes can be modeled for size and fit. Such product experiences can assist in purchasing decisions and lead to increased confidence among customers (Popescu et al., 2022).

Exploring Ownership in the Digital Age: The Emergence of NFTs

As the virtual and metaverse retail continues to evolve, the concept of ownership and the role of non-fungible tokens (NFTs) become increasingly important. While blockchain has the potential to underpin the metaverse and replace existing payment rails, the concept of ownership does not seamlessly transfer from the traditional economy to the new virtual world. Even with blockchain's ability to decentralize digital assets, reviewing the terms of service of the specific metaverse platform where these assets were purchased is still necessary (Marinotti, 2022). For instance, proponents of cryptocurrencies argue that true ownership of NFTs is possible due to decentralization and interoperability. The belief suggests that tokens provide non-fungible proof of ownership of a digital asset that can be used across metaverse environments (Christodoulou et al., 2022). Decentralization is thought to enable the buying and selling of virtual items on the blockchain without requiring permission from an individual or company (Au, 2022; Belk et al., 2022). However, despite claims of ownership, the situation is more complex, as current ownership of metaverse assets is governed by contract law rather than property law. Marinotti (2022) emphasizes that the nature of ownership differs between the physical and virtual worlds, potentially misleading consumers.

When an item is purchased on a virtual platform, the transaction is recorded on a blockchain — a decentralized, digital ledger where records cannot be deleted or altered (Au, 2022). This process assigns ownership of an NFT to the user's digital crypto wallet, which can only be accessed by the owner using the wallet's private key. Though the NFT appears to be inaccessible to anyone other than the owner, a distinction must be made between the NFT and the digital asset. Owning digital objects in a virtual world is not the same as owning objects in the physical world (Belk et al., 2022). The difference between what is purchased, and the token raises questions about the true nature of ownership in the metaverse and highlights the need for a more comprehensive understanding of the legal and practical implications of owning digital assets and NFTs.

The distinction of "ownership" in the burgeoning metaverse is crucial and can be found in the terms and conditions of service. When joining any metaverse platform, users must agree to terms of service, terms of use, or end-user license agreements. These legally binding documents define the legal rights of users. However, most users do not read these terms of service. A study found that only 1.7% of users could locate and question a hidden "child assignment clause" embedded in a terms-of-service document, which required users to give away their firstborn child (Obar & Oeldorf-Hirsch, 2020). The legal nuances of ownership are outlined in these lengthy and dense documents, and, unlike blockchain, the terms of service for each platform are centralized. Since legal ownership is controlled by a single company and the existing multiverse of metaverses is not interconnected, users cannot move avatars or other digital assets between virtual worlds. Platforms often link specific NFTs to proprietary digital assets, meaning that NFTs purchased on a metaverse platform and the digital goods they represent are rarely the same thing. While NFTs exist on the blockchain, the digital assets and virtual real estate are stored and only exist on private servers in inaccessible databases (Marinotti, 2020).

Digital marketers and consumers should be educated on how transactions are conducted and the legalities of ownership to understand the value proposition. For example, companies that own the servers where digital assets are stored have the ability to delete links and decouple assets, disallowing their use by the supposed "owners." These platforms also reserve the right to change their terms of service at any time, often without providing notice to users (Rustad & Onufrio, 2011). To ensure compliance with the terms of service, users would need to continually refresh and reread the terms to detect any added language that could lead to their banishment from the platform and the deletion of their assets. The situation underscores the importance of understanding the intricacies of ownership on fully virtual platforms and raises questions about how the concept of ownership may evolve in this digital environment. The complex interplay between blockchain, NFTs, and centralized terms of service necessitates a more comprehensive approach to defining and protecting digital assets and their ownership in the rapidly developing metaverse (Malik et al., 2022).

ENSURING CONSUMER PRIVACY AND DATA SECURITY IN DIGITAL MARKETING

As metaverse retail continues to expand, encompassing new forms of interaction, commerce, and virtual real estate, the importance of privacy and cybersecurity within this digital landscape becomes increasingly critical. The very nature of a digitally born platform, with rich user interaction and involvement, necessitates a high level of security and trust to ensure that the satisfaction of customers and citizens is maintained while optimizing the efficiency of public service delivery (Kshetri, 2021b). In today's cyber world, there is a significant aversion to centralizing authority (Çubuk et al., 2023), which emphasizes the need for a robust infrastructure that can address privacy and cybersecurity concerns.

Blockchain technology, which underpins popular cryptocurrencies, offers numerous applications that can potentially benefit the virtual world of real estate in the metaverse (Wiederhold & Riva, 2021). This decentralized approach to digital asset management can provide enhanced security, transparency, and trust for users engaging in the virtual real estate market. As the limitations of investing in physical property become more apparent, the new world of virtual real estate is poised to grow and flourish (Tayal et al., 2022). This section delves into the complexities of privacy and cybersecurity within the metaverse, exploring the challenges and opportunities that this new virtual landscape presents. The role of blockchain technology in addressing these concerns shall be examined, as well as the potential implications for the future of digital marketing and the broader metaverse retail ecosystem.

Leveraging Blockchain Technology in Digital Marketing

As metaverse retail continues to evolve, the integration of blockchain technology offers numerous opportunities for improving efficiency, transparency, and trust across various industries. Beyond its well-known applications in finance and metaverse environments, blockchain has been employed in diverse sectors such as healthcare, public service, governance, currency exchange, food supply chain, e-voting, music royalty tracking, and personal identification security on the web. Additionally, blockchain has been proposed for use in agricultural supply chains (popularly known as agribusiness), where customer trust and traceability are often lacking (Kshetri et al., 2021). By enhancing product traceability, efficiency, quality, and customer trust, blockchain technology can revolutionize traditional supply chains in agribusiness and improve supply chain management (SCM) for all stakeholders.

The role of blockchain in the metaverse must consider the infrastructure, analysis, and regulatory challenges associated with different types of blockchain implementations. We will discuss the three primary categories of blockchain—public (permissionless), private (permissioned), and hybrid—along with their financial implications based on the mode of peer participation (Sabry et al, 2019). These blockchain types can be further categorized based on their financial perspectives with respect to business and currency as C2C (Type One), B2C (Type Two), and B2B (Type Three). Furthermore, the critical importance of cybersecurity and cyber defense in the context of the metaverse must be noted. As the internet has grown and evolved, the threat of cyber warfare has become an increasingly pressing concern, particularly in financial and military sectors (Kshetri, 2022). The rapid expansion of online users and devices, as well as the development of the metaverse, creates new avenues for cyber-attacks. To ensure the security and stability of the emerging metaverse infrastructure, it is essential to address these cybersecurity challenges effectively.

The emergence of blockchain technology has led to significant transformations in various sectors, including governments, finance, and businesses, most notably with the introduction of cryptocurrencies such as Bitcoin. To fully leverage the benefits of digital transformation, blockchain can be integrated into cloud-based solutions, such as Blockchain-as-a-Service (BaaS), which is built upon the Infrastructure-as-a-Service (IaaS) platform layer (Treiblmaier & Sillaber, 2020). By hosting blockchain-based solutions in a cloud environment, new opportunities arise for customers to create, host, and utilize smart contracts, applications, and functions that contribute to the ongoing digital revolution. The digitalization process has led to numerous benefits, including increased efficiency, regulatory changes, and a growing demand for end-to-end workflows. However, it has also revealed a lack of trust among individuals in the digital world. Blockchain technology addresses these concerns by acting as a "digital decentralized distributed" ledger, or a D3 database, which provides tamperproof records with powerful features such as immutability, decentralization, consensus mechanisms, verifiability, anonymity, efficiency, flexibility, trust, elimination of intermediaries, and transparency (Murthy et al., 2020). These characteristics make blockchain an ideal solution for the evolving digital retail landscape.

The inherent features of blockchain technology, such as traceability, privacy, immutability, consensus mechanisms, and decentralization, offer a robust foundation for cybersecurity and cyber defense in the realm of data and information security. As the number of cyber-attacks and connected devices continues to rise, there is an increasing risk to information security and the public at large. Addressing cybersecurity challenges in the digital revolution era requires the involvement of not only consumers, governments, and the financial sector, but also the trust and participation of citizens. As the World Wide Web (WWW) increasingly adopts secure HTTP (HTTPS) encryption, there is a long-term need to effectively manage cryptography and digital certification requirements, which can be facilitated and strengthened by blockchain technology (Kshetri et al., 2022). This technology has already found applications in numerous areas, such as digital markets (billing, marketing, retail), government sectors (document digitization, smart contracts, electronic voting), Internet of Things (IoT) (personalized robots, autonomous vehicles, machine learning), finance, accounting, and more.

The digital retail revolution is closely tied to the growth of the digital population (internet users) and the increasing number of connected devices worldwide. The digital revolution, coupled with cybersecurity, has significant implications for computer and cyber ethics, as we can anticipate more social and ethical challenges emerging from Artificial Intelligence, robotics, and autonomous weapons systems. This is because the robotics industry, which encompasses AI and security, is evolving similarly to how the computer industry did in the past (Kshetri, 2021a). As technology continues to progress and advance, humans gain greater command and control over the world, which in turn comes with increased responsibility and oversight.

Digital technology lies at the heart of work, life, and culture, and its growth accelerates every second, especially as more people engage with the digital world following the COVID-19 pandemic. The digital revolution has raised questions about digital security, digital forensics, and the cyber world, along with the impact on nations' digital economies, which are now worth billions. The concept of "cyber" has become the fourth domain, joining land, air, and water. The rapid expansion of the digital gaming industry and digital learning scenarios (e-learning) has contributed to the global trend of increasing email and internet usage in numerous organizations, even in underdeveloped nations that may lack access to clean drinking water but still have access to the web and the digital world (Konyeha, 2020). Looking ahead, these challenges need be addressed to harness the power of blockchain technology, cybersecurity, and digital innovation to create a safer and more equitable digital landscape.

NAVIGATING THE FUTURE OF SOCIAL MEDIA AND BEYOND

As a new era of digital marketing and social media dawns, the landscape of media consumption and creation has undergone significant transformation. Social media platforms have rapidly become the primary conduit for engaging with consumers, outpacing traditional media industries in their ability to capture audience attention and trust (Järvinen et al., 2012). Through a combination of increased smartphone functionality and more accessible tools for media creation, the barriers to entry for content production have been dramatically lowered, allowing for a more "organic" and "authentic" form of messaging that resonates with contemporary audiences (Fulgoni & Lipsman, 2014). The shift in media consumption has had far-reaching implications, influencing not only marketing strategies but also the visual aesthetics of popular films and other visual storytelling formats.

The prevalence of amateur smartphone videos has given rise to a new aesthetic trope that equates realism with a less polished, more "amateur" appearance. This has led to the widespread adoption of shaky cam techniques, even in high-budget films set in alternate dimensions or historical contexts (Keen & Ramage, 2010). The future of digital marketing and social media, examining how the changing landscape will continue to shape the way marketers engage with consumers, as well as the creative and technological innovations that will further transform the media landscape shall be of particular interest for marketers. The implications of this shift for content creators, brands, and businesses seeking to harness the power of digital marketing and social media to connect with their audiences in meaningful and impactful ways are considered.

Digital Marketing Influencers: Opportunities and Challenges

In recent years, the rise of influencer marketing has disrupted the traditional digital marketing landscape. Social media influencers, who are individuals with a large and engaged following on social media, have become powerful marketing tools for brands (Atiq et al., 2022). Influencer marketing relies on the notion that people are more likely to trust recommendations from someone they know or follow rather than from a traditional advertisement (Brown & Hayes, 2008; Vrontis et al., 2021). Influencers are often seen as relatable and trustworthy, which makes them ideal for promoting products and services to their followers. As a result, influencer marketing has become an important part of many brands' digital marketing strategies. With the ability to target specific demographics and niche interests, influencer marketing has leveled the playing field for smaller brands and allows them to compete with larger companies (Masuda et al., 2022). However, as the industry has grown, concerns about transparency and authenticity have arisen, leading to increased scrutiny and regulations from social media platforms and advertising agencies (De Cicco et al., 2021). Despite these challenges, influencer marketing is expected to continue its growth in the future, as brands seek new and innovative ways to reach and engage with their target audiences.

Influencers often have a devoted fan base that trusts and values their opinions and recommendations, which has resulted in brands paying influencers to promote their products or services to their followers. The influencers can create sponsored content that looks like organic content, seamlessly integrating the brand's message into their social media posts. This type of advertising is often perceived as more authentic and trustworthy than traditional advertising methods. The rise of influencer marketing has also led to a shift in the way that brands approach their social media strategies. Rather than solely focusing on creating their own content, brands are now collaborating with influencers to co-create content that resonates with their target audience (Vrontis et al., 2022). Moreover, micro-influencers, those with smaller followings, have also become a popular option for brands as they offer a more affordable option for reaching a targeted audience. These influencers have a smaller but highly engaged following, often with a more niche focus, making them a valuable partner for brands looking to reach a specific audience (Madina et al., 2022).

Exploring the Potential of AI-Generated Content in Digital Marketing

The rise of generative AI and its integration with social media content creation is disrupting the craft of artistic creation, allowing virtually anyone to write and create art regardless of any formal training or experience with the traditional medium (Dwivedi et al., 2023). ChatGPT, Midjourney, Stable Diffusion, and other generative AI tools have made it possible for consumers to create high-quality works with simple text prompts, breaking technical and artistic barriers that were previously insurmountable (Huang & Siddarth, 2023). Previously impenetrable barriers, such as coding and programming, are also being broken with recent integrations of ChatGPT in programs such as Unity (Topsakal & Topsakal, 2023). Moreover, advancements have been made for text-to-video generative AI, which could bring consumers into a reality in which people are able to create and edit video content from their computers without the need for computer graphics skills or even a camera (Gozalo-Brizuela & Garrido-Merchan, 2023). The shift in skills and abilities by the consumer will lead to the emergence of new content formats and ultimately more interest from social media audiences concerning generative AI.

The rise of generative AI is also impacting digital marketing, with AI being used to analyze public opinion through audience-generated content (Louie et al., 2020). Social media audiences create an incredible amount of data, which marketers and advertisers have been able to harvest, collate, and analyze to assist with their messaging. As social media becomes the dominant place for discourse and opinions, these platforms have also become the most accepted metric for gauging public opinion on an event, brand, or individual (McGregor, 2019). By having AI analyze public opinion through audience-generated content, we can gauge consumer sentiment in a nearly real-time timeframe. Harvesting AI prompts and creations from users will further expand the ability to apply sentiment analysis and better gauge the interests and emotions of the audience (Mao et al., 2022). The amount of information that can be gleaned is immense. For instance, at its peak viewership, the round-the-clock Twitch stream *Watch Me Forever* had over 16,000 viewers attentively hanging on every line of dialogue generated, spoken, and (crudely) animated by the generative AI. Adapting the simple concept of a never-ending sitcom, specifically influenced by *Seinfeld, Watch Me Forever* demonstrates the interest audiences have for AI-generated content as more than a mere curiosity or novelty. The new technology grants accessibility of art creation to a much wider audience, allowing for more voices and thus, more data and content to examine to better serve the interests of consumers (Aljedaani, 2022).

The Role of Generative AI in the Metaverse and Beyond

Generative AI technology has immense potential to revolutionize the growing metaverse by enabling the creation of infinite unique assets and environments, all through a simple prompt or algorithm (Ratican et al., 2023). The technology can generate everything from landscapes and buildings to characters and items, all without the need for human input or intervention. In the metaverse, this could lead to an unprecedented level of creative control for users and developers, allowing for endless possibilities and a more dynamic and diverse virtual world. One potential application of generative AI in the metaverse is the creation of personalized avatars (Karaarslan & Altundas, 2022). Currently, most avatars in virtual worlds are limited to a set of pre-made options or require complex 3D modeling skills to create from scratch. However, with generative AI, users could input their preferences and create a unique avatar that truly reflects their identity. The approach is already seen in virtual fashion, where AI generates one-of-a-kind clothing items based on user preferences (Stevenson, 2023).

Another application of generative AI in the metaverse is in the creation of immersive environments. With the ability to generate unique landscapes, buildings, and other environmental elements, the metaverse could offer an infinite variety of virtual spaces for users to explore and interact with. This could also extend to the creation of dynamic and responsive environments that adapt and change based on user input or external factors, creating a more immersive and engaging experience (Hutson et al, 2023). However, the use of generative AI in the metaverse also raises important ethical concerns. With the potential for infinite creation, there is a risk that generative AI could lead to the proliferation of low-quality or even harmful content in the metaverse. There is also the risk of bias and discrimination in AI-generated content, particularly in the creation of avatars and other virtual identities. As the metaverse and digital marketing continue to develop, it will be important to carefully consider the ethical implications of generative AI and its potential impact on the virtual world. By striking a balance between creative freedom and responsible use of technology, there may be the ability to ensure that the metaverse continues to evolve in a positive and inclusive direction.

Enhancing Customer Experience and Privacy Through AI on Digital Retail Platforms

As digital retail platforms become more sophisticated, they are increasingly using AI to improve the customer experience while balancing the need for privacy. AI-powered chatbots and virtual assistants are now commonplace, providing customers with immediate support and assistance in real-time (George & George, 2023). AI algorithms are also being used to personalize the shopping experience by recommending products and services that are tailored to the individual customer's needs and preferences (Rathore, 2023). These personalized recommendations help to increase customer engagement, improve customer satisfaction, and ultimately drive sales.

However, as retailers collect more customer data to fuel these AI algorithms, privacy concerns arise. Customers may feel uneasy about sharing their personal information with retailers and worry about how their data will be used. To address these concerns, retailers must be transparent about their data collection practices and ensure that they are complying with all relevant privacy regulations. Additionally, they should provide customers with control over their data and enable them to easily access, correct, and delete their personal information (Tangari et al., 2021).

To enhance customer experience and privacy further, some digital retail platforms are exploring new technologies such as blockchain. By using a decentralized, tamper-proof ledger, blockchain offers a way to increase transparency and trust in digital transactions, while also ensuring the privacy of sensitive customer data (Kshetri, 2021b). Blockchain technology can also provide customers with greater control over their data, enabling them to determine who has access to their information and for what purposes. The integration of AI, privacy, and customer experience is a crucial aspect of digital retail platforms. As retailers continue to innovate and expand their offerings, they must prioritize these elements to provide customers with personalized and secure shopping experiences. By leveraging emerging technologies like blockchain and being transparent about data collection practices, retailers can build trust with their customers and establish themselves as leaders in the digital retail landscape.

CONCLUSION

The rise of extended reality (XR), blockchain technology, and generative AI are changing the face of digital marketing. The metaverse and its potential for retail theatre and social media engagement provide new avenues for digital marketers to reach their target audience. Blockchain technology promises greater security and transparency, while generative AI allows for more accessible and diverse content creation. However, the landscape of the online world is ever-changing, and digital marketers must be willing to adapt to stay ahead of the curve. As technology continues to advance, keeping up with the latest trends will be essential in order to effectively navigate the digital realm. The future of digital marketing and extended reality may be uncertain, but it presents exciting possibilities for businesses to connect with their audience in new and innovative ways.

Furthermore, the future of digital marketing is not just about technology and trends, but also about ethics and accountability. The rise of social media and the democratization of content creation have given consumers more power than ever before, and marketers need to be aware of the potential consequences of their actions. It is important for brands to be transparent, authentic, and ethical in their marketing practices, and to prioritize the needs and interests of their audience over their own bottom line. As such, the future of digital marketing and XR and AI is full of potential, but it also requires careful consideration and a willingness to adapt. By staying informed, remaining ethical, and putting their audience first, marketers can successfully navigate this ever-changing landscape and build meaningful connections with their target audience.

REFERENCES

Ahn, S. J., Kim, J., & Kim, J. (2022). The bifold triadic relationships framework: A theoretical primer for advertising research in the metaverse. *Journal of Advertising*, *51*(5), 592–607. doi:10.1080/00913367.2022.2111729

Aljedaani, W., Saad, E., Rustam, F., de la Torre Díez, I., & Ashraf, I. (2022). Role of artificial intelligence for analysis of COVID-19 vaccination-related tweets: Opportunities, challenges, and future trends. *Mathematics*, *10*(17), 3199. doi:10.3390/math10173199

Alsukaini, A. K. M., Sumra, K., Khan, R., & Awan, T. M. (2023). New trends in digital marketing emergence during pandemic times. *International Journal of Innovation Science*, *15*(1), 167–185. doi:10.1108/IJIS-08-2021-0139

Alt, R., & Puschmann, T. (2016). Bankmodell. In Digitalisierung der Finanzindustrie (pp. 55-117). Springer Gabler.

Arnold, W. E. IV. (2012). Tax Enforcement In Virtual Worlds-Virtually Impossible. *Syracuse J. Int'l L. & Com.*, *40*, 187.

Atiq, M., Abid, G., Anwar, A., & Ijaz, M. F. (2022). Influencer marketing on Instagram: A sequential mediation model of storytelling content and audience engagement via relatability and Trust. *Information (Basel), 13*(7), 345. doi:10.3390/info13070345

Au, A. (2022). Cryptocurrencies and the promise of individual economic sovereignty in an age of digitalization: A critical appraisal. *The Sociological Review*. doi:10.1177/00380261221127858

Auer, R., & Claessens, S. (2018, Sept.). Regulating cryptocurrencies: Assessing market reactions. *BIS Quarterly Review*.

Avital, M., King, J. L., Beck, R., Rossi, M., & Teigland, R. (2016). Jumping on the Blockchain Bandwagon: Lessons of the Past and Outlook to the Future. *Proceedings of the 37thInternational Conference on Information Systems*, 1-6.

Balakhonskaya, L. V., Balakhonsky, V. V., & Gustokashina, A. A. (2022, April). "Newstalgia" as Digital Marketing Communication Strategy. In 2022 Communication Strategies in Digital Society Seminar (ComSDS) (pp. 134-141). IEEE. doi:10.1109/ComSDS55328.2022.9769130

Ball, M. (2022). *The Metaverse and How It Will Revolutionize Everything*. Liveright Publishing, Co. W.W. Norton & Company.

Belk, R., Humayun, M., & Brouard, M. (2022). Money, possessions, and ownership in the Metaverse: NFTs, cryptocurrencies, Web3 and Wild Markets. *Journal of Business Research, 153*, 198–205. doi:10.1016/j.jbusres.2022.08.031

Berg, C., Davidson, S., & Potts, J. (2019). Blockchain technology as economic infrastructure: Revisiting the electronic markets hypothesis. *Frontiers in Blockchain, 2*, 22. doi:10.3389/fbloc.2019.00022

Bourlakis, M., Papagiannidis, S., & Li, F. (2009). Retail spatial evolution: Paving the way from traditional to metaverse retailing. *Electronic Commerce Research, 9*(1), 135–148. doi:10.100710660-009-9030-8

Brown, D., & Hayes, N. (2008). *Influencer marketing*. Routledge. doi:10.4324/9780080557700

Bruce, N. I., Murthi, B. P. S., & Rao, R. C. (2017). A Dynamic Model for Digital Advertising: The Effects of Creative Format, Message Content, and Targeting on Engagement. *JMR, Journal of Marketing Research, 54*(2), 202–218. doi:10.1509/jmr.14.0117

Butt, A., Ahmad, H., Ali, F., Muzaffar, A., & Shafique, M. N. (2023). Engaging the customer with augmented reality and employee services to enhance equity and loyalty. *International Journal of Retail & Distribution Management, 51*(5), 629–652. doi:10.1108/IJRDM-04-2021-0165

Carstens, A. (2018). *Money in the digital age: what role for central banks?* Lecture at the House of Finance, Goethe University, Frankfurt, Germany.

Catapano, R., Shennib, F., & Levav, J. (2022). Preference Reversals Between Digital and Physical Goods. *JMR, Journal of Marketing Research, 59*(2), 353–373. doi:10.1177/00222437211065020

Christodoulou, K., Katelaris, L., Themistocleous, M., Christodoulou, P., & Iosif, E. (2022). NFTs and the metaverse revolution: research perspectives and open challenges. *Blockchains and the Token Economy*, 139-178.

Çubuk, E. B. S., Zeren, H. E., & Demirdöven, B. (2023). The Role of Data Governance in Cybersecurity for E-Municipal Services: Implications From the Case of Turkey. In *Handbook of Research on Cybersecurity Issues and Challenges for Business and FinTech Applications* (pp. 410–425). IGI Global.

De Cicco, R., Iacobucci, S., & Pagliaro, S. (2021). The effect of influencer–product fit on advertising recognition and the role of an enhanced disclosure in increasing sponsorship transparency. *International Journal of Advertising*, *40*(5), 733–759. doi:10.1080/02650487.2020.1801198

Desai, V., & Vidyapeeth, B. (2019). Digital marketing: A review. *International Journal of Trend in Scientific Research and Development*, *5*(5), 196–200. doi:10.31142/ijtsrd23100

Dhaoui, C., Webster, C. M., & Tan, L. P. (2017). Social Media Sentiment Analysis: Lexicon Versus Machine Learning. *Journal of Consumer Marketing*, *34*(6), 480–488. doi:10.1108/JCM-03-2017-2141

Dodds, T., de Vreese, C., Helberger, N., Resendez, V., & Seipp, T. (2023). Popularity-driven Metrics: Audience Analytics and Shifting Opinion Power to Digital Platforms. *Journalism Studies*, *24*(3), 1–19. doi:10.1080/1461670X.2023.2167104

Du, R.Y., Netzer, O., Schweidel, D.A., & Mitra, D. (2021). Capturing Marketing Information to Fuel Growth. *Journal of Marketing, 85*(1), 163-183.

Dwivedi, Y. K., Kshetri, N., Hughes, L., Slade, E. L., Jeyaraj, A., Kar, A. K., Baabdullah, A. M., Koohang, A., Raghavan, V., Ahuja, M., Albanna, H., Albashrawi, M. A., Al-Busaidi, A. S., Balakrishnan, J., Barlette, Y., Basu, S., Bose, I., Brooks, L., Buhalis, D., ... Wright, R. (2023). "So what if ChatGPT wrote it?" Multidisciplinary perspectives on opportunities, challenges and implications of generative conversational AI for research, practice and policy. *International Journal of Information Management*, *71*, 102642. doi:10.1016/j.ijinfomgt.2023.102642

Fanusie, Y., & Robinson, T. (2018). *Bitcoin laundering: an analysis of illicit flows into digital currency services.* Center on Sanctions and Illicit Finance Memorandum.

Fernandes, A., & Chatterjee, S. (2022). Possibilities of metaverse: The second life. *International Journal of Engineering and Management Research*, *12*(4), 79–82.

Foley, S., Karlsen, J., & Putniņš, T. (2018). Sex, drugs, and bitcoin: How much illegal activity is financed through cryptocurrencies? *Review of Financial Studies.*

Frier, S. (2021). *No filter: The inside story of Instagram.* Simon and Schuster.

Fulgoni, G., & Lipsman, A. (2014). Numbers, please: Digital game changers: How social media will help usher in the era of mobile and multi-platform campaign-effectiveness measurement. *Journal of Advertising Research*, *54*(1), 11–16. doi:10.2501/JAR-54-1-011-016

Gadekallu, T. R., Pham, Q. V., Nguyen, D. C., Maddikunta, P. K. R., Deepa, N., Prabadevi, B., Pathirana, P. N., Zhao, J., & Hwang, W. J. (2022). Blockchain for edge of things: Applications, opportunities, and challenges. *IEEE Internet of Things Journal*, *9*(2), 964–988. doi:10.1109/JIOT.2021.3119639

George, A. S., & George, A. H. (2023). A review of ChatGPT AI's impact on several business sectors. *Partners Universal International Innovation Journal*, *1*(1), 9–23.

Gozalo-Brizuela, R., & Garrido-Merchan, E. C. (2023). *ChatGPT is not all you need. A State of the Art Review of large Generative AI models.* arXiv preprint arXiv:2301.04655.

Hackl, C. (2020). The Metaverse is Coming and It's A Very Big Deal. *Forbes, 2020*(June), 5. https://www.forbes.com/sites/cathyhackl/2020/07/05/the-metaverse-is-coming--its-a-very-big-deal/?sh=1f4c347a440f

Haig, M. (2001). Talking to the teen generation. *Brand Strategy, 30.*

Harris, K., Harris, R., & Baron, S. (2001). Customer participation in retail service: Lessons from Brecht. *International Journal of Retail & Distribution Management, 29*(8), 359–369. doi:10.1108/09590550110396845

Hart, C. B. (2017). Considering the Interaction of Functional Factors in Video Game Design Influencing the Economic Effectiveness of Microtransactions. *The Evolution and Social Impact of Video Game Economics*, 61-80.

Heitner, D. (2016). *Screenwise: Helping kids thrive (and survive) in their digital world.* Routledge. doi:10.4324/9781315213187

Hollensen, S., Kotler, P., & Opresnik, M. O. (2022). Metaverse–the new marketing universe. *The Journal of Business Strategy.*

Huang, S., & Siddarth, D. (2023). *Generative AI and the Digital Commons.* arXiv preprint arXiv:2303.11074.

Hutson, J., Banerjee, G., Kshetri, N., Odenwald, K., & Ratican, J. (2023). Architecting the Metaverse: Blockchain and the Financial and Legal Regulatory Challenges of Virtual Real Estate. *Journal of Intelligent Learning Systems and Applications, 15*(1), 1–23. doi:10.4236/jilsa.2023.151001

Huynh-The, T., Gadekallu, T. R., Wang, W., Yenduri, G., Ranaweera, P., Pham, Q. V., da Costa, D. B., & Liyanage, M. (2023). Blockchain for the metaverse: A Review. *Future Generation Computer Systems, 143*, 401–419. doi:10.1016/j.future.2023.02.008

Järvinen, J., Tollinen, A., Karjaluoto, H., & Jayawardhena, C. (2012). Digital and social media marketing usage in B2B industrial section. *Marketing Management Journal, 22*(2), 102–117.

KaraarslanE.AltundasS. (2022). Cross-platform and Personalized Avatars in the Metaverse: Ready Player Me Case. Available at SSRN 4249064.

Keen, A., & Ramage, M. (2010). The cult of the amateur. *Online Communication and Collaboration. REAd (Porto Alegre)*, 251–255.

Kimble, C., & Milolidakis, G. (2015). Big data and business intelligence: Debunking the myths. *Global Business and Organizational Excellence, 35*(1), 23–34. doi:10.1002/joe.21642

Konyeha, S. (2020). Exploring cybersecurity threats in digital marketing. *NIPES J. Sci. Technol. Res, 2*(3), 12. doi:10.37933/nipes/2.3.2020.2

Kraus, S., Kanbach, D. K., Krysta, P. M., Steinhoff, M. M., & Tomini, N. (2022). Facebook and the creation of the metaverse: Radical business model innovation or incremental transformation? *International Journal of Entrepreneurial Behaviour & Research, 28*(9), 52–77. doi:10.1108/IJEBR-12-2021-0984

Kshetri, N. (2021a). *Blockchain Technology for improving transparency and citizen's trust*. Springer Nature Switzerland AG. doi:10.1007/978-3-030-73100-7_52

Kshetri, N. (2021b). A survey on Computer ethics (w.r.t. Artificial Intelligence, Robot Weaponry, Fuzzy systems, Autonomous Vehicles). *International Journal of Innovative Technology and Exploring Engineering*, *10*(4), 207–210. Advance online publication. doi:10.35940/ijitee.D8582.0210421

Kshetri, N. (2022). The Global Rise of Online Devices, Cyber Crime and Cyber Defense: Enhancing Ethical Actions, Counter Measures, Cyber Strategy, and Approaches. *ProQuest Dissertations Publishing*, DOI: doi:10.13140/RG.2.2.33257.57446

Kshetri, N., Bhushal, C. S., Pandey, P. S., & Dwivedi, V. (2022). BCT-CS: Blockchain technology applications for Cyber defense and Cybersecurity: A survey and solutions. *International Journal of Advanced Computer Science and Applications*, *13*(11). Advance online publication. doi:10.14569/IJACSA.2022.0131140

Landau, J-P. & Genais, A. (2018). *Les crypto-monnaies, rapport au Ministre de l'Économie et des Finances*. Academic Press.

Louie, R., Coenen, A., Huang, C. Z., Terry, M., & Cai, C. J. (2020, April). Novice-AI music co-creation via AI-steering tools for deep generative models. In *Proceedings of the 2020 CHI conference on human factors in computing systems* (pp. 1-13). 10.1145/3313831.3376739

Madina, I. H., Sukmono, F. G., & Junaedi, F. (2022, November). Micro-influencer Marketing Beauty Brand on Social Media. In *HCI International 2022–Late Breaking Posters: 24th International Conference on Human-Computer Interaction, HCII 2022, Virtual Event, June 26–July 1, 2022, Proceedings, Part II* (pp. 40-47). Cham: Springer Nature Switzerland.

Malik, N., Wei, M. Y., Appel, G., & Luo, L. (2022). Blockchain Technology for Creative Industry: Current State and Research Opportunities. *International Journal of Research in Marketing*, *40*(1), 38–48. doi:10.1016/j.ijresmar.2022.07.004

Mao, R., Liu, Q., He, K., Li, W., & Cambria, E. (2022). The biases of pre-trained language models: An empirical study on prompt-based sentiment analysis and emotion detection. *IEEE Transactions on Affective Computing*, 1–11. doi:10.1109/TAFFC.2022.3204972

Marinotti, J. (2020). Tangibility as Technology. *SSRN*, *37*, 671. doi:10.2139srn.3682090

Marinotti, J. (2022). Can you truly own anything in the metaverse? A law professor explains how blockchains and NFTs don't protect virtual property. *Market Watch*. https://www.marketwatch.com/story/can-you-truly-own-anything-in-the-metaverse-a-law-professor-explains-how-blockchains-and-nfts-dont-protect-virtual-property-11650559724#:~:text=When%20you%20buy%20an%20item,a%20unique%20string%20of%20bits

Masuda, H., Han, S. H., & Lee, J. (2022). Impacts of influencer attributes on purchase intentions in social media influencer marketing: Mediating roles of characterizations. *Technological Forecasting and Social Change*, *174*, 121246. doi:10.1016/j.techfore.2021.121246

McGregor, S. C. (2019). Social media as public opinion: How journalists use social media to represent public opinion. *Journalism*, *20*(8), 1070–1086. doi:10.1177/1464884919845458

McRoberts, S. (2020). *From'Social'Media to Collaborative Media: Cooperative Inquiry for Shoulder-To-Shoulder Youth Video Authorship Technologies* [Doctoral dissertation]. University of Minnesota.

Moriuchi, E. (2021). The role of technology in social media. In Cross-Cultural Social Media Marketing: Bridging Across Cultural Differences (pp. 97-107). Emerald Publishing Limited. doi:10.1108/978-1-83867-175-420211009

Möser, M., Böhme, R., & Breuker, D. (2013). An inquiry into money laundering tools in the Bitcoin ecosystem. *Proceedings of the APWG eCrime Researchers Summit (ECRIME)*, 1-14. 10.1109/eCRS.2013.6805780

Mullins, R., & Agnihotri, R. (2022). Digital Selling: Organizational and Managerial Influences for Frontline Readiness and Effectiveness. *Journal of the Academy of Marketing Science*, *50*(4), 800–821. doi:10.100711747-021-00836-5

Murthy, C. V. B., Shri, M. L., Kadry, S., & Lim, S. (2020). Blockchain based cloud computing: Architecture and research challenges. *IEEE Access : Practical Innovations, Open Solutions*, *8*, 205190–205205. doi:10.1109/ACCESS.2020.3036812

Nakamoto, S. (2008). Bitcoin: A peer-to-peer electronic cash system. *Decentralized Business Review*, 21260.

Nandwani, P., & Verma, R. (2021). A review on sentiment analysis and emotion detection from text. *Social Network Analysis and Mining*, *11*(1), 81. doi:10.100713278-021-00776-6 PMID:34484462

Obar, J., & Oeldorf-Hirsch, A. (2020). The biggest lie on the Internet: Ignoring the privacy policies and terms of service policies of social networking services. *Information Communication and Society*, *23*(1), 128–147. doi:10.1080/1369118X.2018.1486870

Palla, P. J., Kyriacou, E., & Zarkada, A. (2023). The Effect of Involvement on Attitude Formation and Strength in the Digital Domain. *Journal of Marketing Communications*, *29*(2), 137–160. doi:10.1080/13527266.2022.2154062

Papagiannidis, S., & Bourlakis, M. A. (2010). Staging the New Retail Drama: At a Metaverse near you! *Journal of Virtual Worlds Research*, *2*(5), 425–446. doi:10.4101/jvwr.v2i5.808

Popescu, G. H., Valaskova, K., & Horak, J. (2022). Augmented Reality Shopping Experiences, Retail Business Analytics, and Machine Vision Algorithms in the Virtual Economy of the Metaverse. *Journal of Self-Governance & Management Economics*, *10*(2), 67–81.

Puntoni, S., Reczek, R. W., Giesler, M., & Botti, S. (2021). Consumers and artificial intelligence: An experiential perspective. *Journal of Marketing*, *85*(1), 131–151. doi:10.1177/0022242920953847

Quach, S., Thaichon, P., Martin, K. D., Weaven, S., & Palmatier, R. W. (2023). Digital Technologies: Tensions in Privacy and Data. *Journal of the Academy of Marketing Science*, *50*(6), 1299–1323. doi:10.100711747-022-00845-y PMID:35281634

Quiroz-Guitierrez, M. (2022). This week in the metaverse: 'Metaverse' could be word of the year, Johnnie Walker launches an NFT, and Mattel creates an NFT marketplace. *Fortune Crypto*. https://fortune.com/crypto/2022/11/25/this-week-in-the-metaverse-johnnie-walker-oxford-rockstar-games/

Ramadan, Z. (2023). Marketing in the metaverse era: Toward an integrative channel approach. *Virtual Reality (Waltham Cross)*, 1–14. doi:10.100710055-023-00783-2 PMID:37360809

Rathore, B. (2023). Integration of Artificial Intelligence& It's Practices in Apparel Industry. *International Journal of New Media Studies*, *10*(1), 25–37.

Ratican, J., Hutson, J., & Wright, A. (2023). A Proposed Meta-Reality Immersive Development Pipeline: Generative AI Models and Extended Reality (XR) Content for the Metaverse. *Journal of Intelligent Learning Systems and Applications*, *15*(1), 24–35. doi:10.4236/jilsa.2023.151002

Rizvanović, B., Zutshi, A., Grilo, A., & Nodehi, T. (2023). Linking the potentials of extended digital marketing impact and start-up growth: Developing a macro-dynamic framework of start-up growth drivers supported by digital marketing. *Technological Forecasting and Social Change*, *186*, 122128. doi:10.1016/j.techfore.2022.122128

Rospigliosi, P. A. (2022). Metaverse or Simulacra? Roblox, Minecraft, Meta and the turn to virtual reality for education, socialisation and work. *Interactive Learning Environments*, *30*(1), 1–3. doi:10.1080/10494820.2022.2022899

Rückeshäuser, N. (2017). Do We Really Want Blockchain-Based Accounting? Decentralized Consensus as Enabler of Management Override of Internal Controls. *Proceedings of the 13th International Conference on Wirtschaftsinformatik*, 16-30.

Rustad, M. L., & Onufrio, M. V. (2011). Reconceptualizing consumer terms of use for a globalized knowledge economy. *University of Pennsylvania Journal of Business Law,* 1085.

Saura, J. R., Palos-Sanchez, P., & Grilo, A. (2019). Detecting indicators for startup business success: Sentiment analysis using text data mining. *Sustainability (Basel)*, *11*(3), 917. doi:10.3390u11030917

Shah, R. (2023). Augmented Reality in E-Commerce: The New Era of Online Shopping. In Intelligent Sustainable Systems: Selected Papers of WorldS4 2022, Volume 2 (pp. 775-783). Springer Nature Singapore.

Sheth, J., Jain, V., & Ambika, A. (2020). Repositioning the customer support services: The next frontier of competitive advantage. *European Journal of Marketing*, *54*(7), 1787–1804. doi:10.1108/EJM-02-2020-0086

Silva, M., Giovanni, L., Fernandes, J., Oliveira, D., & Silva, C. S. (2023). What Makes Disinformation Ads Engaging? A Case Study of Facebook Ads from the Russian Active Measures Campaign. *Journal of Interactive Advertising*, 1–20. Advance online publication. doi:10.1080/15252019.2023.2173991

Solis, B. (2010). *Engage: The complete guide for brands and businesses to build, cultivate, and measure success in the new web*. John Wiley & Sons.

Stevenson, T. (2023). *Virtual Fashion: Digital Representations of Materiality and Time* [Doctoral dissertation]. Open Access Te Herenga Waka-Victoria University of Wellington.

Strobel, J., & Hawkins, C. (2022). Designing in Second Life: Identity construction and learning in a virtual informal environment. *Journal of Online Engineering Education*, *1*(1).

Strycharz, J., van Noort, G., Helberger, N., & Smit, E. (2019). Contrasting perspectives–practitioner's viewpoint on personalised marketing communication. *European Journal of Marketing*, *53*(4), 635–660. doi:10.1108/EJM-11-2017-0896

Tangari, G., Ikram, M., Ijaz, K., Kaafar, M. A., & Berkovsky, S. (2021). Mobile health and privacy: cross sectional study. *BMJ, 373*.

Tayal, S., Rajagopal, K., & Mahajan, V. (2022, March). Virtual Reality based Metaverse of Gamification. In *2022 6th International Conference on Computing Methodologies and Communication (ICCMC)* (pp. 1597-1604). IEEE. 10.1109/ICCMC53470.2022.9753727

Thykier, C. (2022). Immersive technologies are shaping the future of e-commerce right now. *The Drum*. https://www.thedrum.com/opinion/2022/09/20/immersive-technologies-are-shaping-the-future-e-commerce-right-now?utm_campaign=Social%20Media:%20Thought%20leadership&utm_content=240335635&utm_medium=social&utm_source=linkedin&hss_channel=lcp-3290097

Topsakal, O., & Topsakal, E. (2023). Framework for A Foreign Language Teaching Software for Children Utilizing AR, Voicebots and ChatGPT (Large Language Models). *The Journal of Cognitive Systems*, *7*(2), 33–38.

Treiblmaier, H., & Sillaber, C. (2020). A case study of blockchain-induced digital transformation in the public sector. In *Blockchain and Distributed Ledger Technology Use Cases* (pp. 227–244). Springer. doi:10.1007/978-3-030-44337-5_11

Valaskova, K., Machova, V., & Lewis, E. (2022). Virtual Marketplace Dynamics Data, Spatial Analytics, and Customer Engagement Tools in a Real-Time Interoperable Decentralized Metaverse. *Linguistic and Philosophical Investigations*, *21*(0), 105–120. doi:10.22381/lpi2120227

Vrontis, D., Makrides, A., Christofi, M., & Thrassou, A. (2021). Social media influencer marketing: A systematic review, integrative framework and future research agenda. *International Journal of Consumer Studies*, *45*(4), 617–644. doi:10.1111/ijcs.12647

Weber, I., Xu, X., Riveret, R., Governatori, G., Ponomarev, A., & Mendling, J. (2016). Untrusted Business Process Monitoring and Execution. *Proceedings of International Conference on Business Process Management*, 329-347.

Yang, Q., Zhao, Y., Huang, H., Xiong, Z., Kang, J., & Zheng, Z. (2022). Fusing blockchain and AI with metaverse: A survey. *IEEE Open Journal of the Computer Society*, *3*, 122–136. doi:10.1109/OJCS.2022.3188249

Yoo, K., Welden, R., Hewett, K., & Haenlein, M. (2023). The merchants of meta: A research agenda to understand the future of retailing in the metaverse. *Journal of Retailing*, *99*(2), 173–192. doi:10.1016/j.jretai.2023.02.002

ADDITIONAL READING

Chaffey, D., & Ellis-Chadwick, F. (2019). *Digital marketing*. Pearson UK.

Desai, V., & Vidyapeeth, B. (2019). Digital marketing: A review. *International Journal of Trend in Scientific Research and Development*, *5*(5), 196–200. doi:10.31142/ijtsrd23100

Hartanto, Y., Firmansyah, M. A., & Adhrianti, L. (2022, April). Implementation Digital Marketing Pesona 88 Curup in to Build Image for the Decision of Visit Tourist Attraction. In *4th Social and Humanities Research Symposium (SoRes 2021)* (pp. 589-594). Atlantis Press. 10.2991/assehr.k.220407.121

Herhausen, D., Miočević, D., Morgan, R. E., & Kleijnen, M. H. (2020). The digital marketing capabilities gap. *Industrial Marketing Management*, *90*, 276–290. doi:10.1016/j.indmarman.2020.07.022

Jadhav, G. G., Gaikwad, S. V., & Bapat, D. (2023). A systematic literature review: Digital marketing and its impact on SMEs. *Journal of Indian Business Research*, *15*(1), 76–91. doi:10.1108/JIBR-05-2022-0129

Khiong, K. (2022). Impact and Challenges of Digital Marketing in Healthcare Industries during Digital Era and Covid-19 Pandemic. *Journal of Industrial Engineering & Management Research*, *3*(5), 112–118.

Krishen, A. S., Dwivedi, Y. K., Bindu, N., & Kumar, K. S. (2021). A broad overview of interactive digital marketing: A bibliometric network analysis. *Journal of Business Research*, *131*, 183–195. doi:10.1016/j.jbusres.2021.03.061

Mogaji, E., Soetan, T. O., & Kieu, T. A. (2020). The implications of artificial intelligence on the digital marketing of financial services to vulnerable customers. *Australasian Marketing Journal*.

Olson, E. M., Olson, K. M., Czaplewski, A. J., & Key, T. M. (2021). Business strategy and the management of digital marketing. *Business Horizons*, *64*(2), 285–293. doi:10.1016/j.bushor.2020.12.004

Purwanti, Y. (2021). The influence of digital marketing & innovasion on the school performance. *Turkish Journal of Computer and Mathematics Education*, *12*(7), 118–127.

Saura, J. R. (2021). Using data sciences in digital marketing: Framework, methods, and performance metrics. *Journal of Innovation & Knowledge*, *6*(2), 92–102. doi:10.1016/j.jik.2020.08.001

Saura, J. R., Ribeiro-Soriano, D., & Palacios-Marqués, D. (2021). Setting B2B digital marketing in artificial intelligence-based CRMs: A review and directions for future research. *Industrial Marketing Management*, *98*, 161–178. doi:10.1016/j.indmarman.2021.08.006

Shankar, V., Grewal, D., Sunder, S., Fossen, B., Peters, K., & Agarwal, A. (2022). Digital marketing communication in global marketplaces: A review of extant research, future directions, and potential approaches. *International Journal of Research in Marketing*, *39*(2), 541–565. doi:10.1016/j.ijresmar.2021.09.005

Zanubiya, J., Meria, L., & Juliansah, M. A. D. (2023). Increasing Consumers with Satisfaction Application based Digital Marketing Strategies. *Startupreneur Bisnis Digital*, *2*(1), 12–21. doi:10.33050abda.v2i1.266

KEY TERMS AND DEFINITIONS

Artificial Intelligence (AI): The simulation of human intelligence processes by machines, such as learning, reasoning, and self-correction.

Augmented Reality (AR): A technology that overlays digital information onto the physical world, typically viewed through a mobile device or headset.

Blockchain: A decentralized, distributed ledger technology that allows for secure and transparent record-keeping of transactions without the need for a central authority.

Customer Experience: The overall impression and interaction a customer has with a brand, encompassing all touchpoints and interactions throughout the customer journey.

Digital Marketing: The practice of promoting products or services through digital channels, such as search engines, social media, email, and websites.

Digital Retail Platforms: Online platforms that enable the buying and selling of products or services, such as e-commerce websites, mobile apps, and social media platforms.

Immersive Technologies: Technologies that allow users to feel fully immersed in a virtual environment, such as augmented reality (AR) and virtual reality (VR).

Metaverse: A virtual shared space created by the convergence of physical and virtual reality, enabled by advanced technologies and populated by digital representations of users.

Privacy: The ability to control and protect personal information from being disclosed or misused by unauthorized parties.

Virtual Reality (VR): A technology that creates a fully immersive digital environment that simulates a physical world, typically viewed through a headset.

Chapter 4
Trustworthy Artificial Intelligence and Machine Learning:
Implications on Users' Security and Privacy Perceptions

Raquel Maria do Espírito Santo Faria
Universidade do Porto, Portugal

Ana Isabel Torres
https://orcid.org/0000-0002-0621-956X
Universidade de Aveiro, Portugal

Gabriela Beirão
https://orcid.org/0000-0001-7259-1709
Universidade do Porto, Portugal

ABSTRACT

Artificial intelligence (AI) has altered our world in numerous ways. Although its application has benefits, the underlying issues surrounding privacy and security in AI need to be understood, not only by the organizations that use it but also by the users that are susceptible to its vulnerabilities. To better understand the impact of privacy and security in AI, this chapter reviews the current literature on artificial intelligence, trustworthiness, and privacy and security concepts and uses bibliometric techniques to understand and identify current trends in the field. Finally, the authors highlight the challenges facing AI and machine learning and discuss the results obtained from the bibliometric analysis, which provides insight into the several implications for managers and contributions to future research and policy.

DOI: 10.4018/978-1-6684-8958-1.ch004

INTRODUCTION

In the last years, Artificial Intelligence (AI) has increasingly impacted our world, and it has been successfully applied to several areas, including Industry, Engineering, Life Sciences, Business, and Education, just to name a few. AI is a multidisciplinary field combining science and engineering aiming to create intelligent machines (Benaich & Hogart, 2022). The world is becoming more and more digital and data-driven, as such, AI will advance technological progress at a rapid pace. Nowadays, everything around us, from culture to consumer products, is a product of intelligence (Benaich & Hogart, 2022).

Even without knowing, we use AI in various ways daily, making our routines more efficient and accessible. Whenever we use a digital assistant like Google Assistant, Siri, or a map application, AI improves interaction and answers our questions. AI, however, does not restrict only to consumers. The impact of AI in different industries is quite significant, ranging from self-driving cars to financial advisory services. Companies are integrating AI models and applications into their business models as a critical efficiency component (Dwivedi et al., 2021). Companies report that AI fosters revenue in sales and marketing while reducing costs in supply chain management and manufacturing functions (Sadok, n.a).

This has led companies to an overcoming shift that has moved their businesses toward a more technological level rather than a more traditional and personal level. Experts estimate that by 2025, 95% of customer interactions will use AI-assisted channels and that the next generation of consumers will be assisted by chatbot applications (Anica-Popa et al., 2021). With the increasing use of AI applications, people are progressively more dependent on these technologies. For companies, AI technologies entail several benefits: increased revenues, sales reinforcement, price segmentation from the customer database, customer satisfaction, lower product returns, and cost reduction (Syam & Sharma, 2018). Therefore, companies must progress toward digitalizing their processes and functions using AI in service automation.

AI and service automation enables many companies to improve their processes and increase workers' productivity. However, it can also pose a threat, as is reshaping the job industry by replacing workers (Frank et al., 2019). Also, it may impact customers emotional sense as human beings. According to Bolton et al. (2018), customers who feel detached, frustrated, alienated, or isolated rather than involved in the customer experience may limit their adoption of this technology. Organizations have the challenge of balancing the efficiency and efficacy of digital technology while enhancing interactions and relationships with their customers, which must be the focus of their value proposition.

This dependency on AI can raise a significant risk for organizations and customers. Organizations use AI to maintain good customer service and optimize costs and the delivery of services. This way, the customer service is less personalized, might lack transparency, and can raise concerns about privacy and security issues, resulting in unhappy customers. Furthermore, using AI applications in some contexts can result in client harm, especially when AI is applied to medicine and healthcare. For example, questions have arisen about whether or not AI can exercise the same rights as doctors (Sunarti et al., 2021). It is essential to understand how to mitigate this risk and in what contexts they might emerge. As such, we need to know how customers interact with these applications and their trustworthiness, as they are becoming a big part of any company's service infrastructure. Understanding customer privacy and security perceptions around the different AI applications in various fields is important.

The main objective of this chapter is to present a map of privacy and security research in terms of intellectual roots (intellectual structure) to contribute to a better understanding of the numerous privacy and security research streams regarding AI and its evolution in recent research. Using a bibliometric analysis approach, this study aims to understand the current trends in AI-enabled customer experience and, particularly, to examine the impact of security and privacy on users' experience with activities that integrate AI technologies. This method enables a broad comprehension of the field and in-depth insights. Finally, this book chapter focuses on discovering open questions in AI trustworthiness development that might be impacted by security and privacy issues from the user's perception.

LITERATURE REVIEW

Artificial Intelligence and Machine Learning

Artificial intelligence (AI) is a broad discipline aiming to create intelligent machines instead of the natural intelligence that humans and animals demonstrate. AI has become a global term that seizes the long-term ambition of the field to construct machines able to emulate and excel in the full range of human cognition (Benaich & Hogart, 2022). Machine learning (ML) is a part of AI that usually uses statistical methods that let machines "learn" directly from data without explicit instructions on how to do it. This process is known as "training" a "model" using a learning "algorithm" that progressively improves model performance on a specific task (Benaich & Hogart, 2022).

However, there is no consensus around the definition of Artificial Intelligence (AI), with various authors proposing several definitions over the years. One of the early AI definitions was introduced by Bellman (1978) as an automated process associated with human thought, including learning, problem-solving, and decision-making. According to Russell and Norvig (2010), AI is the study of agents that act after taking in environmental cues from their surroundings. Dwivedi et al. (2021) defined AI as the increasing ability of machines to take over specific roles and tasks currently performed by humans in the workplace and society.

The different areas of AI have been divided in various ways over the past years. Mccarthy (2007) divided AI into twelve branches and topics: logical AI, search AI, pattern recognition, representation, inference, common sense knowledge and reasoning, learning from experience, planning, epistemology, ontology, heuristics, and genetic programming. The key point is that these systems use algorithms to gather, examine, compare, and predict as much information as possible. It was also noted that AI still has a long way to progress in reasoning. Zadeh (2008) states that the challenge of reasoning relies on two of humans' outstanding abilities. Firstly, the ability to reason, communicate and act rationally in the face of ambiguity, uncertainty, inadequate information, and partiality of truth. And secondly, the capacity to complete a wide range of physical and mental tasks without any calculations or measurements. Automating these abilities, particularly automating natural language understanding, is required to achieve machine intelligence on par with humans.

A more recent study by Collins et al. (2021) specified a different range of AI branches from Expert Systems, Machine Learning, Robotics, Natural Language Processing, Machine Vision, and Speech Recognition. Expert Systems are defined as systems that try to represent knowledge and simulate human behavior when solving a problem. These authors conclude that machine learning is increasingly used and is a way to improve the method's results as it continuously gets more data. AI can also be applied to robotics, especially in manufacturing (also known as Industry 4.0). Natural Language Processing is a way of converting human language into a representation for computers to understand, and it is the base for AI speech recognition applications. Finally, machine vision is a way of analyzing images using an algorithmic inspection.

AI implementation intrinsically depends on the amount and quality of personal information organizations gather from their customers. However, companies must have ethical considerations and choose the right balance between personalization advantages and privacy risks (Inman & Nikolova, 2017). To take advantage of an AI-powered shopping experience, customers are being increasingly pressured to share private information, which can easily make them mistrust AI and raise privacy issues. Although, privacy concerns regarding the collection and use of personal information for marketing purposes already exist, AI broad use is raising those concerns, as users' data is being collected and processed by machines and algorithms (Anica-Popa et al., 2021).

Machine Learning is a set of algorithms that enable systems to learn. Systems with machine learning capabilities may interact with data, learn from experience, and create intelligent solutions based on prior knowledge (Jarrahi, 2018). Several ways of applying machine learning to applications were found, some of which we use daily and might not even acknowledge. Based on the literature it was identified four main types of machine learning applications: chatbots, virtual assistants, recommender systems, and predictive analytics. Table 1 shows the most relevant privacy and security challenges, barriers of use, and impacts on trust identified in the literature for the four machine learning types.

Table 1. Users' trustiness perceptions of ML artifacts

ML Artifact	Features	Privacy and Security Challenges	Barriers of use	Impacts on Trust	Reference
Voice Based Digital Assistant/ Personal Assistant/ Smart assistant	Real-time observation and processing of complicated data Undertakes tasks on behalf of users Personalization Anthropomorphism	Storage and use of data Continuous analysis of user behavior	The system uses passive listening The user's personal information is not secure. Misunderstanding of the use and storage of data	Those valuing this technology are ready to sacrifice privacy to reap its benefits. Privacy concerns limit the adoption of technology. The tendency for users to only do simple activities with the technology.	(Vimalkumar et al., 2021); (de Barcelos Silva et al., 2020)
Chatbots	The first line of support Available 24/7 No waiting or queue Anthropomorphism	Reduced access to the companies' personnel Storage and use of data Complex operations	Interpretation issues Misunderstanding of use and storage of data transparency	The tendency for users to only do simple activities with the technology. E.g., users will not complete transactions	(Følstad et al., 2018); (Cheng & Jiang 2020); (Hasal et al., 2021)
Recommender System	Personalization Facilitates decisions	Storage and use of data No prevention of the system using feedback/ rating data Continuous analysis of user behavior	Misunderstanding of the use and storage of data Manipulated feedback/ ratings bias and compromised identity	Those valuing this technology are ready to sacrifice privacy to reap its benefits. False/manipulated recommendations can lead to mistrust.	(Schafer et al., 2007); (Knijnenburg et al., 2012): (Pu et al., 2012)
Predictive Analytics/ Big data analytics	Identifies patterns	Storage and use of data No prevention in the system using feedback/ rating data Continuous analysis of user behavior	Users are unaware that this ML artifact is used in their technology. Due to this, there is no reported feedback on Barriers to use.	Due to unawareness, there is no reported feedback on the impacts on trust. This coincides with the ethical concerns of AI.	(McCue 2006); (Glenn & Monteith, 2014); (Mai, 2016)

A chatbot application is a machine learning application known to simulate discussions with humans, which improves over time by constantly learning algorithms from existing data (Moriuchi et al., 2021). For example, daily use of chatbots might include requesting a support ticket for a refund or exchanging an item purchased online. The chatbot with pre-defined conversations can direct the customer to the correct department or even already process the refund or exchange. Like chatbots, virtual assistants or smart assistants are typically composed of three main components, sensors monitoring environmental and physical characteristics, controllers interpreting the information they receive, and actuators carrying out actions (Lau et al., 2018). Known virtual assistants were developed by companies such as Google, Apple, and Amazon, with capabilities like telling you the weather forecast, finding information about a restaurant, helping you plan your agenda, playing musing and podcasts, entertaining, and even telling jokes. Recent research also has shown that chatbots are useful tools to support the online purchase decision making, assisting customers during the (pre)purchase and after-sales support and, particularly, perceived usefulness and rewarding interactions are associated with customer engagement with chatbots which positively affects repurchase intentions (Torres & Delgado, 2023).

Recommender systems are different machine learning applications using software tools that provide suggestions for items a user may find helpful. Recommender systems are primarily intended for those lacking the personal experience or expertise to assess various alternatives (Soediono, 1989). Recommender systems are used, for example, in e-commerce websites that use individuals' previously tracked purchases to predict and suggest future purchases.

Another Machine Learning application is predictive analytics which forecasts future outcomes by combining historical data with statistical modelling, data mining techniques, and machine learning. Businesses use predictive analytics to spot dangers, opportunities, and future trends By analyzing patterns in this data (IBM, 2023). Daily use of predictive analytic tools might include users accessing navigation maps to discover the best routes and estimate arrival times.

Trustworthy AI

AI can potentially bring significant benefits to both users and companies that use this technology. However, we are also confronted with challenges with the continuous use of AI applications. Examples include the impact on labor and the use of untrustworthy and unreliable applications that gather individuals' data and information. To build, deploy, and operate AI systems without fear, trustworthy AI focuses on what principles should be implemented (Wickramasinghe et al., 2020). In AI-enabled customer service, the trust concept is even more complex because trust goes beyond technology and brand, including the process and aim of using AI (Hengstler et al., 2016; Siau & Wang, 2018). Research has shown the complex nature of AI use (Dwivedi et al., 2021) and the uncertainty in several areas, such as security, reliability, and ethics.

Although AI satisfies every criterion of the logical account of trust, it was found that this is a type of reliance rather than trust, as it does not possess emotional states or can be held responsible for its actions (Ryan, 2020). Basing AI as being trustworthy is not compelling because doing so distorts the nature of human relationships, humanizes artificial intelligence, and absolves those who develop and use it of responsibility (Ryan, 2020). However, Glikson and Woolley (2020) showed in their study that (1) the type of trust people build is significantly influenced by machine intelligence and differentiates types of trust depending if it concerns robotic AI or virtual and embedded AI; (2) the degree of machine learning may influence how trust grows, with use and experience showing that a high level of intelligence fosters more trust and, (3) high machine intelligence offers the chance to either preserve the initial high levels of trust (by living up to the high expectations) or minimize the decline of trust for embedded and virtual AI. Also, those authors stated that the trust trajectory for robotic AI is similar to trust development in human relationships, starting low and increasing after the direct hands-on experience. On the other hand, it was observed that significant initial trust declines because of experience with virtual and embedded AI (Glikson & Woolley, 2020).

From a more end-consumer perspective, Ameen et al. (2021) analyze that integrating AI in shopping can lead to a better AI-enabled customer experience. Their findings highlight the central role the concept of trust plays in AI-enabled customer experience, identifying major sacrifices consumers may face, such as a lack of human interaction, loss of privacy, loss of control, time consumption, and possible negative feelings of irritation, all of which can damage AI-enabled service experiences. The authors conclude that when a company offers high-quality, personalized, and convenient AI-enabled services, customers start to trust the brand and its technology. A high level of trust positively impacts service quality.

Hengstler et al. (2016) state that AI technology must be trusted for applied AI to work, the company's role is essential, and communication must also be trusted in the process. As a result, businesses need to start developing trust as technology develops. Significant challenges that emerge from the trustworthiness of AI are personal or organizational privacy and security concerns, the use of biased systems, and even the role AI can take in decision-making processes. A critical AI challenge is guaranteeing that data has consistently high quality since the sources and volume (web, social media, mobile devices, sensors, and IoT) have increased considerably (Anica-Popa et al., 2021). Importantly, in the case of ML algorithms, the underrepresentation of the population in the data used to train the model causes a built-in bias, a vulnerability usually imputed to AI (Shneiderman, 2016). Therefore, trustworthy AI also concerns ML algorithms that tend to incorporate the biases of their human developers, which can induce discrimination in the algorithms and, thus, racist or sexist chatbots (Anica-Popa et al., 2021). For exam,ple, most digital assistants are pictured as young Caucasian women, reflecting the stereotyped perception of women in administrative roles (Spencer et al., 2018).

Also, ML models may be seen as "black boxes" because of algorithms' opacity, thus making it difficult to explain how they arrive at certain predictions or suggestions (Adadi & Berrada, 2018; Miller, 2019). One example is using past consumer behaviors as a base for sales forecasting, which may carry on a bias because it is no longer relevant to a customer's current buying need or preference (Anica-Popa et al., 2021). Thus, the development and training of AI algorithms must be responsible and accurate to avoid costly mistakes.

Moreover, ethical principles need to be implemented when deploying algorithms to foster pricing and promotions since retailers could use AI to socially discriminate against customers by using different messages and prices based on customers' specific profiles (Gerlick & Liozu, 2020). From this perspective, AI emerges as an effective marketing tool and a powerful manipulation tool. However, there is a considerable reputational risk that AI-enabled aggressive strategies can generate that could provoke major financial and operational problems (Anica-Popa et al., 2021).

In discussing AI trustworthiness and impacts on individuals and society, critical areas such as medicine and healthcare are especially important since AI solutions or applications can have negative impacts. The European Commission has acknowledged this topic and has proposed ethical guidelines for trustworthy AI. According to their study, trustworthy AI should be composed of three main characteristics: lawful, ethical, and robust. Trustworthy AI needs to be lawful, with instructions and guidelines on what should be avoided, done, and permissible. Ethical and Robust AI are closely related. Ethics refers to the compliance to ethical principles and values. Robust AI refers to AI systems where safeguards should be anticipated to prevent unanticipated adverse effects from a technical perspective. Depending on their social and environmental context, such systems should operate safely and securely. Each element is needed to build trustworthy AI, as the three principles complement each other in an ideal world and operate close together (European Commission, 2019).

User Privacy and Security

In both physical and digital worlds, privacy and security are crucial. In the digital world, the notions of privacy and security are becoming more and more salient as users deal with these terms and often consent to privacy policies daily, from purchasing an item online to even downloading a simple mobile application. Consequently, external providers can track and use people data in many ways, including customer transaction data from a CRM system, demographic data gleaned from credit card or loyalty card details, survey data linked to an email address, and even visitor data to stores. Additionally, when one considers social media data, which can be connected to individual-level activity, customer-level data becomes very rich and detailed (Bradlow et al., 2017).

Privacy and Security are interconnected, but they are not interchangeable. Privacy can be defined as the level of concern a consumer has regarding a potential infringement of their right to prohibit sharing personal information with third parties (Ischen et al., 2020). Tucker (2018) comments that three factors make privacy challenging: (1) Data may exist for much longer than intended due to the low cost of storage; (2) Data can be repurposed again and utilized for different things than what they were initially meant for; and (3) Data for one person may include information about another person without authorization or knowledge. Since one must have confidence that the entities with whom one has entrusted personal information will protect it effectively, privacy is not only a personal concern but also a security issue in general (Heurix et al., 2015).

However, security entails keeping sensitive data and information safe and protected from unauthorized access (Okta, 2022). Accordingly, Kaur et al. (2018) state that "security is the act of safeguarding data and data resources using technology and procedures preparing from inspections, unauthorized access, recordings, etc." For instance, in China, a local safari park was sued for "violating consumer protection law" after making facial recognition registration mandatory for visitor entrance. The lawsuit focused on the risk of data leaks: "once leaked, illegal misuse will easily endanger the safety of consumers," the safari park has since changed its entrance policy to allow visitors to choose between facial recognition or fingerprint recognition. China's use of facial recognition is incredibly widespread (see coverage in The State of AI 2018 & 2019), but there are some signs that privacy concerns are being taken more seriously.

Sensors are widely used in smart cities, hospitals, and homes, which allows for collecting a massive amount of information from informed and uninformed individuals. To address these issues, is essential to have legislation (Zhang & Tao, 2021). To anticipate various security and privacy threats, currently, there is the existence of laws that protect users regarding information privacy and security compliance. Some of the most known in Europe and the United States of America include the General Data Protection Regulation (GDPR): where organizations worldwide are subject to its requirements as long as they target or gather information about EU citizens, the Health Information Portability and Accountability Act (HIPAA): safeguards user's data held by healthcare professionals, the Fair Credit Reporting Act (FCRA): protects and limits access of credit information and the Family Educational Right and Privacy

Act (FERPA): secures student records held by educational institutions and agencies while allowing authorized students and parents access.

Although we benefit from these passed laws, it is important to notice that these laws are, unfortunately, not enough to hinder organizations that continuously push the boundaries and limits of compliance. Heurix et al. (2015) further observe that companies are increasingly breaking the general rule of data minimization, which states that they should only gather and store as much data as is required to efficiently operate their business processes. Some of the largest Internet-based businesses generate money by obtaining, analyzing, and selling as much personal information about their consumers as possible. Thus, it is important to notice that balancing two competing interests is necessary for a data privacy policy. Customers might not use applications related to AI if there is insufficient protection, and excessive regulation could repress innovation (Davenport et al., 2020).

The scope of AI literature is relatively vast, and users' perceptions of risk and trust with AI cover different research fields. A bibliometric analysis will be performed to map and understand the current trends in AI-enabled customer experience and, particularly, to examine the impact of security and privacy on users' experience with activities that integrate AI technologies. This method broadens the field and gives in-depth insights into users' perceptions of risk and trust concerning AI applications. Following, we describe the method analysis and data collection.

METHODOLOGY

This study utilizes bibliometric methods to analyze the literature on associated risks generated by implementing artificial intelligence on users' security and privacy perceptions and experiences. The bibliometric analysis draws on statistical tools to systematically map and decipher large amounts of scientific data and rigorously assess the contribution and impact of publications in a research field (Donthu et al., 2021).

This paper adopts a systematic literature review based on the guidelines outlined by Donthu et al. (2021). The procedure includes four steps: (1) definition of the aims and scope; (2) choosing the technique for bibliometric analysis; (3) data collection (includes data cleaning); and (4) running the analysis and reporting.

The aim is to map the current state of the literature on users' perceptions of risk and trust with AI. Since AI is relatively recent, the scope of the research was limited to articles published after 2010. The technique chosen for the bibliometric analysis was co-word analysis using VOSviewer (Visualization of similarities viewer) to identify the interlinkages between the keywords and, thus, understand the key research areas and linkages of the published articles.

The co-word analysis technique is based on "the idea that the co-occurrence of keywords describes the contents of the documents" (Callon et al., 1991). Also, the interlinkage between keywords is shown by the co-occurrence of keywords in a particular cluster (Van Eck & Waltman, 2010). Vosviewer clusters the keywords occurring together most frequently into groups shown in maps.

To collect the data, we use the Web of Science (WoS) database, a comprehensive and leading scientific database. The search was performed on the title, abstract, and keywords, including articles from 2010 till March 2023. The relevant keywords for analysis were chosen based on the revision of extant research relating AI, trustworthiness (or similar terms), and user experience and perceptions. The WoS search string included the following keywords: "Artificial Intelligence" AND (security OR safety OR confident* OR harm* OR Trust* OR privacy) AND (perception* OR "user experience"). The search retrieved 814 results. The results were then reviewed based on the following inclusion criteria: the language of publication (English); and the type of publication (article, proceeding paper, review article, early access, and book chapters). Following these steps, 752 papers were used for further analysis. Then, the publications were manually checked for relevance, and four articles were removed because they were reports from conferences, workshops, and tutorials.

The screening process resulted in a sample of 748 articles (614 articles and 134 proceeding papers) published since 2010 in 369 different journals and 77 different countries. Also, researchers with different backgrounds have contributed to the field, as the maximum number of papers per author is seven, and more than 2800 authors have contributed. Figure 1 shows that AI research is still evolving and is in its initial stage. The number of publications remained low from 2010 until 2014; however, since 2015 there has been a sudden and constant increase in the number of publications. The huge rise in publications is attributable to the widespread interest among academics in the Artificial Intelligence privacy and security domains. USA and China are the countries with more publications (see Figure 2). As Haenlein & Kaplan (2021) note, technological advances in AI may even cause a new era of global governance as China and the US emerge as leaders in this field, whereas other international regions, including Europe, are behind. This suggests solid academic research is necessary to support consumer, manager, and public policy decision-making. Figure 3 illustrates the different areas of research that have addressed this topic. The main research areas that tackle this issue are Computer science, Engineering, Business Economics, and Psychology. Importantly, there is an increasing number of research in the healthcare field.

Figure 1. Number of publications published in the period January 2010 - March 2023

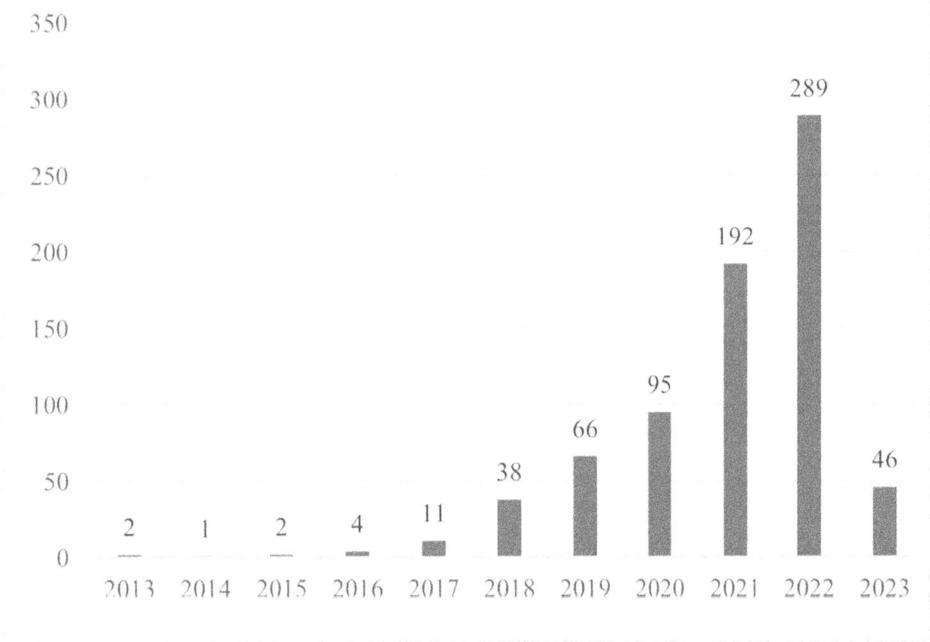

Figure 2. Number of publications per country since 2010 (only countries with more than 20 publications are shown)

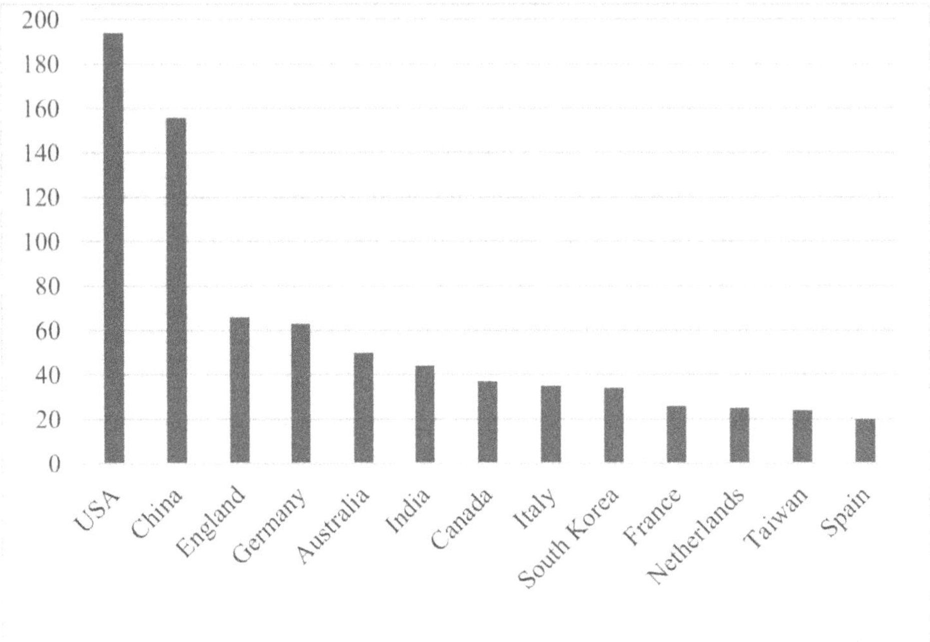

Figure 3. Top research areas by number of publications

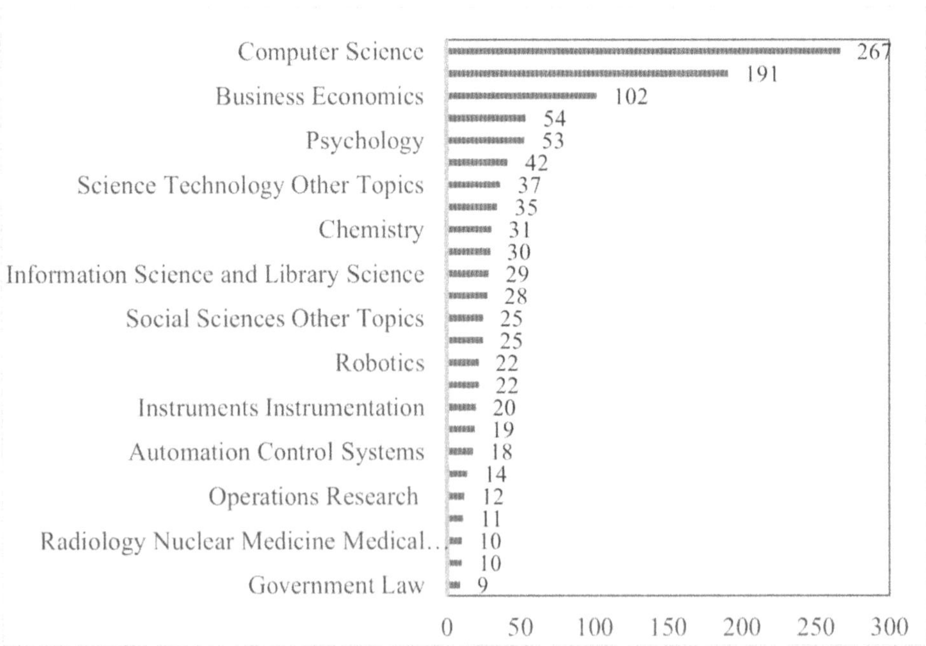

To conduct the bibliometric review using co-word analysis, the bibliographic information was inserted in VOS viewer, which used the keywords that appeared most frequently in the title, abstract and author-provided keywords. A thesaurus file was supplied to VOS viewer during analysis to eliminate keyword inconsistency (e.g., singular vs. plural keywords, UK vs. US English spelling). The network was generated by including keywords that occur at least four times in the sample of articles, which resulted in filtering 3660 keywords to 243 that met the threshold. The keywords irrelevant to our study were deleted, resulting in a final of 241 keywords.

RESULTS ANALYSIS

The papers address many diversified topics; as such, the network created by VOSviewer helped us to understand the emerging research themes and relationships among keywords related to AI and accelerated concerns about trust and safety. Based on the analysis, eight clusters were formed. Table 2 shows the top keywords with more than 30 occurrences. The ones with the highest occurrence are artificial Intelligence, trustworthiness and trust, perceptions, machine learning, acceptance, automated vehicles, robots, and adoption.

Table 2. Top keywords with the highest frequency.

Keywords	Cluster	Occurrence	Cluster colors
AI	5	394	purple
trustworthiness and trust	4	159	yellow
perception	1	113	red
technology	7	68	orange
system	1	62	red
machine learning	1	57	red
acceptance	2	55	green
automated vehicles	1	47	red
robot	3	47	blue
adoption	2	43	green
privacy	6	41	grey
automation	3	38	blue
behavior	4	38	yellow
customer satisfaction	2	36	green
decision making	5	36	purple
neural networks	1	33	red
healthcare	1	31	red
Internet	2	31	green
anthropomorphism	7	31	orange
deep learning	1	30	red
information	3	30	blue

Figures 4 and 5 also depict the visualization (VOS viewer) of the conceptual structure of the publications, that is, the themes and their inter-relations. Larger circles represent the more often used keywords and related concepts. There is a total of seven clusters, which are presented in different colors. The cluster boundaries are fuzzy since they are connected. Table 3 shows the results by themes and sub-themes. Overall, the findings show: 1) concerns about trust and safety within AI are triggering diverse and plural research; 2) privacy and security issues overlap in several research areas, and 3) the complex and vast repercussions of AI on every aspect of our lives, and the huge potential it presents further encourage and calls for more in-depth research investigations.

Figure 4. Network visualization of keywords

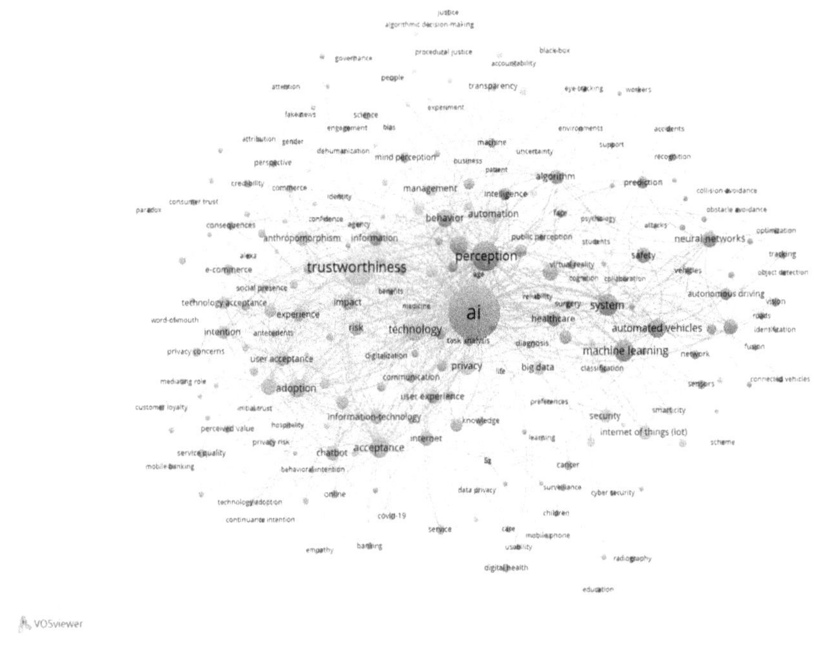

Figure 5. Density visualization of keywords

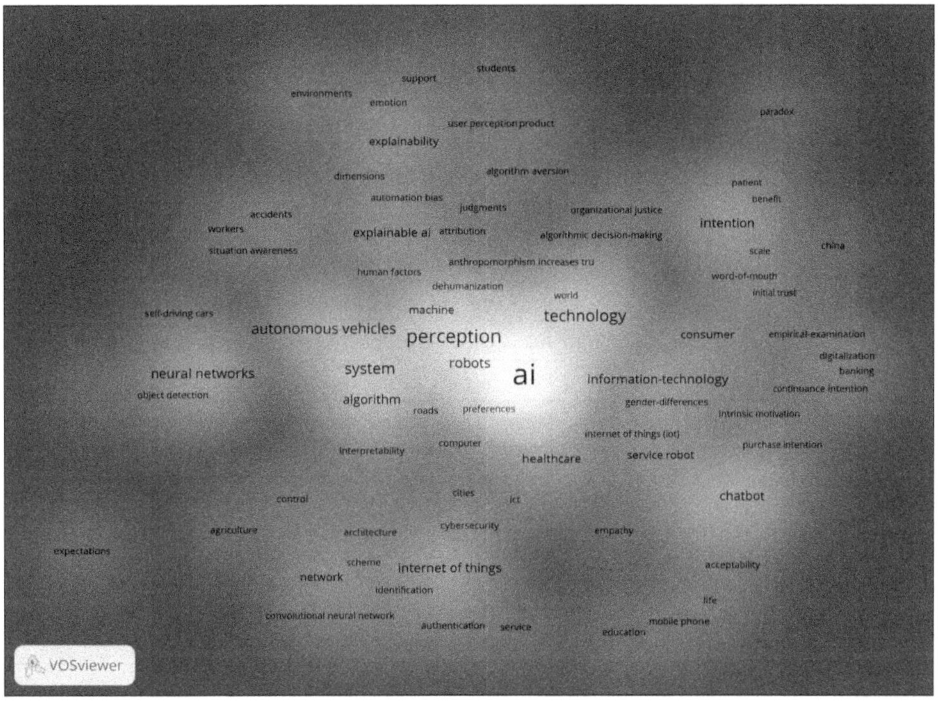

Table 3. Clusters' themes and sub-themes

Cluster	Theme	Sub-Themes
1	AI systems and perceptions	Machine learning, deep learning, and neural networks
		Automated vehicles and autonomous driving
		Healthcare Systems perceptions, safety, phycology Biometric data, face recognition, eye-tracking Collaboration, human-robot collaboration
2	AI acceptance and adoption	Risk perception and privacy concerns
		Perceived value, satisfaction, and loyalty
		Adoption, technology acceptance, easiness of use
		E-commerce, chatbots, conversational agents
3	Information, experience, and human-machine interaction	Robots, agency, behavior, experience, interactions with humans, dehumanization Challenges, consequences, mind perception, machines
		Explainable AI
4	Trustworthiness	Automation, performance, measurement Management, accountability, algorithmic decision-making Attitudes, transparency, justice, fairness, uncertainty
5	AI	Decision-making, errors
		Cyber security and ethics
		AI applications in healthcare Services
6	Internet of Things	Security and privacy
		Big data
		Blockchain Cloud computing, edge computing, architecture
7	Technology and anthropomorphism	Anthropomorphism, social responses, personalization, confidence, user perception Willingness, antecedents, online Technology, service robots, automation bias, benefits
8	Expectations and preferences	Expectations, preferences, and personality Competence, universal dimensions

CONCLUSION

Using bibliometric methodologies, this study selected the most significant published sources and examined the changes that have occurred in the conceptual framework of privacy and security research. From 2010 to 2014 there were no major publications in the field; however, 2015 shows a considerable increase in the number of publications in terms of volume, which only increased since then. Privacy and security are increasingly becoming more critical as technology advances, and academics are now focusing on this issue as the digitalization of services continues to increase. Nonetheless, despite the several benefits for businesses and customers, AI entails several privacy and security risks and challenges for companies and political policies.

AI implementations have managerial implications concerning the technical domain of learning algorithms and big data processing, involving consistent privacy and security risk management. It is important to have a top-down view on the AI context specific to each organization to make informed decisions on key principles concerning the business, IT development, and ethical issues, that is, deciding on how much and how information is going to be used to feed learning algorithms for customer profiling, customer privacy, etc. (Anica-Popa et al., 2021).

The ethical concerns of trustworthy AI previously mentioned are critical to any business system using AI-driven customer profiling. The amount of data collected, tracked, and used by companies enables them to profile customers exploiting their preferences, strongly influencing their buying decision process, and persuading them to purchase. From a customer perspective, these practices entail several risks and increase fears concerning trustful AI applications, affecting companies' brand image. Therefore, from a business perspective, such aggressive strategies produce considerable reputational risks to brand trust that could damage the benefits associated with AI technologies. The key organizational drivers of AI-enabled customer experience investigated by this chapter - trust, security, privacy, transparency, and ethics – could be used to manage AI perceived risk and trustworthiness.

Finally, as AI adoption grows, regulators give developers more to think about. Many actors attempt to define principles for the responsible use of AI: common themes include transparency, auditability, robustness, safety, and fairness. To safeguard data security and privacy, controllers and processors of personal data must take the necessary precautions (Zhang & Tao, 2021). Several governments are imposing rules and legislation. Washington State passed a law requiring government agencies to obtain a warrant to run facial recognition scans, except in an emergency (Dave, 2020). This law requires that the software is independently tested for "accuracy and unfair performance differences" across skin tone, gender, age, and other characteristics. In the EU, the AI Ethics Guidelines from the AI High-Level Expert Group (HLEG) have been developed and are set to shape legislative action in the EU on AI (European Commission, 2019). The Global Partnership on AI is a new initiative from 14 countries and the EU building on top of the OECD work. The Personal Information Security Specifications is a new voluntary standard for data privacy in China that companies, including Tencent and Alipay, are now trialing. Also, companies like Google are leaning into fairness, interpretability, privacy, and security of AI models, aiming to increase educational content and tools through the TensorFlow community to learn how to integrate responsible AI practices.

In sum, organizations need to address the following challenges: (i) Ensuring an appropriate level of explain ability of AI applications; (ii) Using data of good quality, and (iii) Conducting rigorous model validation.

FUTURE RESEARCH DIRECTIONS

Future research initiatives can help to address the shortcomings of this study. The fact that the bibliometric data was generated only from the Web of Science is a research constraint. Hence, different data sources, such as Scopus or SpringerLink, should be used in the next investigations. Based on 748 documents, the study provides an overview of various factors, such as published document categories, publication sources, and VOSviewer-referenced research. Furthermore, a more detailed oriented analysis can be performed to understand the impact of each research area found in this current study. This study also focused solely on user perceptions of privacy and security. However, academics can further research the interconnected areas and interrelate them.

To understand what remains to be discovered regarding these themes and the challenges associated with the field, we uncover future research questions that may help guide academics, as shown in Table 4. This section addresses general research questions in the AI field, the trustworthiness of AI and its implications regarding user perceptions of security and privacy.

Table 4. Future research questions

Category	Research Question	Author
General AI Discussion	Depending on the development of complicated AI abilities, more research can examine the impact on employability, privacy, and security separately.	(Ferreira et al., 2020)
	What kinds of applications should AI be utilized for? Or should it not be used?	(Davenport et al., 2020)
	What are the cultural differences concerning ethical AI?	(Davenport et al., 2020); (Puntoni et al., 2021)
	Can AI be used to create and extract value within ethical bounds, given its ability to permeate nearly every facet of society?	(Mustak et al., 2021)
	How can we prevent societal prejudice brought on by the use of AI?	(Mustak et al., 2021)
	How is AI's ability to exploit affected by the type and source of data it uses?	(Puntoni et al., 2021)
	What makes people react to feelings of exploitation by engaging in actions like deliberately providing false information by creating fictitious user profiles, sabotaging AI by disabling sensor inputs, or donning anti-surveillance outerwear to trick facial recognition algorithms?	(Puntoni et al., 2021)
Trustworthiness impacts privacy and security	What stage of the decision-making process should machines replace humans?	(Mustak et al., 2021)
	How do emotions and affective perception, which in turn affect the adoption of technologies, are impacted by privacy worries and trust?	(Vimalkumar et al., 2021)
	With the ongoing monitoring of consumers (e.g., via biometrics), the ubiquitous collection of consumer data, and the connectivity of service robots to sizable databases, including CRM systems, how can consumer privacy be protected and privacy issues be minimized?	(Wirtz et al., 2018)
	What causes a consumer's initial mistrust in robots, and how can it be dispelled?	(Wirtz et al., 2018)
	Are there any facts to support the idea that biased AI programmers produce biased AI algorithms? Will efforts to increase diversity in the tech industry lessen the possibility of bias?	(Tucker, 2018)
User Experience	What do non-experts believe AI to be, given the presence of AI systems in people's daily lives? Is this likely to influence how they feel about how much regulation or implementation is necessary?	(Bingley et al., 2023)
	Is there a link between satisfaction, continued usage intentions, and customer loyalty regarding AI?	(Cheng & Jiang, 2020)
	How do consumers choose the best trade-off between privacy and the benefits of AI?	(Davenport et al., 2020)
	How does the security and ethics of AI technology look from a user standpoint?	(Ameen et al., 2021)

REFERENCES

Adadi, A., & Berrada, M. (2018). Peeking Inside the Black-Box: A Survey on Explainable Artificial Intelligence (XAI). *IEEE Access : Practical Innovations, Open Solutions*, *6*, 52138–52160. doi:10.1109/ACCESS.2018.2870052

Ameen, N., Tarhini, A., Reppel, A., & Anand, A. (2021). Customer experiences in the age of artificial intelligence. *Computers in Human Behavior*, *114*, 106548. Advance online publication. doi:10.1016/j.chb.2020.106548 PMID:32905175

Anica-Popa, I., Anica-Popa, L., Rădulescu, C., & Vrîncianu, M. (2021). The integration of artificial intelligence in retail: Benefits, challenges and a dedicated conceptual framework. *Amfiteatru Economic*, *23*(56), 120–136. doi:10.24818/EA/2021/56/120

Bellman, R. E. (1978). An introduction to artificial intelligence: Can computers think? Boyd & Fraser Pub.

Ben Schafer, J., Frankowski, D., Herlocker, J., & Sen, S. (2007). Collaborative filtering recommender systems. Lecture Notes in Computer Science, 4321, 291–324. doi:10.1007/978-3-540-72079-9_9

Benaich, N., & Hogart, I. (2022). *State of AI Report 2022*. https://www.stateof.ai/

Bingley, W. J., Curtis, C., Lockey, S., Bialkowski, A., Gillespie, N., Haslam, S. A., Ko, R. K. L., Steffens, N., Wiles, J., & Worthy, P. (2023). Where is the human in human-centered AI? Insights from developer priorities and user experiences. *Computers in Human Behavior*, *141*, 107617. doi:10.1016/j.chb.2022.107617

Bolton, R. N., McColl-Kennedy, J. R., Cheung, L., Gallan, A., Orsingher, C., Witell, L., & Zaki, M. (2018). Customer experience challenges: Bringing together digital, physical and social realms. *Journal of Service Management*, *29*(5), 776–808. doi:10.1108/JOSM-04-2018-0113

Bradlow, E. T., Gangwar, M., Kopalle, P., & Voleti, S. (2017). The role of Big Data and predictive analytics in retailing. *Journal of Retailing*, *93*(1), 79–95. doi:10.1016/j.jretai.2016.12.004

Callon, M., Courtial, J. P., & Laville, F. (1991). Co-word analysis as a tool for describing the network of interactions between basic and technological research: The case of polymer chemistry. *Scientometrics*, *22*(1), 155–205. doi:10.1007/BF02019280

Cheng, Y., & Jiang, H. (2020). How do AI-driven Chatbots impact user experience? Examining gratifications, perceived privacy risk, satisfaction, loyalty, and continued use. *Journal of Broadcasting & Electronic Media*, *64*(4), 592–614. doi:10.1080/08838151.2020.1834296

Collins, C., Dennehy, D., Conboy, K., & Mikalef, P. (2021). Artificial intelligence in information systems research: A systematic literature review and research agenda. *International Journal of Information Management*, *60*, 102383. Advance online publication. doi:10.1016/j.ijinfomgt.2021.102383

Dave, P. (2020). *Washington state adopts facial recognition rules critics view as too loose*. Reuters. https://www.reuters.com/article/us-washington-tech-idUSL1N2BO1XW

Davenport, T., Guha, A., Grewal, D., & Bressgott, T. (2020). How artificial intelligence will change the future of marketing. *Journal of the Academy of Marketing Science, 48*(1), 24–42. doi:10.100711747-019-00696-0

de Barcelos Silva, A., Gomes, M. M., da Costa, C. A., da Rosa Righi, R., Barbosa, J. L. V., Pessin, G., De Doncker, G., & Federizzi, G. (2020). Intelligent personal assistants: A systematic literature review. *Expert Systems with Applications, 147*, 113193. Advance online publication. doi:10.1016/j.eswa.2020.113193

Donthu, N., Kumar, S., Mukherjee, D., Pandey, N., & Lim, W. M. (2021). How to conduct a bibliometric analysis: An overview and guidelines. *Journal of Business Research, 133*, 285–296. doi:10.1016/j.jbusres.2021.04.070

Dwivedi, Y. K., Hughes, L., Ismagilova, E., Aarts, G., Coombs, C., Crick, T., Duan, Y., Dwivedi, R., Edwards, J., Eirug, A., Galanos, V., Ilavarasan, P. V., Janssen, M., Jones, P., Kar, A. K., Kizgin, H., Kronemann, B., Lal, B., Lucini, B., & Williams, M. D. (2021). Artificial Intelligence (AI): Multidisciplinary perspectives on emerging challenges, opportunities, and agenda for research, practice and policy. *International Journal of Information Management, 57*. doi:10.1016/j.ijinfomgt.2019.08.002

European Commission. (2019). Ethics guidelines for trustworthy AI. High-Level Expert Group on Artificial Intelligence. *European Commission*, 1–39. https://ec.europa.eu/futurium/en/ai-alliance-consultation

Ferreira, P., Teixeira, J. G., & Teixeira, L. F. (2020). Understanding the Impact of Artificial Intelligence on Services. *Lecture Notes in Business Information Processing, 377*, 202–213. doi:10.1007/978-3-030-38724-2_15

Følstad, A., Nordheim, C. B., & Bjørkli, C. A. (2018). What makes users trust a chatbot for customer service? An exploratory interview study. Lecture Notes in Computer Science, 11193, 194–208. doi:10.1007/978-3-030-01437-7_16

Frank, M. R., Autor, D., Bessen, J. E., Brynjolfsson, E., Cebrian, M., Deming, D. J., Feldman, M., Groh, M., Lobo, J., Moro, E., Wang, D., Youn, H., & Rahwan, I. (2019). Toward understanding the impact of artificial intelligence on labor. *Proceedings of the National Academy of Sciences of the United States of America, 116*(14), 6531–6539. doi:10.1073/pnas.1900949116 PMID:30910965

Gerlick, J. A., & Liozu, S. M. (2020). Ethical and legal considerations of artificial intelligence and algorithmic decision-making in personalized pricing. *Journal of Revenue and Pricing Management, 19*(2), 85–98. doi:10.105741272-019-00225-2

Glenn, T., & Monteith, S. (2014). Privacy in the Digital World: Medical and Health Data Outside of HIPAA Protections. *Current Psychiatry Reports, 16*(11), 494. doi:10.100711920-014-0494-4 PMID:25218603

Glikson, E., & Woolley, A. W. (2020). Human Trust in Artificial Intelligence: Review of Empirical Research. *The Academy of Management Annals, 14*(2), 627–660. doi:10.5465/annals.2018.0057

Haenlein, M., & Kaplan, A. (2021). Artificial intelligence and robotics: Shaking up the business world and society at large. *Journal of Business Research, 124*, 405–407. doi:10.1016/j.jbusres.2020.10.042

Hasal, M., Nowaková, J., Ahmed Saghair, K., Abdulla, H., Snášel, V., & Ogiela, L. (2021). Chatbots: Security, privacy, data protection, and social aspects. *Concurrency and Computation*, *33*(19). Advance online publication. doi:10.1002/cpe.6426

Hengstler, M., Enkel, E., & Duelli, S. (2016). Applied artificial intelligence and trust-The case of autonomous vehicles and medical assistance devices. *Technological Forecasting and Social Change*, *105*, 105–120. doi:10.1016/j.techfore.2015.12.014

Heurix, J., Zimmermann, P., Neubauer, T., & Fenz, S. (2015). A taxonomy for privacy enhancing technologies. *Computers & Security*, *53*, 1–17. doi:10.1016/j.cose.2015.05.002

IBM. (2023). *What is predictive analytics?* https://www.ibm.com/topics/predictive-analytics

Inman, J. J., & Nikolova, H. (2017). Shopper-Facing Retail Technology: A Retailer Adoption Decision Framework Incorporating Shopper Attitudes and Privacy Concerns. *Journal of Retailing*, *93*(1), 7–28. doi:10.1016/j.jretai.2016.12.006

Ischen, C., Araujo, T., Voorveld, H., van Noort, G., & Smit, E. (2020). Privacy Concerns in Chatbot Interactions. Lecture Notes in Computer Science, 11970, 34–48. doi:10.1007/978-3-030-39540-7_3

Jarrahi, M. H. (2018). Artificial intelligence and the future of work: Human-AI symbiosis in organizational decision making. *Business Horizons*, *61*(4), 577–586. doi:10.1016/j.bushor.2018.03.007

Kaur, P., Sharma, M., & Mittal, M. (2018). Big Data and Machine Learning Based Secure Healthcare Framework. *Procedia Computer Science*, *132*, 1049–1059. doi:10.1016/j.procs.2018.05.020

Knijnenburg, B. P., Willemsen, M. C., Gantner, Z., Soncu, H., & Newell, C. (2012). Explaining the user experience of recommender systems. *User Modeling and User-Adapted Interaction*, *22*(4–5), 441–504. doi:10.100711257-011-9118-4

Lau, J., Zimmerman, B., & Schaub, F. (2018). Alexa, Are You Listening? Privacy Perceptions, Concerns and Privacy-seeking Behaviors with Smart Speakers. *Proceedings of the ACM on Human-Computer Interaction*, *2*(CSCW), 1–31. doi:10.1145/3274371

Mai, J. E. (2016). Big data privacy: The datafication of personal information. *The Information Society*, *32*(3), 192–199. doi:10.1080/01972243.2016.1153010

McCarthy, J. (2007). *What is artificial intelligence?* http://www-formal.stanford.edu/jmc/

McCue, C. (2006). Data mining and predictive analytics in public safety and security. *IT Professional*, *8*(4), 12–18. doi:10.1109/MITP.2006.84

Miller, T. (2019). Explanation in artificial intelligence: Insights from the social sciences. *Artificial Intelligence*, *267*, 1–38. doi:10.1016/j.artint.2018.07.007

Moriuchi, E., Landers, V. M., Colton, D., & Hair, N. (2021). Engagement with chatbots versus augmented reality interactive technology in e-commerce. *Journal of Strategic Marketing*, *29*(5), 375–389. doi:10.1080/0965254X.2020.1740766

Mustak, M., Salminen, J., Plé, L., & Wirtz, J. (2021). Artificial intelligence in marketing: Topic modeling, scientometric analysis, and research agenda. *Journal of Business Research, 124*, 389–404. doi:10.1016/j.jbusres.2020.10.044

Okta. (2022). *Privacy vs. Security: Exploring the Differences & Relationship*. Okta. https://www.okta.com/identity-101/privacy-vs-security/

Pu, P., Chen, L., & Hu, R. (2012). Evaluating recommender systems from the user's perspective: Survey of the state of the art. *User Modeling and User-Adapted Interaction, 22*(4–5), 317–355. doi:10.100711257-011-9115-7

Puntoni, S., Reczek, R. W., Giesler, M., & Botti, S. (2021). Consumers and Artificial Intelligence: An Experiential Perspective. *Journal of Marketing, 85*(1), 131–151. doi:10.1177/0022242920953847

Russell, S., & Norvig, P. (2010). *Artificial Intelligence: A Modern Approach* (3rd ed.). Pearson. doi:10.1017/S0269888900007724

Ryan, M. (2020). In AI We Trust: Ethics, Artificial Intelligence, and Reliability. *Science and Engineering Ethics, 26*(5), 2749–2767. doi:10.100711948-020-00228-y PMID:32524425

Sadok, M. (n.d.). *Artificial Intelligence and Machine Learning in the Insurance Sector*. https://www.strategy-transformation.com/artificial-intelligence-and-machine-learning-in-the-insurance-sector/?cv=1

Shneiderman, B. (2016). The dangers of faulty, biased, or malicious algorithms requires independent oversight. *Proceedings of the National Academy of Sciences of the United States of America, 113*(48), 13538–13540. doi:10.1073/pnas.1618211113 PMID:27911762

Siau, K., & Wang, W. (2018). Building trust in artificial intelligence, machine learning, and robotics. *Cutter Business Technology Journal, 31*(2), 47–53.

Soediono, B. (1989). General structure analysis system. *Journal of Chemical Information and Modeling, 53*, 160. doi:10.1017/CBO9781107415324.004

Spencer, J., Poggi, J., & Gheerawo, R. (2018). Designing out stereotypes in artificial intelligence: Involving users in the personality design of a digital assistant. *Proceedings of the 4th EAI international conference on smart objects and technologies for social good*, 130-135. 10.1145/3284869.3284897

Sunarti, S., Fadzlul Rahman, F., Naufal, M., Risky, M., Febriyanto, K., & Masnina, R. (2021). Artificial intelligence in healthcare: Opportunities and risk for future. *Gaceta Sanitaria, 35*, S67–S70. doi:10.1016/j.gaceta.2020.12.019 PMID:33832631

Syam, N., & Sharma, A. (2018). Waiting for a sales renaissance in the fourth industrial revolution: Machine learning and artificial intelligence in sales research and practice. *Industrial Marketing Management, 69*, 135–146. doi:10.1016/j.indmarman.2017.12.019

Torres, A., & Delgado, C. (2023). Assessing Customer Interactions with Chatbots in Online Shopping Experience: An Empirical Study. In J. Santos & B. Sousa (Eds.), *Promoting Organizational Performance Through 5G and Agile Marketing*. IGI Global., doi:10.4018/978-1-6684-5523-4

Tucker, C. (2018). Privacy, Algorithms, and Artificial Intelligence. University of Chicago Press.

Van Eck, N. J., & Waltman, L. (2010). Software survey: VOSviewer, a computer program for bibliometric mapping. *Scientometrics*, *84*(2), 523–538. doi:10.100711192-009-0146-3 PMID:20585380

Vimalkumar, M., Sharma, S. K., Singh, J. B., & Dwivedi, Y. K. (2021). 'Okay google, what about my privacy?': User's privacy perceptions and acceptance of voice based digital assistants. *Computers in Human Behavior*, *120*, 106763. Advance online publication. doi:10.1016/j.chb.2021.106763

Wickramasinghe, C. S., Marino, D. L., Grandio, J., & Manic, M. (2020). Trustworthy AI development guidelines for human system interaction. *International Conference on Human System Interaction, HSI*, 130–136. 10.1109/HSI49210.2020.9142644

Wirtz, J., Patterson, P. G., Kunz, W. H., Gruber, T., Lu, V. N., Paluch, S., Martins, A., & Lu, N. (2018). Brave new world: Service robots in the frontline. *Journal of Service Management*, *29*(5), 1757–5818. doi:10.1108/JOSM-04-2018-0119

Zadeh, L. A. (2008). Toward human level machine intelligence - Is it achievable? The need for a paradigm shift. *IEEE Computational Intelligence Magazine*, *3*(3), 11–22. doi:10.1109/MCI.2008.926583

Zhang, J., & Tao, D. (2021). Empowering Things with Intelligence: A Survey of the Progress, Challenges, and Opportunities in Artificial Intelligence of Things. *IEEE Internet of Things Journal*, *8*(10), 7789–7817. doi:10.1109/JIOT.2020.3039359

ADDITIONAL READING

Bostrom, N. (2015). *Superintelligence: Paths, Dangers, Strategies*. Oxford University Press.

Brynjolfsson, E., & McAfee, A. (2014). *The second machine age: Work, progress, and prosperity in a time of brilliant technologies*. WW Norton & Company.

Domingos, P. (2015). *The Master Algorithm: How the Quest for the Ultimate Learning Machine Will Remake Our World*. Penguin Books Limited.

Kurzweil, R. (2000). *The Age of Spiritual Machines: When computers exceed human intelligence*. Penguin Putnam Inc.

Oliveira, A. (2017). *The Digital Mind: How Science is Redefining Humanity*. Massachusetts Institute of Technology, MIT Press. doi:10.7551/mitpress/9780262036030.001.0001

KEY TERMS AND DEFINITIONS

Artificial Intelligence (AI): Is a broad discipline aiming to create intelligent machines that emulate and exceed the full range of human cognition.

Chatbot: A chatbot application is a machine learning application known to simulate discussions with humans, which improves over time by constantly learning algorithms from existing data.

Machine Learning (ML): ML is a subset of AI that often uses statistical techniques to give machines the ability to "learn" from data without being explicitly given instructions for how to do so. This process is known as "training" a "model" using a learning "algorithm" that progressively improves model performance on a specific task.

Predictive Analytics: Predictive analytics is another machine learning application that forecasts future outcomes by combining historical data with statistical modelling, data mining techniques, and machine learning. Businesses use predictive analytics to spot dangers, opportunities, and future trends by analyzing trends in this data.

Privacy: Can be defined as the level of concern a consumer has regarding a potential infringement of their right to prohibit sharing personal information with third parties.

Recommender Systems: Recommender systems are different machine learning applications using software tools that provide suggestions for items a user may find useful or for those lacking the personal experience or expertise to assess various alternatives. Recommender systems are used, for example, in e-commerce websites that use our previously tracked purchases to predict and suggest future purchases.

Security: Security is safeguarding data and data resources using technology and procedures preparing for inspections, unauthorized access, recordings, etc.

Trustworthy Artificial Intelligence: Trustworthy AI means that users trust the complex nature of AI use and the ambiguity around use areas, such as security, reliability, and ethics. The trust trajectory for robotic AI is similar to trust development in human relationships, starting low and increasing/decreasing after the direct hands-on experience.

Virtual Assistants: Virtual assistants are smart assistants typically composed of Sensors to monitor environmental and physical characteristics, controllers interpreting the information that they receive, and actuators to carry out actions. Known virtual assistants were developed by companies such as Google, Apple, and Amazon, with capabilities like telling you the weather forecast, finding information about a restaurant, helping you plan your agenda, playing musing and podcasts, entertaining, and even telling jokes.

Chapter 5
Artificial Intelligence and Marketing:
Progressive or Disruptive Transformation? Review of the Literature

Paulo Botelho Pires
https://orcid.org/0000-0003-3786-6783
CEOS.PP, Polytechnic of Porto, Portugal

José Duarte Santos
https://orcid.org/0000-0001-5815-4983
CEOS.PP, Polytechnic of Porto, Portugal & ISCAP, Portugal

ABSTRACT

Recent advances in artificial intelligence have had a growing impact, and the marketing discipline is no exception. This study carries out an analysis of the impact of artificial intelligence, presenting first its different techniques and then the impact of these techniques on marketing areas and activities. A systematic study or literature review was used. The following marketing areas and activities have been identified: product recommendation, brand and trademarks management, purchase decision forecast, price, advertising management, chatbots, distribution and retail, engagement, and planning process. Findings show that artificial intelligence is having a widespread impact across marketing areas and activities, and they also show that this impact is disrupting marketing areas and activities, as well as causing gradual changes.

DOI: 10.4018/978-1-6684-8958-1.ch005

INTRODUCTION

One of the most significant current discussions in marketing is the implications that the development of artificial intelligence has brought to this field, both from a strategic and operational point of view. Indeed, the development of artificial intelligence (AI) has long been a matter of great interest in a wide range of fields. This subject has received considerable critical attention. Understanding this complexity is vitally important to leverage the potential of marketing as a field at the heart of the organization, enabling it to identify and seize opportunities, overcome challenges, and at the same time ensure that actions remain within the bounds of the acceptability of values, morals, and ethics. Recent trends have led to a proliferation of studies that have attempted to show the implications of the advancement of artificial intelligence in marketing. The next sections will focus mainly on several advanced developments with recognized implications, namely artificial intelligence, which includes machine learning, deep learning, artificial neural networks, natural language processing, genetic algorithms, reinforcement learning, support vector machines, and others. The objective was to identify the implications that intelligence has caused in marketing, specifically which areas and which marketing activities have incorporated artificial intelligence. To this end, we first described what artificial intelligence is and its different areas of knowledge, and then reviewed the bibliography, looking for articles that linked artificial intelligence and marketing. The databases consulted were Scopus, Science Direct, and Clarivate. The selection criteria for the articles followed two criteria. The first criterion was the number of citations, and the articles with the most citations were selected. For the second criterion, the date of publication was chosen, because this topic has had significant developments in the last five years. The keywords chosen were "artificial intelligence" and "marketing", which could be in the title, abstract or keywords of the publication.

ARTIFICIAL INTELLIGENCE

Marketing is no exception to how quickly artificial intelligence is changing how firms run. AI has become a powerful tool for enhancing the efficacy and efficiency of marketing efforts in recent years. With its capacity to analyze enormous volumes of data, AI technology may be used in a wide range of activities (Gkikas & Theodoridis, 2019; Mariani et al., 2023; Ruiz-Real et al., 2021; Van Esch & Black, 2021). But the term artificial intelligence is a somewhat heterogeneous and broad set of disciplines (Buchanan, 2005; Frankish & Ramsey, 2014; Xu et al., 2020):

1. Machine Learning is a subset of AI that deals with algorithms that allow systems to improve from experience without being explicitly programmed.
2. Natural Language Processing (NLP) deals with enabling machines to understand, interpret, and generate human language.
3. Reinforcement Learning is a type of machine learning where an agent learns to make decisions by performing actions in an environment and receiving rewards or penalties.
4. Generative Models can generate new data that is similar to previously seen data.
5. Deep Learning is a subfield of machine learning that uses deep neural networks to model complex patterns in data.
6. Neural Networks are a type of machine learning model inspired by the structure and function of the human brain.

7. Evolutionary Computation is a set of techniques for optimization and problem-solving that are inspired by biological evolution.
8. Genetic Algorithms are a type of optimization algorithm inspired by the process of natural selection and genetics that use techniques from evolutionary biology, such as mutation and crossover, to generate new solutions to a problem, and have been applied to a wide range of optimization problems, including but not limited to scheduling, routing, resource allocation, parameter tuning, and design optimization.
9. Genetic Programming (GP) is a form of a genetic algorithm that uses evolution to generate computer programs, rather than just numerical solutions to problems.
10. Fuzzy Logic is a mathematical framework for dealing with uncertainty and imprecision, which has been applied to many AI problems.
11. Bayesian Networks are a probabilistic graphical model that represents relationships among variables and their probabilities.

Starting with machine learning analysis, the literature reveals that it can be applied to the following activities (Borges et al., 2021; Ngai & Wu, 2022; Verma et al., 2021): Product recommendation, brands and trademarks management, purchase decision forecast, price, advertising management, chatbots, distribution and retail, engagement, and planning process.

MARKETING MIX

Product Recommendation

AI can help in product recommendations by using algorithms and machine learning techniques to analyze large amounts of data on customer behavior, preferences, and past purchases and use that information to generate personalized recommendations for each customer, considering their individual needs and interests (Alabdulrahman & Viktor, 2021; Ballestar et al., 2019; Bauer & Nanopoulos, 2014; Borges et al., 2021; Cheung et al., 2003; Chinchanachokchai et al., 2021; Choi et al., 2012; Esmaeilpour et al., 2012; Ghose et al., 2012; Greenstein-Messica & Rokach, 2020; Kim et al., 2001; Lepa et al., 2020; Marchand & Marx, 2020; O'Mahony et al., 2004; Qazi et al., 2020; Siering et al., 2018; Wei et al., 2005). Three approaches can be used to recommend products using AI. The first one is collaborative filtering, where data on customer behavior is used, such as the items they have purchased or viewed, to identify patterns and make recommendations based on the actions of similar customers. The second one is content-based filtering, which uses information about the features and attributes of products to make recommendations based on a customer's previous preferences and selections. The last one, hybrid recommendation systems, combines the strengths of both collaborative and content-based filtering to provide even more accurate recommendations.

Price

Although pricing activities often remain outside the sphere of marketing management, AI can help substantially in this component (Adetunji et al., 2022; Arora et al., 2022; Casamatta et al., 2022; Christen et al., 2022; Foryś, 2022; Kolte et al., 2023; Lahmiri et al., 2023; Potrawa & Tetereva, 2022; Ren et al., 2022; Samunderu & Farrugia, 2022; Soltani et al., 2022; Sueyoshi & Tadiparthi, 2005; Sueyoshi & Tadiparthi, 2008; Thirumuruganathan et al., 2023; Wolkenfelt & Situmeang, 2020; Yang et al., 2020):

1. Price Optimization – AI algorithms can analyze data on consumer behavior, market trends, and competition to determine optimal prices for products and services.
2. Dynamic Pricing – AI can automatically adjust prices in real time based on supply and demand, competitor pricing, and other factors.
3. Price Prediction – AI algorithms can predict future prices based on historical data and current market conditions, helping businesses make informed decisions about pricing strategies.
4. Price Monitoring – AI-powered tools can monitor prices across multiple channels and competitors, providing businesses with valuable market intelligence.
5. Price Personalization – AI can analyze data on individual customer preferences and behaviors to offer personalized prices and promotions that increase customer loyalty and sales.
6. Price Segmentation – AI can analyze customer data to identify different segments and price elasticities, allowing businesses to personalize prices based on customer segments.
7. Price Discrimination – AI algorithms can identify customers who are willing to pay a premium price and offer them personalized pricing, resulting in increased revenue.
8. Price Recommendation – AI can provide businesses with recommendations for pricing strategies based on market trends and customer behavior.
9. Price Testing – AI algorithms can automate price testing, allowing businesses to quickly and easily evaluate the impact of different pricing strategies.
10. Price Compliance – AI can monitor prices to ensure they are compliant with laws, regulations, and company policies.

Advertising Management

Advertising, as one of the components of the marketing mix, has probably changed the most with the emergence and massification of the Internet. Nowadays, internet advertising, through its many forms, prevails over traditional advertising and, consequently, the intervention of the IA is an added value, contributing to the following points (Aswani et al., 2018, Bai et al., 2019; Bochkarev & Smirnov, 2019; Choi & Lim, 2020; Couwenberg et al., 2017; Dalenberg, 2018; Fan & Chang, 2009, 2010, 2011; Goodrich et al., 2015; Haider et al., 2018; Hou et al., 2021; Hu et al., 2020; Kanei et al., 2020; Kaur, 2022; King et al., 2015; Lee et al., 2018; Li et al., 2019; Liang et al., 2019; Liu et al., 2021; Matz et al., 2019; Miralles-Pechuán et al., 2018, 2020; Nengroo & Kuppusamy, 2018; Peng et al., 2020; Popov & Iakovleva, 2018; Quesenberry & Coolsen, 2019; Raphael et al., 2022; Schwartz et al., 2017; Simmonds et al., 2020; Thejas, et al., 2021; Wang et al., 2019; Wang et al., 2020; Xu et al., 2018; Yang et al., 2020; Zappin et al., 2022):

1. Targeted Advertising – AI algorithms can analyze customer data to identify target audiences, allowing businesses to deliver more relevant and personalized advertisements.
2. Campaign Optimization – AI algorithms can optimize advertising campaigns in real-time, making adjustments based on performance data to improve campaign efficiency and reach.

3. Media Planning – AI algorithms can assist in media planning by analyzing data on audience demographics, geographic distribution, and purchase behavior, helping businesses make informed decisions about which media channels to use and how to allocate their advertising budget.
4. Ad Personalization – AI algorithms can personalize advertisements based on individual customer preferences, increasing the impact and effectiveness of ad campaigns.
5. Fraud Detection – AI algorithms can detect fraudulent clicks and impressions in real time, helping businesses protect their advertising investment from fraud.
6. Creative Optimization – AI algorithms can analyze the performance of different advertisements, allowing businesses to make data-driven decisions about which creative elements are most effective and adjust their ad strategies accordingly.

Chatbots

Computer programs known as chatbots are created to mimic conversations with human users, frequently through messaging services, websites, or mobile apps. To comprehend user inquiries and provide automated help and information, they employ natural language processing (NLP) and machine learning techniques. Customer support, sales, and marketing are just a few of the activities that chatbots are capable of handling. They have several advantages over conventional human-based customer care, including 24/7 accessibility, improved efficiency, and cost savings. They are becoming more and more common among companies aiming to boost consumer engagement and enhance the entire customer experience. Chatbots are applied in marketing in a myriad of activities, with different purposes and advantages, such as (Adamopoulou & Moussiades, 2020; Bodu et al., 2022; Chen et al., 2022; Gkinko & Elbanna, 2022; Hsu & Lin, 2023; Illescas-Manzano et al., 2021; Lin & Wu, 2023; Luo et al., 2019; Ma & Sun, 2020; Misischia et al., 2022; Ngai et al., 2021; Pantano & Pizzi, 2020; Rizomyliotis et al., 2022; Sandeep et al., 2022; Shumanov & Johnson, 2021; Tran et al., 2021; Van den Broeck et al., 2019; Volkmar et al., 2022; Wang et al., 2022; Zarouali et al., 2018):

1. Customer Engagement – Chatbots provide businesses with a new channel to engage with customers in real time, allowing them to respond to inquiries, provide information, and resolve issues quickly and efficiently.
2. Personalization – Chatbots can collect and analyze customer data to provide personalized experiences, helping businesses build stronger relationships with their customers.
3. Lead Generation – Chatbots can be used to generate leads by providing potential customers with information about products or services and guiding them through the sales process.
4. Cost Savings – Chatbots can handle a large volume of customer inquiries, reducing the need for human customer support and freeing up resources for other marketing activities.
5. Data Collection – Chatbots can collect valuable data about customer behavior, preferences, and feedback, providing businesses with valuable insights into their target market.
6. Education and Training – Chatbots can be used to deliver educational content and training materials, helping businesses to engage employees and improve their skills.

Distribution and Retail

Businesses may increase productivity, save expenses, and improve customer experience by utilizing AI to optimize the distribution component of the marketing mix (Alboqami, 2023; Bhowmick & Mitra, 2019; Danaher et al., 2020; Guha et al., 2021; Haleem et al., 2022; Hossain et al., 2022; Kamoonpuri & Sengar, 2023; Kelly et al., 2023; Leguina et al., 2020; Loureiro et al., 2021; Mediavilla et al., 2022; Pereira et al., 2022; Toorajipour et al., 2021; Verma et al., 2021):

1. Channel Optimization – AI algorithms can analyze data on customer behavior and purchasing patterns to determine the most effective channels for distributing products or services, allowing businesses to reach their target audiences more efficiently.
2. Inventory Management – AI algorithms can help businesses to optimize inventory levels, reducing the risk of overstocking or stock shortages, and helping to ensure that products are available when and where customers want them.
3. Logistics Optimization – AI algorithms can analyze data on delivery routes, shipping costs, and customer demand to optimize logistics operations, reducing costs and improving delivery times.
4. Personalization – AI algorithms can analyze customer data to personalize the distribution experience, providing customers with relevant and customized recommendations, offers, and experiences.
5. Price Optimization – AI algorithms can analyze data on customer behavior, market trends, and competition to determine the optimal price for products and services, helping retailers to maximize revenue and profitability.
6. Fraud Detection – AI algorithms can analyze transaction data to detect fraudulent activity, helping retailers to protect their businesses and customers.

BRAND AND TRADEMARK MANAGEMENT

Knowing that brands and trademarks are among the most valuable resources for organizations, IA can also help in managing these activities. The bibliography points to a wide range (Balaji et al., 2021; Blankenburg et al., 2015; Bodu et al., 2022; Carpineto & Romano, 2020; Chen et al., 2015; Ducange et al., 2019; Kaiser et al., 2020; Kübler et al., 2020; Liu et al., 2020; Tirunillai & Tellis, 2014; Trappey et al., 2021; Trappey et al., 2022; Charles V. Trappey, Amy J. C. Trappey, & Sam C. C. Lin, 2020; Charles V. Trappey, Amy J. C. Trappey, & Bo-Hung Liu, 2020; Watanuki & Akama, 2022; Wilk et al., 2022; Zhang & Lu, 2021):

1. Trademark Search and Monitoring – AI-powered tools can quickly search large databases and identify potential conflicts or infringements.
2. Brand Management – AI algorithms can analyze the brand perception and customer sentiment, helping businesses make informed decisions on brand strategy.
3. Contract Analysis – AI can automate the review and analysis of contracts, ensuring that brand and trademark usage is consistent with legal agreements.
4. Content Moderation – AI-powered tools can automatically monitor online content for inappropriate use of a brand or trademark, helping businesses protect their intellectual property.

5. Trademark Filing – AI can streamline the trademark application process by automatically generating the necessary documents and forms based on the information provided.
6. Predictive Analytics – AI can help businesses anticipate changes in the marketplace and make proactive decisions to protect their brand and trademark.
7. Image Recognition – AI algorithms can identify and categorize images, making it easier to track the use of a brand or trademark in visual media.
8. Domain Monitoring – AI-powered tools can monitor the use of a brand or trademark in domain names, helping businesses protect their online presence.

CONSUMER BEHAVIOR

Purchase Decision Forecast

Consumer behavior is one of the classic schools of marketing thought, and a consensus model of the behavior has never been found to unite the academic community. Moreover, digital has induced changes in consumer behavior. To this end, IA can help marketing managers (Abolghasemi et al., 2022; Allal-Chérif et al., 2021; Arasu et al., 2020; Chaudhuri et al., 2021; Chen et al., 2021; Elalem et al., 2022; Ghatasheh et al., 2020; Islam et al., 2022; Li et al., 2019; Martínez et al., 2020; Paolanti et al., 2020; Schaeffer & Sanchez, 2020; Steininger & Gatzemeier, 2019; Zhang et al., 2014):

1. Predictive Modeling – AI algorithms can use historical customer data to create predictive models that identify the likelihood of a purchase based on various factors such as demographics, behavior patterns, and past purchases.
2. Recommendation Systems – AI can analyze customer data to generate personalized product recommendations, increasing the likelihood of a purchase.
3. Customer Lifetime Value Prediction – AI can predict a customer's future value to a business based on their past purchases, demographics, and behavior patterns, allowing businesses to prioritize their customer engagement and retention efforts.
4. Customer Behavioral Analysis – AI algorithms can analyze customer data to identify patterns and trends in customer behavior, allowing businesses to better understand their target market and predict future purchase decisions.
5. Sentiment Analysis – AI can analyze customer feedback, social media posts, and other forms of online content to identify changes in customer sentiment and predict shifts in purchase behavior;
6. Personalized Marketing – AI can analyze customer data to generate personalized marketing messages and product recommendations, increasing the likelihood of a purchase.

Engagement

Consumer involvement, along with customer experience, is integral to consumer behavior and has recently been the subject of an extensive effort by marketing researchers because these constructs are known to be related to the satisfaction and loyalty construct. Thus, IA is relevant to consumer engagement and can enhance it (Arora et al., 2019; Cheng & Huang, 2020; Dong et al., 2018; Jung & Jeong, 2020; Kim et al., 2015; Kwok et al., 2020; Luo & Xu, 2019; Nazir et al., 2023; Pantanowitz et al., 2022;

Perez-Vega et al., 2021; Rajamohana & Umamaheswari, 2018; Srivastava & Kalro, 2019; Sung et al., 2021; Taecharungroj & Mathayomchan, 2019; Zhang et al., 2016):

1. Personalization – AI algorithms can analyze customer data to provide personalized recommendations, offers, and experiences, helping to build stronger relationships with customers and increase engagement.
2. Predictive Analytics – AI algorithms can analyze customer data to predict future behaviors and preferences, allowing businesses to create more targeted and relevant marketing campaigns, increasing engagement.
3. Chatbots – AI-powered chatbots can provide customers with quick and personalized responses to questions, helping to build stronger relationships and increase engagement.
4. Content Creation – AI algorithms can analyze customer data to identify the types of content that are most likely to engage customers, allowing businesses to create more relevant and effective content.
5. Ad Optimization – AI algorithms can analyze customer data to determine the best times, channels, and formats for delivering ads, increasing the likelihood that customers will engage with them.
6. Voice-Enabled Technologies – AI algorithms can be integrated into voice-enabled technologies such as Amazon Alexa or Google Home to create voice-activated marketing experiences that are more convenient and engaging for customers.
7. Emotion Detection – AI algorithms can analyze customer data and feedback to identify emotions such as happiness, frustration, or confusion, allowing businesses to respond appropriately and increase engagement.
8. Social Media Monitoring – AI algorithms can monitor social media platforms to identify and respond to customer feedback in real time, helping businesses to build stronger relationships and increase engagement.
9. Virtual Reality – AI algorithms can be integrated into virtual reality experiences, allowing customers to engage with products and services in new and exciting ways, increasing engagement and building stronger relationships.

PLANNING PROCESS

The marketing planning process also gathers help from the application of AI. In this case, the following is highlighted (Arias-Pérez & Vélez-Jaramillo, 2022; Chen et al., 2020; Orsini, 1986; Seeger et al., 2022; Zuiderwijk et al., 2021):

1. Customer Insights – AI algorithms can analyze customer data to provide deep insights into customer behavior, preferences, and trends, helping businesses to make informed decisions about their marketing strategies.
2. Market Analysis – AI algorithms can analyze market data to provide insights into market trends, competition, and opportunities, helping businesses to make informed decisions about their marketing strategies.

3. Budget Optimization – AI algorithms can analyze data on customer behavior and market trends to determine the most effective channels and tactics for reaching customers, helping businesses to optimize their marketing budgets.
4. Campaign Optimization – AI algorithms can analyze data on customer behavior and campaign performance to determine the most effective messages, offers, and channels, helping businesses to optimize their marketing campaigns and increase their impact.
5. Predictive Analytics – AI algorithms can analyze customer data to predict future behaviors and preferences, allowing businesses to create more targeted and effective marketing campaigns.

ANALYSIS AND RESULTS

The previous description contains a detailed and broad overview of the application of artificial intelligence in marketing. The transversality of this application is perceptible, as artificial intelligence is found in a myriad of marketing activities. Table 1 contains an overview of these activities.

Table 1. Overview of the application of artificial intelligence in marketing

Name of the Activity		Description of the Activity
Marketing MIX	Product Recommendation	Use that information to generate personalized recommendations
	Price	Manage all pricing related activities
	Communication	Advertising management
	Chatbots	Customer support, sales assistant, education and training
	Distribution and retail	Manage all distribution related activities
Brand	Brand and trademark management	Manage all brand related activities
Consumer behavior	Purchase decision forecast	Manage the entire consumer decision making process
	Engagement	Manage the entire engagement process
Planning	Planning process	Manage the entire planning process

CONCLUSION

Marketing has been significantly affected by the development of AI, and controlling this convolution is decisive in making the most of marketing's potential as the field at the heart of the business and ensuring that activities are carried out with increased performance. With its ability to analyze vast amounts of information, AI has recently emerged as a potent tool for improving the efficacy and efficiency of marketing initiatives. These include Machine Learning, Natural Language Processing (NLP), Reinforcement Learning, Generative Models, Deep Learning, Neural Networks, Evolutionary Computation, Genetic Algorithms, Genetic Programming, Fuzzy Logic, and Bayesian Networks.

By analyzing consumer behavior, interests, and previous purchases to provide individualized product suggestions for each client, AI may assist in the product recommendation process. Collaborative filtering, content-based filtering, and hybrid recommendation systems are three methods that may be used to provide product recommendations using AI. Through collaborative filtering, patterns in consumer behavior are discovered and suggestions are generated based on the behaviors of comparable customers. Content-based filtering generates suggestions using knowledge of the characteristics and features of the product. For even more precise recommendations, hybrid recommendation systems combine the benefits of both collaborative and content-based filtering.

Businesses may handle brand and trademark operations with the use of AI, including trademark search and monitoring, brand management, contract analysis, content moderation, trademark filing, predictive analytics, picture recognition, domain monitoring, and more. Artificial intelligence (AI)-enabled tools can swiftly scan sizable databases for potential conflicts or infringements, assess brand perception and consumer sentiment, decide on brand strategy with knowledge, automate the review and analysis of contracts, and speed up the trademark application process. AI can aid organizations in anticipating market shifts and taking preemptive measures to safeguard their brand and trademark.

Optimization, dynamic pricing, prediction, monitoring, personalization, segmentation, price discrimination, price suggestion, price testing, and compliance are a few pricing-related tasks that AI may assist with. To establish the best prices for goods and services, AI may evaluate data on customer behavior, market trends, and rivalry. Additionally, it can forecast future prices using historical data and present market conditions, offer organizations useful market knowledge and make pricing strategy suggestions based on market trends and consumer behavior. Additionally, AI can automate price testing, enabling companies to swiftly and simply assess the effects of various pricing schemes.

Predictive models, recommendation systems, forecasting customer lifetime value, customer behavioral analysis, sentiment analysis, and personalized marketing are some of the ways AI may assist marketing managers. The creation of prediction models by AI algorithms using historical consumer data can determine the likelihood of purchase based on a variety of variables, including demographics, behavior patterns, and previous transactions. To detect fluctuations in client sentiment and anticipate changes in purchasing behavior, AI may also monitor customer reviews, social media posts, and other online information.

Targeted advertising, campaign optimization, media planning, ad personalization, fraud detection, and creative optimization are all things that AI algorithms may assist organizations with. They can discover target audiences through consumer data analysis, make modifications based on performance data, and tailor adverts to the tastes of individual customers. The real-time detection of fraudulent clicks and impressions using AI systems can help organizations avoid fraud.

Customer interaction, personalization, lead creation, cost savings, data collecting, education and training, and education and training are just a few of the marketing uses for chatbots. Businesses now have a new way to interact with consumers in real-time using chatbots, which enables them to swiftly and effectively reply to questions, give information, and address problems. To create tailored experiences, generate leads, and offer insightful information about consumer behavior, preferences, and comments, they can also gather and analyze customer data. They may also be used to distribute training materials and instructional information, assisting companies in involving staff members and enhancing their abilities.

By maximizing the distribution element of the marketing mix, AI may assist firms in enhancing customer experience, reducing costs, and increasing productivity. This covers fraud detection, pricing optimization, personalization, inventory management, and logistics optimization, among other things. With the use of AI algorithms, merchants may increase sales and profitability by analyzing consumer behavior, market trends, and competitive pricing to identify the best price for goods and services.

Consumer engagement may be improved by AI in a variety of ways, including customization, predictive analytics, chatbots, content creation, ad optimization, voice-activated technology, emotion recognition, social media monitoring, virtual reality, and more. To give tailored suggestions, offers, and experiences, AI algorithms may evaluate consumer data. This analysis can assist to deepen customer connections and boost engagement. Additionally, they may examine consumer feedback and data to spot emotions like joy, annoyance, or perplexity. They can also keep an eye on social media platforms to see and instantly respond to customer comments.

By offering insights into consumer behavior, preferences, and trends as well as market analysis, budget and campaign optimization, predictive analytics, and other services, AI may assist organizations in making well-informed decisions regarding their marketing strategy. AI may also be used to forecast future preferences and behaviors, enabling companies to develop more specialized and successful marketing efforts.

AI is causing both disruptions and gradual and progressive changes in marketing activities. AI is transforming the marketing landscape, providing businesses with new tools and capabilities that were previously not possible. At the same time, it is also causing significant disruptions to traditional marketing methods, forcing businesses to adapt and evolve their strategies to stay ahead.

REFERENCES

Abolghasemi, M., Tarr, G., & Bergmeir, C. (2022). Machine learning applications in hierarchical time series forecasting: Investigating the impact of promotions. *International Journal of Forecasting*. Advance online publication. doi:10.1016/j.ijforecast.2022.07.004

Adamopoulou, E., & Moussiades, L. (2020). Chatbots: History, technology, and applications. *Machine Learning with Applications*, *2*, 100006. doi:10.1016/j.mlwa.2020.100006

Adetunji, A. B., Akande, O. N., Ajala, F. A., Oyewo, O., Akande, Y. F., & Oluwadara, G. (2022). House Price Prediction using Random Forest Machine Learning Technique. *Procedia Computer Science*, *199*, 806–813. doi:10.1016/j.procs.2022.01.100

Alabdulrahman, R., & Viktor, H. (2021). Catering for unique tastes: Targeting grey-sheep users recommender systems through one-class machine learning. *Expert Systems with Applications*, *166*, 114061. doi:10.1016/j.eswa.2020.114061

Alboqami, H. (2023). Trust me, I'm an influencer! - Causal recipes for customer trust in artificial intelligence influencers in the retail industry. *Journal of Retailing and Consumer Services*, *72*, 103242. doi:10.1016/j.jretconser.2022.103242

Allal-Chérif, O., Simón-Moya, V., & Ballester, A. C. C. (2021). Intelligent purchasing: How artificial intelligence can redefine the purchasing function. *Journal of Business Research*, *124*, 69–76. doi:10.1016/j.jbusres.2020.11.050

Arasu, B. S., Seelan, B. J. B., & Thamaraiselvan, N. (2020). A machine learning-based approach to enhancing social media marketing. *Computers & Electrical Engineering*, *86*, 106723. doi:10.1016/j.compeleceng.2020.106723

Arias-Pérez, J., & Vélez-Jaramillo, J. (2022). Ignoring the three-way interaction of digital orientation, Not-invented-here syndrome and employee's artificial intelligence awareness in digital innovation performance: A recipe for failure. *Technological Forecasting and Social Change*, *174*, 121305. doi:10.1016/j.techfore.2021.121305

Arora, A., Bansal, S., Kandpal, C., Aswani, R., & Dwivedi, Y. (2019). Measuring social media influencer index-insights from Facebook, Twitter and Instagram. *Journal of Retailing and Consumer Services*, *49*, 86–101. doi:10.1016/j.jretconser.2019.03.012

Arora, P., Gupta, H., & Singh, A. (2022). Forecasting resale value of the car: Evaluating the proficiency under the impact of machine learning model. *Materials Today: Proceedings*, *69*, 441–445. doi:10.1016/j.matpr.2022.09.074

Aswani, R., Kar, A. K., & Vigneswara Ilavarasan, P. (2018). Detection of spammers in twitter marketing: A hybrid approach using social media analytics and bio inspired computing. *Information Systems Frontiers*, *20*(3), 515–530. doi:10.100710796-017-9805-8

Bai, X., Abasi, R., Edizel, B., & Mantrach, A. (2019). Position-aware deep character-level CTR prediction for sponsored search. *IEEE Transactions on Knowledge and Data Engineering*, *33*(4), 1722–1736. doi:10.1109/TKDE.2019.2941881

Balaji, T. K., Annavarapu, C. S. R., & Bablani, A. (2021). Machine learning algorithms for social media analysis: A survey. *Computer Science Review*, *40*, 100395. doi:10.1016/j.cosrev.2021.100395

Ballestar, M. T., Grau-Carles, P., & Sainz, J. (2019). Predicting customer quality in e-commerce social networks: A machine learning approach. *Review of Managerial Science*, *13*(3), 589–603. doi:10.100711846-018-0316-x

Bauer, J., & Nanopoulos, A. (2014). Recommender systems based on quantitative implicit customer feedback. *Decision Support Systems*, *68*, 77–88. doi:10.1016/j.dss.2014.09.005

Bhowmick, A. K., & Mitra, B. (2019). Listen to me, my neighbors or my friend? Role of complementary modalities for predicting business popularity in location based social networks. *Computer Communications*, *135*, 53–70. doi:10.1016/j.comcom.2019.01.004

Blankenburg, M., Horn, C., & Krüger, J. (2015). Detection of Counterfeit by the Usage of Product Inherent Features. *Procedia CIRP*, *26*, 430–435. doi:10.1016/j.procir.2014.07.062

Bochkarev, K., & Smirnov, E. (2019). Detecting advertising on building façades with computer vision. *Procedia Computer Science*, *156*, 338–346. doi:10.1016/j.procs.2019.08.210

Boddu, R. S. K., Santoki, A. A., Khurana, S., Vitthal Koli, P., Rai, R., & Agrawal, A. (2022). An analysis to understand the role of machine learning, robotics and artificial intelligence in digital marketing. *Materials Today: Proceedings*, *56*, 2288–2292. doi:10.1016/j.matpr.2021.11.637

Borges, A. F. S., Laurindo, F. J. B., Spínola, M. M., Gonçalves, R. F., & Mattos, C. A. (2021). The strategic use of artificial intelligence in the digital era: Systematic literature review and future research directions. *International Journal of Information Management*, *57*, 102225. doi:10.1016/j.ijinfomgt.2020.102225

Buchanan, B. G. (2005). A (very) brief history of artificial intelligence. *AI Magazine*, *26*(4), 53–53.

Carpineto, C., & Romano, G. (2020). An experimental study of automatic detection and measurement of counterfeit in brand search results. *ACM Transactions on the Web*, *14*(2), 1–35. doi:10.1145/3378443

Casamatta, G., Giannoni, S., Brunstein, D., & Jouve, J. (2022). Host type and pricing on Airbnb: Seasonality and perceived market power. *Tourism Management*, *88*, 104433. doi:10.1016/j.tourman.2021.104433

Chaudhuri, N., Gupta, G., Vamsi, V., & Bose, I. (2021). On the platform but will they buy? Predicting customers' purchase behavior using deep learning. *Decision Support Systems*, *149*, 113622. doi:10.1016/j.dss.2021.113622

Chen, Q., Gong, Y., Lu, Y., & Tang, J. (2022). Classifying and measuring the service quality of AI chatbot in frontline service. *Journal of Business Research*, *145*, 552–568. doi:10.1016/j.jbusres.2022.02.088

Chen, S., Wang, X., Zhang, H.-y., Wang, J., & Peng, J. (2021). Customer purchase forecasting for online tourism: A data-driven method with multiplex behavior data. *Tourism Management*, *87*, 104357. doi:10.1016/j.tourman.2021.104357

Chen, W., Zhao, L., Kang, Q., & Di, F. (2020). Systematizing heterogeneous expert knowledge, scenarios and goals via a goal-reasoning artificial intelligence agent for democratic urban land use planning. *Cities (London, England)*, *101*, 102703. doi:10.1016/j.cities.2020.102703

Chen, Y.-P., Nelson, L. D., & Hsu, M. (2015). From "where" to "what": Distributed representations of brand associations in the human brain. *JMR, Journal of Marketing Research*, *52*(4), 453–466. doi:10.1509/jmr.14.0606 PMID:27065490

Cheng, L.-C., & Huang, C.-L. (2020). Exploring contextual factors from consumer reviews affecting movie sales: An opinion mining approach. *Electronic Commerce Research*, *20*(4), 807–832. doi:10.100710660-019-09332-z

Cheung, K.-W., Kwok, J. T., Law, M. H., & Tsui, K.-C. (2003). Mining customer product ratings for personalized marketing. *Decision Support Systems*, *35*(2), 231–243. doi:10.1016/S0167-9236(02)00108-2

Chinchanachokchai, S., Thontirawong, P., & Chinchanachokchai, P. (2021). A tale of two recommender systems: The moderating role of consumer expertise on artificial intelligence based product recommendations. *Journal of Retailing and Consumer Services*, *61*, 102528. doi:10.1016/j.jretconser.2021.102528

Choi, J.-A., & Lim, K. (2020). Identifying machine learning techniques for classification of target advertising. *ICT Express*, *6*(3), 175–180. doi:10.1016/j.icte.2020.04.012

Choi, K., Yoo, D., Kim, G., & Suh, Y. (2012). A hybrid online-product recommendation system: Combining implicit rating-based collaborative filtering and sequential pattern analysis. *Electronic Commerce Research and Applications*, *11*(4), 309–317. doi:10.1016/j.elerap.2012.02.004

Christen, T., Hess, M., Grichnik, D., & Wincent, J. (2022). Value-based pricing in digital platforms: A machine learning approach to signaling beyond core product attributes in cross-platform settings. *Journal of Business Research*, *152*, 82–92. doi:10.1016/j.jbusres.2022.07.042

Couwenberg, L. E., Boksem, M. A., Dietvorst, R. C., Worm, L., Verbeke, W. J., & Smidts, A. (2017). Neural responses to functional and experiential ad appeals: Explaining ad effectiveness. *International Journal of Research in Marketing*, *34*(2), 355–366. doi:10.1016/j.ijresmar.2016.10.005

Dalenberg, D. J. (2018). Preventing discrimination in the automated targeting of job advertisements. *Computer Law & Security Report, 34*(3), 615–627. doi:10.1016/j.clsr.2017.11.009

Danaher, P. J., Danaher, T. S., Smith, M. S., & Loaiza-Maya, R. (2020). Advertising effectiveness for multiple retailer-brands in a multimedia and multichannel environment. *JMR, Journal of Marketing Research, 57*(3), 445–467. doi:10.1177/0022243720910104

Dong, L.-y., Ji, S., Zhang, C., Zhang, Q., Chiu, D. W., Qiu, L., & Li, D. (2018). An unsupervised topic-sentiment joint probabilistic model for detecting deceptive reviews. *Expert Systems with Applications, 114*, 210–223. doi:10.1016/j.eswa.2018.07.005

Ducange, P., Fazzolari, M., Petrocchi, M., & Vecchio, M. (2019). An effective Decision Support System for social media listening based on cross-source sentiment analysis models. *Engineering Applications of Artificial Intelligence, 78*, 71–85. doi:10.1016/j.engappai.2018.10.014

Elalem, Y. K., Maier, S., & Seifert, R. W. (2022). A machine learning-based framework for forecasting sales of new products with short life cycles using deep neural networks. *International Journal of Forecasting*. Advance online publication. doi:10.1016/j.ijforecast.2022.09.005

Esmaeilpour, M., Naderifar, V., & Shukur, Z. (2012). Cellular learning automata for mining customer behaviour in shopping activity. *International Journal of Innovative Computing, Information, & Control, 8*(4), 2491–2511.

Fan, T.-K., & Chang, C.-H. (2009). Blogger-centric contextual advertising. *Proceedings of the 18th ACM conference on Information and knowledge management*, 1803-1806. 10.1145/1645953.1646234

Fan, T.-K., & Chang, C.-H. (2010). Sentiment-oriented contextual advertising. *Knowledge and Information Systems, 23*(3), 321–344. doi:10.100710115-009-0222-2

Fan, T.-K., & Chang, C.-H. (2011). Blogger-Centric Contextual Advertising. *Expert Systems with Applications, 38*(3), 1777–1788. doi:10.1016/j.eswa.2010.07.105

Foryś, I. (2022). Machine learning in house price analysis: Regression models versus neural networks. *Procedia Computer Science, 207*, 435–445. doi:10.1016/j.procs.2022.09.078

Frankish, K., & Ramsey, W. M. (2014). *The Cambridge handbook of artificial intelligence*. Cambridge University Press. doi:10.1017/CBO9781139046855

Ghatasheh, N., Faris, H., AlTaharwa, I., Harb, Y., & Harb, A. (2020). Business analytics in telemarketing: Cost-sensitive analysis of bank campaigns using artificial neural networks. *Applied Sciences (Basel, Switzerland), 10*(7), 2581. doi:10.3390/app10072581

Ghose, A., Ipeirotis, P. G., & Li, B. (2012). Designing ranking systems for hotels on travel search engines by mining user-generated and crowdsourced content. *Marketing Science, 31*(3), 493–520. doi:10.1287/mksc.1110.0700

Gkikas, D. C., & Theodoridis, P. K. (2019). Artificial intelligence (AI) impact on digital marketing research. In Strategic Innovative Marketing and Tourism: 7th ICSIMAT (pp. 1251-1259). Academic Press.

Gkinko, L., & Elbanna, A. (2022). The appropriation of conversational AI in the workplace: A taxonomy of AI chatbot users. *International Journal of Information Management, 102568*. Advance online publication. doi:10.1016/j.ijinfomgt.2022.102568

Goodrich, K., Schiller, S. Z., & Galletta, D. (2015). Consumer reactions to intrusiveness of online-video advertisements: Do length, informativeness, and humor help (or hinder) marketing outcomes? *Journal of Advertising Research, 55*(1), 37–50. doi:10.2501/JAR-55-1-037-050

Greenstein-Messica, A., & Rokach, L. (2020). Machine learning and operation research based method for promotion optimization of products with no price elasticity history. *Electronic Commerce Research and Applications, 40*, 100914. doi:10.1016/j.elerap.2019.100914

Guha, A., Grewal, D., Kopalle, P. K., Haenlein, M., Schneider, M. J., Jung, H., Moustafa, R., Hegde, D. R., & Hawkins, G. (2021). How artificial intelligence will affect the future of retailing. *Journal of Retailing, 97*(1), 28–41. doi:10.1016/j.jretai.2021.01.005

Haider, C. M. R., Iqbal, A., Rahman, A. H., & Rahman, M. S. (2018). An ensemble learning based approach for impression fraud detection in mobile advertising. *Journal of Network and Computer Applications, 112*, 126–141. doi:10.1016/j.jnca.2018.02.021

Haleem, A., Javaid, M., Asim Qadri, M., Pratap Singh, R., & Suman, R. (2022). Artificial intelligence (AI) applications for marketing: A literature-based study. *International Journal of Intelligent Networks, 3*, 119–132. doi:10.1016/j.ijin.2022.08.005

Hossain, M. A., Agnihotri, R., Rushan, M. R. I., Rahman, M. S., & Sumi, S. F. (2022). Marketing analytics capability, artificial intelligence adoption, and firms' competitive advantage: Evidence from the manufacturing industry. *Industrial Marketing Management, 106*, 240–255. doi:10.1016/j.indmarman.2022.08.017

Hou, Z., Ma, K., Wang, Y., Yu, J., Ji, K., Chen, Z., & Abraham, A. (2021). Attention-based learning of self-media data for marketing intention detection. *Engineering Applications of Artificial Intelligence, 98*, 104118. doi:10.1016/j.engappai.2020.104118

Hsu, C.-L., & Lin, J. C.-C. (2023). Understanding the user satisfaction and loyalty of customer service chatbots. *Journal of Retailing and Consumer Services, 71*, 103211. doi:10.1016/j.jretconser.2022.103211

Hu, J., Li, T., Zhuang, Y., Huang, S., & Dong, S. (2020). GFD: A weighted heterogeneous graph embedding based approach for fraud detection in mobile advertising. *Security and Communication Networks, 2020*, 1–12. doi:10.1155/2020/8810817

Illescas-Manzano, M. D., Vicente López, N., Afonso González, N., & Cristofol Rodríguez, C. (2021). Implementation of Chatbot in Online Commerce, and Open Innovation. *Journal of Open Innovation, 7*(2), 125. doi:10.3390/joitmc7020125

Islam, T., Meade, N., Carson, R. T., Louviere, J. J., & Wang, J. (2022). The usefulness of socio-demographic variables in predicting purchase decisions: Evidence from machine learning procedures. *Journal of Business Research, 151*, 324–338. doi:10.1016/j.jbusres.2022.07.004

Jung, S. H., & Jeong, Y. J. (2020). Twitter data analytical methodology development for prediction of start-up firms' social media marketing level. *Technology in Society*, *63*, 101409. doi:10.1016/j.techsoc.2020.101409

Kaiser, C., Ahuvia, A., Rauschnabel, P. A., & Wimble, M. (2020). Social media monitoring: What can marketers learn from Facebook brand photos? *Journal of Business Research*, *117*, 707–717. doi:10.1016/j.jbusres.2019.09.017

Kamoonpuri, S. Z., & Sengar, A. (2023). Hi, May AI help you? An analysis of the barriers impeding the implementation and use of artificial intelligence-enabled virtual assistants in retail. *Journal of Retailing and Consumer Services*, *72*, 103258. doi:10.1016/j.jretconser.2023.103258

Kanei, F., Chiba, D., Hato, K., Yoshioka, K., Matsumoto, T., & Akiyama, M. (2020). Detecting and understanding online advertising fraud in the wild. *IEICE Transactions on Information and Systems*, *103*(7), 1512–1523. doi:10.1587/transinf.2019ICP0008

Kaur, P. (2022). Sentiment analysis using web scraping for live news data with machine learning algorithms. *Materials Today: Proceedings*, *65*, 3333–3341. doi:10.1016/j.matpr.2022.05.409

Kelly, S., Kaye, S.-A., & Oviedo-Trespalacios, O. (2023). What factors contribute to the acceptance of artificial intelligence? A systematic review. *Telematics and Informatics*, *77*, 101925. doi:10.1016/j.tele.2022.101925

Kim, J. W., Lee, B. H., Shaw, M. J., Chang, H.-L., & Nelson, M. (2001). Application of decision-tree induction techniques to personalized advertisements on internet storefronts. *International Journal of Electronic Commerce*, *5*(3), 45–62. doi:10.1080/10864415.2001.11044215

Kim, Y., Kwon, D. Y., & Jeong, S. R. (2015). Comparing machine learning classifiers for movie WOM opinion mining. *KSII Transactions on Internet and Information Systems*, *9*(8), 3169–3181. doi:10.3837/tiis.2015.08.025

King, M. A., Abrahams, A. S., & Ragsdale, C. T. (2015). Ensemble learning methods for pay-per-click campaign management. *Expert Systems with Applications*, *42*(10), 4818–4829. doi:10.1016/j.eswa.2015.01.047

Kolte, A., Roy, J. K., & Vasa, L. (2023). The impact of unpredictable resource prices and equity volatility in advanced and emerging economies: An econometric and machine learning approach. *Resources Policy*, *80*, 103216. doi:10.1016/j.resourpol.2022.103216

Kübler, R. V., Colicev, A., & Pauwels, K. H. (2020). Social media's impact on the consumer mindset: When to use which sentiment extraction tool? *Journal of Interactive Marketing*, *50*(1), 136–155. doi:10.1016/j.intmar.2019.08.001

Kwok, L., Tang, Y., & Yu, B. (2020). The 7 Ps marketing mix of home-sharing services: Mining travelers' online reviews on Airbnb. *International Journal of Hospitality Management*, *90*, 102616. doi:10.1016/j.ijhm.2020.102616 PMID:32834353

Lahmiri, S., Bekiros, S., & Avdoulas, C. (2023). A comparative assessment of machine learning methods for predicting housing prices using Bayesian optimization. *Decision Analytics Journal*, *6*, 100166. doi:10.1016/j.dajour.2023.100166

Lee, D., Hosanagar, K., & Nair, H. S. (2018). Advertising content and consumer engagement on social media: Evidence from Facebook. *Management Science*, *64*(11), 5105–5131. doi:10.1287/mnsc.2017.2902

Leguina, J. R., Rumín, Á. C., & Rumín, R. C. (2020). Digital Marketing Attribution: Understanding the User Path. *Electronics (Basel)*, *9*(11), 1822. doi:10.3390/electronics9111822

Lepa, S., Herzog, M., Steffens, J., Schoenrock, A., & Egermann, H. (2020). A computational model for predicting perceived musical expression in branding scenarios. *Journal of New Music Research*, *49*(4), 387–402. doi:10.1080/09298215.2020.1778041

Li, J., Pan, S., & Huang, L. (2019). A machine learning based method for customer behavior prediction. *Tehnicki Vjesnik (Strojarski Fakultet)*, *26*(6), 1670–1676.

Li, X., Shi, M., & Wang, X. S. (2019). Video mining: Measuring visual information using automatic methods. *International Journal of Research in Marketing*, *36*(2), 216–231. doi:10.1016/j.ijresmar.2019.02.004

Liang, X., Wang, C., & Zhao, G. (2019). Enhancing content marketing article detection with graph analysis. *IEEE Access : Practical Innovations, Open Solutions*, *7*, 94869–94881. doi:10.1109/ACCESS.2019.2928094

Lin, J.-S., & Wu, L. (2023). Examining the psychological process of developing consumer-brand relationships through strategic use of social media brand chatbots. *Computers in Human Behavior*, *140*, 107488. doi:10.1016/j.chb.2022.107488

Liu, L., Dzyabura, D., & Mizik, N. (2020). Visual listening in: Extracting brand image portrayed on social media. *Marketing Science*, *39*(4), 669–686. doi:10.1287/mksc.2020.1226

Liu, M., Cai, S., Lai, Z., Qiu, L., Hu, Z., & Ding, Y. (2021). A joint learning model for click-through prediction in display advertising. *Neurocomputing*, *445*, 206–219. doi:10.1016/j.neucom.2021.02.036

Loureiro, S. M. C., Guerreiro, J., & Tussyadiah, I. (2021). Artificial intelligence in business: State of the art and future research agenda. *Journal of Business Research*, *129*, 911–926. doi:10.1016/j.jbusres.2020.11.001

Luo, X., Tong, S., Fang, Z., & Qu, Z. (2019). Frontiers: Machines vs. humans: The impact of artificial intelligence chatbot disclosure on customer purchases. *Marketing Science*, *38*(6), 937–947. doi:10.1287/mksc.2019.1192

Luo, Y., & Xu, X. (2019). Predicting the helpfulness of online restaurant reviews using different machine learning algorithms: A case study of yelp. *Sustainability (Basel)*, *11*(19), 5254. doi:10.3390u11195254

Ma, L., & Sun, B. (2020). Machine learning and AI in marketing – Connecting computing power to human insights. *International Journal of Research in Marketing*, *37*(3), 481–504. doi:10.1016/j.ijresmar.2020.04.005

Marchand, A., & Marx, P. (2020). Automated Product Recommendations with Preference-Based Explanations. *Journal of Retailing*, *96*(3), 328–343. doi:10.1016/j.jretai.2020.01.001

Mariani, M. M., Machado, I., & Nambisan, S. (2023). Types of innovation and artificial intelligence: A systematic quantitative literature review and research agenda. *Journal of Business Research*, *155*, 113364. doi:10.1016/j.jbusres.2022.113364

Martínez, A., Schmuck, C., Pereverzyev, S. Jr, Pirker, C., & Haltmeier, M. (2020). A machine learning framework for customer purchase prediction in the non-contractual setting. *European Journal of Operational Research*, *281*(3), 588–596. doi:10.1016/j.ejor.2018.04.034

Matz, S. C., Segalin, C., Stillwell, D., Müller, S. R., & Bos, M. W. (2019). Predicting the personal appeal of marketing images using computational methods. *Journal of Consumer Psychology*, *29*(3), 370–390. doi:10.1002/jcpy.1092

Mediavilla, M. A., Dietrich, F., & Palm, D. (2022). Review and analysis of artificial intelligence methods for demand forecasting in supply chain management. *Procedia CIRP*, *107*, 1126–1131. doi:10.1016/j.procir.2022.05.119

Miralles-Pechuán, L., Ponce, H., & Martínez-Villaseñor, L. (2018). A novel methodology for optimizing display advertising campaigns using genetic algorithms. *Electronic Commerce Research and Applications*, *27*, 39–51. doi:10.1016/j.elerap.2017.11.004

Miralles-Pechuán, L., Ponce, H., & Martínez-Villaseñor, L. (2020). A 2020 perspective on "A novel methodology for optimizing display advertising campaigns using genetic algorithms". *Electronic Commerce Research and Applications*, *40*, 100953. doi:10.1016/j.elerap.2020.100953

Misischia, C. V., Poecze, F., & Strauss, C. (2022). Chatbots in customer service: Their relevance and impact on service quality. *Procedia Computer Science*, *201*, 421–428. doi:10.1016/j.procs.2022.03.055

Nazir, S., Khadim, S., Ali Asadullah, M., & Syed, N. (2023). Exploring the influence of artificial intelligence technology on consumer repurchase intention: The mediation and moderation approach. *Technology in Society*, *72*, 102190. doi:10.1016/j.techsoc.2022.102190

Nengroo, A. S., & Kuppusamy, K. S. (2018). Machine learning based heterogeneous web advertisements detection using a diverse feature set. *Future Generation Computer Systems*, *89*, 68–77. doi:10.1016/j.future.2018.06.028

Ngai, E. W. T., Lee, M. C. M., Luo, M., Chan, P. S. L., & Liang, T. (2021). An intelligent knowledge-based chatbot for customer service. *Electronic Commerce Research and Applications*, *50*, 101098. doi:10.1016/j.elerap.2021.101098

Ngai, E. W. T., & Wu, Y. (2022). Machine learning in marketing: A literature review, conceptual framework, and research agenda. *Journal of Business Research*, *145*, 35–48. doi:10.1016/j.jbusres.2022.02.049

O'Mahony, M., Hurley, N., Kushmerick, N., & Silvestre, G. (2004). Collaborative recommendation: A robustness analysis. *ACM Transactions on Internet Technology*, *4*(4), 344–377. doi:10.1145/1031114.1031116

Orsini, J.-F. (1986). Artificial intelligence: A way through the strategic planning crisis? *Long Range Planning*, *19*(4), 71–77. doi:10.1016/0024-6301(86)90273-6

Pantano, E., & Pizzi, G. (2020). Forecasting artificial intelligence on online customer assistance: Evidence from chatbot patents analysis. *Journal of Retailing and Consumer Services*, *55*, 102096. doi:10.1016/j.jretconser.2020.102096

Pantanowitz, L., Bui, M. M., Chauhan, C., ElGabry, E., Hassell, L., Li, Z., Parwani, A. V., Salama, M. E., Sebastian, M. M., Tulman, D., Vepa, S., & Becich, M. J. (2022). Rules of engagement: Promoting academic-industry partnership in the era of digital pathology and artificial intelligence. *Academic Pathology*, *9*(1), 100026. doi:10.1016/j.acpath.2022.100026 PMID:35669406

Paolanti, M., Pietrini, R., Mancini, A., Frontoni, E., & Zingaretti, P. (2020). Deep understanding of shopper behaviours and interactions using RGB-D vision. *Machine Vision and Applications*, *31*(7-8), 1–21. doi:10.100700138-020-01118-w

Peng, L., Cui, G., & Chung, Y. (2020). Do the pieces fit? Assessing the configuration effects of promotion attributes. *Journal of Business Research*, *109*, 337–349. doi:10.1016/j.jbusres.2019.11.081

Pereira, A. M., Moura, J. A. B., Costa, E. D. B., Vieira, T., Landim, A. R. D. B., Bazaki, E., & Wanick, V. (2022). Customer models for artificial intelligence-based decision support in fashion online retail supply chains. *Decision Support Systems*, *158*, 113795. doi:10.1016/j.dss.2022.113795

Perez-Vega, R., Kaartemo, V., Lages, C. R., Borghei Razavi, N., & Männistö, J. (2021). Reshaping the contexts of online customer engagement behavior via artificial intelligence: A conceptual framework. *Journal of Business Research*, *129*, 902–910. doi:10.1016/j.jbusres.2020.11.002

Popov, A., & Iakovleva, D. (2018). Adaptive look-alike targeting in social networks advertising. *Procedia Computer Science*, *136*, 255–264. doi:10.1016/j.procs.2018.08.264

Potrawa, T., & Tetereva, A. (2022). How much is the view from the window worth? Machine learning-driven hedonic pricing model of the real estate market. *Journal of Business Research*, *144*, 50–65. doi:10.1016/j.jbusres.2022.01.027

Qazi, M., Tollas, K., Kanchinadam, T., Bockhorst, J., & Fung, G. (2020). Designing and deploying insurance recommender systems using machine learning. *Wiley Interdisciplinary Reviews. Data Mining and Knowledge Discovery*, *10*(4), e1363. doi:10.1002/widm.1363

Quesenberry, K. A., & Coolsen, M. K. (2019). Drama goes viral: Effects of story development on shares and views of online advertising videos. *Journal of Interactive Marketing*, *48*(1), 1–16. doi:10.1016/j.intmar.2019.05.001

Rajamohana, S., & Umamaheswari, K. (2018). Hybrid approach of improved binary particle swarm optimization and shuffled frog leaping for feature selection. *Computers & Electrical Engineering*, *67*, 497–508. doi:10.1016/j.compeleceng.2018.02.015

Raphael, J., Madhusudana Rao, N., Bindu, A., & Gao, X.-Z. (2022). Clustering-based Factorization Machines for Advertisement Click prediction. *Procedia Computer Science*, *215*, 546–555. doi:10.1016/j.procs.2022.12.057

Ren, Y.-S., Ma, C.-Q., Kong, X.-L., Baltas, K., & Zureigat, Q. (2022). Past, present, and future of the application of machine learning in cryptocurrency research. *Research in International Business and Finance*, *63*, 101799. doi:10.1016/j.ribaf.2022.101799

Rizomyliotis, I., Kastanakis, M. N., Giovanis, A., Konstantoulaki, K., & Kostopoulos, I. (2022). "How mAy I help you today?" The use of AI chatbots in small family businesses and the moderating role of customer affective commitment. *Journal of Business Research*, *153*, 329–340. doi:10.1016/j.jbusres.2022.08.035

Ruiz-Real, J. L., Uribe-Toril, J., Torres, J. A., & De Pablo, J. (2021). Artificial intelligence in business and economics research: Trends and future. *Journal of Business Economics and Management*, *22*(1), 98–117. doi:10.3846/jbem.2020.13641

Samunderu, E., & Farrugia, M. (2022). Predicting customer purpose of travel in a low-cost travel environment—A Machine Learning Approach. *Machine Learning with Applications*, *9*, 100379. doi:10.1016/j.mlwa.2022.100379

Sandeep, S. R., Ahamad, S., Saxena, D., Srivastava, K., Jaiswal, S., & Bora, A. (2022). To understand the relationship between Machine learning and Artificial intelligence in large and diversified business organisations. *Materials Today: Proceedings*, *56*, 2082–2086. doi:10.1016/j.matpr.2021.11.409

Schaeffer, S. E., & Sanchez, S. V. R. (2020). Forecasting client retention — A machine-learning approach. *Journal of Retailing and Consumer Services*, *52*, 101918. doi:10.1016/j.jretconser.2019.101918

Schwartz, E. M., Bradlow, E. T., & Fader, P. S. (2017). Customer acquisition via display advertising using multi-armed bandit experiments. *Marketing Science*, *36*(4), 500–522. doi:10.1287/mksc.2016.1023

Seeger, P. M., Yahouni, Z., & Alpan, G. (2022). Literature review on using data mining in production planning and scheduling within the context of cyber physical systems. *Journal of Industrial Information Integration*, *28*, 100371. doi:10.1016/j.jii.2022.100371

Shumanov, M., & Johnson, L. (2021). Making conversations with chatbots more personalized. *Computers in Human Behavior*, *117*, 106627. doi:10.1016/j.chb.2020.106627

Siering, M., Deokar, A. V., & Janze, C. (2018). Disentangling consumer recommendations: Explaining and predicting airline recommendations based on online reviews. *Decision Support Systems*, *107*, 52–63. doi:10.1016/j.dss.2018.01.002

Simmonds, L., Bellman, S., Kennedy, R., Nenycz-Thiel, M., & Bogomolova, S. (2020). Moderating effects of prior brand usage on visual attention to video advertising and recall: An eye-tracking investigation. *Journal of Business Research*, *111*, 241–248. doi:10.1016/j.jbusres.2019.02.062

Soltani, A., Heydari, M., Aghaei, F., & Pettit, C. J. (2022). Housing price prediction incorporating spatio-temporal dependency into machine learning algorithms. *Cities (London, England)*, *131*, 103941. doi:10.1016/j.cities.2022.103941

Srivastava, V., & Kalro, A. D. (2019). Enhancing the helpfulness of online consumer reviews: The role of latent (content) factors. *Journal of Interactive Marketing*, *48*(1), 33–50. doi:10.1016/j.intmar.2018.12.003

Steininger, D. M., & Gatzemeier, S. (2019). Digitally forecasting new music product success via active crowdsourcing. *Technological Forecasting and Social Change*, *146*, 167–180. doi:10.1016/j.techfore.2019.04.016

Sueyoshi, T., & Tadiparthi, G. R. (2005). A wholesale power trading simulator with learning capabilities. *IEEE Transactions on Power Systems*, *20*(3), 1330–1340. doi:10.1109/TPWRS.2005.851948

Sueyoshi, T., & Tadiparthi, G. R. (2008). An agent-based decision support system for wholesale electricity market. *Decision Support Systems*, *44*(2), 425–446. doi:10.1016/j.dss.2007.05.007

Sung, E., Bae, S., Han, D.-I. D., & Kwon, O. (2021). Consumer engagement via interactive artificial intelligence and mixed reality. *International Journal of Information Management*, *60*, 102382. doi:10.1016/j.ijinfomgt.2021.102382

Taecharungroj, V., & Mathayomchan, B. (2019). Analysing TripAdvisor reviews of tourist attractions in Phuket, Thailand. *Tourism Management*, *75*, 550–568. doi:10.1016/j.tourman.2019.06.020

Thejas, G. S., Dheeshjith, S., Iyengar, S. S., Sunitha, N. R., & Badrinath, P. (2021). A hybrid and effective learning approach for Click Fraud detection. *Machine Learning with Applications*, *3*, 100016. doi:10.1016/j.mlwa.2020.100016

Thirumuruganathan, S., Emadi, N. A., Jung, S., Salminen, J., Robillos, D. R., & Jansen, B. J. (2023). Will they take this offer? A machine learning price elasticity model for predicting upselling acceptance of premium airline seating. *Information & Management*, *60*(3), 103759. doi:10.1016/j.im.2023.103759

Tirunillai, S., & Tellis, G. J. (2014). Mining marketing meaning from online chatter: Strategic brand analysis of big data using latent dirichlet allocation. *JMR, Journal of Marketing Research*, *51*(4), 463–479. doi:10.1509/jmr.12.0106

Toorajipour, R., Sohrabpour, V., Nazarpour, A., Oghazi, P., & Fischl, M. (2021). Artificial intelligence in supply chain management: A systematic literature review. *Journal of Business Research*, *122*, 502–517. doi:10.1016/j.jbusres.2020.09.009

Tran, A. D., Pallant, J. I., & Johnson, L. W. (2021). Exploring the impact of chatbots on consumer sentiment and expectations in retail. *Journal of Retailing and Consumer Services*, *63*, 102718. doi:10.1016/j.jretconser.2021.102718

Trappey, A., Trappey, C. V., & Hsieh, A. (2021). An intelligent patent recommender adopting machine learning approach for natural language processing: A case study for smart machinery technology mining. *Technological Forecasting and Social Change*, *164*, 120511. doi:10.1016/j.techfore.2020.120511

Trappey, A. J. C., Trappey, C. V., & Lin, E. (2022). Intelligent trademark recognition and similarity analysis using a two-stage transfer learning approach. *Advanced Engineering Informatics*, *52*, 101567. doi:10.1016/j.aei.2022.101567

Trappey, C. V., Trappey, A. J. C., & Lin, S. C. C. (2020). Intelligent trademark similarity analysis of image, spelling, and phonetic features using machine learning methodologies. *Advanced Engineering Informatics*, *45*, 101120. doi:10.1016/j.aei.2020.101120

Trappey, C. V., Trappey, A. J. C., & Liu, B.-H. (2020). Identify trademark legal case precedents - Using machine learning to enable semantic analysis of judgments. *World Patent Information*, *62*, 101980. doi:10.1016/j.wpi.2020.101980

Van den Broeck, E., Zarouali, B., & Poels, K. (2019). Chatbot advertising effectiveness: When does the message get through? *Computers in Human Behavior*, *98*, 150–157. doi:10.1016/j.chb.2019.04.009

Van Esch, P., & Black, J. S. (2021). Artificial intelligence (AI): Revolutionizing digital marketing. *Australasian Marketing Journal*, *29*(3), 199–203. doi:10.1177/18393349211037684

Verma, S., Sharma, R., Deb, S., & Maitra, D. (2021). Artificial intelligence in marketing: Systematic review and future research direction. *International Journal of Information Management Data Insights*, *1*(1), 100002. doi:10.1016/j.jjimei.2020.100002

Volkmar, G., Fischer, P. M., & Reinecke, S. (2022). Artificial Intelligence and Machine Learning: Exploring drivers, barriers, and future developments in marketing management. *Journal of Business Research*, *149*, 599–614. doi:10.1016/j.jbusres.2022.04.007

Wang, X., Lin, X., & Shao, B. (2022). How does artificial intelligence create business agility? Evidence from chatbots. *International Journal of Information Management*, *66*, 102535. doi:10.1016/j.ijinfomgt.2022.102535

Wang, Y., Liu, S., Li, S., Duan, J., Hou, Z., Yu, J., & Ma, K. (2019). Stacking-based ensemble learning of self-media data for marketing intention detection. *Future Internet*, *11*(7), 155. doi:10.3390/fi11070155

Wang, Y., Ma, K., Garcia-Hernandez, L., Chen, J., Hou, Z., Ji, K., Chen, Z., & Abraham, A. (2020). A CLSTM-TMN for marketing intention detection. *Engineering Applications of Artificial Intelligence*, *91*, 103595. doi:10.1016/j.engappai.2020.103595

Watanuki, S., & Akama, H. (2022). Neural substrates of brand equity: Applying a quantitative meta-analytical method for neuroimage studies. *Heliyon*, *8*(6), e09702. doi:10.1016/j.heliyon.2022.e09702 PMID:35734557

Wei, Y. Z., Moreau, L., & Jennings, N. R. (2005). Learning users' interests by quality classification in market-based recommender systems. *IEEE Transactions on Knowledge and Data Engineering*, *17*(12), 1678–1688. doi:10.1109/TKDE.2005.200

Wilk, V., Lambert, C., & Meek, S. (2022). Online brand detraction in an online opinion platform. *International Journal of Hospitality Management*, *107*, 103345. doi:10.1016/j.ijhm.2022.103345

Wolkenfelt, M. R. J., & Situmeang, F. B. I. (2020). Effects of app pricing structures on product evaluations. *Journal of Research in Interactive Marketing*, *14*(1), 89–110. doi:10.1108/JRIM-11-2018-0141

Xu, F., Wang, L., & Gao, J. (2020). Thoughts on Application of Artificial Intelligence in Teaching of Different Disciplines. *2020 15th International Conference on Computer Science & Education (ICCSE)*. doi:10.1109/ACCESS.2018.2861429

Xu, R., Wang, M., & Xie, Y. (2018). Optimally connected deep belief net for click through rate prediction in online advertising. *IEEE Access : Practical Innovations, Open Solutions*, *6*, 43009–43020. doi:10.1109/ACCESS.2018.2861429

Yang, Y., Xu, B., Shen, S., Shen, F., & Zhao, J. (2020). Operation-aware neural networks for user response prediction. *Neural Networks*, *121*, 161–168. doi:10.1016/j.neunet.2019.09.020 PMID:31563699

Zappin, A., Malik, H., Shakshuki, E. M., & Dampier, D. A. (2022). YouTube Monetization and Censorship by Proxy: A Machine Learning Prospective. *Procedia Computer Science*, *198*, 23–32. doi:10.1016/j.procs.2021.12.207

Zarouali, B., Van den Broeck, E., Walrave, M., & Poels, K. (2018). Predicting consumer responses to a chatbot on Facebook. *Cyberpsychology, Behavior, and Social Networking*, *21*(8), 491–497. doi:10.1089/cyber.2017.0518 PMID:30036074

Zhang, C., & Lu, Y. (2021). Study on artificial intelligence: The state of the art and future prospects. *Journal of Industrial Information Integration*, *23*, 100224. doi:10.1016/j.jii.2021.100224

Zhang, D., Zhou, L., Kehoe, J. L., & Kilic, I. Y. (2016). What online reviewer behaviors really matter? Effects of verbal and nonverbal behaviors on detection of fake online reviews. *Journal of Management Information Systems*, *33*(2), 456–481. doi:10.1080/07421222.2016.1205907

Zhang, X., Li, S., Burke, R. R., & Leykin, A. (2014). An examination of social influence on shopper behavior using video tracking data. *Journal of Marketing*, *78*(5), 24–41. doi:10.1509/jm.12.0106

Zuiderwijk, A., Chen, Y.-C., & Salem, F. (2021). Implications of the use of artificial intelligence in public governance: A systematic literature review and a research agenda. *Government Information Quarterly*, *38*(3), 101577. doi:10.1016/j.giq.2021.101577

KEY TERMS AND DEFINITIONS

Bayesian Networks: Also known as Belief Networks or Bayesian Belief Networks are a type of probabilistic graphical model that represents relationships between variables and the uncertainty surrounding those relationships. The basic building block of a Bayesian network is a node, which represents a variable, and the edges between nodes represent the relationships or dependencies between variables. The probability distribution of each variable is modeled using a set of conditional probabilities, which describe how the variable depends on its parent variables in the network. Bayesian networks can be used to perform tasks such as probability inference, which involves computing the probability of a particular event given certain observations, and decision-making, which involves choosing the best course of action based on uncertain information. They are particularly useful in applications where the relationships between variables are complex and there is a high degree of uncertainty.

Deep Learning: Deep learning is a subfield of machine learning that focuses on using artificial neural networks with multiple layers (hence "deep") to learn from and make predictions or decisions based on large amounts of complex and diverse data. Unlike traditional neural networks, deep learning algorithms use multiple layers of interconnected nodes to process and analyze data, allowing them to learn and make decisions at a higher level of abstraction.

Fuzzy Logic: This is a mathematical framework for representing and processing uncertainty and imprecision in information. It was developed as an alternative to classical (or "crisp") logic, which only deals with binary values of true and false. In fuzzy logic, information is represented by degrees of truth, rather than binary values, allowing for more nuanced and flexible representations of uncertainty. In fuzzy logic, variables can take on values between 0 and 1, representing the degree to which they are true or false. These degrees of truth can be combined using fuzzy rules, which are statements that relate the values of multiple variables to each other. The output of a fuzzy system is a fuzzy set, which represents the degree of membership of the system's output in various possible categories. This output can then be defuzzified, or translated into a crisp value, by using various methods, such as the center of gravity or the mean of maximum.

Genetic Algorithm: This is a type of optimization algorithm that is inspired by the process of natural selection and evolution. It is a search-based algorithm that uses principles of genetics and natural selection to find solutions to optimization problems. In a genetic algorithm, a population of potential solutions is generated, and each solution is evaluated based on a fitness function. The solutions with the highest fitness are used to generate new solutions through the process of selection, crossover, and mutation, in which parts of the high-fitness solutions are combined to create new, potentially better solutions. This process is repeated over several generations until a satisfactory solution is found or a stopping criterion is reached. Genetic algorithms are commonly used in a variety of fields, including engineering, finance, and gaming, to solve complex optimization problems that are difficult to solve with traditional optimization methods.

Machine Learning: Machine learning is a subfield of artificial intelligence that focuses on the development of algorithms and statistical models that allow computers to learn from and make predictions or decisions based on data, without being explicitly programmed. In machine learning, an algorithm is trained on a large dataset and uses that data to make predictions or decisions based on new, unseen data. The goal of machine learning is to build models that can automatically improve their accuracy over time, by continuously learning from the data they process.

Natural Language Processing: Is a subfield of artificial intelligence and computer science that focuses on the interaction between computers and humans using natural language. The goal of NLP is to develop algorithms and models that enable computers to understand, interpret, and generate human language. NLP has a wide range of applications, including text classification, sentiment analysis, machine translation, and question-answering.

Neural Networks: A neural network is a type of artificial intelligence model that is inspired by the structure and function of the human brain. It is a collection of interconnected nodes or "neurons" that process and transmits information, allowing the network to learn from examples and make predictions or decisions based on input data. Neural networks can be trained to perform a variety of tasks, such as image recognition, speech recognition, and natural language processing.

Support Vector Machine: SVM is a supervised learning algorithm that uses a boundary, called a hyperplane, to separate the data into different classes. The hyperplane is chosen in such a way that it maximizes the margin, or the distance, between the closest data points from each class, called support vectors. SVM can handle non-linearly separable data by transforming it into a higher dimensional space where a linear boundary can be applied. SVM is commonly used for text classification, image recognition, and bioinformatics, among other applications. It is known for its high accuracy, ability to handle large datasets and robustness to outliers.

Chapter 6
Artificial Intelligence in the Context of Digital Marketing

Suraj Juddoo
Midlesex University, Mauritius

ABSTRACT

This chapter examines the drivers for the adoption of artificial intelligence (AI) in digital marketing and the challenges that organizations face while implementing AI-based marketing strategies. The chapter begins with an overview of the potential applications connected with using AI in digital marketing, including automation. It then explores the key drivers for the adoption of AI in digital marketing. This chapter also provides a framework for greater adoption of AI in digital marketing. The framework has many well-known components relative to other known AI frameworks but is focused upon digital marketing. The chapter discusses the challenges that organizations face when implementing AI-based marketing strategies. The chapter also explores the potential risks associated with using AI in digital marketing, including algorithmic bias and the risk of over-reliance on AI. Overall, this chapter provides insights into the drivers and challenges of using AI in digital marketing and offers recommendations for organizations looking to implement AI-based marketing strategies.

INTRODUCTION

Digital marketing (DM) is currently being impacted by Artificial Intelligence (AI) to such an extent that optimized algorithms can forecast consumer behavior very precisely, provide decisions concerning most adequate offers to be proposed to specific profiles of customers, and even evolve along with other new technologies such as blockchain and cloud computing (Kaponis & Maradougakis, 2022). Digital Marketing is an umbrella term denoting online marketing, internet marketing and mobile marketing. A simple example of application of AI in digital marketing is through the use of intelligent chatbots. By adding value insights through data mining techniques, chatbots are now playing a key role in digital sales by not only automating the communication aspects towards partners but by also allowing fine grained analysis of customers intentions.

DOI: 10.4018/978-1-6684-8958-1.ch006

The emergence of DM can be explained by several factors and two prominent factors are the growing production of data by organisations and secondly the significant concentration of consumers using the internet currently (Miklosik et al.,2019). The digital footprint of internet users is a great opportunity which organisations want to tap unto, and which allows marketing efforts to be more measurable. Analytical tools focused upon machine learning use to learn from historical data and improve planning activities.AI powered DM initiatives can effectively respond to changing demands from stakeholders of an organisation (Malviya et al.,2022).

The goals of this chapter are to discuss in depth, using case studies, the involvement and impact of the of use cases driven by Artificial Intelligence for the broad domain of marketing, with a specific focus on digital marketing (DM). This chapter starts by brushing a broad picture of the different ways AI is applied in the context of marketing processes.

The drivers for the use of AI for DM will then be discussed, followed by a discussion upon specific advantages of applying AI for DM. The readers would also be made aware of the challenges and potential risks of using AI for DM. Clear case studies will be used to support the ideas listed above within the chapter.

BACKGROUND

As most business processes, digital marketing tends to benefit in various ways from the use of information systems in general. With the growing development and adoption in AI since some years, marketing professionals have quickly found out that they can be supported in different ways by AI systems (Malviya et al., 2022). However, in order to understand this wide topic, it would be worthwhile for the readers to understand some of the main drivers which lead to the current state of use of AI for digital marketing. The following list down some of the main factors:

1. **Data Processing and Analysis:** With the enormous amount of data generated every day, AI has become essential in processing and analyzing this data at a faster pace, which is essential in making quick and informed decisions in digital marketing (Miklosik et al.2019).
2. **Personalization:** AI allows for personalized customer experiences by analyzing data from various sources, including social media, web browsing, and purchase history, which helps businesses tailor their marketing strategies and offerings to their customers. E.g, intelligent chatbots may provide personalised content for customers based on large amount of customer related data (Malviya et al., 2022).
3. **Cost-Effectiveness:** AI-powered tools can automate certain marketing tasks, reducing the time and cost associated with manual labor.
4. **Improved Targeting and Segmentation:** AI can identify patterns and trends in customer behavior, allowing marketers to segment their audience better and target them with relevant content. This is the basis for digital content marketing (Hsu & Liou, 2021).
5. **Predictive Analysis:** With the help of AI algorithms, digital marketers can anticipate customer behavior, understand their preferences, and predict their future actions. This helps marketers to tailor their marketing strategies and campaigns accordingly (Hsu & Lious, 2021; Malviya et al., 2022).

6. **Chatbots and Voice Assistants:** AI-powered chatbots and voice assistants are transforming the way customers interact with businesses, providing a personalized and instant response to customer queries.
7. **Data Volume:** The amount of data generated by consumers has increased significantly in recent years, making it difficult for marketers to analyze and make sense of it all. AI can help analyze large volumes of data quickly and efficiently, making it easier to identify patterns and insights that can inform marketing strategies (Gao & Zhang, 2020).
8. **Automation:** AI can automate many of the repetitive tasks involved in digital marketing, such as email marketing, social media scheduling, and ad targeting. This saves marketers time and resources, allowing them to focus on more strategic initiatives (Hsu & Liou, 2021; Malviya et al.,2022).
9. **Real-Time Analysis:** AI can quickly analyze data and provide real-time insights, allowing marketers to make faster, more informed decisions. This is particularly important in today's fast-paced digital environment, where consumer behavior and trends can change rapidly.
10. **Competitive Advantage:** Companies that adopt AI for digital marketing can gain a significant competitive advantage by delivering more personalized, relevant experiences to their customers. This can lead to increased customer loyalty, higher conversion rates, and ultimately, greater revenue.

Overall, AI adoption in digital marketing has improved efficiency, accuracy, and results, leading to increased ROI and customer satisfaction. The above ideas denote that in today's hyper competitive business environment where the need to know customers and other stakeholders extremely well, the use of AI is necessary for an organization's marketing business function to be effective and efficient.

However, the use of AI even for digital marketing is impacted by certain challenges, such as:

1. **Data Privacy:** As AI relies heavily on data, there are concerns around data privacy and security. Marketers must ensure that they are collecting and using data ethically and in compliance with privacy regulations such as GDPR (Sachdev, 2020).
2. **Bias:** AI systems can be biased if they are trained on biased data or programmed with biased algorithms. Marketers must be careful to ensure that their AI systems are not perpetuating bias in their marketing efforts (Molina, 2023).
3. **Consumer Preferences:** Users do not always want to interact with a robot or software. It is thus expected that, in the near future, the need for interaction with a human being will remain preferential, with consumers having greater confidence in such communication (Dubey et al., 2022).

The above discuss the most prominent and frequently cited challenges for AI adoption in general, but also englobing the field of digital marketing. There are several initiatives already in place to attenuate the effect of the challenges mentioned such as the use of anonymised data to maintain some adequate respect for data privacy, improving level of data quality and data pre-processing techniques to cater for potential bias results of AI systems and greater evangelisation of AI solutions to increase societal adoption. However, in spite of all these initiatives, the field is a buoyant one and it is very likely that we would witness many developments in the very short term.

Application of AI in Digital Marketing

Digital transformations of organisations are being enhanced by the use of AI where a mixture of automation and human inputs are expected to improve business processes. Furthermore, with global hyper-competition and the growing use of digital activity of the general public following events such as lock-downs due to Covid19 globally, there is a need for organisations to have a finer grain knowledge about their customers. This chapter starts by discussing the numerous ways AI can be used to support and improve the digital marketing processes.

Automation

With the involvement of smart data capture technology such as the Internet of Things (IOT) combined with AI, it becomes easier for business processes to be partially or even fully automated. The automation of business processes is a key factor allowing organisations to offer better customer experience in terms of both personalized and customized interactions. Online markets businesses typically take customers' feedback into consideration and produce actionable trends to support strategies towards market growth. The resulting data captured from web transactions, searches, purchases, reviews, comments, relishes, posts, is unstructured or semi-structured and rarely structured. AI is very useful to perform different types of analytics based on the combination of all structures of related data in order to extract maximum knowledge (Biswas & Sanyal, 2019).

Improved Decision Support

One of the most well-known applications of AI in the realm of marketing is in terms of predicting dynamic product pricing and therefore maximising from ever changing customer buying behaviours. For example, during request for quotations, fuzzy logic rule mining approaches are applied to help marketers discover the hidden relationships between sales data and customer demand data and therefore recommend the most relevant bid details (Pathak and Muscu, 2020). Another example of application of supervised learning algorithms such as decision trees which have been used to produce a model based on features such as website domain name, keywords, zip code and browser characteristics. The application of the model is used to predict optimised bid prices based upon prevailing feature values (Pathak & Muscu, 2020).

Neuro-Marketing

In a digital ecosystem, relations between consumers might be the source of marketing intelligence for organisations. Aimed at providing active two-way information between organisations and consumers, neuro-marketing helps to understand more deeply how the views of consumers might contribute towards sustainable strategies and green companies. The decryption and understanding of consumers' emotions that can be detected in social media-based interactions can be a used for marketing processes to influence positively consumers' emotions towards an organisation or its products (Wolpe, 2019). Some AI algorithms such as Bayesian neural networks can contribute to this direction and predict customer behaviour to improve in digital marketing decision making and retain valuable customers.

Sentiment analysis is one of the applicable technique to extract information and sentiment from the huge amounts of consumer data. Sentiment analysis is applied to a variety of user segmented data, from customer reviews to social media, in order to increase the capability of organisations to understand consumer needs and behaviours in a more targeted approach.

Conversational Systems

AI capabilities to interact successfully in the real world has increased tremendously these recent years such as with the advent of large language models (LLMs) such as ChatGPT, and they are now playing an influential role in marketing. Several companies have invested in chatbots with the goal of customer satisfaction. The degree of realistic interactions of chatbots with consumers increase the latter's desire to engage with an organisation (Toader et al., 2020). Large language models have proven to be able to handle quite challenging cognitive tasks and thus increase the degree of realistic interactions with potential users. These LLMs are nowadays expected to be able to learn and handle a huge amount of tasks in a multi-modal way involving text, images and videos also. An example of one well-known virtual assistant is called 'Vania', who is a digital insurance clerk, and the empirical research results show that users which interacted with 'Vania' described their experience as enjoyable. Another well-known example is the 'MarkBot' which was designed to respond to a website visitor's browsing the product catalogue and is powered by user generated content.

A third example known as the 'AdRobot' aims to match the right offer with the right customer and therefore collects complex data and information about the target audience using data collected from conversations (Hafaiedh et al, 2021). This strategy consists of performing audience classification by segmenting profiles and conversational restrictions so that a predicted user is matched with the right advertising campaign (Kar & Kushwaha, 2021).

Personalized Marketing

Artificial intelligence techniques are applied in big data marketing and can be analyzed to predict consumer behavior. It is important to apply artificial positioning strategies to effectively target the customer to understand their behavior and find their expectations in relation to product features (Arun Kumar, 2021). Artificial Intelligence and Deep Learning have pushed marketing techniques, opening avenues for more personalized marketing so that the consumer is not the recipient of random advertising. There are two key strategic decisions in the areas of marketing, segmentation, and targeting.

Segmentation means dividing data into several clusters, and in the case of marketing dividing markets into different customer profiles with each one having unique and distinguishable characteristics. An example is the division of the air travel market into segments of economy and premium airline categories. Different mining and clustering techniques are able to recognize the features from the data which distinguishes economy to premium airline categories.

Targeting is choosing the most relevant segments to focus an organisation's marketing activities on. Market slicing is more mechanical and can be done automatically by machine artificial intelligence based on relevant data. Choosing the right segment requires domain knowledge, judgment, and intuition. 'SmarTech' is an email marketing application aimed at personalized marketing (Huang & Rust. 2021). Email marketing as it has now evolved is a very safe and ubiquitous marketing technique that is considered profitable. An improved version of the XGBoost algorithm based on Bayesian network optimization parameters, which can increase the accuracy of digital marketing, improve communication efficiency and increase the social impact of marketing through a combination from intelligent algorithms and data analysis (Li, 2022). Search engines using keywords as well as data analysis of browsing history data are used to target consumers, while targeting is done via social media with customers sharing the same content and same interests. Through historical data, machine learning algorithms can identify ads that are performing best and at which stage of the buying process (Jarek & Mazurek, 2019).

Case Study: Use of AI to Improve Email Click-Throughs

In digital marketing, the designers traditionally created email content based on years of experience to make decisions about most suitable images for a particular campaign, where to place them and most corresponding message associable with particular images. Machine learning algorithms that that learn from a huge amount of data can very precisely predict how likely email recipients are to click urls within different types of email content. However this traditional AI model is applicable and valuable after the email content has been developed. Furthermore, some recommender systems based mostly on deep learning suffer from a lack of transparency in explaining how certain algorithms come to certain specific recommendations. There is an increased call for higher level of ability to explain AI solutions in general, but mostly where the results might suffer from a level of bias (Crawford et al. 2019). A recent more interesting development involving AI in this area aimed to develop a dynamic model that enabled designers to have access to AI based insights while creating email content (Sinha et al., 2020).

This new interactive system is shown in Figure 1. Email designers begin by choosing one of several different image layout configurations (e.g. the six image layout framework in the left panel), then select from a collection of images available under a different tab on the same panel. When an image is placed in a slot, the back-end AI calculates the overall click-likelihood and the contribution from the individual features by a dashboard feature. The email content designer can then optionally add text which is then analyzed dynamically. This realtime feature based dashboard allows the designer to make choices that are informed by AI, but allows them to maintain control and use the recommendations interactively and creatively (Sinha et al., 2020).

Figure 1. Proposed dashboard for authoring: Authors first select from one of several layout templates (left) then choose images and image placements (center) and finally add text. The click probability with relative feature contributions dynamically adjusts as content is added and moved.

For marketing professionals, persuasion is an essential factor and must be embodied within email content, since the purpose of the email is to entice potential customers to click on items to find out more about them. Sinha et al. (2020) related quantifiable features of images, placement, and text to three aspects of persuasion: pathos or emotional persuasion, logos or logical argument and ethos for credibility. They used many features that had been proposed by past research as measuring persuasion: image aesthetics, image memorability, layout design, text readability, text formality and text sentiments. Past email campaigns were used to inform an AI based model using the above features and the AI model predicted the persuasive contribution of each related to past customer click behavior. This amounted roughly to the annotations of labels activity very common as part of many machine learning algorithms. Ultimately, a dashboard showing concisely the results of the AI model formed an interactive user interface.

The features described in the prior paragraph were used to independently train two different types of classifiers namely logistic regression and random forest, to predict how likely a user would be to click on different image, placement and text combinations. The training data consisted of user responses to a targeted campaigns consisting of over three million emails. Of these, there was only "email opened" response for approximately two million emails that were retained for the model training process. Typically, the responses were split for training, validation and testing sets on a ratio of 60%, 20% and 20% respectively. The training set was highly imbalanced since within opened emails, individual image clicks (positive individual responses) relatively scarce (5% of the data). Therefore, there was the need to undersample the negative responses to achieve a balanced ratio. Using the transformed and more balanced data, Sinha et al. (2020) independently trained both a logistic regression classifier and a random forest classifier. The test set was held out and used to evaluate the tuned model. Since the Area Under Curve (AUC) values for both algorithms were quite similar,.78 AUC for logistic regression and .81 AUC for random forest, Sinha et al. (2020) chose to implement the logistic regression classifier in our system for greater computational efficiency.

To evaluate the click through lift that the proposed AI based system would have on novel content, Singh et al. (2020) created a series of A/B preference tests (700 total) and hired 50 master turkers on Amazon Mechanical Turk (AMT) to evaluate them. Each of the tests featured similar options, one of which the AI would recommend over the other. Experiments were designed to evaluate whether the algorithm's feature based recommendations on novel content would likely convert to higher click-through rates, a key performance goal in digital marketing. Table 1 shows the the results of the AMT evaluation.

Table 1. A summary of the A/B preference test results showing the percentage of time the AI-guided content was preferred

A/B Test Type	AI-Guided Content Preferred	Clickrate Lift
Text	57%	7%
Image	66%	16%
Placement	72%	22%

It was found that the AI algorithm's recommendations had the strongest predictions rate with respect to the placement recommendation 72% of the time, resulting in a potential click-through lift of 22%. It had less predictive impact on image and text recommendations, with respective accuracies of 66% and

57%. But even these lower accuracies still resulted in potential click-rate lifts of 16% and 7%, both of which would likely deliver real value to a campaign. Thus, in general, even if the results are not massively impressive, they are undeniably positive and with further optimisation works on the AI algorithm, there is positive justifications that AI could recommend email content during the design stage to enable a higher click through rate.

The above examples provide an indication of the plethora of ways AI has been useful for the digital marketing needs. The benefits of adopting AI for digital marketing can also be highly consequential. This chapter already exposed some of the main drivers for the current boom of AI use. The question is how could AI be used for digital marketing support in the short and medium term? How are the drivers discussed foreseeable to be changing? Would there be some new drivers drastically influencing the AI landscape for digital marketing. These are the broad questions the next section attempts to shed more lights upon.

Adoption and Drivers of AI in Digital Marketing

Miklosik et al. (2019) proposed a framework which consists of two main components: 1) Enablers, i.e. factors of organizational culture and management contributing to the atmosphere and conditions, where such a project can be initiated and successfully finalized, and 2) Process map, i.e. a map of processes of such a project consisting of four main phases as in Figure 2.

Figure 2. Framework for successful adoption of machine learning in digital marketing

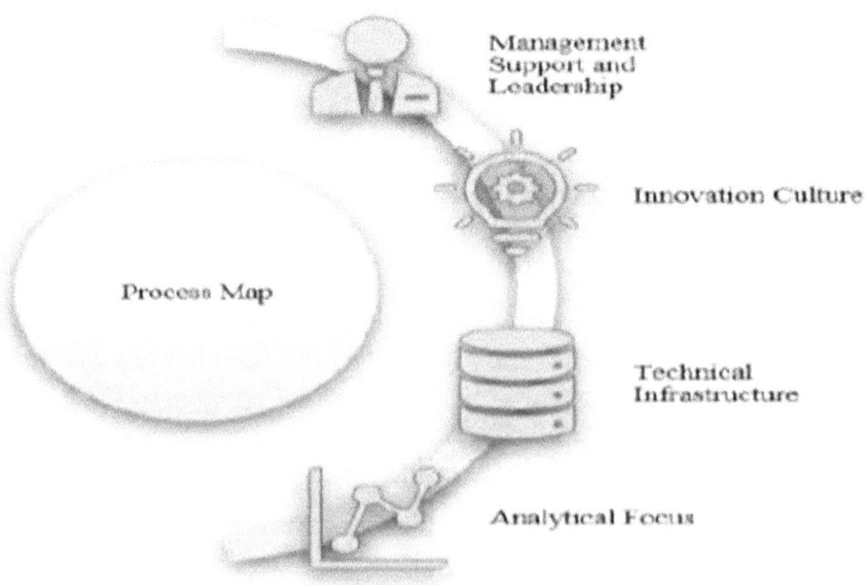

The absence of any of the enablers proposed by Miklosic et al. (2019) could be detrimental to any AI based project adoption for digital marketing. Firstly, as in most IT based projects, top management support is considered critical. Due to its character (cost, cross-departmental reach etc.), adoption of AI based projects with top managers' commitment reduces the silo effect of different departments working separately together. In general, a top-down driven innovative climate is required for such large and complex projects to succeed. The top managers should drill to the rest of the organisation the contribution of detailed analytics to the business and performance of their project teams. They should introduce ideas, adopt new solutions and test them.

Secondly, introducing innovative solutions, measures, and tools needs to be embedded in the company culture and connected with its competitiveness and process efficiency. With the highly increasing rate of development in the AI field, it is expected that organisations advocating AI based solutions will need to be able to rapidly integrate new technological solutions. To achieve this, having the right organisational culture is essential.

Thirdly, organisations need to possess adequate resources in order to enable emerging technologies to form the base for its effective operation success. A knowledgeable CIO and other C-level managers should have at least a high-level understanding of recent technological innovations and their advantages for business. It is advantageous if the company has an internal IT team and/or has developed steady and sustainable relationships with technical partners and developers. Investment in right skillsets and due technical infrastructure are extremely important factors for proper AI based projects adoption.

Lastly, organisations need to be data driven by fostering frequent and detailed use of data for most of its internal and core business processes. Without this component, the initiative to automate data-intensive processes and reporting would not be justifiable by hard data,suggesting huge time savings and efficacy boosts.

Following the process map in figure 2 will serve as a tailor-made project management guideline equipping the organisation through the stages of the project to pay attention to all necessary aspects, enabling the minimization of risk and increasing the chance of an AI project success. The processes of implementation and adoption of AI-based analytical tools in digital marketing are included in one of four main phases of education, audit, design and implementation. The focus of the process map is the identification of periodical, time consuming processes, predominantly in the area of data analysis that might be supplemented by intelligent software solutions, utilizing the power of AI.

The education phase addresses the potential lack of knowledge about the opportunities of utilizing of ML and AI in marketing. This lack prevents companies from developing ideas on deploying these technologies. Companies are encouraged to raise knowledge and acquire know-how in this area, specially to have an idea about what successful projects are and how they were devised. This should be performed by some research department which would be able to map an organisation's business concerns with available research works and case studies.

The Audit phase begins with the identification of processes that consume a signifucant amount of key employees' time. These processes can originate in steps of implementation and evaluation of digital marketing strategies that are typically connected with analyzing large amounts of data. This analysis results in the deployment digital marketing campaigns, understanding the behavior of consumers, their reaction towards the communication message, products, and, in general, their preferences. The identifed processes can be termed as either creative or periodical. The potential of ML-driven analytical tools currently lies greater in the automation of time-consuming periodical analytical processes that are often ineffective when performed solely by humans. Finally, before moving to the next phase, all data sources that are used in each process are identified and closely analyzed.

The Design phase starts with typically with whether to involve external experts and third parties in the process. This would normally be the case for innovative projects where internal resources are lacking.

Following the finalized project team creation, the process of designing, developing and releasing the AI solution starts. Sometimes, existing products and solutions might get chosen and implemented, in other occasions these might need to be customized and integrated. In other cases, custom development needs to happen to satisfy the defined requirements.

In the Deployment phase, the new AI solutions are to be tested and the responsibility of their use will be transferred to dedicated teams. Managers need to monitor their use, resolve upcoming issues and address possible improvement ideas. In case more processes that need attention and automation were identified in the Audit phases, the process returns to evaluate whether these occur periodically. It would also make sense to automate them. However, with AI based projects, due to issues such as model drifts and others, the AI model might continuously be refined and readjusted. Hence, other metrics different from traditional software development methods might need to be used to continuously assess performance of a given version of the AI solution.

The discussions above provide an insight upon phases and steps which might be undertaken to successfully adopt AI for digital marketing activities by an organisation. However, using AI alone as part of a technological stack might not be enough to reap enough competitive advantages, and thus organisations must think of adopting other technologies such as Big Data, Cloud Computing, data science and greater availability of computing power. All these technologies might be considered as complementary for more successful AI adoption and is also relevant for AI in digital marketing. The following sections will introduce those technologies and how they complement AI solutions.

Big Data Analytics

Big Data is considered essential for the promotion of AI in the digital marketing field because AI algorithms rely heavily on data to learn, adapt and make predictions. AI algorithms need vast amounts of data to train and improve their accuracy, and this is where Big Data comes in. Big Data is promoting the use of AI (Artificial Intelligence) because of its unique characteristics that make it suitable for training and optimizing AI algorithms (Marr, 2017). Here are some of the ways Big Data differs from traditional data sources:

1. **Volume:** Big Data refers to large volumes of data that traditional data processing tools cannot handle. This volume is crucial for AI because it provides the large data sets needed to train and optimize AI models accurately.
2. **Velocity:** Big Data is generated at an unprecedented speed, making it difficult for traditional data processing tools to keep up. AI algorithms can handle this velocity and process data in real-time, enabling marketers to optimize their campaigns in real-time.
3. **Variety:** Big Data comes in many different forms, including structured, unstructured, and semi-structured data. AI algorithms can handle this variety, enabling marketers to extract insights from various data sources.
4. **Veracity:** Big Data is often of uncertain quality, making it challenging to extract valuable insights. AI algorithms can handle this veracity and identify patterns in large data sets, enabling marketers to make more accurate predictions.
5. **Value:** Big Data provides value to businesses by enabling them to gain insights into customer behavior, preferences, and needs. AI algorithms can use this data to personalize content, optimize campaigns, and deliver more effective marketing messages, ultimately driving business growth.

In summary, Big Data differs from traditional data sources because of its volume, velocity, variety, veracity, and value, making it essential for training and optimizing AI algorithms. AI-powered marketing solutions rely on Big Data to deliver personalized content, optimize campaigns, and identify new opportunities for growth.

Growth in Data Science

The evolution of data science understanding has played a critical role in promoting the use of AI for marketing. Here are some of the ways in which data science has evolved to support AI-powered marketing solutions (Kordon, 2020):

1. **Data Collection and Storage:** With the rise of big data, businesses have access to vast amounts of data about their customers, products, and markets. Data science has evolved to enable the collection, storage, and processing of this data, making it possible to analyse customer behaviour at scale.
2. **Data Cleaning and Preparation:** Data science has also evolved to support the cleaning and preparation of data. Raw data often contains errors, missing values, and other inconsistencies that can affect the accuracy of AI models. Data science techniques such as data cleaning and feature engineering help ensure that data is clean and well-structured for use in AI algorithms.
3. **Machine Learning Algorithms:** Machine learning is a subset of AI that enables machines to learn from data without being explicitly programmed. Data science has evolved to support the development of machine learning algorithms that can analyze large data sets and identify patterns and insights that are not immediately visible to human analysts.
4. **Deep Learning:** Deep learning is a subset of machine learning that involves the use of neural networks to learn and make predictions. Data science has evolved to support the development of deep learning algorithms that can analyze complex data sets, such as images and videos, and identify patterns and insights that would be difficult for human analysts to identify.

The above provides an overview of the possibilities of data science and how they might help AI based activities for DM. It can be seen that the use of data science is spanned over the whole possible data lifecycle for any type of project.

Cloud Computing

Cloud computing is one of the technologies which has allowed AI to be deployed and implemented for several solutions by providing a suitable platform. It plays a crucial role in supporting the growth and use of AI in several ways (McGuire, 2023):

1. **Scalability:** Cloud computing provides virtually unlimited resources, enabling organizations to scale their AI workloads up or down as needed. This scalability ensures that organizations can accommodate AI workloads that may require a large amount of computing power, such as training complex deep learning models. This is very useful in use cases such as sentiment analysis where hundreds of factors about customers need to be analysed with big volumes of data.

2. **Cost-Effectiveness:** Cloud computing provides an affordable way for organizations to access computing resources required for AI workloads. Organizations do not need to invest in expensive hardware infrastructure as they can leverage cloud computing providers' resources to access AI processing power. This availability of computing power has promoted the use of digital marketing amongst more organizations, specifically the small and medium ones.
3. **Accessibility:** Cloud computing provides accessible and user-friendly interfaces that enable developers and data scientists to quickly set up and deploy AI solutions. This accessibility has significantly reduced the time it takes to create and deploy AI solutions, thereby supporting the growth of AI.
4. **Data Storage and Management:** Cloud computing provides large-scale data storage and management solutions that allow organizations to store and process vast amounts of data needed for AI applications. Cloud providers such as Amazon Web Services (AWS), Microsoft Azure, and Google Cloud provide services like object storage and data lakes that can be used to store and manage data for AI workloads.

Increase in Computing Power

Recent increases in processing power have been a significant driver in the growth and adoption of AI. The following are some of the ways that increased processing power has promoted the use of AI (Fatima et al., 2022):

1. **Faster Training:** With the increase in processing power, training complex deep learning models has become faster and more efficient. The ability to process vast amounts of data in a shorter amount of time allows data scientists to train models more quickly, enabling the development of more sophisticated AI applications.
2. **Larger Datasets:** Increased processing power has allowed data scientists to work with larger datasets, enabling them to extract more meaningful insights from the data. Larger datasets are critical to the development of more accurate AI models, and increased processing power has made it possible to work with more extensive datasets.
3. **Real-Time Inference:** With the increase in processing power, AI models can now make predictions and decisions in real-time, enabling the development of AI applications that can respond to events and situations as they happen.
4. **Complex Applications:** Increased processing power has enabled the development of more complex AI applications, such as natural language processing, computer vision, and autonomous driving. These applications require a significant amount of processing power to operate efficiently and effectively.
5. **Edge Computing:** With the growth of edge computing, processing power is becoming more distributed, allowing AI applications to be deployed closer to where the data is generated. This approach reduces latency and allows for faster response times, enabling the development of new AI applications that require real-time decision-making.

Internet of Things (IoT)

The Internet of Things (IoT) has greatly enhanced the use of Artificial Intelligence (AI) in digital marketing by providing an enormous amount of data from various sources. IoT devices such as smartwatches, fitness trackers, home appliances, and other connected devices generate vast amounts of data that can be used to better understand customer behaviour, preferences, and needs.

With the help of AI, digital marketers can analyse this data and gain insights into how their customers are interacting with their products and services. This enables them to create more targeted and personalized marketing campaigns that are more likely to resonate with their audience. For example, AI-powered analytics can help businesses to predict customer behaviour and preferences, identify trends, and create personalized recommendations based on their interests.

In addition, IoT devices can also be used to collect data on customer interactions with physical spaces, such as retail stores and public spaces. This data can then be used to optimize store layouts and design, improve customer experiences, and enhance marketing efforts. For example, AI-powered cameras and sensors can be used to analyse customer behaviour in a store, such as how long they spend in different sections, which products they interact with, and which areas they avoid.

The combination of the use of AI with IoT has been termed as AIoT. In the following sections, we would discuss applications of AIoT in greater details (Zhang and Tao, 2021) so that a better understanding of the power of merging those two buoyant technologies could be better comprehended. Even though these applications are not specifically connected with the field of digital marketing, it allows to judge the possibilities of AIoT.

Smart Transportation

Smart transportation enabled by AIoT covers traffic participants such as smart IoV (Jiang, H. et al.,2018), traffic infrastructures (Jiang,D. et al., 2018), and industry applications such as smart connected logistics (Lee et al.,2018). Among them, the self-driving car is a typical example empowered by AI, which integrates various perceiving, learning, reasoning, and behaving abilities together. Correct perception of the driving environment is critical for autonomous self-driving cars, such as detecting road markers, traffic sign, estimating the intention of cars and pedestrians and predicting their trajectories. Based on them, the self-driving system can determine its driving policy and interact with other traffic participants. Recently, deep reinforcement learning is leveraged to learn driving rules and techniques from visual input (e.g., front-view images).

AIoT can also enable in-car driver monitoring and interactions as driver behaviors is crucial for preventing traffic accidents. To this end, Kashevnik et al. (2020) developed a mobile application for detecting dangerous driving behaviors, e.g., distraction and drowsiness. It leverages multimodel data for behavior detection, including images for face state detection (e.g., eyes openness and head yaw angles), motion data from IMU sensors for estimating vehicle location and speed, light level for estimating lighting conditions, and speech data for speech state detection (e.g., speech rate and loudness).

Smart Healthcare

AIoT systems for smart healthcare cover several phases, including monitoring, examination, surgery, and rehabilitation. For monitoring, wearable devices with motion sensors and cameras can be used for human activity recognition. Using motion sensors such as accelerometer, human activities can be recognized from time-series motion data based on an AI model. For example, a mobile robot with a camera is used for human activity recognition. Note that the recognition module can be deployed in the edge devices or in the fog node depending on the model size and computational demand, which can be connected to a smart healthcare systems.

AI models are more likely to be deployed on the private cloud of the hospital due to their high computational cost and the privacy concern. Recently, deep reinforcement learning has been used to control the surgical robot (Thananjeyan et al.,2017) for multilateral cutting in 2D orthotropic gauze. Furthermore, AIoT systems can be useful for various rehabilitation monitoring and assessment (Gonzalez-Ortega et al.,2014), e.g., stroke rehabilitation and ankles rehabilitation. Via the connected 3-D AR/VR devices, therapists can assess the rehabilitation and make better treatments accordingly, which is helpful for patients in rural or distant areas.

Smart Agriculture

Precision farming is becoming increasingly popular, referring to observing, measuring, and responding to crop variability through sensors, autonomous agricultural machines, and geographic information systems. For example, crop counting and yield estimation is an important topic of precision agriculture. Unmanned aerial vehicles (UAVs) were used for capturing images of crops and fruits and sending them to the cloud for further counting (Chen at al., 2017). A detection-tracking-counting based method used, resulting in rejection of outliers and double-counted fruits. UAVs can also be used for continuous crop monitoring by capturing crop field images over time and temporally aligning them (Chebrolu et al., 2018). For plant grow control, an AIoT system was set up in a tomato greenhouse and is composed of a wireless sensor network and cloud computing center empowered by AI technologies. Deep RL is used for obtaining the optimal control policy on the illumination, nutrition, and ventilation conditions in the greenhouse.

Thus, the recent growth in development of AI across different industries and business processed, including marketing function, should be regarded as a result in growth in enabling technologies such as Big Data, cloud computing and IoT. In fact, it can be considered that there are some symbiotic interconnections between these technologies such that developments in each inspire growth and improvement in the others. It can be expected that developments in upcoming technologies such as nano and quantum computing would further boost possibilities with AI in general. Simultaneously, there is a changing business landscape. Globalisation and growing competition is pushing for delivering better services to customers, and AI based solutions act as enablers to achieve those aims.

Employment and Other Societal Concerns

The adoption of AI technology is rapidly advancing and has the potential to revolutionize many industries, but there are also concerns about the impact of AI on employment and other social issues that may constrain its adoption (Kelly, 2023). Here are some arguments for both sides:

Constraints on AI adoption due to employment concerns:

1. **Job Displacement:** The adoption of AI technology has the potential to automate many jobs, leading to job displacement for workers in certain industries. This can cause social and economic disruption, as displaced workers may struggle to find new employment.
2. **Skill Gaps:** The development and deployment of AI technology requires a high level of technical expertise, and not all workers will have the necessary skills to work with AI systems. This may

create a skills gap in certain industries, leading to a shortage of qualified workers and slowing down the adoption of AI.

3. **Ethical Concerns:** There are ethical concerns around the use of AI in certain industries, such as the potential for bias in AI decision-making and the impact of AI on privacy and security. These concerns may lead to regulatory constraints on the use of AI, which could slow down its adoption.

Constraints on AI adoption due to other social issues:

1. **Inequality:** The benefits of AI technology may not be equally distributed, which can exacerbate existing social inequalities. This can lead to resistance to the adoption of AI in certain communities or industries.
2. **Trust Issues:** The use of AI in decision-making may erode trust in institutions or organizations, particularly if the decision-making process is not transparent or if the outcomes are perceived as unfair.
3. **Cultural Differences:** The adoption of AI may face cultural barriers, as different societies have varying attitudes towards the use of technology in different areas of life.

However, it's also important to note that there are arguments for why these constraints may not be as significant as some fear, or why they may actually accelerate the adoption of AI:

1. **Job Creation:** While some jobs may be displaced by AI, new jobs may also be created to develop, maintain, and work with AI technology.

These new jobs may require different skills but could also provide new opportunities for workers. In order to encourage societal adoption for AI use, which would also affect the digital marketing sector, the following can be envisaged:

1. **Skill Development:** The need for workers with technical expertise to develop and work with AI technology could lead to increased investment in education and training, which could help to address skill gaps in certain industries.
2. **Incentives:** In some cases, financial or other incentives may be provided to encourage the adoption of AI technology, which could overcome some of the barriers to adoption.
3. **Social Benefits:** The potential benefits of AI technology, such as improved healthcare, more efficient transportation, and increased safety, may outweigh concerns around job displacement and other social issues, leading to greater adoption of AI.

AI: Practical Use in Digital Marketing

In the thorough research carried out by Miklosik et al. (2019), during the in-depth interviews, respondents were asked: ``Can you define marketing analytical tools that are based on the basic principles of AI?'' the following tools were mentioned most often in respondents' responses: Google (AdWords, Search); Google Data Studio; YouTube; Facebook Ada Manager; chat applications; software for programmatic purchase; Echobox; automated webinars; Mailchimp.

Thus, it seems that specialists in the digital marketing fields are aware of some digital marketing tools that are based on AI, but not very accurately. Since 2019, there are much more tools based on AI which are of service to the digital marketing community also.

Other responses indicate that the tools that are based on the principles of Ai will mainly affect the following areas of digital marketing (Miklosik et al., 2019):

- Advertisement systems and the management of advertisement campaigns,
- Automation of reporting processes,
- Partial automation of communication (especially in written form, such as emails or chat communication).

Analytical tools making use of AI can be used to work with data much more effectively from the aforementioned areas. This eliminates the need for human intervention and the software solutions can perform defined actions autonomously.

Respondents identified the following as digital marketing areas where AI is difficult to apply,

- Creative processes,
- Building and maintaining relationships with business stakeholders

These areas mainly work with data in a limited or very specific form. Nowadays, the development of ideas or drawing pictures can also be automated with new generative pre-trained transformer models. The development in AI is so exponential that it is expected that even creative and artistic activities can soon be learnt by AI tools and reproduced to such a level which is comparable of even better compared to human beings (DeCremer et al.,2023).

Another question in the qualitative survey was: ``What activities does your company plan for ML in the near future?''

If the respondent was poorly aware of analytical tools, marketing analysis, big data, data management, etc. and the respondent's company supports the deployment of ML-driven tools only marginally, only very basic or no activities are planned. If the respondents were fully aware of the topics discussed and works in an innovative company, the ML plans were well-developed. Among the most frequent areas where the respondents' companies are planning such activities are:

- Report automation,
- Linking several marketing analytical tools,
- Collection of data generated from marketing activities,
- Automation of the processing of collected data,
- Digital content creation.

The last question was: ``Do you think human work can be replaced by machines in future? If so, how will marketing be affected?'' All respondents agreed that human work certainly can, and almost certainly will, be replaced by machines. However, there will still be areas where machines and automated software will not be able to fully control and manage. According to the respondents, replacement will mostly affect areas that work with data, as well as repetitive work (such as weekly or monthly reporting of campaign results). Employees who have been doing this repetitive work in the past will be able to devote more time to strategic and creative activity that is often required in the digital marketing environment. When asked what percentage of the jobs in digital marketing will be replaced by machines in five years' time, the minimum estimate was 50% and the maximum was 95%.

Following the qualitative study, the questionnaire aimed to identify the barriers and risks of ML and AI application in digital marketing and the anticipated future role of ML-based tools in this industry. The cost of implementation (62%), time required to learn how to deploy and use the tools (47%), and market limitations (market size and lack of opportunities to use ML and AI based tools) (45%) were the three most common barriers. Marketing managers are afraid that using ML-based analytical tools might: result in higher error rate due to lack of know-how (50%); have a negative impact on results and relationships due to missing moral and ethical dimensions of behaviour of the software and its intelligence (41%); or mean losing control over marketing processes (35%). Despite this, 72% of respondents believe that ML and AI represent the future of digital marketing (9% responded that they think these tools will cease to be used and 19% were unsure).

CONCLUSION

AI has brought a significant transformation in digital marketing, providing numerous benefits and challenges. The drivers of AI in digital marketing include increased efficiency, personalization, predictive analytics, improved customer experience, and enhanced decision-making. These drivers are making it more accessible for businesses to reach and engage with their target audiences, increase their ROI, and gain a competitive advantage in their industry. As there more technological developments relative to processing workloads, network transmissions capabilities and data storage/access, there is an expectation that more powerful deep learning-based algorithms could be executed. Therefore, it will not be surprising that AI will be able to carry out a greater plethora of digital marketing tasks in an increasingly automated way. This chapter has also highlighted those impactful applications of AI for digital marketing such as increasing personalisation and targeting abilities of the marketing team, automating routine business processes, being able to interact more efficiently with smart conversational systems which could also be one source of unstructured data capture for improved decision making.

However, AI in digital marketing also poses challenges, such as privacy concerns, the need for skilled personnel, the potential for bias, and the risk of AI taking over jobs that require human interaction. These challenges require continuous attention and management to ensure that AI is used ethically and effectively. There is unsurprisingly a certain level of societal resistance towards greater adoption of AI across different industries. This is true for all disruptive technologies and the point of views of everybody must be taken into account to reduce resistance to change. Hence, communication and education are going to be extremely important for increasing adoption of AI use. Regulations and laws need to be setup and adapted to the increasing use of AI for automated decision making. The impact of AI and other associated technologies such as robotics, IoT and recognition systems would be so thorough within society that it is quite likely to change the whole fabric of society as we know it. Thus, the challenges for AI adoption will be not only technology based, but also more towards understanding its actual capabilities and ways to maximize its uses.

Overall, the increasing demand for AI in digital marketing is expected to continue to grow, as discussed in the last section, as more businesses adopt AI technology to remain competitive in the marketplace. The recent boom in AI based tools are also increasing adoption of AI in society, including by organisations and for digital marketing purposes. By understanding the drivers and challenges of AI in digital marketing, businesses can leverage this technology to their advantage while mitigating any potential risks.

REFERENCES

Arun Kumar, B.R. (2021). AI-Based Digital Marketing Strategies— A Review. *Lecture Notes in Networks and Systems, 173*, 957-969.

Biswas, B., & Sanyal, M. K. (2019). Soft intelligence approaches for selecting products in online market. *Proceedings of the 9th International Conference On Cloud Computing, Data Science and Engineering, Confluence 2019*, 432-437. 10.1109/CONFLUENCE.2019.8776921

Chebrolu, N., Läbe, T., & Stachniss, C. (2018). Robust long-term registration of UAV images of crop fields for precision agriculture. *IEEE Robot. Autom. Lett.*, *3*(4), 3097–3104.

Crawford, K., Dobbe, R., Dryer, T., Fried, G., Green, B., Kaziunas, E., Kak, A., Mathur, V., McElroy, E., Sąnchez, A.N., Raji, D., Rankin, J.L., Richardson, R., Schultz, J., West, S.M., & Whittaker, M. (2019). AI Now 2019 Report. Technical Report. AI Now Institute.

DeCremer, D., Bianzino, N., & Falk, N. (2023). *How Generative AI Could Disrupt Creative Work.* https://hbr.org/2023/04/how-generative-ai-could-disrupt-creative-work

Dubey, G., Hasan, M., & Alam, A. (2022). *Artificial intelligence (AI) and Indian education system: promising applications, potential effectiveness and challenges.* https://hrdc.gujaratuniversity.ac.in/Ejournal

Fatima, S., Dawson, G., Desouza, K., & Denford, J. (2022). *How countries are leveraging computing power to achieve their national artificial intelligence strategies.* https://www.brookings.edu/blog/techtank/2022/01/12/how-countries-are-leveraging-computing-power-to-achieve-their-national-artificial-intelligence-strategies/

Gao, F., & Zhang, L. (2020). Application of Artificial Intelligence and Big Data Technology in Digital Marketing. *Proceedings of ACM ISBDAI conference (ISBDAI 2020).* 10.1145/3436286.3436404

González-Ortega, D., Díaz-Pernas, F., Martínez-Zarzuela, M., & Antón-Rodríguez, M. (2014). A kinect-based system for cognitive rehabilitation exercises monitoring. *Computer Methods and Programs in Biomedicine, 113*(2), 620–631. doi:10.1016/j.cmpb.2013.10.014 PMID:24263055

Hafaiedh, K., Rhouma, M. B., Chargui, F., Haouas, Y., & Kerkeni, A. (2020). AdRobot:A smart segmentation application for automated & personalized marketing campaigns. *ACM International Conference Proceeding Series.*

Hsu, S., & Liou, S. (2021). Artificial Intelligence Impact on Digital Content Marketing Research. *9th International Conference on Orange Technology (ICOT).*

Huang, M.-H., & Rust, R. T. (2021). Engaged to a Robot? The Role of AI in Service. *Journal of Service Research, 24*(1), 30–41. doi:10.1177/1094670520902266

Jarek, K., & Mazurek, G. (2019). Marketing and Artificial Intelligence. *Central European Business Review*. https://cebr.vse.cz/artkey/cbr-201902-0003_marketing-and-artificial-intelligence.php

Jiang, D., Huo, L., Lv, Z., Song, H., & Qin, W. (2018). A joint multi-criteria utility-based network selection approach for vehicle-to-infrastructure networking. *IEEE Transactions on Intelligent Transportation Systems*, *19*(10), 3305–3319. doi:10.1109/TITS.2017.2778939

Jiang, H., Zhang, Z., Dang, J., & Wu, L. (2018). A novel 3-D massive MIMO channel model for vehicle-to-vehicle communication environments. *IEEE Transactions on Communications*, *66*(1), 79–90. doi:10.1109/TCOMM.2017.2751555

Kaponis, A., & Maragoudakis, M. (2022). Data Analysis in Digital Marketing using Machine learning and Artificial Intelligence Techniques, Ethical and Legal Dimensions, State of the Art. In *12th Hellenic Conference on Artificial Intelligence (SETN 2022)*. ACM. 10.1145/3549737.3549756

Kar, A. K., & Kushwaha, A. K. (2021). Facilitators and Barriers of Artificial Intelligence Adoption in Business – Insights from Opinions Using Big Data Analytics. *Information Systems Frontiers*. Advance online publication. doi:10.100710796-021-10219-4

Kashevnik, A., Lashkov, I., & Gurtov, A. (2020). Methodology and mobile application for driver behavior analysis and accident prevention. *IEEE Transactions on Intelligent Transportation Systems*, *21*(6), 2427–2436. doi:10.1109/TITS.2019.2918328

Kelly, P. (2023). *'Why would we employ people?' Experts on five ways AI will change work*. https://www.theguardian.com/global-development/2023/may/12/why-would-we-employ-people-experts-on-five-ways-ai-will-change-work

Kordon, A. (2020). *Data Science Based on Artificial Intelligence*. https://www.researchgate.net/publication/344314160_Data_Science_Based_on_Artificial_Intelligence

Lee, C., Lv, Y., Ng, K., Ho, W., & Choy, K. (2018). Design and application of Internet of Things-based warehouse management system for smart logistics. *International Journal of Production Research*, *56*(8), 2753–2768. doi:10.1080/00207543.2017.1394592

Li, Z. (2022). Accurate Digital Marketing Communication Based on Intelligent Data Analysis. *Scientific Programming*, *2022*, 8294891. doi:10.1155/2022/8294891

Malviya, B., Othman, B., Saxena, K., Sailmadhur, V., & Almasheqbeh, H., (2022). An Empirical Analysis in Measuring the Impact of Artificial Intelligence for Better Marketing Communication to the End-Users Effectively in the Digital Era. *2nd International Conference on Advance Computing and Innovative Technologies in Engineering (ICACITE).*

Maras, M., & Alexandrou, A. (2018). Determining Authenticity of Video Evidence in the Age of Artificial Intelligence and in the Wake of Deepfake Videos. *The International Journal of Evidence & Proof*, 23.

Marr, B. (2017). *Beyond the Big Data buzz*. https://www.linkedin.com/in/bernardmarr/

McGuire, J. (2023). *Cloud and AI Combined: Revolutionizing Tech*. https://www.eweek.com/cloud/cloud-and-ai/

Miklosik, A., Kuchta, M., Evans, N., & Zak, S. (2019). Towards the Adoption of Machine Learning-Based Analytical Tools in Digital Marketing. *IEEE Access : Practical Innovations, Open Solutions, 7*, 85705–85718. Advance online publication. doi:10.1109/ACCESS.2019.2924425

Molina, S. (2023). *Dealing with algorithmic bias in AI solutions for healthcare in Mexico*. https://www.researchgate.net/publication/370592125_Dealing_with_algorithmic_bias_in_AI_solutions_for_healthcare_in_Mexico/citations

Pathak, M. & Musku, U. (2020). Dynamic Bidding with Contextual Bid Decision Trees in Digital Advertisement. *Communications in Computer and Information Science, 1244*, 463-473.

Sachdev, R. (2020). Towards Security and Privacy for Edge AI in IoT/IoE based Digital Marketing Environments. *2020 Fifth International Conference on Fog and Mobile Edge Computing (FMEC)*. 10.1109/FMEC49853.2020.9144755

Sinha, M., Healey, J., & Sengupta, T. (2020). Designing with AI for Digital Marketing. In *Proceedings of Adjunct Proceedings of the 28th ACM Conference on User Modeling, Adaptation and Personalization (UMAP '20 Adjunct)*. ACM. 10.1145/3386392.3397600

Thananjeyan, B., Garg, A., Krishnan, S., Chen, C., Miller, L., & Goldberg, K. (2017). Multilateral surgical pattern cutting in 2D orthotropic gauze with deep reinforcement learning policies for tensioning. *Proc. IEEE Int. Conf. Robot. Autom.*, 2371–2378. 10.1109/ICRA.2017.7989275

Toader, D.-C., Boca, G., Toader, R., Măcelaru, M., Toader, C., Ighian, D., & Rădulescu, A.T. (2020). The effect of social presence and chatbot errors on trust. *Sustainability (Switzerland), 12*(1). doi:10.3390/su12010256

Wolpe, P (2019) Neuromarketing and AI—Powerful Together, but Needing Scrutiny, A JOB. *Neuroscience, 10*(2), 69-70. doi:10.1080/21507740.2019.1618414

Zhang, J., & Tao, D. (2021). Empowering Things With Intelligence: A Survey of the Progress, Challenges, and Opportunities in Artificial Intelligence of Things. IEEE Internet of Things Journal, 8(10).

ADDITIONAL READING

Sterne, J. (2017). *Artificial intelligence for Marketing*. Wiley. doi:10.1002/9781119406341

KEY TERMS AND DEFINITIONS

Big Data: The capacity to use technologies which can work with huge volume of different types of data and in real time basis.

Cloud Computing: The application of pay as you use services over computer networks.

Digital Footprint: Traces of all transactions left after use of any digital technology.

Internet of Things (IoT): The interconnection and interdependence of different devices via the internet.

Personalization: The action of providing tailor made products and services based on individual customer tastes and needs.

Precision Farming: The use of techniques in agriculture which minimizes the use of intrants as no wide-scale method is applied.

Predictive Analysis: The use of analytical techniques in order to be able to guess with a high level of confidence a future occurrence.

Chapter 7
User Perceptions About Online Personal Data Transmissibility

Pedro Pincho
Instituto Universitário de Lisboa (ISCTE-IUL), Portugal

Inês Messias
Instituto Politécnico de Santarém, ISTAR-Iscte, Portugal

Bráulio Alturas
https://orcid.org/0000-0003-0142-3737
Instituto Universitário de Lisboa (ISCTE-IUL), ISTAR-Iscte, Portugal

ABSTRACT

The usage of consumers' personal data is considered by companies as capable of creating immense value in terms of business. The rise of using social networks to access users' shared information, gathering, processing, and using it, has become a normal proceeding by companies. This data represents value to entities that use them to reduce research costs to develop new products, as well as transaction costs while increasing their marketing incomes. The objective of this study is to determine what feelings are related to sharing personal data online. The research questionnaire for this study was developed through a literature review, later shared on social networks, with 103 valid answers having been collected. Data analysis was performed using IBM SPSS Statistics and Excel programs. The results obtained allow us to understand what perceptions the population has regarding data sharing, suggesting that the individual perception of the transmissibility of personal data online is starting to be an area of interest for society since there is a greater awareness of the dangers online.

DOI: 10.4018/978-1-6684-8958-1.ch007

INTRODUCTION

By 2016 the internet had 3 billion users. 2 billion of them were social media users, and 890 million connected to Facebook daily (Aïmeur et al., 2016). According to a study developed by the same author (Aïmeur et al., 2016) when approached about their own perception concerning how their data was protected on social media, only 10% showed trust concerning social networks, 20% stated to trust e-commerce platforms and 22% answered to trust technology companies. A few of years later, in 2022, according to Statista (Buchholz, 2022) the active number of worldwide social media users is estimated at 4.6 billion, corresponding to 60% of the world's population. According to the same source, the projections show that this number is expected to rise by 6 billion in 4 years, by 2027. According to Zuboff (2020) we are living the Era of vigilance capitalism, whereas digital privacy has shown to be a growing concern to all. Understanding how this impacts users' individual perception of their own privacy management is a challenge (Soczka, 2014, in Zyboff, 2020).

On 2016, and to answer concerns regarding regulation of the use of social media and internet consumers' data, the EU has set the General Data Protection Regulation (GDPR) (2016/679), that has been active since 2018. This regulation is based in a proactive principle, whereas the responsible for data processing has to prove that all the phases of the data processing obey to the regulation norms. Created to protect the citizens when it comes to how their information is treated, questions remain about the users' perception about this process.

The virtual hyper exposure noted by Weissman (2021) during the COVID-19 pandemic situation, has marked a transition considering how dependent society has become. The lack of alternatives makes users progressively more dependent on the use of internet for their daily tasks. With It, a growing concern surges, with a raising number of questions that is urgent to give answers to, were privacy and security are central when dealing with the consumers' perception of trust about the personal information shared on social media.

To better understand this issue, a study was made, based on 3 goals: 1) understand the feeling the consumer has when sharing personal information and data online; 2) deepen if the data sharing is in fact the path that should be followed, and if users are available in the future to share more data online as they do today; 3) understand if these approaches to data sharing, with all its pros and cons, are indeed beneficial. Focused on the transmissibility of personal data in the online context, this study had as main objective to understand how a user manages his/her personal data. The study's research question aimed to understand the user's individual perception about the transmissibility of personal data in the online context. Hence, it aimed to 1) identify online shared information's sensitivity; 2) verify the level of satisfaction concerning GDPR; 3) determine the sensation while sharing data online; 4) identify key aspects to determine the construction of trust, in order to set an improvement strategy for the use of information systems to gather such data; 5) understand the perception of the advantages and disadvantages associated with sharing online data.

BACKGROUND

The reason for this study stems from the fact that the chosen theme is current and of extreme relevance to the business world, since it is a Portuguese national objective to empower business structures to achieve the third pillar of the goals stipulated in the 2030 horizon (Innovative Europe). To this end, it is necessary to have a full digital transition, in which the user is proficient in the use of technology in his daily life and professional context, thus enabling him to be a full citizen of the 21st century (European Commission, 2021).

This study also allowed us to better understand the Portuguese modern society in this new digital age, and to understand the influence that digital technology has especially on the lives of young people in this country.

As many processes can be listed in the course of human history, it is at this moment and context, fundamental to make the appreciation of one of the most complete, fast, intuitive and universal tools: the Internet. Analyzing how the users perceive how data circulates on it, perceiving how they carry knowledge, dynamics, energies, dreams, and ambitions to this environment.

Considering the current context, and the digital society in which we live today, it is important to understand the opinion of young people regarding the sharing of personal data online and whether they take into account a set of factors that underlie this issue, such as privacy, security or lack thereof. Moreover, we will try to understand how information systems can help in building trust about the sharing of personal data online.

As stated by Zuboff (2020), we live in the Age of surveillance capitalism. Digital privacy has become a growing concern in the population, and there is a need for refined policies and regulation on this sector to ensure the individual privacy of citizens. "Surveillance capitalists know everything about us, yet their actions are unknown to us. They accumulate vast domains of new knowledge about us, but which is not intended for our use. They predict our future for the benefit of others." (Zuboff, 2020, p. 26).

The inevitability of digital entering our daily lives has never been more evident, it remains for us to know how best to apply it. In a balance between options that will lead us to sustained and sustainable paths of development and evolution, it is important to keep in mind the risks inherent to an unbridled use, irresponsible or sustained in values that in no way dignify the human species.

With the growing number of data collected in scientific academic studies on this topic, it will be possible to have a better understanding of the externalities involved in this new world, thus extending the knowledge chain of this new disruptive business model that is data.

OBJECTIVES

Considering that theme of this dissertation focuses on the transmissibility of personal data in the online context, its aim is to better understand the relationship and the perception of the current digital society with the new world of data.

The main objective of this study was to understand how each individual manages his personal data. Data was collected to understand what feelings are inherent to sharing data online, and how proficiency in the use of information systems can create, or help to support, greater confidence to the users.

Thus, the research question was: "What is the individual's perception of the transferability of personal data online?"

The specific objectives of this study were:

1. Identify the sensitivity of information shared online.
2. Verify the degree of satisfaction regarding the standards in force for the protection of personal data;
3. Determine the existing sentiment during online data sharing.

4. Identify key points in building trust to define a strategy to improve trust of use based on information systems.
5. Understand the perception of advantages and disadvantages associated with online data sharing.

As a research function, it was intended to analyze the existing perception during the sharing of personal data online, considering the existing regulations in view of the risks of exposure, appreciation of inherent problems, difficulties, advantages and disadvantages in the operationalization originated through data sharing and the achievement of the proposed objectives. In the end, in a conclusive tone, essential points or key points are presented, for the creation of trust during the process of online data sharing.

LITERATURE REVIEW

Online Privacy

When online privacy, or the lack of it, is identified as one of the main negative factors about internet, Mekovec and Vrček (2011) confirm that its users have no trust about the guarantees that website owners offer while assuring that their personal information is to remain private. The notion of privacy and the factors that influence the worries about privacy are therefore crucial to understand how users perceive it, to better understand how to avoid and resolve such issues.

Sheehan and Hoy (2000) were among the first to study online privacy concerns and they identified 3 factors that influence the users' concerns. Namely, control over capture and use of user's information, short term operations, i.e. transactions, and the established relationship that approaches questions over client and website relations. The same authors suggest factors that can influence worries about online privacy: a) the consumer intrinsic characteristics; b) their perspectives, beliefs, and attitudes concerning marketing, the control of information mechanisms and processes to acquire data; c) website related variables; d) situational variables.

Showing the same concerns Mekovec and Vrček (2011) propose a model to study online privacy (C.f. Figure 1), based on 5 group of factors, that then subdivide in specific indicators: 1) consumers' intrinsic characteristics; 2) situational factors; 3) website characteristics; 4) the client's relationship to the website, and 5) governmental legislation and privacy protection.

Figure 1. Model proposed by Mekovec and Vrček (2011)

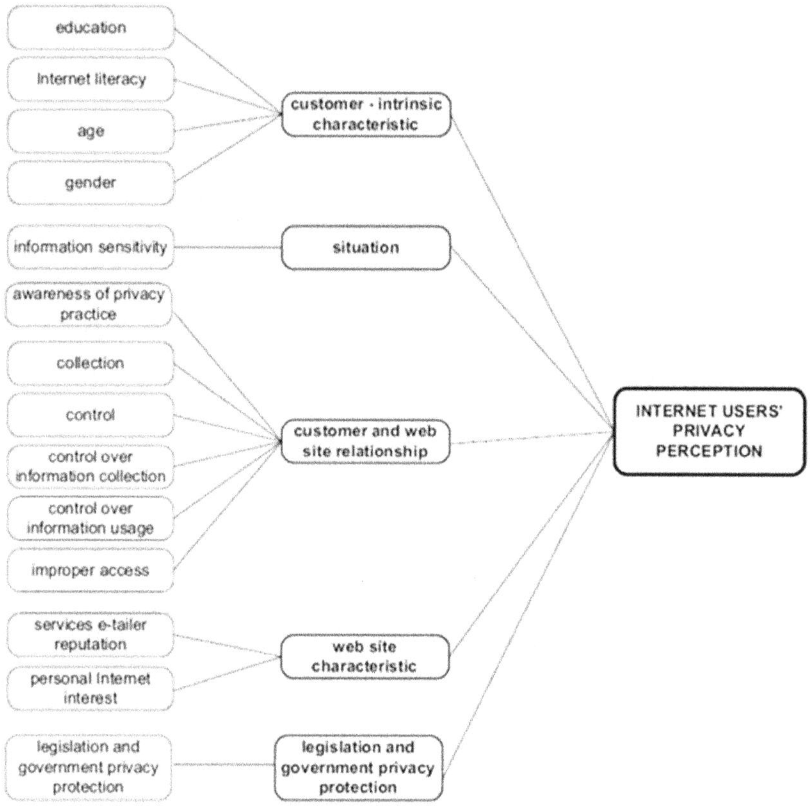

Besides online privacy, risk perception is also crucial to perceive when trying to establish how users understand data privacy concerns. Especially because the users' perceived risk when making the decision to share data online is directly related to its previous experiences. And it diminishes every time it shares information or shops online (Liebermann & Stashevsky, 2002).

The Web and the Corporate World

In the beginning, the Web invented by British scientist Tim Berners-Lee consisted of collecting text through HTML sites hosted on servers, when it appeared around 1989, being quite primitive if we consider the extraordinary progress that has taken place since then.

The web was primarily designed for sharing information between universities and science institutes.

Actually, the computational society is a new state of human civilization, a new way of involving the intensive use of information in all spheres of human activity, implying a severe impact both at a social, economic and environmental level. An example of this has been the recent use of teleworking, due to the pandemic caused by COVID-19, which has shown us the need for an urgent digital transition within companies and institutions, where everyone involved has the essential structures, resources, and skills to do it. Moreover, the modernization of public services, health services, education, culture, environmental management, among others, has become increasingly urgent, where we can add new ways of communicating data and information between government institutions. and the population, to streamline processes and cross-reference data and information that allow reaching two more of the sustainable development objectives: the effectiveness of institutions, and partnerships for the implementation of the objectives.

The implementation of a digital economy does not in itself guarantee sustainable development, but it has a great impact on the quality of public life. The development of these new meanings of communication and technological information are an important factor in increasing economic competitiveness, opening new perspectives regarding methods of organization and creation of new jobs.

However, human rights are not guaranteed, and are vital values in the new digital world, which is why it is important to create conditions for their preservation. From the point of view of Rafisovich et al. (2020), the true progress of humanity in this process of digital development is the capacity for self-development, the development of human consciousness and intelligence along with the improvement of moral qualities.

Jacksi and Abass (2019) indicate that many technologies are being used over the internet for document sharing, each with different characteristics, methods, and protocols. However, for these authors, the most common and easiest to handle is the web, with few and simple features. According to the same authors, web developers want the machine to think more and more like humans, through the addition of new tools, methods, and protocols, being able to define the web as a center for sharing information. Thus, the measurement of user confidence becomes essential, given the role that privacy and security in the handling of online platforms and websites represents so that the companies that own them can continue to collect information that makes it possible to benefit from the potential of convenience in relation to the information that they offer, simultaneously providing that the handling of their products can be done in a safer, clearer and more transparent way.

According to Chin et al. (2012), we must first understand users' attitudes towards smartphone security and privacy and how they may differ from attitudes towards computing systems. To improve the security of mobile systems, we must understand the challenges and concerns that users currently have with performing sensitive operations on their smartphones and identify opportunities to improve the security of systems.

Risk perception

If we consider Rafisovich et al. (2020), the world entered a new development phase, the Era of digital society, ruled by an unprecedented development when it comes to scientific knowledge and their constant usage, something that society has never seen before. This new stage of human development, were world economy and people living standards, have had great changes, much due to technological development. These new technologies that we now consider part of our daily lives, have been substituting and rendering others obsolete, growing naturally with scientific discoveries, resulting in the appearance of new professions and opportunities. Following this transformation Catalina-Garcia et al. (2014), makes a new definition of risk perception as the "cognitive process that is based on the information that each person has about certain subjects…and that each one processes it by organizing their value judgments", which will later conditions their behavior, making the perception of risk a fundamental factor in the acquisition and maintenance of actions related to cybersecurity, mainly as a shield against the present dangers, generally associated with unsafe behavior.

Knowing that the notion of risk perception changes as reality changes, Yap and Selvaratnam (2018) states that the concept of risk has been explained by a set of academic disciplines, namely, sociological, cultural, and psychological, in a study setting that considers environmental, individual, and cognitive factors, capable of contributing to how risk perception varies. Thakur and Srivastava (2015, p. 153) indicate that there are several studies that present online security as a key factor to understand users' attitudes when using web services. Considering this aspect fundamental when promoting integrity, confidentiality, and authentication as well as not recognition of relationships.

According to Leblanc and Biddle (2012), when people choose to engage in an online activity, such as banking or shopping online, they are making a trusting decision about the provider of the website or application in question. Most users usually trust most if not all websites they encounter, causing significant security issues. Hence, any proposed solutions to reduce the threat of online attacks must include consideration of the psychological processes of end users, to improve the way users perceive the risks they are incurring when navigating online. Leblanc and Biddle (2012) also indicate that, in their study's main findings, users reported greater risks perception when associated with finance-related activities, such as banking and online shopping, but attribute lower risk perception to online activities such as using a search engine, or participation in social networks. Knowing that these networks are highly valuable targets for attackers, the risk of unsafe behavior to occur in these platforms is high.

The internet has led to a significant increase in the number of transactions and options for products and services (Zhuang et al., 2018). In this sense, there has been an increase in online commercial transactions in recent years (Raluca, 2018), despite the users' uncertainty regarding the quality of products. Kim and Krishnan (2015) refer that this is caused due to online transactions being more comfortable and perceived as a allowing them to saving time and money for consumers who make purchase decisions through this channel. This allows us to consider that the consumer's perceived risk in decision making is associated with elements related to previous experience and previous purchases, and that this perceived risk decreases as the consumer makes more purchases and goes through more similar shopping experiences (Liebermann & Stashevsky, 2002).

Hence, to minimize purchasing risks for customers, companies must show that they honor their commitments and serve consumers in the best possible way. As for online consumers, they must be offered multiple channels that offer information about these processes, to help them to choose knowing they are making the best decision about the channel they use.

Risk Perception When Using the Web

Anderson et al. (2014), tells us that the internet can provide an excellent forum to discuss any issues that may not be covered by traditional media. Having the potential to interconnect ideas, thoughts, and goals of individuals, however far away they are. Even so, and despite all the positive aspects that web developments bring us, each of them has inherent risks, and it is important to check the perception that users have of the risks they run. Unprecedented amounts of information are shared today by people, appearing therefore new problems of scalability, integrity, and availability of the information in the systems (Monteiro & Alturas, 2012).

Yap and Selvaratnam (2018) advances that the concept of risk has been explained by a set of academic disciplines, namely, sociological, cultural, and psychological, in a context of study considering environmental, individual, and cognitive factors, capable of contribute to the perception of risk variation. Thakur and Srivastava (2015) indicate studies that present online security as a key theme to understand the user's attitude in the use of web services. This being fundamental for the integrity, confidentiality, authentication, and non-recognition of relationships. In the study carried out by these authors, consumers associate security risks with losing money. Heavily influenced by the imagination of stories about hackers, consumers believe that their online accounts are in danger of being accessed by third parties without their consent, and that serious financial implications could ensue. The perception of the risk of privacy is defined by the possibility that, through online business, personal information may be used inappropriately, thus invading the consumer's privacy.

This personal information is largely forwarded to CRM (Customer Relationship Management) business processes, with the aim of optimizing your sales and service provision. CRM, according to Payne and Frow (2005, p. 168), is defined as a strategic approach aimed at increasing value for shareholders, through the development of relationships between entities and their main customers and customer segments, offering thus better opportunities for the use of data and information, so that they have a better understanding of both the customer and the implementation of relationship marketing strategies.

The definition of the concept of data and information is fundamental in approaching this topic and can be defined as a set of symbols that represent a perception of raw facts, that is, and following Debons et al. (1988), they are events from which inferences or conclusions can be drawn. Information is understood as the organization of data seeking to answer the following basic questions: What? Who? When? Where?

For Qi and Zhang (2012), the concepts associated with mass production, first created during the industrial revolution, are being replaced by new ideas where the relationship with the consumer is the center of the business. The focus should be on what the customer needs rather than adding features to products. The old "design-build-sell" model is becoming obsolete, giving rise to the "sell-build-design" model. This means that the cost associated with stimulating customers and acquiring new customers is much lower than previously practiced. To respond to this evolution, companies focus their attention on increasing the customer's business value through analysis, so that the customer can be monitored throughout their life cycle. For this, they use CRM systems, which analyze data using tools such as data warehousing, data mining, customer relationship management, statistics, among others, providing new business opportunities in view of the needs highlighted in the market. All these processes make CRM a process for managing the relationship between the business and the customer.

As Chen and Popovich (2003) refer, CRM is not merely a technological application for marketing, sales and services, because when successfully implemented, it is a multifunctional system, customer-oriented, where strategy and technology integrate in ways that maximize relationships and serve the entire enterprise. The development of Information Technologies and Data Science has enabled companies to understand and predict customer demand more accurately through quantitative approaches (Chong et al., 2017), also contributing to a constant increase in the automation of customer processes. traditionally human-based decision making (Miller, 2018). In this way, one of the conditions to start the CRM process is the possession of customer information, using data that already exists from existing customers, but also that can be acquired through data provided by external sources.

Data Privacy Protection Legislation and Norms

Regulation (EU) 2016/679 of the European Parliament and of the Council, of April 27, 2016 (General Data Protection Regulation – GDPR) applies in Portugal and in the other Member States of the European Union from 25 de Maio de 2018. Thus, establishing a principle of (pro)active responsibility, where the person responsible for the processing of personal data demonstrates that in all stages of the process, this treatment complies with the Regulation.

This regulation establishes the rules regarding the processing of personal data, of a person, company or organization, in the European Union (EU).

Presenting in the general provisions, the main objectives of its existence, namely:

1. Establish the rules regarding the protection of natural persons, regarding the processing of personal data and the free movement of such data.
2. Defend the fundamental rights and freedoms of natural persons, namely their right to the protection of personal data.
3. Clarify that the free movement of personal data within the Union is not restricted or prohibited for reasons related to the protection of natural persons, regarding the processing of personal data.

That said, the definition of personal data becomes fundamental for a better understanding of the subject in question, being defined as information relating to a natural person who can be identified or identifiable by means of an identifier, such as a name, an identification number, location data, or to one or more elements specific to the physical, genetic, mental or social identity of a natural person (European Commission, 2016). For the preservation and confidentiality of this information, it is extremely important that the individual decides what to do with their own personal data. This implies greater transparency, both in the relationship between companies and people, in the way their data is collected and processed. Goddard (2017) presents this concern about privacy in which the European Union has focused its attention, as an opportunity to raise awareness of populations regarding problems related to privacy. The researchers believe that policies related to privacy can bring about confidence in populations regarding the ethical treatment of data and a global impact on the perception of these matters. Not only organizations within the European Union will feel pressure on new methods of applying data processing. Outside the European space, there will also be pressure, as they will have to ensure high GDPR standards reflected in contractual provisions.

It is also possible to add that the RGPD goes beyond the legal process associated with it, as it is also responsible for a normalization and organization of data processing that until now would not have been put into practice, indicates Goddard (2017). According to a study presented on the Statista platform, carried out in January 2021, and in response to the question about the perception of technology companies' control over consumers' personal data, 66% share the feeling that technology companies have too much control over your personal data. The same study reports that respondents in Spain, the United Kingdom and the United States had higher levels of concern about data control, but even those countries that appear to agree least with the statement show more than 50% agreement with over-control over their data. personal.

METHODOLOGY

The study here presented in this paper had as goal to understand the feeling the consumer has when sharing personal information and data online, to deepen if the data sharing is in fact the path that should be followed, and if users are available in the future to share more data online as they do today. It also aimed to understand if these approaches to data sharing, with all its pros and cons, are indeed beneficial.

Hence, considering the objectives set for this study, a questionnaire was designed based on an adaptation of the model proposed and validated by Mekovec and Vrček (2011) on their studies (C.f. Figure 2).

The questions in this present study's questionnaire were created considering an adaptation of this model to the current technological context, and to the study's objectives. This adaptation of the model for this study considers the evaluation of the perception of privacy not only in the context of web pages, as in the original model, but also in the context of mobile applications, games, and online purchases, trying to consider factors that the previously analyzed authors during the literature review indicate as having an impact on individuals' perception of privacy, in the current digital context.

This study's questionnaire was composed by 7 sections, were the first group refers to the consumer's intrinsic characteristics; the second group aims to know the situation factors specific to the consumer's relationship with information technology (IT), including issues related to the usage of social networks; the third group aimed to know the consumer's relationship with the IT, specifically online shopping habits; the fourth group's goal was to know the specific situation factors concerning the usage of e-health apps; the fifth group aimed for a more generic knowledge about societal behavior concerning information systems in order to understand what are the specific areas were consumers feel more and less safe, as well as what are the prevalent feelings during the moments of data sharing online; the sixth group allowed to understand the characteristics of the websites that are most used/consulted; and the seventh group had the focus of getting to know the users' understanding about governmental privacy protection legislation and how this understanding influences their behavior when sharing data online.

Moreover, this questionnaire was subject to the appreciation of an expert in the field, as well as a non-expert, to validate the composition and see if it would be in accordance with the proposed objectives, together with the perception of it for readers before its release to the public.

Figure 2. Model adaptation, about individual perception on data transmissibility of personal data online
Source: Adapted from Mekovec and Vrček (2011)

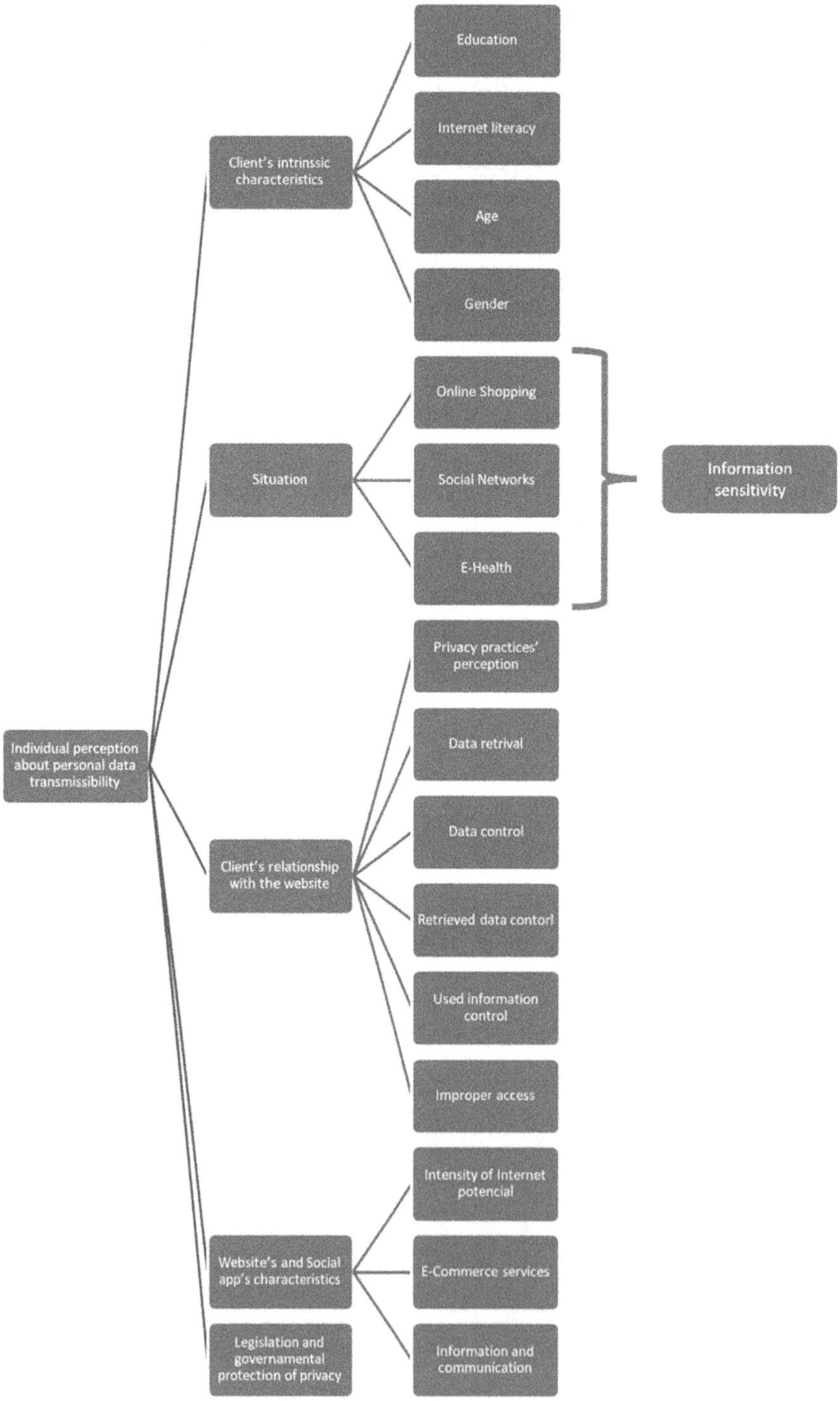

FINDINGS AND DISCUSSION

Considering the research objective and goals, this study's methodological approach included to design a questionnaire, that was implemented via social media. This data gathering instrument was designed considering an adaptation of Mekovec and Vrček model (2011) that was made to encompass today's online reality. The questionnaire's goal was to evaluate the users' perception about the privacy of the data they share online in today's digital context. After its design, the questions were validated by an expert and a non-expert. It was of great importance to know the intrinsic characteristics of the consumer, because as Mekovec and Vrček (2011) advances, when approaching the subject of an individual's perception of privacy, it is important to consider the characteristics of that same individual, given that people share different perspectives, experiences and consequently opinions. To determine the existing feelings of this study's enquiries when sharing personal data online, respondents were asked what feelings they had when sharing personal data online, where the most recurrent feelings were concern, insecurity and distrust. Through the correlation between the degree of awareness when sharing personal data online and what feelings exist while sharing data, it was possible to conclude that there is mostly a level 3 awareness level where it is also possible to observe that at this level of consciousness, there is a greater number of clicks, which in turn translates into a greater number of feelings existing during the sharing (C.f. Figure 3).

Figure 3. Correlation between the level of consciousness when sharing data online with sharing personal data online

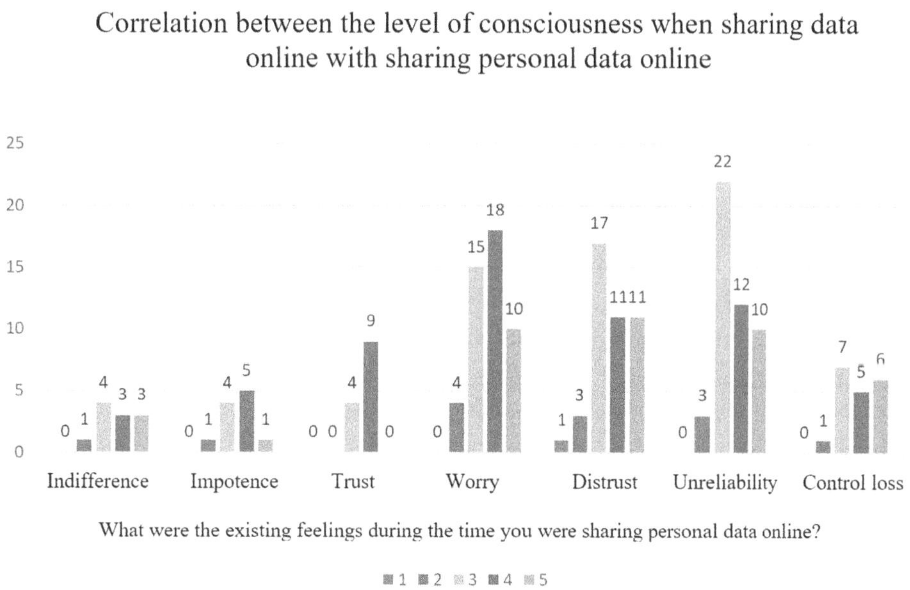

Respondents were also asked about their level of loss of control over data already made available over time, and they were able to conclude that there is a high average perception of loss of control (72.8%). Questioned about the habit of reading the terms and conditions of security and privacy on websites and applications in order to understand the "rules of the game", the answers indicate that there is no frequent practice of reading them. Perhaps for this reason, the question regarding the frequency of adjustment of the definitions of the terms of privacy and security, also indicates that it is not a custom, as more than half of the sample (55.2%) indicate that they do it a few or sometimes. Correlating the qualifications of the respondents with the frequency of adjustment of the definitions of the terms of privacy and security, as shown in Figure 4, we can observe that the respondents do not adjust the definitions of the terms of privacy and security regardless of their qualifications. The highest concentration of responses in terms of frequency of adjustment of definitions of terms of privacy and security, focuses on grade 2.

Regarding transparency in the processing of personal data during the online shopping process, the results indicate that the majority (66.3%) consider the process transparent, evaluating it as having a high average of transparency. To identify key points in building trust in the use of information systems, questions were asked about the degree of confidence they feel in the ability to process personal data by companies that own social networking platforms and websites, where the result indicates a low average confidence (74.5%). Considering that the trust factor is an extremely important point for the relationship between users and information systems, it can be deduced that they feel little confidence in the capacity of data processing by social network companies. When asked about the degree of confidence when making online purchases, the vast majority (80.3%) indicated a medium high level. It should be noted that it is possible to verify that there is a small difference between the trust attributed to social networks and the trust attributed to e-commerce, with e-commerce where users have greater confidence.

When analyzing e-commerce specifically, we tried to understand how safe respondents consider the online shopping process, with 77.7% of the sample responding considering the degree of security as medium high, thus seeing the online shopping process as safe for users. Even so, this degree of trust felt may originate from the lack of knowledge of several factors, leading to a false sense of security, which, as described by Leblanc and Biddle (2012), is observed when most users, generally trust the majority, if not on every site it finds, causing significant security issues. In this way, it should be noted that despite the degree of confidence shown by users regarding the safety of online purchases, this feeling may have several factors, not just the in-depth knowledge of the possible risks during these processes.

With regard to the type of information made available on social networks, it was possible to observe that sharing the real name is the most expressive, together with the date of birth, family members and their relationships. In turn, the least expressive are the address and telephone number, denoting some care in sharing information considered sensitive by most users. As for the type of privacy settings adopted for social networks, the limitation to the public that can access the content is the most evident, together with alert checks for account handling on other devices and limitations on who can see the list. of friends. The least mentioned are search engines outside of social networks, the email or telephone number provided and location tracking. By correlating the participants' educational qualifications with the type of information available on social networks, we observe that the line corresponding to secondary education is where there is the highest concentration of responses, indicating that for individuals with this type of qualifications there is a greater amount of information available online, making these individuals the most exposed segment virtually.

Regarding the information available in online purchases, the real name, address, taxpayer number and email are the most shared information, while financial information and sharing the date of birth are the least considered. Through the correlation between qualifications and the type of information available in online purchases, it was possible to observe that the level of secondary education qualifications continues to be the most exposed segment, despite presenting a slight difference in relation to participants with graduation.

Concerning the sharing of personal data to use e-health apps, our inquires have stated to make available their name, email, number of steps they make during the day, height, weight and heart rate, considering them relevant data for the apps to function properly. The less shared information is relative to personal illnesses, assurance policy number, location, and address. When correlating this information and their academic qualifications, it was possible to conclude that graduates are the ones that share more data for e-health apps. Furthermore, comparing these findings with the other areas that were considered for this study, it is possible to conclude that it's on e-health that users share more personal private data.

When analyzed the responses obtained regarding the pre-disposition of respondents to sharing personal data online on the various topics arranged, it was possible to conclude that the areas where respondents are less willing to share their personal data, were the areas of online games together with social networks, as they present a higher concentration of responses in a very low pre-disposition. If these were the two areas where there was less willingness, on the other hand, e-commerce, education, and the professional context are the areas where there is greater availability for sharing personal data.

Thus, knowing the difficulty in measuring the perception or sensitivity of information shared online, and that it is described as individual privacy concerns for a specific type of information in a specific situation, it was possible to conclude that there is some sensitivity of information shared in Portuguese society, but that the path of instruction and development of digital literacy in our community is still a way to go, and the "seeds" of digital knowledge have been sown. It should be noted that internet users' perception of a website or the digital world depends not only on their current interaction, but also on the consideration of experiences with websites or past contexts.

Regarding the satisfaction level with personal data protection legislation and norms, most respondents were moderately/highly satisfied (73,8%). Correlating this with their academic qualifications it was possible to observe no variation, hence this satisfaction was verified independently of academic qualifications. When inquired about these norms effectiveness, the results were similar, with a slight variation on the moderate level, were 50% of the sample was. Hence, it is possible to conclude that there is a need to contextualize users about their privacy and online security rights, norms, and legislation, for them to feel safer.

To identify the key aspects to build trust in using information systems, respondents were inquired about their confidence level about the treatment companies do of their personal data. Results showed that respondents feel less trust when it comes to websites and social networks (74,5%). However, their level of trust on how e-commerce websites deal with their personal data, our respondents answered to feel they are very trustworthy. Hence, to find out more why this happens, our respondents have stated that they feel that the online shopping process is very safe, allowing to conclude that their level of trust can happen due to the lack of knowledge about several factors, leading to a false sense of security, as Leblanc & Biddle (2012) described.

As such, the presented level of trust by our respondents may have several factors, and not just their profound knowledge about the possible risks they incur into during these processes.

Comparing the level of trust attributed to the areas of social networks, e-commerce, and health, we can conclude that social networks are the area where there is a lower degree of trust and the area of health where there is a higher degree of trust. As for their usage of social networking platforms, online shopping, or health applications, we have that 99% of respondents use social networks, 88.3% shop online and 70.9% use health or physical exercise applications. Thus, it is possible to conclude that although people use social networks more in their daily lives than they shop online or use health or physical exercise applications, this does not mean that they feel more confident in the handling of their data by entities, holders of social media platforms and websites.

To identify key points in building trust with information systems, we can combine this information with the information available for the purpose of identifying existing feelings during data sharing (concern, insecurity and distrust) to seek combat them.

The way to build trust will be by providing information to the user in an open, clear and summarized way about the process of processing their data online. The strategy for improving user confidence involves educating society in handling its data online.

Understanding the perception of the advantages and disadvantages associated with sharing personal data online, we can conclude that in social networks, appreciation is indifferent or a practically remote advantage for about 68% of respondents. As for the usefulness of e-commerce, it appears that the majority (48.6%) consider it advantageous or very advantageous. Finally, in the health area, 57.3% answered that the applicability of sharing their personal data for health purposes is indifferent or advantageous.

In view of these results, we can conclude that there is a difference in the results of e-commerce, compared to social networks and health. Perhaps because in e-commerce there are more situational factors where the process unfolds in an efficient way, leaving the user satisfied for having made the purchase he intended. However, it should be noted that this analysis may not be being carried out at the level of the processing of personal data, but in the provision of the service.

The analysis of the results obtained allowed responding to all the objectives proposed in this study, having been supported by indicators that made it possible to support certain conclusions that help us to understand a little better the relationship of our society with the information systems that we currently have.

It is possible to highlight the fact that the respondents' educational qualifications are not a decisive factor for variations in the degree of satisfaction in relation to the prevailing norms. But that the level of contextualization in relation to the RGPD can be a differentiating indicator of the level of satisfaction with current regulations. It is important to mention the difference in society's willingness to share personal data online, depending on the area for which it is intended. That is, there are areas of our society where the population is more willing to provide more personal data, namely in the areas of e-commerce, education and professional context.

As for the existing feelings when sharing personal data online, we can conclude that the predominant feelings, as stated previously, are concern, insecurity, and distrust.

This is a clear indicator that these could be the feelings or areas to be overcome to build trust in information systems. Following the analysis of the data collected in this study about users' trust, it is possible to infer that this is related to the way society interprets the handling of its data online. It is important to educate people in this regard and give them all the information they need while using websites, not putting information in small print, for example, to generate feelings that something is hidden or hidden beyond the information provided.

According to Chin et al. (2012), the measurement of users' trust privacy and security in the handling of online platforms and websites is extremely important so that the companies that own platforms and websites can have information that allows them to make the handling of their products safer, allowing users to benefit from the security and confidence in together with the convenience potential offered by online platforms and websites.

Finally, to understand the perception of the advantages and disadvantages associated with data sharing, we can conclude that society mostly considers the use of information systems in the areas of social networks, e-commerce, and health to be advantageous.

Considering the digital world, it is essential to consider the perspectives related to this topic to understand the impact that this new world can bring to our society. Namely, through the weighting of values, as the price to be paid for an effective and efficient society can lead to a lack of privacy for those who live in it. Over time, we will encounter situations where the invasion of privacy will prevail over personal interests, and then it will be important to have as much information as possible about our relationship as a society with information systems and how information systems manage to transform as a society, without affecting our individual freedom and privacy.

CONCLUSIONS AND RECOMMENDATIONS

It is a conclusion of this study that although people use social networks more in their daily lives than they shop online or use health or physical exercise applications, this does not mean that they feel more confident in the handling of their data by entities, holders of social media platforms and websites. To identify key points in building trust with information systems, we can add this information, to the one already available, in order to identify the feelings that exist during data sharing (concern, insecurity and distrust) to help combat them. The feeling of trust could be addressed by providing information to the user in an open, clear, and summarized way about the process of processing their data online. The strategy for improving user confidence involves educating society in handling its data online.

More in-depth studies on the areas where there is a greater willingness to share personal data, could be an asset to complement the results of this study. Since a greater willingness to share personal data on a given topic must have a social foundation, normally associated with areas where greater efficiency is sought in the provision of services, such as "health", even this is not a priority area for society according to this study.

The correlation of more variables could also enrich future studies, giving as an example the fact that the different generations that use information systems have different behaviors and preventive measures between them and understand the respective differences in these behaviors.

Another possible future topic of research would be to understand to what extent the intervention of the public or private power should be responsible for the security of the use of the network, to guarantee the confidentiality and integrity of the information available online, so that a relationship of trust can be built with transparency of information systems.

There are several paths that can and should be taken within this area of research. Suggesting a topic for future research, it could be about the price or consequences of a society that is more effective and efficient, through the crossing of data, and to what extent society would or would not be willing to give up its data.

REFERENCES

Aïmeur, E., Lawani, O., & Dalkir, K. (2016). When changing the look of privacy policies affects user trust: An experimental study. *Computers in Human Behavior*, *58*, 368–379. doi:10.1016/j.chb.2015.11.014

Buchholz, K. (2022). *The Rapid Rise of TikTok. Statista, Topics – Social media*. https://www.statista.com/chart/28412/social-media-users-by-network-amo/

Catalina-Garcia, B., López-de-Ayala, M. C., & García, A. (2014). Los riesgos de los adolescentes en Internet: Los menores como actores y víctimas de los peligros de Internet [The risks of teens on the Internet: minors as actors and victims of Internet dangers]. *Revista Latina de Comunicación Social, 69*(69), 462–485. doi:10.4185/RLCS-2014-1020

Chen, I., & Popovich, K. (2003). Understanding customer relationship management (CRM) People, process and technology. *Business Process Management Journal, 9*(5), 672–688. doi:10.1108/14637150310496758

Chin, E., Felt, A. P., Sekar, V., & Wagner, D. (2012). Measuring user confidence in smartphone security and privacy. *SOUPS 2012 - Proceedings of the 8th Symposium on Usable Privacy and Security*, 1. 10.1145/2335356.2335358

Chong, A., Ch'ng, E., Liu, M., & Li, B. (2017). Predicting consumer product demands via Big Data: The roles of online promotional marketing and online reviews. *International Journal of Production Research, 55*(17), 5142–5156. doi:10.1080/00207543.2015.1066519

Debons, A., Horne, E., & Cronenweth, S. (1988). *Information science: An integrated view*. G.K. Hall.

European Commission. (2021). *Horizon Europe, pilar III - Europa inovadora – Apoiar e estabelecer ligações entre os inovadores na Europa*. Publications Office of the European Union Directorate. General for Research and Innovation. https://data.europa.eu/doi/10.2777/831048

European Union. (2016). *Regulation (EU) 2016/679 of the European Parliament and of the Council of 27 April 2016 on the protection of natural persons with regard to the processing of personal data and the free movement of such data. Official Journal of the European Union*. https://eur-lex.europa.eu/legal-content/PT/TXT/PDF/?uri=CELEX:32016R0679&qid=1641839336270&from=PT

Gapsalamov, A. R., Bochkareva, T. N., Akhmetshin, E. M., Vasilev, V. L., & Anisimova, T. I. (2020). Sociedade digital: Novos desafios para a educação. *Periódico Tchê Química, 17*(34), 803–817. doi:10.52571/PTQ.v17.n34.2020.827_P34_pgs_803_816.pdf

Goddard, M. (2017). The EU General Data Protection Regulation (GDPR): European regulation that has a global impact. *International Journal of Market Research, 59*(6), 703–705. doi:10.2501/IJMR-2017-050

Jacksi, K., & Abass, S. M. (2019). Development history of the world wide web. *International Journal of Scientific and Technology Research, 8*(9), 75–79.

Kim, Y., & Krishnan, R. (2015). On product-level uncertainty and online purchase behavior: An empirical analysis. *Management Science, 61*(10), 2449–2467. doi:10.1287/mnsc.2014.2063

LeBlanc, D., & Biddle, R. (2012). Risk perception of internet-related activities. In *2012 Tenth Annual International Conference on Privacy, Security and Trust* (pp. 88–95). IEEE. 10.1109/PST.2012.6297924

Liebermann, Y., & Stashevsky, S. (2002). Perceived risks as barriers to Internet and ecommerce usage. *Qualitative Market Research, 5*(4), 291–300. doi:10.1108/13522750210443245

Mekovec, R., & Vrček, N. (2011). Factors that influence Internet users' privacy perception. In *Proceedings of the ITI 2011, 33rd International Conference on Information Technology Interfaces* (pp. 227–232). IEEE.

Miller, A. (2018). Want Less-Biased Decisions? Use Algorithms. *Harvard Business Review*, 26.

Monteiro, D., & Alturas, B. (2012). Segurança e Privacidade na Web 2.0: Foco nas Redes Sociais. *Egitânia Sciencia*, *10*, 109–133.

Payne, A., & Frow, P. (2005). A Strategic Framework for Customer Relationship Management. *Journal of Marketing*, *69*(4), 167–176. doi:10.1509/jmkg.2005.69.4.167

Qi, L., & Zhang, S. (2012). The Development of Customer Relationship Management System Based on Rough Set. *Communications in Computer and Information Science*, *315*, 328–333. doi:10.1007/978-3-642-34240-0_43

Sheehan, K. B., & Hoy, M. G. (2000). Dimensions of privacy concerns among online consumers. *Journal of Public Policy & Marketing*, *19*(1), 62–73. doi:10.1509/jppm.19.1.62.16949

Soczka, L. B. D. C. (2014). *Gestão da privacidade em redes sociais: perceções de uso de dados e partilha de informação pessoal.* Dissertação de Mestrado, Universidade de Lisboa. Instituto Superior de Economia e Gestão. http://hdl.handle.net/10400.5/12689

Thakur, R., & Srivastava, M. (2015). A study on the impact of consumer risk perception and innovativeness on online shopping in India. *International Journal of Retail & Distribution Management*, *43*(2), 148–166. doi:10.1108/IJRDM-06-2013-0128

Weissman, J. (2021). *The Crowdsourced Panopticon: Conformity and Control on Social Media.* Rowman & Littlefield Publishers.

Yap, K. W., & Selvaratnam, D. P. (2018). Empirical analysis of factors influencing the public health expenditure in Malaysia. *Journal of Emerging Economies and Islamic Research*, *6*(3), 1–14. doi:10.24191/jeeir.v6i3.8783

Zhuang, H., Leszczyc, P. T. L. P., & Lin, Y. (2018). Why is price dispersion higher online than offline? The impact of retailer type and shopping risk on price dispersion. *Journal of Retailing*, *94*(2), 136–153. doi:10.1016/j.jretai.2018.01.003

Zuboff, S. (2020). *A Era do Capitalismo da Vigilância. A Disputa por Um Futuro Humano na Nova Fronteira do Poder.* Relógio D'Água Editores.

ADDITIONAL READING

Alturas, B. (2022). *Introdução aos Sistemas de Informação Organizacionais* (2nd ed.). Edições Sílabo.

Whitman, M. E., & Mattord, H. J. (2021). *Principles of Information Security (MindTap Course List)* (7th ed.). Cengage Learning.

KEY TERMS AND DEFINITIONS

Data Sharing: Data sharing is the ability to make the same data available to one or many consumers. Nowadays, the ever-growing amount of data has become a strategic asset for any company. Sharing data - within your organization or externally - is an enabling technology for new business opportunities.

Internet Security: Internet security is a term that describes security for activities and transactions made over the internet. It's a particular component of the larger ideas of cybersecurity and computer security, involving topics including browser security, online behavior, and network security.

Online Privacy: Online privacy is the level of privacy protection an individual has while connected to the Internet. It covers the amount of online security available for personal and financial data, communications, and preferences.

Social Media: Social media refers to digital platforms and tools that allow users to create, share, and exchange content, opinions, and information with others. Social media platforms enable users to connect with each other and engage in online communication, which can include text, images, videos, and other types of multimedia.

Chapter 8
Examining User Understanding and Perceptions of E-Commerce Data Privacy, Security, and Protection

Jeganathan Gomathi Sankar
https://orcid.org/0000-0002-5077-5109
BSSS Institute of Advanced Studies, Bhopal, India

Arokiaraj David
https://orcid.org/0000-0002-9591-2410
St. Francis Institute of Management and Research, Mumbai, India

P. Valan
VIT Business School, Vellore, India

ABSTRACT

The objective of this study is to investigate the level of understanding that internet users have regarding data privacy, security, and protection. The study aims to determine the extent to which individuals are conscious of the potential hazards of sharing personal information online and the steps they take to secure their data. The research also examines the role of technology companies and government agencies in educating internet users about data privacy and security. The study was conducted in Bhopal using stratified random sampling, and data were collected from employees and students of an educational institution in Bhopal. The findings of this study will give an understanding of the current awareness of internet users and aid in future efforts to enhance data privacy and security for all users.

DOI: 10.4018/978-1-6684-8958-1.ch008

INTRODUCTION

In the era of information technology, privacy is increasingly becoming a concern as technology continues to penetrate personal space. Users of online information technology are faced with numerous dangers, such as spam, cookies, and the clickstream. Advancements in real-time person-location technologies, including geo-location and biometric identification, along with miniaturized processors, embedded in everyday items, pose risks to privacy and security, requiring robust mitigation measures.

The public's general lack of trust in technology is a major hindrance to widespread adoption of electronic commerce (Pavlou & Fygenson, 2006). Trust in the information society is also a crucial issue, as well as the protection of personal information and assets. According to Furger (1999), large data archives about individuals serve as a basis for public and commercial organizations to exercise control over people. Sender-driven technologies, combined with profile data, may also result in individuals being overwhelmed with personalized information, putting undue pressure on their behavior (Chen & Cheung, 2007).

The concerns about privacy and security in the world of information technology continue to be a topic of daily discussion (Jeganathan et al., 2022). While there are many articles and reports about the challenges faced by IT users, there is a lack of scientific studies that thoroughly examine their worries. This study aimed to address this gap by surveying online IT users about their concerns and fears related to privacy and security. Information technology encompasses various aspects, such as e-mail and online commerce, and protecting data from unauthorized access, unintended disclosure, and tampering is critical. Privacy, in this context, refers to a person or organization's right to control the information that is shared with others.

This study is particularly relevant given the growing importance of these technologies in our lives, and the increasing number of businesses that operate online. The participants in the study expressed concerns about internet privacy protection, online security, and the potential consequences of accidentally sending sensitive information to unintended recipients. Companies are investing in developing new technologies to help people protect their personal information, keep their credit card details secure, and avoid websites that may sell their data to third parties (Tertulino et al, 2023). Governments and private organizations are also investing in secure methods for transferring internet data to build trust with customers. When customers trust a secure website, they can feel confident about providing credit card information through encrypted transmission (Kim & Benbasat, 2003; Sankar, & Kiruba Sagar 2020).

The social media has revolutionized social relationships, information exchange, and business potential, attracting over a billion users (Schomakers et al., 2019). This has resulted in the production of vast amounts of data, known as "Big Data", which presents significant opportunities for the healthcare industry, enterprises, and society as a whole (AlAlwan et al., 2017; Kapoor et al., 2018; Shiau et al., 2017). The healthcare sector can leverage Big Data to anticipate and manage epidemics, create user-centered products, and find innovative commercial services. Additionally, real-time data analysis can improve road safety by promoting more cautious driving practices (Nambiar et al., 2013; Sagiroglu & Sinanc, 2013). Although Big Data has potential advantages, individuals are cognizant of the surging volume of information being gathered about them and the potential hazards associated with data manipulation. According to surveys, people are becoming progressively apprehensive about their privacy and the safety of their personal details (O'Neil, 2001). The introduction of the European General Data Protection Regulation (GDPR) in May 2018 has generated considerable attention and discussion regarding online privacy. As individuals become increasingly worried about their online privacy, they are revisiting their internet usage habits and being cautious about providing personal data. (Awad et al., 2006). Individuals' perceptions of data privacy vary based on the sensitivity of the information and the motivations of those who are collecting it (Lee et al., 2022). The subject of what information is considered sensitive and what factors influence this impression arises because different people and countries have varying perceptions of what information is sensitive (Ma, 2022).

REVIEW OF LITERATURE

The concept of privacy impacts our lives in various ways, and Burgoon (1982) distinguishes between different types of privacy, including informational, physical, psychological, and interactional privacy. Information security, also known as cybersecurity, is a critical concern in today's digital world. With the increasing dependence on technology and the Internet, the risk of cyber-attacks and data breaches has become a significant threat to individuals, businesses, and governments. This has led to an increased focus on information security research to identify and mitigate vulnerabilities and threats. Information security is defined as the practice of protecting information by mitigating information risks, information security is not only about protecting data from unauthorized access, but also includes ensuring the confidentiality, integrity, and availability of data (Rekik et al., 2021), Westin (1967) gives more weight to informational privacy and defines it as having control over one's information. In the digital age, where data about us is constantly being collected, informational privacy has become a critical component of all other forms of privacy (Koops et al., 2016; Ma et al., 2020). The 2021 Eurobarometer survey on data protection found that 82% of respondents in the European Union were concerned about not having complete control over their personal data. The survey also revealed that 77% of respondents were concerned about the potential misuse of their personal data and 74% were worried about the security of their personal data. These findings indicate that concerns over information privacy continue to be widespread and significant (European Commission, 2021), and these concerns are frequently used in empirical research to compare intended and actual privacy conditions (Li, 2011b). These worries may be directed at the online community as a whole or at a specific situation (Li, 2011b). Factors such as attitudes and privacy concerns impact information sharing and technology use (Li, 2011b; Smith et al., 2011). Physical security is next important aspect of data security and privacy, as it involves the protection of physical assets, such as hardware, devices, and facilities, that store and process sensitive information. Existing research articles emphasize the importance of physical security measures to prevent unauthorized access, theft, and damage to physical assets. Physical security measures, such as access controls, surveillance cameras, and alarms, are critical to protecting data centers and other facilities that store and process sensitive information (Abbas et al., 2021). Physical security measures should be integrated with other security measures, such as encryption and network security, to ensure comprehensive protection of data assets (Abbas et al., 2021). Alzaqebah et al., 2021) highlights the importance of physical security measures in preventing theft of mobile devices, which often contain sensitive personal and business information. The authors highlight that physical security measures, such as password protection and biometric authentication, can help prevent unauthorized access to mobile devices and protect sensitive data. Tabrizchi et al. (2020) emphasizes the importance of physical security policies and procedures to prevent data breaches and protect sensitive information. The authors suggest that organizations should have clear policies and procedures for physical security, such as access control, visitor management, and incident response, to ensure that physical assets are protected from unauthorized access and other threats. Research articles emphasize the importance of psychological security measures to protect individuals from the negative emotional and psychological impacts of cyber threats and data breaches. It is important that psychological security measures, such as fostering a culture of trust and transparency, can help promote a sense of safety and security among employees and protect against insider threats to data security (Mangku et al., 2021). Nandi et al. (2020) suggests that psychological security measures, such as providing individuals with greater control over their personal data, can help promote a sense of empowerment and increase trust in the digital environment. Authors signify the importance of interactional privacy measures to protect individuals' privacy and autonomy in the digital environment. Individuals' interactions with smart home technology can reveal sensitive personal information, such as their daily routines and habits, and that interactional privacy measures, such as clear and transparent privacy policies and user-friendly privacy settings, are necessary to protect individuals' privacy and autonomy in the smart home environment. So, it is important of interactional privacy in the context of smart homes (Stahl, 2021). Social media companies collect vast amounts of personal information from users and that individuals may not fully understand how their personal information is being used, thus, interactional privacy measures, such as providing clear and accessible privacy settings and allowing individuals to control the use of their personal information, are necessary to protect individuals' privacy and autonomy on social media platforms (Zhang et al., 2019). The proper interactional privacy measures, such as personalized privacy settings and transparent data collection practices, can help promote trust and engagement among individuals using e-commerce platforms (Mangku., 2021)

The level of concern about privacy can vary depending on the context, and one important factor in this variation is the perceived sensitivity of the information being sought. As Li (2011b) notes, individuals are more likely to be concerned about their privacy when they perceive that the information being sought is sensitive or personal. As data is thought to become more sensitive, privacy concerns grow. People are particularly concerned about medical data, according to Slepchuk et al. (2022), while Swani et al. (2021) discovered that people who think that health information is highly sensitive also exhibit increased worry about health information. Studies have shown that building trust with users and being transparent about data usage can help to mitigate privacy concerns and increase the willingness of individuals to share sensitive information (Schomakers et al., 2019; Yakubu & Chen, 2020).

Yakubu and Chen (2020) found that users were more willing to disclose sensitive information when they perceived the organization collecting the information to be trustworthy and transparent about their data usage practices. Schomakers et al. (2019) similarly found that being transparent about data usage and providing individuals with control over their personal information can help to increase trust and mitigate privacy concerns. As per the guidelines laid out in the General Data Protection Regulation (GDPR), sensitive information is classified as any data relating to an individual that identifies or can be linked to a specific and identifiable natural person. The GDPR only applies to personal data, and certain categories of personal data are given heightened protection due to their sensitivity (recital 51 GDPR). Information that pertains to a person's racial or ethnic background, political opinions, religious or philosophical beliefs, union membership, genetic and biometric data, health information, or details about their sexual orientation or sexual history are considered to be particularly sensitive personal data, as defined by Article 9 Section 1 of the General Data Protection Regulation (GDPR). The GDPR strictly forbids the processing of such data unless explicitly authorized by law, such as with the express consent of the user (Art. 6 Sec. 1 lit. a) GDPR) (General Data Protection Regulation (EU) 2016/679).

Schomakers et al. (2019) and Tarhini et al. (2021) both suggest that the perception of threats and the amount of online protection needed can be greatly impacted by the particular circumstances surrounding the usage of digital technologies. Milne et al. (2019) suggest that the risks associated with different types of information can vary depending on various factors, such as the sensitivity of the information and the purpose for which it is being used. Milne et al. (2019) also noted that the perceived risks associated with personal information can depend on the context in which it is being used. For example, individuals may perceive different risks associated with providing personal information for healthcare purposes compared to providing the same information for marketing or advertising purposes. Their findings suggest that the risks associated with personal information can vary depending on the type of information, the purpose for which it is being used, and the context in which it is being shared. This highlights the importance of considering these factors when developing privacy and security policies and strategies for managing personal information. As an example, social media profiles are more closely tied to potential social and psychological consequences, while credit card numbers are more commonly associated with financial risks. Labrecque et al. (2021) conducted a study to assess individuals' perceptions of the sensitivity of different types of personal information and their willingness to disclose that information. They established a ranking of 52 different types of information based on their perceived sensitivity, with information such as financial information and health information being perceived as more sensitive than information such as hobbies or political views. Labrecque et al. (2021) found that individuals were less willing to disclose more sensitive types of personal information, and that this reluctance to disclose was influenced by factors such as the trustworthiness of the organization collecting the information, the intended use of the information, and the perceived benefits of sharing the information. These findings highlight the importance of considering individuals' perceptions of the sensitivity of personal information when developing privacy and security policies and strategies for managing personal data. Organizations can use this information to better understand individuals' concerns and preferences regarding the collection and use of personal information, and to develop more effective approaches for managing and protecting that information. Consequently, the sensitivity of information is dependent on the specific type of data and the person in question and can impact how individuals view their own online privacy (Labrecque et al., 2021; Milne et al., 2019).

Various academic fields have differing interpretations of privacy. For instance, privacy has been described as the "right to solitude" (Warren & Brandeis, 1890, p. 195), Warren and Brandeis (1890) argued that the common law of torts, which was designed to protect property rights, did not provide sufficient protection for the right to privacy. They advocated for the recognition of a new legal principle that would protect individuals' right to control their personal information and prevent unauthorized intrusions into their private lives. In their article, Warren and Brandeis highlighted the importance of privacy in maintaining personal autonomy and dignity, noting that "The intensity and complexity of life, attendant upon advancing civilization, have rendered necessary some retreat from the world, and man, under the refining influence of culture, has become more sensitive to publicity, so that solitude and privacy have become more essential to the individual" (Warren & Brandeis, 1890, p. 196). Their article was a landmark in the development of privacy law and helped to shape the modern understanding of privacy as a fundamental human right. The concept of privacy as the "right to solitude" or the "right to be let alone" continues to resonate with many people today and has been cited in numerous legal cases and scholarly articles as a cornerstone of privacy protection.

Trepte and Masur (2020) argued that privacy can be seen as a form of information management, and that deliberate management of information flow is a crucial factor in protecting privacy. They suggested that privacy should be understood as a dynamic process that involves ongoing management and negotiation of personal information boundaries, rather than a fixed or static state. Trepte and Masur's (2020) perspective underscores the importance of viewing privacy as an ongoing process that requires active management and engagement, rather than a passive state that can be achieved through a one-time action or decision. By framing privacy as a form of management, the authors emphasize the importance of proactive strategies for protecting personal information, rather than simply relying on legal protections or technological solutions. This article places a spotlight on information privacy. In this context, definitions frequently emphasize choosing or exercising control over the distribution of personal information, including who receives or has access to such information, as well as when and how it is shared (Malin, 2005).

RESEARCH METHODOLOGY

The study aimed to evaluate the level of knowledge and understanding that internet users had about data privacy and security. To achieve this, a questionnaire survey was conducted among employees and students at a private educational institute in Bhopal. The survey was conducted over a period of four months, from September to December 2022. The survey was distributed to participants along with a letter of introduction and a protocol statement. The letter of introduction served as a brief introduction to the study and provided background information on the researchers and the purpose of the study. It also explained the importance of the study and why the participants' participation was critical. The protocol statement, on the other hand, was a more detailed document that explained the specifics of the study, including the research questions, the methodology, and the expected outcomes. The protocol statement also explained the participants' rights and provided details on how their data would be collected and analyzed. The purpose of providing the letter of introduction and the protocol statement was to ensure that the participants fully understood the nature and purpose of the study before agreeing to participate. It also aimed to increase the participants' trust in the research and to minimize any potential concerns they might have had about data privacy and security.

The study's approach to gathering data was designed to ensure that participants were fully informed and understood the purpose and importance of the research, as well as to ensure their rights and privacy were protected throughout the study. The questionnaires were distributed among the employees and students at the private educational institute by the administrative staff. The participants were given a four-week timeframe to complete the questionnaires and return them to the administrative staff. To ensure the confidentiality of the collected information, the research team collected all of the questionnaires from the administrative staff after the survey period ended. This process helped to prevent any potential breaches of privacy or unauthorized access to the data, which is essential for maintaining the integrity of the research. By collecting the questionnaires in this way, the research team was able to analyze the data in a secure and confidential manner, which is crucial for any study involving sensitive information.

Researchers employed stratified random sampling to select participants from eight organizations (employees and students of a private educational institute) for a study. 688 questionnaires were distributed, resulting in 436 usable surveys (63.37% response rate). Cronbach's alpha coefficient of 0.92 confirmed questionnaire reliability and internal consistency, surpassing the recommended threshold for acceptable reliability. The collected data is considered consistent, reliable, and suitable for analysis.

RESULTS OF THE STUDY

Table 1 provides information on various demographic and behavioral characteristics of a sample of 150 individuals. The data shows that the sample is evenly split between male (52%) and female (48%) respondents. The majority of the sample is aged 21-30 (84%) and have either undergraduate (48%) or postgraduate (48%) degree. The largest percentage of the sample has an annual income of less than 50,000 (52%) and access the internet primarily through a smartphone (48%). Most of the sample has been using the internet for less than 5 years (36%) and has an email account (96%). The most common email account type is a home account (56%). 40% of respondents expressed their willingness to use their credit card online, while 88% reported having made at least one online purchase. Of those surveyed, 20% reported frequent online purchases occurring more than once a month, while 12% reported never having made an online purchase. Regarding concerns over online privacy and security, 44% of respondents expressed worry over the abuse of their credit card and other personal information.

Table 1. Demographic profile of the internet users

Gender	No. of Respondents	% of Respondents	Cumulative Percent
Male	78	52.0	52.0
Female	72	48.0	100.0
Age			
21-30 years old	126	84.0	84.0
31-40 years old	12	8.0	92.0
41-50 years old	6	4.0	96.0
> 50 years old	6	4.0	100.0
Educational Level			
UG	72	48.0	48.0
PG	72	48.0	96.0
PhD	6	4.0	100.0
Annual Income			
<50 thousand	78	52.0	52.0
1-2 lakhs	18	12.0	64.0
2-4 lakhs	18	12.0	76.0
4-8 lakhs	12	8.0	84.0
8-16 lakhs	12	8.0	92.0
>16 lakhs	12	8.0	100.0
Internet Usage			
Computer	6	4.0	4.0
Smartphone	72	48.0	52.0
Both	72	48.0	100.0
Have a smartphone			
Yes	150	100.0	100.0
Time spend on internet in a day			
< 1 hour	6	4.0	4.0
1-2 hours	42	28.0	32.0
2-4 hours	48	32.0	64.0
4-8 hours	36	24.0	88.0
> 8 hours	18	12.0	100.0
How long used the Internet			
< 5 yrs	54	36.0	36.0
5-10 yrs	48	32.0	68.0
10-20 yrs	42	28.0	96.0
> 20 yrs	6	4.0	100.0
Have an email account			
Yes	144	96.0	96.0
No	6	4.0	100.0

Continued on following page

Table 1. Continued

Gender	No. of Respondents	% of Respondents	Cumulative Percent
Email Account Type			
Home	84	56.0	56.0
work	30	20.0	76.0
college	30	20.0	96.0
Other	6	4.0	100.0
Willing to use your credit card on web			
Yes	60	40.0	40.0
No	90	60.0	100.0
Purchased anything online			
Yes	132	88.0	88.0
No	18	12.0	100.0
Frequently purchase things online			
More than once a month	30	20.0	20.0
Once a month	48	32.0	52.0
At least once in six months	36	24.0	76.0
At least once a year	18	12.0	88.0
Never	18	12.0	100.0
Concerned abuse of credit card and other			
Yes	66	44.0	44.0
no	84	56.0	100.0

Table 2 presents the results of three independent samples t-tests, comparing the means of three groups (Security Awareness, Privacy Awareness, and Protection Awareness) in terms of their variances. The tests were conducted twice: once assuming equal variances between the groups and once without this assumption. The results show that, for all three groups, the assumption of equal variances was not met. The T-test for Equality of Means reveals that the computed T-values for all three groups are statistically significant (with p-values < 0.05), indicating that there exists a notable disparity in the means of these groups. Moreover, a higher T-value signifies a larger discrepancy in the means among the groups.

Table 2. Result of independent sample between gender and the study variables

Gender		Levene's Test for Assumption of Equal Variances		T-Test for Equality of Means		Sig. (2-Tailed)
		F	Sig.	T	df	
Security Awareness	Equal variances assumed	5.275	.023	2.526	148	.013
	Equal variances not assumed			2.502	134.844	.014
Privacy Awareness	Equal variances assumed	1.964	.163	4.782	148	.000
	Equal variances not assumed			4.729	131.424	.000
Protection Awareness	Equal variances assumed	2.698	.103	3.968	148	.000
	Equal variances not assumed			3.908	122.666	.000

Table 3 presents the results of three independent samples t-tests, comparing the means of three groups (Security Awareness, Privacy Awareness, and Protection Awareness) in terms of their variances. The results show that, the T-test for Equality of Means shows that the T-values computed for all three groups are statistically significant, with p-values less than 0.05, indicating a significant contrast in the means of the groups. Additionally, a higher T-value suggests a more significant disparity in the means among the groups.

Table 3. Result of independent sample between email account and the study variables

Email Account		Levene's Test for Assumption of Equal Variances		T-Test for Equality of Means		Sig. (2-Tailed)
		F	Sig.	T	df	
Security Awareness	Equal variances assumed	6.412	.012	3.478	148	.001
	Equal variances not assumed			17.093	143.000	.000
Privacy Awareness	Equal variances assumed	8.013	.005	3.994	148	.000
	Equal variances not assumed			19.632	143.000	.000
Protection Awareness	Equal variances assumed	7.536	.007	4.807	148	.000
	Equal variances not assumed			23.625	143.000	.000

Table 4 shows the results of three independent samples t-tests for "Security Awareness", "Privacy Awareness", and "Protection Awareness". The table includes information on equal variances and Levene's Test. The results indicate a significant difference in means for "Security Awareness" (p=.031, equal variances assumed, p=.056, not assumed), but no significant differences for "Privacy Awareness" (p=.590) and "Protection Awareness" (p=.075).

Table 4. Result of independent sample between credit card users and the study variables

Credit Card Users		Levene's Test for Assumption of Equal Variances		T-Test for Equality of Means		Sig. (2-Tailed)
		F	Sig.	T	df	
Security Awareness	Equal variances assumed	40.556	.000	-2.178	148	.031
	Equal variances not assumed			-1.936	79.934	.056
Privacy Awareness	Equal variances assumed	11.871	.001	-.540	148	.590
	Equal variances not assumed			-.493	89.130	.623
Protection Awareness	Equal variances assumed	16.679	.000	-1.990	148	.048
	Equal variances not assumed			-1.803	86.039	.075

Table 5 shows 3 independent samples t-tests for 3 variables: Security Awareness, Privacy Awareness, and Protection Awareness. The table reports the significance level for each test assuming equal variances among the samples and not assuming equal variances. A significance level of .05 or less is often used to determine statistical significance. Results show that there is a significant difference in means for all 3 variables when not assuming equal variances, but not significant when assuming equal variances. This suggests that there is a significant difference in the means of the 3 awareness variables with unequal variances.

Table 5. Result of independent sample between purchased online and the study variables

Purchased Online		Levene's Test for Assumption of Equal Variances		T-Test for Equality of Means		Sig. (2-Tailed)
		F	Sig.	T	df	
Security Awareness	Equal variances assumed	2.664	.105	6.973	148	.000
	Equal variances not assumed			5.778	19.927	.000
Privacy Awareness	Equal variances assumed	4.877	.029	8.317	148	.000
	Equal variances not assumed			6.262	19.239	.000
Protection Awareness	Equal variances assumed	10.439	.002	10.827	148	.000
	Equal variances not assumed			7.397	18.689	.000

Table 6 reports the outcomes of 3 independent samples t-tests for the variables Security Awareness, Privacy Awareness, and Protection Awareness. Two tests were conducted for each variable assuming equal variances among the samples and not assuming equal variances. The reported significance level (2-tailed) determines statistical significance, and a significance level of .05 or less is often used. The results of both tests, assuming equal variances and not assuming equal variances, are not significant for all 3 variables, suggesting that there is not a statistically significant contrast in the means of the 3 awareness variables, regardless of the assumption of equal variances among the samples.

Table 6. Result of independent sample between concerned about credit card and the study variables

Concerned About Credit Card		Levene's Test for Assumption of Equal Variances		T-Test for Equality of Means		Sig. (2-Tailed)
		F	Sig.	T	df	
Security Awareness	Equal variances assumed	3.207	.075	-.413	148	.680
	Equal variances not assumed			-.415	142.036	.679
Privacy Awareness	Equal variances assumed	1.332	.250	-1.084	148	.280
	Equal variances not assumed			-1.049	118.038	.296
Protection Awareness	Equal variances assumed	.284	.595	-.027	148	.979
	Equal variances not assumed			-.026	122.659	.979

Table 7 shows the results of a one-way ANOVA test, which is used to conduct if there is a significant difference in the mean scores of a dependent variable (security awareness, privacy awareness, and protection awareness) between different levels of an independent variable (internet usage). The results show that there is a significant difference in the mean scores of security awareness, privacy awareness, and protection awareness between the levels of internet usage ($p < 0.05$). This suggests that internet usage has an impact on the level of awareness of security, privacy, and protection of data.

Table 7. Result of one-way ANOVA between internet usage and the study variables

Internet Usage		Sum of Squares	df	Mean Square	F	Sig.
Security Awareness	Between Groups	16.474	2	8.237	16.279	.000
	Within Groups	74.380	147	.506		
	Total	90.854	149			
Privacy Awareness	Between Groups	16.497	2	8.248	18.686	.000
	Within Groups	64.888	147	.441		
	Total	81.384	149			
Protection Awareness	Between Groups	13.953	2	6.976	15.378	.000
	Within Groups	66.688	147	.454		
	Total	80.640	149			

Table 8 shows Duncan's multiple range test results for the awareness level of data security and the method used to access the internet. The test determined significant differences between the mean awareness levels of data security for groups defined by computer, both, and smartphone internet access methods. The mean awareness level of data security is highest for smartphone users (4.35), followed by both users (3.83), and computer users (3.00). The significance level is 1.000 for all comparisons, indicating statistically significant differences between the groups.

Table 8. Duncan result for the awareness level of data security and internet usage

Duncan[a,b]				
Use to Access Internet	N	Subset for Alpha = 0.05		
		1	2	3
Computer	6	3.0000		
Both	72		3.8333	
Smartphone	72			4.3500
Sig.		1.000	1.000	1.000

Table 9 shows the results of Duncan multiple range test between the Awareness level of data Privacy and Internet Usage. The groups compared are Computer, Both, and Smartphone, which are the types of devices used to access the internet. The Sig. column shows the significance level of the difference between the means of each group. For all comparisons, the significance level is 1.000, which is greater than the alpha level of 0.05. This means that there is no significant difference in the Awareness level of data Privacy between the groups of Internet Usage. The means show the average level of Awareness of data Privacy for each group. The group with the highest mean is Smartphone with 4.4167.

Table 9. Duncan result for the awareness level of data privacy and internet usage

Duncan[a,b]				
Use to Access Internet	N	Subset for Alpha = 0.05		
		1	2	3
Computer	6	3.0000		
Both	72		3.9286	
Smartphone	72			4.4167
Sig.		1.000	1.000	1.000

Table 10 shows the results of a Duncan test, which is a statistical test used to compare the means of two or more groups. The test was used to examine the level of awareness about data protection and internet usage. The results indicate that there is a significant difference in the mean awareness level between the group of people who use computers to access the internet and the group of people who use smartphones ($p = 0.231$). The mean awareness level for the computer group is 3.000 and the mean awareness level for the smartphone group is 4.5208. However, there is no significant difference in the mean awareness level between the group of people who use both computers and smartphones to access the internet and the smartphone group ($p = 1.000$). The mean awareness level for each group is 4.2292. It's important to note that the group sizes are unequal, and the harmonic mean of the group sizes was used, so the type I error levels may not be guaranteed.

Table 10. Duncan result for the awareness level of data protection and internet usage

Duncan[a,b]			
Use to Access Internet	N	Subset for Alpha = 0.05	
		1	2
Computer	6	3.0000	
Both	72		4.2292
Smartphone	72		4.5208
Sig.		1.000	.231

Table 11 shows the results of a One-Way ANOVA test, which was performed to examine the relationship between the time spend on the internet and three study variables: Security Awareness, Privacy Awareness, and Protection Awareness. For Security Awareness, the Between Groups SS is 9.352 and the Within Groups SS is 81.503. The F-value of 4.159 and a significance level of .003 indicate that there is a significant relationship between the time spent on the internet and security awareness. Similarly, for Privacy Awareness and Protection Awareness, the F-values of 7.785 and 6.581 respectively, and the significance levels of .000 indicate that there is a significant relationship between the time spent on the internet and privacy and protection awareness.

Table 11. Result of one-way ANOVA between time spend on internet and the study variables

Time Spent on Internet in a Day		Sum of Squares	df	Mean Square	F	Sig.
Security Awareness	Between Groups	9.352	4	2.338		
	Within Groups	81.503	145	.562	4.159	.003
	Total	90.854	149			
Privacy Awareness	Between Groups	14.388	4	3.597		
	Within Groups	66.996	145	.462	7.785	.000
	Total	81.384	149			
Protection Awareness	Between Groups	12.390	4	3.098		
	Within Groups	68.250	145	.471	6.581	.000
	Total	80.640	149			

Table 12 compares mean data security awareness scores for different levels of internet usage. Those who spend <1hr or 2-4hrs have similar scores (3.0000 and 3.9500), while those who spend 1-2hrs or 4-8hrs score higher (4.0571 and 4.2000). Those who spend >8hrs score highest (4.3333). Results indicate no significant difference between <1hr and 2-4hr groups (p=1.000), but significant difference between others (p<.05).

Table 12. Duncan result for the awareness level of data security and internet usage

Duncan[a,b]			
Time Spent on Internet in a Day	N	Subset for Alpha = 0.05	
		1	2
< 1 hour	6	3.0000	
2-4 hours	48		3.9500
1-2 hours	42		4.0571
4-8 hours	36		4.2000
> 8 hours	18		4.3333
Sig.		1.000	.179

Table 13 presents the mean scores of data privacy awareness for different levels of internet usage. Individuals who spend less than 1 hour have a score of 3.0000, while those who spend 1-2 hours or 4-8 hours have similar scores (3.8980 and 4.1667, respectively). Those who spend 2-4 hours or more than 8 hours have higher scores (4.2679 and 4.5714, respectively). There is no significant difference between <1hr and 1-2hr groups (p=1.000), but significant differences exist between other groups (p<.05).

Table 13. Duncan result for the awareness level of data privacy and internet usage

Duncan[a,b]				
Time Spent on Internet in a Day	**N**	**Subset for Alpha = 0.05**		
		1	**2**	**3**
< 1 hour	6	3.0000		
1-2 hours	42		3.8980	
4-8 hours	36		4.1667	4.1667
2-4 hours	48		4.2679	4.2679
> 8 hours	18			4.5714
Sig.		1.000	.137	.103

Table 14 compares the means of different levels of internet usage in relation to data protection awareness. Those who spend less than 1 hour have a score of 3.0000, while those who spend 1-2 hours have a higher score of 4.2500. Those who spend 2-4 hours or 4-8 hours have even higher scores (4.3750 and 4.4167, respectively), and those who spend more than 8 hours have the highest score (4.5833). There is no significant difference between <1hr and 1-2hr groups (p=1.000), but significant differences exist between other groups (p<.05).

Table 14. Duncan result for the awareness level of data protection and internet usage

Duncan[a,b]			
Time Spent on Internet in a Day	**N**	**Subset for Alpha = 0.05**	
		1	**2**
< 1 hour	6	3.0000	
1-2 hours	42		4.2500
2-4 hours	48		4.3750
4-8 hours	36		4.4167
> 8 hours	18		4.5833
Sig.		1.000	.202

Table 15 presents the results of a one-way analysis of variance (ANOVA) examining the relationship between email account type and three study variables: security awareness, privacy awareness, and protection awareness. The ANOVA tests whether the means of the study variables are equal across the different email account types. The "Sig." column provides the p-value, which is the probability of observing the test statistic if the null hypothesis (that the means are equal) is true. In this table, all p-values are less than .05, which suggests that the differences in the study variables between email account types are statistically significant.

Table 15. Result of one-way ANOVA between email account type and the study variables

Email Account Type		Sum of Squares	df	Mean Square	F	Sig.
Security Awareness	Between Groups	10.585	3	3.528	6.417	.000
	Within Groups	80.270	146	.550		
	Total	90.854	149			
Privacy Awareness	Between Groups	7.424	3	2.475	4.885	.003
	Within Groups	73.961	146	.507		
	Total	81.384	149			
Protection Awareness	Between Groups	12.669	3	4.223	9.071	.000
	Within Groups	67.971	146	.466		
	Total	80.640	149			

Table 16 reports results of a Duncan post-hoc test after a one-way ANOVA, comparing different email account types. The "college" type was found significantly different from "work", "home", and "other" types, with a p-value of 1.000. The comparison between "work" and "home" types was not significant, with a p-value of .059.

Table 16. Duncan result for the awareness level of data security and email account type

Duncan[a,b]			
Email Account Type	N	Subset for Alpha = 0.05	
		1	2
Work	30	3.8400	
Home	84	3.9429	
College	30	4.3600	
Other	6		5.0000
Sig.		.059	1.000

Table 17 shows the results of a Duncan test examining data privacy awareness and email account type. The results indicate no significant difference in awareness between work and college accounts (p=0.206), but a significant difference between home and other accounts (p=1.000). The highest mean for awareness was found in the home account group (mean = 4.1939).

Table 17. Duncan result for the awareness level of data privacy and email account type

Duncan[a,b]			
Email Account Type	**N**	**Subset for Alpha = 0.05**	
		1	**2**
Work	30	3.8571	
College	30	4.0286	
Home	84	4.1939	
Other	6		5.0000
Sig.		.206	1.000

Table 18 presents the result of a Duncan test for awareness level of data protection and email account type. The test found that the groups with "Home" and "College" email account type have a higher mean score for awareness level of data protection compared to the group with a "Work" email account type. The group with an "Other" email account type has the highest mean score. However, not all significance level values are below 0.05, indicating some differences in mean scores are not statistically significant.

Table 18. Duncan result for the awareness level of data protection and email account type

Duncan[a,b]				
Email Account Type	**N**	**Subset for Alpha = 0.05**		
		1	**2**	**3**
Work	30	3.8500		
Home	84	4.3214	4.3214	
College	30		4.6500	4.6500
Other	6			5.0000
Sig.		.050	.171	.145

Table 19 presents the results of a one-way ANOVA test between the frequency of purchasing things online and the three study variables: Security Awareness, Privacy Awareness, and Protection Awareness. In conclusion, the results of the one-way ANOVA test suggest that the frequency of purchasing things online has a significant effect on the awareness levels of data security, privacy, and protection.

Table 19. Result of one-way ANOVA between frequently purchase things online and the study variables

Frequently Purchase Things Online		Sum of Squares	df	Mean Square	F	Sig.
Security Awareness	Between Groups	31.142	4	7.786	18.906	.000
	Within Groups	59.712	145	.412		
	Total	90.854	149			
Privacy Awareness	Between Groups	39.115	4	9.779	33.545	.000
	Within Groups	42.269	145	.292		
	Total	81.384	149			
Protection Awareness	Between Groups	42.690	4	10.673	40.778	.000
	Within Groups	37.950	145	.262		
	Total	80.640	149			

DISCUSSION OF THE STUDY

The section of the data analysis report that presents the findings is a crucial part of any research study as it provides insights into the research question and sheds light on the level of awareness of the respondents regarding the topic under investigation. In this particular study, the focus was on data privacy, security, and protection of e-commerce transactions. The study aimed to collect data from a representative sample of individuals, and the results revealed that an equal number of male and female participants responded to the survey. Most respondents were between the ages of 21-30 and held a college degree. The use of both smartphones and desktop computers to access the internet was prevalent among the respondents, and most of them reported owning smartphones and using them for an average of 2-4 hours daily. Furthermore, the majority of respondents reported using the internet for more than two decades. One interesting finding of the study was that despite having email addresses, the respondents were hesitant to use their credit cards for online transactions. This finding indicates that while internet usage has become a part of everyday life for many individuals, there is still a level of distrust when it comes to online transactions, particularly in terms of the security and privacy of their data. Moreover, the study compared the mean scores of different age groups concerning their awareness of data protection and revealed that individuals over the age of 50 had a significantly higher mean score regarding their level of awareness of data protection than the other age groups. This finding emphasizes the importance of raising awareness about data protection and privacy across all age groups to safeguard personal data.

The reluctance of respondents to use their credit cards for online transactions is a cause for concern, as it indicates that there is still a significant level of distrust regarding the security and privacy of personal data online. This finding is in line with previous studies that have shown that consumers are often concerned about the security of their personal data when making online purchases. The reasons behind this distrust may vary, but it could be due to the perception that online transactions are more vulnerable to data breaches or that their personal information is not sufficiently protected. This hesitation to make online purchases could have a significant impact on the growth of e-commerce. To address this issue, e-commerce companies need to take measures to build trust with their customers, such as improving their security systems, being transparent about their data collection and usage policies, and providing clear and concise information about their privacy practices. Additionally, e-commerce companies should invest in educating consumers about the measures they take to ensure the security and privacy of their data, which could help alleviate concerns and increase consumer confidence in online transactions.

The comparison of the mean scores of different age groups in terms of their awareness of data protection is a crucial finding of the study. The study collected data from 150 individuals, with an equal distribution between male and female respondents, most of whom were between the ages of 21-30 and held a college degree. The results of the study revealed that individuals over the age of 50 had a significantly higher mean score regarding their level of awareness of data protection than the other age groups. This finding emphasizes the importance of raising awareness about data protection and privacy across all age groups to safeguard personal data. In addition, the study found that users who spent more than two hours browsing the internet on their smartphones and those who had accessed the internet for less than five years were more aware of data privacy, security, and protection. This suggests that increased exposure to online activities can enhance one's awareness of data privacy and security issues. Respondents with official email accounts and those who made only one online purchase per month were also more concerned about their data privacy, security, and protection, indicating that certain online activities may trigger more awareness about data privacy and security issues. Overall, the insights gained from this study can inform policies and strategies related to data protection and privacy, especially for individuals who are at higher risk of being affected by data breaches and other privacy issues. Policymakers and researchers can use these insights to develop educational programs and awareness campaigns that target specific age groups and online activities to raise awareness about data protection and privacy.

CONCLUSION

In conclusion, the study aimed to understand the awareness level of internet users on data privacy, security, and protection. Results ascertained the significant difference in accordance with the level of awareness of internet users in regard to data privacy, security, and protection. Furthermore, results revealed that different email account types and age groups have an impact on the awareness level of internet users. It was found that home email users were more aware of data privacy and security compared to work, college, and other email users. Additionally, younger internet users were found to have a higher awareness level compared to older users. Furthermore, the results of the one-way ANOVA and Duncan tests showed a significant difference in the awareness level of internet users regarding data privacy, security, and protection.

The study's implications for the general public and policymakers are significant, considering the growing reliance on the internet and big data production. Heightened awareness regarding privacy, security, and protection of personal information is crucial. The findings underscore the need for awareness campaigns. Policymakers, organizations, and businesses can use the study to evaluate privacy policies and enhance user data protection. In summary, this study comprehensively examines internet users' awareness of data privacy, security, and protection, emphasizing the necessity of awareness and measures to safeguard personal data.

Managerial Implications

The study emphasizes the importance of data privacy, security, and protection for organizations and businesses. To achieve this, they should develop and implement effective privacy policies and conduct regular reviews to ensure compliance with regulations and best practices. Adequate training for employees and raising awareness among customers and stakeholders are also crucial. Policymakers should develop more robust data protection regulations and provide regular updates to ensure businesses are aware of their responsibilities. These measures are essential for business growth and sustainability in the digital age.

Academic Implications

The study's academic implications are significant as it contributes to the body of literature on data privacy, security, and protection. The research's findings provide insights into the factors that impact individuals' awareness of data privacy, security, and protection, such as age and email account type. This study can serve as a basis for future research to explore these factors further and identify strategies to increase awareness. The findings also highlight the need for further research to evaluate the effectiveness of awareness-raising campaigns and privacy policies. The study's academic implications extend to the research methodology used, which can be replicated in future research, and the use of statistical analysis tools to draw meaningful conclusions. The study emphasizes the need for further research to explore the factors that influence awareness levels and evaluate the effectiveness of awareness-raising campaigns and privacy policies in protecting personal data. The study's findings can inform policy and practice in this area and provide a foundation for future research.

REFERENCES

Abbas, A., Fatima, A., Arrona-Palacios, A., Haruna, H., & Hosseini, S. (2021). Research ethics dilemma in higher education: Impact of internet access, ethical controls, and teaching factors on student plagiarism. *Education and Information Technologies*, *26*(5), 6109–6121. doi:10.100710639-021-10595-z

Al Omar, A., Jamil, A. K., Khandakar, A., Uzzal, A. R., Bosri, R., Mansoor, N., & Rahman, M. S. (2021). A transparent and privacy-preserving healthcare platform with novel smart contract for smart cities. *IEEE Access : Practical Innovations, Open Solutions*, *9*, 90738–90749. doi:10.1109/ACCESS.2021.3089601

Alalwan, A. A., Rana, N. P., Dwivedi, Y. K., & Algharabat, R. (2017). Social media in marketing: A review and analysis of the existing literature. *Telematics and Informatics*, *34*(7), 1177–1190. doi:10.1016/j.tele.2017.05.008

Altman, I. (1975). *The environment and social behavior: privacy, personal space, territory, and crowding*. Brooks/Cole Publishing Company.

Alzaqebah, M., Jawarneh, S., Mohammad, R. M. A., Alsmadi, M. K., & Almarashdeh, I. (2021). Improved multi-verse optimizer feature selection technique with application to phishing, spam, and denial of service attacks. *International Journal of Communication Networks and Information Security*, *13*(1), 76–81.

Arokiaraj, D., Ganeshkumar, C., & Paul, P. V. (2020). Innovative management system for environmental sustainability practices among Indian auto-component manufacturers. *International Journal of Business Innovation and Research*, *23*(2), 168–182. doi:10.1504/IJBIR.2020.110095

Awad, N. F., & Krishnan, M. S. (2006). The personalization privacy paradox: An empirical evaluation of information transparency and the willingness to be profiled online for personalization. *Management Information Systems Quarterly*, *30*(1), 13–28. doi:10.2307/25148715

Bansal, G., & Gefen, D. (2010). The impact of personal dispositions on information sensitivity, privacy concern and trust in disclosing health information online. *Decision Support Systems*, *49*(2), 138–150. doi:10.1016/j.dss.2010.01.010

Brandeis, L., & Warren, S. (1890). The right to privacy. *Harvard Law Review*, *4*(5), 193–220. doi:10.2307/1321160

Burgoon, J. K. (1982). Privacy and communication. *Annals of the International Communication Association*, *6*(1), 206–249. doi:10.1080/23808985.1982.11678499

Cavoukian, A. (2012). Privacy by design: origins, meaning, and prospects for assuring privacy and trust in the information era. In *Privacy protection measures and technologies in business organizations: aspects and standards* (pp. 170–208). IGI Global. doi:10.4018/978-1-61350-501-4.ch007

Chen, Y., & Cheung, A. S. (2017). The transparent self under big data profiling: Privacy and Chinese legislation on the social credit system. *SSRN*, *12*, 356. doi:10.2139srn.2992537

Choudhary, N., David, A., & Feleen, F. (2021). Employee Engagement and Commitment in Service Sector. *Wesleyan Journal of Research, 13*(4.7), 107-112.

David, A., Ganesh Kumar, C., & Jeganathan, G. S. (2022). Impact of Food Safety and Standards Regulation on Food Business Operators. In *Au Virtual International Conference* (pp. 355-363). Academic Press.

Feleen, F., & David, A. (2021). A Comparative Study of Work From Home vs Work From Office: Preference of Women Employees in IT Industry. *Design Engineering (London)*, *7*(1), 5763–5775.

Feleen, F., David, A., Choudhary, N., & Vivekanand, N. (2021). *Impact of Psychological Capacities on the Work-Life Balance of Entrepreneurs*. Academic Press.

Furger, R. (1999). On the Web You Have No Secrets. *PC World*, *17*(7), 29–31.

Ganeshkumar, C., David, A., Sankar, J. G., & Saginala, M. (2023). Application of Drone Technology in Agriculture: A Predictive Forecasting of Pest and Disease Incidence. In *Applying Drone Technologies and Robotics for Agricultural Sustainability* (pp. 50–81). IGI Global.

Hair, J. F., Black, W. C., Babin, B. J., & Anderson, R. E. (2014). *Multivariate data analysis* (7th ed.). Pearson.

Jeganathan, G. S., & David, A. (2022). Determination of Hospitality Services Quality and Customer Satisfaction-A Holserv Approach. In *Au Virtual International Conference* (pp. 325-334). Academic Press.

Jeganathan, G. S., David, A., & Ganesh Kumar, C. (2022). Adaptation of Blockchain Technology In HRM. *Korea Review of International Studies*, 10-22.

Kalburgi, N. K., David, A., & Muralidhar, L. B. (2023). Understanding the Perceptions of Students towards YouTube as a Learning Tool-An Empirical Approach. *Central European Management Journal,* 2336-2693.

Kapoor, K. K., Tamilmani, K., Rana, N. P., Patil, P., Dwivedi, Y. K., & Nerur, S. (2018). Advances in social media research: Past, present and future. *Information Systems Frontiers*, *20*(3), 531–558. doi:10.100710796-017-9810-y

Kim, D., & Benbasat, I. (2003). Trust-related arguments in internet stores: A framework for evaluation. *Journal of Electronic Commerce Research*, *4*(2), 49–64.

Koops, B. J., Newell, B. C., Timan, T., Skorvanek, I., Chokrevski, T., & Galic, M. (2016). A typology of privacy. *U. Pa. J. Int'l L.*, *38*, 483.

Labrecque, L. I., Markos, E., & Darmody, A. (2021). Addressing online behavioral advertising and privacy implications: A comparison of passive versus active learning approaches. *Journal of Marketing Education*, *43*(1), 43–58. doi:10.1177/0273475319828788

Lakshman, K., & David, A. (n.d.). *Senior Citizens' Perceptions on E-banking Services*. Exceller Books.

Lee, H., Kang, S., & Lee, U. (2022). Understanding privacy risks and perceived benefits in open dataset collection for mobile affective computing. *Proceedings of the ACM on Interactive, Mobile, Wearable and Ubiquitous Technologies*, *6*(2), 1–26. doi:10.1145/3534623

Li, Q. (2011b). Privacy in social networks: An empirical analysis. *The Journal of Privacy and Confidentiality*, *3*(1), 1–23.

Ma, C., Li, J., Ding, M., Yang, H. H., Shu, F., Quek, T. Q., & Poor, H. V. (2020). On safeguarding privacy and security in the framework of federated learning. *IEEE Network*, *34*(4), 242–248. doi:10.1109/MNET.001.1900506

Ma, X. (2022). IS professionals' information security behaviors in Chinese IT organizations for information security protection. *Information Processing & Management*, *59*(1), 102744. doi:10.1016/j.ipm.2021.102744

Madaan, G., Swapna, H. R., Kumar, A., Singh, A., & David, A. (2021). Enactment of sustainable technovations on healthcare sectors. *Asia Pacific Journal of Health Management*, *16*(3), 184–192. doi:10.24083/apjhm.v16i3.989

Malin, B. A. (2005). An evaluation of the current state of genomic data privacy protection technology and a roadmap for the future. *Journal of the American Medical Informatics Association : JAMIA*, *12*(1), 28–34. doi:10.1197/jamia.M1603 PMID:15492030

Mangku, D. G. S., Yuliartini, N. P. R., Suastika, I. N., & Wirawan, I. G. M. A. S. (2021). The Personal Data Protection of Internet Users in Indonesia. *Journal of Southwest Jiaotong University*, *56*(1), 23. doi:10.35741/issn.0258-2724.56.1.23

Markos, E., Milne, G. R., & Peltier, J. W. (2017). Information sensitivity and willingness to provide continua: A comparative privacy study of the United States and Brazil. *Journal of Public Policy & Marketing*, *36*(1), 79–96. doi:10.1509/jppm.15.159

Milne, G. R., Pettinico, G., Hajjat, F. M., & Markos, E. (2017). Information sensitivity typology: Mapping the degree and type of risk consumers perceive in personal data sharing. *The Journal of Consumer Affairs*, *51*(1), 133–161. doi:10.1111/joca.12111

Milne, R., Morley, K. I., Howard, H., Niemiec, E., Nicol, D., Critchley, C., Prainsack, B., Vears, D., Smith, J., Steed, C., Bevan, P., Atutornu, J., Farley, L., Goodhand, P., Thorogood, A., Kleiderman, E., & Middleton, A. (2019). Trust in genomic data sharing among members of the general public in the UK, USA, Canada and Australia. *Human Genetics*, *138*(11-12), 1237–1246. doi:10.100700439-019-02062-0 PMID:31531740

Nambiar, R., Bhardwaj, R., Sethi, A., & Vargheese, R. (2013, October). *A look at challenges and opportunities of big data analytics in healthcare. In 2013 IEEE international conference on Big Data*. IEEE.

Nandi, M. L., Nandi, S., Moya, H., & Kaynak, H. (2020). Blockchain technology-enabled supply chain systems and supply chain performance: A resource-based view. *Supply Chain Management*, *25*(6), 841–862. doi:10.1108/SCM-12-2019-0444

Nihmathullah, Z., Ramasamy, R., & Raj David, A. (2022). *Event Impact Assessment: A Case of Puducherry*. Book Rivers.

Nugent, N., & Rhinard, M. (2015). *The European commission*. Bloomsbury Publishing. doi:10.1007/978-1-137-54333-2

Nunnally, J. C. (1967). *Psychometric theory*. McGraw-Hill.

O'Neil, D. (2001). Analysis of Internet users' level of online privacy concerns. *Social Science Computer Review*, *19*(1), 17–31. doi:10.1177/089443930101900103

ParneM. D.ChandrikaK. G.DavidA. (1979). General Adjustments and Work-Satisfaction Of Indian Expatriates. SSRN.

Pavlou, P. A., & Fygenson, M. (2006). Understanding and predicting electronic commerce adoption: An extension of the theory of planned behavior. *Management Information Systems Quarterly*, *30*(1), 115–143. doi:10.2307/25148720

Renn, O., Laubichler, M., Lucas, K., Kröger, W., Schanze, J., Scholz, R. W., & Schweizer, P. J. (2022). Systemic risks from different perspectives. *Risk Analysis*, *42*(9), 1902–1920. doi:10.1111/risa.13657 PMID:33331037

Rohm, A. J., & Milne, G. R. (2004). Just what the doctor ordered: The role of information sensitivity and trust in reducing medical information privacy concern. *Journal of Business Research*, *57*(9), 1000–1011. doi:10.1016/S0148-2963(02)00345-4

Sagiroglu, S., & Sinanc, D. (2013, May). Big data: A review. In 2013 international conference on collaboration technologies and systems (CTS) (pp. 42-47). IEEE. doi:10.1109/CTS.2013.6567202

Sankar, J. G., & Kiruba Sagar, M, V. (2020). Examining the Risk Factor Associated with UTAUT MODEL. *Solid State Technology*, 1196–1198.

Schomakers, E. M., Lidynia, C., Müllmann, D., & Ziefle, M. (2019). Internet users' perceptions of information sensitivity–insights from Germany. *International Journal of Information Management*, *46*, 142–150. doi:10.1016/j.ijinfomgt.2018.11.018

Shiau, W. L., Dwivedi, Y. K., & Yang, H. S. (2017). Co-citation and cluster analyses of extant literature on social networks. *International Journal of Information Management*, *37*(5), 390–399. doi:10.1016/j.ijinfomgt.2017.04.007

Slepchuk, A. N., Milne, G. R., & Swani, K. (2022). Overcoming privacy concerns in consumers' use of health information technologies: A justice framework. *Journal of Business Research*, *141*, 782–793. doi:10.1016/j.jbusres.2021.11.073

Smith, H. J., Dinev, T., & Xu, H. (2011). Information privacy research: An interdisciplinary review. *Management Information Systems Quarterly*, *35*(4), 989–1016. doi:10.2307/41409970

Srivastava, V., Singh, A. K., David, A., & Rai, N. (2022). Modelling student employability on an academic basis: A supervised machine learning approach with R. In *Handbook of Research on Innovative Management Using AI in Industry 5.0* (pp. 179–191). IGI Global. doi:10.4018/978-1-7998-8497-2.ch012

Stahl, B. C., Andreou, A., Brey, P., Hatzakis, T., Kirichenko, A., Macnish, K., Laulhé Shaelou, S., Patel, A., Ryan, M., & Wright, D. (2021). Artificial intelligence for human flourishing–Beyond principles for machine learning. *Journal of Business Research*, *124*, 374–388. doi:10.1016/j.jbusres.2020.11.030

Sudhakar, B. D., Kattepogu, N., & David, A. (2017). Marketing assistance and digital branding-an insight for technology up-gradation for MSME's. *International Journal of Management Studies & Research*, *5*(1), 2455–1562.

Swani, K., Milne, G. R., & Slepchuk, A. N. (2021). Revisiting trust and privacy concern in consumers' perceptions of marketing information management practices: Replication and extension. *Journal of Interactive Marketing*, *56*(1), 137–158. doi:10.1016/j.intmar.2021.03.001

Tabrizchi, H., & Kuchaki Rafsanjani, M. (2020). A survey on security challenges in cloud computing: Issues, threats, and solutions. *The Journal of Supercomputing*, *76*(12), 9493–9532. doi:10.100711227-020-03213-1

Tarhini, A., Alalwan, A. A., Shammout, A. B., & Al-Badi, A. (2019). An analysis of the factors affecting mobile commerce adoption in developing countries: Towards an integrated model. *Review of International Business and Strategy,* 29(3), 157-179. doi:10.1108/RIBS-10-2018-0092.

Tavani, H. T., & Moor, J. H. (2001). Privacy protection, control of information, and privacy-enhancing technologies. *Computers & Society*, *31*(1), 6–11. doi:10.1145/572277.572278

Tertulino, R., Antunes, N., & Morais, H. (2023). Privacy in electronic health records: A systematic mapping study. *Journal of Public Health (Berlin)*, 1–20. doi:10.100710389-022-01795-z

Trepte, S., & Masur, P. K. (2020). Need for privacy. Encyclopedia of personality and individual differences, 3132-3135.

Westin, A. F. (1967). Special report: Legal safeguards to insure privacy in a computer society. *Communications of the ACM*, *10*(9), 533–537. doi:10.1145/363566.363579

Yakubu, A. M., & Chen, Y. P. P. (2020). Ensuring privacy and security of genomic data and functionalities. *Briefings in Bioinformatics*, *21*(2), 511–526. doi:10.1093/bib/bbz013 PMID:30759195

Zhang, J., & Letaief, K. B. (2019). Mobile edge intelligence and computing for the internet of vehicles. *Proceedings of the IEEE, 108*(2), 246–261. doi:10.1109/JPROC.2019.2947490

ADDITIONAL READING

Chawla, N., & Kumar, B. (2022). E-commerce and consumer protection in India: The emerging trend. *Journal of Business Ethics, 180*(2), 581–604. doi:10.100710551-021-04884-3 PMID:34257470

Gouthier, M. H., Nennstiel, C., Kern, N., & Wendel, L. (2022). The more the better? Data disclosure between the conflicting priorities of privacy concerns, information sensitivity and personalization in e-commerce. *Journal of Business Research, 148*, 174–189. doi:10.1016/j.jbusres.2022.04.034

Haddara, M., Salazar, A., & Langseth, M. (2023). Exploring the Impact of GDPR on Big Data Analytics Operations in the E-Commerce Industry. *Procedia Computer Science, 219*, 767–777. doi:10.1016/j.procs.2023.01.350

Maseeh, H. I., Jebarajakirthy, C., Pentecost, R., Arli, D., Weaven, S., & Ashaduzzaman, M. (2021). Privacy concerns in e-commerce: A multilevel meta-analysis. *Psychology and Marketing, 38*(10), 1779–1798. doi:10.1002/mar.21493

Picoto, W. N., Abreu, J. C., & Martins, P. (2023). Integrating the Internet of Things Into E-Commerce: The Role of Trust, Privacy, and Data Confidentiality Concerns in Consumer Adoption. *International Journal of E-Business Research, 19*(1), 1–18. doi:10.4018/IJEBR.321647

Vinoth, S., Vemula, H. L., Haralayya, B., Mamgain, P., Hasan, M. F., & Naved, M. (2022). Application of cloud computing in banking and e-commerce and related security threats. *Materials Today: Proceedings, 51*, 2172–2175. doi:10.1016/j.matpr.2021.11.121

Wu, Z., Shen, S., Zhou, H., Li, H., Lu, C., & Zou, D. (2021). An effective approach for the protection of user commodity viewing privacy in e-commerce website. *Knowledge-Based Systems, 220*, 106952. doi:10.1016/j.knosys.2021.106952

Yong, S. (2021). The Impact of Big Data Security on E-commerce in the Context of Cloud Data. In *Application of Intelligent Systems in Multi-modal Information Analytics: 2021 International Conference on Multi-modal Information Analytics (MMIA 2021),* Volume 1 (pp. 479-484). Springer International Publishing. 10.1007/978-3-030-74811-1_70

Zhu, R., Srivastava, A., & Sutanto, J. (2020). Privacy-deprived e-commerce: The efficacy of consumer privacy policies on China's e-commerce websites from a legal perspective. *Information Technology & People, 33*(6), 1601–1626. doi:10.1108/ITP-03-2019-0117

KEY TERMS AND DEFINITIONS

Data Privacy: Data privacy refers to the protection and control of an individual's personal information or data, ensuring that it is collected, stored, processed, and used in a manner that respects their rights and maintains confidentiality.

Data Protection: Data protection refers to the practices, policies, and measures put in place to ensure the privacy, integrity, and security of personal data. It involves the safeguarding of personal information from unauthorized access, loss, damage, or misuse.

Data Security: Data security refers to the protection of digital data from unauthorized access, use, disclosure, alteration, or destruction. It involves the implementation of measures and protocols to safeguard data integrity, confidentiality, and availability.

Electronic Commerce: Electronic Commerce, commonly referred to as e-commerce, is the process of conducting business activities such as buying and selling goods, services, and information electronically using computer networks, particularly the internet. It involves the exchange of data and funds between buyers and sellers in a digital format.

General Data Protection Regulation: The General Data Protection Regulation (GDPR) is a comprehensive data protection law that was enacted by the European Union (EU) and came into effect on May 25, 2018. It replaced the previous Data Protection Directive and is designed to harmonize data protection laws across EU member states and enhance the protection of individuals' personal data.

Information Technology: Information Technology (IT) refers to the use, development, and management of computer-based systems, software applications, and networks to store, process, transmit, and retrieve information.

Internet Users: Internet users refer to individuals who have access to and utilize the internet for various purposes such as communication, information retrieval, entertainment, and conducting online transactions.

Sensitive Information: Sensitive information refers to any type of data that, if disclosed or compromised, could cause harm, privacy invasion, or significant damage to individuals, organizations, or systems. This information is typically confidential and requires special protection due to its nature and potential impact if it falls into the wrong hands.

Trust: Trust in data privacy refers to the confidence and assurance that individuals and organizations have in the protection, handling, and use of their personal data by entities that collect and process it.

Chapter 9
Privacy and Intimacy Concerns in Digital Marketing:
Literature Review

Lluc Vila Boix
https://orcid.org/0000-0002-2937-6576
Blanquerna - Ramon Llull University, Spain

Giorgia Miotto
https://orcid.org/0000-0002-0973-6597
Blanquerna - Ramon Llull University, Spain

Alicia Blanco González
https://orcid.org/0000-0002-8509-7993
Rey Juan Carlos University, Spain

ABSTRACT

The ubiquity and demand of sharing content by social networks (SN) led marketers to deal with challenges regarding the perception of privacy and intimacy and to consider dichotomies between preferences and real behaviours. Research is still needed to address how SN impact legitimacy. Also, there is a need to study how the de-definition of privacy and intimacy boundaries has affected the behaviours of SN users. The authors look at the issue from a theoretical point of view, considering authors from different fields of knowledge to break down the challenges for marketers regarding users' perception of privacy and intimacy on SN. The redefinition of privacy and intimacy boundaries has impacted the behaviours of SN users. It so has the effect of privacy and intimacy on the organisational legitimacy of brands advertising on SN. They suggest several techniques to alleviate privacy and intimacy concerns based on the theoretical implications. Ignoring these concerns can cause problems for brands and institutions and lead to a loss of trust and brand reputation, which translates into lower profits.

DOI: 10.4018/978-1-6684-8958-1.ch009

INTRODUCTION

We notice an increase in scholars' interest in social networks, privacy, intimacy and how users manage their privacy boundaries (Baruh et al., 2017). Recent studies show the growing importance of digital technology for marketing; some also highlight the need for research on how social networks can impact organisational legitimacy acquisition processes, as now individuals may be capable of influencing and contributing to the social construction of organisational legitimacy by shaping the public discourse (Grewal et al., 2020). Plangger et al. (2022) highlight the need to study how privacy is becoming increasingly important for consumers in a digital context, becoming a clear need for brands to gain a competitive advantage in the marketplace (Bleier et al., 2020). This chapter analyses how social network users' perceptions of privacy and intimacy affect organisational legitimacy. Legitimacy is a discursive construction created in the public sphere by many individuals; for that reason, it is especially relevant to study it at a networked level (Etter et al., 2018; Illia et al., 2023). Finding a balance between corporate profit and consumer privacy is one of the biggest challenges advertisers face today due to growing privacy concerns over users (Yi et al., 2023). This challenge is reflected in the steady increase in the number of articles on privacy and the growth of the topic (Boerman & Smit, 2022).

Additionally, relevant scholars' findings have highlighted more than once that privacy is one of the top issues for internet users as they are becoming more and more security-conscious consumers (Acquisti et al., 2016). Consumers' emission of digital signs depends on the intention of adopting and using technologies like the internet or social networks, so it is essential to understand why they use them. For example, some consumers may adopt them for purely practical reasons, while others may do so for hedonic and social reasons such as identity construction or interaction (Schweidel et al., 2022).

This book chapter aims to bring forward the growing concern of researchers and managers in different industries about privacy and the invasion of privacy in the networked environment enabled by Web 2.0 and social networks. In parallel, it aims to provide insights into how companies can make decisions and activate concrete tactics to alleviate their customers' or potential customers' perceived privacy or intimacy violations to obtain better relationships that translate into higher profits. In doing so, we aim to provide a theoretical basis with the relevant scientific literature to give rise to new research that considers the variables of privacy and privacy when assessing their role in the proper functioning of digital marketing.

From these proposals and the initial literature review, we propose the following research questions:

- **RQ1:** What are the specific challenges marketers face regarding users' perception of privacy and intimacy on social networks?
- **RQ2:** How does the redefinition of privacy and intimacy boundaries impact the behaviours of social network users?
- **RQ3:** Are there any potential solutions or strategies for marketers to address these challenges and maintain users' trust and engagement on social networks to have more revenue?

LITERATURE REVIEW METHODOLOGY

As the main objective of this research is to gain an in-depth understanding of the topics mentioned earlier, the in-depth review of different sources has given a comprehensive understanding of the issues and subjects we aim to trait and resolve, focusing on giving a managerial approach to our research.

First, we searched what is said about privacy in non-scientific media or journals to have the most current view of how this issue is discussed in the public sphere. Then, we started to make an overview. The first search was to get a broad view of the literature and the issues we wanted to address through Google Scholar, and when we acquired a broader knowledge of the topics and keywords, we did a second search both in Google Scholar and Web Of Science; this last database allowed us to refine topics and complement the first search with more specific keywords that we later addressed to Semantic Scholar, an artificial intelligence search engine for scientific literature, we used this tool to complement the first searches, as it can help to contrast and validate key authors and give an overview on open access research (Fricke, 2018). Furthermore, Semantic Scholar "is designed to identify hidden connections and links between research and links between research topics" (Dardas et al., 2023, p. 3). Hence, it is an excellent tool to double-check the first research findings on relevance and connections between topics and literature.

To do the last searches and select the literature we want to review, we used these descriptors: *privacy, online privacy, intimacy, online intimacy, personalised advertising, social media, social network, self-disclosure, trust, legitimacy* and *online social networks (OSNs).* Based on the results, the most relevant articles were selected for their number of citations and relationship with the variables of the phenomena studied. For the first selection of articles, relevant ones were selected from the last 4–5 years. Then, in addition to the database search, the snowball methodology was applied using the authors and references cited from the first selected relevant articles to find new and relevant articles to review, especially considering those cited in more than one article.

Additional criteria related to adequacy and validity were applied to select or discard articles. For example, we double-checked if the reference was used by other authors or researchers, if the author's information uses well-known references and theories to develop the research or if it cites the leading authors in the fields of our interest. It should also be noted that research from other fields of knowledge was also considered because of the innovative vision they can provide to this literature review.

The researchers of this chapter intend to use this literature review as a literature and reference basis for future research on the effects of the management of privacy and the violation of intimacy in advertising on social networks.

LITERATURE REVIEW

Privacy and Intimacy in Digital Marketing

Before getting into the subject, it is convenient to offer a definition of privacy that aligns with the perspective taken in this text. Burgoon (1982) differentiated four dimensions of privacy: physical, social, psychological, and informational; for social networks, the last three dimensions are particularly relevant. Bleier et al. (2020) state that defining has always been challenging. However, we would take Trepte's and Westin's definitions of Privacy as "selective control of information sharing, where control is key" (Trepte, 2021, p. 1) or "the claim of individuals, groups, or institutions to determine for themselves when, how, and to what extent information about them is communicated to others" (Westin, 1968, p. 7). Control is critical since privacy concerns decrease when users perceive that they have it (Bleier et al., 2020; Schweidel et al., 2022; Tucker, 2014). The networked nature of social networks blurs this individual concept of control, as users cannot control who sees their content and for what purpose they use it (Trepte, 2021). However, at the same time, social networks require more and more content to be shared in order to develop the user's self, becoming known for the elaboration and exhibition of images that increase personal exposure; this exposure ends up modifying intimacy and its boundaries, as well as the division between what it is public and private. The critical point in the redefinition of private and public spaces is that social networks combine solid and weak ties, making it possible to connect and interact with acquaintances, family members or total strangers. Intimacy in this particular context can be defined as a "preferential relationship connecting two or more individuals in an exclusive bond. This formulation differs from the more pervasive psychological understanding of intimacy as a confiding communication style associated with individual self-disclosure" (Kaplan, 2021, p. 596).

The Communication Privacy Management Theory, developed by Petronio (2002), is another relevant theory for privacy scholars as it illustrates how individuals protect their data by establishing privacy rules and boundaries between their information and third parties, as when customers are aware of data collection by firms, they weight the benefits of technology use against costs of sharing personal information (Schweidel et al., 2022; Zhu & Kanjanamekanant, 2021). The perception of these benefits differs depending on the user's characteristics; users have different perceived levels of intimacy concerning their data, and some are less willing than others to provide personal information to companies; it depends on the perceived benefits regarding personalised advertising (Bleier et al., 2020; Gonçalves & de Figueiredo, 2022; Yi et al., 2023). According to Petronio, people decide where their privacy limits lie based on the calculus of the advantages and disadvantages of disclosing their personal information. This scholar understands control as a privacy management tool (Petronio, 2002; Trepte, 2021). Due to the risk associated with social network voluntary personal disclosure practices, people consider the advantages and disadvantages of releasing confidential information and seek to establish boundaries between private and public (Chennamaneni & Taneja, 2015). However, users perceive social networks as private spaces, so when an advertising message hits them, they may feel that a private space is violated (Lin & Kim, 2016). Different studies have found that variables such as perceived privacy turbulence, perceived cost-benefit, perceived risk, perceived privacy control and perceived personalisation are significant determinants of users' perceived sense of privacy, which affects how they interact with the platform and the advertisements displayed (De Keyzer et al., 2015; James et al., 2017; Liu & Wang, 2018; McNealy & Mullis, 2019; Tucker, 2014; Zhu & Kanjanamekanant, 2021).

An example of how intimacy can take place in social networks is how some selfies can be taken in intimate spaces such as a home, giving a glimpse of what was previously considered private. Intimacy is context-dependent, as the appropriateness of what one chooses to show and what one considers intimate depends on context. For example, a user will not show the same photo they display on a dating social network to their friends or family on another social network (Lasén, 2015).

Co-ownership of Data in the Knowledge Economy

Traditional economy has moved towards a new economy based on the production of knowledge and information; this has been boosted by the constant improvement in communication and information technologies; this, in turn, has enlarged the information on individuals that is available and that can be collected and used. However, the adoption of these technologies by consumers has led to always-on involuntary surveillance of user data and the possibility of this being misused, as data has become one of the most valuable assets for companies in every industry (Gonçalves & de Figueiredo, 2022; Soleymanian et al., 2021). One of the most prominent examples of this new paradigm is how implementing social networks in different spheres of our lives has blurred the lines between public and private information; its potential is such that, for example, any user can turn one of their messages into a viral and global message, with the actual capacity to make an impact worldwide. The main characteristic of these social networks is that their growth is based on the generation and sharing of user-generated content, transforming traditional content consumers into prosumers who consume, produce and share content and information at the same time (Acquisti et al., 2016; Chennamaneni & Taneja, 2015; Lee et al., 2022). The need to share content leads to self-disclosure behaviour, as when users share content; they pass it from private to co-owned, transferring the responsibility for the information to the new co-owners (Chennamaneni & Taneja, 2015; Petronio, 2002; Zhu & Kanjanamekanant, 2021). Therefore, everyone willing to spread information about someone else should be subject to restrictions on when, where, and why they can do so. In addition, since information is context-dependent, established relationships or context-related norms will determine whether it is appropriate to share it (Bleier et al., 2020). In this sense, privacy has a behaviour similar to legitimacy according to Suchman (1995) conception of legitimacy, since privacy, like legitimacy, is context-dependant.

Limits of Personalised Advertising

Social networks are now a regular part of the daily routines and activities of many consumers, who spend an average of 2 hours and 22 minutes a day on social networks with the expectation that they will spend more and more time on these platforms (*Global Daily Social Media Usage 2022*, 2022; Setyani et al., 2019; Zhu & Kanjanamekanant, 2021). Spending hours in this pro-self-disclosure environment, users end up sharing content about their daily activities by posting photos and locations, which allows third parties, such as marketing companies consuming this content, to create profiles of individual users to target them with personalised advertising (Gangarde et al., 2019; Lee et al., 2022; Trepte, 2021). The personalisation of advertising is one of the strategies used to encourage impulsive purchases and has become more and more popular over the last few years; as data analytics capabilities enable personalised ads to reflect and address needs that even the user is not aware of, enabling the activation of impulse purchases (Setyani et al., 2019). This technique incorporates information about the person, such as demographic data or data about their online behaviour. Social networks can provide this data since they have a steady stream of it from millions of users; using it has proven to be an effective technique as users are more likely to have a higher intention to purchase the recommended product in personalised ads (Lin et al., 2022; Setyani et al., 2019). However, despite favourable effects on advertising performance, such as increased click-through rates, there is a tipping point where excessive personalisation may become counterproductive and produce unfavourable perceptions because of privacy concerns and perceptions produced by over-customization (Setyani et al., 2019).

Users as Relevant Sources of Information

This ease of sharing content has facilitated what is known as social commerce, which differs from traditional e-commerce as it takes some of the main characteristics of Web 2.0, such as involving communities of consumers engaging in conversations where they share opinions. Social commerce is defined as "forms of Internet-based social media that allow people to participate actively in the marketing and selling of products and services in online marketplaces and communities [...] merge online shopping and social networking" (Stephen & Toubia, 2010, p. 215). The social commerce environment makes making impulsive purchases even easier (Setyani et al., 2019). In these new forms of commerce, dynamics similar to those of social networks are applied, and in this sense, concerns about user privacy also arise. Trust has a similar role in terms of purchase intention and the production of word-of-mouth (Hajli et al., 2017). At the same time, consumers are increasingly relying on social networks as a source of information. Now, some users search for information on them, as they are more likely to rely on peer-generated content, understood as content generated by other users like them. This content can influence their opinions, attitudes and purchasing behaviour as interactions among users emerge as the primary source of value, changing the capabilities of e-vendors on value production, as the dynamics are directed towards co-creation of value; where sellers create value but at the same time users also can create value by giving evaluations on products or services or simply sharing their experience using them (Hajli et al., 2017; Schweidel et al., 2022). Web 2.0 technologies are forcing companies to relinquish some control, handing it over to consumers. We may be moving toward a time when marketing will be more decentralised, and brands will need to emphasise safeguarding the security and privacy of their customers as they transition to the new, even more decentralised paradigm of Web 3.0 (Plangger et al., 2022; Thomaz et al., 2020). Some of the top online marketing platforms in the world, including Google and Meta, have started to offer initiatives to preserve the anonymity of users and, at the same time, provide marketers with a certain level of insights to create segmentations based on various interests, characteristics and past behaviours. These initiatives create walled gardens that, at the same time, reinforce the monopoly of dominance over user data held by these large marketing platforms. For example, Google may combine data from services such as Gmail, YouTube or Google Chrome to build consumer profiles and provide advertisers with precise targeting options (Bleier et al., 2020; Boerman & Smit, 2022; Plangger et al., 2022).

Often, companies collaborate with technology providers that can capture a wide range of digital signals from consumers. They can also interpret and package these signals in an actionable way for businesses by selling this data directly or offering solutions that facilitate its use. A clear example is the technology of platforms such as Meta or Twitter that allows companies to build profiles based on users' psychological characteristics and interests, based on the electronic footprint and traces that users leave when they operate in the digital environment. The current currency for using the services of social networking companies is user information. The value proposition offered to the companies who want to advertise through them is to be able to personalise the targeting of the communication, as it has been proven that communications tailored to individuals are more effective (Acquisti et al., 2016; Hirsh et al., 2012; Lee et al., 2022; Matz et al., 2020; Rimer & Kreuter, 2006; Schweidel et al., 2022). In particular, message personalisation can be beneficial at the consideration and intention stages of the conversion funnel (Lee et al., 2022).

User Data: From Private to Co-Owned

Users' personal information is transferred to the collective privacy boundary, jointly controlled by the user and the social networking platform when they post it on the platform; for example, personalised ads take information from this collective privacy boundary. The problem arises when the new co-owners of the shared information (content shared, likes, reactions or messages) interpret the rules differently than the user does, for example, by assuming that the other party understands them as they do; by way of illustration, undesired disclosure of another person's sensitive information is an invasion of their trust, as this sensitive information has lower disclosure intentions for the owner (Petronio & Reierson, 2009; Zhu & Kanjanamekanant, 2021). Another source of problems is that this co-ownership differs between users, so some users are more likely to view the sharing of information as more of a concern than others; for that reason, visibility of user signals depends on its willingness to share, highly related to its comfortability with the sharing of his signals by third parties (Schweidel et al., 2022; Zhu & Kanjanamekanant, 2021). In addition, this provision is related to consumers' perception that the company will treat their information fairly and reasonably, addressing consumers' concerns and demands (Bleier et al., 2020).

The redefinition of privacy and intimacy boundaries has increased concern from users, media and academics alike (Acquisti et al., 2016; Bria, 2013; Laussel et al., 2022), and so has the use of social networks (Gangarde et al., 2019; Lin et al., 2022). For example, scholars like Choi and Sung (2018) contend that a person's level of concern about online privacy affects their choice of a social network, as it does so the size of social networks, as users are more likely to consent to more extensive networks with a broader reach than to smaller companies (Acquisti et al., 2016). Moreover, privacy concerns increased during the last time (Goldfarb & Tucker, 2011; Schweidel et al., 2022). This increase in the privacy problem has led institutions like the European Union to implement legislative initiatives such as the European Union's General Data Protection Regulation (GDPR). This regulation advocates for transparency and disclosure of what data companies collect and for what purpose, protecting and empowering citizens by giving them options such as the ability to consent or refuse the use of their data in a specific way (Bleier et al., 2020; Matz et al., 2020; Schweidel et al., 2022). For example, this legislation has expanded what is considered personal data, including users' IP addresses helping to establish more unambiguous establishments and boundaries (Bleier et al., 2020; Laussel et al., 2022). However, the fundamental issue is that consumers seldom have a better understanding of their rights, which limits the impact of these regulations. The result is that their existence does not affect the ability of companies to capture digital signals because their effectiveness is questionable, but without them, privacy, in general, could deteriorate and become progressively more difficult for consumers to obtain or maintain (Bleier et al., 2020; Lin et al., 2022; Schweidel et al., 2022).

New Ways of Targeting

In the past, market information was aggregated and based on generalising a group of consumers with specific homogeneously shared characteristics. Now, the advances in data tracking technology allow the consideration of each individual's characteristics (Gonçalves & de Figueiredo, 2022). The differential point in privacy is the before and after that sets the introduction of big data and more advanced techniques of user behaviour-tracking; this new paradigm makes old conceptions of privacy obsolete and allows a few companies to organise unstructured data to facilitate product segmentation so that marketers can target particular people (Boerman & Smit, 2022; Zhu & Kanjanamekanant, 2021). This online advertising techniques are one of the most common examples of how large amounts of user data can be used (Acquisti et al., 2016). Companies can better develop highly detailed customer profiles based on their preferences, interests, and behaviours by tracking their online activity since, in the online environment, virtually all activity generates traces that can be stored, analysed, and used to create knowledge. This digital tracking is made possible by the advancement of information technologies, the proliferation of mobile devices, and the increasingly widespread use of data (Lasén, 2015). With the aid of these contemporary technologies, marketers can record consumer behaviour in various contexts and transform it into informative signals that can be analysed and potentially used to produce income; this is one of the reasons why the number of companies trying to collect data from their customers will increase dramatically in the coming years (Laussel et al., 2022; Schweidel et al., 2022). Now, brands can segment their potential customers using structured data, like demographics or unstructured data, such as users' activities on platforms like social networks or browsing and search traces acquired in a way that users may or may not be aware of. With the recent and constant technological advances, data collection, analysis, and storage costs have been reduced, making it easier for more companies to use individual data for marketing purposes. The data collected can enable accurate price discrimination based on behavioural segmentation, known as a behaviour-based discrimination price model; this segmentation requires large amounts of information about users, and the data obtained from the different platforms, which, correctly processed, allows companies to create customised prices that increase the companies' profits approaching prices to consumer's actual willingness to pay (Lin et al., 2022). The ease of usage of this personal data raises privacy-related challenges as some studies report concerns of users about the invasion of privacy in the context of online advertising (Bleier et al., 2020; Boerman & Smit, 2022; Gonçalves & de Figueiredo, 2022).

User Data as Competitive Advantage

Some studies claim that few users know that firms collect digital traces and data from their online behaviours; e.g. consumer devices may store and share information such as location with third parties (Morey et al., 2015; Schweidel et al., 2022; Zhu & Kanjanamekanant, 2021). The ability to collect data that competitors cannot collect by investing in technological innovations has become a competitive advantage, leading to more and more companies wanting to improve their ability to collect, process, and transform information into insights for their marketing actions. At the same time, experts in business and marketing must be aware of how consumers feel about data and the use of digital technologies because those able to understand the consumer will be the ones who will truly gain a competitive advantage (Bleier et al., 2020; Plangger et al., 2022). Every day, more and more companies can use the information gathered to launch personalised actions such as advertising that uses this data to personalise messages and audiences. This personalised targeting is experiencing a steady increase in popularity as the ability to personalise the messages based on the signals that the consumer emits can help reduce marketing inefficiencies that translate into more flexibility in advertisers' margins, which at the same time can benefit users by allowing companies to offer lower prices and more optimised products or services, as the tension between privacy and marketing efficiency is a matter of negotiation within the logic of the market economy (Zhu & Kanjanamekanant, 2021; Lee et al., 2022; Schweidel et al., 2022; Blattberg & Deighton, 1991). Scholars like Kosinski et al. (2013) have shown that many intimate user characteristics, such as political points of view and inclinations or sexual orientation, can be predicted through digital traces of users, e.g. reactions to the content. Despite this possibility of targeting, there is a paradox in that users perceive personalised ads as more attractive and connected to their real interests, which translates into higher purchase intent. However, it generates privacy concerns. While most consumers express concern about how their data is collected and used (97%), about 20% know that its location, online search traces or interactions in social networks can be transformed and collected into valuable data that can be shared with third parties for other purposes (Schweidel et al., 2022).

The Price Paid for Privacy and Intimacy

There is a diffuse boundary where advertisements can lose effectiveness by triggering users' privacy concerns and provoking negative responses due to over-personalisation (Zhu & Kanjanamekanant, 2021). The ability to track consumers' digital signals makes it easier to understand consumer interests, preferences and activities that can be collected overtly or covertly, and consumers' awareness may vary. In any case, there is tension between the user's intention to receive the expected personalisation and their concern about protecting their privacy. These captured signals arise from a multiplicity of activities consumers perform, and through artificial intelligence and big data analytics techniques, companies can anticipate consumer needs and be used for more personalised, specific, and targeted marketing actions at the specific stage of the consumer's shopping process. These signals can occur even before the consumer enters what we understand to as the "customer journey". The signals make it possible to trace this path both at the individual level and at the level of consumer segments with very similar behaviour (Schweidel et al., 2022). The diff leads users into an asymmetric dominance situation between the user and the advertiser or platform, making users increasingly less able to make privacy decisions as processes and stakeholders increasingly become opaque (Matz et al., 2020). The fact that the user knows less than the brand about how their data is being used creates an asymmetry that puts them at a disadvantage in knowing how their data is being collected, for what purpose and the possible consequences. When sharing or attempting to safeguard their personal information, consumers are rarely fully aware of the dangers and effects on their privacy, nor of the scope of behavioural targeting (Acquisti et al., 2016). The monitoring and processing of data are such that some companies can collect and analyse the signals emitted by users to know the willingness of consumers to pay for a particular product, giving them higher margins (Schweidel et al., 2022).

Moreover, social networks have facilitated the culture of disclosure, and users are more likely than ever to disclose their thoughts, activities and emotions; the technology that invades our privacy is now a part of our daily life (Acquisti et al., 2016). Such is the concern that some consumers will pay a premium price to increase their privacy or may even consider changing brands, providers or platforms. Contrary to the situation where users are willing to pay extra, some companies are willing to pay to obtain user data to alleviate their privacy concerns (Lin et al., 2022). However, good privacy management is advantageous for brands, as it can increase the willingness to pay for a product or service (Bleier et al., 2020; Laussel et al., 2022); and if large numbers of consumers begin to take control of their privacy, it will limit the extent to which companies could collect their digital traces (Schweidel et al., 2022; Tsai et al., 2011). As more and more consumers know how valuable their personal information is, some brands have implemented a positioning focused on defending users' privacy, allowing them to use new tools to protect their privacy as part of the brand experience (Plangger et al., 2022).

Against this trend towards disclosure, some companies such as Apple, through iOS, their widely known mobile user operating system, have given their users tools to safeguard their privacy from third parties, restricting the possibilities of digital signal tracking by giving more power to the user in response to growing concern on the part of users (Bleier et al., 2020; Boerman & Smit, 2022; Schweidel et al., 2022). The aforementioned mobile operating system has implemented questionnaires for users to determine whether or not they want to share specific data, which makes it even more critical for brands to work on establishing a close relationship with consumers, as the more significant the relationship between companies and users, the more personalisation they expect, and the more likely they are to share information and relax their desire for privacy by blurring the barriers to their personal information (Schweidel et al., 2022). The same authors state that this user empowerment by Apple is not for free, as creating this can prevent other companies from getting information from the users and thus secure a competitive advantage by creating entire ecosystems controlled by the company, thus providing customers with an incentive to stay exclusively inside a specific ecosystem by reducing cost and risk and assisting consumers in making decisions. Furthermore, this prevents prospective rivals from receiving consumer signals (Bleier et al., 2020).

To Be or Not to Be in Social Networks

There is also an all-or-nothing situation since the consent mechanisms are virtually binary and force users to accept if they want to use the service (Matz et al., 2020). In this sense, the theory of uses and gratifications has been used to understand how persons use specific media to satisfy their needs, as media use is goal-oriented (Chennamaneni & Taneja, 2015). According to Chennamaneni & Taneja's (2015) research, sharing personal information on social networks can help users establish and sustain relationships, generate social capital, and manage their identities. It is particularly challenging for users to stop utilising social networks since it has a significant role in socialising (Baruh et al., 2017). For this reason, they use it even though they know the privacy control deficits it entails (Trepte, 2021).

The interesting point is that despite the user's concern about privacy and intimacy, researchers' results have found a large gap between individuals' attitudes towards privacy and their actual behaviour. This difference between what is done and what is said is called the privacy paradox (Acquisti et al., 2016; Baruh et al., 2017; Boerman & Smit, 2022; Gonçalves & de Figueiredo, 2022). This paradox is context-dependent since privacy is a process of negotiating between what is private and what is public, a modulation of what a person wishes to protect or communicate at a given moment and in a specific context; it can sometimes lead to measures being taken to safeguard data, or sometimes not to protect data at all because of the high costs involved (Acquisti et al., 2016; Baruh et al., 2017). This paradox occurs because actual behaviour is more liberal than behavioural intentions; then, there is tension between the two (Gonçalves & de Figueiredo, 2022). Some researchers state that users perform a privacy calculation; which is called privacy calculus, and it comes from the so-called Privacy Calculus Theory developed by Laufer & Wolfe (1977); according to this theory, which is grounded in the rationality of decisions, people analyse the societal benefits of releasing their information against the drawbacks, and as a result, they will only do so if the advantages outweigh the risks of losing their privacy. Sometimes, privacy concerns could be activated when companies reuse previous browsing behaviours in a new context. However, the extent to which retargeting makes users privacy-conscious rather than being perceived as providing valuable information (Bleier et al., 2020).

Benefits and dangers are both valued, and this process involves thinking rationally and consciously about how much control an individual is willing to accept over their data and how it is utilised. There is a mismatch between what the user professes to desire and their actual conduct since many procedures contain cognitive biases that hinder people from calculating all pertinent factors. As a result, consumers have a more privacy-oriented inclination to compromise their privacy (Gonçalves & de Figueiredo, 2022). The same authors state another interesting phenomenon related to wearable technology, as the privacy paradox is also imposed in the environments of wearable devices that collect a high amount of user information. Users agree to use these technologies because they are looking for exhaustive monitoring of their vital signs for different reasons, such as fitness tracking and rarely ask for the protection of such intimate data. Users must also perform a privacy calculus when deciding whether to accept or stop using wearable technology. If this data is used for a purpose other than tracking the subject's fitness, such as insurance or credit scoring, the new context of the data is likely to raise privacy concerns (Bleier et al., 2020).

The User Relation With Privacy and Trust

A last aspect that is highly important for business marketing strategies is how targeted advertising on social networks can backfire if the target of the message is worried about their privacy or the degree of control they have over their data, as consumers desire to control their personal information is a precursor to privacy concerns, which in turn reduces purchase intentions, providing competitive advantages to marketers who better protect consumers' privacy (Phelps et al., 2001; Schweidel et al., 2022; Tsai et al., 2011). In this communication, perceived privacy is paramount since when privacy is perceived to be high, it increases the willingness to trust the advertised brand and also affects consumer behaviour through advertising since the attitude towards the advertisement has a direct relationship with the final purchase intention (Zhu & Kanjanamekanant, 2021). Trust is a fundamental part of online transactions, such as online shopping, and even more so in social commerce, and can be defined as an "individual's belief that an exchange will happen in a manner consistent with one's confident expectations" (Hajli et al., 2017, p. 134). This relationship between trust and expectations leads us to legitimacy, as it depends to a large extent on the reputation of the brand and individual expectations towards it. For example, consumers expect their privacy and intimacy to be respected, as they grant legitimacy to the brand based on their previous experiences and expectations (Hajli et al., 2017). Then, users will engage with websites or platforms based on their trust and value; therefore, the degree of trust they place in a social network determines the involvement of users concerning the content, and lack of trust prevents the proper exchange of information; thus, users who trust more in social networks tend to be more willing to exchange information, i.e., be more open in sharing and less concerned about privacy (Hajli et al., 2017).

Concerns may be such that some users perform techniques to become invisible, for example, using fake email addresses, using VPNs, and false information to hinder marketing efforts to track them; more and more skilled technology consumers are using digital tools to engage in identity management activities and hide personal data (Bleier et al., 2020; Laussel et al., 2022; Thomaz et al., 2020). The use of identity management practices by customers can have a privacy cost; those who act to safeguard their privacy are known as active customers, while those who allow the company to collect and store information about them are known as passive customers, so there will be a high number of active customers when the privacy cost is low (Laussel et al., 2022).

In the online environment, message credibility is determined by the accuracy and informative quality of the message itself. Highly personalised advertising better represents the user's needs, generating more relevant recommendations and is more likely to be perceived as being of high quality and informational accuracy. The perceived similarity between user's interests and what the advertisement offers, and perceived usefulness in the sense that an advertisement can help the user find things they like, are particularly likely to be triggered by a high level of personalisation, which translates into a higher perception of credibility given to the advertisement (Setyani et al., 2019). In addition, when excessive targeting of the message is not justified, highly personalised advertising can cause customers to reject the message they receive as intrusive, resulting in a loss of credibility and relevance for the company's communications. They can feel a loss of control over their privacy and intimacy, adversely affecting purchase intentions and moving them to act in a very restrictive manner concerning data sharing, i.e. using ad-blocking add-ons (Acquisti et al., 2016; Bleier et al., 2020; Lee et al., 2022; Tucker, 2014). Therefore, it is essential to highlight that alleviating consumers' concerns about data overuse is fundamental to personalised campaigns' utility (Lee et al., 2022).

ACTIONS TO REDUCE CONCERNS

The Necessity of Data for Effective Marketing

Data-driven marketing can benefit from strategies companies can use to reduce privacy concerns. These strategies can foster privacy innovation and provide a long-term, sustainable competitive advantage. First, marketers need to understand the boundaries and what makes consumers accept or reject using their data to personalise messages and advertisements. Getting closer to expectations in terms of personalisation is an imperative need, as failure to properly understand the boundaries can damage the relationship with the brand by causing an unpleasant sense of privacy or intimacy invasion.

Businesses are affected by consumer privacy concerns in several different ways, including direct revenue losses from lost sales, litigation risks, or the blocking of potentially valuable data. Privacy concerns can also reduce consumers' likelihood of buying, especially in those firms with business models highly connected to customised advertising. As a result, it is becoming increasingly important to review strategies and action plans that lessen these concerns (Bleier et al., 2020). One of the techniques used to decrease privacy concerns is the compensation of consumers for providing their information to marketers because when they are compensated, their expectations of privacy control decrease due to the belief that marketers have legitimate co-ownership and the right to control and use their information (Zhu & Kanjanamekanant, 2021). Another helpful technique to reduce privacy concerns on a sustained basis is to establish emotional connections between the brand and the consumers; these relationships help to establish trust and reduce concerns. Some brands use anthropomorphisation to establish emotional relationships by attributing human values and personality to the brand and its communications (Plangger et al., 2022; Zhu & Kanjanamekanant, 2021). This relationship can be built by delivering appropriate content to consumers; this, finally, may encourage consumers to reveal more information that can be useful for the brand (Schweidel et al., 2022). The degree of mutual trust between the parties is one of the most crucial factors in determining any relationship. This trust in the customer-company context refers to the degree to which customers believe a company is competent, trustworthy and honest in a given situation. In a trust-based relationship, consumers expect the brand to adhere to contextual standards and not misuse their data (Bleier et al., 2020). As trust is fundamental in shaping consumer facilities to provide personal information, brands must establish it to collect consumers' most detailed information while reducing privacy concerns in response to personalised advertising. Then, a company that exercises trust can use certain personal information to create personalised ads more freely than one that the consumer does not trust (Bleier et al., 2020).

Another lever that firms can pull to increase the willingness of the consumer to emit digital signals is their privacy policy, as transparency and control can increase trust (Grosso et al., 2020). Some scholars, such as (Yi et al., 2023) and (Tang & Ning, 2023), are committed to privacy policies fully customised to the user, as users have different needs and perceptions of privacy that must be considered. One of the examples of how transparency materialises in online advertising is the AdChoices program initiated by Google, which shows how consumer browsing data is being used in a concrete banner advertisement (Bleier et al., 2020). This initiative is in line with the responsibility of platforms to respect the boundaries of user information, not crossing the limits between what the user considers public and private, and respecting social boundaries by not exposing and shaming with personalised advertising. Furthermore, by applying techniques of anthropomorphism that induce personification by developing a clear consensus of co-ownership with subscribers, social platforms can secure their revenue stream through a more positive attitude towards the advertisements displayed on them, improving the purchase intent and revenue of their customers, the advertisers (Zhu & Kanjanamekanant, 2021). To respect the limits, platforms should only allow personalised ads based on information shared on the platform, without allowing the use of third-party sources such as browsing and search history, as Zhu & Kanjanamekanant (2021) state that advertisements based on internal data are received better.

Establishing Relations With Consumers

Building relationships with consumers can be part of a strategy to reduce privacy concerns and relax their awareness about collecting private information while allowing brands to collect data from the direct interactions between the firm and the user. This data generally is only available to firms that created the relationship by giving them a competitive advantage over information freely posted by users on social networks, which is available to all competitors. This advantage must be addressed as consumers who share information directly with the company tend to expect more personalisation from the company (Schweidel et al., 2022). The authors explain that users react more favourably to personalised advertising that is customised through openly collected user information; therefore, the company must build trust by being transparent to the extent of allowing greater control over user data, as the perception of control can help alleviate privacy concerns (Lambillotte et al., 2022). Transparency and control are positively related to decreasing privacy concerns. One example is data use notice and consent, also known as informed consent, which asks companies to inform customers about their data practices and that they only use the information for the purposes for which the user has given consent, being transparent about the personal data and information the company uses in its operations can help alleviate privacy concerns (Bleier et al., 2020). Identifying essential data for marketing operations is vital to avoid overreaching the appropriateness of signals collected from consumers, as consumers' expectations about using their data are limited by context; for example, the willingness to accept the disclosure of data may vary with the sensitivity of the data, industry or relationship with the brand (Schweidel et al., 2022). Another vital element of all brands' responsibility is to prevent and manage data breaches, which is critical to avoid consumer privacy protection strategies caused by the concerns that produce these information leaks (Lin et al., 2022). Transparency is a tactic that has shown to be very useful as consumers tend to trust more websites, platforms and brands that disclose what information they collect and how they intend to use it, additionally offering the ability to modify, correct and delete personal information benefits the trust that is established and reduces privacy concerns (Schweidel et al., 2022). Another strategy involving communication tactics is for companies to carry out communication activities to reduce privacy concerns. For example, a good strategy is to conduct direct communications with customers, highlighting the improvement and care taken by the brand in terms of enhancing security and privacy, either within the company or directly in the products it offers, and guiding customers on how to protect their privacy demonstrating that the company is committed to resolving issues raised by customers (Gonçalves & de Figueiredo, 2022). Other authors suggest that customers will alleviate their privacy concerns and be more open to disclosure behaviours when they perceive a high level of privacy guarantee in protecting and collecting personal information (Gong et al., 2020).

New Perspectives and Solutions

Interestingly Bhattacharya et al. (2023) found that the country of origin of e-commerce serves as a sign that can increase trust and help alleviate consumer privacy concerns. In the case of e-commerce, digital technologies create customer value when, for example, they deliver digital experiences comparable to physical ones, improving customer experiences while mitigating privacy concerns. In this regard, businesses that take the initiative are unafraid to try new things and embrace emerging digital technologies have the potential to lead their industries with innovations that encourage the development of customer relationships; because the strength of the customer-firm relationships determines customers' willingness to transmit digital signals that facilitate and enable personalised marketing, this established relationship facilitates the exchange of signals. However, it is also essential for businesses to take action when deploying and implementing new technologies because the data exchange made possible by social networking technology also raises privacy and security concerns. As a result, new tensions relating to users' privacy preferences during the customer journey may arise. To combat them, the brand must offer higher quality products and better services, such as offering and recommending different content and products (Boerman & Smit, 2022; Lin et al., 2022; Plangger et al., 2022; Schweidel et al., 2022).

Finally, Boerman & Smit (2022) propose a paradigm of advertising that may be of interest to use fewer user data, for which proposals such as contextual targeting have given good results since it offers high conversion rates to clicks and returns on investment while having the advantage that they do not harm the user's privacy, since they use data from the context in which the advertisement appears (Table 1).

Table 1. Strategies and techniques to reduce privacy and intimacy concerns

Authors	Proposed Strategy or Technique
Zhu & Kanjanamekanant, 2021	To compensate customers to decrease their privacy control expectations. Use platforms that only use data gathered from their platform, without sharing it with third parties
Plangger et al., 2022; Zhu & Kanjanamekanant, 2021	Build and establish emotional connections between brand and consumer, establishing relationships based on the anthropomorphism of the brand
Schweidel et al., 2022	Deliver appropriate content to consumers to build relationships, encourage them to disclose more information, and personalize advertising only with user information collected openly and transparently.
Bleier et al., 2020	Build trust between the consumer and the brand
Grosso et al., 2020	Push transparency and control through the right privacy policy to increase trust
Lambillotte et al., 2022; Schweidel et al., 2022	Give transparency and permit the management of user information as the perception of control helps to alleviate privacy concerns
Lin et al., 2022	Prevent and fight against data breaches
Gonçalves & de Figueiredo, 2022	Carry out communication campaigns to reduce privacy concerns, communicating the enhancement of security and privacy done by the brand
Boerman & Smit, 2022	Opt for new paradigms and ways to advertise, such as contextual targeting that requires fewer data from users to target the customers
Tang & Ning, 2023; Yi et al., 2023	To have privacy policies fully customizable by the user, to adapt to different necessities, perceptions and contexts
Gong et al., 2020	To transmit and communicate a high level of privacy guarantee in protecting and collecting personal information
Bhattacharya et al., 2023	Use and display country of origin and other attributes that generate trust to reduce privacy concerns

DISCUSSION AND IMPLICATIONS

Understanding the issues related to privacy and intimacy concerns has been an important topic for research; we have observed how the scientific literature reflects its importance and how different authors propose different solutions to alleviate these tensions. To our best knowledge, no previous studies combined the variables of privacy and intimacy in digital marketing, nor the study of the same variables specified in the environment of social networks in these networks, the importance of privacy and intimacy is accentuated as it is an environment of socialisation.

The new perspective provided by this review of the most recent and relevant literature is intended to help establish a theoretical basis for future studies to analyse the impact of the different variables and phenomena mentioned. Future studies may advance the quantitative measurement of the impact of each of these variables on consumer purchase intentions or other management-related metrics.

Likewise, we also intend to list several techniques for managers and decision-makers to act to alleviate consumer concerns related to the study variables for more sustained business development; this list can be found in Table 1.

CONCLUSION AND FUTURE RESEARCH

Privacy concerns are essential in digital marketing, particularly in social networks. As the use of social networks has become an everyday occurrence for many people, companies must recognise the importance of balancing personalised marketing strategies with user privacy concerns as these networks allow for the personalisation of ads, which can be an effective tool for more sales and higher profits; however, excessive personalisation can lead to privacy concerns while also generating negative perceptions of the brand, resulting in a severe loss of trust. To mitigate privacy concerns, companies must understand their customers' boundaries and expectations of privacy and intimacy, establish emotional connections, and build trust. Failure to do so can lead to direct revenue losses, litigation risks, or valuable data blocking. Therefore, privacy innovation by marketers is necessary to provide a sustainable competitive advantage and maintain positive customer relationships. By recognising the importance of privacy and intimacy issues and taking appropriate steps to address them, companies can enhance their brand reputation and legitimacy, increasing their chances of success in the marketplace.

REFERENCES

Acquisti, A., Taylor, C., & Wagman, L. (2016). The economics of privacy. *Journal of Economic Literature*, *54*(2), 442–492. doi:10.1257/jel.54.2.442

Baruh, L., Secinti, E., & Cemalcilar, Z. (2017). Online privacy concerns and privacy management: A meta-analytical review. *Journal of Communication*, *67*(1), 26–53. doi:10.1111/jcom.12276

Bhattacharya, S., Sharma, R. P., & Gupta, A. (2023). Does e-retailer's country of origin influence consumer privacy, trust and purchase intention? *Journal of Consumer Marketing*, *40*(2), 248–259. doi:10.1108/JCM-04-2021-4611

Blattberg, R. C., & Deighton, J. (1991). Interactive marketing: Exploiting the age of addressability. *Sloan Management Review*, *33*(1), 5–15.

Bleier, A., Goldfarb, A., & Tucker, C. (2020). Consumer privacy and the future of data-based innovation and marketing. *International Journal of Research in Marketing*, *37*(3), 466–480. doi:10.1016/j.ijresmar.2020.03.006

Boerman, S. C., & Smit, E. G. (2022). Advertising and privacy: An overview of past research and a research agenda. International Journal of Advertising, 1–9. doi:10.1080/02650487.2022.2122251

Bria, F. (2013). *Social media and their impact on organisations: Building Firm Celebrity and organisational legitimacy through social media*. Imperial College London. doi:10.25560/24944

Burgoon, J. K. (1982). Privacy and communication. *Annals of the International Communication Association*, *6*(1), 206–249. doi:10.1080/23808985.1982.11678499

Chennamaneni, A., & Taneja, A. (2015). Communication Privacy Management and Self-Disclosure on Social Media—A Case of Facebook. *Americas Conference on Information Systems.*

Choi, T. R., & Sung, Y. (2018). Instagram versus Snapchat: Self-expression and privacy concern on social media. *Telematics and Informatics*, *35*(8), 2289–2298. doi:10.1016/j.tele.2018.09.009

Dardas, L. A., Sallam, M., Woodward, A., Sweis, N., Sweis, N., & Sawair, F. A. (2023). Evaluating Research Impact Based on Semantic Scholar Highly Influential Citations, Total Citations, and Altmetric Attention Scores: The Quest for Refined Measures Remains Illusive. *Publications / MDPI*, *11*(1), 1. Advance online publication. doi:10.3390/publications11010005

De Keyzer, F., Dens, N., & De Pelsmacker, P. (2015). Is this for me? How consumers respond to personalized advertising on social network sites. *Journal of Interactive Advertising*, *15*(2), 124–134. doi:10.1080/15252019.2015.1082450

Etter, M., Colleoni, E., Illia, L., Meggiorin, K., & D'Eugenio, A. (2018). Measuring Organizational Legitimacy in Social Media: Assessing Citizens' Judgments With Sentiment Analysis. *Business & Society*, *57*(1), 60–97. doi:10.1177/0007650316683926

Fricke, S. (2018). Semantic Scholar. *Journal of the Medical Library Association: JMLA*, *106*(1). Advance online publication. doi:10.5195/jmla.2018.280

Gangarde, R., Sharma, A., & Pawar, A. (2019). Bibliometric Survey of Privacy of Social Media Network Data Publishing. *Library Philosophy and Practice*, *2019*, 1–21.

Global daily social media usage 2022. (2022, January 26). Statista. https://www-statista-com.eu1.proxy.openathens.net/statistics/433871/daily-social-media-usage-worldwide/

Goldfarb, A., & Tucker, C. (2011). Online display advertising: Targeting and obtrusiveness. *Marketing Science*, *30*(3), 389–404. doi:10.1287/mksc.1100.0583

Gonçalves, R. B., & de Figueiredo, J. C. B. (2022). Effects of perceived risks and benefits in the formation of the consumption privacy paradox: A study of the use of wearables in people practicing physical activities. *Electronic Markets*, *32*(3), 1–15. doi:10.100712525-022-00559-7

Gong, X., Zhang, K. Z., Chen, C., Cheung, C. M., & Lee, M. K. (2020). What drives self-disclosure in mobile payment applications? The effect of privacy assurance approaches, network externality, and technology complementarity. *Information Technology & People*, *33*(4), 1174–1213. doi:10.1108/ITP-03-2018-0132

Grewal, D., Hulland, J., Kopalle, P. K., & Karahanna, E. (2020). The future of technology and marketing: A multidisciplinary perspective. *Journal of the Academy of Marketing Science*, *48*(1), 1–8. doi:10.100711747-019-00711-4

Grosso, M., Castaldo, S., Li, H. A., & Larivière, B. (2020). What information do shoppers share? The effect of personnel-, retailer-, and country-trust on willingness to share information. *Journal of Retailing*, *96*(4), 524–547. doi:10.1016/j.jretai.2020.08.002

Hajli, N., Sims, J., Zadeh, A. H., & Richard, M.-O. (2017). A social commerce investigation of the role of trust in a social networking site on purchase intentions. *Journal of Business Research*, *71*, 133–141. doi:10.1016/j.jbusres.2016.10.004

Hirsh, J. B., Kang, S. K., & Bodenhausen, G. V. (2012). Personalized Persuasion: Tailoring Persuasive Appeals to Recipients' Personality Traits. *Psychological Science*, *23*(6), 578–581. doi:10.1177/0956797611436349 PMID:22547658

Illia, L., Colleoni, E., Etter, M., & Meggiorin, K. (2023). Finding the Tipping Point: When Heterogeneous Evaluations in Social Media Converge and Influence Organizational Legitimacy. *Business & Society*, *62*(1), 117–150. doi:10.1177/00076503211073516

James, T. L., Wallace, L., Warkentin, M., Kim, B. C., & Collignon, S. E. (2017). Exposing others' information on online social networks (OSNs): Perceived shared risk, its determinants, and its influence on OSN privacy control use. *Information & Management*, *54*(7), 851–865. doi:10.1016/j.im.2017.01.001

Kaplan, D. (2021). Public intimacy in social media: The mass audience as a third party. *Media Culture & Society*, *43*(4), 595–612. doi:10.1177/0163443721991087

Kosinski, M., Stillwell, D., & Graepel, T. (2013). Private traits and attributes are predictable from digital records of human behavior. *Proceedings of the National Academy of Sciences of the United States of America*, *110*(15), 5802–5805. doi:10.1073/pnas.1218772110 PMID:23479631

Lambillotte, L., Bart, Y., & Poncin, I. (2022). When Does Information Transparency Reduce Downside of Personalization? Role of Need for Cognition and Perceived Control. *Journal of Interactive Marketing*, *57*(3), 393–420. doi:10.1177/10949968221095557

Lasén, A. (2015). *Digital self-portraits, exposure and the modulation of intimacy. In Mobile and Digital Communication: Approaches to Public and Private*. Livros LabCom. doi:10.4324/9781315399300-8

Laufer, R. S., & Wolfe, M. (1977). Privacy as a Concept and a Social Issue: A Multidimensional Developmental Theory. *The Journal of Social Issues*, *33*(3), 22–42. doi:10.1111/j.1540-4560.1977.tb01880.x

Laussel, D., Van Long, N., & Resende, J. (2022). Profit effects of consumers' identity management: A dynamic model. *Management Science*. Advance online publication. doi:10.1287/mnsc.2022.4511

Lee, J., Kim, C., & Lee, K. C. (2022). Exploring the personalization-intrusiveness-intention framework to evaluate the effects of personalization in social media. *International Journal of Information Management, 66*, 102532. Advance online publication. doi:10.1016/j.ijinfomgt.2022.102532

Lin, C. A., & Kim, T. (2016). Predicting user response to sponsored advertising on social media via the technology acceptance model. *Computers in Human Behavior, 64*, 710–718. doi:10.1016/j.chb.2016.07.027

Lin, X., Huang, X., Liu, S., Li, Y., Luo, H., & Yu, S. (2022). Competitive price-quality strategy of platforms under user privacy concerns. *Journal of Theoretical and Applied Electronic Commerce Research, 17*(2), 571–589. doi:10.3390/jtaer17020030

Liu, Z., & Wang, X. (2018). How to regulate individuals' privacy boundaries on social network sites: A cross-cultural comparison. *Information & Management, 55*(8), 1005–1023. doi:10.1016/j.im.2018.05.006

Matz, S. C., Appel, R. E., & Kosinski, M. (2020). Privacy in the age of psychological targeting. *Current Opinion in Psychology, 31*, 116–121. doi:10.1016/j.copsyc.2019.08.010 PMID:31563799

McNealy, J., & Mullis, M. D. (2019). Tea and turbulence: Communication privacy management theory and online celebrity gossip forums. *Computers in Human Behavior, 92*, 110–118. doi:10.1016/j.chb.2018.10.029

Morey, T., Forbath, T., & Schoop, A. (2015). Customer data: Designing for transparency and trust. *Harvard Business Review, 93*(5), 96–105.

Petronio, S. (2002). *Boundaries of privacy: Dialectics of disclosure*. Suny Press. doi:10.1353/book4588

Petronio, S., & Reierson, J. (2009). *Regulating the privacy of confidentiality: Grasping the complexities through communication privacy management theory.* Academic Press.

Phelps, J. E., D'Souza, G., & Nowak, G. J. (2001). Antecedents and consequences of consumer privacy concerns: An empirical investigation. *Journal of Interactive Marketing, 15*(4), 2–17. doi:10.1002/dir.1019

Plangger, K., Grewal, D., de Ruyter, K., & Tucker, C. (2022). The future of digital technologies in marketing: A conceptual framework and an overview. *Journal of the Academy of Marketing Science, 50*(6), 1125–1134. doi:10.100711747-022-00906-2

Rimer, B. K., & Kreuter, M. W. (2006). Advancing Tailored Health Communication: A Persuasion and Message Effects Perspective. *Journal of Communication, 56*(suppl_1), S184–S201. doi:10.1111/j.1460-2466.2006.00289.x

Schweidel, D. A., Bart, Y., Inman, J. J., Stephen, A. T., Libai, B., Andrews, M., Rosario, A. B., Chae, I., Chen, Z., Kupor, D., Longoni, C., & Thomaz, F. (2022). How consumer digital signals are reshaping the customer journey. *Journal of the Academy of Marketing Science, 50*(6), 1–20. doi:10.100711747-022-00839-w PMID:35221393

Setyani, V., Zhu, Y.-Q., Hidayanto, A. N., Sandhyaduhita, P. I., & Hsiao, B. (2019). Exploring the psychological mechanisms from personalized advertisements to urge to buy impulsively on social media. *International Journal of Information Management, 48*, 96–107. doi:10.1016/j.ijinfomgt.2019.01.007

SoleymanianM.WeinbergC.ZhuT. (2021). Privacy concerns, economic benefits, and consumer decisions: A multi-period panel study of consumer choices in the automobile insurance industry. In *Economic Benefits, and Consumer Decisions: A Multi-Period Panel Study of Consumer Choices in the Automobile Insurance Industry*. doi:10.2139/ssrn.3905034

Stephen, A. T., & Toubia, O. (2010). Deriving value from social commerce networks. *JMR, Journal of Marketing Research*, *47*(2), 215–228. doi:10.1509/jmkr.47.2.215

Suchman, M. C. (1995). Managing Legitimacy: Strategic and Institutional Approaches. *Academy of Management Review*, *20*(3), 571. doi:10.2307/258788

Tang, Y., & Ning, X. (2023). Understanding user misrepresentation behavior on social apps: The perspective of privacy calculus theory. *Decision Support Systems*, *165*, 113881. doi:10.1016/j.dss.2022.113881

Thomaz, F., Salge, C., Karahanna, E., & Hulland, J. (2020). Learning from the Dark Web: Leveraging conversational agents in the era of hyper-privacy to enhance marketing. *Journal of the Academy of Marketing Science*, *48*(1), 43–63. doi:10.100711747-019-00704-3

Trepte, S. (2021). The social media privacy model: Privacy and communication in the light of social media affordances. *Communication Theory*, *31*(4), 549–570. doi:10.1093/ct/qtz035

Tsai, J. Y., Egelman, S., Cranor, L., & Acquisti, A. (2011). The effect of online privacy information on purchasing behavior: An experimental study. *Information Systems Research*, *22*(2), 254–268. doi:10.1287/isre.1090.0260

Tucker, C. E. (2014). Social networks, personalized advertising, and privacy controls. *JMR, Journal of Marketing Research*, *51*(5), 546–562. doi:10.1509/jmr.10.0355

Westin, A. F. (1968). Privacy and freedom. *Washington and Lee Law Review, 25*.

Yi, Y., Zhu, N., He, J., Jurcut, A. D., Ma, X., & Luo, Y. (2023). A privacy-dependent condition-based privacy-preserving information sharing scheme in online social networks. *Computer Communications*, *200*, 149–160. Advance online publication. doi:10.1016/j.comcom.2023.01.010

Zhu, Y.-Q., & Kanjanamekanant, K. (2021). No trespassing: Exploring privacy boundaries in personalized advertisement and its effects on ad attitude and purchase intentions on social media. *Information & Management*, *58*(2), 103314. doi:10.1016/j.im.2020.103314

ADDITIONAL READING

Gerstein, R. S. (1978). Intimacy and Privacy. *Ethics*, *89*(1), 76–81. doi:10.1086/292105

O'Hara, K. (2010). Intimacy 2.0: Privacy rights and privacy responsibilities on the World Wide Web. In University of Southampton Institutional Repository.

Protecting User Privacy in Web Search Utilization. (2023). *Advances in Information Security*. Privacy, and Ethics Book Series. doi:10.4018/978-1-6684-6914-9

KEY TERMS AND DEFINITIONS

Intimacy: An aspect of an individual's private life that depending on context and social norms, is considered private and only shared with those with whom they have a close or emotional connection. It is a multidimensional concept comprising physical, psychological, social, and informational dimensions.

Legitimacy: It is the perception by individuals that an entity is authentic, complies with the law, is truthful, as well as that it operates in an ethical, expected, and appropriate manner in the specific social context in which it operates.

Privacy: A perception of selective control over a set of information that a person considers his private life and has the right to protect and control by choosing with whom and how he shares it.

Privacy Concern: The concern that an individual develops towards the possible misuse or unexpected misuse of their private or intimate information.

Relationship: A connection or bond between two individuals or entities characterised by trust, interactions and mutual understanding, shared interests, values, or experiences.

Social Network: Refers to an online platform based on the ease with which users can create, share and consume content with other people or entities. This content can take different formats and be consumed on multiple devices.

Transparency: It is the quality of a person or entity to be open and honest in responding to other parties involved in any action or decision, smoothly providing information.

Trust: A crucial aspect of any relationship that refers to the belief of certainty and security that someone gives to a person or entity. It is a belief that implies the assurance that the other will act ethically, fairly, and competently as expected. Trust is based on the legitimacy given.

Chapter 10
Security in Digital Marketing: Challenges and Opportunities

Albérico Travassos Rosário
https://orcid.org/0000-0003-4793-4110
GOVCOPP, IADE, Universidade Europeia, Portugal

ABSTRACT

Digital marketing presents both challenges and opportunities when it comes to security. As more and more customer data is collected and stored digitally, the potential for sensitive information to fall into the wrong hands increases. Digital marketing also offers opportunities for improved security. Implementing two-factor authentication and using unique and complex passwords can also minimize the risk of unauthorized access to accounts and personal information. Overall, the key to maintaining security in digital marketing is to be proactive and stay informed about the latest threats and vulnerabilities. This includes staying up to date on best practices for data protection and regularly monitoring and testing your systems for security weaknesses. Based on this research gap, a systematic review of the bibliometric literature was performed, and data were synthesized from 80 documents identified through Scopus indexing. This research aims to assess the challenges and opportunities.

INTRODUCTION

The internet has created digital marketing opportunities that allow companies and their marketing teams to reach broader local and international audiences through eCommerce websites and internet-based platforms, including social media. These opportunities have enabled businesses to increase their revenues and scale up their operations, thus enhancing their financial performance (Krishen et al., 2021). In addition, digital marketing has created channels for marketers to build strong relationships with a company's ideal customers through two-communication, facilitating value co-creation and improved customization of products and services. Thus, digital marketing has increasingly become essential for business survival in the current business environment. However, digital marketing has also increased exposure to cybersecurity issues, such as data breaches, cyberattacks and malware infections (Konyeha, 2020). For instance, completing transactions on an eCommerce website often requires third-party services, such as PayPal,

DOI: 10.4018/978-1-6684-8958-1.ch010

which require customers' financial details, including bank and personal information. Such information is constantly targeted by hackers, increasing an eCommerce website's vulnerability to cyber-attack. Thus, security in digital marketing has become a critical concern.

Cyber insecurity as a threat to digital marketing disproportionally affects digital marketers. For instance, marketers' accounts have higher risks of cyber-attacks since they have higher permissions and access rights. In addition, digital marketers tend to link their social media profiles with links to eCommerce websites they promote to encourage their followers to click through (Manocha et al., 2020). When the link harbours malware, every person who clicks on that link is subjected to a cyber-attack (Konyeha, 2020). These instances show the extent to which digital marketers can be subject to cyber insecurity and the severe consequences they may have on the marketer, their audience, and the overall company. Thus, digital marketers are subjected to the burden of safeguarding a company's and its customer's safety and privacy. Other cyber insecurity issues include attacks targeting content management systems (CMS), such as WordPress, Drupal, and Joomla, which companies use for content marketing to attract and maintain clients (Kumar et al., 2022). Phishing attacks allow hackers to create fake email accounts that match real business accounts to steal personal information such as login credentials or credit card information. In addition, hackers can target business emails used in digital marketing, which can be exploited to send spam messages that include viruses. These cyber insecurity issues require businesses to adopt best practices in digital marketing security, including proactive measures such as regular software updates and security patches, two-factor authentication and strong password policies (Konyeha, 2020).

This research aims to identify the most relevant documents and synthesize their data and findings to provide insights that can aid in developing a practical security framework in digital marketing.

The bibliometric literature review presented synthesizes data from 80 documents identified through Scopus indexing to identify opportunities and challenges in digital marketing security, thus providing practical insights that can be integrated into business to create a robust security framework.

METHODOLOGICAL APPROACH

The researcher conducted a systematic review of the bibliometric literature to gather, summarize, and analyze data from multiple research. This approach helps bring different perspectives into the study topic. Gaffar et al. (2015) recognize comprehensive literature analysis as an effective strategy for creating new knowledge by interpreting and combining existing knowledge. Okoli (2015) further explains that a rigorous standalone literature review should be systematic by following a specific methodological approach, comprehensive in its scope of the study, and explicit in explaining the procedures it was conducted. Following these recommendations makes the study reproducible and results in quality, accurate findings that can be integrated into business practice. The rapidly growing concerns over cyber insecurity in this digital era have attracted the attention of researchers, resulting in the publishing of massive research articles, books, and other materials. The Scopus database was used to index relevant sources. Thus, the LRSB helped filter the most relevant and quality sources for analysis and reporting. Consequently, the methodology can be used to decipher and map cumulative scientific knowledge and emerging variations of a well-established topic (Rosário, 2021; Rosário & Dias, 2022, 2023; Rosário, et al., 2021).

Thus, the use of bibliometric analysis can help understand its development and adoption in businesses to identify potential challenges. The use of the LRSB review process is divided into 3 phases and 6 steps (Table 1), as proposed by Rosário (2021), Rosário and Dias (2022, 2023), and Rosário, et al. (2021).

Table 1. Process of systematic LRSB

Phase	Step	Description
Exploration	Step 1	formulating the research problem
	Step 2	searching for appropriate literature
	Step 3	critical appraisal of the selected studies
	Step 4	data synthesis from individual sources
Interpretation	Step 5	reporting findings and recommendations
Communication	Step 6	presentation of the LRSB report

The database of indexed scientific and/or academic documents used was Scopus, the most important peer review in the scientific and academic world. It is considered to be one of the largest abstract and citation databases, containing over 76 million records and 24,000 peer-reviewed journals from around the world, the Scopus database is an essential tool for researchers and scholars, providing a wealth of information and tools to help advance research and facilitate collaboration across different fields and regions.

However, we consider that the study has the limitation of considering only the Scopus decomposition database, excluding other scientific and academic bases. The literature search includes peer-reviewed scientific and/or academic documents published up to January 2022.

The initial literature search involved using the keyword "security," resulting in 882,224 documents. Most of these documents were not relevant to the study topic. Thus, the researcher added the keyword "digital marketing," reducing the documents to 80 (N=80). The screening process is summarized in Table 2.

Table 2. Screening methodology

Database Scopus	Screening	Publications
Meta-search	keyword: *security*	882,224
First Inclusion Criterion	keyword: security Subject area: business, management and accounting	4578
Second Inclusion Criterion	keyword: security Subject area: business, management and accounting Exactly word: Digital Marketing	80
Screening	keyword: security Subject area: business, management and accounting Exactly word: digital marketing Published until January 2022	

Source: own elaboration

Finally, content and theme analysis techniques were used to identify, analyze, and report the various documents as proposed by Rosário (2021), Rosário and Dias (2022, 2023), and Rosário, et al. (2021). The 80 scientific and/or academic documents indexed in Scopus are later analyzed in a narrative and bibliometric way to deepen the content and possible derivation of common themes that directly respond to the research question (Rosário, 2021; Rosário & Dias, 2022, 2023; Rosário, et al., 2021). Of the 57 selected documents, 30 are Conference Paper; 25 Articles; 11 are Book Chapter; 9 are Conference Review; 3 Book; and 2 are Review.

PUBLICATION DISTRIBUTION

Peer-reviewed articles on marketing management in retail customer satisfaction until January 2022. The year 2021 had the highest number of peer-reviewed publications on the subject, reaching 24.

Figure 1 summarizes the peer-reviewed literature published in January 2022.

The publications were sorted out as follows: Lecture Notes In Networks And Systems (6); Blockchain Technology And Applications For Digital Marketing (4); 2022 2nd International Conference On Advance Computing And Innovative Technologies In Engineering Icacite 2022 (3); Communications In Computer And Information Science (3); International Journal Of Advanced Science And Technology (3); 2020 5th International Conference On Fog And Mobile Edge Computing Fmec 2020 (2); Lecture Notes In Computer Science Including Subseries Lecture Notes In Artificial Intelligence And Lecture Notes In Bioinformatics (2); Smart Innovation Systems And Technologies (2); Sustainability Switzerland (2); the remaining publications with 1. Interest in the topic with a positive evolution since 2013.

Figure 1. Documents by year
Source: Own elaboration

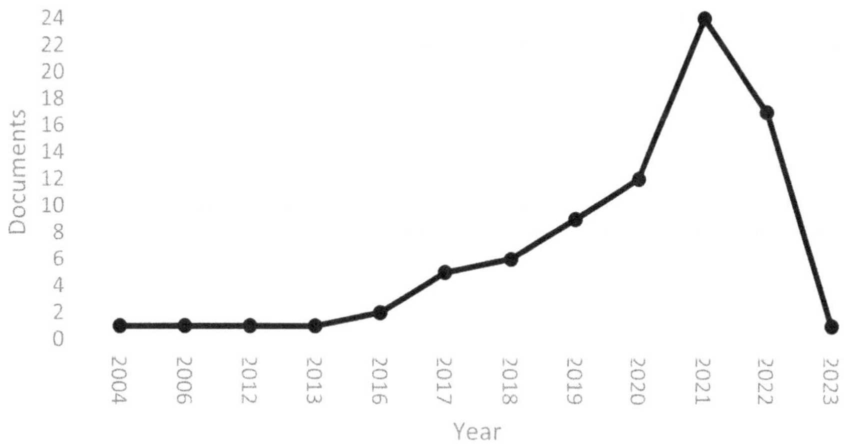

In Table 3 we analyze the Scimago Journal & Country Rank (SJR), the best quartile and the H index by publication Application Of Machine Learning In Agriculture is the most quoted publication with 2,470 (SJR), Q1 and H Index 6. There is a total of 10 publications in Q1, 5 publications in Q2 and 8 publications, in Q3 and 4 publications in Q4. Publications from best quartile Q1 represent 16% of the publications on titles; best quartile Q2 represents 8%, best quartile Q3 represents 13%, and best Q4 represents 6% of each of the titles of 62 publications, finally, 35 publications still do not have data available, representing 56% of publications.

As shown in Table 3, the significant majority of publications still do not have indexed data.

Table 3. Scimago journal and country rank impact factor

Title	SJR	Best Quartile	H Index
Application Of Machine Learning In Agriculture	2,470	Q1	6
Land Use Policy	1,640	Q1	125
Internet Of Things	1,610	Q1	27
Computer Networks	1,590	Q1	139
IEEE Access	0,930	Q1	158
Marketing Intelligence And Planning	0,930	Q2	75
Computational Intelligence And Neuroscience	0,860	Q1	61
Applied Mathematics And Nonlinear Sciences	0,840	Q1	14
Journal Of Librarianship And Information Science	0,760	Q1	33
Security And Communication Networks	0,730	Q2	50
Sustainability	0,660	Q1	109
MIT Sloan Management Review	0,650	Q2	109
Agriculture Switzerland	0,530	Q2	43
Synthesis Lectures On Human Language Technologies	0,390	Q1	23
International Review On Public And Nonprofit Marketing	0,360	Q3	19
Iaes International Journal Of Artificial Intelligence	0,350	Q3	11
Lecture Notes In Business Information Processing	0,300	Q3	52
Informing Science	0,270	Q2	25
ACM International Conference Proceeding Series	0,230	-*	128
Emerald Emerging Markets Case Studies	0,230	Q3	7
Smart Innovation Systems And Technologies	0,220	Q3	27
Advances In Intelligent Systems And Computing	0,220	Q4	48
Communications In Computer And Information Science	0,210	Q4	55
African Journal Of Hospitality Tourism And Leisure	0,210	Q3	14
Iop Conference Series Earth And Environmental Science	0,200	-*	34
Journal Of Intellectual Property Rights	0,180	Q3	14
Journal Of Computational And Theoretical Nanoscience	0,170	Q4	53
Lecture Notes In Networks And Systems	0,150	Q4	22
Lecture Notes In Civil Engineering	0,130	Q4	13
International Journal Of Advanced Science And Technology	0	-*	17
1st International Conference On Computer Applications And Information Security Iccais 2018	0	-*	7
2019 IEEE 9th International Conference On System Engineering And Technology Icset 2019 Proceeding	0	-*	6
International Conference On Advanced Communication Technology Icact	0	-*	37

Continued on following page

Table 3. Continued

Title	SJR	Best Quartile	H Index
International Conference On Communication Technologies Comtech 2017	0	-*	7
International Journal Of Economic Research	0	-*	22
Journal Of Direct Data And Digital Marketing Practice	0	-*	16
Journal Of Physics Conference Series	0	-*	10
Opcion	0	-*	20
Printing News	0	-*	2
Proceedings Of The 2017 International Conference Quality Management Transport And Information Security Information Technologies IT And Qm And Is 2017	0	-*	11
Proceedings Of The 31st International Business Information Management Association Conference Ibima 2018 Innovation Management And Education Excellence Through Vision 2020	0	-*	13
Proceedings Of The 5th International Conference On Management Leadership And Governance Icmlg 2017	0	-*	3
Blockchain Technology And Applications For Digital Marketing	-*	-*	-*
2022 2nd International Conference On Advance Computing And Innovative Technologies In Engineering Icacite 2022	-*	-*	-*
2020 5th International Conference On Fog And Mobile Edge Computing Fmec 2020	-*	-*	-*
Lecture Notes In Computer Science Including Subseries Lecture Notes In Artificial Intelligence And Lecture Notes In Bioinformatics	-*	-*	-*
2020 8th International Conference On Information And Communication Technology Icoict 2020	-*	-*	-*
2021 9th International Conference On Reliability Infocom Technologies And Optimization Trends And Future Directions Icrito 2021	-*	-*	-*
2022 IEEE German Education Conference Gecon 2022	-*	-*	-*
4th International Conference On Innovative Computing Icic 2021	-*	-*	-*
Customer Relationship Management Concepts And Technologies Fourth Edition	-*	-*	-*
Cyber Warfare And Terrorism Concepts Methodologies Tools And Applications	-*	-*	-*
Developments In Marketing Science Proceedings Of The Academy Of Marketing Science	-*	-*	-*
Future Of E Commerce	-*	-*	-*
Improving Business Performance Through Innovation In The Digital Economy	-*	-*	-*
Proceedings 2017 2nd International Conference On Recent Trends And Challenges In Computational Models Icrtccm 2017	-*	-*	-*
Proceedings 2021 2nd International Conference On Computer Science And Management Technology Iccsmt 2021	-*	-*	-*
Proceedings Of The 2020 IEEE International Conference Quality Management Transport And Information Security Information Technologies IT And Qm And Is 2020	-*	-*	-*
Proceedings Of The 5th International Conference On Electronics Communication And Aerospace Technology Iceca 2021	-*	-*	-*
Research Anthology On Machine Learning Techniques Methods And Applications	-*	-*	-*
Routledge Companion To Marketing Research	-*	-*	-*
Springer Proceedings In Business And Economics	-*	-*	-*

Note: *data not available.

Source: Own elaboration

The subject areas covered by the 80 scientific and/or academic documents were: Computer Science (45); Engineering (28); Business, Management and Accounting (23); Decision Sciences (17); Economics, Econometrics and Finance (14); Mathematics (13); Social Sciences (13); Energy (8); Agricultural and Biological Sciences (5); Environmental Science (4); Medicine (4); Physics and Astronomy (4); Chemical Engineering (3); Materials Science (2); Arts and Humanities (1); Chemistry (1); Earth and Planetary Sciences (1); and Neuroscience (1).

The most cited article was "E-agricultural supply chain management coupled with blockchain effect and cooperative strategies" by Mohammed et al. (2021). with 22 citations published in the Sustainability 0,660 (SJR), the best quartile (Q1), and with an H-index (109), this article is " the research has incorporated the blockchain effect by web design elements into the agricultural supply chain management (Agri-SCM) study".

In Figure 2 we can analyze the evolution of citations of the documents published until January 2022. The number of citations shows a positive net growth with R2 of 42% for the period ≤2013-2023, with 2023 reaching 221 citations.

Figure 2. Evolution of citations between ≤2013 and 2023
Source: Own elaboration

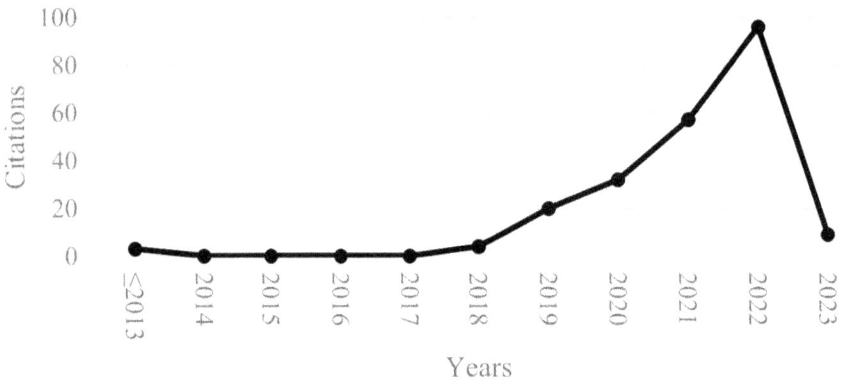

The h-index was used to ascertain the productivity and impact of the published work, based on the largest number of articles included that had at least the same number of citations. Of the documents considered for the h-index, 9 have been cited at least 9 times.

Citations of all scientific and/or academic documents from the period ≤2013 to January 2022, with a total of 221 citations, of the 80 documents 26 were not cited. The self-citation of documents in the period ≤2013 to January 2023, 2022 was self-cited 96 times.

The bibliometric study was carried out to investigate and identify indicators of the dynamics and evolution of scientific and/or academic information in documents based on the main keywords (Figure 3). The results were extracted from the scientific software VOSviewe, which aims to identify the main search keywords "Security" and "Digital Marketing".

Figure 3. a network of all keywords
Source: Own elaboration

The research was based on scientific and/or academic documents on future challenges of Security in Digital Marketing. In Figure 4, we can examine the linked keywords, and thus, it is possible to highlight the network of keywords that appear together / linked in each scientific article, allowing us to identify the topics studied by research and identify trends in future research. Finally, in Figure 5, a profusion of bibliographic coupling with a unit of analysis of the cited references is presented.

Figure 4. A network of linked keywords
Source: Own elaboration

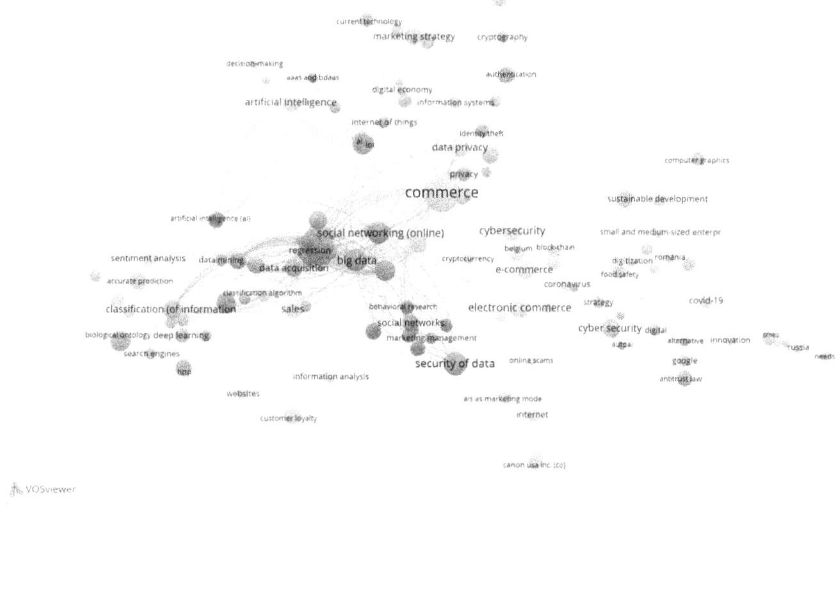

Figure 5. A network of bibliographic coupling
Source: Own elaboration

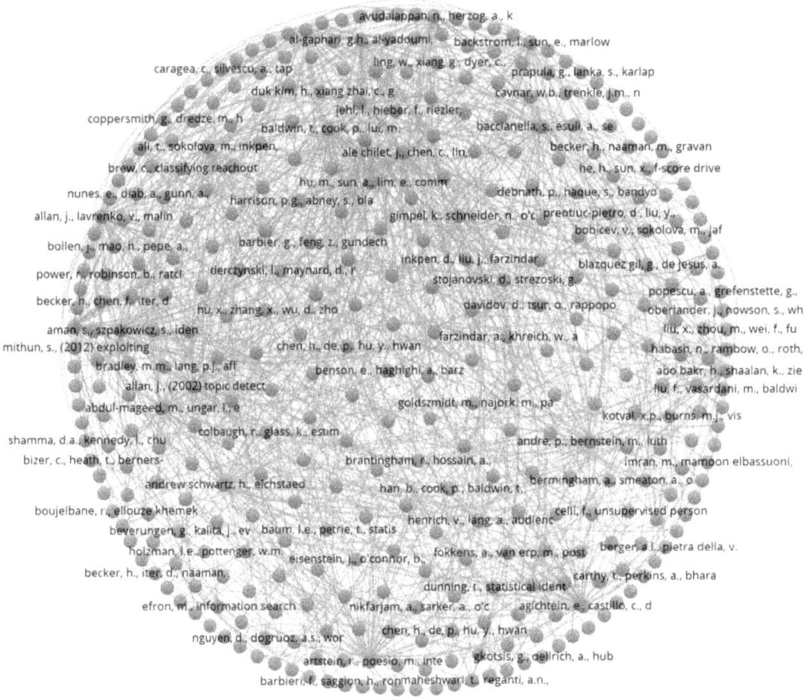

THEORETICAL PERSPECTIVES

The need to integrate digital marketing strategies into current core business practices has become very critical. This is because contemporary digital marketing approaches provide opportunities for businesses to communicate with their ideal customers, build trust, establish and maintain relationships, enter new markets, and increase organizational competitiveness (Marinho et al., 2021). The modern client demands active interactions, personalization, and value co-creation, requiring digital marketers to leverage emerging information and communication technologies (Aftab et al., 2021). However, this increased use of technologies in digital marketing increases vulnerability to cyber-attacks. For instance, online transactions require sharing sensitive personal information such as banking and personal address. Hackers often target this information to commit financial fraud or impersonate a client for ulterior motives such as access to certain information. Reports show that data breaches and ID theft cases have multiplied, affecting millions of consumers and causing approximately $6 trillion in losses (Kumar et al., 2022). These issues make it essential to study and analyze data on security in digital marketing to provide information that can aid improvements.

Definition and Evolution of Digital Marketing

Digital marketing comprises marketing initiatives that use an electronic device or the internet to communicate an organization's offerings or brand value. In this case, businesses leverage digital channels such as search engines, social media, email, and their websites to interact and engage with existing and prospective clients (Al Mansoori & Ahmad, 2021). As a result, digital marketing is known as 'online marketing,' 'internet marketing,' or 'web marketing'. With the increasing penetration of social media, smart devices, and the internet, companies are using multiple digital methods and platforms to interact with clients where they spend the majority of their time: online (Milton Ganesh et al., 2017). Digital marketing encompasses various approaches, including using a company's website for its online branding assets, such as digital advertising, email marketing, and online brochures. Other methods of digital marketing include Search Engine Optimization (SEO), Search Engine Marketing (SEM), e-commerce marketing, influencer marketing, content marketing, campaign marketing, content automation, data-driven marketing, social media marketing, social media optimization, and gamified marketing (Ali & Xia, 2022; Mahendru & Singh, 2023). The diversity of the marketing approaches allows companies to adopt multichannel marketing to ensure that marketing initiatives reach a broad audience, thus increasing the probability of achieving the desired outcomes. For example, a company can combine email marketing with social media marketing, thus reaching a wider audience.

Although digital marketing has become increasingly popular recently, its history dates back to 1971 when Ray Tomlinson sent the first email. Tomlinson's technology allowed users to send and receive files via different devices. In addition, the 1980s saw an expansion of computer storage that allowed companies to store customer information (Arellano et al., 2022). With these technologies, companies began to choose online tools such as database marketing instead of limited broker listing. As a result, they leveraged these innovations to improve buyer-seller relationships by tracking customer information through databases (Perdices et al., 2021). However, the term' digital marketing' was coined in the 1990s following the development of server or client architecture and the popularity of personal computers (Desai & Vidyapeeth, 2019). In addition, during this period, Customer Relationship Management (CRM) applications were increasingly becoming popular in most companies and were integrated into marketing strategies. The increased adoption of technologies led to intense competition that compelled suppliers to incorporate more services into their software, such as marketing, sales, and customer service (Bansal et al., 2021; Pînzaru et al., 2017). Moreover, marketers had more control over massive amounts of online consumer data following the internet's inception attributable to eCRM software. This software enabled companies to update client requirements data and determine and prioritize their experience, leading to higher adoption.

The evolution of digital marketing since the 1990s and 2000s has altered how companies and organizations utilize technology for marketing. Digital marketing efforts are growing more widespread and efficient as digital channels are more integrated into marketing strategies and everyday life (Huaraca Aparco et al., 2022; Khan & Kushwah, 2021). In addition, individuals worldwide are increasingly utilizing digital gadgets instead of visiting physical stores, increasing the need for marketers to embrace digital communication channels to reach and engage them (Desai & Vidyapeeth, 2019). The rise of social media platforms such as Facebook, LinkedIn, YouTube, and Twitter facilitates this transition to digital marketing and eCommerce. Besides, consumers increasingly rely on digital gadgets in their everyday lives, which translates to increased anticipation of consistent user experience across many platforms while seeking product information (Magano & Cunha, 2020; Hoang et al., 2019). As a result, changes in customer behavior have aided the diversity of marketing technologies as companies are prompted to adjust their marketing strategies and tools to match clients' standards, requirements, and expectations.

Definition of Security in Digital Marketing

The digital world is rapidly growing, with businesses and marketers utilizing emerging platforms to expand their reach and increase their sales and revenues. As a result, digital marketing has become a vital and integral component of organizational strategy, assisting firms in reaching a larger audience through online platforms (Soldatova et al., 2020). Online presence has become critical for all businesses aiming to strengthen their competitive status in their respective industry, as online interactions and engagement with clients are crucial (Soares & Sousa, 2022; Ramadan, 2019). However, with the advent of new tools and technologies utilized by digital marketers daily, the possibility of security breaches and privacy violations is equally alarming. In addition, organizations attempting to take advantage of every opportunity presented by the digital world have increased exposure to cyber security risk. Thus, Velinov et al. (2022) define marketing security as real-time control and management of company and customer data in ways that prevent leakages and access by unauthorized persons. The rise of cyber insecurity and threats in digital marketing indicates the challenges hindering the full realization of marketing security. The extent of the problem is evidenced in Kumar et al.'s research, which estimates that cybercrimes caused $6 trillion in losses in 2021. Similarly, Liu et al. (2022) indicate that 83% of retailers in the US are vulnerable to cyber-attacks and can be easily attacked. In addition, the scholars noted that cybercrimes increased by 600% during the Covid-19 pandemic as businesses transitioned into online models due to increased dependence on technology. These statistics show the significance of cybersecurity for businesses and organizations leveraging digital technologies to increase efficiency, performance, and productivity in the current digital and technological era.

Since the digital marketing environment is interconnected, digital marketers must not overlook the value of data protection or underestimate the importance of cybersecurity applications beyond networking. A minor flaw can result in a massive disaster, resulting in financial loss and customer confidence (Farzindar & Inkpen, 2018). For example, digital marketers have higher permission and access rights, which give them access to sensitive information within a company's information that aids their marketing planning and implementation processes (Watson et al., 2022; Gregory & Bentall, 2012). Therefore, the information can land on unauthorized persons, including hackers, in a case where their accounts are compromised. In addition, content management systems (CMS) such as WordPress and Joomla are susceptible to cyber-attacks because most hackers are familiar with their procedures (Al-Azani & El-Alfy, 2020). As a result, they can effortlessly spread malware if not blocked. Email marketing is another digital marketing tool vulnerable to cyber-attacks (Buttle & Maklan, 2019). Hackers might exploit organization email accounts to disseminate spam messages containing viruses, leading sites to be blocked by the system of the organization responsible for the security of other websites on their server. This digital marketing security threat can have multiple negative consequences, including halting the email marketing campaign and the sites being banned or prohibited (Bishop & Rowley, 2013; Suleiman et al., 2021). The other challenge is identity theft, leading to illegal downloads, hacked passwords, and unauthorized money transactions (Almabdy, 2018). Therefore, continuous monitoring and tracking of internet activities and risk assessments are essential in cybersecurity. Digital marketers should collaborate with other relevant departments, such as IT, to prioritize strengthening the company's security protocols. Solid cybersecurity tactics can enhance data protection and ensure security in payment gateways, social media pages, and other platforms.

Importance of Security in Digital Marketing

Digital marketing leverages online channels to build a brand's image, promote company values, and convey its ethos. In addition, it strengthens customer relationships and makes information accessible to all key stakeholders, thus making the company stand out in the competitive business environment (Dvir & Gafni, 2018). Therefore, a single cyber-attack or malicious activity can have severe consequences, such as a negative reputation and low customer confidence and trust (Rabby et al., 2022). Thus, security in digital marketing is critical to organizational success in the current digital and technological era. This sub-section explores the various benefits of enhancing digital marketing security.

Improved Customer Trust and Confidence

Having the proper security measures in place can strengthen customer trust and confidence in a company. With the rise in data breaches worldwide, customers' are more sceptical about organizations' capability to protect their sensitive information (Indrawati & Shabila, 2020). These concerns slow down digital marketing campaigns leading to less success as customers are afraid of sharing personal information to complete online transactions or engage with digital marketers online (Mukherjee et al., 2021; Rabby et al., 2022). As a result, digital marketers and their organizations can consider incorporating high-tech security features such as voice biometrics, fingerprint ID, moving data to the cloud, and machine learning to detect suspicious activities (Klien et al., 2018). Communicating these practices to the customers proves that the digital markers are going beyond standard requirements to strengthen security measures and protect customer data, thus winning their trust and building confidence.

Increased Brand Reputation and Loyalty

Companies work hard to build and protect their reputation by making a safe option for their target customers. Brand loyalty requires trust. Loyal customers trust that the company can protect their personal and sensitive data. In the case of digital marketing, brand reputation and loyalty are directly linked to brand trust (Robin et al., 2021; Swetha et al., 2019). This is because customers are more likely to have positive brand perceptions and build long-term relationships if they can trust the company to protect their confidential and sensitive information. On the other hand, customers can interpret inadequate data security measures as a lack of respect for their privacy and a company's unwillingness to address their concerns (Bozhuk & Krasnov, 2017). As a result, a breach exposing personal or private information shows that the company did not prioritize the data entrusted to them by their customers. This situation results in a negative brand reputation and a lack of trust and loyalty. This notion is evidenced in a FireEye survey, which revealed that 75% of consumers were inclined to cease purchasing from a firm if a data breach was connected to its failure to prioritize cybersecurity (Security Compass, 2020). In addition, the same study indicates that 81% of surveyed executives revealed that a data breach that results in the loss of confidential customer information leads to a 21% loss of an organization's economic value of its reputation and image. This lost reputation takes approximately 11.8 months to restore. Security Compass (2020) also reveals that 77% of consumers consider data privacy and cybersecurity as the top reasons to select a seller, indicating the impact of security on loyalty. Therefore, it is critical for businesses and digital marketers to prioritize security and communicate best practices to the audiences to enhance brand reputation and build loyalty.

New Business Opportunities Through Enhanced Security Measures

More businesses today rely on technologies to operate, making cybersecurity a critical issue in the modern business world. With the increasing threat of cyber-attacks and data breaches, companies are investing heavily in enhanced security measures to protect organizational and customer data and systems (Notta & Kitta, 2021). As a result, these initiatives have created new business opportunities in the cybersecurity market. For instance, there is a demand for cybersecurity professionals with expertise in advanced security solutions such as artificial intelligence and machine learning-based security systems (Oncioiu, 2019). Companies worldwide are increasingly adopting these systems due to their ability to automatically detect and respond to security threats. Consequently, they are associated with multiple benefits, such as reducing the time and effort required to conduct manual threat assessment and intervention.

The second business opportunity relates to the growth in the provision of managed security services, which allow companies to outsource their security needs to experts. This development has led to the rapid emergence of cybersecurity solutions firms, which focuses on handling organizations' security issues (Rath, 2022). Consequently, executives and their teams, including digital marketers, can focus on other core business activities and let professionals handle their security. The demand for managed security services providers will continue to increase as more firms prioritize reducing security risks (Simion et al., 2018). Moreover, cloud security solutions have emerged as a new business opportunity due to the growing popularity of cloud computing (Radha & Nelson Kennedy Babu, 2018; Vatsa et al., 2021). Companies are embracing cloud-based security solutions as an effective way of securing their data and applications in a way that can be easily integrated into their existing infrastructure (Singer, 2006). Thus, companies specializing in security solutions and services are leveraging the growing need for enhanced cybersecurity measures to create revenue-generating opportunities, create jobs for cybersecurity professionals, and develop trustable brands in the global cybersecurity market.

Challenges in Digital Marketing Security

The increased adoption of advanced technologies in digital marketing has expanded opportunities for malicious cyber-attacks. Digital marketers are now equally vulnerable to cyber-attacks as other professionals working with clients online (Sheresheva et al., 2021). Thus, identifying and analyzing the various security issues threatening digital marketing can effectively protect digital marketers and their target audiences from potentially malicious actors (Taheam et al., 2016). This section provided data on the most common challenges in digital marketing, including data breaches, phishing scams, malware infections, and social engineering.

Data Breaches

A data breach occurs when secure or private/confidential information is intentionally or unintentionally released to an untrusted environment. It can also be defined as a security violation in which sensitive, confidential data is stolen, accessed, transmitted, or used by unauthorized persons (Hameed & Rahman, 2017). Data breaches result in multiple negative impacts, including financial losses, legal consequences, reputational damage, and loss of trust. The extent of data breaches as a security threat is shown in Srinivas and Liang's (2022) research, which indicates that the number of data breach events has increased from 785 in 2015 to 1108 in 2020. These security issues have exposed 300,562,519 records and are increasingly becoming more common and inflicting substantial damage to businesses. Srinivas and Liang (2022) projected that a company would be the target of a cyber threat every 11 seconds and pay an average of $3.86 million per incident in 2021. Other than the financial impact, data breaches in marketing can have other challenges, such as losing confidence in a brand, since some customers may become reluctant to transact with a breached firm (Kirk & Noguera, 2019). While this reluctance could be temporary or long-term, its impact may be severe since building the lost trust and confidence may take causing loss of revenues.

Social Engineering

Social engineering is the most popular type of fraud used by hackers. It involves any malicious activity that impacts a person's behavior in doing something that is not necessarily in their best interests (Heartfield & Loukas, 2015). In this regard, the attackers use psychological manipulation to convince clients to accomplish various tasks or activities and disclose or leak sensitive information, such as login details. Whether it is a one-step technique or a series of stages, the primary goal of social engineering scams is to obtain conditional details or access the system. Liu et al. (2022) identify the "forget password" option as the most basic form of social engineering, which can be manipulated to direct the user to a malicious link and provide the attackers access to the user account or system. Other types of social engineering attacks included phishing, vishing, impersonation and smishing. Phishing occurs when the attacker sends emails posing as a reputable source, such as a bank, to obtain personal information (Salahdine & Kaabouch, 2019). Vishing involves using telephone calls to compel individuals to take action that provides the attacker with valuable information. Liu et al. (2022) noted that these attacks increased by 554% in 2021. Impersonation occurs when an attacker presents themselves as another person or firm and socializes with a target individual to obtain confidential information, while smishing involves sending messages on the phone to encourage the victims to take specific actions that provide attackers access to desired personal information. The targeting of humans in these types of cyber-attacks makes it the most dangerous since people are more likely to trust other people than technologies and computers (Koyun & Al Janabi, 2017). This makes humans the weakest link in any organization's security system since they can be easily manipulated. For instance, the human interactions in these attacks make it impossible to prevent them from using hardware or software solutions unless people are trained to identify and avoid them. However, a simple mistake or confusion can lead to enormous losses, thus threatening all systems and networks.

While social engineering attacks are a global problem, developed countries record more cases. For instance, the U.S. Department of Justice identified social engineering attacks as the most dangerous cybercrimes in the world (Koyun & Al Janabi, 2017). Similarly, a 2016 study by Cyence, cyber security Analyst Company, found that the U.S. was the country most targeted by social engineers and had the highest attack cost at $121.22 billion, followed by Germany and Japan (Salahdine & Kaabouch, 2019). In addition, the FBI found an emerging trend of CEO fraud, where attackers send emails to employees posing as their boss and asking them to transfer payments, resulting in more than $2.3 billion in losses. Digital marketers, as employees, can be vulnerable to such attacks (He, 2021). Given their high access permissions and controls that allow them access to sensitive information, such as customer data, it is crucial to create awareness and train digital marketers on social engineering attacks (Srivastav & Gupta, 2021). Besides, Salahdine and Kaabouch (2019) found that social engineering attacks have high success rates of approximately 84%. These statistics indicate the need to detect and mitigate these cyber-attacks of cyber-attacks to strengthen security initiatives.

Phishing Scams

Recent years have seen a major increase in phishing scams, making them a significant concern for digital marketers and consumers. Singh and Mittal (2022) define a phishing scam as a type of cybercrime where an attacker tricks a digital marketer or a consumer into revealing confidential information such as passwords, credit card numbers, or social security numbers. In most cases, scammers send emails using emails that appear to come from reputable organizations and ask for information (Alkhalil et al., 2021). The similarity between the fake email used by the attacker and the actual corporate email confuses the targeted individual, prompting them to provide the required information, thus falling for the scam. Liu et al. (2022) indicate that 70% of companies worldwide were victims of phishing scams in 2020, resulting in approximately $1.8 billion in losses. Various strategies are used to carry out phishing scams in digital marketing, including fake emails, websites, or social media messages that mimic a reputable organization. For example, in an email scam, a hacker can send an email impersonating a trustworthy source such as a bank or a retailer (Sachdev, 2020). The impersonation allows the hacker to gain the trust of unsuspecting recipients, thus requesting them to share personal information.

Additionally, some phishing scams involve creating fake websites that mimic legitimate sites and deceiving people into providing their personal information. Other scammers leverage social media phishing scams, where they create fake profiles that match a particular reputable individual or organization and send messages to collect personal information illegally (Alkhalil et al., 2021). Therefore, digital marketers and consumers must be cautious of websites, emails, or messages sent from unknown sources or ones that contain typos or grammatical errors requesting personal information. One major way of overcoming this challenge is verifying the website's or email's authenticity by checking the URL and sender's domain name or hovering over links (Gupta et al., 2017). Other strategies for avoiding phishing scams include providing education to enhance awareness, leveraging anti-phishing tools and software, and frequently assessing systems for suspicious activities.

Malware Infections

Malware infections are another cybersecurity challenge affecting digital marketing. It refers to any software that may infect computers, and hackers use it by implanting it on target websites. Hackers use malware to acquire personal data such as passwords and account information, steal money, or prevent the system owner from accessing the website or account (Qamar et al., 2019). In addition, malware attacks are commonly used to carry out illicit operations on the victim's system and might be ransomware, device control, or malware. There are various reasons hackers may use malware to conduct cyber-attacks, including disrupting or malfunctioning a server, computer, or computer network or gaining unauthorized access to the system (Rudd et al., 2016; Selvaganapathy et al., 2021). In digital marketing, these illegal activities violate the marketer's privacy and security while simultaneously providing the attacker access to sensitive information such as customer data. Examples of common malware include ransomware, worms, rogue software, viruses, horses, spyware, trojans, scareware, and adware (Liu et al., 2022). Addressing these security issues in digital marketing can be challenging since each threat requires its protection method, such as antivirus, firewalls, and algorithms. With the number of malware cases rapidly increasing as companies embrace advanced technologies for data-driven marketing initiatives and business decision-making, it is critical to place comprehensive measures capable of tackling different threats.

Attacks on Customer Personal Data

One of the most significant issues the digital marketing industry currently faces is targeting customers' data. As the world transitions into the digital era, the amount of firm and consumer data collected, shared, stored, and preserved on systems and online has significantly grown in volume (Jain et al., 2022; Ramirez-Asis et al., 2022). In addition, data and network access and consumption are increasing as companies leverage emerging technologies to enhance performance and operational efficiency (Revett et al., 2016). While this digital transition has created opportunities for business growth and better marketing and targeting, it has increased the danger of cybercrime. In this case, attempts to get personal data have significantly increased, reducing consumer and corporate confidence in one another. For example, in digital marketing for online businesses, the client must share private information with the business, such as a home address, phone number, and bank card number (Rahim et al., 2019). While this information is necessary for completing transactions, it allows companies to know and record massive customer data, which becomes the target for cyber-attacks. The extent of this problem is evidenced in Liu et al.'s (2022) research, which indicates that approximately 15 billion data records were compromised in 2019. This makes attacks on customer data one of the biggest challenges in digital marketing and eCommerce. There are two primary attacks on customer personal data characterizing the digital marketing industry; 1) where the marketers or organizations use customer personal information without consent, and 2) when cyber attackers illegally access confidential information.

Opportunities to Improve Security in Digital Marketing

Cybersecurity has become increasingly important in digital marketing as it strengthens the security of the marketing and overall corporate systems used to deliver customer value. In addition, cybersecurity issues can have a significant impact on customer trust and loyalty and can influence purchasing decisions (Bhargava et al., 2020). Given the importance of customer relationships in marketing and the need to build customer confidence through guaranteed security and privacy (Rahman, 2021), it is important to explore various opportunities to help overcome the cyber security threats in digital marketing. The opportunities explored in this section include using encryption technologies, strong password policies and two-factor authentication, regular security audits and vulnerability assessments, and employee training and awareness programs.

Use of Encryption Technologies

Digital marketers and organizations should adopt encryption technologies since they provide a secure method of protecting sensitive data during transmission and storage. This opportunity can help strengthen security in digital marketing by preventing data breaches, unauthorized access, and other security threats (Duan, 2022). Besides, some encryption algorithms such as AES and RSA can encrypt customer personal data, such as payment information, email addresses, and browsing history, making it difficult for cyber attackers to access or use this information for malicious intents (Alloghani et al., 2019). Given the growing consumer concerns over collecting and using their data, these encryption technologies provide digital marketers with solutions to guarantee improved security and privacy. Therefore, by using encryption technologies, digital marketers strengthen company and customers' security and increase their credibility and trust among their target clientele. As a result, leveraging these innovations can increase brand loyalty and enhance business growth.

Strong Password Policies and Two-Factor Authentication

Strong password policies and two-factor authentication are critical in enhancing digital marketing security. An organization with a firm password policy requires users to create complex passwords regularly updated with letters, symbols, and numbers (Parkinson et al., 2021). On the other hand, two-factor authentication adds an extra layer of security by requiring users to enter a unique code shared through their phone or email after entering their password (Wang & Wang, 2016). Combining these security methods strengthen protection against a threat such as password hacking and theft. Besides improving security, implementing strong password policies and two-factor authentication is also suitable for business. For example, customers are more likely to work with companies that take security measures seriously since it builds a sense of safety and trust (Narayanasamy et al., 2019; Paul et al., 2020). When customers feel that their sensitive data, such as their home address or banking information, is safe, they will be more willing to transact, build, and maintain long-term relationships. Therefore, strong password policies and two-factor authentication can help build customer trust and protect a company's reputation while reducing data breach costs and minimizing the risk of lawsuits and regulatory fines.

Regular Security Audits and Vulnerability Assessments

Companies must protect their digital marketing strategies with the growing rate of cyber threats and data breaches. Regular security audits and vulnerability assessments are effective strategies for improving security in digital marketing (Rathod et al., 2020). For instance, security audits facilitate the identification of potential weaknesses in a company's systems, evaluate the risk level of its current security frameworks, and determine the best strategies to improve its security posture (Fernández-Caramés & Fraga-Lamas, 2020). On the other hand, vulnerability assessments help identify and evaluate the vulnerabilities in a company's systems and networks. These assessments provide valuable information that aids an organization's efforts to determine the best ways to prevent or mitigate potential security threats. In addition, these evaluations are crucial in identifying areas that need improvement and providing recommendations to reduce the risk of data breaches and other cyber-attacks (Coffey et al., 2018; Boujrad & lamlili, 2021). Companies can leverage regular security audits and vulnerability assessments to stay ahead of emerging threats and ensure adequate protection of their digital marketing strategies.

Employee Training and Awareness Programs

Research identifies social engineering attacks using human interactions as a significant security challenge in digital marketing. These attacks target employees and involve manipulating them into taking specific actions that provide attackers access to a company's sensitive data or the marketer's accounts (Altukhova et al., 2022; Ly et al., 2019). Given their role in an organization, marketers tend to have higher access permissions and controls within an organization's systems and processes, meaning that their vulnerability to social engineering attacks can have severe consequences. These perspectives have made training and awareness programs increasingly crucial in improving security in digital marketing (Li et al., 2019). This is because the approach helps ensure that digital marketers are updated on the latest security measures and threats. In addition, regular training and awareness sessions increase their understanding of the importance of data security and their role in keeping sensitive information secure (Eisenschink et al., 2022). For example, training sessions can provide information on password management, email security, and social media usage policies. As a result, it can improve marketers' understanding of the consequences of a data breach, the significance of maintaining privacy, and their individual and collective roles in preventing it (Jayashree et al., 2022). Investing in employee training and awareness programs improves employees' sense of responsibility, knowledge, and confidence in protecting sensitive information and reducing the likelihood of cyber-attacks.

CONCLUSION

Technological advancements have transformed digital marketing by providing tools and techniques to reach broader local and international audiences through eCommerce websites and internet-based platforms, including social media. One significant development linked with this growth is the increased adoption of advanced ICT technologies that facilitates consumer data collection and analysis for data-driven decision-making and strategizing. As a result, digital marketers have increasingly relied on consumer data to build and maintain relationships, value co-creation, building brand reputation, trust, and loyalty. Despite these benefits, the rapid adoption of technologies in digital marketing has increased exposure to cyber-attacks, thus threatening the sector's security. For instance, cyber attackers target and steal customer data, either sold to third-party companies or used for malicious activities such as illegally transferring a customer's money. Recent years have seen an increase in these activities, indicating the need to develop more robust digital marketing security measures.

The various security issues threatening the stability of digital marketing include data breaches, social engineering attacks, phishing scams, malware infections, and attacks on customers' data. Data breaches occur when attackers steal, access, or transmit confidential data. It can have multiple negative consequences, including financial loss, reputational damage, loss of customer trust and confidence in the company, legal consequences, and regulatory fines. On the other hand, social engineering attacks refer to psychological manipulation to convince individuals of tasks or activities that result in the disclosure of confidential information. In this case, the attackers can impersonate an influential person, such as the CEO, or fake a reputable organization's email or website to encourage digital marketers to take specific tasks that give them access to the system. Phishing scams are a type of social engineering attack where the attacker uses fake emails that appear to come from a reputable source to convince a digital marketer or consumer to reveal confidential information. Malware infections occur when an attacker implants software into a victim's website to access personal data such as passwords and account information, allowing them to block the website owner or transfer money, among other malicious activities. The severity of the consequences of these security challenges requires digital marketers and organizations to embrace best practices to strengthen their security measures. Examples of these practices include using encryption technologies, implementing strong password policies and two-factor authentication measures, conducting regular security audits and vulnerability assessments, and providing employee training and awareness programs.

The theoretical and practical implications of security in digital marketing can be significant for both businesses and consumers. Here are some of the main implications theoretical: (i) trust (security in digital marketing can help establish trust between businesses and their customers. When customers feel secure about their personal information and transactions, they are more likely to trust a company and continue to do business with them); (ii) reputation (a company's reputation can be affected by security breaches. If a company's security is compromised, it can damage their reputation, causing customers to lose trust in them and potentially leading to a loss of business); (iii) legal (there are legal implications for companies that do not take security seriously. Companies that do not properly secure customer data may face legal action and fines).

The main practical implications are: (i) customer data (digital marketing often involves collecting and storing customer data. It is important to properly secure this data to prevent it from falling into the wrong hands); (ii) cyber-attacks (cyber-attacks can result in the loss of customer data, financial loss, and damage to a company's reputation. It is important for businesses to have strong security measures in place to protect against these attacks); (iii) compliance (companies must comply with various regulations and standards to protect customer data. For example, the General Data Protection Regulation (GDPR) in the European Union requires companies to take measures to protect personal data).

In conclusion, security is a critical aspect of digital marketing that can have significant implications for both businesses and customers. By taking security seriously, businesses can establish trust with customers, protect their reputations, and avoid legal and financial consequences.

As already mentioned, the main limitation is to consider only the Scopus indexing database, excluding other scientific and academic databases.

As digital marketing continues to grow and evolve, security concerns will become increasingly important. Here are some potential future research lines on security in digital marketing: (i) authentication and Authorization (research could be conducted on how to better secure user accounts and access to digital marketing platforms. This could include exploring the use of two-factor authentication, biometric authentication, and other methods to enhance security); (ii) data privacy (with the increasing concerns around data privacy, future research could focus on developing better ways to protect user data. This could include exploring the use of encryption, anonymization, and other methods to secure personal data); (iii) cybersecurity threats (research could be conducted on identifying and mitigating cyber threats such as phishing attacks, malware, and ransomware in the digital marketing space. This research could help marketers to better protect their systems and data); (iv) compliance and regulations (as data protection regulations continue to evolve, the research could focus on how to ensure compliance with laws such as GDPR, CCPA, and others. This could include exploring ways to simplify compliance processes and automate data protection measures); (v) emerging technologies (as new technologies such as blockchain, artificial intelligence, and the Internet of Things (IoT) continue to gain traction, the research could be conducted on the potential security implications of these technologies in the digital marketing space. This could help marketers to better understand how to secure their systems and data in an increasingly complex environment). Overall, the goal of future research in security in digital marketing would be to develop innovative and effective solutions that enable marketers to protect their systems and data from cyber threats while also complying with data protection regulations.

ACKNOWLEDGMENT

I would like to express gratitude to the Editor and the Arbitrators. They offered extremely valuable suggestions or improvements. The author was supported by the GOVCOPP Research Center of the University of Aveiro.

REFERENCES

Aftab, M. O., Ahmad, U., Khalid, S., Saud, A., Hassan, A., & Farooq, M. S. (2021). Sentiment analysis of customer for ecommerce by applying AI. *4th International Conference on Innovative Computing, ICIC 2021*. 10.1109/ICIC53490.2021.9693026

Al-Azani, S., & El-Alfy, E. M. (2020). Enhanced video analytics for sentiment analysis based on fusing textual, auditory and visual information. *IEEE Access : Practical Innovations, Open Solutions*, *8*, 136843–136857. doi:10.1109/ACCESS.2020.3011977

Al Mansoori, M. S., & Ahmad, S. Z. (2021). Adapting to the "new normal" post-pandemic consumer behavior: The case of Rafeeg's strategy of service marketing. *Emerald Emerging Markets Case Studies*, *11*(3), 1–17. doi:10.1108/EEMCS-08-2020-0311

Ali, A., & Xia, C. (2022). Current and prospective impacts of digital marketing on the small agricultural stakeholders in the developing countries. Application of machine learning in agriculture, 91-112. doi:10.1016/B978-0-323-90550-3.00012-6

Alkhalil, Z., Hewage, C., Nawaf, L., & Khan, I. (2021). Phishing attacks: A recent comprehensive study and a new anatomy. *Frontiers of Computer Science*, *3*, 563060. doi:10.3389/fcomp.2021.563060

Alloghani, M., Alani, M. M., Al-Jumeily, D., Baker, T., Mustafina, J., Hussain, A., & Aljaaf, A. J. (2019). A systematic review on the status and progress of homomorphic encryption technologies. *Journal of Information Security and Applications*, *48*, 102362. doi:10.1016/j.jisa.2019.102362

Almabdy, S. (2018). Comparative analysis of relational and graph databases for social networks. *1st International Conference on Computer Applications and Information Security, ICCAIS 2018*. 10.1109/CAIS.2018.8441982

Altukhova, E. V., Nikeryasova, V. V., Ivanova, Y. Y., Markov, M. A., & Romanchenko, O. V. (2022). *Transformation of educational space in the system of digitalization of the economy*. doi:10.1007/978-3-030-94245-8_22

Arellano, P. R., Aguilar, F. D., Quintana Bornot, A., & Carrera, L. A. (2022). *Contexts of digital tools in marketing management in MSMEs for their permanence in the market*. doi:10.1007/978-3-031-11438-0_42

Bansal, R., Malyadri, P., Singh, A., & Pervez, A. (2021). Blockchain technology and applications for digital marketing. Blockchain technology and applications for digital marketing. doi:10.4018/978-1-7998-8081-3

Bhargava, N., Palvadi, S. K., Kumar, A., & Rathore, P. S. (2020). An economical methodology to rhetorical identifications in cloud victimization virtual machine snapshots. Cyber warfare and terrorism: Concepts, methodologies, tools, and applications, 395-409. doi:10.4018/978-1-7998-2466-4.ch025

Bishop, T., & Rowley, J. (2013). Digital marketing in independent libraries in the United Kingdom. *Journal of Librarianship and Information Science*, *45*(4), 323–334. doi:10.1177/0961000612453473

Boujrad, M., & lamlili, Y. E. M. N. (2021). A New Artificial Intelligence-Based Strategy for Digital Marketing Reinforcement. In *Innovations in Smart Cities Applications Volume 4: The Proceedings of the 5th International Conference on Smart City Application* (pp. 689-699). Springer International Publishing.

Bozhuk, S. G., & Krasnov, A. S. (2017). Methodics of research of consumers psychographic characteristics in the internet. *Proceedings of the 2017 International Conference "Quality Management, Transport and Information Security, Information Technologies", IT and QM and IS 2017*, 166-172. 10.1109/ITMQIS.2017.8085790

Buttle, F., & Maklan, S. (2019). Customer relationship management: Concepts and technologies (4th ed.). doi:10.4324/9781351016551

Coffey, K., Maglaras, L.A., Smith, R., Janicke, H., Ferrag, M.A., Derhab, A., Mukherjee, M., Rallis, S. & Yousaf, A. (2018). Vulnerability assessment of cyber security for SCADA systems. *Guide to Vulnerability Analysis for Computer Networks and Systems: An Artificial Intelligence Approach*, 59-80. doi:10.1007/978-3-319-92624-7_3

Desai, V., & Vidyapeeth, B. (2019). Digital marketing: A review. *International Journal of Trend in Scientific Research and Development*, *5*(5), 196–200. doi:10.31142/ijtsrd23100

Duan, B. (2022). *Digital marketing solutions based on consumer data and homomorphic encryption.* Applied Mathematics and Nonlinear Sciences. doi:10.2478/amns.2021.2.00253

Dvir, N., & Gafni, R. (2018). When less is more: Empirical study of the relation between consumer behavior and information provision on commercial landing pages. *Informing Science*, *21*, 19–39. doi:10.28945/4015

Eisenschink, M., Gluck, C., Maier, M., Scheuchenpflug, E., Timinger, H., & Martens, M. (2022). A new trend in further education? micro degrees as a contribution to deal with new paradigms in small and medium-sized enterprises. *2022 IEEE German Education Conference, GeCon 2022.* 10.1109/GeCon55699.2022.9942738

Farzindar, A., & Inkpen, D. (2017). Natural language processing for social media. *Synthesis Lectures on Human Language Technologies*, *10*(2), 1–195. doi:10.1007/978-3-031-02167-1

Fernández-Caramés, T. M., & Fraga-Lamas, P. (2020). Teaching and learning iot cybersecurity and vulnerability assessment with shodan through practical use cases. *Sensors (Basel)*, *20*(11), 3048. doi:10.339020113048 PMID:32471252

Gaffar, A., Deshpande, A., Bandara, W., & Mathiesen, P. (2015). Importance of literature profiling: An archival analysis with illustrative examples for IS researchers. In *Proceedings of the 19th Pacific Asia Conference on Information Systems (PACIS)* (pp. 1-13). Association for Information Systems (AIS). https://eprints.qut.edu.au/85249/

Gregory, A., & Bentall, L. (2012). Data governance protecting and managing the value of your customer data assets: Stage 3: Identifying and controlling the risk in using third-party processors. *Journal of Direct, Data and Digital Marketing Practice*, *13*(4), 335–344. doi:10.1057/dddmp.2012.5

Gupta, B. B., Tewari, A., Jain, A. K., & Agrawal, D. P. (2017). Fighting against phishing attacks: State of the art and future challenges. *Neural Computing & Applications*, *28*(12), 3629–3654. doi:10.100700521-016-2275-y

Hameed, K., & Rahman, N. (2017). Today's social network sites: An analysis of emerging security risks and their counter measures. *International Conference on Communication Technologies, ComTech 2017,* 143-148. 10.1109/COMTECH.2017.8065764

He, Q. (2021). Research on the advantage strategy of social network big data in marketing. *ACM International Conference Proceeding Series,* 923-926. 10.1145/3456887.3457106

Heartfield, R., & Loukas, G. (2015). A taxonomy of attacks and a survey of defense mechanisms for semantic social engineering attacks. *ACM Computing Surveys*, *48*(3), 1–39. doi:10.1145/2835375

Hoang, S. N., Nguyen, L. V., Huynh, T., & Pham, V. T. (2019). *An efficient model for sentiment analysis of electronic product reviews in Vietnamese*. doi:10.1007/978-3-030-35653-8_10

Huaraca Aparco, R., Del Carmen Delgado Lime, M., Tapia Tadeo, F., Taipe Pardo, F., Palomino Rincón, H., Mescco Cáceres, E., ... Guzmán, N. P. (2022). Sustainability of rural agribusiness through e-commerce information systems. *IOP Conference Series: Earth and Environmental Science, 968*(1). 10.1088/1755-1315/968/1/012002

Indrawati, & Shabila, A. M. (2020). The influence of website-based and company-based quality toward loyalty with perceived website trust as antecedents. *2020 8th International Conference on Information and Communication Technology, ICoICT 2020.* doi:10.1109/ICoICT49345.2020.9166408

Jain, A., Ramachandran, K. K., Sharma, S., Sharma, T., Pareek, P., & Pant, B. (2022). Detailed investigation of influence of machine learning (ML) and big data on digital transformation in marketing. *2022 2nd International Conference on Advance Computing and Innovative Technologies in Engineering, ICACITE 2022* (pp. 1061-1065). 10.1109/ICACITE53722.2022.9823810

Jayashree, S., Sidana, N., Pham, L. T., Kunju, L. M., Ratnavalli, B., & Gangodkar, D. (2022). The progressive role of machine learning in enhancing the effectiveness of digital marketing in emerging economies. *2022 2nd International Conference on Advance Computing and Innovative Technologies in Engineering, ICACITE 2022*, 1640-1645. 10.1109/ICACITE53722.2022.9823438

Khan, H., & Kushwah, K. K. (2021). Blockchain and the future of digital marketing. Blockchain technology and applications for digital marketing, 250-275. doi:10.4018/978-1-7998-8081-3.ch016

Kirk, G., & Noguera, J. (2019). Strategic marketing and cybersecurity: The case of data breaches. *Issues in Information Systems, 20*(3), 165–174. doi:10.48009/3_iis_2019_165-174a

Klien, J. A., Rao, P. M., & Dalvi, M. (2018). Competition and consumer privacy in the cyberspace market. *Journal of Intellectual Property Rights, 23*(2-3), 70–85.

Konyeha, S. (2020). Exploring cybersecurity threats in digital marketing. *NIPES Journal of Science and Technology Research, 2*(3), 12–20. doi:10.37933/nipes/2.3.2020.2

Koyun, A., & Al Janabi, E. (2017). Social engineering attacks. *Journal of Multidisciplinary Engineering Science and Technology, 4*(6), 7533–7538.

Krishen, A. S., Dwivedi, Y. K., Bindu, N., & Kumar, K. S. (2021). A broad overview of interactive digital marketing: A bibliometric network analysis. *Journal of Business Research, 131*, 183–195. doi:10.1016/j.jbusres.2021.03.061

Kumar, S., Pallathadka, H., & Pallathadka, L. K. (2022). An analysis of cyber security threats in digital marketing. *Journal of Critical Reviews, 9*(03), 85–94. www.jcreview.com/admin/Uploads/Files/626bc981113797.49051701.pdf

Li, L., He, W., Xu, L., Ash, I., Anwar, M., & Yuan, X. (2019). Investigating the impact of cybersecurity policy awareness on employees' cybersecurity behavior. *International Journal of Information Management, 45*, 13–24. doi:10.1016/j.ijinfomgt.2018.10.017

Liu, X., Ahmad, S. F., Anser, M. K., Ke, J., Irshad, M., Ul-Haq, J., & Abbas, S. (2022). Cyber security threats: A never-ending challenge for e-commerce. *Frontiers in Psychology, 13*, 927398. Advance online publication. doi:10.3389/fpsyg.2022.927398 PMID:36337532

Liu, Y., & Huang, X. (2021). Brand digital marketing under intranet security control based on the machine learning classification algorithm. *Security and Communication Networks, 2021*, 1–10. Advance online publication. doi:10.1155/2021/9977221

Ly, N. Q., Do, T. K., & Nguyen, B. X. (2019). Large-scale coarse-to-fine object retrieval ontology and deep local multitask learning. *Computational Intelligence and Neuroscience, 2019*, 1–40. Advance online publication. doi:10.1155/2019/1483294 PMID:31396268

Magano, J., & Cunha, M. N. (2020). Digital marketing impact on tourism in Portugal: A quantitative study. *African Journal of Hospitality, Tourism and Leisure, 9*(1), 1–19.

Mahendru, M., & Singh, A. (2022). Exploratory Analysis of AI Automation in Various Horizons. In *ICT Systems and Sustainability: Proceedings of ICT4SD 2022* (pp. 301–311). Springer Nature Singapore. doi:10.1007/978-981-19-5221-0_29

Manocha, P., Som, S., & Chanana, L. (2020). Relational delivery model and impact for leveraging blockchain to deliver e-governance services via social media. *International Journal of Advanced Science and Technology, 29*(3), 8908–8921.

Marinho, J., Almeida, S., & Neto, C. (2021). *Exploration of 3 W's of web marketing in the hotel sector – A study conducted at the Casa da Calçada hotel.* doi:10.1007/978-3-030-90241-4_55

Milton Ganesh, S., Vijayakumar, P., & Jegatha Deborah, L. (2017). A secure gesture based authentication scheme to unlock the smartphones. *Proceedings - 2017 2nd International Conference on Recent Trends and Challenges in Computational Models, ICRTCCM 2017,* 153-158. 10.1109/ICRTCCM.2017.31

Mukherjee, S., Chittipaka, V., & Baral, M. M. (2021). Developing a model to highlight the relation of digital trust with privacy and security for the blockchain technology. Blockchain technology and applications for digital marketing, 110-125. doi:10.4018/978-1-7998-8081-3.ch007

Narayanasamy, S. S. A. L., Hajamydeen, A. I., & Ishak, Z. (2019). Theoretical framework of digital marketing and the future availability in Malaysia. *2019 IEEE 9th International Conference on System Engineering and Technology, ICSET 2019 - Proceeding,* 277-280. 10.1109/ICSEngT.2019.8906342

Notta, O., & Kitta, A. (2021). Factors affecting e-marketing adoption and implementation in food firms: An empirical investigation of Greek food and beverage firms. *Springer Proceedings in Business and Economics,* 509-526. 10.1007/978-3-030-63970-9_35

Okoli, C. (2015). A guide to conducting a standalone systematic literature review. *Communications of the Association for Information Systems, 37.* Advance online publication. doi:10.17705/1CAIS.03743

Oncioiu, I. (2019). Improving business performance through innovation in the digital economy. Improving business performance through innovation in the digital economy, 1-272.

Parkinson, S., Khan, S., Crampton, A., Xu, Q., Xie, W., Liu, N., & Dakin, K. (2021). Password policy characteristics and keystroke biometric authentication. *IET Biometrics*, *10*(2), 163–178. doi:10.1049/bme2.12017

Paul, A. K., Bhoi, S. K., Srivasthva, V., & Lakshmi, P. (2020). Ideal host for digital marketing: A multi criterion decision model approach. *International Journal of Advanced Science and Technology*, *29*(3), 8365–8373.

Perdices, D., Ramos, J., García-Dorado, J. L., González, I., & López de Vergara, J. E. (2021). Natural language processing for web browsing analytics: Challenges, lessons learned, and opportunities. *Computer Networks*, *198*, 108357. Advance online publication. doi:10.1016/j.comnet.2021.108357

Pînzaru, F., Anghel, L., & Mihalcea, A. (2017). Sustainable management in the new economy: Are Romanian companies ready for the digital challenge? *Proceedings of the 5th International Conference on Management Leadership and Governance, ICMLG 2017,* 346-352.

Qamar, A., Karim, A., & Chang, V. (2019). Mobile malware attacks: Review, taxonomy & future directions. *Future Generation Computer Systems*, *97*, 887–909. doi:10.1016/j.future.2019.03.007

Rabby, F., Chimhundu, R., & Hassan, R. (2022). *Blockchain-enabled trust management for digital marketing in the industry 4.0 era.* doi:10.1007/978-3-030-93646-4_14

Radha, S., & Nelson Kennedy Babu, C. (2018). An enhancement of cloud based sentiment analysis an bdaas using SVM based lexicon dictionary and adaptive resource scheduling. *Journal of Computational and Theoretical Nanoscience*, *15*(2), 437–445. doi:10.1166/jctn.2018.7107

Rahim, R., Nguyen, P. T., Nurwita, E. L., & Shankar, K. (2019). Green data science in cyber security: Network security threat detection and prevention techniques [Un estudio sobre herramientas y técnicas para modelos de negocio]. *Opcion, 35*(20), 2899-2921.

Rahman, K. T. (2021). Applications of blockchain technology for digital marketing: A systematic review. Blockchain technology and applications for digital marketing, 16-31. doi:10.4018/978-1-7998-8081-3.ch002

Ramadan, Z. (2019). The democratization of intangible luxury. *Marketing Intelligence & Planning, 37*(6), 660–673. doi:10.1108/MIP-11-2018-0490

Ramirez-Asis, H., Silva-Zapata, M., Ramirez-Asis, E., Sharma, T., Durga, S., & Pant, B. (2022). A conceptual analysis on the impact of big data analytics toward on digital marketing transformation. *2022 2nd International Conference on Advance Computing and Innovative Technologies in Engineering, ICACITE 2022,* 1651-1655. 10.1109/ICACITE53722.2022.9823874

Rath, M. (2022). Machine learning and its use in e-commerce and e-business. Research anthology on machine learning techniques, methods, and applications, 1193-1209. doi:10.4018/978-1-6684-6291-1.ch062

Rathod, A. Y., Pandya, S., & Doshi, N. (2020). IoT and modern marketing: Its social implications. *International Conference on Advanced Communication Technology, ICACT, 2020*, 407-413. 10.23919/ICACT48636.2020.9061210

Revett, K., de Magalhães, S. T., Magalhães, M. J., & Jahankhani, H. (2016). *Balancing targeted delivery of content and personal freedom in the digital on-line video marketing landscape*. doi:10.1007/978-3-319-51064-4_8

Robin, R., Gaber, H., & Wright, L. T. (2021). Encouraging information disclosure on social media platforms in consumer marketing research. In The routledge companion to marketing research (pp. 132-146). Routledge.

Rosário, A., Vilaça, F., Raimundo, R., & Cruz, R. (2021). Literature review on Health Knowledge Management in the last 10 years (2009-2019). *The Electronic Journal of Knowledge Management, 18*(3), 338-355. doi:10.34190/ejkm.18.3.2120

Rosário, A. T. (2021). The Background of articial intelligence applied to marketing. *Academy of Strategic Management Journal, 20*(6), 1–19.

Rosário, A. T., & Dias, J. C. (2022). Sustainability and the Digital Transition: A Literature Review. *Sustainability (Basel), 14*(7), 4072. doi:10.3390u14074072

Rosário, A. T., & Dias, J. C. (2023). How Industry 4.0 and Sensors Can Leverage Product Design: Opportunities and Challenges. *Sensors (Basel), 23*(3), 1165. doi:10.339023031165 PMID:36772206

Rudd, E. M., Rozsa, A., Günther, M., & Boult, T. E. (2016). A survey of stealth malware attacks, mitigation measures, and steps toward autonomous open world solutions. *IEEE Communications Surveys and Tutorials, 19*(2), 1145–1172. doi:10.1109/COMST.2016.2636078

Sachdev, R. (2020). Towards security and privacy for edge AI in IoT/IoE based digital marketing environments. *2020 5th International Conference on Fog and Mobile Edge Computing, FMEC 2020*, 341-346. 10.1109/FMEC49853.2020.9144755

Salahdine, F., & Kaabouch, N. (2019). Social engineering attacks: A survey. *Future Internet, 11*(4), 89. doi:10.3390/fi11040089

Security Compass. (2020). *Security compass whitepaper: why cybersecurity is important for your brand reputation*. www.securitycompass.com/wp-content/uploads/why-cybersecurity-is-important-for-your-brand-reputation.pdf

Selvaganapathy, S., Sadasivam, S., & Ravi, V. (2021). A review on android malware: Attacks, countermeasures and challenges ahead. *Journal of Cyber Security and Mobility*, 177-230. doi:10.13052/jcsm2245-1439.1017

Sheresheva, M., Efremova, M., Valitova, L., Polukhina, A., & Laptev, G. (2021). Russian tourism enterprises' marketing innovations to meet the covid-19 challenges. *Sustainability (Basel), 13*(7), 3756. Advance online publication. doi:10.3390u13073756

Simion, C. P., Militaru, G., Popescu, M., & Popescu, A. (2018). Security of digital marketing operations to improve small business performance. *Proceedings of the 31st International Business Information Management Association Conference, IBIMA 2018: Innovation Management and Education Excellence through Vision*, 6644–6653.

Singer, J. G. (2006). Systems marketing for the information age. *MIT Sloan Management Review, 48*(1).

Singh, A., & Mittal, S. (2022). Traditional to digital commerce: Impact of scams on consumer's attitude towards online shopping. In The future of E-commerce (pp. 197-209).

Soares, D. B., & Sousa, B. B. (2022). The role of communication in consumer behavior in social and nonprofit marketing: The case of PSP in Portugal. *International Review on Public and Nonprofit Marketing, 19*(1), 1–13. doi:10.100712208-021-00294-3

Soldatova, A. V., Budrin, A. G., Budrina, E. V., Solovieva, D. V., & Semenov, V. P. (2020). Information technologies in the management of digital marketing communications. *Proceedings of the 2020 IEEE International Conference "Quality Management, Transport and Information Security, Information Technologies", IT and QM and IS 2020*, 534-537. 10.1109/ITQMIS51053.2020.9322990

Srinivas, S., & Liang, H. (2022). Being digital to being vulnerable: Does digital transformation allure a data breach? *Journal of Electronic Business & Digital Economics, 1*(1/2), 111–137. doi:10.1108/JEBDE-08-2022-0026

Srivastav, P., & Gupta, H. (2021). Role and applications of digital marketing in digital era: A review. *2021 9th International Conference on Reliability, Infocom Technologies and Optimization (Trends and Future Directions), ICRITO 2021*. 10.1109/ICRITO51393.2021.9596087

Suleiman, D. A., Awan, T. M., & Javed, M. (2021). Enhancing digital marketing performance through usage intention of ai-powered websites. *IAES International Journal of Artificial Intelligence, 10*(4), 810–817. doi:10.11591/ijai.v10.i4.pp810-817

Swetha, M. S., Buvaneswari, P. S., & Kottaisamy, U. (2019). An empirical study on consumer awareness on digital footprints. *International Journal of Advanced Science and Technology*, *28*(17), 759–768.

Taheam, K., Sharma, R., & Goswami, S. (2016). Drivers of digital wallet usage: Implications for leveraging digital marketing. *International Journal of Economic Research*, *13*(1), 175–186.

Vatsa, M., Rastogi, S., Tiwari, A., & Jain, S. (2021). Impacts of cloud computing in digital marketing. *Proceedings of the 5th International Conference on Electronics, Communication and Aerospace Technology, ICECA 2021*, 1170-1174. 10.1109/ICECA52323.2021.9676043

Velinov, E., Leroy, I., & Cetlova, H. (2022, April). Marketing Process in Information Security Context: Comparison Between Czech Republic and Belgium. In *Proceedings of the International Conference Engineering Innovations and Sustainable Development* (pp. 567-577). Cham: Springer International Publishing. 10.1007/978-3-030-90843-0_64

Wang, D., & Wang, P. (2016). Two birds with one stone: Two-factor authentication with security beyond conventional bound. *IEEE Transactions on Dependable and Secure Computing*, *15*(4), 708–722. doi:10.1109/TDSC.2016.2605087

Watson, A., Syrdal, H., Osborn, J., McGrath, R., Ringleb, A., Botten, T., . . . Waller, M. (2022). *Special session: The University of Google? A panel discussion about the disruptive changes in marketing education and what programs may look like in the not-so-distant future: An abstract.* . doi:10.1007/978-3-030-95346-1_54

ADDITIONAL READING

Adenew, B. (2004). The food security role of agriculture in Ethiopia. *eJADE: electronic Journal of Agricultural and Development Economics, 1*, 138-153.

Agbo, C. C., & Mahmoud, Q. H. (2020). Blockchain in healthcare: Opportunities, challenges, and possible solutions. *International Journal of Healthcare Information Systems and Informatics*, *15*(3), 82–97. doi:10.4018/IJHISI.2020070105

Cook, J., Rehman, S. U., & Khan, M. A. (2023). Security and Privacy for Low Power IoT Devices on 5G and Beyond Networks: Challenges and Future Directions. *IEEE Access : Practical Innovations, Open Solutions*, *11*, 39295–39317. doi:10.1109/ACCESS.2023.3268064

Dai, H., Zheng, Z., & Zhang, Y. (2019). Blockchain for internet of things: a survey. *IEEE Internet Things Journal, 6*, 8076-8094. doi:10.1109/JIOT.2019.2920987

Grover, P., Kar, A. K., Janssen, M., & Ilavarasan, P. V. (2019). Perceived usefulness, ease of use and user acceptance of blockchain technology for digital transactions–insights from user-generated content on Twitter. *Enterprise Information Systems*, *13*(6), 771–800. doi:10.1080/17517575.2019.1599446

Kshetri, N. (2017). Blockchain's roles in strengthening cybersecurity and protecting privacy. *Telecommunications Policy*, *41*(10), 1027–1038. doi:10.1016/j.telpol.2017.09.003

Kuznetsova, I. G., Voronkova, O. Y., Nimatulaev, M. M., Ruiga, I. R., Zhuruli, G. N., & Levichev, V. E. (2019). Ensuring the national security of agriculture in the digital era through the formation of human capital. *Int. J. Econ. Bus. Adm.*, *7*(1), 558–569. doi:10.35808/ijeba/301

Taghizadeh-Hesary, F., Rasoulinezhad, E., & Yoshino, N. (2019). Energy and food security: Linkages through price volatility. *Energy Policy*, *128*, 796–806. doi:10.1016/j.enpol.2018.12.043

KEY TERMS AND DEFINITIONS

Content Management Systems (CMS): Solutions to significantly simplify the creation, management, publishing, distribution, and archiving processes of content.

Digital Marketing: Communication actions that companies can use through the internet, mobile phones and other digital means, to publicize and market their products or services, gaining new customers and improving their relationship network.

Hacker: Is an individual who dedicates himself, with unusual intensity, to knowing and modifying the innermost aspects of devices, programs, and computer networks.

Search Engine Marketing (SEM): A term that triggers the display of an ad when fetched from a search engine or presented on a content network site where the ad is intended to be served.

Search Engine Optimization (SEO): Is the set of strategies to enhance and improve the positioning of a website on the pages of organic results - disregarding sponsored links - on search engines generating conversions, whether they are a lead, a purchase, a form submission, scheduling an appointment and others.

Social Engineering: In the context of information security, it refers to the psychological manipulation of people to perform actions or to disclose confidential information.

Chapter 11
Exploring Mixed Reality: Enhancing Consumer Interaction

Rana Salah Nasr
The German University in Cairo, Egypt

Sara El-Deeb
The German University in Cairo, Egypt

ABSTRACT

Researchers recently became interested in mixed reality (MR) because of the availability of hardware that integrates the advantages of two worlds. As an immersive and innovative technological solution for consumers and brands, research has provided insights into the implementation of MR. This technology is promising to transform business models and consumer behavior. Studies have revealed how MR boosts consumer engagement and purchase intentions. In this chapter, the diverse concepts and techniques of recent technological breakthroughs are reviewed. This includes the differences between augmented reality (AR), virtual reality (VR), and MR. Also, MR will be explored to understand the fusion of reality and virtuality, challenges, and limitations in emerging trends. Thus, providing insights from the perspective of digital marketing that results in better interaction with consumers due to the immersive and interactive experiences it offers.

INTRODUCTION

It has been traditional for humans since the mid-1950s to blur the lines between physical and digital realities (Rinf.tech, 2022). This mission resulted in the emergence of digital technologies, where disruptive innovations created a distinct identity for humans. The identity has perfectly suited the dawning era of immersive technologies (Dehghani et al., 2020; Trunfio et al., 2022).

Immersive technologies, such as AR, VR, and MR, have revolutionized industries and shaped new environments (Dwivedi et al., 2022; Sung et al., 2021; Trunfio et al., 2022). Thus, establishing the real-virtual continuum phenomenon, which impacts the way people experience virtual worlds (Dehghani et al., 2020; Flavián et al., 2019).

DOI: 10.4018/978-1-6684-8958-1.ch011

With immersive technologies on the rise, MR is the least explored. Nonetheless, it is gaining popularity in a wide range of industries due to its ability to seamlessly integrate realistic-looking 3D content with the users' physical environment and enable mutual benefits (Bekele & Champion, 2019; Buhalis & Karatay, 2022; Dwivedi et al., 2022; Speicher et al.,, 2019).

There are two main types of MR: augmented reality and augmented virtuality (Howard & Davis, 2022). Unlike AR, which provides limited spatial and visual immersion, VR sets limit their users' ability to view the real world. However, MR offers an innovative solution to these problems (Bekele & Champion, 2019; Buhalis & Karatay, 2022; Dwivedi et al., 2022; Speicher et al., 2019).

MR has distinctive features that contribute to a delightful user experience, such as interactivity and vividness. Interactivity creates a sense of enjoyment and increased presence, enabling users to manipulate the virtual environment in real time. This results in an immersive and interactive experience (Bae et al., 2020).

MR technologies may provide realistic and effective outcomes. That is through their technical characteristics in terms of ambient sounds and lighting, user movements and positions, objects and physical locations, and objects surfaces and boundaries (Bae et al., 2020; Rinf.tech, 2022). However, there are still some challenges to overcome. This includes technical challenges such as short battery life, the discomfort of wearing it for an extended period, its strong dependence on coverage and speed of connection, and the relatively narrow field of view. Also of concern are latency, accuracy, and privacy issues (Chai et al., 2022; Knierim et al., 2018; Rinf.tech, 2022; Sung et al., 2021).

This chapter aims to provide a comprehensive review of the current state of MR and explore its potential for enhancing consumer interaction. By synthesizing the different definitions of MR and its theories, this chapter seeks to gain insight into the potential of MR. It will revolutionize the way consumers interact with products and services. In addition, it provides an appropriate focus and direction for future studies by addressing disputes in existing knowledge about MR.

METHODOLOGY

We conducted a thorough, systematic review of articles on MR technology investigation and related marketing-related technologies. It, therefore, used a two-step search procedure. First, performing a manual search of journals in the areas of Human-Computer Interaction, Technology Marketing, and related journals. Second, a comprehensive web-based search for relevant terms (i.e., MR technology, AR, VR, immersive experiences, and disruptive innovations). This study also used several electronic databases, including Google Scholar, Science Direct, Emerald Publishing, Elsevier, Wiley, and Taylor & Francis Group. These databases are for articles published between 1994 and 2023.

All in all, the author integrated research streams comprising previous research papers that introduced the concept of "virtuality continuum" to formulate a taxonomy of the different approaches in which; the real and virtual aspects of MR worlds can be realized (Bekele & Champion, 2019; Milgram & Kishino, 1994; Speicher et al.,, 2019). In addition, recent research efforts have been directed toward understanding the potential of MR technology in various applications, including the Metaverse (Bae et al., 2020; Buhalis & Karatay, 2022; Dehghani et al., 2020; Nevelsteen, 2018; Rauschnabel et al., 2018; Trunfio et al., 2022).

LITERATURE REVIEW

Overview of the Existing Research on MR

MR has emerged as a highly disruptive innovation that has transformed various industries, from entertainment to healthcare. As outlined above, it enables the integration of the physical and virtual worlds, creating a seamless and engaging user experience that was once unimaginable. As Milgram and Kishino (1994) defined it, MR is the merging of real and virtual environments, allowing users to interact with and manipulate both. Although MR continues to gain popularity, there is still a lack of consensus on its definition.

Several studies have addressed the inconsistencies found in the numerous definitions and interpretations of MR to overcome the conceptual confusion hindering the development of the field (Bae et al., 2020; Bekele & Champion, 2019; Dwivedi et al., 2022; Rauschnabel et al., 2018). However, the vagueness remains, and issues for managers and practitioners are intensifying. The reason for this is that user experience can be adversely affected (Rauschnabel et al., 2022). In this regard, implementing MR technology in different contexts can be challenging (Speicher et al., 2019).

The author aims to consolidate the arguments found in research into a more manageable and comprehensible form, with the intention of enhancing clarity for both researchers and practitioners. Given that, the author adopted the "Reality-Virtuality Continuum" introduced by Milgram and Kishino (1994) as a starting point for consolidating the several perspectives on the concept of MR (Bekele & Champion, 2019; Rauschnabel et al., 2022; Speicher et al., 2019).

Similar to the confusion of MR's definition, some authors argue that the continuum is not as universally accepted. It was claimed that the continuum focused primarily on visual elements. More specifically, MR originated in the computer graphics field. Hence, most MR concepts, which date back to 1994, are limited to graphical aspects without regard to technological advancements, design techniques, and attitudes toward the development of MR (Speicher et al., 2019).

Bekele & Champion (2019) noted that in the technology field, definitions and scientific theories evolve continuously to keep up with current advancements. Accordingly, revitalizing the continuum is crucial to understand the relationship between users, reality, and virtuality. That requires incorporating users' experience needs since it is an essential segment of any system or app design. Thus, identifying the effectiveness of interaction interfaces that enhance the characteristics of MR technology. Altogether, the user-reality-virtuality interaction creates a real-virtual environment, which refines our perception of MR.

MR, therefore, refers to a highly realistic improvement of the real world for users. It is extremely realistic that users cannot differentiate virtual elements from actual physical objects. It creates a seamless transition between real and digitally constructed environments (Bekele & Champion, 2019; Buhalis & Karatay, 2022; Rauschnabel et al., 2022). As mentioned previously, MR-based applications are becoming more prevalent in business contexts (Sung et al., 2021). It has been reported by (Rinf.Tech, 2022) that 75% of MR apps will be integrated with smartphones and 40% will be social media based. The study done by Juniper Research forecasts that the MR market will be valued at $43.8 billion by the end of 2024.

To take advantage of such disruptive innovation, it is critical to first explore its unique characteristics. Next, the author consolidates literature streams into MR key characteristics to serve as a reference for researchers and practitioners.

MR Characteristics

User experience is becoming more driven and even enhanced by technology. The world has witnessed the rapidity of data transfer, minimal delays, and significant advancements that 5G provides. As a result, there is a massive rise in MR content creation that is user-accepted. Given that, it is imperative to note the technical characteristics of MR, as it plays an essential role in making the experience more immersive and comprehensive (Bae et al., 2020; Buhalis et al., 2022; Borsci et al., 2015).

In this respect, some of the key technical characteristics that are emphasized in scholarly work include Interactivity, Vividness, Technological Embodiment, Contextual Embedding, and Multisensory stimulation, Usability, Dynamic Displays. These features distinguish MR technology from other technologies and are considered significant to highlight (Bae et al., 2020; Chai et al., 2022; Dehghani et al., 2020; Flavián et al., 2019; Holt, 2023; Rauschnabel et al., 2022; Speicher et al., 2019; Sung et al., 2021; Trunfio et al., 2022; Wedel et al., 2020).

These characteristics, which will be discussed later, play a leading role in shaping the user experience. They develop varying levels of immersion and feelings of presence. Immersion causes feelings of presence, and both are often used interchangeably. The qualities of immersion and feelings of presence are based on the user's perception of virtual worlds. This means that the more engaging the content is due to technological capabilities, the stronger the feeling of being present in the experience (Flavián et al., 2019; Nevelsteen, 2018; Wedel et al., 2020).

According to Dehghani et al., (2020) and Sung et al., (2021), *immersion* refers to the deep engagement of users with the virtual world. That is, feeling completely absorbed in virtual stimuli. As a result, users feel detached from the real world. Delving into the world of MR experiences, *spatial presence* is described as the degree to which a user is absorbed in the environment where the experience occurs. Therefore, users cannot distinguish between what is real and what is virtual (Ogunseiju et al., 2022; Wedel et al., 2020).

Interactivity

To start with, *interactivity* is one of the significant factors that contribute to enjoyment in interactive systems. Scholars define it as the user's capability to control and manipulate the virtual environment in real-time, which has an impact on consumers' decisions (Bae et al., 2020; Rauschnabel et al., 2022). It is important to point out that interactivity is classified into "internally-based self-efficacy" and "externally-based system efficacy".

The former allows users to control their position and direction in space, whereas the latter refers to how responsive a system is to their actions. Both result in human-technology interaction. A unique example of interactivity is when a user can interact with a virtual light switch that operates a real lamp in the environment (Flavián et al., 2019; Rauschnabel et al., 2022; Speicher et al., 2019).

Vividness

The growing popularity of MR devices is driven by the *vividness* of the virtual content offered to their users. Vividness refers to the level of richness, clarity, and detail. It incorporates sensory cues that create a sense of realism and immersion in the simulated environment. The more vivid the virtual content is, the more likely the user feels immersed in the experience. Results from existing literature also show that vividness contributes to the enjoyment of the experience. This seamless experience of vivid content creates a convincing sense of realism that is a key factor for MR (Bae et al., 2020; Ogunseiju et al., 2022; Trunfio et al., 2022).

Technological Embodiment

Technological embodiment depicts how technology can serve as an extension of a user's body. This key factor for the MR environment determines the degree of immersion and presence a user feels. Through wearable devices such as HMD, users can have a more seamless and natural experience. As it creates a 3D visual experience by presenting a distinct image to each eye. That is achieved through head-based rendering, where sensors track the head position of the user, orientation, and movement. Also, the user can zoom in and out or rotate 360°. Thus, enabling users a real-time interaction in virtual environments (Flavián et al., 2019; Holt, 2023; Rauschnabel et al., 2022; Wedel et al., 2020).

Contextual Embedding

Contextual embedding describes the positioning and interpretation of cues in the surrounding environment in a specific context. MR technology can recognize and identify objects in the environment and track the progress of the user in a task, adjusting the display accordingly based on the physical context (Rauschnabel et al., 2022). In an experiment done in a study, users rated snacks in three different settings. These settings were a sensory booth, an actual cafe, and a virtual cafe experience developed using HoloLens, an MR device, while seated in the sensory booth. The findings indicated that MR technology could provide relevant experiences to users as in the real-life cafe (Chai et al., 2022).

Multisensory Stimulation, Usability, Dynamic Displays

MR enriches the user experience by incorporating *multisensory modalities* such as video, audio, touch, and scent (Bae et al., 2020). It is evident that the quality of graphic design, audio, and the use of multiple senses generates deep feelings of presence (Holt, 2023). As a technical feature of MR devices, *usability* refers to the ease of use of a system in terms of the comfort of the wearable device, the potential to browse, store, filter data, and use multiple languages (Buhalis & Karatay, 2022). Thus, leading to a more engaging and fulfilling experience by minimizing limitations and maximizing interaction with the multimedia and physical-digital environment (Dehghani et al., 2020). *Dynamic Displays* enable real-time modifications and changes to both the real and virtual environments (Chai et al., 2022). All things considered, Multisensory stimulation, Usability, and Dynamic Displays are imperative features as they generate a high level of immersion (Bae et al., 2020).

Existing Theories on MR

MR is a rapidly evolving discipline that has the potential to reshape how consumers interact with the digital and physical worlds. Accordingly, there is a growing body of research on MR that addresses various topics, ranging from the technical characteristics of MR technology to user experience. After reviewing the extant literature on MR and synthesizing key aspects of MR, it is imperative to identify the main theories and conceptual frameworks used to explore the technology. Thus, the author will examine these theories and gain insight into the fundamentals that create the optimal consumer experience. Furthermore, identifying areas where there are research gaps.

Just like other innovative technologies such as AI, there is an absence of clarity about the theoretical implications of MR in the marketing field. This emphasizes the need for researchers and practitioners to receive guidance and direction to advance this emerging research domain (Flavián et al., 2019). This section offers an overview of the key concepts and theories that underpin this research.

The technology acceptance in digital retail environments is closely related to consumers' positive experience. For decades, researchers have employed the Technology Acceptance Model (TAM) to investigate the user acceptance and the user experience of MR systems in digital retail. Although TAM is commonly used for examining technology acceptance, there may be other models that better capture the unique user experience of MR. Several authors have argued that when consumers are incorporated, physically embodied, and extended, their experiences become more realistic (Dehghani et al., 2020; Flavián et al., 2019; Jain & Werth, 2019). This suggests that the user experience of MR may not be fully captured by traditional acceptance models such as TAM, and that alternative models may be required.

Stimulus-Organism-Response (S-O-R) Model

The *stimulus-organism-response (S-O-R) model* (See Figure 1) is widely used as a theoretical framework in immersive technology research to understand how consumers react to various stimuli in their environment. The model suggests that a stimuli (S) has the potential to affect an organism (O), which in turn affects behavior (R). In other words, using immersive technologies (S) can create cognitive and emotional states in users (O), leading to behavioral responses (Bae et al., 2020; Chai et al., 2022; Sung et al., 2021).

Figure 1. Conceptual framework of S-O-R theory

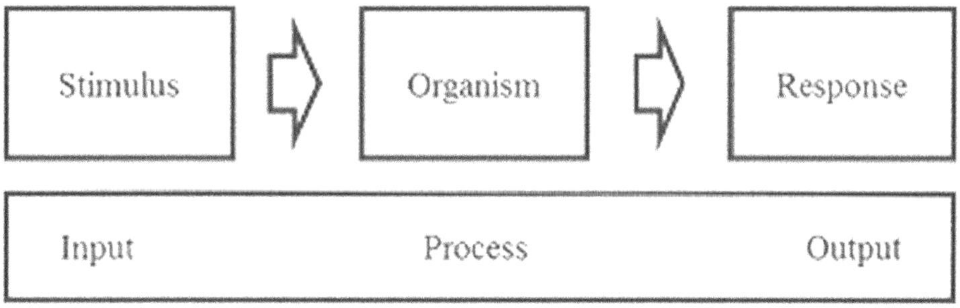

Academics have identified a gap in the analysis of disruptive innovations and their related constructs such as acceptance, engagement, immersion, presence, and awareness. To provide insight into the underlying principles of MR, they have applied the *S-O-R model* to understand consumers' intentions in particular contexts. Drawing upon this, interactivity and vividness are two main characteristics of MR that have been considered stimulus (S) that affect consumers' behavior and satisfaction (R) through their emotional states (O), including perceived immersion, enjoyment, and novel experiences. The research revealed that the technical characteristics of MR (i.e., interactivity and vividness) in the context of a specific cultural and artistic exhibition influenced the MR experience. That included perceived immersion and enjoyment as well as visitor satisfaction (Bae et al., 2020; Chen et al., 2022; Sung et al., 2021).

Studies, however, are calling for scholars to extend literature-consolidated constructs using additional functional features to investigate the effects of immersive experiences (MR) on behavior. Furthermore, consider barriers, limitations, and constraints as they affect the enhancement of MR devices' design and performance (Trunfio et al., 2022).

Embodied Social Presence Theory (ESP)

Some authors proposed novel theoretical implications to gain insights into the effect of MR technology on the consumer experience. That extended the conceptual frameworks to incorporate technological (embodiment), psychological (presence), and behavioral (interactivity) perspectives (Flavián et al., 2019). In this vein, *Embodied Social Presence (ESP) Theory* is adopted to assist managers in creating immersive experiences that enable users to feel physically present with other people in a shared virtual environment.

ESP generates technology-mediated interactions where people experience a strong sense of presence and connectedness with others. This phenomenon occurs due to its ability to engage and stimulate the human senses through physical embodiment. The theory suggests that the higher level to which technology allows people to feel present, the more influential that technology will be in enhancing a sense of social presence. It will also facilitate effective communication and social interaction. On this basis, this theory can better capture the immersive experiences developed by emerging MR technology (Dehghani et al., 2020; Flavián et al., 2019).

Two key elements represent the notion of technological embodiment: immersion and sensory simulation; both concepts were outlined above. It is proposed that when technology is more strongly embodied, it generates a greater sense of closeness between technology and the senses, resulting in more immersive experiences. This sense of presence and improved experiences is enhanced by the fact that MR devices are not only compact and mobile, but they are also wearable and sometimes built into the human body. That is, technological devices serve as a mediator between the user's experience and the technology, resulting in the technology becoming an extension of the human body. As a result of this adaptation, the user can interpret, perceive, and interact with the user's immediate surroundings (Flavián et al., 2019). Essentially, *ESP* presents a holistic approach to understanding the significance of the virtual body and, consequently, the physical body in the context of communication (Mennecke et al., 2011).

Uses and Gratification Theory (U&GT)

To gain a deeper understanding of how MR technology affects the consumer experience and intention, Dehghani et al., (2020) has integrated the *Uses and gratification theory (U&GT)* with *ESP* to examine potential applications for Windows Mixed Reality (WMR) devices as well as consumer perceptions and behavior-related intentions. Even though previous studies have considered TAM/UTAUT models similar, traditional technology acceptance theories such as TAM cannot fully capture MR's unique characteristics.

In their study, the authors formulated a framework that includes factors that promote and hinder the adoption of WMR devices. This is in an effort to better gain insights into consumer behavior. This empirical study is among the first attempts to examine ongoing advancements in WMR devices. Its goal was to comprehensively understand consumer behavioral intentions and explore areas that need further investigation. Accordingly, the proposed variables were Perceived Functional Benefits, Perceived

Trust, Perceived Visual Appeal, Perceived Immersion, Perceived Autonomy, and Perceived Interactivity (Dehghani et al., 2020).

By reviewing the findings, the study demonstrates that the functionality, trust, and visual appeal of WMR devices promote satisfied users. More specifically, the mass adoption of devices depends mainly on the increased levels of functional benefits and trust they provide (Trunfio et al., 2022). Also, the higher the degree of engagement, involvement, and total immersion, the more satisfied users are. Despite all odds, some claim that interactivity contributes indirectly to adoption. According to Dehghani et al., (2020), the insignificance of interactivity on user intentions could be due to individual preferences and the environment in which an event is held, thus affecting the level of responsiveness of WMR devices. Nevertheless, other research on VR shopping platforms (Chen et al., 2022) and MR in the tourism industry (Bae et al., 2020) showed significant results regarding the impact of interactivity on satisfaction. Therefore, it is necessary to investigate this factor in more depth.

As for the relationship between interactivity and immersion, the authors found that users need to have a sense of freedom and realistic interaction with virtual objects to experience immersion (Dehghani et al., 2020). Overall, the *U&GT model* supports our understanding of why individuals adopt specific technologies. That is by exploring their motivations and the gratifications they seek from using the technology (Rauschnabel et al., 2018).

Self-Determination Theory (SDT)

Self-Determination Theory (SDT) is a motivation theory that focuses on intrinsic and extrinsic factors, which covers the essential components of competence, autonomy, and relatedness (Elford et al., 2022). The theory is accepted to illustrate how activities can satisfy consumers' motivational needs and has been employed to develop interventions to modify behavior. It has been argued that it may not be a reliable predictor of behavior in industries such as tourism and leisure (Buhalis & Karatay, 2022). However, Holt (2023) used these motivational needs, such as relatedness, self-expansion, and enjoyment, to explore how feelings of presence and activities relate to the psychological benefits of users of social VR platforms. Consequently, findings revealed that social VR could offer psychological benefits.

According to the theory, *perceived autonomy* refers to individuals' sense of having absolute control over their actions without any external interference in a given situation. They experience psychological freedom and are intrinsically motivated when they feel their choices are based on autonomous decisions. Whereas, external factors such as rewards or punishments can decrease their sense of autonomy and intrinsic motivation (Elford et al., 2022; Rauschnabel et al.,, 2018).

In the acceptance and usage of new technologies, notably self-service technology, the degree of control perceived by consumers significantly influences their behaviors. Research suggests that users' confidence in utilizing available technology to meet their desired outcomes influences their propensity to accept and use the technology (Rauschnabel et al.,, 2018). By contrast, Dehghani et al., (2020) findings produced an insignificant relationship between perceived autonomy and user satisfaction when utilizing WMR. Thus, claiming that users do not anticipate or desire complete autonomy over a technology.

Competence is a fundamental human need that encompasses acquiring adequate knowledge and skills by overcoming difficulties and creating opportunities to grow. Simply put, individuals' perception of their competency drives them intrinsically to pursue learning. Ultimately, *perceived relatedness* is how emotionally connected an individual feels to other people or objects. When individuals perceive a stronger sense of belonging and connection, such as towards others, it leads to a higher level of integration

(Elford et al., 2022; Kam et al., 2020). Alternatively, specific outcomes, such as gaining social status, do not drive feelings of relatedness (Proulx et al., 2017).

Privacy Concerns

According to most research on technology acceptance, scholars discuss the factors that explain the actions users need to take to use a specific technology (Rauschnabel & Ro, 2016). Although, the willingness to adopt an innovation may vary among consumers. It is of equal importance to point out the rise of consumer concerns with the widespread availability of computing technology and its unbounded possibilities for gathering, processing, sharing, and using personal data (Smith et al., 2011).

Studies have found that big technology firms such as Google and Facebook have faced significant criticism for their data misuse of users. As a result, that affects the behaviors of users on these platforms. In the context of disruptive innovations, *privacy concerns* have gained interest among authors as technologies become more personal, ubiquitous, and pervasive (Rauschnabel et al., 2018; Rauschnabel & Ro, 2016).

AR devices employ various sensors, such as cameras, to collect and process digital data with real-world data. On this premise, users avoid the usage of these technologies. Despite privacy being considered imperative in consumer research, it is scarce in the context of AR (Rauschnabel et al., 2018). Accordingly, scholars were interested in investigating privacy concerns with AR devices' adoption.

Privacy concerns refer to the belief that users' personal privacy is at risk because of the growing and extensive capabilities of information technology. These capabilities enable information technology to collect large amounts of data about users without their awareness or consent. It is imperative to note that privacy concerns and the perceived trustworthiness of technology are related. That is to say, the privacy concerns create a sense of vulnerability and uncertainty that can make people hesitant to adopt it (Rauschnabel et al., 2018).

It is evident from existing literature that AR devices can potentially harm the privacy of the user and those around them. These devices can automatically analyze and interpret the user's environment. Thus, users often consider how their actions may affect others. Accordingly, the intention to adopt these systems depends on various factors, such as the people involved and the situational context in which an action takes place (Rauschnabel et al., 2018; Rauschnabel & Ro, 2016).

Surprisingly, results in previous studies claimed that the tendency to which people are influenced by the potential threat to the privacy of others is higher than their privacy. The belief that the potential risk to their privacy is unlikely to occur shortly is reflected in the fact that few strategies can minimize these risks. Nevertheless, threatening other people's privacy can have immediate consequences, such as reacting negatively toward users of AR (Rauschnabel et al., 2018).

DISCUSSION

The current literature on MR technology lacks not only knowledge of privacy issues, but also attention to other antecedents that have not been studied extensively. Previous research has primarily examined various behavioral outcomes such as product knowledge, attitude towards products and platforms, willingness to purchase, and purchase intention regarding virtual commerce (Chen et al., 2022). This chapter seeks to summarize the existing MR literature and synthesize the relevant findings of each stream to provide insight into relationships that need to be explored.

Several studies studying cutting-edge technologies notably focused on AR and its distinctive characteristics, such as the innovative aspect of the technology, the fashion-design component, the potential social interaction with non-users, and the potential risk of misuse. Thus, arguing that it is challenging to rely on a single theory to explain consumers' responses (Rauschnabel et al., 2018). Even though several studies used the terminologies of MR and AR interchangeably (Chai et al., 2022), it is critical to consider the unique characteristics of MR as independent from other technologies. Identify the factors that drive consumers' adoption behavior. In addition, there has not been much research on how privacy concerns about MR may hinder adoption (Trunfio et al., 2022). Future research should consider multiple factors, including motivations and perceptions of risk. While focusing on how other people's privacy matters.

Drawing from the existing body of literature on *SDT*, *U&GT*, and privacy risks, the author highlights the factors that can drive and hinder users from using MR. That is because academics and practitioners have not given sufficient attention to the application of MR. According to Buhalis & Karatay (2022), the scholars noted that Gen Z is willing to interact in an immersive environment as long as it provides them with speedy and engaging experiences that satisfy their curiosity and deliver immediate gratification. Scholars should explore the contextual applicability of MR to the Metaverse. In light of that, the Metaverse is considered the next disruptive force (Buhalis et al., 2022).

THEORETICAL IMPLICATIONS

Researchers and practitioners have struggled to explore MR in depth (Flavián et al., 2019; Speicher et al., 2019). The majority of articles discuss MR and AR interchangeably since they both seem to result from a virtual environment (Dwivedi et al., 2022). However, each has its own qualities that make them unique. Thus, contributing differently (Bekele & Champion, 2019; Buhalis & Karatay, 2022). This emerging area of research therefore requires guidance for researchers and practitioners.

While MR is still in its infancy and challenging, this chapter offers academics practical insights into developing MR theories regarding its real-virtual characteristics and functions. It makes use of various theoretical developments to advance the debate on MR (Bekele & Champion, 2019) and other immersive technologies, including AI. Furthermore, it opens the door to further scholarly investigations into the potential role of MR and AI as immersive technologies. Although Chat GPT, generative AI, is not considered a type of MR, it is possible in the near future that MR experiences will incorporate Chat GPT. Thus, enabling more sophisticated and interactive virtual environments.

This chapter also fills numerous gaps in MR research, revealing previously unexplored causal relationships between MR capabilities and the Metaverse. The novelty and unique characteristics of MR technology continue to attract consumers, as it offers features that cannot be found in other forms of media (Buhalis & Karatay, 2022).

To address some unanswered questions found in previous research and identify opportunities for future work, the author proposed two research questions. First, how do users' motivation and MR characteristics influence consumer experiences in the Metaverse? Secondly, what characteristics of MR technology make privacy concerns more or less likely to affect the adoption rate? To answer these questions, the author extended the *UG&T model* with *Self-determination Theory (SDT)* to integrate areas of study related to privacy concerns and motivation. Ultimately, to understand the consumer's willingness to adopt MR technology.

U&GT is a flexible and adaptable theory that can be adapted to different contexts and combined with other theoretical approaches (Rauschnabel et al., 2018). Thus, it can be integrated into the Metaverse context while identifying the potential factors that affect an individual's intrinsic motivation through *SDT* (Elford et al., 2022).

PRACTICAL IMPLICATIONS

MR creates an immersive and personalized experience that allows companies to foster a strong connection with consumers. MR overcomes challenges by providing benefits related to visual appeal, favorable settings, and language options. Also, its features for browsing, storing and filtering data. Its natural and real-time interaction with the physical world enables the audience to feel part of the experience rather than just observers. Enhanced accessibility of this technology is evident as consumers can access digital content from any location and at any time, resulting in an overall improved experience (Buhalis & Karatay, 2022; Knierim et al., 2018; Sung et al., 2021).

However, MR are still relatively rare in conventional retail settings. Accordingly, practitioners need to create effective marketing strategies that make the shopping experience more enjoyable. Therefore, they need to incorporate advanced AI technologies such as speech recognition and speech synthesis into MR. Thus, making the whole consumer experience more engaging and informative by providing information on the spot. Furthermore, resulting in the increased acceptance of MR technology in retail environments (Dehghani et al., 2020; Sung et al., 2021).

As one of the early adopters of hologram technology in retail, chocolate company Kit Kat has used mobile holograms to provide consumers with an immersive and delightful shopping experience. This is done by showcasing their variety of flavors on a virtual conveyor belt that customers can view in 3D through their mobile phones. This emerging applied technology trend is just one example of how MR can be used to improve the customer experience and create engagement in retail environments (Sung et al., 2021).

It is recommended that practitioners consider such a trend to be light years ahead of competition. Building on that, trust is still a key factor for consumers to adopt MR devices while shopping. To do so, developers need to make consumers feel more present by designing a platform that allows WMR to adapt when unpredictable situations arise, namely, when people try to gain unauthorized access to information that could reveal a user's interests and actions. In this respect, they can add value by creating promotional campaigns that boost customer loyalty (Dehghani et al., 2020; Flavián et al., 2019).

In order to provide the most optimal customer experience, companies must consider the level of technological embodiment that might be incorporated into the experience. Similarly, companies need to optimize the entire consumer journey by creating memorable and enduring experiences. Hence, generating positive cognitive, affective, emotional, social, and physical responses (Flavián et al., 2019). In the end, MR offers a promising future for businesses seeking to integrate physical and virtual worlds to create more engaging and immersive experiences for their customers.

The fusion of physical and virtual worlds presents an opportunity for a fresh iteration of the internet, known as the Metaverse, which utilizes blockchain technology, VR headsets, and avatars. This recently coined term seamlessly blends the two realms, offering businesses the potential to improve experiences and create novel opportunities. Through the integration of MR, the Metaverse is gaining popularity among users, allowing them to merge resources and enjoy holistic experiences (Buhalis et al., 2022; Dwivedi et al., 2022).

IMPLICATIONS FOR FUTURE RESEARCH

The goal of this chapter is to provide clarity on the application of MR technology in digital marketing while synthesizing pertinent theories and establishing meaningful relationships. That contributes to future studies since it presents unique solutions and maximizes the potential benefits of this disruptive innovation.

The advancement of MR practices may require researchers to re-evaluate current concepts and theories related to consumer behavior. Consumers' perceptions of their environment and interactions with brands are evolving due to the fast pace of technological developments (Buhalis & Karatay, 2022; Flavián et al., 2019). This chapter can serve as a reference for future studies which aim to investigate advancements in MR devices, thereby advancing theoretical understanding. Accordingly, it can help researchers examine the impact of major MR characteristics, including interactivity, vividness, technological embodiment, contextual embedding, multisensory stimulation, usability, and dynamic displays, on consumer behavior.

It would also be worthwhile to consider concepts such as perceived autonomy, relatedness, and competence, to understand to what extent motivation influences consumers in new technology. Along with two key aspects: technical characteristics and privacy concerns. All of which could be further examined and tested in the metaverse.

Dehghani et al., (2020) claimed that extended reality (XR) technology would be marketed as a means of accessing the metaverse. In addition, future designs of the metaverse are expected to support all types of XR, notably AR, VR, and MR. Specifically, the metaverse is expected to rely mainly on MR in the context of tourism to bring together all necessary needs and participants in a shared 3D virtual environment, thereby revolutionizing the internet to a parallel virtual universe. Given that, researchers and practitioners can explore numerous possibilities to interact and connect with customers in a metaverse using MR technology.

Although, the metaverse presents promising potential opportunities for interaction between the virtual and real worlds. In addition, it has the potential to introduce novel business models. It demonstrates significant obstacles for all individuals, including ensuring safety and security, promoting acceptable behaviors, and protecting privacy. Thus, hindering widespread adoption (Dwivedi et al., 2022). It is recommended that researchers use this study as a roadmap. So that a more comprehensive understanding of the adoption/avoidance of MR technology, which is a widely practiced but not extensively researched topic, can be achieved.

CONCLUSION

VR, AR, and MR are the foundations of many emerging technologies (Dwivedi et al., 2022). These devices are paving the way for the rise of novel hybrid experiences, causing a shift in the customer experience environment (Flavián et al., 2019). Even though MR is becoming more popular and paramount, there is still a lack of agreement on what it means (Speicher et al., 2019). Considering all the arguments about perceiving MR and AR as synonyms, this study reviewed existing literature and theories to create a clearer unified view of MR and its implementation in various contexts. Through the use of key identifying factors, the author is thus able to gain a better understanding of MR experiences.

Buhalis & Karatay (2022) revealed in their study that respondents have limited awareness of all the capabilities of MR. However, they appreciate the significance of MR in co-creating tourism and heritage experiences. Accordingly, this study focused on this marketing trend. The objective was to clarify the concept and provide valuable information about the development of MR theory for researchers and practitioners. In particular, about the characteristics that underlie immersive experiences in various contexts and the barriers to adoption.

MR devices are advanced technological interfaces encompassing hardware, software, mobile computing, and visualization techniques such as 3D, holograms, spatial mapping, and sensors. These devices feature the highest levels of technical quality, vividness, technological embodiment, multisensory stimulation, usability, and dynamic displays that combine physical and digital content. Accordingly, they produce immersive experiences (Rauschnabel et al., 2018; Trunfio et al., 2022) that can disrupt marketing (Dehghani et al., 2020).

Based on theoretical perspectives, perceived autonomy can result in users having a sense of freedom and internal motivation to proceed (Dehghani et al., 2020). Furthermore, when they perceive functional, technical, and emotional benefits, it boosts their motivation and positively impacts their behavior (Dehghani et al., 2020). On the contrary, findings of (Rauschnabel et al., 2018) found an insignificant effect on the relationship between reduced autonomy and consumers' willingness to use AR smart glasses. Given that, users may still experience dissatisfaction and reduced responsiveness despite the freedom they gain with the devices, under the condition of their inability to do some things in their virtual lives. Therefore, the author encourages researchers to explore this relationship in MR technology.

According to competence as outlined above, individuals' perception of their competency drives them intrinsically to pursue learning (Elford et al., 2022; Kam et al., 2020). Findings showed that people more interested in new technologies tend to have a better expectation of their knowledge and skills regarding using those technologies. As a result, people's willingness to adopt cutting-edge technologies increase (Rauschnabel & Ro, 2016).

Trunfio et al., (2022) found that interactivity is influential in predicting cognitive engagement, which is critical to driving outcomes in immersive environments. Scholars in the study highlighted the success of MR in the context of museums, given its technological and functional characteristics. Accordingly, these factors encourage visitors to engage in dynamic and autonomous interactions with the museum and its content. Consequently, they feel a heightened sense of technological embodiment and presence in a hybrid environment. Given that, future work can explore other industries where MR is suitable.

To address Rauschnabel et al., (2018) question, this study expanded the research by considering privacy concerns with MR devices. While highlighting the new aspect, which is the extent to which the use of MR technology can pose a risk to the privacy of other individuals. Empirical findings on the use of AR devices revealed that people are more likely to consider privacy concerns related to other people rather than their own. Altogether, this risk harms their reactions.

Following the research of Buhalis and Karatay (2022), developers should invest significantly in equipment, design, and production of MR technology to become more prevalent. With the COVID-19 pandemic, the world has witnessed the acceleration of the digitization of experiences that allowed the creation of more innovative forms of co-creating experiences. Accordingly, businesses should adjust to this ever-changing era and prepare for future trends by employing MR technologies to promote consumer engagement and offer immersive and memorable experiences.

In conclusion, an immersive MR environment can enrich customer experiences by incorporating physical embodiment. As a result, this can produce positive action and increase engagement, enjoyment, and satisfaction. The fundamental factors contributing to this positive outcome include hedonic experience, functional experience, and virtual experience (Jain & Werth, 2019). Retailers can leverage MR to create more immersive and engaging environments that offer customers value while minimizing their privacy concerns. Traditionally, MR has been employed for various purposes such as games, education, training, tourism, and cultural exhibits, as outlined by Bae et al., (2020). In this chapter, however, the author highlights the metaverse as the next disruptive technology, with MR expected to serve as the primary method. This raises the question of whether the metaverse is a lasting phenomenon or merely a fad.

REFERENCES

Bae, S., Jung, T. H., Moorhouse, N., Suh, M., & Kwon, O. (2020). The influence of mixed reality on satisfaction and brand loyalty in cultural heritage attractions: A brand equity perspective. *Sustainability (Basel)*, *12*(7), 2956. doi:10.3390u12072956

Bekele, M. K., & Champion, E. (2019). Redefining mixed reality: User-reality-virtuality and virtual heritage perspectives. In *24th Annual Conference of the Association for Computer-Aided Architectural Design Research in Asia (CAADRIA 2019)* (pp. 675-68). CuminCAD. 10.52842/conf.caadria.2019.2.675

Borsci, S., Lawson, G., & Broome, S. (2015). Empirical evidence, evaluation criteria and challenges for the effectiveness of virtual and mixed reality tools for training operators of car service maintenance. *Computers in Industry*, *7*, 17–26. doi:10.1016/j.compind.2014.12.002

Buhalis, D., & Karatay, N. (2022). Mixed Reality (MR) for generation Z in cultural heritage tourism towards metaverse. In *Information and Communication Technologies in Tourism 2022: Proceedings of the ENTER 2022 eTourism Conference*. Springer International Publishing.

Buhalis, D., Lin, M. S., & Leung, D. (2022). Metaverse as a driver for customer experience and value co-creation: implications for hospitality and tourism management and marketing. *International Journal of Contemporary Hospitality Management, 35*(2), 701–716.

Chai, J. J., O'Sullivan, C., Gowen, A. A., Rooney, B., & Xu, J. L. (2022). Augmented/mixed reality technologies for food: A review. *Trends in Food Science & Technology*, *124*, 182–194. doi:10.1016/j.tifs.2022.04.021

Chen, J. V., Ha, Q. A., & Vu, M. T. (2022). The Influences of Virtual Reality Shopping Characteristics on Consumers' Impulse Buying Behavior. *International Journal of Human-Computer Interaction*, 1–19. doi:10.1080/10447318.2022.2098566

Cheng, X., Zhang, S., Fu, S., Liu, W., Guan, C., Mou, J., ... Huang, C. (2022). Exploring the metaverse in the digital economy: an overview and research framework. *Journal of Electronic Business & Digital Economics, 1*(1/2), 206-224.

Dehghani, M., Lee, S. H. M., & Mashatan, A. (2020). Touching holograms with windows mixed reality: Renovating the consumer retailing services. *Technology in Society*, *63*, 101394. doi:10.1016/j.techsoc.2020.101394

Dwivedi, Y. K., Hughes, L., Baabdullah, A. M., Ribeiro-Navarrete, S., Giannakis, M., Al-Debei, M. M., Dennehy, D., Metri, B., Buhalis, D., Cheung, C. M. K., Conboy, K., Doyle, R., Dubey, R., Dutot, V., Felix, R., Goyal, D. P., Gustafsson, A., Hinsch, C., Jebabli, I., ... Wamba, S. F. (2022). Metaverse beyond the hype: Multidisciplinary perspectives on emerging challenges, opportunities, and agenda for research, practice and policy. *International Journal of Information Management*, *66*, 102542. doi:10.1016/j.ijinfomgt.2022.102542

Elford, D., Lancaster, S. J., & Jones, G. A. (2022). Fostering Motivation toward Chemistry through Augmented Reality Educational Escape Activities. A Self-Determination Theory Approach. *Journal of Chemical Education*, *99*(10), 3406–3417. doi:10.1021/acs.jchemed.2c00428

Flavián, C., Ibáñez-Sánchez, S., & Orús, C. (2019). The impact of virtual, augmented and mixed reality technologies on the customer experience. *Journal of Business Research*, *100*, 547–560. doi:10.1016/j.jbusres.2018.10.050

Holt, S. (2023). Virtual reality, augmented reality and mixed reality: For astronaut mental health; and space tourism, education and outreach. *Acta Astronautica*, *203*, 436–446. doi:10.1016/j.actaastro.2022.12.016

Howard, M. C., & Davis, M. M. (2022). A meta-analysis and systematic literature review of mixed reality rehabilitation programs: Investigating design characteristics of augmented reality and augmented virtuality. *Computers in Human Behavior*, *130*, 107197. doi:10.1016/j.chb.2022.107197

Jain, S., & Werth, D. (2019). Current state of mixed reality technology for digital retail: a literature review. In *HCI in Business, Government and Organizations. eCommerce and Consumer Behavior: 6th International Conference, HCIBGO 2019, Held as Part of the 21st HCI International Conference, HCII 2019.* Springer International Publishing. 10.1007/978-3-030-22335-9_2

Kam, H. J., Menard, P., Ormond, D., & Crossler, R. E. (2020). Cultivating cybersecurity learning: An integration of self-determination and flow. *Computers & Security*, *96*, 101875. doi:10.1016/j.cose.2020.101875

Knierim, P., Kosch, T., Hoppe, M., & Schmidt, A. (2018). Challenges and opportunities of mixed reality systems in education. *Mensch und Computer 2018-Workshopband*, 325-330.

Mennecke, B. E., Triplett, J. L., Hassall, L. M., Conde, Z. J., & Heer, R. (2011). An examination of a theory of embodied social presence in virtual worlds. *Decision Sciences*, *42*(2), 413–450. doi:10.1111/j.1540-5915.2011.00317.x

Milgram, P., & Kishino, F. (1994). A taxonomy of mixed reality visual displays. *IEICE Transactions on Information and Systems*, *77*(12), 1321–1329.

Nevelsteen, K. J. (2018). Virtual world, defined from a technological perspective and applied to video games, mixed reality, and the Metaverse. *Computer Animation and Virtual Worlds*, *29*(1), 1–22. doi:10.1002/cav.1752

Ogunseiju, O. R., Gonsalves, N., Akanmu, A. A., Bairaktarova, D., Bowman, D. A., & Jazizadeh, F. (2022). Mixed reality environment for learning sensing technology applications in Construction: A usability study. *Advanced Engineering Informatics*, *53*, 101637. doi:10.1016/j.aei.2022.101637

Proulx, J. N., Romero, M., & Arnab, S. (2017). Learning mechanics and game mechanics under the perspective of self-determination theory to foster motivation in digital game based learning. *Simulation & Gaming*, *48*(1), 81–97. doi:10.1177/1046878116674399

Rauschnabel, P. A., Felix, R., Hinsch, C., Shahab, H., & Alt, F. (2022). What is XR? Towards a framework for augmented and virtual reality. *Computers in Human Behavior*, *133*, 107289. doi:10.1016/j.chb.2022.107289

Rauschnabel, P. A., He, J., & Ro, Y. K. (2018). Antecedents to the adoption of augmented reality smart glasses: A closer look at privacy risks. *Journal of Business Research*, *92*, 374–384. doi:10.1016/j.jbusres.2018.08.008

Rauschnabel, P. A., & Ro, Y. K. (2016). Augmented reality smart glasses: An investigation of technology acceptance drivers. *International Journal of Technology Marketing*, *11*(2), 123–148. doi:10.1504/IJTMKT.2016.075690

Rinf.tech. (2022). *Mixed Reality Use Cases and Challenges in 2022*. https://www.rinf.tech/mixed-reality-use-cases-and-challenges-in-2022

Smith, H. J., Dinev, T., & Xu, H. (2011). Information privacy research: An interdisciplinary review. *Management Information Systems Quarterly*, *35*(4), 989–1015. doi:10.2307/41409970

Speicher, M., Hall, B. D., & Nebeling, M. (2019). What is mixed reality? In *Proceedings of the 2019 CHI conference on human factors in computing systems (CHI 2019)*. ACM. 10.1145/3290605.3300767

Sung, E. C., Bae, S., Han, D. I. D., & Kwon, O. (2021). Consumer engagement via interactive artificial intelligence and mixed reality. *International Journal of Information Management*, *60*, 102382. doi:10.1016/j.ijinfomgt.2021.102382

Trunfio, M., Jung, T., & Campana, S. (2022). Mixed reality experiences in museums: Exploring the impact of functional elements of the devices on visitors' immersive experiences and post-experience behaviours. *Information & Management*, *59*(8), 103698. doi:10.1016/j.im.2022.103698

Wedel, M., Bigné, E., & Zhang, J. (2020). Virtual and augmented reality: Advancing research in consumer marketing. *International Journal of Research in Marketing*, *37*(3), 443–465. doi:10.1016/j.ijresmar.2020.04.004

ADDITIONAL READINGS

Benford, S., Greenhalgh, C., Reynard, G., Brown, C., & Koleva, B. (1998). Understanding and constructing shared spaces with mixed-reality boundaries. *ACM Transactions on computer-human interaction (TOCHI)*, *5*(3), 185–223.

Gao, Y., & Liu, H. (2022). Artificial intelligence-enabled personalization in interactive marketing: a customer journey perspective. *Journal of Research in Interactive Marketing*, (ahead-of-print), 1–18.

Japutra, A., Bilro, R. G., & Loureiro, S. M. C. (2020). Beyond virtual and augmented reality: AI-assisted mixed reality and its impacts on society. In *Managerial challenges and social impacts of virtual and augmented reality* (pp. 252–265). IGI Global. doi:10.4018/978-1-7998-2874-7.ch015

Meegahapola, L., & Perera, I. (2017, September). Enhanced in-store shopping experience through smart phone based mixed reality application. In *2017 Seventeenth international conference on advances in ICT for emerging regions (ICTer)* (pp. 1–8). IEEE. 10.1109/ICTER.2017.8257810

Murphy, K. M., Cash, J., & Kellinger, J. J. (2018). Learning with avatars: Exploring mixed reality simulations for next-generation teaching and learning. In *Handbook of research on pedagogical models for next-generation teaching and learning* (pp. 1–20). IGI Global. doi:10.4018/978-1-5225-3873-8.ch001

Nah, F. F. H., & Xiao, B. (2020). *HCI in business, government and organizations*. Springer International Publishing. doi:10.1007/978-3-030-50341-3

Sala, N. (2021). Virtual reality, augmented reality, and mixed reality in education: A brief overview. *Current and prospective applications of virtual reality in higher education*, 48–73.

Schroeder, R. (2008). Defining virtual worlds and virtual environments. *Journal of Virtual Worlds Research, 1*(1). Advance online publication. doi:10.4101/jvwr.v1i1.294

Venditti, C. P., & Mele, P. (2020). How to Combine Virtual and Reality in Archaeology Communication: A Brief Overview of Mixed Reality and "Its Surroundings". *Developing Effective Communication Skills in Archaeology*, 245–258.

KEY TERMS AND DEFINITIONS

Augmented Reality (AR): A technology that overlays digital content on the real world, improving the user's experience of the physical world.

Immersion: A state of being entirely engaged or absorbed in an experience, often facilitated by technologies like MR.

Immersive Experience: Characterized by an environment that is sensory-rich and fully engages the user's attention and emotions, creating a sense of presence and immersion in a virtual or mixed reality environment.

Immersive Technologies: Such as VR, AR, and MR. They are hardware and software that create a sense of immersion in virtual environments. They aim to enhance the user's sensory experience.

Metaverse: A fully digital world in which users, represented by avatars, can use immersive technologies to interact with each other and digital objects.

Mixed Reality (MR): A technology that combines the physical and virtual worlds to create a new environment in which physical and virtual objects can coexist and interact in real time.

Privacy Concerns: Worries or fears about the protection and management of personal information, data, and communication. They occur when people believe that their personal information is being collected or used without their consent.

User Interaction: The manner in which users engage and interact with a virtual or mixed reality environment. This may include gestures, voice commands, or physical movements.

Virtual Reality (VR): A technology that uses a headset and other sensory inputs to immerse the user in a digital world.

Chapter 12
Mixed Reality in Confronting Consumer Security and Privacy Issues in Digital Marketing:
Integrating the Best of Both Worlds for Better Interaction With Users

Mercy Dube
https://orcid.org/0000-0003-0429-8441
Midlands State University, Zimbabwe

Samuel Musungwini
https://orcid.org/0000-0002-9315-6252
Midlands State University, Zimbabwe

Edward Mudzimba
Midlands State University, Zimbabwe

Noreen Watyoka
Midlands State University, Zimbabwe

ABSTRACT

The developments in technology have presented many opportunities as well as threats to businesses in interacting with their customers. Mixed reality (MR) technology is one of those disruptive technological developments that many organizations have taken advantage of in order to enhance interaction with consumers. Consumers are not always eager to interact with organizations through the internet due to security and privacy concerns associated with the use of the internet. On the other hand, mixed reality technologies combine the physical and digital worlds allowing better interaction with consumers. Mixed reality technology allows effective consumer interaction, improved consumer experiences and enhanced engagement. There are however challenges associated with the use of mixed reality technologies which include costs, privacy, and security issues; hence, the adoption of these technologies in developed countries is minimal. It can be recommended that there is a need for companies to invest in infrastructure that promotes the full implementation of mixed reality technologies.

DOI: 10.4018/978-1-6684-8958-1.ch012

INTRODUCTION

Over the past three decades, Information and Communication Technologies have permeated every facet of society from politics, religion, socioeconomic and the business world (Sanskar & Rejo, 2020; Turner & Welch, 2019). In recent years this technology has increasingly become pervasive and highly disruptive in nature and this resulted in the birth of many new ways of doing things as postulated by Musungwini et al. (2023). Among the emergence of disruptive technologies is the concept of Mixed reality (MR) this is an emerging technology that combines the physical and digital worlds to fashion out a novel reality as suggested by Speicher et al. (2019). MR encapsulates characteristics of augmented reality (AR) and integrates them with virtual reality (VR) and this consequently enables the users to interact with the physical and digital world in a seamless and immersive way Flavian et al. (2019). That is why MR is viewed as offering the potential to revolutionize the way people work, play, communicate, and learn (Sanskar & Rejo, 2020). From interactive gaming experiences to virtual classrooms, MR is already being used in a variety of applications across the Globe, especially the developed countries (Sung et al., 2021),

It is because of its potential to bridge the gap between the physical and digital worlds which positions MR on the cusps to have a major impact on the way we live and interact with the world around us subsequently creating a hybrid environment. It is the perfect combination of virtual reality (VR) and augmented reality (AR), blending physical and digital elements to create a more immersive experience (Sung et al., 2021). MR has the potential to revolutionize the way we interact with our physical environment and the digital world, providing a new way to interact with data and information (Flavian et al., 2019). This book chapter intends to review the literature on disruptive technologies like augmented reality, virtual reality and mixed reality areas of application and explore the positives and challenges that are inherent in mixed reality and make appropriate recommendations for measures to be taken by business organizations when they want to implement MR in their operations.

BACKGROUND

Mixed Reality (MR) is a concept that has been around for many years, but only recently has it become more widely used. The term was first coined in 1994 by Paul Milgram and Fumio Kishino, who defined it as “a class of environments that includes both virtual and real elements, where physical and digital objects co-exist and interact in real-time.” The concept of MR has evolved over the years, as technology has advanced and become more widely available. In the early 2000s, the term was used to describe a range of technologies, including augmented reality (AR), virtual reality (VR), and a combination of both (Speicher et al., 2019). In recent years, MR has become more widely known due to the success of products such as the Microsoft HoloLens and the Oculus Rift and these products are leading the way in the development of MR, as they allow users to interact with virtual objects in a physical environment (Rauschnabel, 2021). MR has a wide range of applications, and it now straddles various fields such as entertainment, education, healthcare, and industry, and it has the potential to revolutionize the way people interact with the world around them, and it is expected to continue to grow in popularity in the years to come.

Mixed Reality (MR) is an emerging technology that combines the physical and digital worlds, allowing users to interact with the environment in a more natural and immersive way. It is a combination of virtual reality (VR) and augmented reality (AR) and is set to revolutionize the way we interact with our environment. MR has a wide range of applications in various fields, ranging from entertainment and gaming to healthcare, education, and industry (Gattullo et al., 2022). In entertainment and gaming, MR can be used to create immersive virtual experiences. For example, users can interact with virtual objects in a 3D environment, allowing them to explore and interact with their environment more naturally. In the healthcare field, MR can be used to create virtual simulations of medical procedures, allowing doctors to practice and train in a safe environment as asserted by Flavián et al. (2019).

This disruptive technology which is evolving can also be used to create interactive patient education tools, allowing patients to learn more about their condition engagingly. In academic circles, MR can be utilized to design interactive lessons that enable students to explore and engage with digital objects and settings to improve the learning experience. This use can be extended to distance learning, enabling interaction between students and instructors in a virtual setting. Engineers can test and experiment in a secure setting by using MR to build virtual simulations of industrial processes. Also, it can be utilized to develop compelling interactive training materials for employees to learn more about their jobs. Overall, MR has numerous uses across a wide range of industries and is poised to completely change how we interact with our surroundings. It can be used to produce interactive patient education tools, immersive virtual experiences, interactive learning scenarios, and virtual simulations of industrial processes.

Mixed Reality is revolutionizing the field of marketing in the world and can be harnessed to provide such impetus in developing contexts like Zimbabwe. MR combines digital technology with the physical environment to create a unique and immersive customer experience for this technology user (Sung et al., 2021). Because it is transforming the way marketing practitioners engage with their customers and build good relationships which are beneficial to both parties, MR has enabled marketers to create interactive and engaging experiences for customers (Flavian et al., 2019). It allows them to create immersive experiences that are tailored to their individual needs and preferences thereby unleashing great fulfilling experiences. As a result, we believe that Marketing practitioners in the developing world like Zimbabwe can use MR technology to create virtual stores which can allow their customers to explore the products on offer in a virtualized environment in sync with the dictates of Lacoche et al. (2019). This allows customers to interact with products in a more personal way, hence it can be used to create interactive experiences such as virtual tours or augmented reality experiences as suggested by Njerekai (2020) and echoed by Pan and Zhang (2021). MR is also being used to create more personalized advertising campaigns.

Marketing professionals can leverage the use of MR to create interactive adverts that are tailored to the individual customer (Alcañiz et al., 2019). This allows marketers to target specific customers with offers and promotions that are contextually relevant and economically suitable to them [customers] (Sung et al., 2019). As a result, MR can be used to generate more engaging customer experiences by allowing customers to explore products, services, and experiences in a more appealing way. This can help to increase customer engagement and generate customer loyalty towards the business. Research has also shown that MR is being used to create data-driven insights for businesses and on this front Marketing, practitioners can use MR to track customer behaviour and preferences to gain deeper and more intimate insights into how to better target customers (Krafft et al., 2020). As a result, we believe that this can help marketers create more effective campaigns and increase their return on investments (ROI). Overall, MR can transform the discipline and practice of marketing and we strongly believe this can be more beneficial in developing contexts like Zimbabwe.

By enabling marketing practitioners to create more interactive and engaging experiences for customers and providing data-driven insights into customer behavior, MR is revolutionizing the way marketers engage with customers and build their relationships and is sure to continue to have a major impact on the marketing landscape in the years to come (Hoyer et al., 2020). The growth of MR in developing contexts is being driven by the increasing availability of affordable hardware and software, as well as the emergence of new applications (Lacoche et al., 2019). As more people become aware of the potential of MR, more organizations are investing in the technology and developing new applications. This is leading to increased demand for MR-related skills and expertise, which is helping to drive the growth of the MR industry. At the same time, MR is being used to address a range of development-related issues in the creation of virtual simulations of complex environments, such as cities, which can be used to study urban dynamics and plan for future development (Um et al., 2022). It can thus be used to create virtual models of infrastructure, such as roads and bridges, which can be used to optimize the design and construction of such projects. In the next subsection, we look at the application of mixed reality in different areas and environments.

APPLICATIONS OF MIXED REALITY

Technological developments have presented many opportunities for organizations, be they profit-oriented or non-profit oriented. MR has been gaining traction in recent years, as advancements in technology have enabled more sophisticated applications to be developed which has seen it being used in a variety of fields, from entertainment to education, and it has the potential to revolutionize the way we interact with the world around us, especially the business world (Farshid et al., 2018). In the business and marketing world, MR has the potential to revolutionize the customer experience in the creation of interactive, immersive experiences for customers. This could include the creation of virtual showrooms, where customers can explore products and services in a 3D environment, or virtual reality (VR) tours of factories and offices. MR can also be used to create interactive advertisements, such as AR ads that appear in the real world (Kadavasal et al., 2007).

Technological developments are the basis for the growth of mixed reality technologies. These technologies have enabled the development of intelligent application tools that can be used as decision–making tools resulting in fast, efficient, and effective decision-making processes (Rokhsaritalemi et al., 2020). However, consumers still have privacy and security challenges in interacting with companies through the use of these different technologies (De Guzman et al., 2019). Mixed reality (MR) has emerged as an innovative technology for businesses to engage with consumers by creating immersive experiences that combine virtual and real-world environments. The use of mixed reality technology platforms can enhance consumer interaction and counteract the different challenges (De Guzman et al., 2019).

Speicher et al. (2019), assert that mixed reality has varied applications in different sectors and these include visualization, collaboration, simulation, and navigation among others. They went on further to say that complex issues are simplified and made easy by visualization through mixed reality technology. Mixed reality (MR) has varied applications in education, healthcare, and businesses. The most important developments in educational environments are reality technologies and mixed reality offers the most promising opportunities in that regard (Dick, 2021). Mixed reality involves the merging of virtual and physical worlds enabling users to interact with both digital and real-world objects simultaneously affording learners to interact with more potential mixed learning realities in their learning processes (Dick 2021). One of the primary advantages of MR in education is its ability to enhance learning experiences

(Gattullo et al., 2022). The authors further assert that mixed reality technology offers students unique experiences to interact with 3D models, simulations, and other immersive environments.

Kizilcec et al. (2021) found that mixed reality simulations of natural disasters significantly improved students' engagement and learning outcomes. Similarly, Kim et al. (2019) found that mixed reality-based simulations of chemistry experiments improved students' understanding of chemical reactions and concepts. Mixed reality also facilitates collaborative learning and group work among students. Kim et al. (2021) explored the use of mixed reality platforms for group projects in a college-level computer science course and the findings showed that mixed reality-based collaboration facilitated teamwork, improved communication, and increased motivation among students. In addition to these benefits, mixed reality also promotes accessibility and inclusivity in education. This is because mixed reality technologies can provide students with disabilities or mobility impairments with an opportunity to engage with learning materials, they would not typically have access to (Lombard et al., 2021).

The health sector has started exploring the potential of mixed reality to enhance interaction with clients, improve diagnosis and treatment and provide education and training to healthcare professionals (Sahija, 2022). Mixed reality technology can be used to create interactive simulations and educational modules to help patients understand their conditions and manage their symptoms. Alghadir et al. (2021) used mixed reality to develop a hand therapy application that provided patients with exercises and visual feedback to improve their hand function after a stroke. This shows the effectiveness of mixed reality for the health sector. Mixed reality is also applicable to medical training and simulations. It can be used to provide medical students and healthcare professionals with realistic simulations of complex medical procedures and surgeries. Chua et al. (2021) used mixed reality to simulate laparoscopic surgery and found that it improved the trainees' performance compared to traditional training methods. The health sector is also using mixed reality technologies for telemedicine and remote consultations. The technology can be used for remote visits with healthcare professionals (Navarro-Newbal et al., 2022).

Mixed reality technology has gained increasing attention from businesses as a means to enhance consumer interaction and engagement (Mehler-Bicher et al., 2022). One of the primary areas where mixed reality technology is being used by businesses is in retail environments. Retailers are using mixed reality technology to create immersive shopping experiences such as virtual-try-on systems for clothing or make-up, interactive product displays, and virtual storefronts. Wang et al. (2021) found that mixed reality can improve consumers' engagements and purchase intentions as well as their perception of products' quality and value. Another study by Gao et al. (2021) explored the use of mixed reality in e-commerce. They found that mixed reality improved customers' perception of the shopping experience, enhanced their purchase intention, and increased their willingness to pay a premium for products. The study also suggested that mixed reality could help businesses to differentiate themselves from competitors and build stronger customer relationships.

Mixed reality is also being used in the entertainment industry. For example, parks and museums are incorporating MR technology to enhance visitors' experiences by providing interactive and immersive environments. A study by Lee and Kim (2020) found that mixed reality can significantly increase visitors' enjoyment and satisfaction with the experience. Another study by Egger and Neuburger (2020) examined the use of mixed reality in tourism. They found that mixed reality enhanced tourists' experience by providing an immersive environment that enrich their knowledge of the destination. The study also highlighted the potential for mixed reality to create new revenue streams for tourism businesses through the sale of mixed-reality experiences. The automotive industry is also enjoying the use of mixed reality to enhance the design and sales process (Boboc et al., 2020). Car manufacturers can provide virtual tours of their vehicles, allow customers to customize their cars, allows customers to customize cars in real-time, and provide interactive product demonstrations (Boboc et al., 2020). A study by Bae et al. (2021) found that mixed-reality technologies can improve consumers' satisfaction with purchase processes and their perception of service quality. In addition to enhancing interaction, mixed reality technology can also provide businesses with valuable data and insight into consumer behavior (Sung et al., 2021). The authors went on further to assert that through mixed reality organizations can track how consumers interact with products and environments, providing businesses with information on consumer preferences and behaviour.

Overall, the discussion suggests that MR technology has significant potential for businesses to enhance consumer interaction and engagement across a range of industries. While the technology is still relatively new and expensive, businesses that invest in MR technology may gain a competitive advantage by providing consumers with unique and immersive experiences that improve satisfaction, engagement and purchase intention. It must be noted that while the concept of mixed reality offers widespread opportunities to many human endeavors, it equally has some risks and limitations. The next subsection looks at the benefits of MR in general but primacy will be given to customer service.

BENEFITS OF MIXED REALITY

As alluded to in the section above mixed reality remains among the best emerging technology-driven solution which has significantly altered how businesses across the broad spectrum of industries can interact with customers. Along the reality-virtuality continuum, there is a plethora of technologies with the potential to enable a business to connect emotionally with targeted customers. In this section, we review the literature regarding the main benefits of mixed reality to customers.

Improved Customer Experiences

Scholars among then Flavian et al. (2019) as well as Sung et al. (2021), concur with the idea that enhanced customer experiences are one of the main benefits which customers stand to benefit from through the utilization of mixed reality platforms. Customer experience is a multifaceted dimension encompassing the customer's cognitive, emotional, behavioral, sensory, and social reactions to a company's offering across the entire customer journey (Lemon & Veroef, 2016). These experiences are built through interaction with the business directly or indirectly through various touch points (Dehghani, et al., 2020).

The marketing profession is alive to the need to provide good customer experiences and normally relies on the role of technologies in designing seamless customer experiences. Mixed reality has emerged as yet another platform through which firms can provide better experiences to consumers. This immersive technology has been proven to be capable of improving how customers interact with goods and services by superimposing virtual or real-world settings, giving them a more immersive and engaging experience (Jessen et al., 2020). In reality, by utilizing affective, physical, cognitive, and social stimuli, this technological platform promotes holistic client experiences (Dehghani et al., 2020). It offers customers an unforgettable real-world experience, in the retail industry, for example, mixed reality enables clients to virtually try on new items or envision how furniture will look in their homes before making a purchase (Flavian et al., 2019). The aforementioned is proof that mixed reality makes life easier for customers by providing a unique experience that considerably enhances their shopping experience.

The importance of providing memorable experiences to customers cannot be underestimated. Sung et al. (2021) claim that the novelty of mixed reality encounters increases consumer intention to share them in their social circles and their propensity to make a purchase. Also, it strongly influences how customers perceive value (Jessen et al., 2020).

Enhanced Interaction Opportunities

Apart from improving user experiences and ensuring customer engagement, mixed reality has also been credited for providing customers with interaction opportunities and also significantly transforming the nature of such interactions (Wedel et al., 2020). In contrast to augmented reality (AR) systems, the goal of creating MR systems is to enable physical interaction and/or manipulation with the digital overlay or object (Maas & Hughes, 2020). It is important to highlight at this point that, in our context, we take consumer interaction in its broader and holistic perspective which encompasses interactions not only with service providers but also with other product users and also with the product or service. Furthermore, our focus on interaction covers the interactions between the customers and the form or content of the mediated environment. The latter form of interaction is commonly referred to as interactivity and has been pitted as one of the important media features of mixed reality platforms which in turn enhances customer interaction with services or products and other users (Wedel et al., 2020). More so, Wedel et al. (2020) opined that this feature of mixed reality permits interactive processes that allow dynamic adjustments in product viewing, trial, and also usage. Similarly, other scholars such as Duan et al. (2019), and Silva et al. (2022) have noted that interactivity can also allow for social interactions around a virtual product employing Avatars or telepresence. This is in contrast to consumer-product interactions in the past through traditional media like print media, which was entirely static with no multiple-angle manipulation of the product (Alcañiz et al., 2019).

The enhanced interaction opportunity availed to consumers through mixed reality platforms has been found to present numerous opportunities to both customers and the business. The Service-dominant logic propounded by Vargo and Lusch (2008), led Alcañiz et al. (2019), to conclude that consumers through their interactions with products and sellers via augmented reality and virtual reality platforms have elevated consumer role to become co-creators of value which reducing customer perceived risk while increasing trust. Within the education sector, Gattullo et al. (2022), indicated that interactivity contributed to enhanced learning effectiveness and also student satisfaction with the learning environment. Additionally, Alcañiz et al. (2019), claim that interactivity helps buyers to participate, act and learn and improves on the feedback which is given to the retailers and retailers can access customer feedback in real-time. On top of the above, it enhances perceived enjoyment (Sung et al., 2019; Turner & Welch, 2019). From the above, it can thus be concluded that the enhanced interaction opportunities which are availed to customers through a blended environment of mixed reality transform the nature of interactions and to a larger extent goes a long way in improving the experiences of the company and its brands.

Increased Customer Engagement

Apart from the above benefits, mixed reality has also been found to be capable of opening up new avenues for customer engagement (Sung et al., 2021). Engagement is typically increased by all immersive technologies (Wedel et al., 2020). Within the marketing field, customer engagement has been described as a cornerstone (Sung et al., 2021). This concept is also multidimensional, comprising behavioral, cognitive, as well as emotional dimensions, similar to the idea of customer experiences as noted earlier (Lemon & Veroef, 2016). Furthermore, it is closely related to customer experiences and customer interaction, Garg et al. (2020) expressed the view that customer engagement is psychological and is based on interactive and co-creative experiences in a service relationship. Customer engagement is vital for business and according to Sung et al. (2021), it contributes positively to positive consumer behavioral intentions such as unpaid brand endorsement. Other scholars among them, Blut et al. (2020), have also argued that engaged customers co-develop products and services and produce and disseminate positive word of mouth.

CHALLENGES FOR MIXED REALITY (COST, SECURITY, AND PRIVACY)

As alluded to in the sections above, mixed reality has emerged as a useful tool which can provide businesses with opportunities for enhanced interaction opportunities with customers. Like other technological applications, mixed reality is not without challenges. This section presents the major challenges confronting mixed reality usage in the digital marketing field.

Costs

As has been noted above, MR application in various field requires the availability of specialized application and hardware (Sanskar & Rejo, 2020). The costs of mixed reality infrastructure can be a hindrance to its wide usage. For instance, one of the most advanced HMDs, Microsoft Hololens2 costs $3,500 (Microsoft, 2021). In addition to that other devices required include components such as cameras and sensors so that mixed-reality experiences can be created. Software development costs for the MR are also on the higher side depending on the complexity of the projects. The average cost of developing an MR app can range from 50 000 to 500 000 for a basic application and for specialized or complex projects costing up to $1 million dollars (Digital Capital, 2018). From a company perspective, the development of software costs emanate from the platform, customization, content creation and integration with other systems (AR Insider, 2019)

Security and Privacy

Research has shown that while the potential applications of MR are vast and wide-ranging, it is equally important to consider the security and privacy implications of this technology. De Guzman et al. (2019) suggested that the proliferation of immersive technologies across industries may entail security implications that may yet be known. De Guzman et al. (2019) expressed the fear that mixed reality can result in the theft of customer personal information through face-matching applications. MR devices collect a vast amount of data about users, including their behavior patterns, location and personal information. This data can be used for advertising or sold to third-party companies without the user`s consent. Sixty-eight per cent (68%) of consumers are worried about their personal information being collected by MR devices (IAPP, 2019). MR devices are also vulnerable to cyber-attacks due to their connectivity with other devices and networks. Hackers can exploit vulnerabilities in MR software or hardware to gain access to sensitive information or control the device remotely. Cybercriminals are increasingly targeting MR devices as they become more popular among consumers (Mcfee, 2019).

Physical security is also another problem when MR devices are not properly secured or monitored. For example, if an MR headset is left unattended in a public place, some can steal and have access to information stored (De Guzman, 2019) There is also a challenge in the usage as MR experiences can be so immersive resulting in users lose track of their surrounding and put themselves in danger. For example, a user wearing an MR headset while walking in a street might not notice oncoming traffic or other hazards. Content integrity can also be another challenge since in the MR environment it is not easy to differentiate real from virtual objects or people. Users can be misled into believing that something is real when it is a counterfeit.

DISCUSSION, REFLECTIONS, AND RECOMMENDATIONS FOR A DEVELOPING CONTEXT

The challenges confronting the application of mixed reality on the way forward for businesses in developing countries are numerous and complex. These range from inadequate infrastructure to limited access to technology, these countries face a unique set of obstacles in their pursuit of digital transformation as reported by Musungwini et al. (2022). Therefore, for businesses in these countries to make the most of the potential of mixed reality there must first address these challenges. This includes investing in the necessary infrastructure, such as high-speed internet, to support the implementation of mixed reality solutions. Additionally, businesses must ensure that their employees are equipped with the necessary skills and knowledge to effectively use and maintain the technology so there is a need to provide financial resources for their training. Businesses in developing contexts must also consider the cost implications of incorporating mixed reality into their operations, as the technology can be expensive to implement.

We have identified that the cost of implementing MR technology can be prohibitive for businesses in developing countries especially as the developing countries are characterized by the sprouting of Small and Medium Enterprises (SMEs). Hence, we believe that the hardware and software required to create and maintain an MR environment can be expensive, and the cost of training personnel to use the technology can add to the overall cost which may be huge for SMEs. Additionally, businesses may need to invest in additional infrastructure, such as high-speed internet connections, to ensure that the MR environment is properly maintained. MR technology can be vulnerable to security threats, such as malware and data breaches. That is why businesses must ensure that the MR environment is properly secured to protect sensitive data and prevent unauthorized access, and this may be daunting for businesses in developing contexts. Businesses in developing countries may not have the resources or expertise to properly secure their MR environment.

We have also established that MR technology can also be used to collect and store personal data, which can be a major concern for businesses in developing countries. Businesses must ensure that they are compliant with local laws and regulations regarding the collection and use of personal data and that they have adequate measures in place to protect the privacy of their customers. The way forward for businesses in developing countries is to invest in the necessary infrastructure and training to ensure that they can properly implement and maintain MR technology. Additionally, businesses should ensure that they are compliant with local laws and regulations regarding the collection and use of personal data and that they have adequate measures in place to protect the privacy of their customers. Finally, businesses should ensure that their MR environment is properly secured to protect sensitive data and prevent unauthorized access. These authors believe that by tackling these challenges head-on, businesses in developing countries like Zimbabwe can leverage the power of mixed reality to unlock new opportunities and drive innovation. Therefore, the application of MR has the potential to revolutionize the way businesses in developing countries operate and by leveraging the power of virtual and augmented reality, businesses can create immersive experiences that can help them reach new markets, increase efficiency, and reduce costs. However, several challenges must be addressed for businesses to successfully apply MR in developing countries.

SOLUTIONS AND RECOMMENDATIONS

It is our humble submission that MR applications should be developed with a focus on the needs of the local population, considering the local context and cultural norms. We believe that this will ensure that the MR applications are tailored to the specific needs of the local population and are more likely to be accepted and adopted. Businesses should also consider the cost of developing and deploying MR applications as well as the cost of training personnel to use and maintain the applications. This will ensure that the applications are cost-effective and can be implemented on time. Businesses should invest in research and development or partner with research institutions like universities to ensure that the applications are secure and reliable. This will ensure that the applications are not vulnerable to malicious attacks and can be used safely.

Business organizations in developing countries should concentrate on creating appropriate applications for those with disabilities. This will guarantee that all people can use the applications and that they are inclusive. Companies should concentrate on creating applications that are compatible with current platforms and systems. By ensuring that the apps can be incorporated into current systems and platforms, they will become more effective and helpful. Using MR applications may have ethical repercussions, which businesses should think about. This will guarantee that the applications are utilized sensibly and do not violate anyone's or any group's rights. Companies should also think about how using MR applications can affect the business operating environment. This will ensure that the applications are developed and used in a way that is sustainable and does not harm the environment. Finally, businesses should consider the potential economic benefits of using MR applications. This will ensure that the applications are developed in a way that maximizes the economic benefits for the local population.

FUTURE RESEARCH DIRECTIONS

The chapter provides valuable insights in the characterization of mixed reality and its role in enhancing consumer interaction, future research may explore on how MR applications can be adapted in different set ups. More so, ethical implications of the application of mixed reality technologies can also be an important area for future studies.

CONCLUSION

In conclusion, Mixed Reality is an emerging technology with a wide range of potential applications in developing contexts. It has the potential to improve access to resources and services, as well as to address a range of development-related issues. The history of MR has been a fascinating one, from its genesis in the 1980s to its current state as a rapidly growing field of technology. Its potential for application in a variety of areas is immense, offering the potential for novel and innovative solutions to existing problems in various areas. The potential benefits of MR include improved user experience, increased efficiency, and enhanced collaboration. However, its development is not without its challenges, particularly in terms of the complexity of the technology and the need for specialized skills, user data security and privacy concerns, and the cost of acquiring this technology. However, as technology continues to evolve and become more widely available, it is likely to become an increasingly important tool for development in the years to come. By combining physical and virtual elements, it [MR] has opened a range of possibilities for applications in areas such as education, entertainment, healthcare, and more. Its potential benefits include improved user experience, enhanced collaboration, and increased efficiency. Hence, the future of mixed reality looks bright and its potential to revolutionize the way we interact with the world is undeniable, especially in a developing context. With continued research and development, the possibilities of mixed reality are sure to be explored and realized in the years to come. Our book chapter is in sync with the theme of the book which is Confronting Security and Privacy Challenges in Digital Marketing, although our chapter gave primacy to the developing world context.

REFERENCES

Alcañiz, M., Bigne, E., & Guixeres, J. (2019). Virtual reality in marketing: A framework, review and research agenda. *Frontiers in Psychology*, *10*, 1530. [REMOVED HYPERLINK FIELD] doi:10.3389/fpsyg.2019.01530 PMID:31333548

Alghadir, A. H., Beg, R. I., Shaphe, M. A., & Ahmad, F. (2021). Intermanual Transfer Effects on Performance Gain Following Dominant Hand Training in Community-Dwelling Healthy Adults: A Preliminary Study. *Journal of Multidisciplinary Healthcare*, *14*, 1007–1016. Advance online publication. doi:10.2147/JMDH.S298991 PMID:33958874

Bae, S., Jung, T. H., Moorhouse, N., Suh, M., & Kwon, O. (2020). The influence of mixed reality on satisfaction and brand loyalty in cultural heritage attractions: A brand equity perspective. *Sustainability (Basel)*, *12*(7), 2956. doi:10.3390u12072956

Ben, D. (2016). *5 authentication methods put passwords to shame*. The Next Web. https://thenextweb.com/insider/2016/03/31/5-technologies-will-is-world-authentication-head

Blut, M., Heirati, N., & Schoefer, K. (2020). The dark side of customer participation: When customer participation in service co-development leads to role stress. *Journal of Service Research*, *23*(2), 156–173. doi:10.1177/1094670519894643

Boboc, R. G., Gîrbacia, F., & Butilă, E. V. (2020). The application of augmented reality in the automotive industry: A systematic literature review. *Applied Sciences (Basel, Switzerland)*, *10*(12), 4259. doi:10.3390/app10124259

Chang, Y. J., Chen, C. H., Huang, W. T., & Huang, W. S. (2011, July). *Investigating students' perceived satisfaction, behavioral intention, and effectiveness of English learning using augmented reality. In 2011 IEEE international conference on multimedia and Expo*. IEEE.

De Guzman, J. A., Thilakarathna, K., & Seneviratne, A. (2019). Security and privacy approaches in mixed reality: A literature survey. *ACM Computing Surveys*, *52*(6), 1–37. doi:10.1145/3359626

Dehghani, M., Lee, S. H. M., & Mashatan, A. (2020). Touching holograms with windows mixed reality: Renovating the consumer retailing services. *Technology in Society*, *63*, 101394. doi:10.1016/j.techsoc.2020.101394

Dick, E. (2021). *The Promise of Immersive Learning: Augmented and Virtual Reality's Potential in Education*. ITIF. https://itif.org/publications/2021/08/30/promise-immersive-learning-augmented-and-virtual-reality-potential

Duan, Y., Edwards, J. S., & Dwivedi, Y. K. (2019). Artificial intelligence for decision making in the era of big data—Evolution, challenges and research agenda. *International Journal of Information Management*, *48*, 63–71. doi:10.1016/j.ijinfomgt.2019.01.021

Egger, R., & Neuburger, L. (2020). Augmented, virtual, and mixed reality in tourism. Handbook of e-Tourism, 1-25.

Flavián, C., Ibáñez-Sánchez, S., & Orús, C. (2019). The impact of virtual, augmented and mixed reality technologies on the customer experience. *Journal of Business Research*, *100*, 547–560. doi:10.1016/j.jbusres.2018.10.050

Gao, L., Cai, H., & Bai, R. (2021). *Real-time visual representations for mobile mixed reality remote collaboration*. Semantic Scholar. doi:10.1145/3275495.3275515

Garg, P., Gupta, B., Dzever, S., Sivarajah, U., & Kumar, V. (2020). Examining the relationship between social media analytics practices and business performance in the Indian retail and IT industries: The mediation role of customer engagement. *International Journal of Information Management*, *52*, 102069. doi:10.1016/j.ijinfomgt.2020.102069

Gattullo, M., Laviola, E., Boccaccio, A., Evangelista, A., Fiorentino, M., Manghisi, V. M., & Uva, A. E. (2022). Education Laboratories. *Computers*, *11*(50), 1–24.[REMOVED HYPERLINK FIELD] PMID:36407564

Hoyer, W. D., Kroschke, M., Schmitt, B., Kraume, K., & Shankar, V. (2020). Transforming the Customer Experience Through New Technologies. *Journal of Interactive Marketing*, *51*, 57–71. doi:10.1016/j.intmar.2020.04.001

Jessen, A., Hilken, T., Chylinski, M., Mahr, D., Heller, J., Keeling, D. I., & de Ruyter, K. (2020). The playground effect: How augmented reality drives creative customer engagement. *Journal of Business Research*, *116*, 85–98. doi:10.1016/j.jbusres.2020.05.002

Kadavasal, M. S., Dhara, K. K., Wu, X., & Krishnaswamy, V. (2007). Mixed reality for enhancing business communications using virtual worlds. *Proceedings of the ACM Symposium on Virtual Reality Software and Technology, VRST*, (pp. 233–234). ACM. 10.1145/1315184.1315236

Kim, G. J. (2005). *Designing Virtual Reality Systems: The Structured Approach*. Springer.

Kim, S. J., Laine, T. H., & Suk, H. J. (2021). Presence Effects in Virtual Reality Based on User Characteristics: Attention, Enjoyment, and Memory. *Electronics (Basel), 10*(9), 1051. doi:10.3390/electronics10091051

Kizilcec, R. F., Anderson, F., & Cho, Y. J. (2021). *Delivery Ghost: Effects of Language Immersion and Interactivity in a Language Learning Game.* ACM Digital Library.

Krafft, M., Sajtos, L., & Haenlein, M. (2020). Challenges and Opportunities for Marketing Scholars in Times of the Fourth Industrial Revolution. *Journal of Interactive Marketing, 51*, 1–8. doi:10.1016/j.intmar.2020.06.001

Lacoche, J., Le Chénéchal, M., Villain, E., & Foulonneau, A. (2019, September). Model and tools for integrating iot into mixed reality environments: Towards a virtual-real seamless continuum. In *ICAT-EGVE 2019-International Conference on Artificial Reality and Telexistence and Eurographics Symposium on Virtual Environments.* Dig Lib. 10.2312/egve.20191286

Lee, S. J., Ahn, C., Song, K. M., & Ahn, H. (2018). Trust and distrust in e-commerce. *Sustainability (Basel), 10*(4), 1015. doi:10.3390u10041015

Lemon, K. N., & Verhoef, P. C. (2016). Understanding customer experience throughout the customer journey. *Journal of Marketing, 80*(6), 69–96. doi:10.1509/jm.15.0420

Maas, M. J., & Hughes, J. M. (2020). Virtual, augmented and mixed reality in K–12 education: A review of the literature. *Technology, Pedagogy and Education, 29*(2), 231–249. doi:10.1080/1475939X.2020.1737210

Mehler-Bicher, A., Steiger, L., & Wetzel, D. (2020). Mixed Reality Applications in Business Contexts. In Holography - Recent Advances and Applications. IntechOpen.

Microsoft. (2021). *Microsoft HoloLens 2: Technical specifications.* Microsoft. https://www.microsoft.com/en-us/hololens/hardware

Musungwini, S., Gavai, P. V., Furusa, S. S., & Gumbo, R. (2022). Inclusive Digital Transformation for the Marginalized Communities in a Developing Context. In *Digital Transformation for Promoting Inclusiveness in Marginalized Communities* (pp. 95–122). IGI Global. doi:10.4018/978-1-6684-3901-2.ch005

Musungwini, S., Gavai, P. V., Munyoro, B., & Chare, A. (2023). Emerging ICT Technologies for Agriculture, Training, and Capacity Building for Farmers in Developing Countries: A Case Study in Zimbabwe. In Applying Drone Technologies and Robotics for Agricultural Sustainability (pp. 12-30). IGI Global.

Navarro-Newbal, A. A., Velez, J. A., Satzabal, J. E., Munera, L. E., & Bernabe, G. (2022). *Virtual surgical tele-simulations in ophthalmology* (Vol. 1256). International Congress Series. Elsevier.

Njerekai, C. (2020). An application of the virtual reality 360° concept to the Great Zimbabwe monument. *Journal of Heritage Tourism, 15*(5), 567–579. doi:10.1080/1743873X.2019.1696808

Pan, Y., & Zhang, L. (2021). Roles of artificial intelligence in construction engineering and management: A critical review and future trends. *Automation in Construction, 122*, 103517. doi:10.1016/j.autcon.2020.103517

Pansari, A., & Kumar, V. (2017). Customer engagement: The construct, antecedents, and Consequences. *Journal of the Academy of Marketing Science*, *45*(3), 294–311. doi:10.100711747-016-0485-6

Rauschnabel, P. A. (2021). Augmented reality is eating the real world! The substitution of physical products by holograms. *International Journal of Information Management*, *57*, 102279. doi:10.1016/j.ijinfomgt.2020.102279

Rokhsaritalemi, S., Sadeghi-Niaraki, A., & Choi, M. (2020). A Review on Mixed Reality: Current Trends, Challenges and Prospects. *Applied Sciences (Basel, Switzerland)*, *10*(2), 636. doi:10.3390/app10020636

Sahija, D. (2022). A critical review of mixed reality integration with medical devices for patient care. *International Journal for Innovative Research in Multidisciplinary Field*, *8*(1), 100–105. doi:10.2015/IJIRMF/202201017

Sanska, S., & Rejo, M. (2020). Threats by mixed reality and counter measures. *Procedia Computer Science*, *171*, 2720–2728. doi:10.1016/j.procs.2020.04.295

Silva, M. J. B., Lorena, O. R. D., Cerqueira, K. A., & Campos, P. O. (2022). Avatar marketing: A study on the engagement and authenticity of virtual influencers on Instagram. *Social Network Analysis and Mining*, *12*(1), 130. doi:10.100713278-022-00966-w

Speicher, M., Hall, B. D., & Nebeling, M. (2019, May). What is mixed reality? In *Proceedings of the 2019 CHI conference on human factors in computing systems* (pp. 1-15). ACM. 10.1145/3290605.3300767

Sung, E. (2020). Brand experience via mobile AR app marketing. Augmented reality and virtual reality: Progress in IS, 3–9. Springer. doi:10.1007/978-3-030-37869-1_1

Sung, E. C., Bae, S., Han, D. I. D., & Kwon, O. (2021). Consumer engagement via interactive artificial intelligence and mixed reality. *International Journal of Information Management*, *60*, 102382. doi:10.1016/j.ijinfomgt.2021.102382

Turner, F., & Welch, I. (2019). The Mixed Reality Toolkit as the Next Step in the Mass Customization Co-Design Experience. *International Journal of Industrial Engineering and Management*, *10*(2), 191–199. doi:10.24867/IJIEM-2019-2-239

Um, T., Kim, H., Kim, H., Lee, J., Koo, C., & Chung, N. (2022). Travel Incheon as a Metaverse: Smart Tourism Cities Development Case in Korea. In Information and Communication Technologies in Tourism 2022. Springer. doi:10.1007/978-3-030-94751-4_20

Vargo, S. L., & Lusch, R. F. (2008). Service-dominant logic: Continuing the evolution. *Journal of the Academy of Marketing Science*, *36*(1), 1–10. doi:10.100711747-007-0069-6

Wang, W., Wang, F., Song, W., & Su, S. (2020). Application of augmented reality (AR) technologies in inhouse logistics. In E3S Web of Conferences (Vol. 145, p. 02018). EDP Sciences. doi:10.1051/e3sconf/202014502018

Wedel, M., Bign'e, E., & Zhang, J. (2020). Virtual and augmented reality: Advancing research in consumer marketing. *International Journal of Research in Marketing*, *37*(3), 443–465. doi:10.1016/j.ijresmar.2020.04.004

ADDITIONAL READING

Alimamy, S., & Gnoth, J. (2022). I want it my way! The effect of perceptions of personalization through augmented reality and online shopping on customer intentions to co-create value. *Computers in Human Behavior, 128*, 107105. doi:10.1016/j.chb.2021.107105

Deng, X., Unnava, H. R., & Lee, H. (2019). "Too true to be good?" When virtual reality decreases interest in actual reality. *Journal of Business Research, 100*, 561–570. doi:10.1016/j.jbusres.2018.11.008

Hammady, R., Ma, M., & Strathearn, C. (2020). Ambient information visualisation and visitors' technology acceptance of mixed reality in museums. *Journal on Computing and Cultural Heritage, 13*(2), 1–22. doi:10.1145/3359590

Jain, S., Schweiss, T., Bender, S., & Werth, D. (2021). Omnichannel retail customer experience with mixed-reality shopping assistant systems. In *Advances in Visual Computing: 16th International Symposium Proceedings, Part I* (pp. 504–517). Springer International Publishing. 10.1007/978-3-030-90439-5_40

Moorhouse, N., tom Dieck, M. C., & Jung, T. (2019). An experiential view to children learning in museums with augmented reality. *Museum Management and Curatorship, 34*(4), 402–418. doi:10.1080/09647775.2019.1578991

Pfeifer, P., Hilken, T., Heller, J., Alimamy, S., & Di Palma, R. (2023). More than meets the eye: In-store retail experiences with augmented reality smart glasses. *Computers in Human Behavior, 146*, 107816. doi:10.1016/j.chb.2023.107816

Shin, D. (2019). How does immersion work in augmented reality games? A user-centric view of immersion and engagement. *Information Communication and Society, 22*(9), 1212–1229. doi:10.1080/1369118X.2017.1411519

Trunfio, M., & Campana, S. (2020). A visitors' experience model for mixed reality in the museum. *Current Issues in Tourism, 23*(9), 1053–1058. doi:10.1080/13683500.2019.1586847

KEY TERMS AND DEFINITIONS

Augmented Reality: Is when digital content is superimposed on users' real surroundings.

Consumer Engagement: Refers to the creation of seamless relationships with customers.

Consumer Experience: The totality of interactions that the customer has with a brand.

Immersive Technology: Is a collective name for all disruptive technology applications such as virtual reality, augmented reality and mixed reality that create experiences by merging the physical and virtual worlds.

Information Communication Technology: Refers to all technological tools and resources that can be used to send, store, create or share information.

Real Environment: Natural or physical environment.

Virtual Environment: Refers to a computer-generated environment that mimics the real world.

Virtual Reality: Is a computer-generated environment allowing users to navigate and interact triggering real time simulation of senses.

Chapter 13
Immersive Marketing on Metaverse:
Development of Metrics for Performance Analysis and Security-Related Challenges

Amaresh Jha
https://orcid.org/0000-0002-6083-1610
UPES, Dehradun, India

ABSTRACT

Measuring immersive marketing experiences in the metaverse is a new area of study and it includes a wide range of algorithms to make better assessments and predictions. Any algorithm or metrics to measure the effectiveness of metaverse marketing will require a large amount of data, and then comes the challenge of data security and privacy. This study primarily aims at providing a framework for measuring the effectiveness of metaverse marketing considering the key drivers of virtual-commerce experiences and the metrics like engagement rates, conversion rates, customer acquisition costs, and the privacy and security-related changes in metaverse data analytics.

INTRODUCTION

In the context of the metaverse, immersive marketing has the potential to create even more engaging and memorable experiences for consumers for a complete immersion in a virtual-commerce environment that allows them to interact with products and services in a more natural and intuitive way. Brands can create virtual storefronts or experiences within the metaverse that allow consumers to fully engage with their products and services, leading to increased brand awareness, loyalty, and sales. Recent inventions have a great focus on human centered interactive and immersive technologies (Jerald, 2017). Virtual Commerce (Jin & Bolebruch, 2009) is a 3D extension of e-commerce where the purpose is to give the users or the consumers more immersive experience of the products and services. Immersive marketing relies heavily on storytelling (Cummings et al., 2022; Gill et al., 2022) to create an emotional connection

DOI: 10.4018/978-1-6684-8958-1.ch013

with the audience. The story should be engaging, memorable, and aligned with the brand message. It evokes emotions and feelings that are associated with the brand or product. The immersive experience for a product or service should be interactive and encourage active participation from the audience. This can be achieved using sensory stimuli such as sound, touch, and smell (Harley et al., 2018; Jha et al., 2022). This can be achieved using virtual or augmented reality, gamification, or other interactive technologies. Measuring the success of immersive marketing experiences is important to understand how the audience is engaging with the brand or product, and to optimize future campaigns. The "Engagement' metric measures the level of interaction and participation of the audience with immersive experience. It includes metrics such as the number of clicks, views, shares, or likes. The "Conversion rate" metric measures the percentage of users who complete a desired action, such as making a purchase or signing up for a newsletter, after engaging with the immersive experience. The "Brand recall" metric measures the audience's ability to recall the brand or product after engaging with the immersive experience. It can be measured through surveys, focus groups, or by tracking website visits and social media engagement (Pollák & Markovič, 2022). The "Time Spent" metric measures the amount of time the audience spends engaging with the immersive experience. Longer engagement times indicate a higher level of interest and engagement. The "User Feedback" collected through surveys, social media, or user testing provides valuable insights into the audience's perception of the immersive experience and can be used to improve future campaigns. The "Cost per engagement" metric measures the cost of each engagement or interaction with the immersive experience. It can be used to evaluate the return on investment of the immersive marketing campaign and to optimize future campaigns.

RESEARCH QUESTIONS

The broad research questions under this study pertaining to metrics of immersive marketing experience are:

- What are the most effective metrics for measuring the success of immersive marketing experiences, and how do they differ from traditional marketing metrics?
- How do engagement metrics for immersive marketing experiences compare to engagement metrics for traditional marketing campaigns, and what factors contribute to differences in engagement rates?
- How do immersive marketing experiences impact brand recall, and what factors contribute to differences in brand recall rates between immersive and traditional marketing campaigns?
- How can user feedback be effectively incorporated into the evaluation of immersive marketing experiences, and what insights can be gained from user feedback that can inform future campaigns?
- What are the key drivers of conversion rates for immersive marketing experiences, and how do these differ from traditional marketing campaigns?
- What is the relationship between the time spent engaging with an immersive marketing experience and the level of brand awareness, and how can this relationship be leveraged to optimize future campaigns?
- How can cost per engagement be effectively used to evaluate the ROI of immersive marketing campaigns, and what factors should be considered when calculating the cost per engagement?
- How can immersive marketing experiences be optimized to maximize engagement rates, brand recall, and conversion rates, and what role do metrics play in this optimization process?

REVIEW OF LITERATURE

Rose (2012) in his book titled "The Art of Immersion: How the Digital Generation Is Remaking Hollywood, Madison Avenue, and the Way We Tell Stories", provide a comprehensive account on how digital media has transformed storytelling and how immersive experiences are changing the way we engage with brands and products. The book "Experiential Marketing: Secrets, Strategies, and Success Stories from the World's Greatest Brands" by Smith and Hanover (2016) provides an overview of experiential marketing, including immersive marketing techniques, and features case studies from successful experiential marketing campaigns. Heath and Heath (2017) in their book "The Power of Moments: Why Certain Experiences Have Extraordinary Impact" explore the power of creating memorable experiences and how to create moments that leave a lasting impact on the audience. Lukashevich and Lugano (2020) in their work "Virtual and Augmented Reality in Education, Art, and Museums" provide a detailed account on how virtual and augmented reality can be used in various settings, including marketing, and how these technologies can be used to create immersive and engaging experiences for audiences (Burke, 1997). Smilansky (2018) has provided a comprehensive overview of experiential marketing, including the use of immersive marketing techniques, and includes practical advice and case studies in the book "Experiential Marketing: A Practical Guide to Interactive Brand Experiences". Metaverse will be using an adaptive network (Gill et al., 2022) which is more dynamic in nature and hence there is a probability that the immersive marketing on metaverse will use more dynamic networks.

Barrera and Shah (2023) in their article provide a detailed account of conceptual framework and on marketing in the metaverse. The authors recommend that firms can utilize immersiveness, sociability, and environmental fidelity to design and characterize consumer experiences in the metaverse. A comprehensive study of the potential impact of metaverse on society, commerce, and culture has been done by Smart et al. (2008) and has been published as a book titled "The Metaverse Roadmap: Pathways to the 3D Web". Cline (2020) in his novel "Ready Player Two: A Novel" provides a vivid depiction of a fully realized metaverse and explores the potential impact of this technology on society and commerce. Andjelic (2021) in her book "The Business of Aspiration: How Social, Cultural, and Environmental Capital Change Brands" provides a blueprint of the changing nature of branding and marketing in the age of the metaverse, and the importance of social, cultural, and environmental capital in building successful brands. The level of immersion that a marketing campaign provides is a crucial factor in measuring effectiveness (Weinhardt et al., 2021). This could include the use of virtual or augmented reality, the level of interactivity, and the extent to which the user is transported ınto the virtual experience. As the metaverse continues to evolve and grow, it is likely that immersive marketing will become an increasingly important aspect of digital marketing strategies for many brands. However, it is important to note that as with any new technology, there are also ethical and privacy concerns that must be considered and addressed. The goal of immersive marketing is to provide an unforgettable experience that inspires and motivates customers to engage with the brand or product. Personalization is key to creating a memorable experience. The immersive experience should be tailored to the individual, considering their preferences and interests (Karaarslan et al., 2023). It's important to measure the effectiveness of the immersive marketing campaign to determine its impact on the audience and its overall ROI. This study looks at the possible metrics such as engagement rates, conversion rates, and brand recall which can be used to evaluate the success of the immersive marketing campaigns in the metaverse. As the metaverse continues to develop, brands will have more opportunities to create immersive and engaging experiences for their customers, which can lead to greater brand loyalty and increased sales. Metaverse marketing can open new revenue streams for brands by allowing them to sell virtual goods and experiences to their customers. The metaverse has the potential to connect people from all over the world, allowing brands to reach a global audience with their marketing campaigns (Catherine, 2022). With the use of data analytics and machine learning, brands can create personalized metaverse experiences for their customers, tailoring their marketing messages to everyone's preferences and interests. The metaverse can provide a platform for social engagement between brands and their customers, allowing for more interactive and collaborative experiences. The metaverse can provide a sustainable alternative to traditional marketing methods by reducing the need for physical materials and minimizing the carbon footprint of marketing campaigns. In conclusion, the prospects for metaverse marketing in the next 10 years look promising, with the potential for increased adoption, enhanced brand experiences, new revenue streams, global reach, personalization, social engagement, and sustainability. Brands that embrace metaverse marketing and adapt to the evolving landscape are likely to see significant benefits in terms of customer engagement and business growth (Palmatier et al., 2018). With the growth of virtual and augmented reality technologies, more people are likely to become familiar with the metaverse, leading to increased adoption of metaverse marketing by brands.

In comparison to traditional marketing metrics, metrics for measuring the success of immersive marketing experiences tend to be more focused on engagement, brand recall, and conversion, as opposed to reach and frequency (Batat, 2019). Immersive marketing experiences are designed to create deeper connections with audiences, so measuring the level of engagement and the impact on brand awareness and conversion are critical in evaluating the success of the campaign. Additionally, immersive marketing can be analyzed to provide insights into the audience's behavior and preferences, allowing for further optimization of the experience. The most effective metrics for measuring the success of immersive marketing experiences depend on the goals of the specific campaign (Figure 1).

Figure 1. Measuring immersive marketing experience

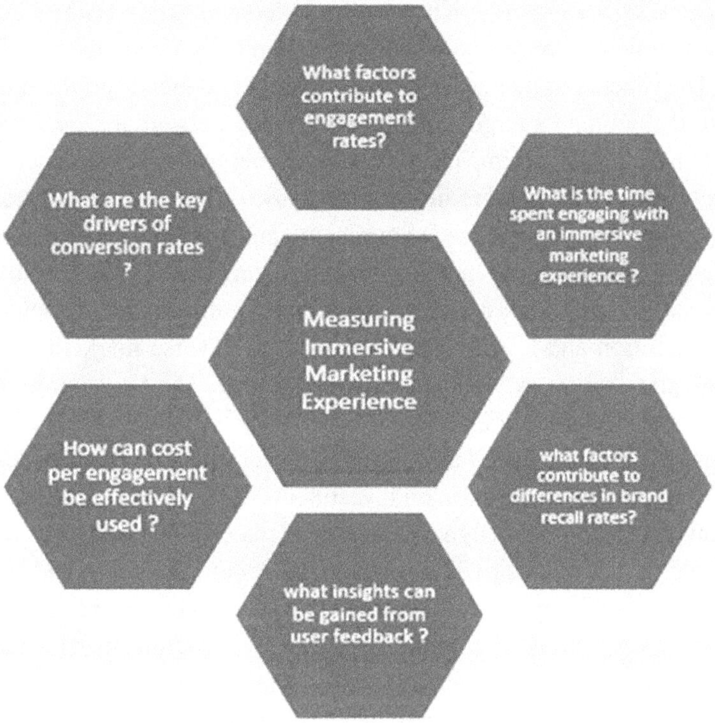

Engagement metrics for immersive marketing experiences can differ from engagement metrics for traditional marketing campaigns due to the nature of the experience and the level of interactivity with the audience (Falchuk et al., 2018). The metaverse engagement metrics has certain attributes which is like other engagement metrics like identifying key performance indicators, data collection and analysis, evaluating the results and reviewing the strategies for enhancing the metrics (Alfaro et al., 2019). The first step is to identify the KPIs which may include metrics such as user retention, click-through rates, conversion rates, and social engagement. The second step is collecting data on the selected KPIs from the metaverse platform and any associated analytics tools. The third step is analyzing the collected data to identify patterns and trends in user behavior, such as which areas of the metaverse are most popular, which activities are most engaging, and which marketing messages are most effective. The third step is to evaluate the results of the data analysis to determine the overall level of metaverse engagement. This may involve comparing current data to previous periods, as well as benchmarking against industry standards. Based on the results of the evaluation, the metaverse marketing strategy is adjusted as necessary to optimize engagement. This may involve revising messaging, targeting different user segments, or modifying the metaverse experience. Continuously monitoring and refining the metaverse engagement strategy based on ongoing data analysis and feedback from users is the next step. By following this process brands can measure and optimize their metaverse engagement, ultimately leading to more effective marketing campaigns and increased ROI.

Metaverse marketing can be defined as the practice of promoting products or services in virtual or augmented reality environments, where users can interact with the brand and experience its offerings in an immersive way (Prieto, 2019). The effectiveness of metaverse marketing can be influenced by several factors, including target audience, immersive experience, brand alignment, technical infrastructure, and legal considerations. The success of metaverse marketing largely depends on the relevance of the target audience to the brand. If the brand's target audience is already present and engaged in the metaverse, then it is more likely to have a positive impact. The more immersive the experience, the more likely the audience is to engage with the brand and remember the marketing message. This can include elements such as interactive environments, personalized experiences, and emotional connections (Van Rijmenam, 2022). The messaging and branding used in metaverse marketing campaigns should be aligned with the overall brand strategy and image. Consistency across all marketing channels, including the metaverse, can increase brand recognition and loyalty. The success of metaverse marketing also depends on the technical infrastructure and support available to deliver a seamless and engaging experience. This can include high-quality graphics, stable servers, and user-friendly interfaces. Measuring the effectiveness of metaverse marketing requires the use of appropriate metrics and analysis. This can include tracking user engagement, conversion rates, and return on investment (ROI) to determine the effectiveness of the campaign. As with any marketing campaign, metaverse marketing must comply with applicable laws and regulations, including those related to data privacy, intellectual property, and consumer protection. In summary, the effectiveness of metaverse marketing is influenced by various factors such as the target audience, immersive experience, brand alignment, technical infrastructure, metrics and analysis, and legal considerations. Brands that carefully consider and address these factors can create successful metaverse marketing campaigns that engage users and drive business results.

Metaverse marketing has the potential to revolutionize the way brands interact with their customers and prospects. With the growth of virtual and augmented reality technologies, more people are likely to become familiar with the metaverse, leading to increased adoption of metaverse marketing by brands (de Brito Silva et al. 2022). Metaverse marketing presents several security-related challenges that brands and marketers need to address to protect user data and prevent fraud. By implementing robust security measures and complying with legal and regulatory requirements, brands can build trust with their users and ensure the success of their metaverse marketing efforts. Data encryption and decryption (Jha & Jha, 2022) related challenges are going to be there with 3D internet-based platforms as well. The metaverse collects a lot of user data, which can be used to target ads and personalize experiences. However, brands need to ensure that this data is collected and stored securely, and that users have control over how their data is used. In the metaverse, users can create multiple identities and personas, which can be used to commit fraud and engage in malicious activities. Brands need to implement identity verification processes to ensure that users are who they claim to be. The metaverse is vulnerable to cybersecurity threats, such as hacking, phishing, and malware. Brands need to implement robust cybersecurity measures to protect user data and prevent unauthorized access to their systems. In the metaverse, users can purchase and trade virtual assets, such as digital currencies, digital goods, and virtual real estate. These assets are vulnerable to theft and fraud, so brands need to implement measures to protect them. The metaverse allows users to create and share content, which can include offensive or inappropriate material. Brands need to implement content moderation processes to ensure that their brand is not associated with harmful or offensive content. Metaverse marketing may be subject to various legal and regulatory requirements, such as data protection laws and advertising standards. Brands need to ensure that they are compliant with these requirements, which can be complex and vary by jurisdiction.

RESEARCH METHODOLOGY

The metaverse has emerged as a promising platform for marketing and advertising, providing immersive and interactive experiences for brands and consumers. In this exploratory analysis, the researcher conducted interviews with industry experts and professionals to get answers of the nine broad questions under study pertaining to immersive marketing experiences.

Participant Selection: We interviewed a diverse group of 43 professionals involved in metaverse marketing, including marketers (17), developers (21), and strategists (5).

Interview Process: Semi-structured interviews were conducted seeking responses to the broad research questions allowing participants to provide detailed responses based on their experiences and observations.

Data Analysis: Interview transcripts were carefully analyzed to identify recurring themes, patterns, and noteworthy insights.

ANALYSIS OF FINDINGS

On the question of metrics for measuring the success of immersive marketing, participants emphasized the importance of measuring engagement metrics, such as time spent, interactions, and click-through rates as well as tracking the number of interactions within immersive experiences and the duration of user engagement provided insights into campaign effectiveness. The other emphasis was made on analyzing click-through rates and conversion rates which helps assess the impact of immersive marketing on driving desired actions. Participants highlighted the need to evaluate brand perception and sentiment as an indicator of campaign success. Assessing changes in brand awareness, brand sentiment, and brand perception pre- and post-campaign offered insights into the effectiveness of immersive marketing in shaping consumer perceptions. The participants also emphasized monitoring social media mentions, sentiment analysis, and brand sentiment surveys and termed these metrices as valuable tools for measuring brand perception.

On the question that how the metrices of measuring immersive marketing are different from the metrices of measuring the traditional marketing experiences the interview analysis revealed notable differences. While traditional marketing focuses on capturing attention within limited time frames and tracking interactions like clicks and conversions, immersive marketing allows for extended user interaction time, diverse interactions within virtual environments, and emotional responses. Metrics such as time spent, interactions, click-through rates, social media engagement, emotional response, and data analytics play a vital role in evaluating the effectiveness of both marketing approaches. Marketers can leverage these insights to design and optimize their campaigns according to the specific engagement metrics associated with each approach.

On the question that how brand recall is different for immersive marketing compared to traditional marketing, the interview analysis demonstrates that immersive marketing experiences have a significant impact on brand recall. The immersive nature, emotional connection, interactivity, multisensory experience, and personalization contribute to higher brand recall rates in immersive marketing campaigns. In contrast, traditional marketing relies more on repetition and frequency of exposure. Understanding these factors enables marketers to design effective campaigns that leverage the unique features of immersive marketing to enhance brand recall.

The next question put before the respondents was how valuable is the user feedback incorporation in evaluation of immersive marketing experience? The analysis of interview highlighted that early and ongoing feedback collection, diverse feedback channels, qualitative and quantitative analysis, actionable insights, and establishing a feedback loop with users are key elements to consider. By embracing user feedback and incorporating it into the evaluation process, marketers can optimize immersive marketing experiences, enhance user satisfaction, and drive greater success in their campaigns.

On the question pertaining to key drivers in conversion rates the analysis of interviews highlights that the specific drivers of conversion rates for immersive marketing experiences can vary depending on the target audience, industry, and campaign objectives. Analyzing real-time data and conducting A/B testing can provide deeper insights into the unique factors driving conversions in a particular context.

The next question put for response was how time spent relates to brand awareness and how it can be interpreted for developing an insight. The respondents suggested that one can start by examining quantitative data related to the time spent engaging with the immersive marketing experience and the level of brand awareness. This can include metrics such as session duration, average time per user, or specific time intervals during the immersive experience. Cross-reference this data with metrics related to brand awareness, such as pre- and post-campaign surveys, brand recognition surveys, or social media sentiment analysis. To assess the correlation between the time spent engaging with immersive experience and the level of brand awareness, statistical methods can be used to determine if there is a significant relationship between these variables. This analysis can help identify whether longer engagement duration are associated with higher brand awareness or if there is no substantial correlation.

The next question was how cost per engagement could measure the return on investment of an immersive marketing campaign. The respondents said that it's important to consider that cost per engagement should be used in conjunction with other relevant metrics and insights to gain a comprehensive understanding of the overall impact and success of immersive marketing initiatives.

On the question of optimizing the immersive marketing experiences for maximizing engagement rates, the respondents suggested a mixed strategy comprising of audience research, creating interactive elements within the immersive experience to increase engagement rates, incorporating features such as gamification, quizzes, polls, or challenges that encourage active participation. The other suggestions included crafting a compelling and immersive narrative that captures the attention of participants, developing a story arc that unfolds throughout the experience, leveraging suspense, surprise, or emotional triggers to maintain engagement. Some respondents suggested incorporating multi-sensory elements within the immersive experience to heighten engagement. This can involve leveraging audio, visuals, tactile sensations, or even scent to create a more immersive and memorable experience. By stimulating multiple senses, you create a richer and more engaging environment that captivates participants. Incorporating features that encourage participants to share their immersive experiences on social media or with their networks was another suggestion by strategist. On the specific question of optimization, the respondents suggest the strategy of regularly tracking and analyzing engagement metrics during and after the immersive marketing campaign.

Development of Metrics

The detailed analysis of the interview and the literature on immersive marketing has led to a conclusion that quality of metaverse experiences can be measured using mathematical modeling of metaverse marketing (Du et al., 2023). It involves using mathematical equations and algorithms to analyze and optimize the effectiveness of metaverse marketing campaigns. Some potential mathematical models that could be used for metaverse marketing are:

- Regression Analysis: Regression analysis can be used to identify the relationship between different variables and outcomes in metaverse marketing campaigns. For example, regression analysis could be used to identify the correlation between ad placement and click-through rates.
- Predictive Modeling: Predictive modeling can be used to forecast the impact of different marketing strategies on user behavior. For example, predictive modeling could be used to determine the likelihood that a particular message or offer will result in a purchase.
- Game Theory: Game theory can be used to analyze the behavior of users in the metaverse and determine the optimal marketing strategies to maximize engagement and conversion rates. For example, game theory could be used to model the behavior of users in a virtual store and determine the optimal pricing and promotion strategies to maximize revenue.
- Network Analysis: Network analysis can be used to analyze the connections and relationships between different users and groups in the metaverse. For example, network analysis could be used to identify influencers and key opinion leaders who are most likely to promote a brand or product.
- Optimization Algorithms: Optimization algorithms can be used to optimize different aspects of metaverse marketing campaigns, such as ad placement, message targeting, and user segmentation. For example, optimization algorithms could be used to identify the optimal combination of targeting parameters to maximize engagement and conversion rates.

In conclusion, mathematical modeling can be a powerful tool for analyzing and optimizing metaverse marketing campaigns (Kulshrestha et al., 2021). By using these models, brands can gain a deeper understanding of user behavior, identify optimal marketing strategies, and ultimately increase the effectiveness of their metaverse marketing efforts (Figure 2).

Figure 2. Engagement metrics for immersive marketing

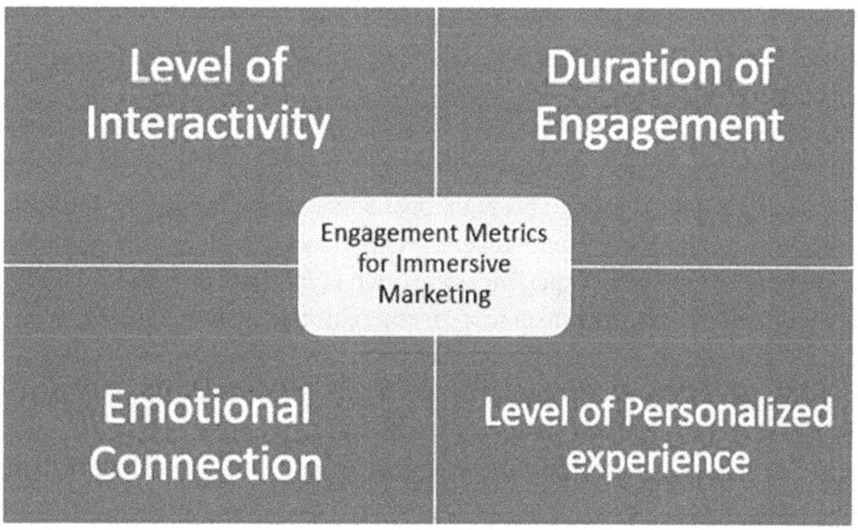

The factors that can contribute to differences in engagement rates are:

- Level of interactivity: Immersive marketing experiences are designed to be more interactive and engaging than traditional marketing campaigns, which often rely on one-way communication. Immersive experiences allow audiences to actively participate in the experience, making it more memorable and impactful.
- Duration of engagement: Immersive marketing experiences often require a longer time commitment from the audience compared to traditional marketing campaigns. This can lead to higher engagement rates as the audience is more invested in the experience and more likely to spend more time engaging with it.
- Emotional connection: Immersive marketing experiences can create a stronger emotional connection with the audience than traditional marketing campaigns, as they often involve storytelling, personalization, and interactivity. This emotional connection can lead to higher engagement rates and a stronger impact on brand perception.
- Unique value proposition: Immersive marketing experiences offer a unique value proposition compared to traditional marketing campaigns. They often provide exclusive content or experiences that are not available elsewhere, which can be a significant draw for audiences.
- Technical requirements: Immersive marketing experiences often require specific technology or equipment to fully participate, such as VR headsets or mobile devices. This can limit the potential audience and affect engagement rates.

Impact of Immersive Marketing on Brand Recall

Immersive marketing experiences can have a significant impact on brand recall by creating memorable and immersive experiences that are more likely to be remembered by the audience. Here are a few factors that can contribute to differences in brand recall rates between immersive and traditional marketing campaigns:

- Multi-sensory experience: Immersive marketing experiences often engage multiple senses, including sight, sound, and touch, creating a more memorable and impactful experience. This multi-sensory experience can lead to higher brand recall rates as the audience is more likely to remember the experience.
- Emotional connection: Immersive marketing experiences can create a stronger emotional connection with the audience than traditional marketing campaigns, as they often involve storytelling, personalization, and interactivity. This emotional connection can lead to higher brand recall rates as the audience is more likely to remember the experience and the brand associated with it.
- Novelty: Immersive marketing experiences are often unique and different from traditional marketing campaigns, which can make them more memorable and lead to higher brand recall rates.
- Repetition: Repetition can also impact brand recall rates. Immersive marketing experiences often provide multiple touchpoints with the audience, which can increase the number of times the audience is exposed to the brand and improve brand recall.
- Relevance: The relevance of the immersive experience to the brand and the audience can also impact brand recall rates. If the immersive experience is not closely related to the brand or is not of interest to the target audience, it may not be as effective in increasing brand recall rates.

User Feedback as a Measure of Immersive Marketing

User feedback is a valuable tool for evaluating the effectiveness of immersive marketing experiences and can provide insights that can inform future campaigns. Some ways to effectively incorporate user feedback into the evaluation of immersive marketing experiences can be:

- Collect feedback at multiple touchpoints: Immersive marketing experiences often involve multiple touchpoints with the audience, from pre-event marketing to the actual experience to post-event follow-up. Collecting feedback at each touchpoint can provide a more comprehensive understanding of the audience's experience.
- Use a mix of quantitative and qualitative feedback: Quantitative feedback, such as surveys or ratings, can provide numerical data that can be analyzed to identify trends and patterns. Qualitative feedback, such as open-ended questions or comments, can provide deeper insights into the audience's thoughts and feelings about the experience.
- Analyze feedback in context: It's essential to analyze user feedback in the context of the specific campaign goals and target audience. For example, feedback from a group of early adopters may be different from feedback from a more general audience, and the evaluation should take that into account.
- Look for patterns and themes: Analyzing user feedback for patterns and themes can provide valuable insights into what worked well and what could be improved in future campaigns. For example, if multiple users provide feedback about a specific aspect of the experience, such as difficulty navigating the experience, it may be an area that needs improvement in future campaigns.

Insights that can be gained from user feedback include:

- Audience preferences: User feedback can provide insights into the audience's preferences and what they find most engaging or memorable about the experience. This information can be used to inform future campaigns and tailor the experience to the audience's preferences.
- Effectiveness of messaging: User feedback can provide insights into the effectiveness of the messaging and whether it resonated with the audience.
- Areas for improvement: User feedback can identify areas for improvement in the experience, such as technical difficulties or confusing navigation.
- Overall impact: User feedback can provide insights into the overall impact of the experience on the audience and the effectiveness of the campaign in achieving its goals.

Overall, incorporating user feedback into the evaluation of immersive marketing experiences can provide valuable insights that can inform future campaigns and help improve the effectiveness of immersive marketing.

Key Drivers of Conversion Rate for Immersive Marketing

The key drivers of conversion rates for immersive marketing experiences can differ from traditional marketing campaigns due to the unique aspects of the immersive experience. Figure 3 shows the four main drivers of conversion.

Figure 3. Drivers of conversion

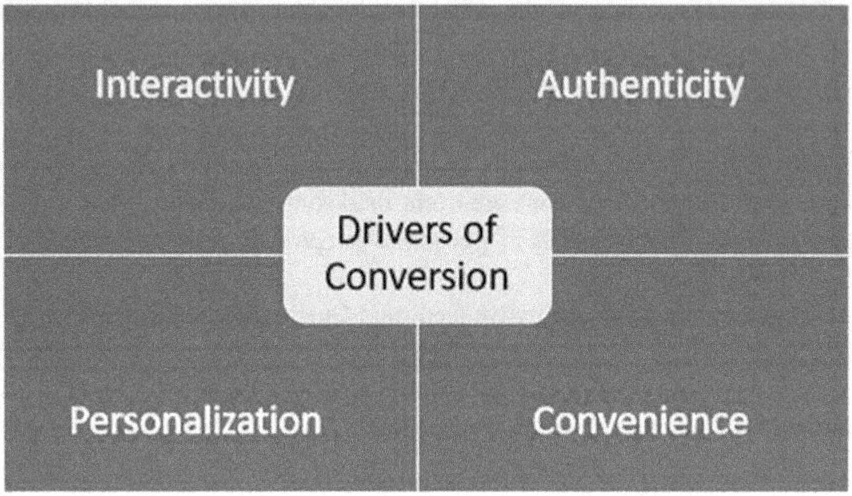

Some few drivers that can impact conversion rates for immersive marketing experiences:

- Interactivity: Immersive marketing experiences often involve interactivity, allowing the audience to engage with the experience and the brand. This interactivity can lead to higher conversion rates, as the audience is more likely to feel connected to the brand and more motivated to act.
- Authenticity: Immersive marketing experiences that are perceived as authentic and genuine can lead to higher conversion rates. Authenticity can be achieved through factors such as real-time interactions, user-generated content, or partnerships with trusted organizations.
- Personalization: Immersive marketing experiences can be highly personalized, creating a more individualized and tailored experience for the audience. This personalization can lead to higher conversion rates, as the audience is more likely to feel that the experience is designed specifically for them.
- Emotional connection: Immersive marketing experiences can create a stronger emotional connection with the audience than traditional marketing campaigns. This emotional connection can lead to higher conversion rates, as the audience is more likely to feel a sense of loyalty and attachment to the brand.
- Unique value proposition: Immersive marketing experiences that offer a unique value proposition can be more effective in driving conversions. The immersive experience should offer something that cannot be found elsewhere, such as exclusive access, personalized content, or a memorable experience.
- Convenience: Immersive marketing experiences that are easy to access and participate in can be more effective in driving conversions. This can include factors such as accessible locations, clear instructions, and simple technology.

Time Spent as a Measure of Success of Immersive Marketing

The relationship between the time spent engaging with an immersive marketing experience and the level of brand awareness can be a critical factor in the success of the campaign. The longer the audience spends engaging with the experience, the greater the opportunity for the brand to make an impression and increase brand awareness. Some ways to leverage this relationship to optimize future campaigns include:

- Measure engagement time: To understand the relationship between engagement time and brand awareness, it is essential to measure the time the audience spends engaging with the immersive marketing experience. This can be done using tools such as heat maps, surveys, and tracking of social media engagement.
- Use engaging content: To increase engagement time, it is essential to have engaging content that keeps the audience interested and involved in the experience. This can include interactive elements, personalized content, and immersive storytelling.
- Create multiple touchpoints: Immersive marketing experiences can involve multiple touchpoints, including pre-event marketing, the actual experience, and post-event follow-up. Creating multiple touchpoints can increase engagement time and create a more memorable and lasting impression of the brand.
- Personalize the experience: Personalizing the immersive marketing experience can help increase engagement time by creating a more tailored experience for the audience. This can include personalized content, messaging, and interactive elements.
- Analyze the data: Analyzing data on engagement time and brand awareness can provide insights into the effectiveness of the campaign and inform future campaigns. This can include identifying patterns in engagement time, comparing engagement time across different touchpoints, and measuring the impact on brand awareness.

Cost Per Engagement (CPE) as a Metric of Immersive Marketing

Cost per engagement (CPE) can be an effective way to evaluate the return on investment (ROI) of immersive marketing campaigns. CPE measures the cost of each engagement with the campaign, which can provide valuable insights into the effectiveness of the campaign and help optimize future marketing efforts. Here are some factors to consider when calculating the cost per engagement for immersive marketing campaigns:

- Definition of engagement: It is important to define what constitutes an engagement in the context of the immersive marketing campaign. Engagement can include various actions, such as clicking on a link, attending an event, sharing content on social media, or completing a purchase. Defining the engagement criteria is critical to accurately calculating the CPE.
- Measurement methods: The methods used to measure engagement should be consistent and reliable. This can include tracking website analytics, using social media monitoring tools, or conducting surveys to measure engagement.
- Cost factors: The cost factors for immersive marketing campaigns can be more complex than for traditional campaigns. These can include the cost of creating the immersive experience, the cost

of hardware and software, the cost of hosting events or activations, and the cost of personnel to manage and run the campaign.

- Timeframe: The timeframe over which engagement is measured can impact the calculation of the CPE. For example, engagement over a shorter timeframe may be more expensive per engagement than engagement over a longer timeframe.
- Audience size: The size of the audience can impact the calculation of the CPE. Larger audiences may require more resources and therefore a higher cost per engagement.
- Business objectives: The business objectives of the campaign should be considered when calculating the CPE. For example, if the objective of the campaign is to increase brand awareness, the cost per engagement for social media shares may be more relevant than the cost per engagement for purchases.

Measuring the Virtual Commerce on Metaverse

Virtual commerce in the metaverse can be measured in several ways. Some possible metrics to consider when evaluating the effectiveness of virtual commerce in the metaverse are represented in Figure 4.

Figure 4. Metaverse metrics

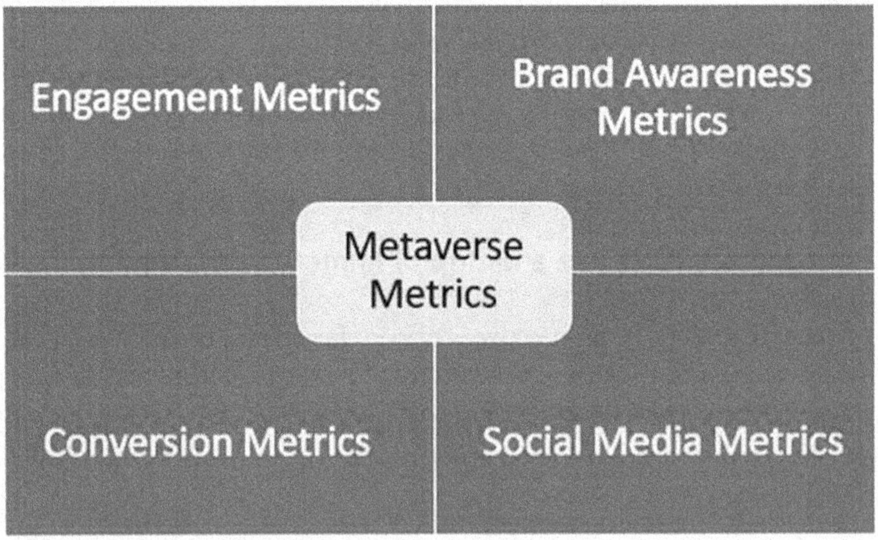

Some possible metrics:

- Conversion rate: This metric measures the percentage of visitors to a virtual store who make a purchase. A high conversion rate indicates that the store is effective at convincing visitors to buy its products.
- Average order value (AOV): AOV measures the average amount spent per transaction. An increasing AOV indicates that customers are buying more items or higher-priced items.

- Customer acquisition cost (CAC): This metric measures the cost of acquiring a customer. In the context of virtual commerce, this could include advertising costs, platform fees, or the cost of creating virtual products. A lower CAC indicates that the store is able to attract customers more efficiently.
- Repeat purchase rate: This metric measures the percentage of customers who return to make another purchase. A high repeat purchase rate indicates that customers are satisfied with their initial purchase and are likely to become loyal customers.
- Engagement: Engagement metrics measure how active users are in the virtual world. This could include measures such as time spent in the virtual store, number of visits, or interactions with virtual products. High engagement indicates that users find the virtual world interesting and engaging, which may lead to more sales.
- Brand awareness: This metric measures how well-known a virtual store or brand is within the virtual world. This could be measured by surveying users or by tracking social media mentions. Higher brand awareness may lead to more traffic and sales.

Algorithmic Application of Findings

The Algorithm for Calculating Average Order Value (AOV)

The following steps lead to the development of algorithm for calculating the average order value:

- Define a variable to hold the total order value (TOV), initialized to 0.
- Define a variable to hold the number of orders (NO), initialized to 0.
- For each order in the dataset: a. Add the order value to the TOV variable. b. Increment the NO variable by 1.
- Calculate the AOV by dividing the TOV variable by the NO variable.
- Round the AOV to the nearest two decimal places if necessary.
- Output the AOV as the result.

This algorithm can be implemented in Python as below:

```
orders = [50.00, 25.00, 30.00, 75.00, 20.00]
TOV = 0
NO = 0
for order in orders:
    TOV += order
    NO += 1
AOV = round(TOV/NO, 2)
print("Average Order Value: $" + str(AOV))
```

In this example, the input data is a list of order values. The algorithm calculates the total order value and the number of orders in the list, then divides the total order value by the number of orders to calculate the AOV. The AOV is then rounded to two decimal places and output as a string.

The Algorithm for Calculating Customer Acquisition Cost (CAC)

The following steps are essential for developing an algorithm to calculate the customer acquisition cost in metaverse marketing:

Define a variable to hold the total cost of customer acquisition (TCA), initialized to 0.

Define a variable to hold the number of customers acquired (NCA), initialized to 0.

For each customer acquisition campaign in the dataset: a. Add the cost of the campaign to the TCA variable. b. Increment the NCA variable by the number of customers acquired from the campaign.

Calculate the CAC by dividing the TCA variable by the NCA variable.

Round the CAC to the nearest two decimal places if necessary.

Output the CAC as the result.

This algorithm can be implemented in python as below:

```
campaigns = [{'cost': 1000.00, 'customers': 50}, {'cost': 500.00, 'customers': 25}, {'cost': 1500.00, 'customers': 75}]
TCA = 0
NCA = 0
for campaign in campaigns:
    TCA += campaign['cost']
    NCA += campaign['customers']
CAC = round(TCA/NCA, 2)
print("Customer Acquisition Cost: $" + str(CAC))
```

In this example, the input data is a list of customer acquisition campaigns, each containing the cost of the campaign and the number of customers acquired from the campaign. The algorithm calculates the total cost of customer acquisition and the total number of customers acquired from all campaigns, then divides the total cost by the total number of customers to calculate the CAC. The CAC is then rounded to two decimal places and output as a string.

The Algorithm for Calculating Conversion Rate

The algorithm for calculating the conversion rate is developed following the below steps:

Define a variable to hold the number of visitors to the virtual store (NV), initialized to 0.

Define a variable to hold the number of purchases made (NP), initialized to 0.

For each visitor to the virtual store: a. Increment the NV variable by 1. b. If the visitor makes a purchase, increment the NP variable by 1.

Calculate the conversion rate by dividing the NP variable by the NV variable and multiplying by 100 to get a percentage.

Round the conversion rate to the nearest two decimal places if necessary.

Output the conversion rate as the result.

The above algorithm can be implemented using python as below:

```
visitors = 1000
purchases = 50
```

```
NV = visitors
NP = purchases
conversion_rate = round(NP/NV*100, 2)
print("Conversion Rate: " + str(conversion_rate) + "%")
```

Input data, in this example, is the number of visitors to the virtual store and the number of purchases made. The algorithm calculates the number of visitors and the number of purchases, then divides the number of purchases by the number of visitors and multiplies by 100 to get a percentage. The conversion rate is then rounded to two decimal places and output as a string with a percentage symbol.

The Algorithm for Calculating Repeat Purchase Rate (RPR)

The algorithm for calculating the repeat purchase rate can be developed as below:

Define a variable to hold the number of customers who made a repeat purchase (NRP), initialized to 0.

Define a variable to hold the number of customers who made an initial purchase (NIP), initialized to 0.

For each customer in the dataset: a. If the customer made more than one purchase, increment the NRP variable by 1. b. Otherwise, increase the NIP variable by 1.

Calculate the repeat purchase rate by dividing the NRP variable by the NIP variable and multiplying by 100 to get a percentage.

Round the repeat purchase rate to the nearest two decimal places if necessary.

Output the repeat purchase rate as the result.

Implementation of this algorithm in Python:

```
customers = [{'purchases': 1}, {'purchases': 2}, {'purchases': 1}, {'purchas-
es': 3}]
NRP = 0
NIP = 0
for customer in customers:
    if customer['purchases'] > 1:
        NRP += 1
    else:
        NIP += 1
repeat_purchase_rate = round(NRP/NIP*100, 2)
print("Repeat Purchase Rate: " + str(repeat_purchase_rate) + "%")
```

The input data, in the above python program, is a list of customers, each containing the number of purchases made by the customer. The algorithm calculates the number of customers who made a repeat purchase and the number of customers who made an initial purchase, then divides the number of customers who made a repeat purchase by the number of customers who made an initial purchase and multiplies by 100 to get a percentage. The repeat purchase rate is then rounded to two decimal places and output as a string with a percentage symbol.

The Algorithm for Measuring Brand Awareness

The algorithm for measuring brand awareness is as below:

Define a variable to hold the number of people who are aware of the brand (NA), initialized to 0.

Define a variable to hold the number of people in the target audience (NT), initialized to 0.

For each person in the target audience: a. If the person is aware of the brand, increment the NA variable by 1. b. Increment the NT variable by 1.

Calculate the brand awareness by dividing the NA variable by the NT variable and multiplying by 100 to get a percentage.

Round the brand awareness to the nearest two decimal places if necessary.

Output the brand awareness as the result.

Here's an example of implementation of this algorithm in Python:

```
target_audience = 1000
brand_awareness = 550
NA = brand_awareness
NT = target_audience
brand_awareness_percentage = round(NA/NT*100, 2)
print("Brand Awareness: " + str(brand_awareness_percentage) + "%")
```

In this example, the input data is the number of people in the target audience and the number of people who are aware of the brand. The algorithm calculates the number of people who are aware of the brand and the total number of people in the target audience, then divides the number of people who are aware of the brand by the total number of people in the target audience and multiplies by 100 to get a percentage. The brand awareness percentage is then rounded to two decimal places and output as a string with a percentage symbol.

The Algorithm for Calculating Overall Engagement

The following steps lead to development of an algorithm for measuring the overall engagement:

Define a variable to hold the number of people who engaged with the content (NE), initialized to 0.

Define a variable to hold the number of people who were exposed to the content (NX), initialized to 0.

For each piece of content: a. If the content was clicked, liked, shared, or commented on, increase the NE variable by 1. b. Increment the NX variable by the number of people who were exposed to the content.

Calculate the engagement rate by dividing the NE variable by the NX variable and multiplying by 100 to get a percentage.

Round the engagement rate to the nearest two decimal places if necessary.

Output the engagement rate as the result.

The above algorithm can be implemented in Python as below:

```
content = [{'exposure': 1000, 'engagement': 100},{'exposure': 500, 'engage-
ment': 50},{'exposure': 2000, 'engagement': 150}]
NE = 0
NX = 0
```

```
for c in content:
    NE += c['engagement']
    NX += c['exposure']
engagement_rate = round(NE/NX*100, 2)
print("Engagement Rate: " + str(engagement_rate) + "%")
```

The Algorithm for Measuring Metaverse Marketing Effectiveness

The following steps can be followed for developing a general algorithm for measuring the overall effectiveness of metaverse marketing:

Define a variable to hold the number of conversions (NC), initialized to 0.

Define a variable to hold the number of people who were exposed to the marketing campaign (NX), initialized to 0.

For each marketing campaign: a. If the campaign resulted in a conversion (e.g., a sale, a sign-up), increase the NC variable by 1. b. Increment the NX variable by the number of people who were exposed to the campaign.

Calculate the conversion rate by dividing the NC variable by the NX variable and multiplying by 100 to get a percentage.

Define a variable to hold the total cost of the marketing campaign (TC).

Calculate the cost per conversion by dividing the total cost of the campaign by the number of conversions.

Output the conversion rate and cost per conversion as the result.

The above algorithm can be implemented in python as below:

```
marketing_campaigns = [{'exposure': 1000, 'conversions': 50, 'cost':
10000},{'exposure': 500, 'conversions': 30, 'cost': 5000},{'exposure': 2000,
'conversions': 100, 'cost': 20000}]
NC = 0
NX = 0
TC = 0
for c in marketing_campaigns:
    NC += c['conversions']
    NX += c['exposure']
    TC += c['cost']
conversion_rate = round(NC/NX*100, 2)
cost_per_conversion = round(TC/NC, 2)
print("Conversion Rate: " + str(conversion_rate) + "%")
print("Cost Per Conversion: $" + str(cost_per_conversion))
```

In this example, the input data is a list of marketing campaigns, each containing the number of people who were exposed to the campaign, the number of conversions resulting from the campaign, and the total cost of the campaign. The algorithm calculates the total number of conversions resulting from all campaigns, the total number of people who were exposed to all campaigns, and the total cost of all campaigns, then divides the total number of conversions by the total number of people who were exposed to all campaigns and multiplies by 100 to get a percentage. The algorithm also calculates the cost per conversion by dividing the total cost of all campaigns by the total number of conversions. The conversion rate and cost per conversion are then rounded to two decimal places and output as strings.

CONCLUSION

A conceptual framework for measuring the effectiveness of immersive marketing campaigns would comprise of clearly defining the objectives of the immersive marketing campaign, brand awareness, engagement, conversions, or any other desired outcomes. The level of immersion that the campaign provides is an important factor in measuring effectiveness. This could include the use of virtual or augmented reality, the level of interactivity, and the extent to which the user is transported into the virtual experience. Defining specific metrics that will be used to measure the success of the campaign is critical (Luo, 2020). These could include metrics such as click-through rates, time spent in the immersive experience, social media engagement, or conversions. Understanding the target audience for the immersive marketing campaign is important in determining its effectiveness. Demographic information, as well as user behavior data, can be used to tailor the experience to the specific needs and preferences of the audience. The context in which the immersive marketing campaign is experienced is also important. This includes factors such as the platform on which the experience is delivered, the time of day, and the user's location. Finally, the budget allocated to the campaign can be used as a factor in measuring its effectiveness. By comparing the campaign's return on investment (ROI) with the amount of money spent on the campaign, the effectiveness of the campaign can be evaluated.

The meta-analysis of the current practices and the available knowledge on metrics for measuring the effectiveness of the immersive marketing campaigns leads to a conclusion that it is important to use a data-driven approach that incorporates metrics and user feedback. By setting clear objectives, defining the target audience, using engaging and immersive content, personalizing the experience, measuring, and analyzing data, using feedback to make improvements, and continuously testing and iterating, immersive marketing experiences can be optimized to achieve the best possible results. Defining the target audience is critical to creating an immersive marketing experience that resonates with the intended audience. This can include considering factors such as demographics, interests, and behaviors. Engaging and immersive content is critical to maximizing engagement rates and brand recall. This can include using interactive elements, personalized content, and immersive storytelling.

REFERENCES

Alfaro, L., Rivera, C., Luna-Urquizo, J., Zuniga, J. C., Portocarrero, A., & Raposo, A. B. (2019). Immersive technologies in marketing: State of the art and a software architecture proposal. *International Journal of Advanced Computer Science and Applications*, *10*(10), 482–490. doi:10.14569/IJACSA.2019.0101064

Andjelic, A. (2021). *The Business of Aspiration: How Social, Cultural, and Environmental Capital Changes Brands*. Routledge.

Barrera, K. G., & Shah, D. (2023). Marketing in the Metaverse: Conceptual understanding, framework, and research agenda. *Journal of Business Research*, *155*, 113420. doi:10.1016/j.jbusres.2022.113420

Batat, W. (2019). *The new luxury experience: creating the ultimate customer experience*. Springer., doi:10.1007/978-3-030-01671-5

Burke, R. R. (1997). Do you see what I see? The Future of Virtual Shopping. *Journal of the Academy of Marketing Science*, *25*(4), 352–360. doi:10.1177/0092070397254007

Catherine, B. (2022). *Converge: a futurist's insights into the potential of our world as technology and humanity collide*. Major Street Publishing.

Cline, E. (2020). *Ready player two: a novel*. Ballantine Books.

Cummings, J. J., Tsay-Vogel, M., Cahill, T. J., & Zhang, L. (2022). Effects of immersive storytelling on affective, cognitive, and associative empathy: The mediating role of presence. *New Media & Society*, *24*(9), 2003–2026. doi:10.1177/1461444820986816

de Brito Silva, M. J., de Oliveira Ramos Delfino, L., Alves Cerqueira, K., & de Oliveira Campos, P. (2022). Avatar marketing: A study on the engagement and authenticity of virtual influencers on Instagram. *Social Network Analysis and Mining*, *12*(1), 130. doi:10.100713278-022-00966-w

Du, H., Ma, B., Niyato, D., Kang, J., Xiong, Z., & Yang, Z. (2023). Rethinking quality of experience for metaverse services: A consumer-based economics perspective. *IEEE Network*, 1–8. doi:10.1109/MNET.131.2200503

Falchuk, B., Loeb, S., & Neff, R. (2018). The social metaverse: Battle for privacy. *IEEE Technology and Society Magazine*, *37*(2), 52–61. doi:10.1109/MTS.2018.2826060

Gill, K. S., Assvlbekova, A., Addanke, S., Jha, A., Mishra, I., & Nurkusheva, L. (2022, April). Multimedia Systems and its Role in Adaptive Network Management. In *2022 International Conference on Sustainable Computing and Data Communication Systems (ICSCDS)* (pp. 1547-1553). IEEE. 10.1109/ICSCDS53736.2022.9760752

Gimpel, H., Krämer, J., Neumann, D., Pfeiffer, J., Seifert, S., Teubner, T., & Weidlich, A. (2021). Market Engineering: Insights from Two Decades of Research on Markets and Information. doi:10.1007/978-3-030-66661-3

Guazzaroni, G., & Pillai, A. S. (Eds.). (2019). *Virtual and augmented reality in Education, Art, and Museums*. IGI Global. doi:10.4018/978-1-7998-1796-3

Harley, D., Verni, A., Willis, M., Ng, A., Bozzo, L., & Mazalek, A. (2018, March). Sensory vr: Smelling, touching, and eating virtual reality. In *Proceedings of the Twelfth International Conference on Tangible, Embedded, and Embodied Interaction* (pp. 386-397). 10.1145/3173225.3173241

Heath, C., & Heath, D. (2017). *The power of moments: why certain experiences have extraordinary impact*. Simon & Schuster.

Jerald, J. (2017, March). *Human-centered design for immersive interactions. In 2017 IEEE Virtual Reality (VR)*. IEEE.

Jha, A., & Jha, A. (2022). Data Encryption Dispute Resolutions under Intermediary Guidelines of Information Technology Act: Challenges and Future Framework. *DESIDOC Journal of Library and Information Technology*, *42*(3), 201–207. doi:10.14429/djlit.42.3.17869

Jha, A., Singh, S. R., & Dr Meenakshi. (2022). Human-Machine Convergence and Disruption of Socio-Cognitive Capabilities. *International Journal of Next-Generation Computing*, *13*(3). doi:10.47164/ijngc.v13i3.893

Jha, A., & Sudhakar, P. kumar Lokhande, S. A., Ishodzhanova, G., Venkatrao, K., & Zhakupova, A. (2022, September). Facial Recognition Impact in Smartphone Sector. In *2022 4th International Conference on Inventive Research in Computing Applications (ICIRCA)* (pp. 1566-1571). IEEE. 10.1109/ICIRCA54612.2022.9985766

Jin, S. A. A., & Bolebruch, J. (2009). Virtual commerce (v-commerce) in Second Life: The roles of physical presence and brand-self connection. *Journal of Virtual Worlds Research*, *2*(4). Advance online publication. doi:10.4101/jvwr.v2i4.760

Karaarslan, E., Aydin, Ö., Cali, Ü., & Challenger, M. (Eds.). (2023). *Digital Twin Driven Intelligent Systems and Emerging Metaverse*. Springer Nature. doi:10.1007/978-981-99-0252-1

Kulshrestha, R., Shekhar, C., Jain, M., & Chakravarthy, S. R. (2021). *Mathematical modeling and computation of real-time problems: an interdisciplinary approach*. CRC Press. doi:10.1201/9781003055037

Luo, L. (2020). *Temporal modelling of customer behaviour*. Palgrave Macmillan. doi:10.1007/978-3-030-18289-2

Palmatier, R. W., Kumar, V., & Harmeling, C. M. (2018). *Customer engagement marketing*. Palgrave Macmillan. doi:10.1007/978-3-319-61985-9

Pollák, F. (2022). Introductory Chapter: Brand Management as Part of Corporate Identity. In Brand Management. IntechOpen.

Prieto, W. T. (Ed.). (2019). *Promoting investment and protecting commerce online: legitimate sites v. parasites. (part i and ii)*. Nova Science Publishers.

Rosa, N., & Furness, T. (2022). *Understanding the metaverse a business and ethical guide*. John Wiley & Sons.

Rose, F. (2012). *The art of immersion: how the digital generation is remaking hollywood madison avenue and the way we tell stories*. W.W. Norton.

Smart, J., Jamais, C., & Paffendorf, J. (2008). *Metaverse roadmap: pathways to the 3D web*. W3. https://www.w3.org/2008/WebVideo/Annotations/wiki/images/1/19/MetaverseRoadmapOverview.pdf

Smilansky, S. (2018). *Experiential marketing: a practical guide to interactive brand experiences*. Kogan Page.

Smith, K., & Hanover, D. (2016). *Experiential marketing: secrets strategies and success stories from the world's greatest brands*. John Wiley & Sons. doi:10.1002/9781119176688

Van Rijmenam, M. (2022). *Step into the metaverse: How the immersive Internet will unlock a trillion-dollar social economy*. John Wiley & Sons.

ADDITIONAL READING

Griffin, D., & van der Meer, A. (2020). *Press Start: Using gamification to power-up your marketing*. Bloomsbury Publishing.

Hackl, C., Lueth, D., & Di Bartolo, T. (2022). *Navigating the metaverse: A guide to limitless possibilities in a Web 3.0 world*. John Wiley & Sons.

Kreutzer, R. T., & Klose, S. (2023). *Next Stop Metaverse: A Quick Guide to Concepts, Uses, and Potential for Research and Practice*. Springer Nature. doi:10.1007/978-3-658-41180-0

Moro-Visconti, R. (2022). *The Valuation of Digital Intangibles: Technology, Marketing, and the Metaverse*. Springer Nature. doi:10.1007/978-3-031-09237-4

Smilansky, S. (2018). *Experiential marketing: A practical guide to interactive brand experiences* (2nd ed.). Kogan Page Publishers.

Wang, C. (2023). *The palgrave handbook of interactive marketing*. Palgrave Macmillan. doi:10.1007/978-3-031-14961-0

Yang, K. C. (Ed.). (2019). *Cases on immersive virtual reality techniques*. IGI Global. doi:10.4018/978-1-5225-5912-2

KEY TERMS AND DEFINITIONS

Brand Awareness: It is a measure of how well consumers can identify and recall a brand, its logo, products, or other distinctive elements associated with a brand.

Brand Recall: Brand recall is an essential metric in assessing how well the brand has made an impression on consumers and how easily it comes to their mind when they consider a particular product or service category.

Conversion Rate: It is a key metric used in digital marketing and e-commerce to measure the effectiveness of a marketing campaign. It is the percentage of customers, or prospects who take a desired action or complete a specific goal within a predetermined period.

Engagement Metrics: Engagement metrics provide valuable insights into user behavior and help businesses assess the effectiveness of their content, marketing campaigns, and user experience.

Immersive Marketing: It is a marketing approach that aims to create highly interactive and engaging experiences for consumers.

Metaverse: It is a virtual universe or interconnected network of digital spaces where people can interact with each other and computer-generated environments in real-time.

Performance Analysis: Is an ongoing and iterative process that enables organizations and individuals to measure progress, make data-driven decisions, and drive performance improvements.

Chapter 14
The Role of Blockchain in C2C E-Commerce Business Models

Marija Duranović
Faculty of Organizational Sciences, University of Belgrade, Serbia

Aleksandra Labus
Faculty of Organizational Sciences, University of Belgrade, Serbia

Zorica Bogdanović
Faculty of Organizational Sciences, University of Belgrade, Serbia

Dušan Barać
Faculty of Organizational Sciences, University of Belgrade, Serbia

Marijana Despotović-Zrakić
Faculty of Organizational Sciences, University of Belgrade, Serbia

ABSTRACT

This chapter analyses the role and potential applications that blockchain as a technology can bring to C2C e-commerce business models. The main goal is to present a systematic analysis of potential applications of blockchain in C2C e-commerce, presenting the expected benefits and the main challenges. As a proof-of-concept, the chapter will specifically address the aspect of developing a C2C market based on blockchain, addressing the specifics of the business model, implementation aspects, and interest of potential customers. The authors propose a design of a C2C platform based on blockchain, that enables efficient and secure C2C transactions without intermediaries. The authors also present the results of a preliminary readiness study, based on the UTAUT2 model of assessing technological readiness. The results point out the importance of the effect of social influence on behavioral intention. The results aim to help business and technical developers shape their blockchain-based e-commerce business models.

DOI: 10.4018/978-1-6684-8958-1.ch014

INTRODUCTION

E-commerce means buying and selling on the Internet, but it is not only a financial transaction between a user and an organization. E-commerce also includes non-financial transactions that customers have with a company. If the world wide web or another internet service is used at any point in the life cycle of a transaction, the transaction is called electronic or e-commerce (Bulsara & Vaghela, 2020). Since the 90s, e-commerce has been continuously evolving and has existed in various forms, such as B2B, B2C, C2C, and various business models, such as storefront, portals, auctions, and others (Gupta, 2014).

Among other trends, trust and privacy have been identified as top priorities for modern e-commerce development (Leonard & Jones, 2021). The key point is to enable customers to have transparent control of their data. For this purpose, blockchain has already been recognized as a suitable technology. Blockchain technology is used in e-commerce to ensure the security of data exchange and the immutability of data in distributed ledgers (Zheng & Lu, 2022). Distributed ledger technology enables a reliable distributed database, which is suitable for e-commerce (Kannengießer et al., 2020). Distributed ledger technology is an append-only database that operates in an untrusted environment, providing efficient and secure data exchange between individuals or organizations. Several applications of distributed ledger technology have developed in various domains, some of them are supply chain management, finance, health care, and others (Kannengießer et al., 2020). Another important part of the blockchain is related to smart contracts - executable codes that have been launched to make the formation of agreements as simple as possible without the need for a third party. This type of automation offers contracting parties more secure contracts programmed to cover all possibilities without oversight by responsible authorities (Khan et al., 2021). There is also a great impact on transactions that are carried out without an intermediary with a reduced duration of the transaction itself.

All types of e-commerce are facing different problems that may be solved using blockchain. For example, eBay as one example of C2C e-commerce, has elements of a business model that negatively affect customer satisfaction. Seller usually has to wait a long time for the transaction to be finished, and a buyer has problems choosing the right quality product with adequate and timely delivery. The company is trying to ensure a safe and positive relationship with its customers and ensure customer loyalty through smooth transactions (Dubosson-Torbay et al., 2002). However, the model requires a high level of trust in the C2C platform, as well as between a buyer and a seller.

This article is focused on C2C e-commerce problems and the possibilities of solving them using blockchain technology. The main problem discussed is the lack of trust between buyers and sellers. Users of e-commerce platforms have trust problems because of scams, frauds, and the possibility of low-quality products. Both parties also have problems with long periods of transferring money (Joshi & Kumar, 2020), frequently because of specifics of the intermediary's business model. As a possible solution, we propose a C2C business model implemented using blockchain technology. We also analyze the readiness of users to accept the proposed model and technology, with the goal to obtain preliminary insights into the factors influencing the acceptance of the proposed solution.

The rest of the paper is organized as follows. Section 2 presents a literature review, analyzing the role of blockchain in e-commerce, as well as the role of cryptocurrencies in e-commerce models. Section 3 gives a proposal for a C2C e-commerce business model based on blockchain technologies. In section 4, we present the methodology and the results of a preliminary study on the assessment of the readiness of potential users of the proposed C2C model. Finally, we give concluding remarks.

LITERATURE REVIEW

Application of Blockchain in C2C e-Commerce Models

C2C e-commerce is business between individuals in an online environment, using the Internet (Mäkeläinen, 2006). With the development of the Internet and the global network, C2C business has begun to expand significantly into the online domain.

Blockchain technologies have found applications in various e-commerce models, including B2B, B2C and C2C (Treiblmaier & Sillaber, 2021; Taherdoost & Madanchian, 2023; Verma & Kulkarni, 2023). Each of the models has some specifics, but there are general benefits that blockchain brings to the e-commerce in general. For example, the main challenges of the fast growing B2B e-commerce (Gupta, 2014), such as relationships between businesses, faster fulfillment of orders, selling through third-party marketplaces, social commerce, personalization, solving supply chain disruptions, and better inventory management (Shopify, n.d.) affect B2C and C2C e-commerce models as well. By applying blockchain technology, we can provide a safe and reliable user interface for consumers and participants in business processes. Blockchain can be used within organizations to create a secure accounting system in real-time, optimize processes and improve trust in international trade; legal and procedural standards for detecting suspicious transactions; optimize supply chains, and increase trust between partners in the supply chain.

Some of the most important functionalities that blockchain-based platforms should offer users are the security of data transmission during the transaction and the safe storage and preservation of data. Blockchain allows participants to access all stored documents about transactions made on the blockchain (Lahkani et al., 2020). To ensure the security of their data, platforms implemented on the blockchain use encrypted data, and private and public keys. Blockchain is tasked with protecting data from possible security breaches. Anyone within the supply chain can use this data. The B2B blockchain platform also has a strong impact on users outside the B2B supply chain, including B2C and C2C participants. The transparent database can be used for various product tracking activities that are of interest to users, for the whole product life cycle. International supply chains have become typical in many organizations (Liu & Li, 2020; Mettler, 2016), and in this context blockchain can significantly help in establishing an upper level of trust between partners, and provide an infrastructure for standardized data exchange. All participants in the supply chain could obtain relevant data from other parts of the chain, while also enabling end customers to get data about product origins.

Within the supply chain, companies create many copies of documents (Zamani & Giaglis, 2018). The problem of a copy of the documentation can lead to errors, delays, wrong processes, and in the worst case, fraud. Blockchain improves supply chain activities, leading to more efficient and cost-effective processes. Any problems that may occur can be avoided or reduced (Zamani & Giaglis, 2018). The problem of duplication of documents can be eliminated, the delay of upcoming processes is reduced and the time required to provide the necessary documentation is reduced. The use of blockchain has a positive impact on the future of business, avoiding disagreements, conflicts, fines, etc. (Lahkani et al., 2020). Due to all the positive factors of blockchain technology, the use potential is great (White, 2017).

The main use cases of blockchain in B2C include trusted user interfaces, instant payments, incentive systems, and traceability of goods (Grover et al., 2018), but many of those are applicable to C2C. C2C, as well as B2C e-commerce consists of collecting information about customers, products, and data from various sources. Using blockchain, transaction costs can be reduced, users provided with access to all information, market entry barriers removed, and website creation and maintenance costs reduced

(Gupta, 2014). Blockchain offers its users reliable user interfaces that should be easy to use (Tapscott & Tapscott, 2017), although technology adoption period is needed. By using the blockchain, the user can manage their data such as proof of identity, various data records, and similar (Grover et al., 2018). Blockchain has also been recognized in the context of smart retail and various services based on internet of things (Zhang & Wen, 2017).

A more extensive application of blockchain technologies in e-commerce is related to the stakeholders' adoption of cryptocurrencies as a payment method, and instant payments that can be ensured through their usage. The existence of cryptocurrencies eliminates the need for intermediaries in payment process and provides a possibility for secure P2P payments, where transactions can be carried out in a very short period.

The main benefits of using blockchain within the C2C model are peer-to-peer transactions without intermediaries; payment without additional commissions, although the transaction fees exist in the blockchain systems as well; higher trust between sellers and buyers; faster money exchange -elimination of the intermediary reduces the time that money spends at the intermediary's account. Transactions without intermediaries free users from additional payments for services to banks or notaries. All transactions are carried out without commission and intermediaries, while contracts are valid without notarization. The transaction of money is faster and faster due to the absence of intermediaries in this process (Shorman et al., 2019).

By signing smart contracts, it improves trust between the two contracting parties, which is a very typical problem in C2C models (Mäkeläinen, 2006). The buying and selling process is clearly defined and regulated. This gives users confidence for current and future purchases. Companies establish quality control using blockchain technology. All transactions carried out are secure and have a guarantee of execution, and users can track transactions within their purchase (Zott & Amit, 2008).

The increase in the business allows the creation of jobs for everyone and frees users from paying additional fees to brokerage firms. The ability to confirm the quality and details of the offered goods provides users with all the necessary information in smart contracts. Manufacturers have the ability to track products from the moment they leave production until they are delivered to the consumer (Shorman et al., 2019).

To sum up, by using blockchain, C2C-based businesses can offer consumers (Gomber et al., 2018):

- Reliable user interface, in a form of a platform that is easy to use and that gives consumers all relevant information.
- Possibility of immediate payment for goods, by providing infrastructure for transactions without payment intermediary.
- Incentive income system, as a profits or compensation earned by any entity.
- Traceability of goods, from production to delivery.

Cryptocurrencies in e-Commerce

In the last decade, the cryptocurrency market developed quickly and strongly. Although it develops rapidly, this market has strong foundations that can hardly lead to a collapse. Bitcoin is considered as the pioneer of cryptocurrency, but after its release in 2009, over 500 cryptos with different successes were developed (Farell, 2015). Blockchain is the main technology of digital cryptocurrencies (Monrat et al., 2019).

Cryptocurrency is completely different from other currencies. The main difference is the absence of physical appearance. We can use currency through mobile payment, but fundamentally we use bills and coins to pay. Cryptocurrencies were not created by banks; they were formed as computer files. The process of creating cryptocurrencies is called mining, and this process requires the power of electricity as well as the necessary equipment. By spending energy, ledgers of transactions are created, which contain all the information about the transactions of the mined cryptocurrency (Leherbauer, 2019).

To ensure that ledgers are sustainable in different nodes, consensus protocols are used. In the following text, we will present some of the most frequently used protocols.

Proof-of-work (PoW) is a proof-based consensus algorithm. The main feature of this algorithm is the identification of a node, which is to connect a newly formed block with an already formed chain. Another characteristic is that the production of this algorithm is expensive for the user. Many cryptocurrencies are modeled after Bitcoin, so most cryptocurrencies that use the PoW mechanism are direct copies of this protocol. An alternative mechanism of PoW is Proof-of-Stake (PoS) (Farell, 2015). One of the characteristics of PoS is that it is energy efficient and saves more energy than PoW (Monrat et al., 2019). Another consensus protocol that may be relevant for this work is Pure-proof-of-stake, as a consensus protocol implemented within the Algorand blockchain platform (Chen & Micali, 2019). This approach is considered to be energy efficient and fast, which makes it suitable for application in C2C platforms. In addition to the listed procedures, there are also Delegated proof-of-stake (DPoS), Byzantine fault tolerance (BFT), and other consensus algorithms.

The cryptocurrency market is developing and expanding every day. Some of the cryptocurrencies are developing but some don't stand well at the market. Based on their general acceptance only several cryptocurrencies are notable. The most important cryptocurrencies include Bitcoin, Ether, Litecoin, and others. All transactions made through Bitcoin are collected into a block. The collected information is transmitted to all nodes connected to the Bitcoin network. The process of the nodes is called mining as it is the node that receives the transaction (Farell, 2015). In 2015, the Ethereum platform developed a cryptocurrency called Ethereum. The basic unit of portability is ether. Nodes within this platform may have compensation, in these situations ether is transferred from account to account. Litecoin is one of the aforementioned cryptocurrencies that are based on the same protocol as Bitcoin. An essential feature of the Dash cryptocurrency, short from digital cash, is privacy during transactions (Leherbauer, 2019). Within the Algorand platform, Algo cryptocurrency is used.

Cryptocurrencies have a positive impact on various business models. The benefit of cryptocurrency is B2B transfer. Central banks could avoid complications by introducing this technology (Ng & Griffin, 2018). There is no need for central control authority in secure electronic transactions (Mendoza-Tello et al., 2019). Companies are more and more ready to accept cryptocurrencies and more and more transactions are done using cryptocurrencies.

The Unified Theory of Acceptance and Use of Technology

Throughout history, several models have been developed, both within psychology and sociology, that have been used to analyze the acceptance and use of technology. The unified theory of acceptance and use of technology (UTAUT) was created as a synthesis of several models. The main function of the UTAUT model is to reveal the critical factors and circumstances that influence the readiness to use technology. Theories that focus on a specific context, identifying relevant predictors and mechanisms are significantly improved compared to previous general theories (Neufeld et al., 2007). Four main constructs form the core of the UTAUT model. These constructs should be adapted to the needs of consumers. The constructs are:

- Expected performance, which is defined as the degree of benefit that users will have from using the technology,
- Expected effort, the level of effort that should be invested in using the technology,
- Social impact of system users and
- Facilitating conditions related to resources and benefits available by using of technology

According to UTAUT, expected performance, expected effort and social influence have an effect on behavioral intentions, while behavioral intention and facilitating conditions define the use of technology (Venkatesh et al., 2012).

As an extension of the original UTAUT model, The UTAUT2 model contains additional constructs and relations that should be integrated into the original model, adapting them to research needs. This was achieved by identifying new constructs, revising existing relationships in the original model, and introducing new relationships. New constructs include:

- Satisfaction, i.e. hedonic motivation, which proved to be the most successful predictor of consumer behavior. Hedonic motivation has a direct impact on consumer acceptance and use of technology (Van der Heijden, 2004; Venkatesh et al., 2003).
- Cost structure, i.e. price, as another important factor influencing use of technology. If the benefits of using the technology are greater than the monetary expenditure, then the significance of the price is positive.

UTAUT was improved with two more constructs, intention and habit. These two constructs are theoretically different, but similar enough to complete the model. Intention has been shown to have less influence on technology use than habit (Limayem et al., 2007).

UTAUT2 as a model for studying technology acceptance has been used in numerous studies. Researchers typically adjust the model to the specific needs of the research, by adding or modifying selected constructs with respect to other research models and findings.

AN EXAMPLE OF AN APPLICATION OF BLOCKCHAIN IN C2C E-COMMERCE

As a proof-of-concept, in this chapter, we propose a C2C e-commerce platform based on blockchain. Specifically, the goal of our platform is to create a large network of participants who want to sell and buy products. Users can log in to the platform as sellers and buyers. The platform should store data about products and transactions. Every transaction must be authentic and secure. Blockchain can offer security, interoperability, and joint action between P2P organizations and individuals.

The platform is described by using Business Model Canvas, as a strategic approach frequently used to describe business ideas (Osterwalder & Pigneur, 2013). This model consists of nine blocks that should be filled in based on the primary activities of the company, infrastructure, partners and other business participants. With the model filled out in detail, all the advantages and disadvantages of a company's business can be easily determined (Joyce & Paquin, 2016). Table 1 shows the business model canvas, while table 2 presents more details about the canvas elements.

Table 1. Business model canvas for the proposed C2C model

<table>
<tr>
<td rowspan="2">Key Partners
-Blockchain platform provider
-Payment Gateway Company
-Companies inside the supply chain
-Marketing partners
-Shipping Companies</td>
<td>Key Activities
-Development of C2C Platform
-Marketing and Promotion Strategy
-Sales
-Payment processing
- Shipping</td>
<td rowspan="2" colspan="2">Value Proposition
-Smart Contracts
-Secure transmission of data
- Fast purchase
- Short time until completion of transaction
-Product Quality
-Fast and safe delivery
-Trust</td>
<td>Customer Relationships
-Customer Support
-Communication with customers
-Customer Assistance</td>
<td rowspan="2">Customer Segments
-Customers interested to buy or sell products online
-Customers who are prepared to pay for products online</td>
</tr>
<tr>
<td>Key Resources
-Security system
-Human Resources
-Physical Assets
-Web Services</td>
<td>Channels
-Web-sites
-Social media platforms
-Mobile app
-Newsletter</td>
</tr>
<tr>
<td colspan="3">Cost Structure
-Employee Cost
-Marketing Cost
-Software Development
-Storage and transportation
-Transaction costs</td>
<td colspan="3">Revenue Streams
-Open Marketplace
-Sales of products
-Space for advertising
-Premium users</td>
</tr>
</table>

Table 2. Detail description of the proposed model

Key Partners	Partners are companies in the supply chain. One of the most important partners is the user. Users can buy or sell products online. To promote our platform, we should also have marketing partners. Marketing partners should help us to find new customers through social media and promotions. Shipping companies are also key partners of our model. Their job is safe and reliable delivery to customers. This relationship would be based on mutual recommendation and cooperation.
Key Activities	In our case, one of the key activities is the development of the platform. The platform prototype will be created on the Algorand platform, using the Pyteal language for backend development, and the React framework for front-end development (Chen & Micali, 2019). After all the activities related to the creation of the platform, it is necessary to create a quality marketing strategy. Of course, the application should be regularly maintained. Another activity is the safe money transfer process that the application offers.
Key Resources	The key resources of our model are human resources, physical assets, security systems, and web services. Physical assets include all devices, software, databases, buildings, and tangible products. Human resources are all participants in the supply chain. Customers can use our application for selling and buying product, so one of the key resources are also Web Services.
Value Propositions	The value is faster and more reliable C2C trade without intermediaries, as well as better protection of buyer and seller data. This is achieved through the application of smart contracts. The process of purchasing is arranged and defined through smart contracts. The process of sending products to customers should be reliable. That's why our value proposition is fast and secure delivery. Data about purchases and transactions are available to users at any time. We should offer good quality and reliable products.
Customer Relationships	Maintaining relationships with clients to foster loyalty through customer service. All our clients can count on customer support and communication with our staff.
Channels	Our model channels are social media, website, and app. The content published on all platforms should be of high quality and representative. In addition to the active maintenance of the website and social networks, users will be sent a newsletter with selected product offers.
Customer Segments	In our model, the consumer segment consists of people whose goal is to sell certain products. The app offers them an easy way to post their offer. Another target group is people who want to buy the product. Based on the wide assortment, they have a large choice, a detailed display of the product and all the necessary information about the seller and the transaction.
Cost Structure	In the beginning, our costs would be high, because we need to develop the software, pay all the employees and invest some money in marketing. The costs within our business model are the costs of implementing the platform. A transaction fee for a blockchain network is charged during each transaction, which is standard for all blockchain networks.
Revenue Streams	The platform includes multiple revenue streams. Premium users will pay the fee for additional features. In addition, there is an advertisement section on the website, where interested companies can advertise their products and services.

Implementation

The overview of the architecture of the proposed C2C e-commerce platform is presented in Figure 1.

Figure 1. Overview of the architecture of the proposes C2C e-commerce platform

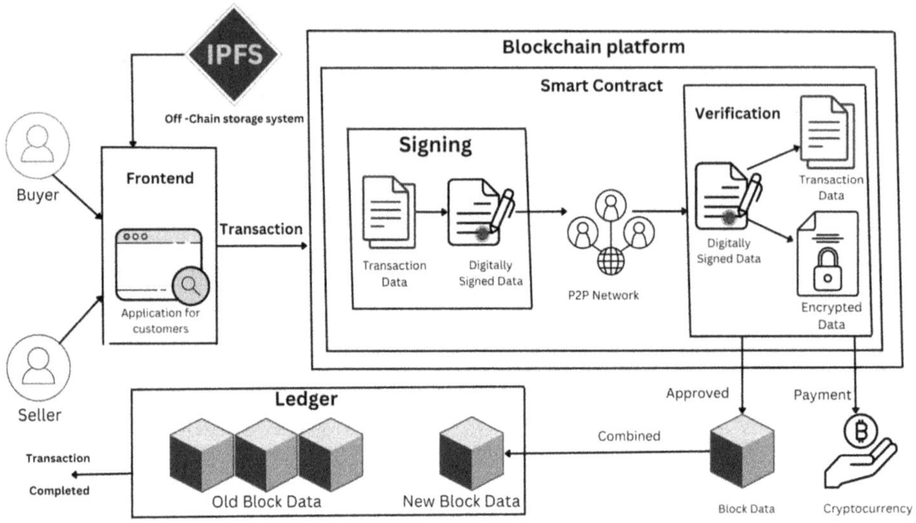

The seller publishes an ad for the sale of the product on the platform. The ad should contain all relevant information about the product. The customer can filter the search and find the desired products. The search can be performed using a keyword as well as already generated filters. In the proposed C2C platform, the main roles are a seller and a buyer, each of them storing the relevant data in the blockchain database. A blockchain database contains information about products and transactions. In this way, all the relevant stakeholders can monitor the supply chain, and determine if there are any problems. All transaction information is encrypted with keys and signatures, and all changes are recorded and available to all participants. Each of the participants has an account, connected to their digital wallet so that the transactions can be secured and conducted using cryptocurrencies. When both the seller and buyer accept the conditions of the transaction, a smart contract is executed, and the funds are locked from the buyer's digital wallet and transferred to the seller when the delivery is completed. In this scenario, there is no intermediary in the transaction, i.e. the bank, while the platform cannot lock the funds longer than needed. The buyer and the seller are the main user roles shown in the figure, but the platform will have additional roles for various administration tasks.

For storing the media files, such as images or videos of the products, posted by sellers within their offer or by buyers within the review section, we propose using peer-to-peer decentralized data storage such as Interplanetary file system (IPFS). IPFS connects all computing devices within the same file system and provides a high throughput block storage model, with addressed hyperlinks. All information about the location of files in IPFS is in the blockchain ledger. Identification is performed using hashes transmitted by smart contracts (Daniel & Tschorsch, 2022).

A simplified model of the proposed business process is presented in Figure 2.

Figure 2. Simplified model of the proposed business process

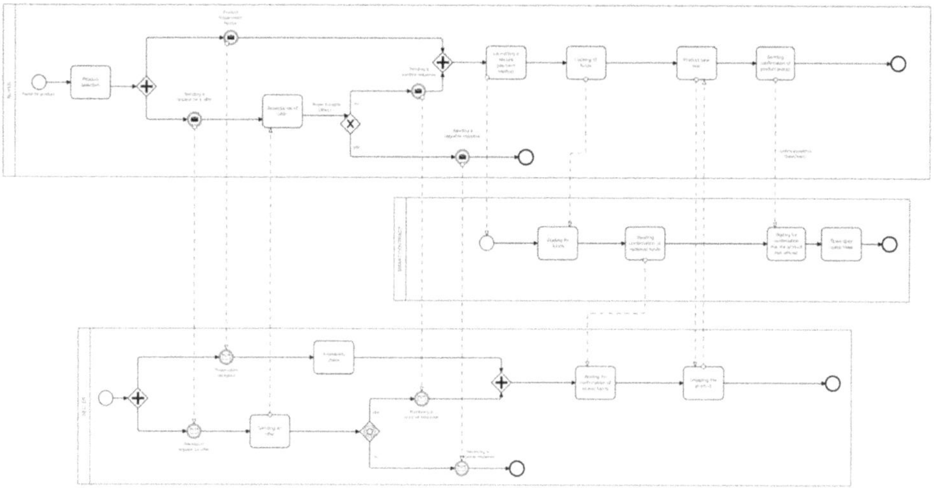

In the following text, we present the algorithms that describe the main smart contracts within the proposed C2C plaftorm.

Algorithm 1 represents the situation where the Buyer is asking for Product Offer. We have two possible scenarios, one where the price is already set and the other where Seller needs to offer a price.

Algorithm 1: Buyer Asking for Product Offer

```
input: Buyer_ID, Seller_ID, Product_ID, Buyer-Product-Decision
if Requester == Buyer_ID then
        Product(Buyer-Product-Decision) = Buyer-Product-Decision.
                if Buyer-Product-Decision == True then
                        if Seller_ID owner == Virtual Inventory then
        Event: The Product is On Virtual Inventory Asking For an Offer.
else
Event: The Product is Approved Asking For an Offer.
else
Product is Rejected.
else
return error.
```

The seller sets the Price Offer in Algorithm 2. If the seller doesn't offer the price, the algorithm returns an error.

Algorithm 2: Seller Price Offer

```
input: Seller_ID, Product_ID
if Requester == Seller_ID then
Product(Price) = Price.
Event: The seller's offer is ready.
```

```
else
return error.
```

In Algorithm 3 Seller is Asking for a Decision. To issue an announcement (Event) that the Seller is asking for the Buyer's decision, the Product ID needs to match Product-IPFS Hash.

Algorithm 3: Seller Asking for Decision

```
input: Seller_ID, Product_ID, Product-Hash
if Requester == Seller_ID then
Product_ID = Product-Hash.
Issue an announcement (Event) that the Seller is asking for the Buyer's deci-
sion.
else
return error.
```

The Algorithm 4 explains the situation where Buyer Approves or Rejects Products. If the Buyer's final decision is "true" the Buyer accepts the final product. Otherwise, the Buyer rejects the product offer.

Algorithm 4: Buyer Approves/Rejects Product

```
input: Buyer_ID, Product_ID, Buyer-Product-Final-Decision
if Requester == Buyer_ID then
         Product(Buyer-Product-Decision) = Buyer-Product-Final-Decision.
 if Buyer-Product-Decision== True then
Event: The Buyer accepted the final Product offer.
                  else
 Even: The Buyer rejected the final Product offer
else
return error.
```

ASSESSING READINESS OF CUSTOMERS FOR ADOPTION OF THE PROPOSED MODEL

Many C2C marketplaces exist worldwide, some operating globally, like eBay or Craigslist, and many operating on local markets. A new platform would have to provide significant improvements to be adopted by a relevant number of users.

The initial readiness of the customers to use the proposed platform has been investigated using the adapted UTAUT2 (Venkatesh et al., 2012). The conducted research aims to point out the main issues that are relevant to customers so that the prototype can be developed focusing on those issues. At this phase, the readiness assessment is aimed at a lower number of participants, to assess the questionnaire and gain preliminary insights.

Research Methodology

For this research, we created a survey on the readiness to use the blockchain-based C2C model of e-commerce. The questions are formulated in such a way as to gather relevant information about the user's preferences. The survey was based on the well-known and widely used UTAUT2 model, for assessing the acceptance of technology (Alalwan et al., 2017). We have kept all the constructs proposed in the original UTAUT2 model: performance expectancy (PE), effort expectancy (EE), social influence (SE), facilitating conditions (FC), price value (PV), habit (HAB), and behavioral intention (BI) (Venkatesh et al., 2012).

The following hypotheses were put forward:

- H1: Performance Expectancy affects the user's willingness to use the featured blockchain-based C2C e-commerce application.
- H2: Effort Expectancy affects the user's willingness to use the featured blockchain-based C2C e-commerce application.
- H3: Social Influence affects the user's willingness to use the featured blockchain-based C2C e-commerce application.
- H4: Facilitating Conditions affects the user's willingness to use the featured blockchain-based C2C e-commerce application.
- H5: Price Value affects the user's willingness to use the featured blockchain-based C2C e-commerce application.
- H6: Habit affects the user's willingness to use the featured blockchain-based C2C e-commerce application.

The UTAUT2 model in the context of research is presented in Figure 3.

Figure 3. UTAUT2 model in the context of research

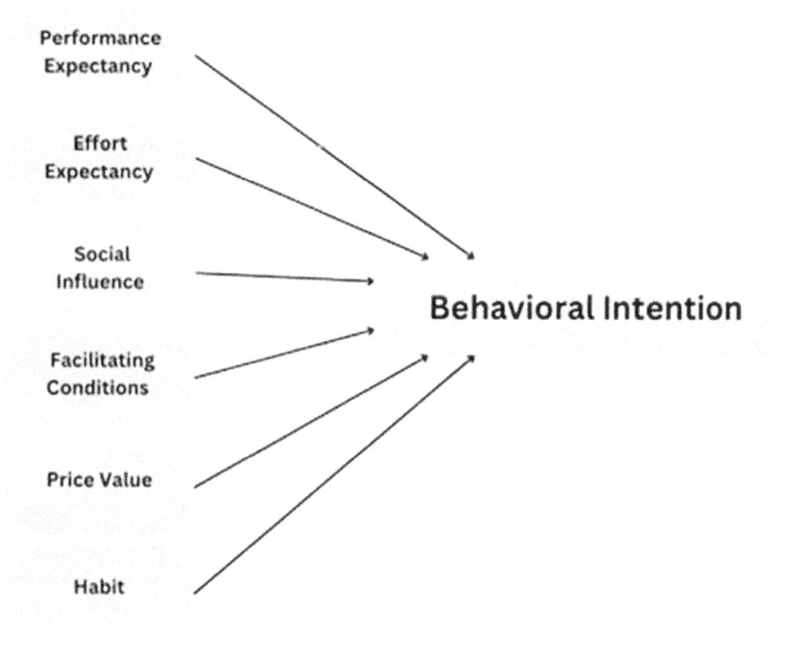

The questions in the survey were focused on collecting opinions about secure transactions without intermediaries and using cryptocurrency payments. Based on the survey, we can assess what factors are the main drivers that can positively affect the use of this technology.

In this phase, 89 participants filled out the questionnaire. The demographic data about participants are shown in Table 3.

Table 3. Demographic data about participants

Age	<20	14
	20-25	37
	25-35	23
	>35	15
Gender	Male	28
	Female	61
Employment status	High school student	14
	Student	19
	Employed	41
	Unemployed	11
	Retiree	4
Education	Primary Education	0
	Secondary Education	36
	College	42
	Postgraduate studies	11
Experience with buying online	Yes	85
	No	4
Experience with selling online	Yes	70
	No	19

Results

The analysis was conducted using the SmartPLS software (Ringle et al., 2022) and the PLS-SEM algorithm. The initial model included a higher number of indicators for each of the constructs, but some of them were removed after correlation analysis. This contributes to lowering the number of questions in the survey for future data collection. The final model and the results of the analysis are presented in Figure 4.

Figure 4. Results of PLS-SEM

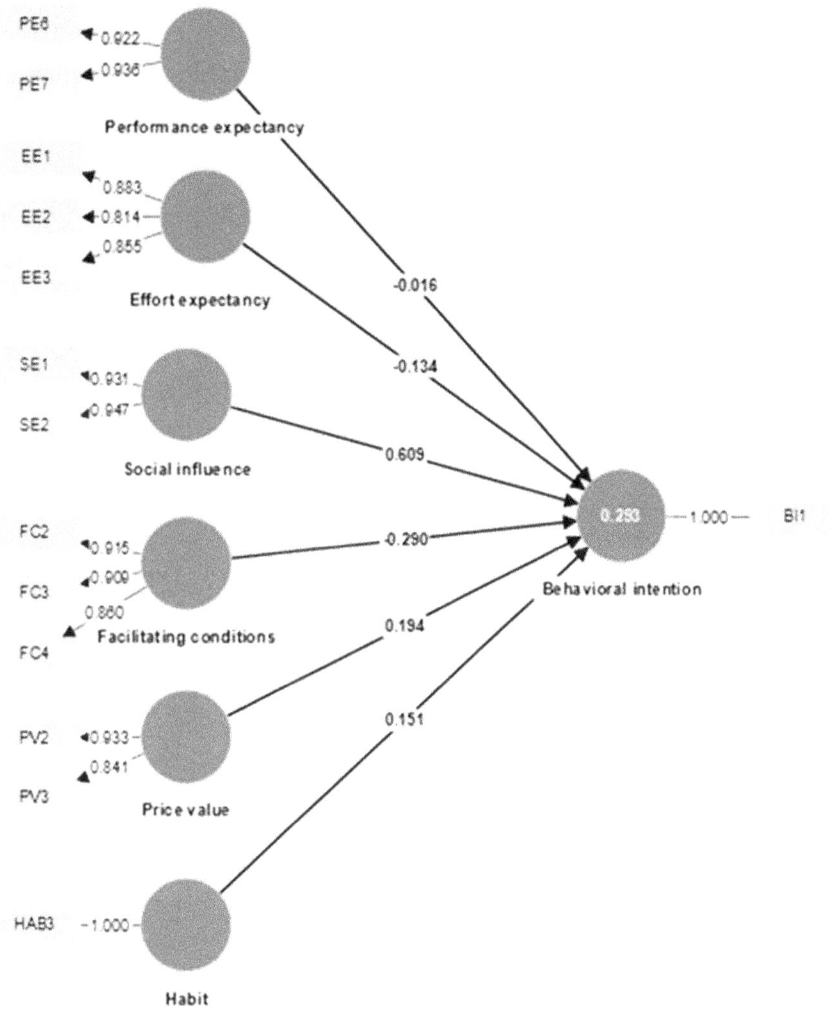

The influence of individual variables on behavioral intention was assessed using path coefficients, where higher positive values indicate a high influence of a construct on behavioral intention, values close to zero indicate that there is no influence, and negative values indicate negative effects. The path coefficients given in Figure 5 indicate that the greatest influence on behavioral intention comes from the social influence variable, meaning that social influence is expected to significantly motivate customers to adopt the proposed model, at least in the initial adoption phase and with the early adopters. These results may be surprising, and the explanation may lie in the great popularity of blockchain technologies and blockchain-based business models. Previous studies have already pointed out the importance of social influence in adopting blockchain solutions (Albayati et al., 2020; AlShamsi et al., 2022; Wamba & Queiroz, 2019).

Price value also shows a relatively high influence, which is consistent with many technology acceptance research results. The users are more likely to adopt the platform if the price is affordable and in accordance with the value of the service. Negative effects of effort expectancy and facilitating conditions most likely come from the formulations of questions, which were given in a negative context.

The assessment of construct reliability and validity is shown in Table 4. All values of Cronbach's alpha, Composite reliability (rho_a), Composite reliability (rho_c), and Average variance extracted (AVE) are considered acceptable.

Table 4. Construct reliability and validity

	Cronbach's alpha	Composite reliability (rho_a)	Composite reliability (rho_c)	Average variance extracted (AVE)
Effort expectancy	0.816	0.855	0.888	0.725
Facilitating conditions	0.875	0.875	0.923	0.801
Performance expectancy	0.842	0.848	0.927	0.863
Price value	0.741	0.828	0.881	0.789
Social influence	0.866	0.877	0.937	0.882

Table 5 shows the assessment of discriminant validity using the Fornell-Larcker criterion. All the values at the diagonal cells are higher than those below them, which means that discriminant validity is acceptable.

Table 5. Discriminant validity: Fornell-Larcker criterion

	Behavioral intention	Effort expectancy	Facilitating conditions	Habit	Performance expectancy	Price value	Social influence
Behavioral intention	1						
Effort expectancy	0.109	0.851					
Facilitating conditions	0.283	0.353	0.895				
Habit	0.311	0.207	0.759	1			
Performance expectancy	0.232	0.202	0.462	0.399	0.929		
Price value	0.325	0.045	0.334	0.361	0.315	0.888	
Social influence	0.465	0.505	0.736	0.567	0.473	0.303	0.939

Table 6 shows VIF values, in order to assess multicollinearity. In many studies, values below 5 are considered acceptable, so we can conclude that the model has no problem with multicollinearity.

Table 6. VIF values

	VIF
BI1	1
EE1	1.975
EE2	1.97
EE3	1.619
FC2	3.106
FC3	2.92
FC4	1.902
HAB3	1
PE6	2.12
PE7	2.12
PV2	1.532
PV3	1.532
SE1	2.405
SE2	2.405

Table 7 shows the results of bootstrapping, where we test the statistical significance of path coefficients. From the obtained values, we can conclude that only the influence of social influence variables on behavioral intention can be considered statistically significant. The p values of hypotheses that test the influence of facilitating conditions and price value on behavioral intention are close to the typically used value of 0.05, so it may happen that these two constructs could have a statistically significant influence on the improvement of the number and structure of participants. All the other correlations were not found to be statistically significant.

Table 7. Bootstrapping results

	Original sample (O)	Sample mean (M)	Standard deviation (STDEV)	T statistics (|O/STDEV|)	P values
Effort expectancy -> Behavioral intention	-0.134	-0.091	0.128	1.047	0.295
Facilitating conditions -> Behavioral intention	-0.29	-0.263	0.169	1.715	0.086
Habit -> Behavioral intention	0.151	0.132	0.166	0.905	0.366
Performance expectancy -> Behavioral intention	-0.016	-0.014	0.114	0.143	0.886
Price value -> Behavioral intention	0.194	0.21	0.107	1.819	0.069
Social influence -> Behavioral intention	0.609	0.57	0.144	4.234	0

DISCUSSION AND CONCLUSION

This chapter presents an overview of the impact of blockchain technologies on the transformation and development of C2C e-commerce business models, where blockchain is expected to provide more secure transactions, increase the speed of funds transfer from buyer to seller, and improve trust. The results point out the key factors that are expected to influence the user adoption of the proposed model.

As the main driver for the adoption of blockchain-based C2C e-commerce platforms, we have identified social influence. This is not surprising, since other studies have already identified the importance of social influence for blockchain adoption (Wamba & Queiroz, 2019). Further investigations are needed to determine the specifics of this influence, but this result can help platform developers to boost customer interest in the C2C platform. One possible approach would be related to employing a model of social visibility of customers, such as providing badges, creating featured member sections on the website, engaging customers in social responsibility activities, or similar. Future work is needed to create better profiles of customers and determine the acceptance drivers for various market segments.

Although this study did not recognize the statistically significant influence of price value on behavioral intention, the obtained path coefficients suggest that this relation should be considered and analyzed with more details. The costs related to the adoption of new C2C platform need to be in line with the value that the platform offers. In addition, the adoption of the blockchain in C2C models is likely to depend in the adoption of cryptocurrencies, the legal aspects of cryptocurrencies application, both local and global, as well as the development of business models and infrastructure of leaders in C2C e-commerce. Finally, the role of trust, as an important factor of C2C e-commerce (Leonard & Jones, 2021), should be investigated with more details.

The main limitation of the conducted research lies in the small number of respondents, and this will be improved in future work. However, the obtained results have contributed to improving the questionnaire and gaining preliminary insights into the expected behavioral intention of potential users of a blockchain-based C2C platform.

ACKNOWLEDGMENT

This work was supported by the Algorand Centres of Excellence program managed by the Algorand Foundation. Any opinions, findings, conclusions, or recommendations expressed in this material are those of the author(s) and do not necessarily reflect the views of the Algorand Foundation.

REFERENCES

Alalwan, A. A., Dwivedi, Y. K., & Rana, N. P. (2017). Factors influencing adoption of mobile banking by Jordanian bank customers: Extending UTAUT2 with trust. *International Journal of Information Management*, *37*(3), 99–110. doi:10.1016/j.ijinfomgt.2017.01.002

Albayati, H., Kim, S. K., & Rho, J. J. (2020). Accepting financial transactions using blockchain technology and cryptocurrency: A customer perspective approach. *Technology in Society*, *62*, 101320. doi:10.1016/j.techsoc.2020.101320

AlShamsi, M., Al-Emran, M., & Shaalan, K. (2022). A systematic review on blockchain adoption. *Applied Sciences (Basel, Switzerland)*, *12*(9), 4245. doi:10.3390/app12094245

Bulsara, H. P., & Vaghela, P. S. (2020). Blockchain Technology for E-commerce Industry E-commerce trends View project Techno-innovations to Techno-Entrepreneurship and completed one project on Development of Course in Pedagogy framework: Industrial Management, National Mission Project on Educati. *International Journal of Advanced Science and Technology*, *29*(5), 3793–3798.

Chen, J., & Micali, S. (2019). Algorand: A secure and efficient distributed ledger. *Theoretical Computer Science*, *777*, 155–183. doi:10.1016/j.tcs.2019.02.001

Daniel, E., & Tschorsch, F. (2022). IPFS and Friends: A Qualitative Comparison of Next Generation Peer-to-Peer Data Networks. *IEEE Communications Surveys and Tutorials*, *24*(1), 31–52. doi:10.1109/COMST.2022.3143147

Dubosson-Torbay, M., Osterwalder, A., & Pigneur, Y. (2002). E-business model design, classification, and measurements. *Thunderbird International Business Review*, *44*(1), 5–23. doi:10.1002/tie.1036

Farell, R. (2015). An analysis of the cryptocurrency industry. *Wharton Research Scholars, 130*. https://repository.upenn.edu/wharton_research_scholars/130

Gomber, P., Kauffman, R. J., Parker, C., & Weber, B. W. (2018). On the Fintech Revolution: Interpreting the Forces of Innovation, Disruption, and Transformation in Financial Services. *Journal of Management Information Systems*, *35*(1), 220–265. doi:10.1080/07421222.2018.1440766

Grover, P., Kar, A. K., & Vigneswara Ilavarasan, P. (2018). Blockchain for businesses: A systematic literature review. Lecture Notes in Computer Science (Including Subseries Lecture Notes in Artificial Intelligence and Lecture Notes in Bioinformatics), 11195 LNCS, 325–336. doi:10.1007/978-3-030-02131-3_29

Gupta, A. (2014). E-Commerce: Role of E-Commerce in today's business. *International Journal of Computing and Corporate Research*, *4*(1), 1–8.

Joshi, P., & Kumar, A. (2020, July). A novel framework for decentralized c2c e-commerce using smart contract. In *2020 11th International Conference on Computing, Communication and Networking Technologies (ICCCNT)* (pp. 1-5). IEEE. 10.1109/ICCCNT49239.2020.9225377

Joyce, A., & Paquin, R. L. (2016). The triple layered business model canvas: A tool to design more sustainable business models. *Journal of Cleaner Production*, *135*, 1474–1486. doi:10.1016/j.jclepro.2016.06.067

Kannengießer, N., Lins, S., Dehling, T., & Sunyaev, A. (2020). Trade-offs between distributed ledger technology characteristics. *ACM Computing Surveys*, *53*(2), 1–37. doi:10.1145/3379463

Khan, S. N., Loukil, F., Ghedira-Guegan, C., Benkhelifa, E., & Bani-Hani, A. (2021). Blockchain smart contracts: Applications, challenges, and future trends. *Peer-to-Peer Networking and Applications*, *14*(5), 2901–2925. doi:10.100712083-021-01127-0 PMID:33897937

Lahkani, M. J., Wang, S., Urbański, M., & Egorova, M. (2020). Sustainable B2B E-commerce and blockchain-based supply chain finance. *Sustainability (Basel)*, *12*(10), 3968. doi:10.3390u12103968

Leherbauer, P. (2019). *Cryptomoney and its' Applications in B2C Markets: Status quo and future Trends/ submitted by Philipp Leherbauer, B. Sc* [Doctoral dissertation, Universität Linz].

Leonard, L. N., & Jones, K. (2021). Trust in C2C electronic commerce: Ten years later. *Journal of Computer Information Systems*, *61*(3), 240–246. doi:10.1080/08874417.2019.1598829

Limayem, M., Hirt, S. G., & Cheung, C. M. K. (2007). How habit limits the predictive power of intention: The case of information systems continuance. *Management Information Systems Quarterly*, *31*(4), 705–737. doi:10.2307/25148817

Liu, Z., & Li, Z. (2020). A blockchain-based framework of cross-border e-commerce supply chain. *International Journal of Information Management*, *52*, 102059. doi:10.1016/j.ijinfomgt.2019.102059

Mäkeläinen, S. I. (2006). *From B2C to C2C e-commerce. Course Essay*. Department of Computer Science, University of Helsinki.

Mendoza-Tello, J. C., Mora, H., Pujol-López, F. A., & Lytras, M. D. (2019). Disruptive innovation of cryptocurrencies in consumer acceptance and trust. *Information Systems and e-Business Management*, *17*(2), 195–222. doi:10.100710257-019-00415-w

Mettler, M. (2016, September). Blockchain technology in healthcare: The revolution starts here. In *2016 IEEE 18th international conference on e-health networking, applications, and services (Healthcom)* (pp. 1-3). IEEE. 10.1109/HealthCom.2016.7749510

Monrat, A. A., Schelén, O., & Andersson, K. (2019). A Survey of Blockchain From the Perspectives of Applications, Challenges, and Opportunities. *IEEE Access : Practical Innovations, Open Solutions*, *7*, 117134–117151. doi:10.1109/ACCESS.2019.2936094

Neufeld, D. J., Dong, L., & Higgins, C. (2007). Charismatic leadership and user acceptance of information technology. *European Journal of Information Systems*, *16*(4), 494–510. doi:10.1057/palgrave.ejis.3000682

Ng, D., & Griffin, P. (2018). The wider impact of a national cryptocurrency. *Global Policy*, 1.

Osterwalder, A., & Pigneur, Y. (2013). *Business Model Generation: A Handbook for Visionaries, Game Changers, and Challengers*. John Wiley & Sons.

Ringle, C. M., Wende, S., & Becker, J.-M. (2022). SmartPLS 4. Oststeinbek: SmartPLS. https://www.smartpls.com

Shopify. (n.d.). *12 B2B Ecommerce Trends To Shape Your Business in 2023*. Shopify. https://www.shopify.com/enterprise/b2b-ecommerce-trends-statistics#2

Shorman, S., Allaymoun, M., Hamid, O., & Sciences, F. (2019). Developing the E-Commerce Model a Consumer To Consumer Using Blockchain. [IJMIT]. *International Journal of Managing Information Technology*, *11*(2), 55–64. doi:10.5121/ijmit.2019.11204

Taherdoost, H., & Madanchian, M. (2023). Blockchain-Based E-Commerce: A Review on Applications and Challenges. *Electronics (Basel)*, *12*(8), 1889. doi:10.3390/electronics12081889

Tapscott, D., & Tapscott, A. (2017). How blockchain will change organizations. *MIT Sloan Management Review*, *58*(2), 10.

Treiblmaier, H., & Sillaber, C. (2021). The impact of blockchain on e-commerce: A framework for salient research topics. *Electronic Commerce Research and Applications*, *48*, 101054. doi:10.1016/j.elerap.2021.101054

Van der Heijden, H. (2004). User acceptance of hedonic information systems. *Management Information Systems Quarterly*, *28*(4), 695–704. doi:10.2307/25148660

Venkatesh, V., Morris, M. G., Davis, G. B., & Davis, F. D. (2003). User acceptance of information technology: Toward a unified view. *Management Information Systems Quarterly*, *47*(3), 425–478. doi:10.2307/30036540

Venkatesh, V., Thong, J. Y. L., & Xu, X. (2012). Consumer acceptance and use of information technology: Extending the unified theory of acceptance and use of technology. *Management Information Systems Quarterly*, *36*(1), 157–178. doi:10.2307/41410412

Verma, N., & Kulkarni, P. (2023). Impact of Blockchain Technology on E-Commerce. In *2023 International Conference on Innovative Data Communication Technologies and Application (ICIDCA)* (pp. 668-672). IEEE. 10.1109/ICIDCA56705.2023.10100222

Wamba, S. F., & Queiroz, M. M. (2019). The Role of Social Influence in Blockchain Adoption: The Brazilian Supply Chain Case. *IFAC-PapersOnLine*, *52*(13), 1715–1720. doi:10.1016/j.ifacol.2019.11.448

White, G. R. T. (2017). Future applications of blockchain in business and management: A Delphi study. *Strategic Change*, *26*(5), 439–451. doi:10.1002/jsc.2144

Zamani, E. D., & Giaglis, G. M. (2018). With a little help from the miners: Distributed ledger technology and market disintermediation. *Industrial Management & Data Systems*, *118*(3), 637–652. doi:10.1108/IMDS-05-2017-0231

Zhang, Y., & Wen, J. (2017). The IoT electric business model: Using blockchain technology for the internet of things. *Peer-to-Peer Networking and Applications*, *10*(4), 983–994. doi:10.100712083-016-0456-1

Zheng, X. R., & Lu, Y. (2022). Blockchain technology–recent research and future trend. *Enterprise Information Systems*, *16*(12), 1939895. doi:10.1080/17517575.2021.1939895

Zott, C., & Amit, R. (2008). The fit between product market strategy and business model: Implications for firm performance. *Strategic Management Journal*, *29*(1), 1–26. doi:10.1002mj.642

ADDITIONAL READING

Abdellatif, T., & Brousmiche, K.-L. (2018). Formal verification of smart contracts based on users and blockchain behaviors models. *2018 9th IFIP International Conference on New Technologies, Mobility and Security (NTMS)*, 1–5.

Antonopoulos, A. M. (2014). *Mastering Bitcoin: unlocking digital cryptocurrencies*. O'Reilly Media, Inc.

Antonopoulos, A. M. (2017). *Mastering Bitcoin: Programming the open blockchain*. O'Reilly Media, Inc.

Crosby, M., Pattanayak, P., Verma, S., & Kalyanaraman, V. (2016). Blockchain technology: Beyond bitcoin. *Applied Innovation*, *2*(6–10), 71.

Narayanan, A., Bonneau, J., Felten, E., Miller, A., & Goldfeder, S. (2016). *Bitcoin and cryptocurrency technologies: a comprehensive introduction*. Princeton University Press.

Swan, M. (2015). *Blockchain: Blueprint for a new economy*. O'Reilly Media, Inc.

Tapscott, D., & Tapscott, A. (2016). *Blockchain revolution: how the technology behind bitcoin is changing money, business, and the world*. Penguin.

Yuan, Y., & Wang, F.-Y. (2018). Blockchain and Cryptocurrencies: Model, Techniques, and Applications. *IEEE Transactions on Systems, Man, and Cybernetics. Systems*, *48*(9), 1421–1428. doi:10.1109/TSMC.2018.2854904

KEY TERMS AND DEFINITIONS

Blockchain: A distributed database, it provides transparency of data to participants of transactions.

C2C Model: A e-business model where participants can buy and sell products with each other.

Cryptocurrency: A digital currency, by using it we can pay online without need of third-party. Data is stored in blocks that are connected in chain.

E-commerce: A online commerce that represent all activities of buying and selling products online.

Smart Contracts: A transaction protocol which runs automatically, and participants need to fulfil the terms of smart contract.

UTAUT Model: The Unified Theory of Acceptance and Use of Technology is a theory that explains why people accept and use technology, considering factors like usefulness, ease of use, social influence, and available resources.

Chapter 15
Consumerism and Blockchain Technology:
The Application of Technology to Improve Market Equalization

Michael Nobre Martins
Universidade Lusíada, Portugal

Nuno Baptista
https://orcid.org/0000-0001-7130-0543
Escola Superior de Comunicação Social, Instituto Politécnico de Lisboa, Portugal

Anna Carolina Boechat
https://orcid.org/0000-0002-9252-6602
IADE, Portugal & Universidade Católica Portuguesa, Portugal

ABSTRACT

Consumerism is an ancient concept that is capturing much attention in recent literature. The consumerism movement was developed in response to power imbalances between companies and the consumer in an increasingly marketized world. It is focused on promoting consumers' rights, market transparency, and consumer freedom of choice. Consumerism aims for market equalization, meaning well-balanced markets, in which market inequalities are reduced, providing a better functioning market environment for both companies and consumers. Being initially designed to revolutionize transactions in the financial system, blockchain is a disruptive technology with potential applications in many different areas. Blockchain is a public, immutable, and permanent ledger, which works as database in a decentralized network, using cryptographic codes. Framed by consumerism literature, this chapter explores the potential applications of blockchain technology, by focusing on key consumerism claims, including marketing ethics, the security of e-commerce transactions, and supply chain traceability and transparency.

DOI: 10.4018/978-1-6684-8958-1.ch015

INTRODUCTION

The consumer's movement was formed in response to power imbalances between companies and the consumer in an increasingly marketized world. It is focused on promoting consumers' rights. Consumers aim for market equalization, meaning well-balanced markets, in which market inequalities are reduced, providing a better functioning market environment for both companies and consumers Kucuk (2016). The term consumerism has multiple meanings - while it can refer to what has been broadly understood as the consumer movement, focused on consumer rights and choice (Hemais & dos Santos, 2021), consumerism also carries a very different meaning within social science literature, one that gives accent to consumerism as a logic of consumer culture, being synonymous with capitalist consumer culture (Kim, 2022). In this chapter the focus is on the first perspective of the concept, consumerism as consumer activism. Kotler (1972, p. 42) seminally defined consumerism as "a social movement seeking to augment the rights and power of buyers in relation to sellers". For Kotler (1972) consumerism is inevitable, pro-marketing and beneficial. Consumers seek fair markets, on which consumer empowerment is enhanced and vulnerabilities on the part of consumers are eliminated - an idea that was termed as "market equalization" by Kucuk (2016). To achieve market equalization consumers demand additional rights, such as the right to have adequate information about the product, the right to additional protection against counterfeit and questionable products and unethical marketing practices, as well as the right to participate in the development of products by co-creating them and influencing companies in directions that will increase the quality of life (Kucuk, 2016).

Blockchain is a public, immutable, and permanent ledger, that works as database in a decentralized network, using cryptographic codes. In its essence, it is a combination of cryptographic technology and peer-to-peer computing (Ertemel, 2018). The notion was first introduced by Satoshi Nakamoto in his article "Bitcoin: A peer-to-peer eletronic cash system" (Nakamoto, 2008), in the context of bitcoin, the first cryptocoin. The term blockchain refers to a distributed database of digital data that can be verified at any time. The chain is created by encrypting transaction data in chronological sequence to secure unalterable records and the integrity of transactions (Hassoun et al., 2023). Blockchain operates as a chain of blocks of sequential data, in which it is only possible to add one block at a time, and a mathematical equation serves as a test, allowing the sequence of the current to be constructed (Ertemel, 2018). Each new data that is inserted into the network is stamped with the date of introduction and other information, thus becoming tamper-proof. It is this verification process, in which blocks are included in the system with high-level encryption, that makes blockchain highly secure and less subject to fraudulent transactions (Nakamoto, 2008; Yontar, 2023)

Technological advances, can provide opportunities to achieve more equitable and socially responsible market structures (Althawadi et al., 2021). This chapter aims to explore the potential of blockchain technology in responding to some claims of the consumerism movement, including the need for increased ethics in market transactions, security of e-commerce, and supply chain transparency.

ETHICAL CONSUMERISM AND BLOCKCHAIN

The consumerism literature typically identifies three waves of consumerism: i) the first wave was characterized by consumer movements focusing on the value of money, product information, labeling and consumer choice; ii) the second comprised product safety and corporate accountability and; iii) the third and most recent wave consists in ethical consumerism as a combination of environmentalism and citizenship (Kotler 1972; Koos, 2021; Lang & Hines, 1993). Ethical consumerism involves a conscious choice to use products selectively based on personal and moral beliefs and can be understood as an expression of ethical concerns about products and organizations (Cho & Krasser, 2011).

The traditional 'capitalist' consumerism form has been criticized over the years, due to its associations with a constant need, an excess of materialism, addictive behaviors, selfishness, and its debatable relation with happiness (Contemporary & Filos, 2010). As a natural consequence, consumers changed over the years and have been each time more conscious about topics such as energy consumption, environmental sustainability, labor issues, animal welfare (Le Grand et al., 2021), poverty, unsustainable resources use and social inequities (Coffin & Egan-Wyer, 2022), bringing a new perspective to consumerism. As an example, according to Coffin and Egan-Wyer (2022), more than 68% of European citizens feel that environmental issues are more important now than before, leading to a perspective where consumption must be seen as a responsible act, with moral choices.

While it is really clear that consumers are demanding a high level of accountability from companies regarding social and environmental practices (Jones, 2019), there is not a consensus in academia about solid accountable behavior from consumers (e.g. Adamkiewicz et al., 2022). Briefly, although there is a high intention to consume in a more ethical way (e.g. Arouri et al., 2021), this intention might not be fulfilled as desired: it seems that there is a gap between how consumers think that their consumption should be and how it is, in fact – which can be explained due to several factors, as financial capability, for example (Coffin & Egan-Wyer, 2022; Lu & Sinha, 2019). Goodwin et al. (2020) give an interesting contribution to the debate regarding this consumer duality: 'shallow' green consumerism represents consumers that value ecological or ethical goods but do not make any robust change regarding their consumption levels and, on the other hand, a 'deep' green consumerism not only values those types of goods but also reduce their consumption levels. Tan et al. (2022), in its turn, expand this dichotomy and mention a societal benefit value (oriented to consumers' altruistic values and behaviors) and a protester or epistemic value (representing a consumer behavior that empowers unconventional purchasing systems to deflect the focus from traditional commercial platforms). Both perspectives help to create an understanding that changing consumer behavior towards an ethical path is still a work in progress, with different layers and actors involved.

Although consumer behavior keeps evolving, it can be safely stated that firms are taking this growing green/ethical 'movement' into consideration and making a real effort to satisfy consumer's desires regarding more conscious consumption (Shanor & Light, 2022), which can be seen through 'sustainable', 'eco-friendly', 'recyclable' (Lee & Raschke, 2023), 'green' or 'organic' (Schmuck et al., 2018) labels. This whole dynamic evolving planet, companies, and consumers can help to understand the ethical consumerism concept, which represents a form of consumption based on morals, ethics, political knowledge, and environmental support, essentially (Suzuki et al., 2019). Ethical consumption embodies an individual self-awareness about consumption behaviors (Suzuki et al., 2019), a voluntary decision to buy products and/or services that are recognized as ethical or sustainable (Antoni & Faillo, 2022). This social phenomenon that takes into consideration environmental issues in purchase decision situations (Le Grand et al., 2021) can be seen through a large range of actions (Goodwin et al., 2020) representing, thus, a certain lifestyle (Jones, 2019).

Interestingly, ethical consumerism can be positively seen by companies, and society, but also in relation to social policies: Le Grand et al. (2021) defends that when customer behaviors are based on ethical aspects it creates a mechanism to regulate markets, reducing negative practices, enhancing competition, improving best practices and revenues, being a civic expression. By building connections between different social groups (Le Grand et al., 2021), ethical consumerism can create movements with probable effects on public policies.

An interesting way to understand ethical consumption is to observe some social dynamics as the circular or sharing economy, for example. Kouhizadeh et al. (2019) analyzed the circular economy addressing that this concept represents a social innovation that contributes to minimizing social, economic, and environmental issues. Based on the idea of recycling, reusing, and remanufacturing, the circular economy provides several benefits to those involved in it, including logistics and supply chain issues through the use of blockchain technology (Kouhizadeh et al., 2019).

The same perspective can be applied to the sharing economy concept, which can be represented by peer-to-peer (P2P) platforms (Tan et al., 2022). These type of platforms – as the ones used to commercialize second-hand products, for example – helps to provide well-being outcomes, avoid waste, and generate social and economic impact. They are based on a clear change regarding consumer behavior, following thus an ethical path (Tan et al., 2022). Like the previous example, blockchain emerges in this case as a technology that provides support for this dynamic, once it "includes a distributed ledger, peer-to-peer connectivity, cryptography, and other reputable technologies" (Fernando & Saravannan, 2021, p. 88) and is able to change financial transactions, impacting the interaction between individuals and the whole society (Ronaghi & Mosakhani, 2022). Thus, considering both examples of ethical consumption dynamics and based on the blockchain capabilities, it can be stated that blockchain is not only related to these types of economies (e.g. Tan et al., 2022) but also a tool than can enhance ethical consumerism in general.

First, it is important to highlight that transparency has been pointed out as one of the most important characteristics of blockchain technology (e.g. Schahczenski & Schahczenski, 2020), elevating it as a social value tool. Blockchain transparency provides clear information about products, brings authenticity to any type of transaction, guarantees security (Schahczenski & Schahczenski, 2020), helps to create adequate consumers expectations regarding products' sustainability, provides a competitive advantage (Dierksmeier & Seele, 2018), and bring positive outcomes to the supply chain management, benefiting different stakeholders (EU Blockchain Observatory and Forum, 2022), between other advantages found on literature. In sum, the social aspect of blockchain transparency can be represented in the United Nations' definition (2014) of this topic: [Transparency is the] "ability to identify and trace the history, distribution, location, and application of products, parts, and materials, to ensure the reliability of sustainability claims, in the areas of human rights, labor (including health and safety), the environment, and anti-corruption" (Nygaard & Silkoset, 2022, p. 5).

Lapointe and Fishbane (2019) developed a very interesting and detailed research by describing blockchain's ethical framework. The authors identify this technology as (i) a democratic tool that allows individuals to have more control over information in purchasing situations – by creating a digital identity social goods can be provided, as a digital identity system that facilitates homeless people to have access to services, as provided by Blockchain for Change organization; (ii) an asset tracker – Lapointe and Fishbane (2019) present the example of De Beers, a company that is using blockchain technology to trace diamonds from conflicting /non-conflicting sources; and as (iii) an enabler of enterprise efficiency – once it deals with a robust amount of data, blockchain can offer efficient data-share processes, mitigating fraud (Lemos et al., 2022). The same authors (2019) associate blockchain with ethical consumerism by indicating that this technology is helping to generate microeconomies: as pointed out by Dierksmeier and Seele (2018), creating an own website is not a difficult task and anyone can do it; additionally, there are companies offering programs to enlarge blockchain's usage. Thus, the collaborative perspective offered by blockchain technology brings empowerment to individuals (Dierksmeier & Seele, 2018), accelerating the emergence of new businesses and the enhancement of more ethical practices (Dierksmeier & Seele, 2020).

Following the same reasoning line, Ronaghi and Mosakhani (2022) indicate that blockchain impact business ethics, management, and social equity. They note that blockchain has the ability to improve economic processes due to its security and data reliability, creating a greater balance between people, firms, and the ecosystem (Ronaghi & Mosakhani, 2022). Blockchain can be seen as "an engagement-facilitating technology platform" (p. 6), transforming the consumer into a producer (Tan et al., 2022). By allowing the 'prosumer' perspective (Tan et al., 2022), blockchain technology makes room for inclusion and also for the fulfillment of some Sustainable Development Goals (SDGs) (Tham & Sigala, 2020).

Studies regarding blockchain and ethical consumerism also bring some insights into specific industries. Tham and Sigala (2020) focused on the tourism industry and presented interesting information: first, several restaurants and hotels are adopting blockchain platforms to enhance cryptocurrency transactions, bringing more dynamic to these businesses; second, the small and medium tourism operators can also benefit from this strategy, once the blockchain technology can bring them more advantage to compete with bigger competitors, reducing the current asymmetry between firms; third, blockchain browsers and blockchain social media networks can give more power to tourists, once it will allow them to own their of transactional data; fourth, by owning this data, consumers won't depend on banks to authorize transactions (Tham & Sigala, 2020), gaining thus more power of choice and independence.

The food industry was also observed considering the proximity between ethical consumerism and blockchain. Schahczenski and Schahczenski (2020) defend, in general, that blockchain technology could really change the current way that food is consumed and distributed. In addition to a lower cost of transactions, it gives more control to farmers and buyers by showing the whole path of food from point A to point B, besides presenting information through specific platforms regarding carbon and biofuel production. Blockchain can also enhance the fair-trade movement, by showing to the final consumer the benefits of purchasing a certain good from a particular producer (Schahczenski & Schahczenski, 2020).

Blockchain's potential was identified in other industries, such as medicine, education, and real estate (Tham & Sigala, 2020). While in the first blockchain can help to protect medical records, for example, in the second it can enhance academic research by verifying scientific records or emphasizing intellectual property. Real estate can be benefited from blockchain technology due to an easier process of documents and data validation (Tham & Sigala, 2020). It is understood that the ethical perspective is considered as a common ground between them, once blockchain ensures fairness, trust, and transparency.

The EU Blockchain Observatory and Forum (2022) brought some interesting examples regarding blockchain applicability toward an ethical path. Blockchain technology can help to protect workers from developing countries by creating and protecting their identity documentation, preventing slave labor, eradicating illegal fishing, bringing more transparency to recruitment processes, and helping to minimize the chances of exploitation of migrant workers (EU Blockchain Observatory and Forum, 2022). Keeping this social sense, Dierksmeier and Seele (2020, p. 350) affirm that blockchain can "… deliver notary services, certify compliance and audit processes, manage records, establish voting procedures as well as bring transparency to value holdings and transfers". Very much in line with Dierksmeier and Seele (2020) perspective, Lapointe and Fishbane (2019) also listed some possibilities that can arise (or are already arising) from blockchain technology through an ethical point of view. According to them, blockchain can expand access to services, creating inclusivity (especially considering people that don't have formal documentation or credit information); it can protect vital records (they highlight Estonia's government example, which is using blockchain technology to secure people's health records); record public transactions (though applications that register property titles); enable public secure voting (reducing barriers to voting processes); prevent human trafficking (according to the authors, there is a pilot project being developed between the United Nations and the World Identity Network in this extent); improving medical research and healthcare (once again, by guaranteeing data protection and security) (Lapointe & Fishbane, 2019).

Finally, it is important to note the outcomes of Sharif and Ghodoosi's research (2022): according to these authors, although blockchain has been increasingly adopted by companies in order to enhance their production and supply chain issues activities (such as Walmart, Amazon, JPMorgan, and BP), in general only few organizations are using this technology to improve human resources practices. In sum, it seems that both ethical consumer behavior and blockchain usage for ethical purposes are in a development stage, but certainly with good expectations involved.

THE SECURITY OF E-COMMERCE TRANSACTIONS

One of the major trends in the post-pandemic era is the growth of online commerce. The pandemic reinforced some pre-existing trends, with an increase in demand in e-commerce and also for locally produced food, while nutritional quality, origin, and health concerns became more prevalent in consumers' choices (Baptista et al., 2022). These trends are likely to persist. However, e-commerce faces a number of challenges, including the risk of fraud, theft of personal data, and sale of counterfeit products, that affect consumers' trust (Ertemel, 2018). Online companies are targeting online consumers with increased precision through the combined use of Big Data and Artificial Intelligence, rising concerns about companies abuse of such enhanced power over the consumer (Hutchinson, 2022). On the other side, reducing the number of clicks and not losing the consumer through complicated purchasing processes it is imperative for companies to establish themselves in this competitive environment (Stallone et al., 2021). Therefore, it becomes crucial to find tools that guarantee the security and reliability of online platform purchases, thus reinforcing the trust of customers.

In a marketplace sustained by blockchain technology, the identity and legitimacy of each actor is validated at the network level, enhancing market trust. Smart contracts can be instrumental in providing greater consumer confidence. Contract automation is an essential functionality of blockchain that allows to transform clauses of a given contract into code, using automation, that is, from the moment the conditions are fulfilled, the contract is automatically executed (Stallone et al., 2021). For example, dispute processes for damaged material, or delivered items that do not correspond to the order, are simplified through the use of smart contracts. Because of its distributed and decentralized nature, blockchain helps to ensure the integrity and authenticity of transactions. All data, including events, records, and transactions can be stored and permanently accessed by system participants, facilitating warranty activation procedures (Rejeb et al., 2023).

In relation to the control of counterfeiting and pirating, blockchain technology has the potential to minimize such problems through digital authentication. Counterfeit products are loathed by consumers and can cause huge losses in a wide range of businesses. Through blockchain companies can create a certificate of authenticity and associate the digital certificate with the public digital record of the product on the network. Thus, in cases where the product is not sold directly by the brand, the consumer can still confirm its origin and whether it is genuine. Since registration is permanent, even in pre-owned products the consumer is capable to verify the authenticity of the product (Chen et al., 2022). Product data cannot be tampered with once it reaches the blockchain system. Consequently, product information data is secure and consumers can obtain all relevant information about products, enabling consumers to learn about product authenticity (Isaja et al., 2023).

In addition, blockchain also contributes to consumer´s personal data protection. It is essential for the consumer to feel secure when making an online purchase. Although blockchain is a digital and public record, anonymity is a characteristic of the technology. Each user is attributed a unique ID address generated by the system (Zarrin et al., 2021) and cryptography technologies are used to construct the blockchain and guarantee the security of all data (Zhang & Ling, 2023). This functionality allows users to control whom they provide their personal data to, thereby preserving and securing personal data and this feature can prevent sensitive information from being compromised in the event of a data breach or a cyber-attack. In addition, decentralization is undoubtedly the main characteristic that defines the blockchain. Transactions are conducted by nodes through secure cryptography provided by the technology, thus eliminating the need for validation by intermediaries (Zarrin et al., 2021). While centralization is associated with order, decentralization offers flexible, robust, more efficient, and secure systems (Davidson et al., 2016). More efficient in the sense that a centralized system is managed by organizations/people/governments, which implies higher costs compared to a decentralized system. Also, immutability, another key characteristic, can be leveraged by providing a tamper-proof ledger of every transaction recorded in the blockchain. Since every block of data added to the chain is timestamped, there is no room for any modification. The impossibility of reversing the digital ledger makes blockchain a manipulation-free technology (Ertemel, 2018).

Marketing efforts may not provide the necessary information for rational purchase leaving the customer with basic information which is insufficient to dictate a preferred choice and therefore turning into a cause of consumerism (Burskirk & Rothe, 1970). With the growth of e-commerce, consumers have increasingly more choices at their disposal, and their preference is impacted by word-of-mouth processes, including the reviews that can be found in e-commerce platforms and online stores. In addition to playing an important role in decision-making, reviews are also used as a source of information for a better understanding of the product or service (Jha & Shah, 2021). However, is very likely that not all reviews are trustworthy. In marketplaces such as Amazon, eBay or AliExpress, in which the same product is sold by multiple sellers, consumers tend to choose the one with a higher number of reviews or a higher rating, as it conveys the trust that the seller is credible (Ertemel, 2018). This happens because in a distance sale, where the identity of the individual or the company on the counterpart is unknown, it leads the consumer to question their legitimacy. In a marketplace sustained by the blockchain technology, the identity and legitimacy of each actor is validated at the network level, enhancing market trust, thus the technology can be used to provide a more transparent platforms for online transactions.

Smart Contracts are also a key aspect of blockchain and can be instrumental in providing greater consumer confidence. A smart contract is a set of digitally defined rules based on a protocol in which contract participants can automatically enforce these rules. After smart contracts are established the blockchain, once a transaction meets the contract conditions, its terms are automatically executed without third party involvement (Zhang & Ling, 2023). In Blockchain, contract automation is an essential functionality that allows to transform clauses of a given contract into code, using automation, that is, from the moment the previous conditions set by both parties are fulfilled, the contract is automatically self-executed (Stallone et al., 2021). The potential applications of smart contracts in online commerce are significant, and include warranty activation, price promotions activation, automated reverse logistics for returned products and financial transactions. For example, smart contracts can enhance payment processing in e-commerce. Once a buyer and a seller agree to certain terms of a sale, the smart contract is only executed, and the payment released when the buyer confirms the delivery of the product or the service that was previously agreed. This system helps in preventing fraudulent purchases and scams schemes.

In addition, blockchain technology also has the potential to address counterfeiting and pirating through digital authentication. For example, companies or manufacturers can create a digital certificate of authenticity for their products and associate that digital certificate within the ledger. Those products can also be verified and tracked throughout the entire supply chain, so even in cases where the product is not sold directly by the brand, the consumer can still confirm its origin and whether the product is genuine. And since registration on blockchain is permanent, consumers can also verify if the product has been tampered with over time. Even in cases of pre-owned products the consumer is capable to confirm the authenticity of the product by tracing back to its source (Chen et al., 2022).

SUPPLY CHAIN TRACEABILITY AND TRANSPARENCY

Consumers are becoming increasingly concerned about the traceability, of products since industrialized production and globalized long supply chains suffer from a confidence crisis, and have weak affiliated values (Baptista et al., 2022). The social and environmental responsibility that a company communicates has an increasing impact on consumer choice. Supply chain transparency provides consumers with a mechanism to verify the veracity of companies positioning in relation to ethical issues.

Supply chain transparency and traceability have been identified as an effective mechanism for companies to overcome consumers' skepticism of companies' social responsibility claims by improving consumer trust (Kraft et al., 2022). For example, if a company claims to have concerns about environmental sustainability by announcing that exclusively recurs to organic inputs and short supply chains, through supply chain transparency the consumer can potentially track the origins of the products, and verify if the company really acts in accordance with the declared stance, and is not simply greenwashing (Delmas & Burbano, 2011). Consumerism is about companies providing consumers with enough information so they can make decisions, and for this to happen, corporations need to become more transparent and provide consumers with the needed information so that consumers can make sound decisions (Uusitalo & Oksanen, 2004).

Supply chain traceability involves tracking and obtaining information on the origins, flow, state, and location of products in the supply chain (Zhang & Ling, 2023). Dominant supply chain systems are mostly based on centralized configurations, in which individual nodes are responsible for manipulating private databases, leading to information asymmetry among supply chain participants (Li et al., 2023). Information generated through the supply chain is recorded dispersedly in the private systems of each actor, resulting in the problem of "information silos" (Zhang & Ling, 2023). These closed systems lack transparency and are fragile to data manipulation and tampering since they usually involve a significant number of participants dispersed along the chain, that may conceal or misreport accurate information (Hassoun et al., 2023; Zhang & Ling, 2023). Legacy systems also make it difficult for supervisor and regulatory authorities, that are responsible to secure consumers' safety, to supervise product quality and compliance timely and accurately (Li et al., 2023).

Blockchain solutions with a data security system using smart contracts allow supply chain transparency and traceability, potentially impacting consumers' trust in product suppliers and affecting customers' purchase intentions (Hassoun et al., 2023; Isaja et al., 2023; Li et al., 2023). According to Zhang and Ling (2023), blockchain can achieve reliable and efficient supply chains because of three main characteristics: decentralization, traceability and transparency. Blockchain consists in a distributed ledger in which all nodes in the system hold the unique copy of the ledger and share equal status. As such, a decentralized blockchain will not be subject to node failures, being more resistant to malicious intentions. Blockchain information can be audited using timestamps, and examining the links between blocks, so blockchain facilitates traceability. Finally, all nodes in the system can consult the data recorded on the blockchain in real time, and database changes are highly visible. The hash entanglement between chain blocks and the consensus mechanisms make tampering with data particularly difficult, preventing forgery (Li et al., 2023).

Blockchain technologies are based on shared distributed databases, in which all members of the supply chain, including consumers, can access and track the complete history of delivery activities (Li et al., 2023), and smart contracts secure that the data is automatically transmitted from its source, without human interference, ensuring authenticity, integrity and immutability (Rowan, 2022; Isaja et al., 2023). Information leakage and tampering are avoided, with the immutability of records in the ledger, and the credibility of historical data in the supply chain can be guaranteed (Li et al., 2023). Besides supply chain operators, the system can be accessed by other interested stakeholders. For example, Tian (2016) proposed a model that combines radio-frequency identification (RFID) and blockchain technology for agri-food products that considers the suppliers, the government, and third-party organizations as nodes in the traceability system, and that allows actors to access authentic data of production, processing, warehousing and distribution (Zhang & Ling, 2023). Decentralization is a key feature of blockchain technology. Transactions are carried out by nodes through secure encryption provided by technology, thus eliminating the need for intermediary validation (Zarrin et al., 2021). Being decentralized, tamper-proof, and transparent, blockchain technology can address the problems of unreliable data and low tracking efficiency in traditional supply chain systems and provide better information to consumers (Zhang & Ling, 2023).

Blockchain technologies can also bring significant operational benefits, improving efficiency and productivity by providing predictive insights, that facilitate forecasting and supply chain management, helping real-time decisions, reducing waste and contamination, and controlling the efficient use of products and materials in the entire supply chain system (Hassoun et al., 2023; Rowan, 2022; Yontar, 2023). Gains in efficiency by using blockchain technology in supply chain management enable cost savings for companies that can be passed on to the consumer (Hidayati et al., 2023; Rejeb et al., 2023). For example, many suppliers of fresh agricultural products recur to cold chain systems to maintain the freshness of agricultural products. However, cold systems require significant investments in technology to control temperature, humidity, and light. Suppliers can adopt blockchain to better control cold chain systems throughout the supply chain ensuring the quality of fresh agricultural products in the delivery network, improving waste prevention activities and thereby reducing the cost of cold chain logistics (Li et al., 2023).

Ethical consumers appreciate sustainable business models that provide access to trustworthy information concerning product quality, and the economic, social, and environmental impacts of production, processing and distribution (Zhu et al., 2023). Blockchain can support the development of more sustainable business models that promote energy efficiency, improve the management of waste along the chain, and help consumers in the process of tracking sustainability values in materials and product history (Yontar,

2023). Blockchain can also foster cleaner production and improve carbon emissions by contributing to transportation management optimization (Rejeb et al., 2023; Yontar, 2023;). For example, blockchain can be applied in the context of short food supply chains, to optimize transportation, reducing the carbon footprint of these alternative models of supply (Baptista et al., 2022). Blockchain potential role in reverse logistics and recycling activities has also been explored in the literature, by authors such as Khadke et al. (2021), Gong et al. (2022) and Rejeb et al. (2023). These authors concluded that efficiency of recycling activities could be significantly improved with blockchain technology through enhanced waste flow monitoring, tracking and the integration of recycling chains, reducing the degree of unpredictability involved in reverse logistics, while contributing to customer satisfaction by facilitating the process of returning waste, damaged and undesired products, and materials.

In the broader context of the circular economy, blockchain is considered a critical enabler for accelerating transition by relieving some of the barriers that prevent the circular economy from being properly implemented, including information and trust barriers, and lack of collaboration among stakeholders, enhancing information and transparency and promoting innovation (Rejeb et al., 2023). As noted by Yontar (2023), supply chain-driven challenges such as product traceability, material flow optimization, and supplier collaboration are crucial in the adoption of the circular economy.

CONCLUSION

The consumerism movement was developed in response to power imbalances between companies and the consumers. Consumers seek a well-balanced markets, in which consumer empowerment is enhanced and vulnerabilities on the part of consumers are eliminated, such that it provides better and more functioning market environments for both companies and consumers. Consumerism although it represents a movement of empowerment of the consumer it is not incompatible with the marketing concept. On the contrary, it can be considered an opportunity for marketing. The causes of consumerism are generally attributed to a lack of information on consumers side, which disrupts their ability to make informed purchases and, in some cases, results in anti-consumption decisions and actions that hurt companies' interests.

Existing mechanisms to combat counterfeiting and pirating are mostly based on radio frequency identification (RFID) technology and on closed proprietary software and database systems. While current traceability and quality verification technologies are based on bioinformatics to trace and access the genetic authenticity of food products, such as DNA barcoding (Barcaccia et al., 2020; Thomé et al., 2021). Thus far, these solutions have not been effective, since they present several drawbacks, including the clonability of tags, risks of data tampering, asymmetry of information along the supply chain and insufficient validation procedures (Isaja et al., 2023), affecting consumers' trust in the system. This chapter explores the potential of blockchain technology in responding to critics of the consumerism movement, including the need for increased ethics in market transactions, the need to improve the security of e-commerce, and supply chain transparency.

In relation to ethical consumerism claims, it is argued that ethical concerns about products and organizations (energy consumption, environmental sustainability, labor issues, animal welfare, poverty, unsustainable resources use, social inequities) can be answered by blockchain, through increased market transparency, and by facilitating market models based on the sharing and circular economies. The efficiency of recycling activities can be significantly improved with blockchain technology through enhanced waste flow monitoring, tracking and the integration of recycling chains, reducing the degree of unpredictability involved in reverse logistics. Concerning the security of e-commerce models, blockchain contract automation and cryptography technologies can minorize the risks of fraud, theft of personal data and complex sale processes. Smart contracts, facilitate payment activities, dispute processes, warranty activation procedures, price promotions and reverse logistics for returned products. Finally, it is argued that blockchain technology can help to overcome some fragilities of the legacy supply chain system by facilitating regulatory supervision and by allowing cost savings that can be passed on to the consumer. Regulatory market supervision can be improved since blockchain information can be easily audited using timestamps and examining the links between blocks. Businesses' improved forecasting and better control of material flows allow cost savings that can be passed on to the consumer. Table 1 synthesizes the main arguments presented in this chapter.

Table 1. The contribution of blockchain to improve market equalization.

Consumer claims	Blockchain solution
Ethical consumerism	
Ethical concerns about products and organizations	Through blockchain companies can prove their sustainable positioning. Increased accountability from companies.
Difficulties in implementing the circular economy	Improved control of recycling, reusing, and remanufacturing cycles. Collaborative perspective brings empowerment to individuals involved in the circular economy.
Difficulties in implementing sharing economy market models	Increased trust about the origins of second-hand products traded on P2P platforms. Peer-to-peer direct connectivity.
Security of e-commerce transactions	
Risk of fraud and theft of personal data	Decentralized blockchain is not subject to node failures, being more resistant to malicious intentions. Smart contracts secure that the data is automatically transmitted from its source, without human interference. Each user is attributed a unique identification generated by the system and cryptography technologies are used to guarantee the security of all data.
Complex sale and post-sale processes	Smart contracts, facilitate payment, dispute processes, warranty activation procedures, price promotions and reverse logistics for returned products.
Need to improve supply chain transparency	
Information asymmetry among supply chain participants	Blockchain technologies can be based on shared distributed databases, in which all supply chain participants, including the consumer, can access and track the complete history of delivering activities.
Difficulties for regulatory entities to adequately supervise product quality and compliance	Blockchain information can be audited using timestamps and examining the links between blocks. Information tampering is avoided, with the immutability of records in the ledger.
Supply chain efficiency and productivity	Blockchain facilitates forecasting and real-time decisions, reducing waste and contamination, and controlling the efficient use of materials.

Source: Authors

This chapter identifies the potential that blockchain technology has to offer in improving the relationship between the company and the consumer and in responding to the consumer movement aims of equalized markets. The contribution of this study is twofold. First, this research offers a synthesis that can be influential for practice, while also serving to set the stage for future studies analyzing the contribution of blockchain technology to consumerism objectives. It is possible to identify potential applications that can help consumers to verify business ethics, improve transaction security, and increase supply chain trust. The immutability and transparency of blockchain technology create value for any legitimate activity. Paradoxically, decentralization as a main function of blockchain can be seen at this moment in time as the greatest barrier to acceptance by organizations, governments and the consumer. The fact that there is no controlling entity that serves as a guarantee of the system may raise doubts and fears about its use. Other barriers that affect blockchain adoption include the immaturity of blockchain technology, scalability problems, lack of knowledge and management support, and development costs (Rejeb et al., 2023). However, the experience of the COVID pandemic and the consequent supply chain disruptions presented a momentous opportunity to further explore this technology. On the other side, in an increasingly digitized, dynamic market that needs speed and efficiency, it is difficult to deny the usefulness that this technology will have for companies and the potential benefits for the consumer. In terms of limitations, the chapter offers a theoretical discussion. No empirical research was applied to evaluate the application of blockchain in specific markets and to measure consumers' satisfaction.

ACKNOWLEDGMENTS

The authors would like to express their gratitude to the Instituto Politécnico de Lisboa (IPL) for financing the research project BIGTECHCon (IPL/2022/BIGTECHCon_ESCS).

REFERENCES

Adamkiewicz, J., Kochańska, E., Adamkiewicz, I., & Łukasik, R. M. (2022). Greenwashing and sustainable fashion industry. *Current Opinion in Green and Sustainable Chemistry*, *38*, 1–8. doi:10.1016/j.cogsc.2022.100710

Althawadi, O., Fraedrich, J., & Farha, A. A. (2021). Understanding consumerism within Western and Muslim based societies: Twitter usage of Saudi and American consumers. *Journal for Global Business Advancement*, *14*(2), 192–215. doi:10.1504/JGBA.2021.115743

Antoni, G. D., & Faillo, M. (2022). Ethical consumerism and wage levels: Evidence from an experimental market. *Business Ethics, the Environment & Responsibility*, *31*(3), 875–887. doi:10.1111/beer.12447

Arouri, M., El Ghoul, S., & Gomes, M. (2021). Greenwashing and product market competition. *Finance Research Letters*, *42*(January), 101927. doi:10.1016/j.frl.2021.101927

Baptista, N., Alves, H., & Matos, N. (2022). Scoping Challenges and Opportunities Presented by COVID-19 for the Development of Sustainable Short Food Supply Chains. *Sustainability (Basel)*, *14*(21), 14475. doi:10.3390u142114475

Barcaccia, G., D'Agostino, V., Zotti, A., & Cozzi, B. (2020). Impact of the SARS-CoV-2 on the Italian agri-food sector: An analysis of the quarter of pandemic lockdown and clues for a socio-economic and territorial restart. *Sustainability (Basel), 12*(14), 5651. Advance online publication. doi:10.3390u12145651

Burskirk, R. H., & Rothe, J. T. (1970). Consumerism, patient empowerment and changing clinical work-patient awareness and treatment demands on the rise. *Duodecim, 127*(8), 777–783.[REMOVED HYPERLINK FIELD] PMID:21568105

Chen, R., Dai, H., Gao, Y., Fu, B., & Chen, J. (2022). Electronic degree certificate data protection and sharing method based on blockchain. *Computer Engineering, 48*(4), 50–60. doi:10.19678/j.issn.1000-3428.0061193

Cho, S., & Krasser, A. H. (2011). What makes us care? The impact of cultural values, individual factors, and attention to media content on motivation for ethical consumerism. *International Social Science Review, 86*(1/2).

Coffin, J., & Egan–Wyer, C. (2022). The ethical consumption cap and mean market morality. *Marketing Theory, 22*(1), 105–123. doi:10.1177/14705931211058772

Contemporary, A., & Filos, A. (2010). *an Assessment of Some Common Criticisms. 2*, 279–296.

DavidsonS.De FilippiP.PottsJ. (2016). *Economics of Blockchain*. SSRN. doi:10.2139/ssrn.2744751

Delmas, M. A., & Burbano, V. C. (2011). The drivers of greenwashing. *California Management Review, 54*(1), 64–87. doi:10.1525/cmr.2011.54.1.64

Dierksmeier, C., & Seele, P. (2018). Cryptocurrencies and Business Ethics. *Journal of Business Ethics, 152*(1), 1–14. [REMOVED HYPERLINK FIELD] doi:10.100710551-016-3298-0 PMID:30930508

Dierksmeier, C., & Seele, P. (2020). Blockchain and business ethics. *Business Ethics (Oxford, England), 29*(2), 348–359. doi:10.1111/beer.12259

Ertemel, A. V. (2018). Implications of Blockchain Technology on Marketing. *Journal of International Trade, Logistics and Law, 4*(2), 35–45. http://jital.org/index.php/jital/article/view/98

EU Blockchain Observatory and Forum. (2022). *Blockchain for Supply Chain Transparency*. 48.

Fernando, Y., & Saravannan, R. (2021). Blockchain Technology: Energy Efficiency and Ethical Compliance. *Journal of Governance and Integrity, 4*(2), 88–95. doi:10.15282/jgi.4.2.2021.5872

Gong, Y., Wang, Y., Frei, R., Wang, B., & Zhao, C. (2022). Blockchain application in circular marine plastic debris management. *Industrial Marketing Management, 102*(9), 164–176. doi:10.1016/j.indmarman.2022.01.010

Goodwin, N., Harris, J., Nelson, J., Roach, B., & Torras, M. (2020). Consumption and the Consumer Society. *Microeconomics in Context*, 188–216. doi:10.4324/9781315702414-19

Hassoun, A., Kamiloglu, S., Garcia-Garcia, G., Parra-López, C., Trollman, H., Jagtap, S., Aadil, R. M., & Esatbeyoglu, T. (2023). Implementation of relevant fourth industrial revolution innovations across the supply chain of fruits and vegetables: A short update on Traceability 4.0. *Food Chemistry, 409*. doi:10.1016/j.foodchem.2022.135303

Hemais, M. W., & dos Santos, R. B. F. (2021). Understanding the Brazilian consumerism movement from a decolonial perspective: The case of Proteste. *Journal of Macromarketing*, *41*(2), 315–331. doi:10.1177/0276146720960220

Hidayati, J., Vamelia, R., Hammami, J., & Endri, E. (2023). Transparent distribution system design of halal beef supply chain. *Uncertain Supply Chain Management*, *11*(1), 31–40. doi:10.5267/j.uscm.2022.12.003

Hutchinson, C. S. (2022). Potential abuses of dominance by big tech through their use of Big Data and AI. *Journal of Antitrust Enforcement*, *10*(3), 443–468. doi:10.1093/jaenfo/jnac004

Isaja, M., Nguyen, P., Goknil, A., Sen, S., Husom, E. J., Tverdal, S., Anand, A., Jiang, Y., Pedersen, K. J., Myrseth, P., Stang, J., Niavis, H., Pfeifhofer, S., & Lamplmair, P. (2023). A blockchain-based framework for trusted quality data sharing towards zero-defect manufacturing. *Computers in Industry*, *146*(January), 103853. doi:10.1016/j.compind.2023.103853

Jha, A. K., & Shah, S. (2021). Disconfirmation effect on online review credibility: An experimental analysis. *Decision Support Systems, 145*, 113519. / doi:10.1016/j.dss.2021.113519

Jones, E. (2019). Rethinking Greenwashing: Corporate Discourse, Unethical Practice, and the Unmet Potential of Ethical Consumerism. *Sociological Perspectives*, *62*(5), 728–754. doi:10.1177/0731121419849095

Khadke, S., Gupta, P., Rachakunta, S., Mahata, C., Dawn, S., Sharma, M., Verma, D., Pradhan, A., Krishna, A. M. S., Ramakrishna, S., Chakrabortty, S., Saianand, G., Sonar, P., Biring, S., Dash, J. K., & Dalapati, G. K. (2021). Efficient plastic recycling and remolding circular economy using the technology of trust–blockchain. *Sustainability (Basel)*, *13*(16), 1–15. doi:10.3390u13169142

Kim, W. (2022). Television and American consumerism. *Journal of Public Economics*, *208*, 1–17. doi:10.1016/j.jpubeco.2022.104609

Koos, S. (2021). Moralising markets, marketizing morality. The fair trade movement, product labeling and the mergence of ethical consumerism in europe. *Journal of Nonprofit & Public Sector Marketing*, *33*(2), 168–192. doi:10.1080/10495142.2020.1865235

Kotler, P. (1972). What consumerism means for marketers. *Harvard Business Review*, *50*(3), 48–57.

Kouhizadeh, M., Sarkis, J., & Zhu, Q. (2019). At the nexus of blockchain technology, the circular economy, and product deletion. *Applied Sciences*, *9*(8), 1712. Advance online publication. doi:10.3390/app9081712

Kraft, T., Valdés, L., & Zheng, Y. (2022). Consumer trust in social responsibility communications: The role of supply chain visibility. *Production and Operations Management*, *31*(11), 4113–4130. doi:10.1111/poms.13808

Kucuk, S. U. (2016). Consumerism in the digital age. *The Journal of Consumer Affairs*, *50*(3), 515–538. doi:10.1111/joca.12101

Lang, T., & Hines, C. (1993). *The new protectionism: Protecting the future against free trade*. Earthscan Ltd.

Lapointe, C., & Fishbane, L. (2019). The Blockchain Ethical Design Framework. *Innovations: Technology, Governance, Globalization*, *12*(3–4), 50–71. doi:10.1162/inov_a_00275

Le Grand, J., Roberts, J., & Chandra, G. (2021). Buying for good: Altruism, ethical consumerism and social policy. *Social Policy and Administration*, *55*(7), 1341–1355. doi:10.1111pol.12729

Lee, M. T., & Raschke, R. L. (2023). Stakeholder legitimacy in firm greening and financial performance: What about greenwashing temptations?. *Journal of Business Research, 155*. doi:10.1016/j.jbusres.2022.113393

Lemos, C., Ramos, R. F., Moro, S., & Oliveira, P. M. (2022). Stick or Twist—The Rise of Blockchain Applications in Marketing Management. *Sustainability*, *14*(7), 1–16. [REMOVED HYPERLINK FIELD] doi:10.3390u14074172 PMID:36090804

Li, J., Han, D., Wu, Z., Wang, J., Li, K. C., & Castiglione, A. (2023). A novel system for medical equipment supply chain traceability based on alliance chain and attribute and role access control. *Future Generation Computer Systems*, *142*, 195–211. doi:10.1016/j.future.2022.12.037

Li, Y., Tan, C., Ip, W. H., & Wu, C. H. (2023). Dynamic blockchain adoption for freshness-keeping in the fresh agricultural product supply chain. *Expert Systems with Applications*, *217*, 119494. Advance online publication. doi:10.1016/j.eswa.2022.119494

Lu, F. C., & Sinha, J. (2019). Dichotomous Thinking and Ethical Consumerism: Overcoming the Negative Effects of Self-Interest Bias through Third-Person Narrative Persuasion. *Journal of Advertising*, *48*(3), 271–283. doi:10.1080/00913367.2019.1597788

Nakamoto, S. (2008). *Bitcoin: A Peer-to-Peer Electronic Cash System*. Bitcoin. https://bitcoin.org/bitcoin.pdf

Nygaard, A., & Silkoset, R. (2022). Sustainable development and greenwashing: How blockchain technology information can empower green consumers. *Business Strategy and the Environment*, (December), 1–13. doi:10.1002/bse.3338

Rejeb, A., Appolloni, A., Rejeb, K., Treiblmaier, H., Iranmanesh, M., & Keogh, J. G. (2023). The role of blockchain technology in the transition toward the circular economy: Findings from a systematic literature review. *Resources, Conservation and Recycling Advances, 17*, 200126. doi:10.1016/j.rcradv.2022.200126

Ronaghi, M. H., & Mosakhani, M. (2022). The effects of blockchain technology adoption on business ethics and social sustainability: Evidence from the Middle East. *Environment, Development and Sustainability*, *24*(5), 6834–6859. [REMOVED HYPERLINK FIELD] doi:10.100710668-021-01729-x PMID:34393620

Rowan, N. J. (2022, May). The role of digital technologies in supporting and improving fishery and aquaculture across the supply chain – Quo Vadis? *Aquaculture and Fisheries*, *8*(4), 365–374. doi:10.1016/j.aaf.2022.06.003

Schahczenski, J., & Schahczenski, C. (2020). Blockchain and the Resurrection of Consumer Sovereignty in a Sustainable Food Economy. *Journal of Agriculture, Food Systems, and Community Development*, *9*(3), 1–6. doi:10.5304/jafscd.2020.093.028

Schmuck, D., Matthes, J., & Naderer, B. (2018). Misleading Consumers with Green Advertising? An Affect–Reason–Involvement Account of Greenwashing Effects in Environmental Advertising. *Journal of Advertising*, *47*(2), 127–145. doi:10.1080/00913367.2018.1452652

Shanor, A., & Light, S. E. (2022). Greenwashing and the First Amendment. *Columbia Law Review*, *122*(7), 2033–2118.

Sharif, M. M., & Ghodoosi, F. (2022). The Ethics of Blockchain in Organizations. *Journal of Business Ethics*, *178*(4), 1009–1025. [REMOVED HYPERLINK FIELD] doi:10.100710551-022-05058-5 PMID:35125568

Stallone, V., Wetzels, M., & Klaas, M. (2021). Applications of blockchain technology in marketing—A systematic review of marketing technology companies. *Blockchain: Research and Applications*, *2*(3), 100023. Advance online publication. doi:10.1016/j.bcra.2021.100023

Suzuki, J., Okubo, T., Oki, H., & Fukui, T. (2019). *System for Motivating Ethical Consumption Behavior Using Dongle Interface Application*. 162–169. doi:10.3233/AISE190038

Tan, T. M., Makkonen, H., Kaur, P., & Salo, J. (2022). How do ethical consumers utilize sharing economy platforms as part of their sustainable resale behavior? The role of consumers' green consumption values. *Technological Forecasting and Social Change, 176*. doi:10.1016/j.techfore.2021.121432

Tham, A., & Sigala, M. (2020). Road block(chain): Bit(coin)s for tourism sustainable development goals? *Journal of Hospitality and Tourism Technology*, *11*(1), 203–222. doi:10.1108/JHTT-05-2019-0069

Thomé, K. M., Cappellesso, G., Ramos, E. L. A., & Duarte, S. C. de L. (2021). Food Supply Chains and Short Food Supply Chains: Coexistence conceptual framework. *Journal of Cleaner Production*, *278*, 123207. doi:10.1016/j.jclepro.2020.123207

Tian, F. (2016). An agri-food supply chain traceability system for China based on RFID & blockchain technology. *2016 13th International Conference on Service Systems and Service Management (ICSSSM)*, 1–6. 10.1109/ICSSSM.2016.7538424

Uusitalo, O., & Oksanen, R. (2004). Ethical consumerism: A view from Finland. *International Journal of Consumer Studies*, *28*(3), 214–221. doi:10.1111/j.1470-6431.2003.00339.x

Yontar, E. (2023). Critical success factor analysis of blockchain technology in agri-food supply chain management: A circular economy perspective. *Journal of Environmental Management, 330*(October 2022), 117173. doi:10.1016/j.jenvman.2022.117173

Zarrin, J., Phang, H. W., Saheer, L. B., & Zarrin, B. (2021). Blockchain for decentralization of internet: Prospects, trends, and challenges. *Cluster Computing*, *24*(4), 2841–2866. [REMOVED HYPERLINK FIELD] doi:10.100710586-021-03301-8 PMID:34025209

Zhang, X., & Ling, L. (2023). A Review of blockchain solutions in supply chain traceability. *Tsinghua Science and Technology*, *28*(3), 500–510. doi:10.26599/TST.2022.9010030

Zhu, S., Li, J., Wang, S., Xia, Y., & Wang, Y. (2023). The role of blockchain technology in the dual-channel supply chain dominated by a brand owner. *International Journal of Production Economics*, *258*(January), 108791. doi:10.1016/j.ijpe.2023.108791

ADDITIONAL READING

Carrington, M. J., Neville, B. A., & Whitwell, G. J. (2014). Lost in translation: Exploring the ethical consumer intention-behavior gap. *Journal of Business Research*, *67*(1), 2759–2767. doi:10.1016/j.jbusres.2012.09.022

Carrington, M. J., Zwick, D., & Neville, B. (2016). The ideology of the ethical consumption gap. *Marketing Theory*, *16*(1), 21–38. doi:10.1177/1470593115595674

Hobson, K. (2002). Competing discourses of sustainable consumption: Does the "rationalisation of lifestyles" make sense? *Environmental Politics*, *11*(2), 95–120. doi:10.1080/714000601

Holt, D. B. (2012). Constructing Sustainable Consumption: From Ethical Values to the Cultural Transformation of Unsustainable Markets. *The Annals of the American Academy of Political and Social Science*, *644*(1), 236–255. doi:10.1177/0002716212453260

Sesini, G., Castiglioni, C., & Lozza, E. (2020). New trends and patterns in sustainable consumption: A systematic review and research agenda. *Sustainability (Basel)*, *12*(15), 5935. doi:10.3390u12155935

Staniškis, J. K. (2012). Sustainable consumption and production: How to make it possible. *Clean Technologies and Environmental Policy*, *14*(6), 1015–1022. doi:10.100710098-012-0535-9

Trentmann, F. (2004). Beyond consumerism: New historical perspectives on consumption. *Journal of Contemporary History*, *39*(3), 373–401. doi:10.1177/0022009404044446

KEY TERMS AND DEFINITIONS

Blockchain: A public, immutable and permanent ledger, which works as database in a decentralized network, using cryptographic codes.

Circular Economy: An economic model based on recycling, reusing, and remanufacturing, as a means of achieving sustainability objectives.

Consumerism: The pro-consumer movement, meaning a social movement focused on consumers' interests, rights, and welfare.

Ethical Consumerism: Consumers' decision to consume products or services selectively based on personal and moral ethical beliefs.

Market Equalization: A fair and well-functioning market structure based on the equalization of market power between companies and the consumer.

Sharing Economy: An economic model in which assets or services are shared between consumers in a peer-to-peer system.

Smart Contracts: A set of digitally defined rules based on protocols in which participants can decide to automatically enforce these rules.

Compilation of References

Abbas, A., Fatima, A., Arrona-Palacios, A., Haruna, H., & Hosseini, S. (2021). Research ethics dilemma in higher education: Impact of internet access, ethical controls, and teaching factors on student plagiarism. *Education and Information Technologies*, *26*(5), 6109–6121. doi:10.100710639-021-10595-z

Abolghasemi, M., Tarr, G., & Bergmeir, C. (2022). Machine learning applications in hierarchical time series forecasting: Investigating the impact of promotions. *International Journal of Forecasting*. Advance online publication. doi:10.1016/j.ijforecast.2022.07.004

Acquisti, A., Taylor, C., & Wagman, L. (2016). The economics of privacy. *Journal of Economic Literature*, *54*(2), 442–492. doi:10.1257/jel.54.2.442

Adadi, A., & Berrada, M. (2018). Peeking Inside the Black-Box: A Survey on Explainable Artificial Intelligence (XAI). *IEEE Access : Practical Innovations, Open Solutions*, *6*, 52138–52160. doi:10.1109/ACCESS.2018.2870052

Adamkiewicz, J., Kochańska, E., Adamkiewicz, I., & Łukasik, R. M. (2022). Greenwashing and sustainable fashion industry. *Current Opinion in Green and Sustainable Chemistry*, *38*, 1–8. doi:10.1016/j.cogsc.2022.100710

Adamopoulou, E., & Moussiades, L. (2020). Chatbots: History, technology, and applications. *Machine Learning with Applications*, *2*, 100006. doi:10.1016/j.mlwa.2020.100006

Adetunji, A. B., Akande, O. N., Ajala, F. A., Oyewo, O., Akande, Y. F., & Oluwadara, G. (2022). House Price Prediction using Random Forest Machine Learning Technique. *Procedia Computer Science*, *199*, 806–813. doi:10.1016/j.procs.2022.01.100

Aftab, M. O., Ahmad, U., Khalid, S., Saud, A., Hassan, A., & Farooq, M. S. (2021). Sentiment analysis of customer for ecommerce by applying AI. *4th International Conference on Innovative Computing, ICIC 2021*. 10.1109/ICIC53490.2021.9693026

Ahn, S. J., Kim, J., & Kim, J. (2022). The bifold triadic relationships framework: A theoretical primer for advertising research in the metaverse. *Journal of Advertising*, *51*(5), 592–607. doi:10.1080/00913367.2022.2111729

Aïmeur, E., Lawani, O., & Dalkir, K. (2016). When changing the look of privacy policies affects user trust: An experimental study. *Computers in Human Behavior*, *58*, 368–379. doi:10.1016/j.chb.2015.11.014

Al Mansoori, M. S., & Ahmad, S. Z. (2021). Adapting to the "new normal" post-pandemic consumer behavior: The case of Rafeeg's strategy of service marketing. *Emerald Emerging Markets Case Studies*, *11*(3), 1–17. doi:10.1108/EEMCS-08-2020-0311

Al Omar, A., Jamil, A. K., Khandakar, A., Uzzal, A. R., Bosri, R., Mansoor, N., & Rahman, M. S. (2021). A transparent and privacy-preserving healthcare platform with novel smart contract for smart cities. *IEEE Access : Practical Innovations, Open Solutions*, *9*, 90738–90749. doi:10.1109/ACCESS.2021.3089601

Alabdulrahman, R., & Viktor, H. (2021). Catering for unique tastes: Targeting grey-sheep users recommender systems through one-class machine learning. *Expert Systems with Applications*, *166*, 114061. doi:10.1016/j.eswa.2020.114061

Alafeef, M. A. M. I. (2015). The impact of marketing information system to increase the marketing efficiency of stores in KSA (case study-Al-baha and Beljarshy city). *British Journal of Marketing Studies*, *3*(5), 22–33.

Alalwan, A. A., Dwivedi, Y. K., & Rana, N. P. (2017). Factors influencing adoption of mobile banking by Jordanian bank customers: Extending UTAUT2 with trust. *International Journal of Information Management*, *37*(3), 99–110. doi:10.1016/j.ijinfomgt.2017.01.002

Alalwan, A. A., Rana, N. P., Dwivedi, Y. K., & Algharabat, R. (2017). Social media in marketing: A review and analysis of the existing literature. *Telematics and Informatics*, *34*(7), 1177–1190. doi:10.1016/j.tele.2017.05.008

Al-Azani, S., & El-Alfy, E. M. (2020). Enhanced video analytics for sentiment analysis based on fusing textual, auditory and visual information. *IEEE Access : Practical Innovations, Open Solutions*, *8*, 136843–136857. doi:10.1109/ACCESS.2020.3011977

Albayati, H., Kim, S. K., & Rho, J. J. (2020). Accepting financial transactions using blockchain technology and cryptocurrency: A customer perspective approach. *Technology in Society*, *62*, 101320. doi:10.1016/j.techsoc.2020.101320

Alboqami, H. (2023). Trust me, I'm an influencer! - Causal recipes for customer trust in artificial intelligence influencers in the retail industry. *Journal of Retailing and Consumer Services*, *72*, 103242. doi:10.1016/j.jretconser.2022.103242

Alcañiz, M., Bigne, E., & Guixeres, J. (2019). Virtual reality in marketing: A framework, review and research agenda. *Frontiers in Psychology*, *10*, 1530. [REMOVED HYPERLINK FIELD] doi:10.3389/fpsyg.2019.01530 PMID:31333548

Alfaro, L., Rivera, C., Luna-Urquizo, J., Zuniga, J. C., Portocarrero, A., & Raposo, A. B. (2019). Immersive technologies in marketing: State of the art and a software architecture proposal. *International Journal of Advanced Computer Science and Applications*, *10*(10), 482–490. doi:10.14569/IJACSA.2019.0101064

Alghadir, A. H., Beg, R. I., Shaphe, M. A., & Ahmad, F. (2021). Intermanual Transfer Effects on Performance Gain Following Dominant Hand Training in Community-Dwelling Healthy Adults: A Preliminary Study. *Journal of Multidisciplinary Healthcare*, *14*, 1007–1016. Advance online publication. doi:10.2147/JMDH.S298991 PMID:33958874

Ali, A., & Xia, C. (2022). Current and prospective impacts of digital marketing on the small agricultural stakeholders in the developing countries. Application of machine learning in agriculture, 91-112. doi:10.1016/B978-0-323-90550-3.00012-6

Aljedaani, W., Saad, E., Rustam, F., de la Torre Díez, I., & Ashraf, I. (2022). Role of artificial intelligence for analysis of COVID-19 vaccination-related tweets: Opportunities, challenges, and future trends. *Mathematics*, *10*(17), 3199. doi:10.3390/math10173199

Alkhalil, Z., Hewage, C., Nawaf, L., & Khan, I. (2021). Phishing attacks: A recent comprehensive study and a new anatomy. *Frontiers of Computer Science*, *3*, 563060. doi:10.3389/fcomp.2021.563060

Allal-Chérif, O., Simón-Moya, V., & Ballester, A. C. C. (2021). Intelligent purchasing: How artificial intelligence can redefine the purchasing function. *Journal of Business Research*, *124*, 69–76. doi:10.1016/j.jbusres.2020.11.050

Alloghani, M., Alani, M. M., Al-Jumeily, D., Baker, T., Mustafina, J., Hussain, A., & Aljaaf, A. J. (2019). A systematic review on the status and progress of homomorphic encryption technologies. *Journal of Information Security and Applications*, *48*, 102362. doi:10.1016/j.jisa.2019.102362

Almabdy, S. (2018). Comparative analysis of relational and graph databases for social networks. *1st International Conference on Computer Applications and Information Security, ICCAIS 2018.* 10.1109/CAIS.2018.8441982

AlShamsi, M., Al-Emran, M., & Shaalan, K. (2022). A systematic review on blockchain adoption. *Applied Sciences (Basel, Switzerland)*, *12*(9), 4245. doi:10.3390/app12094245

Alshurideh, D. M. (2019). Do electronic loyalty programs still drive customer choice and repeat purchase behaviour? *International Journal of Electronic Customer Relationship Management*, *12*(1), 40–57. doi:10.1504/IJECRM.2019.098980

Alshurideh, M., Kurdi, B. H. A., Masa'deh, R., Alzoubi, H. M., & Salloum, S. (2023). *The Effect of Information Technology on Business and Marketing Intelligence Systems*. Springer International Publishing. doi:10.1007/978-3-031-12382-5

Alsukaini, A. K. M., Sumra, K., Khan, R., & Awan, T. M. (2023). New trends in digital marketing emergence during pandemic times. *International Journal of Innovation Science*, *15*(1), 167–185. doi:10.1108/IJIS-08-2021-0139

Alt, R., & Puschmann, T. (2016). Bankmodell. In Digitalisierung der Finanzindustrie (pp. 55-117). Springer Gabler.

Althawadi, O., Fraedrich, J., & Farha, A. A. (2021). Understanding consumerism within Western and Muslim based societies: Twitter usage of Saudi and American consumers. *Journal for Global Business Advancement*, *14*(2), 192–215. doi:10.1504/JGBA.2021.115743

Altman, I. (1975). *The environment and social behavior: privacy, personal space, territory, and crowding*. Brooks/Cole Publishing Company.

Altukhova, E. V., Nikeryasova, V. V., Ivanova, Y. Y., Markov, M. A., & Romanchenko, O. V. (2022). *Transformation of educational space in the system of digitalization of the economy*. doi:10.1007/978-3-030-94245-8_22

Alvim, D., & Alturas, B. (2021). Impact on organisations of changes in information systems: The case of two Lisbon universities. *International Journal of Information and Operations Management Education*, *7*(2), 137. doi:10.1504/IJIOME.2021.119105

Alzaqebah, M., Jawarneh, S., Mohammad, R. M. A., Alsmadi, M. K., & Almarashdeh, I. (2021). Improved multi-verse optimizer feature selection technique with application to phishing, spam, and denial of service attacks. *International Journal of Communication Networks and Information Security*, *13*(1), 76–81.

Ambler, T., Kokkinaki, F., & Puntoni, S. (2004). Assessing Marketing Performance: Reasons for Metrics Selection. *Journal of Marketing Management*, *20*(3–4), 475–498. doi:10.1362/026725704323080506

Ameen, N., Tarhini, A., Reppel, A., & Anand, A. (2021). Customer experiences in the age of artificial intelligence. *Computers in Human Behavior*, *114*, 106548. Advance online publication. doi:10.1016/j.chb.2020.106548 PMID:32905175

Andjelic, A. (2021). *The Business of Aspiration: How Social, Cultural, and Environmental Capital Changes Brands*. Routledge.

Anica-Popa, I., Anica-Popa, L., Rădulescu, C., & Vrîncianu, M. (2021). The integration of artificial intelligence in retail: Benefits, challenges and a dedicated conceptual framework. *Amfiteatru Economic*, *23*(56), 120–136. doi:10.24818/EA/2021/56/120

An, S., Choi, Y., & Lee, C.-K. (2021). Virtual travel experience and destination marketing: Effects of sense and information quality on flow and visit intention. *Journal of Destination Marketing & Management*, *19*, 19. doi:10.1016/j.jdmm.2020.100492

Antoni, G. D., & Faillo, M. (2022). Ethical consumerism and wage levels: Evidence from an experimental market. *Business Ethics, the Environment & Responsibility*, *31*(3), 875–887. doi:10.1111/beer.12447

Arasu, B. S., Seelan, B. J. B., & Thamaraiselvan, N. (2020). A machine learning-based approach to enhancing social media marketing. *Computers & Electrical Engineering*, *86*, 106723. doi:10.1016/j.compeleceng.2020.106723

Arellano, P. R., Aguilar, F. D., Quintana Bornot, A., & Carrera, L. A. (2022). *Contexts of digital tools in marketing management in MSMEs for their permanence in the market*. doi:10.1007/978-3-031-11438-0_42

Arias-Pérez, J., & Vélez-Jaramillo, J. (2022). Ignoring the three-way interaction of digital orientation, Not-invented-here syndrome and employee's artificial intelligence awareness in digital innovation performance: A recipe for failure. *Technological Forecasting and Social Change*, *174*, 121305. doi:10.1016/j.techfore.2021.121305

Arnold, W. E. IV. (2012). Tax Enforcement In Virtual Worlds-Virtually Impossible. *Syracuse J. Int'l L. & Com.*, *40*, 187.

Arokiaraj, D., Ganeshkumar, C., & Paul, P. V. (2020). Innovative management system for environmental sustainability practices among Indian auto-component manufacturers. *International Journal of Business Innovation and Research*, *23*(2), 168–182. doi:10.1504/IJBIR.2020.110095

Arora, A., Bansal, S., Kandpal, C., Aswani, R., & Dwivedi, Y. (2019). Measuring social media influencer index-insights from Facebook, Twitter and Instagram. *Journal of Retailing and Consumer Services*, *49*, 86–101. doi:10.1016/j.jretconser.2019.03.012

Arora, P., Gupta, H., & Singh, A. (2022). Forecasting resale value of the car: Evaluating the proficiency under the impact of machine learning model. *Materials Today: Proceedings*, *69*, 441–445. doi:10.1016/j.matpr.2022.09.074

Arouri, M., El Ghoul, S., & Gomes, M. (2021). Greenwashing and product market competition. *Finance Research Letters*, *42*(January), 101927. doi:10.1016/j.frl.2021.101927

Arun Kumar, B.R. (2021). AI-Based Digital Marketing Strategies— A Review. *Lecture Notes in Networks and Systems, 173*, 957-969.

Aswani, R., Kar, A. K., & Vigneswara Ilavarasan, P. (2018). Detection of spammers in twitter marketing: A hybrid approach using social media analytics and bio inspired computing. *Information Systems Frontiers*, *20*(3), 515–530. doi:10.100710796-017-9805-8

Atiq, M., Abid, G., Anwar, A., & Ijaz, M. F. (2022). Influencer marketing on Instagram: A sequential mediation model of storytelling content and audience engagement via relatability and Trust. *Information (Basel)*, *13*(7), 345. doi:10.3390/info13070345

Au, A. (2022). Cryptocurrencies and the promise of individual economic sovereignty in an age of digitalization: A critical appraisal. *The Sociological Review*. doi:10.1177/00380261221127858

Auer, R., & Claessens, S. (2018, Sept.). Regulating cryptocurrencies: Assessing market reactions. *BIS Quarterly Review*.

Avital, M., King, J. L., Beck, R., Rossi, M., & Teigland, R. (2016). Jumping on the Blockchain Bandwagon: Lessons of the Past and Outlook to the Future. *Proceedings of the 37thInternational Conference on Information Systems*, 1-6.

Awad, N. F., & Krishnan, M. S. (2006). The personalization privacy paradox: An empirical evaluation of information transparency and the willingness to be profiled online for personalization. *Management Information Systems Quarterly*, *30*(1), 13–28. doi:10.2307/25148715

Bae, S., Jung, T. H., Moorhouse, N., Suh, M., & Kwon, O. (2020). The influence of mixed reality on satisfaction and brand loyalty in cultural heritage attractions: A brand equity perspective. *Sustainability (Basel)*, *12*(7), 2956. doi:10.3390u12072956

Bai, X., Abasi, R., Edizel, B., & Mantrach, A. (2019). Position-aware deep character-level CTR prediction for sponsored search. *IEEE Transactions on Knowledge and Data Engineering*, *33*(4), 1722–1736. doi:10.1109/TKDE.2019.2941881

Balaji, T. K., Annavarapu, C. S. R., & Bablani, A. (2021). Machine learning algorithms for social media analysis: A survey. *Computer Science Review*, *40*, 100395. doi:10.1016/j.cosrev.2021.100395

Balakhonskaya, L. V., Balakhonsky, V. V., & Gustokashina, A. A. (2022, April). "Newstalgia" as Digital Marketing Communication Strategy. In 2022 Communication Strategies in Digital Society Seminar (ComSDS) (pp. 134-141). IEEE. doi:10.1109/ComSDS55328.2022.9769130

Ballestar, M. T., Grau-Carles, P., & Sainz, J. (2019). Predicting customer quality in e-commerce social networks: A machine learning approach. *Review of Managerial Science*, *13*(3), 589–603. doi:10.100711846-018-0316-x

Ball, M. (2022). *The Metaverse and How It Will Revolutionize Everything*. Liveright Publishing, Co. W.W. Norton & Company.

Baltes, L. P. (2015). Content marketing - the fundamental tool of digital marketing. *Bulletin of the Transilvania University of Brasov. Series V, Economic Sciences*, *8*(2), 111–118.

Bansal, R., Malyadri, P., Singh, A., & Pervez, A. (2021). Blockchain technology and applications for digital marketing. Blockchain technology and applications for digital marketing. doi:10.4018/978-1-7998-8081-3

Bansal, G., & Gefen, D. (2010). The impact of personal dispositions on information sensitivity, privacy concern and trust in disclosing health information online. *Decision Support Systems*, *49*(2), 138–150. doi:10.1016/j.dss.2010.01.010

Baptista, N., Alves, H., & Matos, N. (2022). Scoping Challenges and Opportunities Presented by COVID-19 for the Development of Sustainable Short Food Supply Chains. *Sustainability (Basel)*, *14*(21), 14475. doi:10.3390u142114475

Barcaccia, G., D'Agostino, V., Zotti, A., & Cozzi, B. (2020). Impact of the SARS-CoV-2 on the Italian agri-food sector: An analysis of the quarter of pandemic lockdown and clues for a socio-economic and territorial restart. *Sustainability (Basel)*, *12*(14), 5651. Advance online publication. doi:10.3390u12145651

Barr, A., Feigenbaum, E. A., & Cohen, P. R. (1981). *The Handbook of Artificial Intelligence*. HeurisTech Press.

Barrera, K. G., & Shah, D. (2023). Marketing in the Metaverse: Conceptual understanding, framework, and research agenda. *Journal of Business Research*, *155*, 113420. doi:10.1016/j.jbusres.2022.113420

Baruh, L., Secinti, E., & Cemalcilar, Z. (2017). Online privacy concerns and privacy management: A meta-analytical review. *Journal of Communication*, *67*(1), 26–53. doi:10.1111/jcom.12276

Batat, W. (2019). *The new luxury experience: creating the ultimate customer experience*. Springer., doi:10.1007/978-3-030-01671-5

Bauer, J., & Nanopoulos, A. (2014). Recommender systems based on quantitative implicit customer feedback. *Decision Support Systems*, *68*, 77–88. doi:10.1016/j.dss.2014.09.005

Bekele, M. K., & Champion, E. (2019). Redefining mixed reality: User-reality-virtuality and virtual heritage perspectives. In *24th Annual Conference of the Association for Computer-Aided Architectural Design Research in Asia (CAADRIA 2019)* (pp. 675-68). CuminCAD. 10.52842/conf.caadria.2019.2.675

Belk, R., Humayun, M., & Brouard, M. (2022). Money, possessions, and ownership in the Metaverse: NFTs, cryptocurrencies, Web3 and Wild Markets. *Journal of Business Research*, *153*, 198–205. doi:10.1016/j.jbusres.2022.08.031

Bellman, R. E. (1978). An introduction to artificial intelligence: Can computers think? Boyd & Fraser Pub.

Ben Schafer, J., Frankowski, D., Herlocker, J., & Sen, S. (2007). Collaborative filtering recommender systems. Lecture Notes in Computer Science, 4321, 291–324. doi:10.1007/978-3-540-72079-9_9

Ben, D. (2016). *5 authentication methods put passwords to shame*. The Next Web. https://thenextweb.com/insider/2016/03/31/5-technologies-will-is-world-authentication-head

Benaich, N., & Hogart, I. (2022). *State of AI Report 2022*. https://www.stateof.ai/

Berg, C., Davidson, S., & Potts, J. (2019). Blockchain technology as economic infrastructure: Revisiting the electronic markets hypothesis. *Frontiers in Blockchain*, *2*, 22. doi:10.3389/fbloc.2019.00022

Bhargava, N., Palvadi, S. K., Kumar, A., & Rathore, P. S. (2020). An economical methodology to rhetorical identifications in cloud victimization virtual machine snapshots. Cyber warfare and terrorism: Concepts, methodologies, tools, and applications, 395-409. doi:10.4018/978-1-7998-2466-4.ch025

Bhattacharya, S., Sharma, R. P., & Gupta, A. (2023). Does e-retailer's country of origin influence consumer privacy, trust and purchase intention? *Journal of Consumer Marketing*, *40*(2), 248–259. doi:10.1108/JCM-04-2021-4611

Bhowmick, A. K., & Mitra, B. (2019). Listen to me, my neighbors or my friend? Role of complementary modalities for predicting business popularity in location based social networks. *Computer Communications*, *135*, 53–70. doi:10.1016/j.comcom.2019.01.004

Bingley, W. J., Curtis, C., Lockey, S., Bialkowski, A., Gillespie, N., Haslam, S. A., Ko, R. K. L., Steffens, N., Wiles, J., & Worthy, P. (2023). Where is the human in human-centered AI? Insights from developer priorities and user experiences. *Computers in Human Behavior*, *141*, 107617. doi:10.1016/j.chb.2022.107617

Bishop, T., & Rowley, J. (2013). Digital marketing in independent libraries in the United Kingdom. *Journal of Librarianship and Information Science*, *45*(4), 323–334. doi:10.1177/0961000612453473

Biswas, B., & Sanyal, M. K. (2019). Soft intelligence approaches for selecting products in online market. *Proceedings of the 9th International Conference On Cloud Computing, Data Science and Engineering, Confluence 2019*, 432-437. 10.1109/CONFLUENCE.2019.8776921

Blankenburg, M., Horn, C., & Krüger, J. (2015). Detection of Counterfeit by the Usage of Product Inherent Features. *Procedia CIRP*, *26*, 430–435. doi:10.1016/j.procir.2014.07.062

Blattberg, R. C., & Deighton, J. (1991). Interactive marketing: Exploiting the age of addressability. *Sloan Management Review*, *33*(1), 5–15.

Bleier, A., Goldfarb, A., & Tucker, C. (2020). Consumer privacy and the future of data-based innovation and marketing. *International Journal of Research in Marketing*, *37*(3), 466–480. doi:10.1016/j.ijresmar.2020.03.006

Blut, M., Heirati, N., & Schoefer, K. (2020). The dark side of customer participation: When customer participation in service co-development leads to role stress. *Journal of Service Research*, *23*(2), 156–173. doi:10.1177/1094670519894643

Boboc, R. G., Gîrbacia, F., & Butilă, E. V. (2020). The application of augmented reality in the automotive industry: A systematic literature review. *Applied Sciences (Basel, Switzerland)*, *10*(12), 4259. doi:10.3390/app10124259

Bochkarev, K., & Smirnov, E. (2019). Detecting advertising on building façades with computer vision. *Procedia Computer Science*, *156*, 338–346. doi:10.1016/j.procs.2019.08.210

Boddu, R. S. K., Santoki, A. A., Khurana, S., Koli, P., Rai, R., & Agrawal, A. (2022). An analysis to understand the role of machine learning, robotics and artificial intelligence in digital marketing. *Materials Today: Proceedings*, *56*, 2288–2292. doi:10.1016/j.matpr.2021.11.637

Boerman, S. C., & Smit, E. G. (2022). Advertising and privacy: An overview of past research and a research agenda. International Journal of Advertising, 1–9. doi:10.1080/02650487.2022.2122251

Bolton, R. N., McColl-Kennedy, J. R., Cheung, L., Gallan, A., Orsingher, C., Witell, L., & Zaki, M. (2018). Customer experience challenges: Bringing together digital, physical and social realms. *Journal of Service Management*, *29*(5), 776–808. doi:10.1108/JOSM-04-2018-0113

Borges, A. F. S., Laurindo, F. J. B., Spínola, M. M., Gonçalves, R. F., & Mattos, C. A. (2021). The strategic use of artificial intelligence in the digital era: Systematic literature review and future research directions. *International Journal of Information Management*, *57*, 102225. doi:10.1016/j.ijinfomgt.2020.102225

Borsci, S., Lawson, G., & Broome, S. (2015). Empirical evidence, evaluation criteria and challenges for the effectiveness of virtual and mixed reality tools for training operators of car service maintenance. *Computers in Industry*, *7*, 17–26. doi:10.1016/j.compind.2014.12.002

Boujrad, M., & lamlili, Y. E. M. N. (2021). A New Artificial Intelligence-Based Strategy for Digital Marketing Reinforcement. In *Innovations in Smart Cities Applications Volume 4: The Proceedings of the 5th International Conference on Smart City Application* (pp. 689-699). Springer International Publishing.

Bourlakis, M., Papagiannidis, S., & Li, F. (2009). Retail spatial evolution: Paving the way from traditional to metaverse retailing. *Electronic Commerce Research*, *9*(1), 135–148. doi:10.100710660-009-9030-8

Bozhuk, S. G., & Krasnov, A. S. (2017). Methodics of research of consumers psychographic characteristics in the internet. *Proceedings of the 2017 International Conference "Quality Management, Transport and Information Security, Information Technologies", IT and QM and IS 2017*, 166-172. 10.1109/ITMQIS.2017.8085790

Bradlow, E. T., Gangwar, M., Kopalle, P., & Voleti, S. (2017). The role of Big Data and predictive analytics in retailing. *Journal of Retailing*, *93*(1), 79–95. doi:10.1016/j.jretai.2016.12.004

Brandeis, L., & Warren, S. (1890). The right to privacy. *Harvard Law Review*, *4*(5), 193–220. doi:10.2307/1321160

Braun, V., & Clarke, V. (2006). Using thematic analysis in psychology Virginia. *Qualitative Research in Psychology*, *2*(3), 77–101. doi:10.1191/1478088706qp063oa

Bria, F. (2013). *Social media and their impact on organisations: Building Firm Celebrity and organisational legitimacy through social media*. Imperial College London. doi:10.25560/24944

Brown, D., & Hayes, N. (2008). *Influencer marketing*. Routledge. doi:10.4324/9780080557700

Bruce, N. I., Murthi, B. P. S., & Rao, R. C. (2017). A Dynamic Model for Digital Advertising: The Effects of Creative Format, Message Content, and Targeting on Engagement. *JMR, Journal of Marketing Research*, *54*(2), 202–218. doi:10.1509/jmr.14.0117

Buchanan, B. G. (2005). A (very) brief history of artificial intelligence. *AI Magazine*, *26*(4), 53–53.

Buchholz, K. (2022). *The Rapid Rise of TikTok. Statista, Topics – Social media*. https://www.statista.com/chart/28412/social-media-users-by-network-amo/

Buhalis, D., & Karatay, N. (2022). Mixed Reality (MR) for generation Z in cultural heritage tourism towards metaverse. In *Information and Communication Technologies in Tourism 2022: Proceedings of the ENTER 2022 eTourism Conference*. Springer International Publishing.

Buhalis, D., Lin, M. S., & Leung, D. (2022). Metaverse as a driver for customer experience and value co-creation: implications for hospitality and tourism management and marketing. *International Journal of Contemporary Hospitality Management, 35*(2), 701–716.

Bulsara, H. P., & Vaghela, P. S. (2020). Blockchain Technology for E-commerce Industry E-commerce trends View project Techno-innovations to Techno-Entrepreneurship and completed one project on Development of Course in Pedagogy framework: Industrial Management, National Mission Project on Educati. *International Journal of Advanced Science and Technology*, *29*(5), 3793–3798.

Burgoon, J. K. (1982). Privacy and communication. *Annals of the International Communication Association*, *6*(1), 206–249. doi:10.1080/23808985.1982.11678499

Burke, R. R. (1997). Do you see what I see? The Future of Virtual Shopping. *Journal of the Academy of Marketing Science*, *25*(4), 352–360. doi:10.1177/0092070397254007

Burskirk, R. H., & Rothe, J. T. (1970). Consumerism, patient empowerment and changing clinical work-patient awareness and treatment demands on the rise. *Duodecim*, *127*(8), 777–783.[REMOVED HYPERLINK FIELD] PMID:21568105

Butt, A., Ahmad, H., Ali, F., Muzaffar, A., & Shafique, M. N. (2023). Engaging the customer with augmented reality and employee services to enhance equity and loyalty. *International Journal of Retail & Distribution Management*, *51*(5), 629–652. doi:10.1108/IJRDM-04-2021-0165

Buttle, F., & Maklan, S. (2019). Customer relationship management: Concepts and technologies (4th ed.). doi:10.4324/9781351016551

Callon, M., Courtial, J. P., & Laville, F. (1991). Co-word analysis as a tool for describing the network of interactions between basic and technological research: The case of polymer chemistry. *Scientometrics*, *22*(1), 155–205. doi:10.1007/BF02019280

Campbell, C., Sands, S., Ferraro, C., Tsao, H.-Y., & Mavrommatis, A. (2020). From data to action: How marketers can leverage AI. *Business Horizons*, *63*(2), 227–243. doi:10.1016/j.bushor.2019.12.002

Carpineto, C., & Romano, G. (2020). An experimental study of automatic detection and measurement of counterfeit in brand search results. *ACM Transactions on the Web*, *14*(2), 1–35. doi:10.1145/3378443

Carstens, A. (2018). *Money in the digital age: what role for central banks?* Lecture at the House of Finance, Goethe University, Frankfurt, Germany.

Casamatta, G., Giannoni, S., Brunstein, D., & Jouve, J. (2022). Host type and pricing on Airbnb: Seasonality and perceived market power. *Tourism Management*, *88*, 104433. doi:10.1016/j.tourman.2021.104433

Catalina-Garcia, B., López-de-Ayala, M. C., & García, A. (2014). Los riesgos de los adolescentes en Internet: Los menores como actores y víctimas de los peligros de Internet [The risks of teens on the Internet: minors as actors and victims of Internet dangers]. *Revista Latina de Comunicación Social*, *69*(69), 462–485. doi:10.4185/RLCS-2014-1020

Catapano, R., Shennib, F., & Levav, J. (2022). Preference Reversals Between Digital and Physical Goods. *JMR, Journal of Marketing Research*, *59*(2), 353–373. doi:10.1177/00222437211065020

Catherine, B. (2022). *Converge: a futurist's insights into the potential of our world as technology and humanity collide.* Major Street Publishing.

Cavoukian, A. (2012). Privacy by design: origins, meaning, and prospects for assuring privacy and trust in the information era. In *Privacy protection measures and technologies in business organizations: aspects and standards* (pp. 170–208). IGI Global. doi:10.4018/978-1-61350-501-4.ch007

Chai, J. J., O'Sullivan, C., Gowen, A. A., Rooney, B., & Xu, J. L. (2022). Augmented/mixed reality technologies for food: A review. *Trends in Food Science & Technology*, *124*, 182–194. doi:10.1016/j.tifs.2022.04.021

Chambers, L. D. (2019). *The Practical Handbook of Genetic Algorithms: New Frontiers* (Vol. II). CRC Press.

Chang, Y. J., Chen, C. H., Huang, W. T., & Huang, W. S. (2011, July). *Investigating students' perceived satisfaction, behavioral intention, and effectiveness of English learning using augmented reality. In 2011 IEEE international conference on multimedia and Expo*. IEEE.

Chaudhuri, N., Gupta, G., Vamsi, V., & Bose, I. (2021). On the platform but will they buy? Predicting customers' purchase behavior using deep learning. *Decision Support Systems, 149*, 113622. doi:10.1016/j.dss.2021.113622

Chebrolu, N., Läbe, T., & Stachniss, C. (2018). Robust long-term registration of UAV images of crop fields for precision agriculture. *IEEE Robot. Autom. Lett., 3*(4), 3097–3104.

Cheng, X., Zhang, S., Fu, S., Liu, W., Guan, C., Mou, J., ... Huang, C. (2022). Exploring the metaverse in the digital economy: an overview and research framework. *Journal of Electronic Business & Digital Economics, 1*(1/2), 206-224.

Cheng, L.-C., & Huang, C.-L. (2020). Exploring contextual factors from consumer reviews affecting movie sales: An opinion mining approach. *Electronic Commerce Research, 20*(4), 807–832. doi:10.100710660-019-09332-z

Cheng, Y., & Jiang, H. (2020). How do AI-driven Chatbots impact user experience? Examining gratifications, perceived privacy risk, satisfaction, loyalty, and continued use. *Journal of Broadcasting & Electronic Media, 64*(4), 592–614. doi:10.1080/08838151.2020.1834296

Chen, I., & Popovich, K. (2003). Understanding customer relationship management (CRM) People, process and technology. *Business Process Management Journal, 9*(5), 672–688. doi:10.1108/14637150310496758

Chen, J. V., Ha, Q. A., & Vu, M. T. (2022). The Influences of Virtual Reality Shopping Characteristics on Consumers' Impulse Buying Behavior. *International Journal of Human-Computer Interaction*, 1–19. doi:10.1080/10447318.2022.2098566

Chen, J., & Micali, S. (2019). Algorand: A secure and efficient distributed ledger. *Theoretical Computer Science, 777*, 155–183. doi:10.1016/j.tcs.2019.02.001

Chennamaneni, A., & Taneja, A. (2015). Communication Privacy Management and Self-Disclosure on Social Media—A Case of Facebook. *Americas Conference on Information Systems.*

Chen, Q., Gong, Y., Lu, Y., & Tang, J. (2022). Classifying and measuring the service quality of AI chatbot in frontline service. *Journal of Business Research, 145*, 552–568. doi:10.1016/j.jbusres.2022.02.088

Chen, R., Dai, H., Gao, Y., Fu, B., & Chen, J. (2022). Electronic degree certificate data protection and sharing method based on blockchain. *Computer Engineering, 48*(4), 50–60. doi:10.19678/j.issn.1000-3428.0061193

Chen, S., Tamilmani, K., Tran, K. T., Waseem, D., & Weerakkody, V. (2022). How privacy practices affect customer commitment in the sharing economy: A study of Airbnb through an institutional perspective. *Industrial Marketing Management, 107*, 161–175. doi:10.1016/j.indmarman.2022.08.020

Chen, S., Wang, X., Zhang, H.-y., Wang, J., & Peng, J. (2021). Customer purchase forecasting for online tourism: A data-driven method with multiplex behavior data. *Tourism Management, 87*, 104357. doi:10.1016/j.tourman.2021.104357

Chen, W., Zhao, L., Kang, Q., & Di, F. (2020). Systematizing heterogeneous expert knowledge, scenarios and goals via a goal-reasoning artificial intelligence agent for democratic urban land use planning. *Cities (London, England), 101*, 102703. doi:10.1016/j.cities.2020.102703

Chen, Y., & Cheung, A. S. (2017). The transparent self under big data profiling: Privacy and Chinese legislation on the social credit system. *SSRN, 12*, 356. doi:10.2139srn.2992537

Chen, Y.-P., Nelson, L. D., & Hsu, M. (2015). From "where" to "what": Distributed representations of brand associations in the human brain. *JMR, Journal of Marketing Research*, *52*(4), 453–466. doi:10.1509/jmr.14.0606 PMID:27065490

Cheung, K.-W., Kwok, J. T., Law, M. H., & Tsui, K.-C. (2003). Mining customer product ratings for personalized marketing. *Decision Support Systems*, *35*(2), 231–243. doi:10.1016/S0167-9236(02)00108-2

Chin, E., Felt, A. P., Sekar, V., & Wagner, D. (2012). Measuring user confidence in smartphone security and privacy. *SOUPS 2012 - Proceedings of the 8th Symposium on Usable Privacy and Security*, 1. 10.1145/2335356.2335358

Chinchanachokchai, S., Thontirawong, P., & Chinchanachokchai, P. (2021). A tale of two recommender systems: The moderating role of consumer expertise on artificial intelligence based product recommendations. *Journal of Retailing and Consumer Services*, *61*, 102528. doi:10.1016/j.jretconser.2021.102528

Chittenden, L., & Rettie, R. (2003). An evaluation of e-mail marketing and factors affecting response. *Journal of Targeting. Measuring and Analysis for Marketing*, *11*(3), 203–217. doi:10.1057/palgrave.jt.5740078

Chohan, R., & Paschen, J. (2023). NFT marketing: How marketers can use nonfungible tokens in their campaigns. *Business Horizons*, *66*(1), 43–50. doi:10.1016/j.bushor.2021.12.004

Choi, J.-A., & Lim, K. (2020). Identifying machine learning techniques for classification of target advertising. *ICT Express*, *6*(3), 175–180. doi:10.1016/j.icte.2020.04.012

Choi, K., Yoo, D., Kim, G., & Suh, Y. (2012). A hybrid online-product recommendation system: Combining implicit rating-based collaborative filtering and sequential pattern analysis. *Electronic Commerce Research and Applications*, *11*(4), 309–317. doi:10.1016/j.elerap.2012.02.004

Choi, T. R., & Sung, Y. (2018). Instagram versus Snapchat: Self-expression and privacy concern on social media. *Telematics and Informatics*, *35*(8), 2289–2298. doi:10.1016/j.tele.2018.09.009

Chong, A., Ch'ng, E., Liu, M., & Li, B. (2017). Predicting consumer product demands via Big Data: The roles of online promotional marketing and online reviews. *International Journal of Production Research*, *55*(17), 5142–5156. doi:10.1080/00207543.2015.1066519

Cho, S., & Krasser, A. H. (2011). What makes us care? The impact of cultural values, individual factors, and attention to media content on motivation for ethical consumerism. *International Social Science Review*, *86*(1/2).

Choudhary, N., David, A., & Feleen, F. (2021). Employee Engagement and Commitment in Service Sector. *Wesleyan Journal of Research, 13*(4.7), 107-112.

Christen, T., Hess, M., Grichnik, D., & Wincent, J. (2022). Value-based pricing in digital platforms: A machine learning approach to signaling beyond core product attributes in cross-platform settings. *Journal of Business Research*, *152*, 82–92. doi:10.1016/j.jbusres.2022.07.042

Christodoulou, K., Katelaris, L., Themistocleous, M., Christodoulou, P., & Iosif, E. (2022). NFTs and the metaverse revolution: research perspectives and open challenges. *Blockchains and the Token Economy*, 139-178.

Cline, E. (2020). *Ready player two: a novel.* Ballantine Books.

Cloarec, J. (2022). Privacy controls as an information source to reduce data poisoning in artificial intelligence-powered personalization. *Journal of Business Research*, *152*, 144–153. doi:10.1016/j.jbusres.2022.07.045

Coffey, K., Maglaras, L.A., Smith, R., Janicke, H., Ferrag, M.A., Derhab, A., Mukherjee, M., Rallis, S. & Yousaf, A. (2018). Vulnerability assessment of cyber security for SCADA systems. *Guide to Vulnerability Analysis for Computer Networks and Systems: An Artificial Intelligence Approach*, 59-80. doi:10.1007/978-3-319-92624-7_3

Coffin, J., & Egan–Wyer, C. (2022). The ethical consumption cap and mean market morality. *Marketing Theory*, *22*(1), 105–123. doi:10.1177/14705931211058772

Collins, C., Dennehy, D., Conboy, K., & Mikalef, P. (2021). Artificial intelligence in information systems research: A systematic literature review and research agenda. *International Journal of Information Management*, *60*, 102383. Advance online publication. doi:10.1016/j.ijinfomgt.2021.102383

Contemporary, A., & Filos, A. (2010). *an Assessment of Some Common Criticisms*. *2*, 279–296.

Costa, C. J., Ferreira, E., Bento, F., & Aparicio, M. (2016). Enterprise resource planning adoption and satisfaction determinants. *Computers in Human Behavior*, *63*, 659–671. doi:10.1016/j.chb.2016.05.090

Couwenberg, L. E., Boksem, M. A., Dietvorst, R. C., Worm, L., Verbeke, W. J., & Smidts, A. (2017). Neural responses to functional and experiential ad appeals: Explaining ad effectiveness. *International Journal of Research in Marketing*, *34*(2), 355–366. doi:10.1016/j.ijresmar.2016.10.005

Crawford, K., Dobbe, R., Dryer, T., Fried, G., Green, B., Kaziunas, E., Kak, A., Mathur, V., McElroy, E., Sąnchez, A.N., Raji, D., Rankin, J.L., Richardson, R., Schultz, J., West, S.M., & Whittaker, M. (2019). AI Now 2019 Report. Technical Report. AI Now Institute.

Çubuk, E. B. S., Zeren, H. E., & Demirdöven, B. (2023). The Role of Data Governance in Cybersecurity for E-Municipal Services: Implications From the Case of Turkey. In *Handbook of Research on Cybersecurity Issues and Challenges for Business and FinTech Applications* (pp. 410–425). IGI Global.

Cummings, J. J., Tsay-Vogel, M., Cahill, T. J., & Zhang, L. (2022). Effects of immersive storytelling on affective, cognitive, and associative empathy: The mediating role of presence. *New Media & Society*, *24*(9), 2003–2026. doi:10.1177/1461444820986816

Dalenberg, D. J. (2018). Preventing discrimination in the automated targeting of job advertisements. *Computer Law & Security Report*, *34*(3), 615–627. doi:10.1016/j.clsr.2017.11.009

Danaher, P. J., Danaher, T. S., Smith, M. S., & Loaiza-Maya, R. (2020). Advertising effectiveness for multiple retailer-brands in a multimedia and multichannel environment. *JMR, Journal of Marketing Research*, *57*(3), 445–467. doi:10.1177/0022243720910104

Daniel, E., & Tschorsch, F. (2022). IPFS and Friends: A Qualitative Comparison of Next Generation Peer-to-Peer Data Networks. *IEEE Communications Surveys and Tutorials*, *24*(1), 31–52. doi:10.1109/COMST.2022.3143147

Dardas, L. A., Sallam, M., Woodward, A., Sweis, N., Sweis, N., & Sawair, F. A. (2023). Evaluating Research Impact Based on Semantic Scholar Highly Influential Citations, Total Citations, and Altmetric Attention Scores: The Quest for Refined Measures Remains Illusive. *Publications / MDPI*, *11*(1), 1. Advance online publication. doi:10.3390/publications11010005

Dave, P. (2020). *Washington state adopts facial recognition rules critics view as too loose*. Reuters. https://www.reuters.com/article/us-washington-tech-idUSL1N2BO1XW

Davenport, T., Guha, A., Grewal, D., & Bressgott, T. (2020). How artificial intelligence will change the future of marketing. *Journal of the Academy of Marketing Science*, *48*(1), 24–42. doi:10.100711747-019-00696-0

David, A., Ganesh Kumar, C., & Jeganathan, G. S. (2022). Impact of Food Safety and Standards Regulation on Food Business Operators. In *Au Virtual International Conference* (pp. 355-363). Academic Press.

DavidsonS.De FilippiP.PottsJ. (2016). *Economics of Blockchain*. SSRN. doi:10.2139/ssrn.2744751 de Barcelos Silva, A., Gomes, M. M., da Costa, C. A., da Rosa Righi, R., Barbosa, J. L. V., Pessin, G., De Doncker, G., & Federizzi, G. (2020). Intelligent personal assistants: A systematic literature review. *Expert Systems with Applications*, *147*, 113193. Advance online publication. doi:10.1016/j.eswa.2020.113193

De Bruyn, A., Viswanathan, V., Beh, Y. S., Brock, J. K.-U., & von Wangenheim, F. (2020). Artificial Intelligence and Marketing: Pitfalls and Opportunities. *Journal of Interactive Marketing*, *51*, 91–105. doi:10.1016/j.intmar.2020.04.007

De Cicco, R., Iacobucci, S., & Pagliaro, S. (2021). The effect of influencer–product fit on advertising recognition and the role of an enhanced disclosure in increasing sponsorship transparency. *International Journal of Advertising*, *40*(5), 733–759. doi:10.1080/02650487.2020.1801198

De Guzman, J. A., Thilakarathna, K., & Seneviratne, A. (2019). Security and privacy approaches in mixed reality: A literature survey. *ACM Computing Surveys*, *52*(6), 1–37. doi:10.1145/3359626

De Keyzer, F., Dens, N., & De Pelsmacker, P. (2015). Is this for me? How consumers respond to personalized advertising on social network sites. *Journal of Interactive Advertising*, *15*(2), 124–134. doi:10.1080/15252019.2015.1082450

Debons, A., Horne, E., & Cronenweth, S. (1988). *Information science: An integrated view*. G.K. Hall.

DeCremer, D., Bianzino, N., & Falk, N. (2023). *How Generative AI Could Disrupt Creative Work*. https://hbr.org/2023/04/how-generative-ai-could-disrupt-creative-work

Dehghani, M., Lee, S. H. M., & Mashatan, A. (2020). Touching holograms with windows mixed reality: Renovating the consumer retailing services. *Technology in Society*, *63*, 101394. doi:10.1016/j.techsoc.2020.101394

Del Vecchio, P., Secundo, G., & Garzoni, A. (2023). Phygital technologies and environments for breakthrough innovation in customers' and citizens' journey. A critical literature review and future agenda. *Technological Forecasting and Social Change*, *189*, 189. doi:10.1016/j.techfore.2023.122342

Delmas, M. A., & Burbano, V. C. (2011). The drivers of greenwashing. *California Management Review*, *54*(1), 64–87. doi:10.1525/cmr.2011.54.1.64

Desai, V., & Vidyapeeth, B. (2019). Digital marketing: A review. *International Journal of Trend in Scientific Research and Development*, *5*(5), 196–200. doi:10.31142/ijtsrd23100

DesAutels, P., Salehi-Sangari, E., Berthon, P., Rabinovich, T., & Pitt, L. (2014). It is emergent: Five propositions on the relationship between creative consumers and technology. *International Journal of Technology Marketing*, *9*(1), 72–85. doi:10.1504/IJTMKT.2014.058084

Dhaoui, C., Webster, C. M., & Tan, L. P. (2017). Social Media Sentiment Analysis: Lexicon Versus Machine Learning. *Journal of Consumer Marketing*, *34*(6), 480–488. doi:10.1108/JCM-03-2017-2141

Dick, E. (2021). *The Promise of Immersive Learning: Augmented and Virtual Reality's Potential in Education*. ITIF. https://itif.org/publications/2021/08/30/promise-immersive-learning-augmented-and-virtual-reality-potential

Dierksmeier, C., & Seele, P. (2018). Cryptocurrencies and Business Ethics. *Journal of Business Ethics*, *152*(1), 1–14. [REMOVED HYPERLINK FIELD] doi:10.100710551-016-3298-0 PMID:30930508

Dierksmeier, C., & Seele, P. (2020). Blockchain and business ethics. *Business Ethics (Oxford, England)*, *29*(2), 348–359. doi:10.1111/beer.12259

Dodds, T., de Vreese, C., Helberger, N., Resendez, V., & Seipp, T. (2023). Popularity-driven Metrics: Audience Analytics and Shifting Opinion Power to Digital Platforms. *Journalism Studies*, *24*(3), 1–19. doi:10.1080/1461670X.2023.2167104

Dong, L.-y., Ji, S., Zhang, C., Zhang, Q., Chiu, D. W., Qiu, L., & Li, D. (2018). An unsupervised topic-sentiment joint probabilistic model for detecting deceptive reviews. *Expert Systems with Applications*, *114*, 210–223. doi:10.1016/j.eswa.2018.07.005

Donthu, N., Kumar, S., Mukherjee, D., Pandey, N., & Lim, W. M. (2021). How to conduct a bibliometric analysis: An overview and guidelines. *Journal of Business Research*, *133*, 285–296. doi:10.1016/j.jbusres.2021.04.070

Du, R.Y., Netzer, O., Schweidel, D.A., & Mitra, D. (2021). Capturing Marketing Information to Fuel Growth. *Journal of Marketing, 85*(1), 163-183.

Duan, B. (2022). *Digital marketing solutions based on consumer data and homomorphic encryption*. Applied Mathematics and Nonlinear Sciences. doi:10.2478/amns.2021.2.00253

Duan, Y., Edwards, J. S., & Dwivedi, Y. K. (2019). Artificial intelligence for decision making in the era of big data—Evolution, challenges and research agenda. *International Journal of Information Management*, *48*, 63–71. doi:10.1016/j.ijinfomgt.2019.01.021

Dubey, G., Hasan, M., & Alam, A. (2022). *Artificial intelligence (AI) and Indian education system: promising applications, potential effectiveness and challenges.* https://hrdc.gujaratuniversity.ac.in/Ejournal

Dubosson-Torbay, M., Osterwalder, A., & Pigneur, Y. (2002). E-business model design, classification, and measurements. *Thunderbird International Business Review*, *44*(1), 5–23. doi:10.1002/tie.1036

Ducange, P., Fazzolari, M., Petrocchi, M., & Vecchio, M. (2019). An effective Decision Support System for social media listening based on cross-source sentiment analysis models. *Engineering Applications of Artificial Intelligence*, *78*, 71–85. doi:10.1016/j.engappai.2018.10.014

Du, H., Ma, B., Niyato, D., Kang, J., Xiong, Z., & Yang, Z. (2023). Rethinking quality of experience for metaverse services: A consumer-based economics perspective. *IEEE Network*, 1–8. doi:10.1109/MNET.131.2200503

Dvir, N., & Gafni, R. (2018). When less is more: Empirical study of the relation between consumer behavior and information provision on commercial landing pages. *Informing Science*, *21*, 19–39. doi:10.28945/4015

Dwesar, R., & Kashyap, R. (2022). IOT in Marketing: Current Applications and Future Opportunities. In S. N. Mohanty, J. M. Chatterjee, & S. Satpathy (Eds.), *Internet of Things and Its Applications* (pp. 539–553). Springer. doi:10.1007/978-3-030-77528-5_29

Dwivedi, Y. K., Hughes, L., Ismagilova, E., Aarts, G., Coombs, C., Crick, T., Duan, Y., Dwivedi, R., Edwards, J., Eirug, A., Galanos, V., Ilavarasan, P. V., Janssen, M., Jones, P., Kar, A. K., Kizgin, H., Kronemann, B., Lal, B., Lucini, B., & Williams, M. D. (2021). Artificial Intelligence (AI): Multidisciplinary perspectives on emerging challenges, opportunities, and agenda for research, practice and policy. *International Journal of Information Management, 57*. doi:10.1016/j.ijinfomgt.2019.08.002

Dwivedi, Y. K., Hughes, L., Baabdullah, A. M., Ribeiro-Navarrete, S., Giannakis, M., Al-Debei, M. M., Dennehy, D., Metri, B., Buhalis, D., Cheung, C. M. K., Conboy, K., Doyle, R., Dubey, R., Dutot, V., Felix, R., Goyal, D. P., Gustafsson, A., Hinsch, C., Jebabli, I., ... Wamba, S. F. (2022). Metaverse beyond the hype: Multidisciplinary perspectives on emerging challenges, opportunities, and agenda for research, practice and policy. *International Journal of Information Management*, *66*, 102542. doi:10.1016/j.ijinfomgt.2022.102542

Dwivedi, Y. K., Kshetri, N., Hughes, L., Slade, E. L., Jeyaraj, A., Kar, A. K., Baabdullah, A. M., Koohang, A., Raghavan, V., Ahuja, M., Albanna, H., Albashrawi, M. A., Al-Busaidi, A. S., Balakrishnan, J., Barlette, Y., Basu, S., Bose, I., Brooks, L., Buhalis, D., ... Wright, R. (2023). "So what if ChatGPT wrote it?" Multidisciplinary perspectives on opportunities, challenges and implications of generative conversational AI for research, practice and policy. *International Journal of Information Management*, *71*, 102642. doi:10.1016/j.ijinfomgt.2023.102642

Egger, R., & Neuburger, L. (2020). Augmented, virtual, and mixed reality in tourism. Handbook of e-Tourism, 1-25.

Eisenschink, M., Gluck, C., Maier, M., Scheuchenpflug, E., Timinger, H., & Martens, M. (2022). A new trend in further education? micro degrees as a contribution to deal with new paradigms in small and medium-sized enterprises. *2022 IEEE German Education Conference, GeCon 2022.* 10.1109/GeCon55699.2022.9942738

Elalem, Y. K., Maier, S., & Seifert, R. W. (2022). A machine learning-based framework for forecasting sales of new products with short life cycles using deep neural networks. *International Journal of Forecasting*. Advance online publication. doi:10.1016/j.ijforecast.2022.09.005

Elford, D., Lancaster, S. J., & Jones, G. A. (2022). Fostering Motivation toward Chemistry through Augmented Reality Educational Escape Activities. A Self-Determination Theory Approach. *Journal of Chemical Education*, *99*(10), 3406–3417. doi:10.1021/acs.jchemed.2c00428

Ertemel, A. V. (2018). Implications of Blockchain Technology on Marketing. *Journal of International Trade, Logistics and Law, 4*(2), 35–45. http://jital.org/index.php/jital/article/view/98

Esmaeilpour, M., Naderifar, V., & Shukur, Z. (2012). Cellular learning automata for mining customer behaviour in shopping activity. *International Journal of Innovative Computing, Information, & Control*, *8*(4), 2491–2511.

Etter, M., Colleoni, E., Illia, L., Meggiorin, K., & D'Eugenio, A. (2018). Measuring Organizational Legitimacy in Social Media: Assessing Citizens' Judgments With Sentiment Analysis. *Business & Society*, *57*(1), 60–97. doi:10.1177/0007650316683926

EU Blockchain Observatory and Forum. (2022). *Blockchain for Supply Chain Transparency*. 48.

European Commission. (2019). Ethics guidelines for trustworthy AI. High-Level Expert Group on Artificial Intelligence. *European Commission*, 1–39. https://ec.europa.eu/futurium/en/ai-alliance-consultation

European Commission. (2021). *Horizon Europe, pilar III - Europa inovadora – Apoiar e estabelecer ligações entre os inovadores na Europa*. Publications Office of the European Union Directorate. General for Research and Innovation. https://data.europa.eu/doi/10.2777/831048

European Union. (2016). *Regulation (EU) 2016/679 of the European Parliament and of the Council of 27 April 2016 on the protection of natural persons with regard to the processing of personal data and the free movement of such data. Official Journal of the European Union.* https://eur-lex.europa.eu/legal-content/PT/TXT/PDF/?uri=CELEX:32016R0679&qid=1641839336270&from=PT

Falchuk, B., Loeb, S., & Neff, R. (2018). The social metaverse: Battle for privacy. *IEEE Technology and Society Magazine*, *37*(2), 52–61. doi:10.1109/MTS.2018.2826060

Fan, T.-K., & Chang, C.-H. (2009). Blogger-centric contextual advertising. *Proceedings of the 18th ACM conference on Information and knowledge management*, 1803-1806. 10.1145/1645953.1646234

Fan, T.-K., & Chang, C.-H. (2010). Sentiment-oriented contextual advertising. *Knowledge and Information Systems*, *23*(3), 321–344. doi:10.100710115-009-0222-2

Fan, T.-K., & Chang, C.-H. (2011). Blogger-Centric Contextual Advertising. *Expert Systems with Applications*, *38*(3), 1777–1788. doi:10.1016/j.eswa.2010.07.105

Fanusie, Y., & Robinson, T. (2018). *Bitcoin laundering: an analysis of illicit flows into digital currency services*. Center on Sanctions and Illicit Finance Memorandum.

Far, S. B., Asaar, M. R., & Haghbin, A. (2023). A privacy-preserving framework for blockchain-based multi-level marketing. *Computers & Industrial Engineering*, *177*, 177. doi:10.1016/j.cie.2023.109095

Far, S. B., Rad, A. I., & Asaar, M. R. (2022). ACR-MLM: A privacy-preserving framework for anonymous and confidential rewarding in blockchain-based multi-level marketing. *Data Science and Management*, *5*(4), 219–231. doi:10.1016/j.dsm.2022.09.003

Farell, R. (2015). An analysis of the cryptocurrency industry. *Wharton Research Scholars, 130*. https://repository.upenn.edu/wharton_research_scholars/130

Fariborzi, E., & Zahedifard, M. (2012). E-mail Marketing: Advantages, Disadvantages and Improving Techniques. *International Journal of E-Education, e-Business, e-. Management Learning*, *2*(3), 232–236. doi:10.7763/IJEEEE.2012.V2.116

Farzindar, A., & Inkpen, D. (2017). Natural language processing for social media. *Synthesis Lectures on Human Language Technologies*, *10*(2), 1–195. doi:10.1007/978-3-031-02167-1

Fatima, S., Dawson, G., Desouza, K., & Denford, J. (2022). *How countries are leveraging computing power to achieve their national artificial intelligence strategies*. https://www.brookings.edu/blog/techtank/2022/01/12/how-countries-are-leveraging-computing-power-to-achieve-their-national-artificial-intelligence-strategies/

Feleen, F., David, A., Choudhary, N., & Vivekanand, N. (2021). *Impact of Psychological Capacities on the Work-Life Balance of Entrepreneurs*. Academic Press.

Feleen, F., & David, A. (2021). A Comparative Study of Work From Home vs Work From Office: Preference of Women Employees in IT Industry. *Design Engineering (London)*, *7*(1), 5763–5775.

Fernandes, A., & Chatterjee, S. (2022). Possibilities of metaverse: The second life. *International Journal of Engineering and Management Research*, *12*(4), 79–82.

Fernández-Caramés, T. M., & Fraga-Lamas, P. (2020). Teaching and learning iot cybersecurity and vulnerability assessment with shodan through practical use cases. *Sensors (Basel)*, *20*(11), 3048. doi:10.339020113048 PMID:32471252

Fernando, Y., & Saravannan, R. (2021). Blockchain Technology: Energy Efficiency and Ethical Compliance. *Journal of Governance and Integrity, 4*(2), 88–95. doi:10.15282/jgi.4.2.2021.5872

Ferreira, P., Teixeira, J. G., & Teixeira, L. F. (2020). Understanding the Impact of Artificial Intelligence on Services. *Lecture Notes in Business Information Processing, 377*, 202–213. doi:10.1007/978-3-030-38724-2_15

Figueiredo, F., Gonçalves, M. J. A., & Teixeira, S. (2021). Information technology adoption on digital marketing: A literature review. *Informatics (MDPI)*, *8*(4), 74. doi:10.3390/informatics8040074

Flavián, C., Ibáñez-Sánchez, S., & Orús, C. (2019). The impact of virtual, augmented and mixed reality technologies on the customer experience. *Journal of Business Research*, *100*, 547–560. doi:10.1016/j.jbusres.2018.10.050

Foley, S., Karlsen, J., & Putniņš, T. (2018). Sex, drugs, and bitcoin: How much illegal activity is financed through cryptocurrencies? *Review of Financial Studies*.

Følstad, A., Nordheim, C. B., & Bjørkli, C. A. (2018). What makes users trust a chatbot for customer service? An exploratory interview study. Lecture Notes in Computer Science, 11193, 194–208. doi:10.1007/978-3-030-01437-7_16

Foryś, I. (2022). Machine learning in house price analysis: Regression models versus neural networks. *Procedia Computer Science*, *207*, 435–445. doi:10.1016/j.procs.2022.09.078

Frankish, K., & Ramsey, W. M. (2014). *The Cambridge Handbook of Artificial Intelligence*. Cambridge University Press. doi:10.1017/CBO9781139046855

Frank, M. R., Autor, D., Bessen, J. E., Brynjolfsson, E., Cebrian, M., Deming, D. J., Feldman, M., Groh, M., Lobo, J., Moro, E., Wang, D., Youn, H., & Rahwan, I. (2019). Toward understanding the impact of artificial intelligence on labor. *Proceedings of the National Academy of Sciences of the United States of America*, *116*(14), 6531–6539. doi:10.1073/pnas.1900949116 PMID:30910965

Fricke, S. (2018). Semantic Scholar. *Journal of the Medical Library Association: JMLA*, *106*(1). Advance online publication. doi:10.5195/jmla.2018.280

Frier, S. (2021). *No filter: The inside story of Instagram*. Simon and Schuster.

Fulgoni, G., & Lipsman, A. (2014). Numbers, please: Digital game changers: How social media will help usher in the era of mobile and multi-platform campaign-effectiveness measurement. *Journal of Advertising Research*, *54*(1), 11–16. doi:10.2501/JAR-54-1-011-016

Furger, R. (1999). On the Web You Have No Secrets. *PC World*, *17*(7), 29–31.

Gadekallu, T. R., Pham, Q. V., Nguyen, D. C., Maddikunta, P. K. R., Deepa, N., Prabadevi, B., Pathirana, P. N., Zhao, J., & Hwang, W. J. (2022). Blockchain for edge of things: Applications, opportunities, and challenges. *IEEE Internet of Things Journal*, *9*(2), 964–988. doi:10.1109/JIOT.2021.3119639

Gaffar, A., Deshpande, A., Bandara, W., & Mathiesen, P. (2015). Importance of literature profiling: An archival analysis with illustrative examples for IS researchers. In *Proceedings of the 19th Pacific Asia Conference on Information Systems (PACIS)* (pp. 1-13). Association for Information Systems (AIS). https://eprints.qut.edu.au/85249/

Ganeshkumar, C., David, A., Sankar, J. G., & Saginala, M. (2023). Application of Drone Technology in Agriculture: A Predictive Forecasting of Pest and Disease Incidence. In *Applying Drone Technologies and Robotics for Agricultural Sustainability* (pp. 50–81). IGI Global.

Gangarde, R., Sharma, A., & Pawar, A. (2019). Bibliometric Survey of Privacy of Social Media Network Data Publishing. *Library Philosophy and Practice*, *2019*, 1–21.

Gao, F., & Zhang, L. (2020). Application of Artificial Intelligence and Big Data Technology in Digital Marketing. *Proceedings of ACM ISBDAI conference (ISBDAI 2020)*. 10.1145/3436286.3436404

Gao, L., Cai, H., & Bai, R. (2021). *Real-time visual representations for mobile mixed reality remote collaboration*. Semantic Scholar. doi:10.1145/3275495.3275515

Gapsalamov, A. R., Bochkareva, T. N., Akhmetshin, E. M., Vasilev, V. L., & Anisimova, T. I. (2020). Sociedade digital: Novos desafios para a educação. *Periódico Tchê Química*, *17*(34), 803–817. doi:10.52571/PTQ.v17.n34.2020.827_P34_pgs_803_816.pdf

Garg, P., Gupta, B., Dzever, S., Sivarajah, U., & Kumar, V. (2020). Examining the relationship between social media analytics practices and business performance in the Indian retail and IT industries: The mediation role of customer engagement. *International Journal of Information Management*, *52*, 102069. doi:10.1016/j.ijinfomgt.2020.102069

Gattullo, M., Laviola, E., Boccaccio, A., Evangelista, A., Fiorentino, M., Manghisi, V. M., & Uva, A. E. (2022). Education Laboratories. *Computers, 11*(50), 1–24.[REMOVED HYPERLINK FIELD] PMID:36407564

George, A. S., & George, A. H. (2023). A review of ChatGPT AI's impact on several business sectors. *Partners Universal International Innovation Journal, 1*(1), 9–23.

Gerlick, J. A., & Liozu, S. M. (2020). Ethical and legal considerations of artificial intelligence and algorithmic decision-making in personalized pricing. *Journal of Revenue and Pricing Management, 19*(2), 85–98. doi:10.105741272-019-00225-2

Ghatasheh, N., Faris, H., AlTaharwa, I., Harb, Y., & Harb, A. (2020). Business analytics in telemarketing: Cost-sensitive analysis of bank campaigns using artificial neural networks. *Applied Sciences (Basel, Switzerland), 10*(7), 2581. doi:10.3390/app10072581

Ghose, A., Ipeirotis, P. G., & Li, B. (2012). Designing ranking systems for hotels on travel search engines by mining user-generated and crowdsourced content. *Marketing Science, 31*(3), 493–520. doi:10.1287/mksc.1110.0700

Gill, K. S., Assvlbekova, A., Addanke, S., Jha, A., Mishra, I., & Nurkusheva, L. (2022, April). Multimedia Systems and its Role in Adaptive Network Management. In *2022 International Conference on Sustainable Computing and Data Communication Systems (ICSCDS)* (pp. 1547-1553). IEEE. 10.1109/ICSCDS53736.2022.9760752

Gimpel, H., Krämer, J., Neumann, D., Pfeiffer, J., Seifert, S., Teubner, T., & Weidlich, A. (2021). Market Engineering: Insights from Two Decades of Research on Markets and Information. doi:10.1007/978-3-030-66661-3

Gkikas, D. C., & Theodoridis, P. K. (2019). Artificial intelligence (AI) impact on digital marketing research. In Strategic Innovative Marketing and Tourism: 7th ICSIMAT (pp. 1251-1259). Academic Press.

Gkinko, L., & Elbanna, A. (2022). The appropriation of conversational AI in the workplace: A taxonomy of AI chatbot users. *International Journal of Information Management, 102568*. Advance online publication. doi:10.1016/j.ijinfomgt.2022.102568

Glenn, T., & Monteith, S. (2014). Privacy in the Digital World: Medical and Health Data Outside of HIPAA Protections. *Current Psychiatry Reports, 16*(11), 494. doi:10.100711920-014-0494-4 PMID:25218603

Glikson, E., & Woolley, A. W. (2020). Human Trust in Artificial Intelligence: Review of Empirical Research. *The Academy of Management Annals, 14*(2), 627–660. doi:10.5465/annals.2018.0057

Global daily social media usage 2022. (2022, January 26). Statista. https://www-statista-com.eu1.proxy.openathens.net/statistics/433871/daily-social-media-usage-worldwide/

Goddard, M. (2017). The EU General Data Protection Regulation (GDPR): European regulation that has a global impact. *International Journal of Market Research, 59*(6), 703–705. doi:10.2501/IJMR-2017-050

Godin, S. (1999). *Permission Marketing: Turning Strangers into Friends, and Friends into Customers*. Simon and Schuster.

Goldfarb, A., & Tucker, C. (2011). Online display advertising: Targeting and obtrusiveness. *Marketing Science, 30*(3), 389–404. doi:10.1287/mksc.1100.0583

Gomber, P., Kauffman, R. J., Parker, C., & Weber, B. W. (2018). On the Fintech Revolution: Interpreting the Forces of Innovation, Disruption, and Transformation in Financial Services. *Journal of Management Information Systems, 35*(1), 220–265. doi:10.1080/07421222.2018.1440766

Gonçalves, R. B., & de Figueiredo, J. C. B. (2022). Effects of perceived risks and benefits in the formation of the consumption privacy paradox: A study of the use of wearables in people practicing physical activities. *Electronic Markets, 32*(3), 1–15. doi:10.100712525-022-00559-7

Gong, X., Zhang, K. Z., Chen, C., Cheung, C. M., & Lee, M. K. (2020). What drives self-disclosure in mobile payment applications? The effect of privacy assurance approaches, network externality, and technology complementarity. *Information Technology & People*, *33*(4), 1174–1213. doi:10.1108/ITP-03-2018-0132

Gong, Y., Wang, Y., Frei, R., Wang, B., & Zhao, C. (2022). Blockchain application in circular marine plastic debris management. *Industrial Marketing Management*, *102*(9), 164–176. doi:10.1016/j.indmarman.2022.01.010

González-Ortega, D., Díaz-Pernas, F., Martínez-Zarzuela, M., & Antón-Rodríguez, M. (2014). A kinect-based system for cognitive rehabilitation exercises monitoring. *Computer Methods and Programs in Biomedicine*, *113*(2), 620–631. doi:10.1016/j.cmpb.2013.10.014 PMID:24263055

Goodrich, K., Schiller, S. Z., & Galletta, D. (2015). Consumer reactions to intrusiveness of online-video advertisements: Do length, informativeness, and humor help (or hinder) marketing outcomes? *Journal of Advertising Research*, *55*(1), 37–50. doi:10.2501/JAR-55-1-037-050

Goodwin, N., Harris, J., Nelson, J., Roach, B., & Torras, M. (2020). Consumption and the Consumer Society. *Microeconomics in Context*, 188–216. doi:10.4324/9781315702414-19

Gorla, N., Somers, T. M., & Wong, B. (2010). Organizational impact of system quality, information quality, and service quality. *The Journal of Strategic Information Systems*, *19*(3), 207–228. doi:10.1016/j.jsis.2010.05.001

Gounaris, S. P., Panigyrakis, G. G., & Chatzipanagiotou, K. C. (2007). Measuring the effectiveness of marketing information systems: An empirically validated instrument. *Marketing Intelligence & Planning*, *25*(6), 612–631. doi:10.1108/02634500710819978

Goyal, P., Pandey, S., & Jain, K. (2018). *Deep Learning for Natural Language Processing: Creating Neural Networks with Python*. Apress. doi:10.1007/978-1-4842-3685-7

Gozalo-Brizuela, R., & Garrido-Merchan, E. C. (2023). *ChatGPT is not all you need. A State of the Art Review of large Generative AI models*. arXiv preprint arXiv:2301.04655.

Greenstein-Messica, A., & Rokach, L. (2020). Machine learning and operation research based method for promotion optimization of products with no price elasticity history. *Electronic Commerce Research and Applications*, *40*, 100914. doi:10.1016/j.elerap.2019.100914

Gregory, A., & Bentall, L. (2012). Data governance protecting and managing the value of your customer data assets: Stage 3: Identifying and controlling the risk in using third-party processors. *Journal of Direct, Data and Digital Marketing Practice*, *13*(4), 335–344. doi:10.1057/dddmp.2012.5

Grewal, D., Hulland, J., Kopalle, P. K., & Karahanna, E. (2020). The future of technology and marketing: A multidisciplinary perspective. *Journal of the Academy of Marketing Science*, *48*(1), 1–8. doi:10.100711747-019-00711-4

Grønholdt, L., & Martensen, A. (2006). Key Marketing Performance Measures. *The Marketing Review*, *6*(3), 243–252. doi:10.1362/146934706778605287

Grosso, M., Castaldo, S., Li, H. A., & Larivière, B. (2020). What information do shoppers share? The effect of personnel-, retailer-, and country-trust on willingness to share information. *Journal of Retailing*, *96*(4), 524–547. doi:10.1016/j.jretai.2020.08.002

Grover, P., Kar, A. K., & Vigneswara Ilavarasan, P. (2018). Blockchain for businesses: A systematic literature review. Lecture Notes in Computer Science (Including Subseries Lecture Notes in Artificial Intelligence and Lecture Notes in Bioinformatics), 11195 LNCS, 325–336. doi:10.1007/978-3-030-02131-3_29

Guazzaroni, G., & Pillai, A. S. (Eds.). (2019). *Virtual and augmented reality in Education, Art, and Museums.* IGI Global. doi:10.4018/978-1-7998-1796-3

Guha, A., Grewal, D., Kopalle, P. K., Haenlein, M., Schneider, M. J., Jung, H., Moustafa, R., Hegde, D. R., & Hawkins, G. (2021). How artificial intelligence will affect the future of retailing. *Journal of Retailing, 97*(1), 28–41. doi:10.1016/j.jretai.2021.01.005

Gupta, A. (2014). E-Commerce: Role of E-Commerce in today's business. *International Journal of Computing and Corporate Research, 4*(1), 1–8.

Gupta, B. B., Tewari, A., Jain, A. K., & Agrawal, D. P. (2017). Fighting against phishing attacks: State of the art and future challenges. *Neural Computing & Applications, 28*(12), 3629–3654. doi:10.100700521-016-2275-y

Hackl, C. (2020). The Metaverse is Coming and It's A Very Big Deal. *Forbes, 2020*(June), 5. https://www.forbes.com/sites/cathyhackl/2020/07/05/the-metaverse-is-coming--its-a-very-big-deal/?sh=1f4c347a440f

Haenlein, M., & Kaplan, A. (2021). Artificial intelligence and robotics: Shaking up the business world and society at large. *Journal of Business Research, 124*, 405–407. doi:10.1016/j.jbusres.2020.10.042

Hafaiedh, K., Rhouma, M. B., Chargui, F., Haouas, Y., & Kerkeni, A. (2020). AdRobot:A smart segmentation application for automated & personalized marketing campaigns. *ACM International Conference Proceeding Series.*

Haider, C. M. R., Iqbal, A., Rahman, A. H., & Rahman, M. S. (2018). An ensemble learning based approach for impression fraud detection in mobile advertising. *Journal of Network and Computer Applications, 112*, 126–141. doi:10.1016/j.jnca.2018.02.021

Haig, M. (2001). Talking to the teen generation. *Brand Strategy, 30.*

Hair, J. F., Black, W. C., Babin, B. J., & Anderson, R. E. (2014). *Multivariate data analysis* (7th ed.). Pearson.

Hair, J. F. Jr, Harrison, D. E., & Risher, J. J. (2018). Marketing research in the 21st century: Opportunities and challenges. *Revista Brasileira de Marketing, 17*(5), 666–699. doi:10.5585/bjm.v17i5.4173

Hajli, N., Sims, J., Zadeh, A. H., & Richard, M.-O. (2017). A social commerce investigation of the role of trust in a social networking site on purchase intentions. *Journal of Business Research, 71*, 133–141. doi:10.1016/j.jbusres.2016.10.004

Hakkarainen, T., & Colicev, A. (2023). Blockchain-enabled advances (BEAs): Implications for consumers and brands. *Journal of Business Research, 160*, 160. doi:10.1016/j.jbusres.2023.113763

Haleem, A., Javaid, M., Asim Qadri, M., Pratap Singh, R., & Suman, R. (2022). Artificial intelligence (AI) applications for marketing: A literature-based study. *International Journal of Intelligent Networks, 3*, 119–132. doi:10.1016/j.ijin.2022.08.005

Hameed, K., & Rahman, N. (2017). Today's social network sites: An analysis of emerging security risks and their counter measures. *International Conference on Communication Technologies, ComTech 2017,* 143-148. 10.1109/COMTECH.2017.8065764

Harley, D., Verni, A., Willis, M., Ng, A., Bozzo, L., & Mazalek, A. (2018, March). Sensory vr: Smelling, touching, and eating virtual reality. In *Proceedings of the Twelfth International Conference on Tangible, Embedded, and Embodied Interaction* (pp. 386-397). 10.1145/3173225.3173241

Harris, K., Harris, R., & Baron, S. (2001). Customer participation in retail service: Lessons from Brecht. *International Journal of Retail & Distribution Management, 29*(8), 359–369. doi:10.1108/09590550110396845

Hart, C. B. (2017). Considering the Interaction of Functional Factors in Video Game Design Influencing the Economic Effectiveness of Microtransactions. *The Evolution and Social Impact of Video Game Economics*, 61-80.

Hasal, M., Nowaková, J., Ahmed Saghair, K., Abdulla, H., Snášel, V., & Ogiela, L. (2021). Chatbots: Security, privacy, data protection, and social aspects. *Concurrency and Computation*, *33*(19). Advance online publication. doi:10.1002/cpe.6426

Hassoun, A., Kamiloglu, S., Garcia-Garcia, G., Parra-López, C., Trollman, H., Jagtap, S., Aadil, R. M., & Esatbeyoglu, T. (2023). Implementation of relevant fourth industrial revolution innovations across the supply chain of fruits and vegetables: A short update on Traceability 4.0. *Food Chemistry, 409*. doi:10.1016/j.foodchem.2022.135303

Heartfield, R., & Loukas, G. (2015). A taxonomy of attacks and a survey of defense mechanisms for semantic social engineering attacks. *ACM Computing Surveys*, *48*(3), 1–39. doi:10.1145/2835375

Heath, C., & Heath, D. (2017). *The power of moments: why certain experiences have extraordinary impact*. Simon & Schuster.

Heitner, D. (2016). *Screenwise: Helping kids thrive (and survive) in their digital world*. Routledge. doi:10.4324/9781315213187

Hemais, M. W., & dos Santos, R. B. F. (2021). Understanding the Brazilian consumerism movement from a decolonial perspective: The case of Proteste. *Journal of Macromarketing*, *41*(2), 315–331. doi:10.1177/0276146720960220

Hengstler, M., Enkel, E., & Duelli, S. (2016). Applied artificial intelligence and trust-The case of autonomous vehicles and medical assistance devices. *Technological Forecasting and Social Change*, *105*, 105–120. doi:10.1016/j.techfore.2015.12.014

He, Q. (2021). Research on the advantage strategy of social network big data in marketing. *ACM International Conference Proceeding Series,* 923-926. 10.1145/3456887.3457106

Heurix, J., Zimmermann, P., Neubauer, T., & Fenz, S. (2015). A taxonomy for privacy enhancing technologies. *Computers & Security*, *53*, 1–17. doi:10.1016/j.cose.2015.05.002

Hidayati, J., Vamelia, R., Hammami, J., & Endri, E. (2023). Transparent distribution system design of halal beef supply chain. *Uncertain Supply Chain Management*, *11*(1), 31–40. doi:10.5267/j.uscm.2022.12.003

Hill, S. R., & Zubielqui, G. C. d. (2022). Managing Privacy in B2B Marketing: A Systematic Literature Review. *Journal of Computer Information Systems*, 1–18.

Hirsh, J. B., Kang, S. K., & Bodenhausen, G. V. (2012). Personalized Persuasion: Tailoring Persuasive Appeals to Recipients' Personality Traits. *Psychological Science*, *23*(6), 578–581. doi:10.1177/0956797611436349 PMID:22547658

Hoang, S. N., Nguyen, L. V., Huynh, T., & Pham, V. T. (2019). *An efficient model for sentiment analysis of electronic product reviews in Vietnamese*. doi:10.1007/978-3-030-35653-8_10

Hollensen, S., Kotler, P., & Opresnik, M. O. (2022). Metaverse–the new marketing universe. *The Journal of Business Strategy*.

Holt, S. (2023). Virtual reality, augmented reality and mixed reality: For astronaut mental health; and space tourism, education and outreach. *Acta Astronautica*, *203*, 436–446. doi:10.1016/j.actaastro.2022.12.016

Hossain, M. A., Agnihotri, R., Rushan, M. R. I., Rahman, M. S., & Sumi, S. F. (2022). Marketing analytics capability, artificial intelligence adoption, and firms' competitive advantage: Evidence from the manufacturing industry. *Industrial Marketing Management*, *106*, 240–255. doi:10.1016/j.indmarman.2022.08.017

Hou, Z., Ma, K., Wang, Y., Yu, J., Ji, K., Chen, Z., & Abraham, A. (2021). Attention-based learning of self-media data for marketing intention detection. *Engineering Applications of Artificial Intelligence*, *98*, 104118. doi:10.1016/j.engappai.2020.104118

Howard, M. C., & Davis, M. M. (2022). A meta-analysis and systematic literature review of mixed reality rehabilitation programs: Investigating design characteristics of augmented reality and augmented virtuality. *Computers in Human Behavior*, *130*, 107197. doi:10.1016/j.chb.2022.107197

Hoyer, W. D., Kroschke, M., Schmitt, B., Kraume, K., & Shankar, V. (2020). Transforming the Customer Experience Through New Technologies. *Journal of Interactive Marketing*, *51*, 57–71. doi:10.1016/j.intmar.2020.04.001

Hsu, S., & Liou, S. (2021). Artificial Intelligence Impact on Digital Content Marketing Research. *9th International Conference on Orange Technology (ICOT).*

Hsu, C.-L., & Lin, J. C.-C. (2023). Understanding the user satisfaction and loyalty of customer service chatbots. *Journal of Retailing and Consumer Services*, *71*, 103211. doi:10.1016/j.jretconser.2022.103211

Huang, S., & Siddarth, D. (2023). *Generative AI and the Digital Commons.* arXiv preprint arXiv:2303.11074.

Huang, M.-H., & Rust, R. T. (2021). Engaged to a Robot? The Role of AI in Service. *Journal of Service Research*, *24*(1), 30–41. doi:10.1177/1094670520902266

Huang, T.-L., & Liu, B. S. C. (2021). Augmented reality is human-like: How the humanizing experience inspires destination brand love. *Technological Forecasting and Social Change*, *170*, 170. doi:10.1016/j.techfore.2021.120853

Huaraca Aparco, R., Del Carmen Delgado Lime, M., Tapia Tadeo, F., Taipe Pardo, F., Palomino Rincón, H., Mescco Cáceres, E., ... Guzmán, N. P. (2022). Sustainability of rural agribusiness through e-commerce information systems. *IOP Conference Series: Earth and Environmental Science*, *968*(1). 10.1088/1755-1315/968/1/012002

Hu, J., Li, T., Zhuang, Y., Huang, S., & Dong, S. (2020). GFD: A weighted heterogeneous graph embedding based approach for fraud detection in mobile advertising. *Security and Communication Networks*, *2020*, 1–12. doi:10.1155/2020/8810817

Hutchinson, C. S. (2022). Potential abuses of dominance by big tech through their use of Big Data and AI. *Journal of Antitrust Enforcement*, *10*(3), 443–468. doi:10.1093/jaenfo/jnac004

Hutson, J., Banerjee, G., Kshetri, N., Odenwald, K., & Ratican, J. (2023). Architecting the Metaverse: Blockchain and the Financial and Legal Regulatory Challenges of Virtual Real Estate. *Journal of Intelligent Learning Systems and Applications*, *15*(1), 1–23. doi:10.4236/jilsa.2023.151001

Huynh-The, T., Gadekallu, T. R., Wang, W., Yenduri, G., Ranaweera, P., Pham, Q. V., da Costa, D. B., & Liyanage, M. (2023). Blockchain for the metaverse: A Review. *Future Generation Computer Systems*, *143*, 401–419. doi:10.1016/j.future.2023.02.008

IBM. (2023). *What is predictive analytics?* https://www.ibm.com/topics/predictive-analytics

Illescas-Manzano, M. D., Vicente López, N., Afonso González, N., & Cristofol Rodríguez, C. (2021). Implementation of Chatbot in Online Commerce, and Open Innovation. *Journal of Open Innovation*, *7*(2), 125. doi:10.3390/joitmc7020125

Illia, L., Colleoni, E., Etter, M., & Meggiorin, K. (2023). Finding the Tipping Point: When Heterogeneous Evaluations in Social Media Converge and Influence Organizational Legitimacy. *Business & Society*, *62*(1), 117–150. doi:10.1177/00076503211073516

Indrawati, & Shabila, A. M. (2020). The influence of website-based and company-based quality toward loyalty with perceived website trust as antecedents. *2020 8th International Conference on Information and Communication Technology, ICoICT 2020.* doi:10.1109/ICoICT49345.2020.9166408

Inman, J. J., & Nikolova, H. (2017). Shopper-Facing Retail Technology: A Retailer Adoption Decision Framework Incorporating Shopper Attitudes and Privacy Concerns. *Journal of Retailing, 93*(1), 7–28. doi:10.1016/j.jretai.2016.12.006

Isaja, M., Nguyen, P., Goknil, A., Sen, S., Husom, E. J., Tverdal, S., Anand, A., Jiang, Y., Pedersen, K. J., Myrseth, P., Stang, J., Niavis, H., Pfeifhofer, S., & Lamplmair, P. (2023). A blockchain-based framework for trusted quality data sharing towards zero-defect manufacturing. *Computers in Industry, 146*(January), 103853. doi:10.1016/j.compind.2023.103853

Ischen, C., Araujo, T., Voorveld, H., van Noort, G., & Smit, E. (2020). Privacy Concerns in Chatbot Interactions. Lecture Notes in Computer Science, 11970, 34–48. doi:10.1007/978-3-030-39540-7_3

Islam, T., Meade, N., Carson, R. T., Louviere, J. J., & Wang, J. (2022). The usefulness of socio-demographic variables in predicting purchase decisions: Evidence from machine learning procedures. *Journal of Business Research, 151*, 324–338. doi:10.1016/j.jbusres.2022.07.004

Ismail, S. T. (2011). The Role of Marketing Information System on Decision Making: An Applied study on Royal Jordanian Air Lines (RJA). *International Journal of Business and Social Science, 2*(3), 175–185.

Jacksi, K., & Abass, S. M. (2019). Development history of the world wide web. *International Journal of Scientific and Technology Research, 8*(9), 75–79.

Jacobson, J., Gruzd, A., & Hernández-García, Á. (2020). Social media marketing: Who is watching the watchers? *Journal of Retailing and Consumer Services, 53*, 53. doi:10.1016/j.jretconser.2019.03.001

Jain, A., Ramachandran, K. K., Sharma, S., Sharma, T., Pareek, P., & Pant, B. (2022). Detailed investigation of influence of machine learning (ML) and big data on digital transformation in marketing. *2022 2nd International Conference on Advance Computing and Innovative Technologies in Engineering, ICACITE 2022* (pp. 1061-1065). 10.1109/ICACITE53722.2022.9823810

Jain, S., & Werth, D. (2019). Current state of mixed reality technology for digital retail: a literature review. In *HCI in Business, Government and Organizations. eCommerce and Consumer Behavior: 6th International Conference, HCIBGO 2019, Held as Part of the 21st HCI International Conference, HCII 2019.* Springer International Publishing. 10.1007/978-3-030-22335-9_2

Jain, D., Dash, M. K., Kumar, A., & Luthra, S. (2021). How is Blockchain used in marketing: A review and research agenda. *International Journal of Information Management Data Insights, 1*(2), 100044. doi:10.1016/j.jjimei.2021.100044

James, T. L., Wallace, L., Warkentin, M., Kim, B. C., & Collignon, S. E. (2017). Exposing others' information on online social networks (OSNs): Perceived shared risk, its determinants, and its influence on OSN privacy control use. *Information & Management, 54*(7), 851–865. doi:10.1016/j.im.2017.01.001

Jarek, K., & Mazurek, G. (2019). Marketing and Artificial Intelligence. *Central European Business Review.* https://cebr.vse.cz/artkey/cbr-201902-0003_marketing-and-artificial-intelligence.php

Jarrahi, M. H. (2018). Artificial intelligence and the future of work: Human-AI symbiosis in organizational decision making. *Business Horizons, 61*(4), 577–586. doi:10.1016/j.bushor.2018.03.007

Järvinen, J., Tollinen, A., Karjaluoto, H., & Jayawardhena, C. (2012). Digital and social media marketing usage in B2B industrial section. *Marketing Management Journal, 22*(2), 102–117.

Jayashree, S., Sidana, N., Pham, L. T., Kunju, L. M., Ratnavalli, B., & Gangodkar, D. (2022). The progressive role of machine learning in enhancing the effectiveness of digital marketing in emerging economies. *2022 2nd International Conference on Advance Computing and Innovative Technologies in Engineering, ICACITE 2022*, 1640-1645. 10.1109/ICACITE53722.2022.9823438

Jeganathan, G. S., & David, A. (2022). Determination of Hospitality Services Quality and Customer Satisfaction-A Holserv Approach. In *Au Virtual International Conference* (pp. 325-334). Academic Press.

Jeganathan, G. S., David, A., & Ganesh Kumar, C. (2022). Adaptation of Blockchain Technology In HRM. *Korea Review of International Studies*, 10-22.

Jerald, J. (2017, March). *Human-centered design for immersive interactions. In 2017 IEEE Virtual Reality (VR).* IEEE.

Jessen, A., Hilken, T., Chylinski, M., Mahr, D., Heller, J., Keeling, D. I., & de Ruyter, K. (2020). The playground effect: How augmented reality drives creative customer engagement. *Journal of Business Research, 116*, 85–98. doi:10.1016/j.jbusres.2020.05.002

Jha, A. K., & Shah, S. (2021). Disconfirmation effect on online review credibility: An experimental analysis. *Decision Support Systems, 145*, 113519. / doi:10.1016/j.dss.2021.113519

Jha, A., & Sudhakar, P. kumar Lokhande, S. A., Ishodzhanova, G., Venkatrao, K., & Zhakupova, A. (2022, September). Facial Recognition Impact in Smartphone Sector. In *2022 4th International Conference on Inventive Research in Computing Applications (ICIRCA)* (pp. 1566-1571). IEEE. 10.1109/ICIRCA54612.2022.9985766

Jha, A., & Jha, A. (2022). Data Encryption Dispute Resolutions under Intermediary Guidelines of Information Technology Act: Challenges and Future Framework. *DESIDOC Journal of Library and Information Technology, 42*(3), 201–207. doi:10.14429/djlit.42.3.17869

Jha, A., Singh, S. R., & Dr Meenakshi. (2022). Human-Machine Convergence and Disruption of Socio-Cognitive Capabilities. *International Journal of Next-Generation Computing, 13*(3). doi:10.47164/ijngc.v13i3.893

Jiang, D., Huo, L., Lv, Z., Song, H., & Qin, W. (2018). A joint multi-criteria utility-based network selection approach for vehicle-to-infrastructure networking. *IEEE Transactions on Intelligent Transportation Systems, 19*(10), 3305–3319. doi:10.1109/TITS.2017.2778939

Jiang, H., Zhang, Z., Dang, J., & Wu, L. (2018). A novel 3-D massive MIMO channel model for vehicle-to-vehicle communication environments. *IEEE Transactions on Communications, 66*(1), 79–90. doi:10.1109/TCOMM.2017.2751555

Jindal, T., Sheoliha, N., Kishore, K., Uike, D., Khurana, S., & Verma, D. (2022, April). A Conceptual Analysis on the Impact of Internet of Things (IOT) Towards on Digital Marketing Transformation. In *2022 2nd International Conference on Advance Computing and Innovative Technologies in Engineering (ICACITE)* (pp. 1943-1947). IEEE.

Jin, S. A. A., & Bolebruch, J. (2009). Virtual commerce (v-commerce) in Second Life: The roles of physical presence and brand-self connection. *Journal of Virtual Worlds Research, 2*(4). Advance online publication. doi:10.4101/jvwr.v2i4.760

Jones, E. (2019). Rethinking Greenwashing: Corporate Discourse, Unethical Practice, and the Unmet Potential of Ethical Consumerism. *Sociological Perspectives, 62*(5), 728–754. doi:10.1177/0731121419849095

Joshi, P., & Kumar, A. (2020, July). A novel framework for decentralized c2c e-commerce using smart contract. In *2020 11th International Conference on Computing, Communication and Networking Technologies (ICCCNT)* (pp. 1-5). IEEE. 10.1109/ICCCNT49239.2020.9225377

Joyce, A., & Paquin, R. L. (2016). The triple layered business model canvas: A tool to design more sustainable business models. *Journal of Cleaner Production, 135*, 1474–1486. doi:10.1016/j.jclepro.2016.06.067

Jung, S. H., & Jeong, Y. J. (2020). Twitter data analytical methodology development for prediction of start-up firms' social media marketing level. *Technology in Society*, *63*, 101409. doi:10.1016/j.techsoc.2020.101409

Kadavasal, M. S., Dhara, K. K., Wu, X., & Krishnaswamy, V. (2007). Mixed reality for enhancing business communications using virtual worlds. *Proceedings of the ACM Symposium on Virtual Reality Software and Technology, VRST,* (pp. 233–234). ACM. 10.1145/1315184.1315236

Kaiser, C., Ahuvia, A., Rauschnabel, P. A., & Wimble, M. (2020). Social media monitoring: What can marketers learn from Facebook brand photos? *Journal of Business Research*, *117*, 707–717. doi:10.1016/j.jbusres.2019.09.017

Kalburgi, N. K., David, A., & Muralidhar, L. B. (2023). Understanding the Perceptions of Students towards YouTube as a Learning Tool-An Empirical Approach. *Central European Management Journal,* 2336-2693.

Kalyanam, K., & McIntyre, S. (2002). The e-marketing mix: A contribution of the e-tailing wars. *Journal of the Academy of Marketing Science*, *30*(4), 487–499. doi:10.1177/009207002236924

Kam, H. J., Menard, P., Ormond, D., & Crossler, R. E. (2020). Cultivating cybersecurity learning: An integration of self-determination and flow. *Computers & Security*, *96*, 101875. doi:10.1016/j.cose.2020.101875

Kamoonpuri, S. Z., & Sengar, A. (2023). Hi, May AI help you? An analysis of the barriers impeding the implementation and use of artificial intelligence-enabled virtual assistants in retail. *Journal of Retailing and Consumer Services*, *72*, 103258. doi:10.1016/j.jretconser.2023.103258

Kanei, F., Chiba, D., Hato, K., Yoshioka, K., Matsumoto, T., & Akiyama, M. (2020). Detecting and understanding online advertising fraud in the wild. *IEICE Transactions on Information and Systems*, *103*(7), 1512–1523. doi:10.1587/transinf.2019ICP0008

Kannengießer, N., Lins, S., Dehling, T., & Sunyaev, A. (2020). Trade-offs between distributed ledger technology characteristics. *ACM Computing Surveys*, *53*(2), 1–37. doi:10.1145/3379463

Kaplan, D. (2021). Public intimacy in social media: The mass audience as a third party. *Media Culture & Society*, *43*(4), 595–612. doi:10.1177/0163443721991087

Kaponis, A., & Maragoudakis, M. (2022). Data Analysis in Digital Marketing using Machine learning and Artificial Intelligence Techniques, Ethical and Legal Dimensions, State of the Art. In *12th Hellenic Conference on Artificial Intelligence (SETN 2022).* ACM. 10.1145/3549737.3549756

Kapoor, K. K., Tamilmani, K., Rana, N. P., Patil, P., Dwivedi, Y. K., & Nerur, S. (2018). Advances in social media research: Past, present and future. *Information Systems Frontiers*, *20*(3), 531–558. doi:10.100710796-017-9810-y

Kapoor, R., & Kapoor, K. (2021). The transition from traditional to digital marketing: A study of the evolution of e-marketing in the Indian hotel industry. *Worldwide Hospitality and Tourism Themes*, *13*(2), 199–213. doi:10.1108/WHATT-10-2020-0124

Kar, A. K., & Kushwaha, A. K. (2021). Facilitators and Barriers of Artificial Intelligence Adoption in Business – Insights from Opinions Using Big Data Analytics. *Information Systems Frontiers*. Advance online publication. doi:10.100710796-021-10219-4

KaraarslanE.AltundasS. (2022). Cross-platform and Personalized Avatars in the Metaverse: Ready Player Me Case. Available at SSRN 4249064.

Karaarslan, E., Aydin, Ö., Cali, Ü., & Challenger, M. (Eds.). (2023). *Digital Twin Driven Intelligent Systems and Emerging Metaverse*. Springer Nature. doi:10.1007/978-981-99-0252-1

Kashevnik, A., Lashkov, I., & Gurtov, A. (2020). Methodology and mobile application for driver behavior analysis and accident prevention. *IEEE Transactions on Intelligent Transportation Systems*, *21*(6), 2427–2436. doi:10.1109/TITS.2019.2918328

Kaur, P. (2022). Sentiment analysis using web scraping for live news data with machine learning algorithms. *Materials Today: Proceedings*, *65*, 3333–3341. doi:10.1016/j.matpr.2022.05.409

Kaur, P., Sharma, M., & Mittal, M. (2018). Big Data and Machine Learning Based Secure Healthcare Framework. *Procedia Computer Science*, *132*, 1049–1059. doi:10.1016/j.procs.2018.05.020

Keen, A., & Ramage, M. (2010). The cult of the amateur. *Online Communication and Collaboration. REAd (Porto Alegre)*, 251–255.

Kelly, P. (2023). *'Why would we employ people?' Experts on five ways AI will change work*. https://www.theguardian.com/global-development/2023/may/12/why-would-we-employ-people-experts-on-five-ways-ai-will-change-work

Kelly, S., Kaye, S.-A., & Oviedo-Trespalacios, O. (2023). What factors contribute to the acceptance of artificial intelligence? A systematic review. *Telematics and Informatics*, *77*, 101925. doi:10.1016/j.tele.2022.101925

Khadke, S., Gupta, P., Rachakunta, S., Mahata, C., Dawn, S., Sharma, M., Verma, D., Pradhan, A., Krishna, A. M. S., Ramakrishna, S., Chakrabortty, S., Saianand, G., Sonar, P., Biring, S., Dash, J. K., & Dalapati, G. K. (2021). Efficient plastic recycling and remolding circular economy using the technology of trust–blockchain. *Sustainability (Basel)*, *13*(16), 1–15. doi:10.3390u13169142

Khan, H., & Kushwah, K. K. (2021). Blockchain and the future of digital marketing. Blockchain technology and applications for digital marketing, 250-275. doi:10.4018/978-1-7998-8081-3.ch016

Khan, S. N., Loukil, F., Ghedira-Guegan, C., Benkhelifa, E., & Bani-Hani, A. (2021). Blockchain smart contracts: Applications, challenges, and future trends. *Peer-to-Peer Networking and Applications*, *14*(5), 2901–2925. doi:10.100712083-021-01127-0 PMID:33897937

Kimble, C., & Milolidakis, G. (2015). Big data and business intelligence: Debunking the myths. *Global Business and Organizational Excellence*, *35*(1), 23–34. doi:10.1002/joe.21642

Kim, D., & Benbasat, I. (2003). Trust-related arguments in internet stores: A framework for evaluation. *Journal of Electronic Commerce Research*, *4*(2), 49–64.

Kim, G. J. (2005). *Designing Virtual Reality Systems: The Structured Approach*. Springer.

Kim, J. W., Lee, B. H., Shaw, M. J., Chang, H.-L., & Nelson, M. (2001). Application of decision-tree induction techniques to personalized advertisements on internet storefronts. *International Journal of Electronic Commerce*, *5*(3), 45–62. doi:10.1080/10864415.2001.11044215

Kim, S. J., Laine, T. H., & Suk, H. J. (2021). Presence Effects in Virtual Reality Based on User Characteristics: Attention, Enjoyment, and Memory. *Electronics (Basel)*, *10*(9), 1051. doi:10.3390/electronics10091051

Kim, W. (2022). Television and American consumerism. *Journal of Public Economics*, *208*, 1–17. doi:10.1016/j.jpubeco.2022.104609

Kim, Y., & Krishnan, R. (2015). On product-level uncertainty and online purchase behavior: An empirical analysis. *Management Science*, *61*(10), 2449–2467. doi:10.1287/mnsc.2014.2063

Kim, Y., Kwon, D. Y., & Jeong, S. R. (2015). Comparing machine learning classifiers for movie WOM opinion mining. *KSII Transactions on Internet and Information Systems*, *9*(8), 3169–3181. doi:10.3837/tiis.2015.08.025

King, M. A., Abrahams, A. S., & Ragsdale, C. T. (2015). Ensemble learning methods for pay-per-click campaign management. *Expert Systems with Applications*, *42*(10), 4818–4829. doi:10.1016/j.eswa.2015.01.047

Kirk, G., & Noguera, J. (2019). Strategic marketing and cybersecurity: The case of data breaches. *Issues in Information Systems*, *20*(3), 165–174. doi:10.48009/3_iis_2019_165-174a

Kizilcec, R. F., Anderson, F., & Cho, Y. J. (2021). *Delivery Ghost: Effects of Language Immersion and Interactivity in a Language Learning Game*. ACM Digital Library.

Klaus, P., & Zaichkowsky, J. (2020). AI voice bots: A services marketing research agenda. *Journal of Services Marketing*, *34*(3), 389–398. doi:10.1108/JSM-01-2019-0043

Klien, J. A., Rao, P. M., & Dalvi, M. (2018). Competition and consumer privacy in the cyberspace market. *Journal of Intellectual Property Rights*, *23*(2-3), 70–85.

Knierim, P., Kosch, T., Hoppe, M., & Schmidt, A. (2018). Challenges and opportunities of mixed reality systems in education. *Mensch und Computer 2018-Workshopband*, 325-330.

Knijnenburg, B. P., Willemsen, M. C., Gantner, Z., Soncu, H., & Newell, C. (2012). Explaining the user experience of recommender systems. *User Modeling and User-Adapted Interaction*, *22*(4–5), 441–504. doi:10.100711257-011-9118-4

Koiso-Kanttila, N. (2004). Digital Content Marketing: A Literature Synthesis. *Journal of Marketing Management*, *20*(1–2), 45–65. doi:10.1362/026725704773041122

Kolte, A., Roy, J. K., & Vasa, L. (2023). The impact of unpredictable resource prices and equity volatility in advanced and emerging economies: An econometric and machine learning approach. *Resources Policy*, *80*, 103216. doi:10.1016/j.resourpol.2022.103216

Konyeha, S. (2020). Exploring cybersecurity threats in digital marketing. *NIPES J. Sci. Technol. Res*, *2*(3), 12. doi:10.37933/nipes/2.3.2020.2

Koops, B. J., Newell, B. C., Timan, T., Skorvanek, I., Chokrevski, T., & Galic, M. (2016). A typology of privacy. *U. Pa. J. Int'l L.*, *38*, 483.

Koos, S. (2021). Moralising markets, marketizing morality. The fair trade movement, product labeling and the mergence of ethical consumerism in europe. *Journal of Nonprofit & Public Sector Marketing*, *33*(2), 168–192. doi:10.1080/10495142.2020.1865235

Kopalle, P. K., Gangwar, M., Kaplan, A., Ramachandran, D., Reinartz, W., & Rindfleisch, A. (2022). Examining artificial intelligence (AI) technologies in marketing via a global lens: Current trends and future research opportunities. *International Journal of Research in Marketing*, *39*(2), 522–540. doi:10.1016/j.ijresmar.2021.11.002

Kordon, A. (2020). *Data Science Based on Artificial Intelligence*. https://www.researchgate.net/publication/344314160_Data_Science_Based_on_Artificial_Intelligence

Kosinski, M., Stillwell, D., & Graepel, T. (2013). Private traits and attributes are predictable from digital records of human behavior. *Proceedings of the National Academy of Sciences of the United States of America*, *110*(15), 5802–5805. doi:10.1073/pnas.1218772110 PMID:23479631

Kotler, P. (1972). What consumerism means for marketers. *Harvard Business Review*, *50*(3), 48–57.

Kotler, P., Kartajaya, H., & Setiawan, I. (2017). *Marketing 4.0: Moving from Traditional to Digital*. John Wiley & Sons.

Kouhizadeh, M., Sarkis, J., & Zhu, Q. (2019). At the nexus of blockchain technology, the circular economy, and product deletion. *Applied Sciences*, *9*(8), 1712. Advance online publication. doi:10.3390/app9081712

Koyun, A., & Al Janabi, E. (2017). Social engineering attacks. *Journal of Multidisciplinary Engineering Science and Technology*, *4*(6), 7533–7538.

Krafft, M., Arden, C. M., & Verhoef, P. C. (2017). Permission Marketing and Privacy Concerns — Why Do Customers (Not) Grant Permissions? *Journal of Interactive Marketing*, *39*(1), 39–54. doi:10.1016/j.intmar.2017.03.001

Krafft, M., Sajtos, L., & Haenlein, M. (2020). Challenges and Opportunities for Marketing Scholars in Times of the Fourth Industrial Revolution. *Journal of Interactive Marketing*, *51*, 1–8. doi:10.1016/j.intmar.2020.06.001

Kraft, T., Valdés, L., & Zheng, Y. (2022). Consumer trust in social responsibility communications: The role of supply chain visibility. *Production and Operations Management*, *31*(11), 4113–4130. doi:10.1111/poms.13808

Kraus, S., Kanbach, D. K., Krysta, P. M., Steinhoff, M. M., & Tomini, N. (2022). Facebook and the creation of the metaverse: Radical business model innovation or incremental transformation? *International Journal of Entrepreneurial Behaviour & Research*, *28*(9), 52–77. doi:10.1108/IJEBR-12-2021-0984

Krishen, A. S., Dwivedi, Y. K., Bindu, N., & Kumar, K. S. (2021). A broad overview of interactive digital marketing: A bibliometric network analysis. *Journal of Business Research*, *131*, 183–195. doi:10.1016/j.jbusres.2021.03.061

Kshetri, N. (2022). The Global Rise of Online Devices, Cyber Crime and Cyber Defense: Enhancing Ethical Actions, Counter Measures, Cyber Strategy, and Approaches. *ProQuest Dissertations Publishing*, Doi:10.13140/RG.2.2.33257.57446

Kshetri, N. (2021a). *Blockchain Technology for improving transparency and citizen's trust*. Springer Nature Switzerland AG. doi:10.1007/978-3-030-73100-7_52

Kshetri, N. (2021b). A survey on Computer ethics (w.r.t. Artificial Intelligence, Robot Weaponry, Fuzzy systems, Autonomous Vehicles). *International Journal of Innovative Technology and Exploring Engineering*, *10*(4), 207–210. Advance online publication. doi:10.35940/ijitee.D8582.0210421

Kshetri, N., Bhushal, C. S., Pandey, P. S., & Dwivedi, V. (2022). BCT-CS: Blockchain technology applications for Cyber defense and Cybersecurity: A survey and solutions. *International Journal of Advanced Computer Science and Applications*, *13*(11). Advance online publication. doi:10.14569/IJACSA.2022.0131140

Kübler, R. V., Colicev, A., & Pauwels, K. H. (2020). Social media's impact on the consumer mindset: When to use which sentiment extraction tool? *Journal of Interactive Marketing*, *50*(1), 136–155. doi:10.1016/j.intmar.2019.08.001

Kucuk, S. U. (2016). Consumerism in the digital age. *The Journal of Consumer Affairs*, *50*(3), 515–538. doi:10.1111/joca.12101

Kulshrestha, R., Shekhar, C., Jain, M., & Chakravarthy, S. R. (2021). *Mathematical modeling and computation of real-time problems: an interdisciplinary approach*. CRC Press. doi:10.1201/9781003055037

Kumar, A. B. R. (2021). AI-Based Digital Marketing Strategies - A Review. In S. Smys, V. E. Balas, K. A. Kamel and P. Lafata (Eds), *Inventive Computation and Information Technologies: Proceedings of ICICIT 2020* (pp. 957-969). Springer.

Kumar, S., Pallathadka, H., & Pallathadka, L. K. (2022). An analysis of cyber security threats in digital marketing. *Journal of Critical Reviews*, *9*(03), 85–94. www.jcreview.com/admin/Uploads/Files/626bc981113797.49051701.pdf

Kumar, V., Ramachandran, D., & Kumar, B. (2021). Influence of new-age technologies on marketing: A research agenda. *Journal of Business Research*, *125*, 864–877. doi:10.1016/j.jbusres.2020.01.007

Kwok, L., Tang, Y., & Yu, B. (2020). The 7 Ps marketing mix of home-sharing services: Mining travelers' online reviews on Airbnb. *International Journal of Hospitality Management*, *90*, 102616. doi:10.1016/j.ijhm.2020.102616 PMID:32834353

Labrecque, L. I., Markos, E., & Darmody, A. (2021). Addressing online behavioral advertising and privacy implications: A comparison of passive versus active learning approaches. *Journal of Marketing Education*, *43*(1), 43–58. doi:10.1177/0273475319828788

Lacoche, J., Le Chénéchal, M., Villain, E., & Foulonneau, A. (2019, September). Model and tools for integrating iot into mixed reality environments: Towards a virtual-real seamless continuum. In *ICAT-EGVE 2019-International Conference on Artificial Reality and Telexistence and Eurographics Symposium on Virtual Environments*. Dig Lib. 10.2312/egve.20191286

Lahkani, M. J., Wang, S., Urbański, M., & Egorova, M. (2020). Sustainable B2B E-commerce and blockchain-based supply chain finance. *Sustainability (Basel)*, *12*(10), 3968. doi:10.3390u12103968

Lahmiri, S., Bekiros, S., & Avdoulas, C. (2023). A comparative assessment of machine learning methods for predicting housing prices using Bayesian optimization. *Decision Analytics Journal*, *6*, 100166. doi:10.1016/j.dajour.2023.100166

Lakshman, K., & David, A. (n.d.). *Senior Citizens' Perceptions on E-banking Services*. Exceller Books.

Lambillotte, L., Bart, Y., & Poncin, I. (2022). When Does Information Transparency Reduce Downside of Personalization? Role of Need for Cognition and Perceived Control. *Journal of Interactive Marketing*, *57*(3), 393–420. doi:10.1177/10949968221095557

Landau, J-P. & Genais, A. (2018). *Les crypto-monnaies, rapport au Ministre de l'Économie et des Finances*. Academic Press.

Lang, T., & Hines, C. (1993). *The new protectionism: Protecting the future against free trade*. Earthscan Ltd.

Lapointe, C., & Fishbane, L. (2019). The Blockchain Ethical Design Framework. *Innovations: Technology, Governance, Globalization*, *12*(3–4), 50–71. doi:10.1162/inov_a_00275

Lasén, A. (2015). *Digital self-portraits, exposure and the modulation of intimacy. In Mobile and Digital Communication: Approaches to Public and Private*. Livros LabCom. doi:10.4324/9781315399300-8

Laufer, R. S., & Wolfe, M. (1977). Privacy as a Concept and a Social Issue: A Multidimensional Developmental Theory. *The Journal of Social Issues*, *33*(3), 22–42. doi:10.1111/j.1540-4560.1977.tb01880.x

Lau, J., Zimmerman, B., & Schaub, F. (2018). Alexa, Are You Listening? Privacy Perceptions, Concerns and Privacy-seeking Behaviors with Smart Speakers. *Proceedings of the ACM on Human-Computer Interaction*, *2*(CSCW), 1–31. doi:10.1145/3274371

Laukkanen, T., Xi, N., Hallikainen, H., Ruusunen, N., & Hamari, J. (2022). Virtual technologies in supporting sustainable consumption: From a single-sensory stimulus to a multi-sensory experience. *International Journal of Information Management*, *63*, 102455. doi:10.1016/j.ijinfomgt.2021.102455

Laussel, D., Van Long, N., & Resende, J. (2022). Profit effects of consumers' identity management: A dynamic model. *Management Science*. Advance online publication. doi:10.1287/mnsc.2022.4511

Layton, R. A. (2007). Marketing systems - A core macromarketing concept. *Journal of Macromarketing*, *27*(3), 227–242. doi:10.1177/0276146707302836

Le Grand, J., Roberts, J., & Chandra, G. (2021). Buying for good: Altruism, ethical consumerism and social policy. *Social Policy and Administration*, *55*(7), 1341–1355. doi:10.1111pol.12729

LeBlanc, D., & Biddle, R. (2012). Risk perception of internet-related activities. In *2012 Tenth Annual International Conference on Privacy, Security and Trust* (pp. 88–95). IEEE. 10.1109/PST.2012.6297924

Lee, M. T., & Raschke, R. L. (2023). Stakeholder legitimacy in firm greening and financial performance: What about greenwashing temptations?. *Journal of Business Research, 155*. doi:10.1016/j.jbusres.2022.113393

Lee, C., Lv, Y., Ng, K., Ho, W., & Choy, K. (2018). Design and application of Internet of Things-based warehouse management system for smart logistics. *International Journal of Production Research*, *56*(8), 2753–2768. doi:10.1080/00207543.2017.1394592

Lee, D., Hosanagar, K., & Nair, H. S. (2018). Advertising content and consumer engagement on social media: Evidence from Facebook. *Management Science*, *64*(11), 5105–5131. doi:10.1287/mnsc.2017.2902

Leeflang, P. S. H., Verhoef, P. C., Dahlström, P., & Freundt, T. (2014). Challenges and solutions for marketing in a digital era. *European Management Journal*, *32*(1), 1–12. doi:10.1016/j.emj.2013.12.001

Lee, H., Kang, S., & Lee, U. (2022). Understanding privacy risks and perceived benefits in open dataset collection for mobile affective computing. *Proceedings of the ACM on Interactive, Mobile, Wearable and Ubiquitous Technologies*, *6*(2), 1–26. doi:10.1145/3534623

Lee, J., Kim, C., & Lee, K. C. (2022). Exploring the personalization-intrusiveness-intention framework to evaluate the effects of personalization in social media. *International Journal of Information Management*, *66*, 66. doi:10.1016/j.ijinfomgt.2022.102532

Lee, S. J., Ahn, C., Song, K. M., & Ahn, H. (2018). Trust and distrust in e-commerce. *Sustainability (Basel)*, *10*(4), 1015. doi:10.3390u10041015

Lee, Y.-I., & Trim, P. R. J. (2022). Enhancing Marketing Provision through Increased Online Safety That Imbues Consumer Confidence: Coupling AI and ML with the AIDA Model. *Big Data and Cognitive Computing*, *6*(3), 78. doi:10.3390/bdcc6030078

Leguina, J. R., Rumín, Á. C., & Rumín, R. C. (2020). Digital Marketing Attribution: Understanding the User Path. *Electronics (Basel)*, *9*(11), 1822. doi:10.3390/electronics9111822

Leherbauer, P. (2019). *Cryptomoney and its' Applications in B2C Markets: Status quo and future Trends/submitted by Philipp Leherbauer, B. Sc* [Doctoral dissertation, Universität Linz].

Lemon, K. N., & Verhoef, P. C. (2016). Understanding customer experience throughout the customer journey. *Journal of Marketing*, *80*(6), 69–96. doi:10.1509/jm.15.0420

Lemos, C., Ramos, R. F., Moro, S., & Oliveira, P. M. (2022). Stick or Twist—The Rise of Blockchain Applications in Marketing Management. *Sustainability*, *14*(7), 1–16. [REMOVED HYPERLINK FIELD] doi:10.3390u14074172 PMID:36090804

Leonard, L. N., & Jones, K. (2021). Trust in C2C electronic commerce: Ten years later. *Journal of Computer Information Systems*, *61*(3), 240–246. doi:10.1080/08874417.2019.1598829

Lepa, S., Herzog, M., Steffens, J., Schoenrock, A., & Egermann, H. (2020). A computational model for predicting perceived musical expression in branding scenarios. *Journal of New Music Research*, *49*(4), 387–402. doi:10.1080/09298215.2020.1778041

Leximancer. (2021). *Leximancer User Guide: Vol. Release 4*. Leximancer Pty Ltd.

Liang, X., Wang, C., & Zhao, G. (2019). Enhancing content marketing article detection with graph analysis. *IEEE Access : Practical Innovations, Open Solutions*, *7*, 94869–94881. doi:10.1109/ACCESS.2019.2928094

Liebermann, Y., & Stashevsky, S. (2002). Perceived risks as barriers to Internet and ecommerce usage. *Qualitative Market Research*, *5*(4), 291–300. doi:10.1108/13522750210443245

Li, J., Han, D., Wu, Z., Wang, J., Li, K. C., & Castiglione, A. (2023). A novel system for medical equipment supply chain traceability based on alliance chain and attribute and role access control. *Future Generation Computer Systems*, *142*, 195–211. doi:10.1016/j.future.2022.12.037

Li, J., Pan, S., & Huang, L. (2019). A machine learning based method for customer behavior prediction. *Tehnicki Vjesnik (Strojarski Fakultet)*, *26*(6), 1670–1676.

Li, L., He, W., Xu, L., Ash, I., Anwar, M., & Yuan, X. (2019). Investigating the impact of cybersecurity policy awareness on employees' cybersecurity behavior. *International Journal of Information Management*, *45*, 13–24. doi:10.1016/j.ijinfomgt.2018.10.017

Limański, A., Popławska, Ż., & Drabik, I. (2018). Marketing information system and risk reduction in managing a company on foreign markets. *Ekonomia i Prawo*, *17*(1), 43. doi:10.12775/EiP.2018.004

Limayem, M., Hirt, S. G., & Cheung, C. M. K. (2007). How habit limits the predictive power of intention: The case of information systems continuance. *Management Information Systems Quarterly*, *31*(4), 705–737. doi:10.2307/25148817

Lin, C. A., & Kim, T. (2016). Predicting user response to sponsored advertising on social media via the technology acceptance model. *Computers in Human Behavior*, *64*, 710–718. doi:10.1016/j.chb.2016.07.027

Lin, J.-S., & Wu, L. (2023). Examining the psychological process of developing consumer-brand relationships through strategic use of social media brand chatbots. *Computers in Human Behavior*, *140*, 107488. doi:10.1016/j.chb.2022.107488

Lin, X., Huang, X., Liu, S., Li, Y., Luo, H., & Yu, S. (2022). Competitive price-quality strategy of platforms under user privacy concerns. *Journal of Theoretical and Applied Electronic Commerce Research*, *17*(2), 571–589. doi:10.3390/jtaer17020030

Li, Q. (2011b). Privacy in social networks: An empirical analysis. *The Journal of Privacy and Confidentiality*, *3*(1), 1–23.

Liu, L., Dzyabura, D., & Mizik, N. (2020). Visual listening in: Extracting brand image portrayed on social media. *Marketing Science*, *39*(4), 669–686. doi:10.1287/mksc.2020.1226

Liu, M., Cai, S., Lai, Z., Qiu, L., Hu, Z., & Ding, Y. (2021). A joint learning model for click-through prediction in display advertising. *Neurocomputing*, *445*, 206–219. doi:10.1016/j.neucom.2021.02.036

Liu-Thompkins, Y., Okazaki, S., & Li, H. (2022). Artificial empathy in marketing interactions: Bridging the human-AI gap in affective and social customer experience. *Journal of the Academy of Marketing Science*, *50*(6), 1198–1218. doi:10.100711747-022-00892-5

Liu, X., Ahmad, S. F., Anser, M. K., Ke, J., Irshad, M., Ul-Haq, J., & Abbas, S. (2022). Cyber security threats: A never-ending challenge for e-commerce. *Frontiers in Psychology*, *13*, 927398. Advance online publication. doi:10.3389/fpsyg.2022.927398 PMID:36337532

Liu, Y., & Huang, X. (2021). Brand digital marketing under intranet security control based on the machine learning classification algorithm. *Security and Communication Networks*, *2021*, 1–10. Advance online publication. doi:10.1155/2021/9977221

Liu, Y., & Wang, T. (2022). Quality factors and performance outcome of cloud-based marketing system. *Kybernetes*, *51*(1), 485–503. doi:10.1108/K-11-2020-0778

Liu, Z., & Li, Z. (2020). A blockchain-based framework of cross-border e-commerce supply chain. *International Journal of Information Management*, *52*, 102059. doi:10.1016/j.ijinfomgt.2019.102059

Liu, Z., & Wang, X. (2018). How to regulate individuals' privacy boundaries on social network sites: A cross-cultural comparison. *Information & Management*, *55*(8), 1005–1023. doi:10.1016/j.im.2018.05.006

Li, X., Shi, M., & Wang, X. S. (2019). Video mining: Measuring visual information using automatic methods. *International Journal of Research in Marketing*, *36*(2), 216–231. doi:10.1016/j.ijresmar.2019.02.004

Li, Y., Tan, C., Ip, W. H., & Wu, C. H. (2023). Dynamic blockchain adoption for freshness-keeping in the fresh agricultural product supply chain. *Expert Systems with Applications*, *217*, 119494. Advance online publication. doi:10.1016/j.eswa.2022.119494

Li, Z. (2022). Accurate Digital Marketing Communication Based on Intelligent Data Analysis. *Scientific Programming*, *2022*, 8294891. doi:10.1155/2022/8294891

Ljepava, N. (2022). AI-Enabled Marketing Solutions in Marketing Decision Making: AI Application in Different Stages of Marketing Process. *TEM Journal*, *11*(3), 1308–1315. doi:10.18421/TEM113-40

Lo, F.-Y., & Campos, N. (2018). Blending Internet-of-Things (IoT) solutions into relationship marketing strategies. *Technological Forecasting and Social Change*, *137*, 10–18. doi:10.1016/j.techfore.2018.09.029

Louie, R., Coenen, A., Huang, C. Z., Terry, M., & Cai, C. J. (2020, April). Novice-AI music co-creation via AI-steering tools for deep generative models. In *Proceedings of the 2020 CHI conference on human factors in computing systems* (pp. 1-13). 10.1145/3313831.3376739

Loureiro, S. M. C., Guerreiro, J., & Tussyadiah, I. (2021). Artificial intelligence in business: State of the art and future research agenda. *Journal of Business Research*, *129*, 911–926. doi:10.1016/j.jbusres.2020.11.001

Lu, F. C., & Sinha, J. (2019). Dichotomous Thinking and Ethical Consumerism: Overcoming the Negative Effects of Self-Interest Bias through Third-Person Narrative Persuasion. *Journal of Advertising*, *48*(3), 271–283. doi:10.1080/00913367.2019.1597788

Luo, L. (2020). *Temporal modelling of customer behaviour*. Palgrave Macmillan. doi:10.1007/978-3-030-18289-2

Luo, X., Tong, S., Fang, Z., & Qu, Z. (2019). Frontiers: Machines vs. humans: The impact of artificial intelligence chatbot disclosure on customer purchases. *Marketing Science*, *38*(6), 937–947. doi:10.1287/mksc.2019.1192

Luo, Y., & Xu, X. (2019). Predicting the helpfulness of online restaurant reviews using different machine learning algorithms: A case study of yelp. *Sustainability (Basel)*, *11*(19), 5254. doi:10.3390u11195254

Ly, N. Q., Do, T. K., & Nguyen, B. X. (2019). Large-scale coarse-to-fine object retrieval ontology and deep local multitask learning. *Computational Intelligence and Neuroscience*, *2019*, 1–40. Advance online publication. doi:10.1155/2019/1483294 PMID:31396268

Maas, M. J., & Hughes, J. M. (2020). Virtual, augmented and mixed reality in K–12 education: A review of the literature. *Technology, Pedagogy and Education*, *29*(2), 231–249. doi:10.1080/1475939X.2020.1737210

Ma, C., Li, J., Ding, M., Yang, H. H., Shu, F., Quek, T. Q., & Poor, H. V. (2020). On safeguarding privacy and security in the framework of federated learning. *IEEE Network*, *34*(4), 242–248. doi:10.1109/MNET.001.1900506

Madaan, G., Swapna, H. R., Kumar, A., Singh, A., & David, A. (2021). Enactment of sustainable technovations on healthcare sectors. *Asia Pacific Journal of Health Management*, *16*(3), 184–192. doi:10.24083/apjhm.v16i3.989

Madina, I. H., Sukmono, F. G., & Junaedi, F. (2022, November). Micro-influencer Marketing Beauty Brand on Social Media. In *HCI International 2022–Late Breaking Posters: 24th International Conference on Human-Computer Interaction, HCII 2022, Virtual Event, June 26–July 1, 2022, Proceedings, Part II* (pp. 40-47). Cham: Springer Nature Switzerland.

Magano, J., & Cunha, M. N. (2020). Digital marketing impact on tourism in Portugal: A quantitative study. *African Journal of Hospitality, Tourism and Leisure*, *9*(1), 1–19.

Mahendru, M., & Singh, A. (2022). Exploratory Analysis of AI Automation in Various Horizons. In *ICT Systems and Sustainability: Proceedings of ICT4SD 2022* (pp. 301–311). Springer Nature Singapore. doi:10.1007/978-981-19-5221-0_29

Mai, J. E. (2016). Big data privacy: The datafication of personal information. *The Information Society*, *32*(3), 192–199. doi:10.1080/01972243.2016.1153010

Mäkeläinen, S. I. (2006). *From B2C to C2C e-commerce. Course Essay.* Department of Computer Science, University of Helsinki.

Ma, L., & Sun, B. (2020). Machine learning and AI in marketing – Connecting computing power to human insights. *International Journal of Research in Marketing*, *37*(3), 481–504. doi:10.1016/j.ijresmar.2020.04.005

Malgieri, G. (2021). In/acceptable marketing and consumers' privacy expectations: Four tests from EU data protection law. *Journal of Consumer Marketing*, *40*(2), 209–223. doi:10.1108/JCM-03-2021-4571

Malik, N., Wei, M. Y., Appel, G., & Luo, L. (2022). Blockchain Technology for Creative Industry: Current State and Research Opportunities. *International Journal of Research in Marketing*, *40*(1), 38–48. doi:10.1016/j.ijresmar.2022.07.004

Malik, N., Wei, Y. M., Appel, G., & Luo, L. (2022). Blockchain technology for creative industries: Current state and research opportunities. *International Journal of Research in Marketing*.

Malin, B. A. (2005). An evaluation of the current state of genomic data privacy protection technology and a roadmap for the future. *Journal of the American Medical Informatics Association : JAMIA*, *12*(1), 28–34. doi:10.1197/jamia.M1603 PMID:15492030

Malviya, B., Othman, B., Saxena, K., Sailmadhur, V., & Almasheqbeh, H., (2022). An Empirical Analysis in Measuring the Impact of Artificial Intelligence for Better Marketing Communication to the End-Users Effectively in the Digital Era. *2nd International Conference on Advance Computing and Innovative Technologies in Engineering (ICACITE).*

Mangku, D. G. S., Yuliartini, N. P. R., Suastika, I. N., & Wirawan, I. G. M. A. S. (2021). The Personal Data Protection of Internet Users in Indonesia. *Journal of Southwest Jiaotong University*, *56*(1), 23. doi:10.35741/issn.0258-2724.56.1.23

Manis, K. T., & Madhavaram, S. (2023). AI-Enabled marketing capabilities and the hierarchy of capabilities: Conceptualization, proposition development, and research avenues. *Journal of Business Research*, *157*, 113485. doi:10.1016/j.jbusres.2022.113485

Manocha, P., Som, S., & Chanana, L. (2020). Relational delivery model and impact for leveraging blockchain to deliver e-governance services via social media. *International Journal of Advanced Science and Technology*, *29*(3), 8908–8921.

Mao, R., Liu, Q., He, K., Li, W., & Cambria, E. (2022). The biases of pre-trained language models: An empirical study on prompt-based sentiment analysis and emotion detection. *IEEE Transactions on Affective Computing*, 1–11. doi:10.1109/TAFFC.2022.3204972

Maras, M., & Alexandrou, A. (2018). Determining Authenticity of Video Evidence in the Age of Artificial Intelligence and in the Wake of Deepfake Videos. *The International Journal of Evidence & Proof*, 23.

Marchand, A., & Marx, P. (2020). Automated Product Recommendations with Preference-Based Explanations. *Journal of Retailing*, *96*(3), 328–343. doi:10.1016/j.jretai.2020.01.001

Mariani, M. M., Machado, I., & Nambisan, S. (2023). Types of innovation and artificial intelligence: A systematic quantitative literature review and research agenda. *Journal of Business Research*, *155*, 113364. doi:10.1016/j.jbusres.2022.113364

Mariani, M. M., Perez-Vega, R., & Wirtz, J. (2021). AI in marketing, consumer research and psychology: A systematic literature review and research agenda. *Psychology and Marketing*, *39*(4), 755–776. doi:10.1002/mar.21619

Marinho, J., Almeida, S., & Neto, C. (2021). *Exploration of 3 W's of web marketing in the hotel sector – A study conducted at the Casa da Calçada hotel.* doi:10.1007/978-3-030-90241-4_55

Marinotti, J. (2022). Can you truly own anything in the metaverse? A law professor explains how blockchains and NFTs don't protect virtual property. *Market Watch.* https://www.marketwatch.com/story/can-you-truly-own-anything-in-the-metaverse-a-law-professor-explains-how-blockchains-and-nfts-dont-protect-virtual-property-11650559724#:~:text=When%20you%20buy%20an%20item,a%20unique%20string%20of%20bits

Marinotti, J. (2020). Tangibility as Technology. *SSRN*, *37*, 671. doi:10.2139srn.3682090

Marinova, A., Murphy, J., & Massey, B. L. (2002). Permission E-mail marketing as a means of targeted promotion. *The Cornell Hotel and Restaurant Administration Quarterly*, *43*(1), 61–69. doi:10.1177/0010880402431006

Markos, E., Milne, G. R., & Peltier, J. W. (2017). Information sensitivity and willingness to provide continua: A comparative privacy study of the United States and Brazil. *Journal of Public Policy & Marketing*, *36*(1), 79–96. doi:10.1509/jppm.15.159

Marr, B. (2017). *Beyond the Big Data buzz.* https://www.linkedin.com/in/bernardmarr/

Marthews, A., & Tucker, C. (2022). What blockchain can and can't do: Applications to marketing and privacy. *International Journal of Research in Marketing*, *40*(1), 49–53. doi:10.1016/j.ijresmar.2022.09.001

Martínez, A., Schmuck, C., Pereverzyev, S. Jr, Pirker, C., & Haltmeier, M. (2020). A machine learning framework for customer purchase prediction in the non-contractual setting. *European Journal of Operational Research*, *281*(3), 588–596. doi:10.1016/j.ejor.2018.04.034

Martin, K. D., & Murphy, P. E. (2016). The role of data privacy in marketing. *Journal of the Academy of Marketing Science*, *45*(2), 135–155. doi:10.100711747-016-0495-4

Martins, A. R., & Alturas, B. (2016). Impacto organizacional da implementação de um módulo ERP em PME portuguesas [Organizational impact of implementing an ERP module in Portuguese SME*]. 11th Iberian Conference on Information Systems and Technologies*, 33–38. 10.1109/CISTI.2016.7521542

Marwala, T. (2018). Handbook Of Machine Learning - Volume 1: Foundation Of Artificial Intelligence. World Scientific Publishing Company.

Masuda, H., Han, S. H., & Lee, J. (2022). Impacts of influencer attributes on purchase intentions in social media influencer marketing: Mediating roles of characterizations. *Technological Forecasting and Social Change*, *174*, 121246. doi:10.1016/j.techfore.2021.121246

Mathur, M. (2018). Where is the Security Blanket? Developing Social Media Marketing Capability as a Shield from Perceived Cybersecurity Risk. *Journal of Promotion Management*, *25*(2), 200–224. doi:10.1080/10496491.2018.1443310

Matz, S. C., Appel, R. E., & Kosinski, M. (2020). Privacy in the age of psychological targeting. *Current Opinion in Psychology*, *31*, 116–121. doi:10.1016/j.copsyc.2019.08.010 PMID:31563799

Matz, S. C., Segalin, C., Stillwell, D., Müller, S. R., & Bos, M. W. (2019). Predicting the personal appeal of marketing images using computational methods. *Journal of Consumer Psychology*, *29*(3), 370–390. doi:10.1002/jcpy.1092

Ma, X. (2022). IS professionals' information security behaviors in Chinese IT organizations for information security protection. *Information Processing & Management*, *59*(1), 102744. doi:10.1016/j.ipm.2021.102744

McCarthy, J. (2007). *What is artificial intelligence?* http://www-formal.stanford.edu/jmc/

McCue, C. (2006). Data mining and predictive analytics in public safety and security. *IT Professional*, *8*(4), 12–18. doi:10.1109/MITP.2006.84

McGregor, S. C. (2019). Social media as public opinion: How journalists use social media to represent public opinion. *Journalism*, *20*(8), 1070–1086. doi:10.1177/1464884919845458

McGuire, J. (2023). *Cloud and AI Combined: Revolutionizing Tech*. https://www.eweek.com/cloud/cloud-and-ai/

McLeod, R. Jr, & Rogers, J. C. (1985). Marketing Information Systems: Their Current Status in Fortune 1000 Companies. *Journal of Management Information Systems*, *1*(4), 57–75. doi:10.1080/07421222.1985.11517715

McNealy, J., & Mullis, M. D. (2019). Tea and turbulence: Communication privacy management theory and online celebrity gossip forums. *Computers in Human Behavior*, *92*, 110–118. doi:10.1016/j.chb.2018.10.029

McRoberts, S. (2020). *From 'Social' Media to Collaborative Media: Cooperative Inquiry for Shoulder-To-Shoulder Youth Video Authorship Technologies* [Doctoral dissertation]. University of Minnesota.

Mediavilla, M. A., Dietrich, F., & Palm, D. (2022). Review and analysis of artificial intelligence methods for demand forecasting in supply chain management. *Procedia CIRP*, *107*, 1126–1131. doi:10.1016/j.procir.2022.05.119

Mehler-Bicher, A., Steiger, L., & Wetzel, D. (2020). Mixed Reality Applications in Business Contexts. In Holography - Recent Advances and Applications. IntechOpen.

Mekovec, R., & Vrček, N. (2011). Factors that influence Internet users' privacy perception. In *Proceedings of the ITI 2011, 33rd International Conference on Information Technology Interfaces* (pp. 227–232). IEEE.

Mendoza-Tello, J. C., Mora, H., Pujol-López, F. A., & Lytras, M. D. (2019). Disruptive innovation of cryptocurrencies in consumer acceptance and trust. *Information Systems and e-Business Management*, *17*(2), 195–222. doi:10.100710257-019-00415-w

Mennecke, B. E., Triplett, J. L., Hassall, L. M., Conde, Z. J., & Heer, R. (2011). An examination of a theory of embodied social presence in virtual worlds. *Decision Sciences*, *42*(2), 413–450. doi:10.1111/j.1540-5915.2011.00317.x

Merisavo, M., & Raulas, M. (2004). The impact of e-mail marketing on brand loyalty. *Journal of Product and Brand Management*, *13*(7), 498–505. doi:10.1108/10610420410568435

Mettler, M. (2016, September). Blockchain technology in healthcare: The revolution starts here. In *2016 IEEE 18th international conference on e-health networking, applications, and services (Healthcom)* (pp. 1-3). IEEE. 10.1109/HealthCom.2016.7749510

Microsoft. (2021). *Microsoft HoloLens 2: Technical specifications*. Microsoft. https://www.microsoft.com/en-us/hololens/hardware

Mikalef, P., Conboy, K., & Krogstie, J. (2021). Artificial intelligence as an enabler of B2B marketing: A dynamic capabilities micro-foundations approach. *Industrial Marketing Management*, *98*, 80–92. doi:10.1016/j.indmarman.2021.08.003

Miklosik, A., Kuchta, M., Evans, N., & Zak, S. (2019). Towards the Adoption of Machine Learning-Based Analytical Tools in Digital Marketing. *IEEE Access : Practical Innovations, Open Solutions*, *7*, 85705–85718. Advance online publication. doi:10.1109/ACCESS.2019.2924425

Milgram, P., & Kishino, F. (1994). A taxonomy of mixed reality visual displays. *IEICE Transactions on Information and Systems*, *77*(12), 1321–1329.

Milichovsky, F., & Simberova, I. (2015). Marketing effectiveness: Metrics for effective strategic marketing. *The Engineering Economist*, *26*(2), 211–219. doi:10.5755/j01.ee.26.2.3826

Miller, A. (2018). Want Less-Biased Decisions? Use Algorithms. *Harvard Business Review*, 26.

Miller, T. (2019). Explanation in artificial intelligence: Insights from the social sciences. *Artificial Intelligence*, *267*, 1–38. doi:10.1016/j.artint.2018.07.007

Milne, G. R., Pettinico, G., Hajjat, F. M., & Markos, E. (2017). Information sensitivity typology: Mapping the degree and type of risk consumers perceive in personal data sharing. *The Journal of Consumer Affairs*, *51*(1), 133–161. doi:10.1111/joca.12111

Milne, R., Morley, K. I., Howard, H., Niemiec, E., Nicol, D., Critchley, C., Prainsack, B., Vears, D., Smith, J., Steed, C., Bevan, P., Atutornu, J., Farley, L., Goodhand, P., Thorogood, A., Kleiderman, E., & Middleton, A. (2019). Trust in genomic data sharing among members of the general public in the UK, USA, Canada and Australia. *Human Genetics*, *138*(11-12), 1237–1246. doi:10.100700439-019-02062-0 PMID:31531740

Milton Ganesh, S., Vijayakumar, P., & Jegatha Deborah, L. (2017). A secure gesture based authentication scheme to unlock the smartphones. *Proceedings - 2017 2nd International Conference on Recent Trends and Challenges in Computational Models, ICRTCCM 2017,* 153-158. 10.1109/ICRTCCM.2017.31

Miralles-Pechuán, L., Ponce, H., & Martínez-Villaseñor, L. (2018). A novel methodology for optimizing display advertising campaigns using genetic algorithms. *Electronic Commerce Research and Applications*, *27*, 39–51. doi:10.1016/j.elerap.2017.11.004

Miralles-Pechuán, L., Ponce, H., & Martínez-Villaseñor, L. (2020). A 2020 perspective on "A novel methodology for optimizing display advertising campaigns using genetic algorithms". *Electronic Commerce Research and Applications*, *40*, 100953. doi:10.1016/j.elerap.2020.100953

Misischia, C. V., Poecze, F., & Strauss, C. (2022). Chatbots in customer service: Their relevance and impact on service quality. *Procedia Computer Science*, *201*, 421–428. doi:10.1016/j.procs.2022.03.055

Molina, S. (2023). *Dealing with algorithmic bias in AI solutions for healthcare in Mexico.* https://www.researchgate.net/publication/370592125_Dealing_with_algorithmic_bias_in_AI_solutions_for_healthcare_in_Mexico/citations

Mondal, T., Mugaloremutt Jayadeva, S., Pani, R., Subramanian, M., P, A., & Sumana, B. (2022). E marketing strategy in health care using IoT and Machine Learning. *Materials Today: Proceedings*, *56*, 2087–2091. doi:10.1016/j.matpr.2021.11.417

Monrat, A. A., Schelén, O., & Andersson, K. (2019). A Survey of Blockchain From the Perspectives of Applications, Challenges, and Opportunities. *IEEE Access : Practical Innovations, Open Solutions*, *7*, 117134–117151. doi:10.1109/ACCESS.2019.2936094

Monteiro, D., & Alturas, B. (2012). Segurança e Privacidade na Web 2.0: Foco nas Redes Sociais. *Egitânia Sciencia*, *10*, 109–133.

Moradi, M., & Dass, M. (2022). Applications of artificial intelligence in B2B marketing: Challenges and future directions. *Industrial Marketing Management*, *107*, 300–314. doi:10.1016/j.indmarman.2022.10.016

Morey, T., Forbath, T., & Schoop, A. (2015). Customer data: Designing for transparency and trust. *Harvard Business Review*, *93*(5), 96–105.

Moriuchi, E. (2021). The role of technology in social media. In Cross-Cultural Social Media Marketing: Bridging Across Cultural Differences (pp. 97-107). Emerald Publishing Limited. doi:10.1108/978-1-83867-175-420211009

Moriuchi, E., Landers, V. M., Colton, D., & Hair, N. (2021). Engagement with chatbots versus augmented reality interactive technology in e-commerce. *Journal of Strategic Marketing*, *29*(5), 375–389. doi:10.1080/0965254X.2020.1740766

Möser, M., Böhme, R., & Breuker, D. (2013). An inquiry into money laundering tools in the Bitcoin ecosystem. *Proceedings of the APWG eCrime Researchers Summit (ECRIME)*, 1-14. 10.1109/eCRS.2013.6805780

Mouro, C., & Alturas, B. (2016). Fatores que influenciam o consumidor a aceitar publicidade via e-mail [Factors influencing the consumer to accept advertising by e-mail]. *11th Iberian Conference on Information Systems and Technologies*, 27–32. 10.1109/CISTI.2016.7521365

Mukherjee, S., Chittipaka, V., & Baral, M. M. (2021). Developing a model to highlight the relation of digital trust with privacy and security for the blockchain technology. Blockchain technology and applications for digital marketing, 110-125. doi:10.4018/978-1-7998-8081-3.ch007

Mullins, R., & Agnihotri, R. (2022). Digital Selling: Organizational and Managerial Influences for Frontline Readiness and Effectiveness. *Journal of the Academy of Marketing Science*, *50*(4), 800–821. doi:10.100711747-021-00836-5

Murthy, C. V. B., Shri, M. L., Kadry, S., & Lim, S. (2020). Blockchain based cloud computing: Architecture and research challenges. *IEEE Access : Practical Innovations, Open Solutions*, *8*, 205190–205205. doi:10.1109/ACCESS.2020.3036812

Mustak, M., Salminen, J., Plé, L., & Wirtz, J. (2021). Artificial intelligence in marketing: Topic modeling, scientometric analysis, and research agenda. *Journal of Business Research*, *124*, 389–404. doi:10.1016/j.jbusres.2020.10.044

Musungwini, S., Gavai, P. V., Munyoro, B., & Chare, A. (2023). Emerging ICT Technologies for Agriculture, Training, and Capacity Building for Farmers in Developing Countries: A Case Study in Zimbabwe. In Applying Drone Technologies and Robotics for Agricultural Sustainability (pp. 12-30). IGI Global.

Musungwini, S., Gavai, P. V., Furusa, S. S., & Gumbo, R. (2022). Inclusive Digital Transformation for the Marginalized Communities in a Developing Context. In *Digital Transformation for Promoting Inclusiveness in Marginalized Communities* (pp. 95–122). IGI Global. doi:10.4018/978-1-6684-3901-2.ch005

Najafi, S. E., Nozari, H., & Edalatpanah, S. A. (2022). Investigating the Key Parameters Affecting Sustainable IoT-Based Marketing. In J. L. Verdegay, J. Brito, & C. Cruz (Eds.), *Computational Intelligence Methodologies Applied to Sustainable Development Goals* (pp. 51–61). Springer. doi:10.1007/978-3-030-97344-5_4

Nakamoto, S. (2008). *Bitcoin: A Peer-to-Peer Electronic Cash System*. Bitcoin. https://bitcoin.org/bitcoin.pdf

Nakamoto, S. (2008). Bitcoin: A peer-to-peer electronic cash system. *Decentralized Business Review*, 21260.

Nambiar, R., Bhardwaj, R., Sethi, A., & Vargheese, R. (2013, October). *A look at challenges and opportunities of big data analytics in healthcare. In 2013 IEEE international conference on Big Data*. IEEE.

Nandi, M. L., Nandi, S., Moya, H., & Kaynak, H. (2020). Blockchain technology-enabled supply chain systems and supply chain performance: A resource-based view. *Supply Chain Management*, *25*(6), 841–862. doi:10.1108/SCM-12-2019-0444

Nandwani, P., & Verma, R. (2021). A review on sentiment analysis and emotion detection from text. *Social Network Analysis and Mining*, *11*(1), 81. doi:10.100713278-021-00776-6 PMID:34484462

Narayanasamy, S. S. A. L., Hajamydeen, A. I., & Ishak, Z. (2019). Theoretical framework of digital marketing and the future availability in Malaysia. *2019 IEEE 9th International Conference on System Engineering and Technology, ICSET 2019 - Proceeding,* 277-280. 10.1109/ICSEngT.2019.8906342

Navarro-Newbal, A. A., Velez, J. A., Satzabal, J. E., Munera, L. E., & Bernabe, G. (2022). *Virtual surgical tele-simulations in ophthalmology* (Vol. 1256). International Congress Series. Elsevier.

Nazir, S., Khadim, S., Ali Asadullah, M., & Syed, N. (2023). Exploring the influence of artificial intelligence technology on consumer repurchase intention: The mediation and moderation approach. *Technology in Society*, *72*, 102190. doi:10.1016/j.techsoc.2022.102190

Nedeva, V. I. (2004). Concept of an Integrated. *Trakia Journal of Sciences*, *2*(4), 17–21.

Nengroo, A. S., & Kuppusamy, K. S. (2018). Machine learning based heterogeneous web advertisements detection using a diverse feature set. *Future Generation Computer Systems*, *89*, 68–77. doi:10.1016/j.future.2018.06.028

Neufeld, D. J., Dong, L., & Higgins, C. (2007). Charismatic leadership and user acceptance of information technology. *European Journal of Information Systems*, *16*(4), 494–510. doi:10.1057/palgrave.ejis.3000682

Nevelsteen, K. J. (2018). Virtual world, defined from a technological perspective and applied to video games, mixed reality, and the Metaverse. *Computer Animation and Virtual Worlds*, *29*(1), 1–22. doi:10.1002/cav.1752

Ngai, E. W. T., Lee, M. C. M., Luo, M., Chan, P. S. L., & Liang, T. (2021). An intelligent knowledge-based chatbot for customer service. *Electronic Commerce Research and Applications*, *50*, 101098. doi:10.1016/j.elerap.2021.101098

Ngai, E. W. T., & Wu, Y. (2022). Machine learning in marketing: A literature review, conceptual framework, and research agenda. *Journal of Business Research*, *145*, 35–48. doi:10.1016/j.jbusres.2022.02.049

Ng, D., & Griffin, P. (2018). The wider impact of a national cryptocurrency. *Global Policy*, 1.

Nihmathullah, Z., Ramasamy, R., & Raj David, A. (2022). *Event Impact Assessment: A Case of Puducherry*. Book Rivers.

Njerekai, C. (2020). An application of the virtual reality 360° concept to the Great Zimbabwe monument. *Journal of Heritage Tourism*, *15*(5), 567–579. doi:10.1080/1743873X.2019.1696808

Notta, O., & Kitta, A. (2021). Factors affecting e-marketing adoption and implementation in food firms: An empirical investigation of Greek food and beverage firms. *Springer Proceedings in Business and Economics*, 509-526. 10.1007/978-3-030-63970-9_35

Nugent, N., & Rhinard, M. (2015). *The European commission*. Bloomsbury Publishing. doi:10.1007/978-1-137-54333-2

Nunnally, J. C. (1967). *Psychometric theory*. McGraw-Hill.

Nygaard, A., & Silkoset, R. (2022). Sustainable development and greenwashing: How blockchain technology information can empower green consumers. *Business Strategy and the Environment*, (December), 1–13. doi:10.1002/bse.3338

O'Mahony, M., Hurley, N., Kushmerick, N., & Silvestre, G. (2004). Collaborative recommendation: A robustness analysis. *ACM Transactions on Internet Technology*, *4*(4), 344–377. doi:10.1145/1031114.1031116

O'Neil, D. (2001). Analysis of Internet users' level of online privacy concerns. *Social Science Computer Review*, *19*(1), 17–31. doi:10.1177/089443930101900103

O'Sullivan, D., & Abela, A. (2007). Marketing performance measurement ability and firm performance. *Journal of Marketing*, *71*(2), 79–93. doi:10.1509/jmkg.71.2.079

Obar, J., & Oeldorf-Hirsch, A. (2020). The biggest lie on the Internet: Ignoring the privacy policies and terms of service policies of social networking services. *Information Communication and Society*, *23*(1), 128–147. doi:10.1080/1369118X.2018.1486870

Ogunseiju, O. R., Gonsalves, N., Akanmu, A. A., Bairaktarova, D., Bowman, D. A., & Jazizadeh, F. (2022). Mixed reality environment for learning sensing technology applications in Construction: A usability study. *Advanced Engineering Informatics*, *53*, 101637. doi:10.1016/j.aei.2022.101637

Okoli, C. (2015). A guide to conducting a standalone systematic literature review. *Communications of the Association for Information Systems*, *37*. Advance online publication. doi:10.17705/1CAIS.03743

Okta. (2022). *Privacy vs. Security: Exploring the Differences & Relationship.* Okta. https://www.okta.com/identity-101/privacy-vs-security/

Oncioiu, I. (2019). Improving business performance through innovation in the digital economy. Improving business performance through innovation in the digital economy, 1-272.

Opreana, A., & Vinerean, S. (2015). A New Development in Online Marketing Introducing Digital Inbound Marketing. *Expert Journal of Marketing*, *3*(1), 29–34.

Orsini, J.-F. (1986). Artificial intelligence: A way through the strategic planning crisis? *Long Range Planning*, *19*(4), 71–77. doi:10.1016/0024-6301(86)90273-6

Osterwalder, A., & Pigneur, Y. (2013). *Business Model Generation: A Handbook for Visionaries, Game Changers, and Challengers*. John Wiley & Sons.

Palla, P. J., Kyriacou, E., & Zarkada, A. (2023). The Effect of Involvement on Attitude Formation and Strength in the Digital Domain. *Journal of Marketing Communications*, *29*(2), 137–160. doi:10.1080/13527266.2022.2154062

Palmatier, R. W., Kumar, V., & Harmeling, C. M. (2018). *Customer engagement marketing*. Palgrave Macmillan. doi:10.1007/978-3-319-61985-9

Pansari, A., & Kumar, V. (2017). Customer engagement: The construct, antecedents, and Consequences. *Journal of the Academy of Marketing Science*, *45*(3), 294–311. doi:10.100711747-016-0485-6

Pantano, E., & Pizzi, G. (2020). Forecasting artificial intelligence on online customer assistance: Evidence from chatbot patents analysis. *Journal of Retailing and Consumer Services*, *55*, 102096. doi:10.1016/j.jretconser.2020.102096

Pantanowitz, L., Bui, M. M., Chauhan, C., ElGabry, E., Hassell, L., Li, Z., Parwani, A. V., Salama, M. E., Sebastian, M. M., Tulman, D., Vepa, S., & Becich, M. J. (2022). Rules of engagement: Promoting academic-industry partnership in the era of digital pathology and artificial intelligence. *Academic Pathology*, *9*(1), 100026. doi:10.1016/j.acpath.2022.100026 PMID:35669406

Pan, Y., & Zhang, L. (2021). Roles of artificial intelligence in construction engineering and management: A critical review and future trends. *Automation in Construction*, *122*, 103517. doi:10.1016/j.autcon.2020.103517

Paolanti, M., Pietrini, R., Mancini, A., Frontoni, E., & Zingaretti, P. (2020). Deep understanding of shopper behaviours and interactions using RGB-D vision. *Machine Vision and Applications*, *31*(7-8), 1–21. doi:10.100700138-020-01118-w

Papagiannidis, S., & Bourlakis, M. A. (2010). Staging the New Retail Drama: At a Metaverse near you! *Journal of Virtual Worlds Research*, *2*(5), 425–446. doi:10.4101/jvwr.v2i5.808

Parise, S., Guinan, P. J., & Kafka, R. (2016). Solving the crisis of immediacy: How digital technology can transform the customer experience. *Business Horizons*, *59*(4), 411–420. doi:10.1016/j.bushor.2016.03.004

Parkinson, S., Khan, S., Crampton, A., Xu, Q., Xie, W., Liu, N., & Dakin, K. (2021). Password policy characteristics and keystroke biometric authentication. *IET Biometrics*, *10*(2), 163–178. doi:10.1049/bme2.12017

ParneM. D.ChandrikaK. G.DavidA. (1979). General Adjustments and Work-Satisfaction Of Indian Expatriates. SSRN.

Pathak, M. & Musku, U. (2020). Dynamic Bidding with Contextual Bid Decision Trees in Digital Advertisement. *Communications in Computer and Information Science, 1244*, 463-473.

Paul, S. P., Aggarwal, S., & Jha, S. (2022, October). A survey on the use of artificial intelligence (AI)-enabled techniques in digital marketing. In AIP Conference Proceedings (Vol. 2555, No. 1, p. 050003). AIP Publishing LLC.

Paul, A. K., Bhoi, S. K., Srivasthva, V., & Lakshmi, P. (2020). Ideal host for digital marketing: A multi criterion decision model approach. *International Journal of Advanced Science and Technology*, *29*(3), 8365–8373.

Pavlou, P. A., & Fygenson, M. (2006). Understanding and predicting electronic commerce adoption: An extension of the theory of planned behavior. *Management Information Systems Quarterly*, *30*(1), 115–143. doi:10.2307/25148720

Pavlou, P. A., & Stewart, D. W. (2000). Measuring the Effects and Effectiveness of Interactive Advertising : A Research Agenda. *Journal of Interactive Advertising*, *1*(1), 62–78. doi:10.1080/15252019.2000.10722044

Payne, A., & Frow, P. (2005). A Strategic Framework for Customer Relationship Management. *Journal of Marketing*, *69*(4), 167–176. doi:10.1509/jmkg.2005.69.4.167

Peng, L., Cui, G., & Chung, Y. (2020). Do the pieces fit? Assessing the configuration effects of promotion attributes. *Journal of Business Research*, *109*, 337–349. doi:10.1016/j.jbusres.2019.11.081

Perdices, D., Ramos, J., García-Dorado, J. L., González, I., & López de Vergara, J. E. (2021). Natural language processing for web browsing analytics: Challenges, lessons learned, and opportunities. *Computer Networks*, *198*, 108357. Advance online publication. doi:10.1016/j.comnet.2021.108357

Pereira, A. M., Moura, J. A. B., Costa, E. D. B., Vieira, T., Landim, A. R. D. B., Bazaki, E., & Wanick, V. (2022). Customer models for artificial intelligence-based decision support in fashion online retail supply chains. *Decision Support Systems*, *158*, 113795. doi:10.1016/j.dss.2022.113795

Peres, R., Schreier, M., Schweidel, D. A., & Sorescu, A. (2022). Blockchain meets marketing: Opportunities, threats, and avenues for future research. *International Journal of Research in Marketing*, *40*(1), 1–11. doi:10.1016/j.ijresmar.2022.08.001

Perez-Vega, R., Kaartemo, V., Lages, C. R., Borghei Razavi, N., & Männistö, J. (2021). Reshaping the contexts of online customer engagement behavior via artificial intelligence: A conceptual framework. *Journal of Business Research*, *129*, 902–910. doi:10.1016/j.jbusres.2020.11.002

Petrescu, M., Krishen, A. S., Kachen, S., & Gironda, J. T. (2022). AI-based innovation in B2B marketing: An interdisciplinary framework incorporating academic and practitioner perspectives. *Industrial Marketing Management*, *103*, 61–72. doi:10.1016/j.indmarman.2022.03.001

Petronio, S., & Reierson, J. (2009). *Regulating the privacy of confidentiality: Grasping the complexities through communication privacy management theory.* Academic Press.

Petronio, S. (2002). *Boundaries of privacy: Dialectics of disclosure*. Suny Press. doi:10.1353/book4588

Pham, H. C., Brennan, L., Parker, L., Phan-Le, N. T., Ulhaq, I., Nkhoma, M. Z., & Nhat Nguyen, M. (2019). Enhancing cyber security behavior: An internal social marketing approach. *Information and Computer Security*, *28*(2), 133–159. doi:10.1108/ICS-01-2019-0023

Phelps, J. E., D'Souza, G., & Nowak, G. J. (2001). Antecedents and consequences of consumer privacy concerns: An empirical investigation. *Journal of Interactive Marketing*, *15*(4), 2–17. doi:10.1002/dir.1019

Pînzaru, F., Anghel, L., & Mihalcea, A. (2017). Sustainable management in the new economy: Are Romanian companies ready for the digital challenge? *Proceedings of the 5th International Conference on Management Leadership and Governance, ICMLG 2017,* 346-352.

Plangger, K., Grewal, D., de Ruyter, K., & Tucker, C. (2022). The future of digital technologies in marketing: A conceptual framework and an overview. *Journal of the Academy of Marketing Science*, *50*(6), 1125–1134. doi:10.100711747-022-00906-2

Pollák, F. (2022). Introductory Chapter: Brand Management as Part of Corporate Identity. In Brand Management. IntechOpen.

Pomirleanu, N., Schibrowsky, J., Peltier, J., & Nill, A. (2013). A review of internet marketing research over the past 20 years and future research direction. *Journal of Research in Interactive Marketing*, *7*(3), 166–181. doi:10.1108/JRIM-01-2013-0006

Pope, J. A., & Lowen, A. M. (2009). Marketing implications of privacy concerns in the US and Canada. *Direct Marketing (Bradford)*, *3*(4), 301–326. doi:10.1108/17505930911000883

Popescu, G. H., Valaskova, K., & Horak, J. (2022). Augmented Reality Shopping Experiences, Retail Business Analytics, and Machine Vision Algorithms in the Virtual Economy of the Metaverse. *Journal of Self-Governance & Management Economics*, *10*(2), 67–81.

Popov, A., & Iakovleva, D. (2018). Adaptive look-alike targeting in social networks advertising. *Procedia Computer Science*, *136*, 255–264. doi:10.1016/j.procs.2018.08.264

Potrawa, T., & Tetereva, A. (2022). How much is the view from the window worth? Machine learning-driven hedonic pricing model of the real estate market. *Journal of Business Research*, *144*, 50–65. doi:10.1016/j.jbusres.2022.01.027

Prieto, W. T. (Ed.). (2019). *Promoting investment and protecting commerce online: legitimate sites v. parasites. (part i and ii)*. Nova Science Publishers.

Proulx, J. N., Romero, M., & Arnab, S. (2017). Learning mechanics and game mechanics under the perspective of self-determination theory to foster motivation in digital game based learning. *Simulation & Gaming*, *48*(1), 81–97. doi:10.1177/1046878116674399

Puntoni, S., Reczek, R. W., Giesler, M., & Botti, S. (2021). Consumers and artificial intelligence: An experiential perspective. *Journal of Marketing*, *85*(1), 131–151. doi:10.1177/0022242920953847

Pu, P., Chen, L., & Hu, R. (2012). Evaluating recommender systems from the user's perspective: Survey of the state of the art. *User Modeling and User-Adapted Interaction*, *22*(4–5), 317–355. doi:10.100711257-011-9115-7

Qamar, A., Karim, A., & Chang, V. (2019). Mobile malware attacks: Review, taxonomy & future directions. *Future Generation Computer Systems*, *97*, 887–909. doi:10.1016/j.future.2019.03.007

Qazi, M., Tollas, K., Kanchinadam, T., Bockhorst, J., & Fung, G. (2020). Designing and deploying insurance recommender systems using machine learning. *Wiley Interdisciplinary Reviews. Data Mining and Knowledge Discovery*, *10*(4), e1363. doi:10.1002/widm.1363

Qi, L., & Zhang, S. (2012). The Development of Customer Relationship Management System Based on Rough Set. *Communications in Computer and Information Science*, *315*, 328–333. doi:10.1007/978-3-642-34240-0_43

Quach, S., Thaichon, P., Martin, K. D., Weaven, S., & Palmatier, R. W. (2023). Digital Technologies: Tensions in Privacy and Data. *Journal of the Academy of Marketing Science*, *50*(6), 1299–1323. doi:10.100711747-022-00845-y PMID:35281634

Quesenberry, K. A., & Coolsen, M. K. (2019). Drama goes viral: Effects of story development on shares and views of online advertising videos. *Journal of Interactive Marketing*, *48*(1), 1–16. doi:10.1016/j.intmar.2019.05.001

Quiroz-Guitierrez, M. (2022). This week in the metaverse: 'Metaverse' could be word of the year, Johnnie Walker launches an NFT, and Mattel creates an NFT marketplace. *Fortune Crypto*. https://fortune.com/crypto/2022/11/25/this-week-in-the-metaverse-johnnie-walker-oxford-rockstar-games/

Rabby, F., Chimhundu, R., & Hassan, R. (2022). *Blockchain-enabled trust management for digital marketing in the industry 4.0 era.* doi:10.1007/978-3-030-93646-4_14

Radha, S., & Nelson Kennedy Babu, C. (2018). An enhancement of cloud based sentiment analysis an bdaas using SVM based lexicon dictionary and adaptive resource scheduling. *Journal of Computational and Theoretical Nanoscience*, *15*(2), 437–445. doi:10.1166/jctn.2018.7107

Rahim, R., Nguyen, P. T., Nurwita, E. L., & Shankar, K. (2019). Green data science in cyber security: Network security threat detection and prevention techniques [Un estudio sobre herramientas y técnicas para modelos de negocio]. *Opcion, 35*(20), 2899-2921.

Rahman, K. T. (2021). Applications of blockchain technology for digital marketing: A systematic review. Blockchain technology and applications for digital marketing, 16-31. doi:10.4018/978-1-7998-8081-3.ch002

Rajamohana, S., & Umamaheswari, K. (2018). Hybrid approach of improved binary particle swarm optimization and shuffled frog leaping for feature selection. *Computers & Electrical Engineering*, *67*, 497–508. doi:10.1016/j.compeleceng.2018.02.015

Ramadan, Z. (2019). The democratization of intangible luxury. *Marketing Intelligence & Planning*, *37*(6), 660–673. doi:10.1108/MIP-11-2018-0490

Ramadan, Z. (2023). Marketing in the metaverse era: Toward an integrative channel approach. *Virtual Reality (Waltham Cross)*, 1–14. doi:10.100710055-023-00783-2 PMID:37360809

Ramirez-Asis, H., Silva-Zapata, M., Ramirez-Asis, E., Sharma, T., Durga, S., & Pant, B. (2022). A conceptual analysis on the impact of big data analytics toward on digital marketing transformation. *2022 2nd International Conference on Advance Computing and Innovative Technologies in Engineering, ICACITE 2022,* 1651-1655. 10.1109/ICACITE53722.2022.9823874

Raphael, J., Madhusudana Rao, N., Bindu, A., & Gao, X.-Z. (2022). Clustering-based Factorization Machines for Advertisement Click prediction. *Procedia Computer Science*, *215*, 546–555. doi:10.1016/j.procs.2022.12.057

Rath, M. (2022). Machine learning and its use in e-commerce and e-business. Research anthology on machine learning techniques, methods, and applications, 1193-1209. doi:10.4018/978-1-6684-6291-1.ch062

Rathod, A. Y., Pandya, S., & Doshi, N. (2020). IoT and modern marketing: Its social implications. *International Conference on Advanced Communication Technology, ICACT, 2020*, 407-413. 10.23919/ICACT48636.2020.9061210

Rathore, B. (2023). Integration of Artificial Intelligence& It's Practices in Apparel Industry. *International Journal of New Media Studies*, *10*(1), 25–37.

Ratican, J., Hutson, J., & Wright, A. (2023). A Proposed Meta-Reality Immersive Development Pipeline: Generative AI Models and Extended Reality (XR) Content for the Metaverse. *Journal of Intelligent Learning Systems and Applications*, *15*(1), 24–35. doi:10.4236/jilsa.2023.151002

Rauschnabel, P. A. (2021). Augmented reality is eating the real-world! The substitution of physical products by holograms. *International Journal of Information Management*, *57*, 57. doi:10.1016/j.ijinfomgt.2020.102279

Rauschnabel, P. A., Babin, B. J., tom Dieck, M. C., Krey, N., & Jung, T. (2022). What is augmented reality marketing? Its definition, complexity, and future. *Journal of Business Research, 142*, 1140–1150. doi:10.1016/j.jbusres.2021.12.084

Rauschnabel, P. A., Felix, R., Hinsch, C., Shahab, H., & Alt, F. (2022). What is XR? Towards a framework for augmented and virtual reality. *Computers in Human Behavior, 133*, 107289. doi:10.1016/j.chb.2022.107289

Rauschnabel, P. A., He, J., & Ro, Y. K. (2018). Antecedents to the adoption of augmented reality smart glasses: A closer look at privacy risks. *Journal of Business Research, 92*, 374–384. doi:10.1016/j.jbusres.2018.08.008

Rauschnabel, P. A., & Ro, Y. K. (2016). Augmented reality smart glasses: An investigation of technology acceptance drivers. *International Journal of Technology Marketing, 11*(2), 123–148. doi:10.1504/IJTMKT.2016.075690

Rejeb, A., Appolloni, A., Rejeb, K., Treiblmaier, H., Iranmanesh, M., & Keogh, J. G. (2023). The role of blockchain technology in the transition toward the circular economy: Findings from a systematic literature review. *Resources, Conservation and Recycling Advances, 17*, 200126. doi:10.1016/j.rcradv.2022.200126

Renn, O., Laubichler, M., Lucas, K., Kröger, W., Schanze, J., Scholz, R. W., & Schweizer, P. J. (2022). Systemic risks from different perspectives. *Risk Analysis, 42*(9), 1902–1920. doi:10.1111/risa.13657 PMID:33331037

Ren, Y.-S., Ma, C.-Q., Kong, X.-L., Baltas, K., & Zureigat, Q. (2022). Past, present, and future of the application of machine learning in cryptocurrency research. *Research in International Business and Finance, 63*, 101799. doi:10.1016/j.ribaf.2022.101799

Revett, K., de Magalhães, S. T., Magalhães, M. J., & Jahankhani, H. (2016). *Balancing targeted delivery of content and personal freedom in the digital on-line video marketing landscape*. doi:10.1007/978-3-319-51064-4_8

Rimer, B. K., & Kreuter, M. W. (2006). Advancing Tailored Health Communication: A Persuasion and Message Effects Perspective. *Journal of Communication, 56*(suppl_1), S184–S201. doi:10.1111/j.1460-2466.2006.00289.x

Rinf.tech. (2022). *Mixed Reality Use Cases and Challenges in 2022*. https://www.rinf.tech/mixed-reality-use-cases-and-challenges-in-2022

Ringle, C. M., Wende, S., & Becker, J.-M. (2022). SmartPLS 4. Oststeinbek: SmartPLS. https://www.smartpls.com

Rizomyliotis, I., Kastanakis, M. N., Giovanis, A., Konstantoulaki, K., & Kostopoulos, I. (2022). "How mAy I help you today?" The use of AI chatbots in small family businesses and the moderating role of customer affective commitment. *Journal of Business Research, 153*, 329–340. doi:10.1016/j.jbusres.2022.08.035

Rizvanović, B., Zutshi, A., Grilo, A., & Nodehi, T. (2023). Linking the potentials of extended digital marketing impact and start-up growth: Developing a macro-dynamic framework of start-up growth drivers supported by digital marketing. *Technological Forecasting and Social Change, 186*, 122128. doi:10.1016/j.techfore.2022.122128

Robin, R., Gaber, H., & Wright, L. T. (2021). Encouraging information disclosure on social media platforms in consumer marketing research. In The routledge companion to marketing research (pp. 132-146). Routledge.

Rohm, A. J., & Milne, G. R. (2004). Just what the doctor ordered: The role of information sensitivity and trust in reducing medical information privacy concern. *Journal of Business Research, 57*(9), 1000–1011. doi:10.1016/S0148-2963(02)00345-4

Rokhsaritalemi, S., Sadeghi-Niaraki, A., & Choi, M. (2020). A Review on Mixed Reality: Current Trends, Challenges and Prospects. *Applied Sciences (Basel, Switzerland), 10*(2), 636. doi:10.3390/app10020636

Ronaghi, M. H., & Mosakhani, M. (2022). The effects of blockchain technology adoption on business ethics and social sustainability: Evidence from the Middle East. *Environment, Development and Sustainability*, *24*(5), 6834–6859. [REMOVED HYPERLINK FIELD] doi:10.100710668-021-01729-x PMID:34393620

Rosa, N., & Furness, T. (2022). *Understanding the metaverse a business and ethical guide*. John Wiley & Sons.

Rosário, A., Vilaça, F., Raimundo, R., & Cruz, R. (2021). Literature review on Health Knowledge Management in the last 10 years (2009-2019). *The Electronic Journal of Knowledge Management, 18*(3), 338-355. doi:10.34190/ejkm.18.3.2120

Rosário, A. T. (2021). E-Mail Marketing: Research and Challenges. *International Journal of Online Marketing*, *11*(4), 63–83. doi:10.4018/IJOM.2021100104

Rosário, A. T. (2021). The Background of articial intelligence applied to marketing. *Academy of Strategic Management Journal*, *20*(6), 1–19.

Rosário, A. T., & Dias, J. C. (2022). Sustainability and the Digital Transition: A Literature Review. *Sustainability (Basel)*, *14*(7), 4072. doi:10.3390u14074072

Rosário, A. T., & Dias, J. C. (2023). How Industry 4.0 and Sensors Can Leverage Product Design: Opportunities and Challenges. *Sensors (Basel)*, *23*(3), 1165. doi:10.339023031165 PMID:36772206

Rose, F. (2012). *The art of immersion: how the digital generation is remaking hollywood madison avenue and the way we tell stories*. W.W. Norton.

Rospigliosi, P. A. (2022). Metaverse or Simulacra? Roblox, Minecraft, Meta and the turn to virtual reality for education, socialisation and work. *Interactive Learning Environments*, *30*(1), 1–3. doi:10.1080/10494820.2022.2022899

Rowan, N. J. (2022, May). The role of digital technologies in supporting and improving fishery and aquaculture across the supply chain – Quo Vadis? *Aquaculture and Fisheries*, *8*(4), 365–374. doi:10.1016/j.aaf.2022.06.003

Rowley, J. (2008). Understanding digital content marketing. *Journal of Marketing Management*, *24*(5–6), 517–540. doi:10.1362/026725708X325977

Rückeshäuser, N. (2017). Do We Really Want Blockchain-Based Accounting? Decentralized Consensus as Enabler of Management Override of Internal Controls. *Proceedings of the 13th International Conference on Wirtschaftsinformatik*, 16-30.

Rudd, E. M., Rozsa, A., Günther, M., & Boult, T. E. (2016). A survey of stealth malware attacks, mitigation measures, and steps toward autonomous open world solutions. *IEEE Communications Surveys and Tutorials*, *19*(2), 1145–1172. doi:10.1109/COMST.2016.2636078

Ruiz-Real, J. L., Uribe-Toril, J., Torres, J. A., & De Pablo, J. (2021). Artificial intelligence in business and economics research: Trends and future. *Journal of Business Economics and Management*, *22*(1), 98–117. doi:10.3846/jbem.2020.13641

Russell, S., & Norvig, P. (2010). *Artificial Intelligence: A Modern Approach* (3rd ed.). Pearson. doi:10.1017/S0269888900007724

Rustad, M. L., & Onufrio, M. V. (2011). Reconceptualizing consumer terms of use for a globalized knowledge economy. *University of Pennsylvania Journal of Business Law,* 1085.

Ryan, M. (2020). In AI We Trust: Ethics, Artificial Intelligence, and Reliability. *Science and Engineering Ethics*, *26*(5), 2749–2767. doi:10.100711948-020-00228-y PMID:32524425

Sachdev, R. (2020). Towards Security and Privacy for Edge AI in IoT/IoE based Digital Marketing Environments. *2020 Fifth International Conference on Fog and Mobile Edge Computing (FMEC).* 10.1109/FMEC49853.2020.9144755

Sachdev, R. (2020, April 20-23). Towards Security and Privacy for Edge AI in IoT/IoE based Digital Marketing Environments. *2020 Fifth International Conference on Fog and Mobile Edge Computing (FMEC).*

Sadok, M. (n.d.). *Artificial Intelligence and Machine Learning in the Insurance Sector.* https://www.strategy-transformation.com/artificial-intelligence-and-machine-learning-in-the-insurance-sector/?cv=1

Sáez-Ortuño, L., Forgas-Coll, S., Huertas-Garcia, R., & Sánchez-García, J. (2023). Online cheaters: Profiles and motivations of internet users who falsify their data online. *Journal of Innovation & Knowledge, 8*(2).

Sagiroglu, S., & Sinanc, D. (2013, May). Big data: A review. In 2013 international conference on collaboration technologies and systems (CTS) (pp. 42-47). IEEE. doi:10.1109/CTS.2013.6567202

Sahija, D. (2022). A critical review of mixed reality integration with medical devices for patient care. *International Journal for Innovative Research in Multidisciplinary Field, 8*(1), 100–105. doi:10.2015/IJIRMF/202201017

Salahdine, F., & Kaabouch, N. (2019). Social engineering attacks: A survey. *Future Internet, 11*(4), 89. doi:10.3390/fi11040089

Salehi, M., Mirzaei, H., Aghaei, M., & Abyari, M. (2012). Dissimilarity of E-marketing VS traditional marketing. *International Journal of Business and Social Science, 2*(1), 510–515.

Samunderu, E., & Farrugia, M. (2022). Predicting customer purpose of travel in a low-cost travel environment—A Machine Learning Approach. *Machine Learning with Applications, 9*, 100379. doi:10.1016/j.mlwa.2022.100379

Sandeep, S. R., Ahamad, S., Saxena, D., Srivastava, K., Jaiswal, S., & Bora, A. (2022). To understand the relationship between Machine learning and Artificial intelligence in large and diversified business organisations. *Materials Today: Proceedings, 56*, 2082–2086. doi:10.1016/j.matpr.2021.11.409

Sands, S., Campbell, C. L., Plangger, K., & Ferraro, C. (2022). Unreal influence: Leveraging AI in influencer marketing. *European Journal of Marketing, 56*(6), 1721–1747. doi:10.1108/EJM-12-2019-0949

Sankar, J. G., & Kiruba Sagar, M, V. (2020). Examining the Risk Factor Associated with UTAUT MODEL. *Solid State Technology*, 1196–1198.

Sanska, S., & Rejo, M. (2020). Threats by mixed reality and counter measures. *Procedia Computer Science, 171*, 2720–2728. doi:10.1016/j.procs.2020.04.295

Saura, J. R., Palos-Sanchez, P., & Grilo, A. (2019). Detecting indicators for startup business success: Sentiment analysis using text data mining. *Sustainability (Basel), 11*(3), 917. doi:10.3390u11030917

Saura, J. R., Palos-Sánchez, P., & Suárez, L. M. C. (2017). Understanding the digital marketing environment with kpis and web analytics. *Future Internet, 9*(4), 1–13. doi:10.3390/fi9040076

Schaeffer, S. E., & Sanchez, S. V. R. (2020). Forecasting client retention — A machine-learning approach. *Journal of Retailing and Consumer Services, 52*, 101918. doi:10.1016/j.jretconser.2019.101918

Schahczenski, J., & Schahczenski, C. (2020). Blockchain and the Resurrection of Consumer Sovereignty in a Sustainable Food Economy. *Journal of Agriculture, Food Systems, and Community Development, 9*(3), 1–6. doi:10.5304/jafscd.2020.093.028

Schmuck, D., Matthes, J., & Naderer, B. (2018). Misleading Consumers with Green Advertising? An Affect–Reason–Involvement Account of Greenwashing Effects in Environmental Advertising. *Journal of Advertising, 47*(2), 127–145. doi:10.1080/00913367.2018.1452652

Scholz, J., & Smith, A. N. (2016). Augmented reality: Designing immersive experiences that maximize consumer engagement. *Business Horizons*, *59*(2), 149–161. doi:10.1016/j.bushor.2015.10.003

Schomakers, E. M., Lidynia, C., Müllmann, D., & Ziefle, M. (2019). Internet users' perceptions of information sensitivity–insights from Germany. *International Journal of Information Management*, *46*, 142–150. doi:10.1016/j.ijinfomgt.2018.11.018

Schwartz, E. M., Bradlow, E. T., & Fader, P. S. (2017). Customer acquisition via display advertising using multi-armed bandit experiments. *Marketing Science*, *36*(4), 500–522. doi:10.1287/mksc.2016.1023

Schweidel, D. A., Bart, Y., Inman, J. J., Stephen, A. T., Libai, B., Andrews, M., Rosario, A. B., Chae, I., Chen, Z., Kupor, D., Longoni, C., & Thomaz, F. (2022). How consumer digital signals are reshaping the customer journey. *Journal of the Academy of Marketing Science*, *50*(6), 1–20. doi:10.100711747-022-00839-w PMID:35221393

Security Compass. (2020). *Security compass whitepaper: why cybersecurity is important for your brand reputation.* www.securitycompass.com/wp-content/uploads/why-cybersecurity-is-important-for-your-brand-reputation.pdf

Seeger, P. M., Yahouni, Z., & Alpan, G. (2022). Literature review on using data mining in production planning and scheduling within the context of cyber physical systems. *Journal of Industrial Information Integration*, *28*, 100371. doi:10.1016/j.jii.2022.100371

Selvaganapathy, S., Sadasivam, S., & Ravi, V. (2021). A review on android malware: Attacks, countermeasures and challenges ahead. *Journal of Cyber Security and Mobility*, 177-230. doi:10.13052/jcsm2245-1439.1017

Sestino, A., Prete, M. I., Piper, L., & Guido, G. (2020). Internet of Things and Big Data as enablers for business digitalization strategies. *Technovation*, *98*, 102173. doi:10.1016/j.technovation.2020.102173

Setyani, V., Zhu, Y.-Q., Hidayanto, A. N., Sandhyaduhita, P. I., & Hsiao, B. (2019). Exploring the psychological mechanisms from personalized advertisements to urge to buy impulsively on social media. *International Journal of Information Management*, *48*, 96–107. doi:10.1016/j.ijinfomgt.2019.01.007

Shah, R. (2023). Augmented Reality in E-Commerce: The New Era of Online Shopping. In Intelligent Sustainable Systems: Selected Papers of WorldS4 2022, Volume 2 (pp. 775-783). Springer Nature Singapore.

Shanor, A., & Light, S. E. (2022). Greenwashing and the First Amendment. *Columbia Law Review*, *122*(7), 2033–2118.

Sharif, M. M., & Ghodoosi, F. (2022). The Ethics of Blockchain in Organizations. *Journal of Business Ethics*, *178*(4), 1009–1025. [REMOVED HYPERLINK FIELD] doi:10.100710551-022-05058-5 PMID:35125568

Sheehan, K. B., & Hoy, M. G. (2000). Dimensions of privacy concerns among online consumers. *Journal of Public Policy & Marketing*, *19*(1), 62–73. doi:10.1509/jppm.19.1.62.16949

Sheresheva, M., Efremova, M., Valitova, L., Polukhina, A., & Laptev, G. (2021). Russian tourism enterprises' marketing innovations to meet the covid-19 challenges. *Sustainability (Basel)*, *13*(7), 3756. Advance online publication. doi:10.3390u13073756

Sheth, J., Jain, V., & Ambika, A. (2020). Repositioning the customer support services: The next frontier of competitive advantage. *European Journal of Marketing*, *54*(7), 1787–1804. doi:10.1108/EJM-02-2020-0086

Shiau, W. L., Dwivedi, Y. K., & Yang, H. S. (2017). Co-citation and cluster analyses of extant literature on social networks. *International Journal of Information Management*, *37*(5), 390–399. doi:10.1016/j.ijinfomgt.2017.04.007

Shneiderman, B. (2016). The dangers of faulty, biased, or malicious algorithms requires independent oversight. *Proceedings of the National Academy of Sciences of the United States of America, 113*(48), 13538–13540. doi:10.1073/pnas.1618211113 PMID:27911762

Shopify. (n.d.). *12 B2B Ecommerce Trends To Shape Your Business in 2023.* Shopify. https://www.shopify.com/enterprise/b2b-ecommerce-trends-statistics#2

Shorman, S., Allaymoun, M., Hamid, O., & Sciences, F. (2019). Developing the E-Commerce Model a Consumer To Consumer Using Blockchain. [IJMIT]. *International Journal of Managing Information Technology, 11*(2), 55–64. doi:10.5121/ijmit.2019.11204

Shumanov, M., & Johnson, L. (2021). Making conversations with chatbots more personalized. *Computers in Human Behavior, 117*, 106627. doi:10.1016/j.chb.2020.106627

Siau, K., & Wang, W. (2018). Building trust in artificial intelligence, machine learning, and robotics. *Cutter Business Technology Journal, 31*(2), 47–53.

Siering, M., Deokar, A. V., & Janze, C. (2018). Disentangling consumer recommendations: Explaining and predicting airline recommendations based on online reviews. *Decision Support Systems, 107*, 52–63. doi:10.1016/j.dss.2018.01.002

Silva, C. F. d., & Moro, S. (2021). Blockchain technology as an enabler of consumer trust: A text mining literature analysis. *Telematics and Informatics, 60*, 102430.

Silva, E. S., & Bonetti, F. (2021). Digital humans in fashion: Will consumers interact? *Journal of Retailing and Consumer Services, 60*, 60. doi:10.1016/j.jretconser.2020.102430

Silva, M. J. B., Lorena, O. R. D., Cerqueira, K. A., & Campos, P. O. (2022). Avatar marketing: A study on the engagement and authenticity of virtual influencers on Instagram. *Social Network Analysis and Mining, 12*(1), 130. doi:10.100713278-022-00966-w

Silva, M., Giovanni, L., Fernandes, J., Oliveira, D., & Silva, C. S. (2023). What Makes Disinformation Ads Engaging? A Case Study of Facebook Ads from the Russian Active Measures Campaign. *Journal of Interactive Advertising*, 1–20. Advance online publication. doi:10.1080/15252019.2023.2173991

Simion, C. P., Militaru, G., Popescu, M., & Popescu, A. (2018). Security of digital marketing operations to improve small business performance. *Proceedings of the 31st International Business Information Management Association Conference, IBIMA 2018: Innovation Management and Education Excellence through Vision*, 6644–6653.

Simmonds, L., Bellman, S., Kennedy, R., Nenycz-Thiel, M., & Bogomolova, S. (2020). Moderating effects of prior brand usage on visual attention to video advertising and recall: An eye-tracking investigation. *Journal of Business Research, 111*, 241–248. doi:10.1016/j.jbusres.2019.02.062

Singer, J. G. (2006). Systems marketing for the information age. *MIT Sloan Management Review, 48*(1).

Singh, A., & Mittal, S. (2022). Traditional to digital commerce: Impact of scams on consumer's attitude towards online shopping. In The future of E-commerce (pp. 197-209).

Sinha, M., Healey, J., & Sengupta, T. (2020). Designing with AI for Digital Marketing. In *Proceedings of Adjunct Proceedings of the 28th ACM Conference on User Modeling, Adaptation and Personalization (UMAP '20 Adjunct)*. ACM. 10.1145/3386392.3397600

Slepchuk, A. N., Milne, G. R., & Swani, K. (2022). Overcoming privacy concerns in consumers' use of health information technologies: A justice framework. *Journal of Business Research, 141*, 782–793. doi:10.1016/j.jbusres.2021.11.073

Smart, J., Jamais, C., & Paffendorf, J. (2008). *Metaverse roadmap: pathways to the 3D web*. W3. https://www.w3.org/2008/WebVideo/Annotations/wiki/images/1/19/MetaverseRoadmapOverview.pdf

Smilansky, S. (2018). *Experiential marketing: a practical guide to interactive brand experiences*. Kogan Page.

Smith, H. J., Dinev, T., & Xu, H. (2011). Information privacy research: An interdisciplinary review. *Management Information Systems Quarterly*, *35*(4), 989–1016. doi:10.2307/41409970

Smith, K., & Hanover, D. (2016). *Experiential marketing: secrets strategies and success stories from the world's greatest brands*. John Wiley & Sons. doi:10.1002/9781119176688

Soares, D. B., & Sousa, B. B. (2022). The role of communication in consumer behavior in social and nonprofit marketing: The case of PSP in Portugal. *International Review on Public and Nonprofit Marketing*, *19*(1), 1–13. doi:10.100712208-021-00294-3

Soczka, L. B. D. C. (2014). *Gestão da privacidade em redes sociais: perceções de uso de dados e partilha de informação pessoal*. Dissertação de Mestrado, Universidade de Lisboa. Instituto Superior de Economia e Gestão. http://hdl.handle.net/10400.5/12689

Soediono, B. (1989). General structure analysis system. *Journal of Chemical Information and Modeling*, *53*, 160. doi:10.1017/CBO9781107415324.004

Soldatova, A. V., Budrin, A. G., Budrina, E. V., Solovieva, D. V., & Semenov, V. P. (2020). Information technologies in the management of digital marketing communications. *Proceedings of the 2020 IEEE International Conference "Quality Management, Transport and Information Security, Information Technologies", IT and QM and IS 2020*, 534-537. 10.1109/ITQMIS51053.2020.9322990

SoleymanianM.WeinbergC.ZhuT. (2021). Privacy concerns, economic benefits, and consumer decisions: A multi-period panel study of consumer choices in the automobile insurance industry. In *Economic Benefits, and Consumer Decisions: A Multi-Period Panel Study of Consumer Choices in the Automobile Insurance Industry*. doi:10.2139/ssrn.3905034

Solis, B. (2010). *Engage: The complete guide for brands and businesses to build, cultivate, and measure success in the new web*. John Wiley & Sons.

Soltani, A., Heydari, M., Aghaei, F., & Pettit, C. J. (2022). Housing price prediction incorporating spatio-temporal dependency into machine learning algorithms. *Cities (London, England)*, *131*, 103941. doi:10.1016/j.cities.2022.103941

Speicher, M., Hall, B. D., & Nebeling, M. (2019). What is mixed reality? In *Proceedings of the 2019 CHI conference on human factors in computing systems (CHI 2019)*. ACM. 10.1145/3290605.3300767

Spencer, J., Poggi, J., & Gheerawo, R. (2018). Designing out stereotypes in artificial intelligence: Involving users in the personality design of a digital assistant. *Proceedings of the 4th EAI international conference on smart objects and technologies for social good*, 130-135. 10.1145/3284869.3284897

Srinivas, S., & Liang, H. (2022). Being digital to being vulnerable: Does digital transformation allure a data breach? *Journal of Electronic Business & Digital Economics*, *1*(1/2), 111–137. doi:10.1108/JEBDE-08-2022-0026

Srivastav, P., & Gupta, H. (2021). Role and applications of digital marketing in digital era: A review. *2021 9th International Conference on Reliability, Infocom Technologies and Optimization (Trends and Future Directions), ICRITO 2021*. 10.1109/ICRITO51393.2021.9596087

Srivastava, V., & Kalro, A. D. (2019). Enhancing the helpfulness of online consumer reviews: The role of latent (content) factors. *Journal of Interactive Marketing*, *48*(1), 33–50. doi:10.1016/j.intmar.2018.12.003

Srivastava, V., Singh, A. K., David, A., & Rai, N. (2022). Modelling student employability on an academic basis: A supervised machine learning approach with R. In *Handbook of Research on Innovative Management Using AI in Industry 5.0* (pp. 179–191). IGI Global. doi:10.4018/978-1-7998-8497-2.ch012

Stahl, B. C., Andreou, A., Brey, P., Hatzakis, T., Kirichenko, A., Macnish, K., Laulhé Shaelou, S., Patel, A., Ryan, M., & Wright, D. (2021). Artificial intelligence for human flourishing–Beyond principles for machine learning. *Journal of Business Research*, *124*, 374–388. doi:10.1016/j.jbusres.2020.11.030

Stallone, V., Wetzels, M., & Klaas, M. (2021). Applications of Blockchain Technology in marketing—A systematic review of marketing technology companies. *Blockchain: Research and Applications, 2*(3).

Stallone, V., Wetzels, M., & Klaas, M. (2021). Applications of blockchain technology in marketing—A systematic review of marketing technology companies. *Blockchain: Research and Applications*, *2*(3), 100023. Advance online publication. doi:10.1016/j.bcra.2021.100023

Steininger, D. M., & Gatzemeier, S. (2019). Digitally forecasting new music product success via active crowdsourcing. *Technological Forecasting and Social Change*, *146*, 167–180. doi:10.1016/j.techfore.2019.04.016

Stephen, A. T., & Toubia, O. (2010). Deriving value from social commerce networks. *JMR, Journal of Marketing Research*, *47*(2), 215–228. doi:10.1509/jmkr.47.2.215

Stevenson, T. (2023). *Virtual Fashion: Digital Representations of Materiality and Time* [Doctoral dissertation]. Open Access Te Herenga Waka-Victoria University of Wellington.

Stone, M., Aravopoulou, E., Ekinci, Y., Evans, G., Hobbs, M., Labib, A., Laughlin, P., Machtynger, J., & Machtynger, L. (2020). Artificial intelligence (AI) in strategic marketing decision-making: A research agenda. *The Bottom Line (New York, N.Y.)*, *33*(2), 183–200. doi:10.1108/BL-03-2020-0022

Strobel, J., & Hawkins, C. (2022). Designing in Second Life: Identity construction and learning in a virtual informal environment. *Journal of Online Engineering Education*, *1*(1).

Strycharz, J., van Noort, G., Helberger, N., & Smit, E. (2019). Contrasting perspectives–practitioner's viewpoint on personalised marketing communication. *European Journal of Marketing*, *53*(4), 635–660. doi:10.1108/EJM-11-2017-0896

Suchman, M. C. (1995). Managing Legitimacy: Strategic and Institutional Approaches. *Academy of Management Review*, *20*(3), 571. doi:10.2307/258788

Sudhakar, B. D., Kattepogu, N., & David, A. (2017). Marketing assistance and digital branding-an insight for technology up-gradation for MSME's. *International Journal of Management Studies & Research*, *5*(1), 2455–1562.

Sueyoshi, T., & Tadiparthi, G. R. (2005). A wholesale power trading simulator with learning capabilities. *IEEE Transactions on Power Systems*, *20*(3), 1330–1340. doi:10.1109/TPWRS.2005.851948

Sueyoshi, T., & Tadiparthi, G. R. (2008). An agent-based decision support system for wholesale electricity market. *Decision Support Systems*, *44*(2), 425–446. doi:10.1016/j.dss.2007.05.007

Suleiman, D. A., Awan, T. M., & Javed, M. (2021). Enhancing digital marketing performance through usage intention of AI-powered websites. *IAES International Journal of Artificial Intelligence, 10*(4).

Suleiman, D. A., Awan, T. M., & Javed, M. (2021). Enhancing digital marketing performance through usage intention of ai-powered websites. *IAES International Journal of Artificial Intelligence*, *10*(4), 810–817. doi:10.11591/ijai.v10.i4.pp810-817

Sunarti, S., Fadzlul Rahman, F., Naufal, M., Risky, M., Febriyanto, K., & Masnina, R. (2021). Artificial intelligence in healthcare: Opportunities and risk for future. *Gaceta Sanitaria, 35*, S67–S70. doi:10.1016/j.gaceta.2020.12.019 PMID:33832631

Sung, E. (2020). Brand experience via mobile AR app marketing. Augmented reality and virtual reality: Progress in IS, 3–9. Springer. doi:10.1007/978-3-030-37869-1_1

Sung, E., Bae, S., Han, D.-I. D., & Kwon, O. (2021). Consumer engagement via interactive artificial intelligence and mixed reality. *International Journal of Information Management, 60*, 102382. doi:10.1016/j.ijinfomgt.2021.102382

Suzuki, J., Okubo, T., Oki, H., & Fukui, T. (2019). *System for Motivating Ethical Consumption Behavior Using Dongle Interface Application*. 162–169. doi:10.3233/AISE190038

Swani, K., Milne, G. R., & Slepchuk, A. N. (2021). Revisiting trust and privacy concern in consumers' perceptions of marketing information management practices: Replication and extension. *Journal of Interactive Marketing, 56*(1), 137–158. doi:10.1016/j.intmar.2021.03.001

Swetha, M. S., Buvaneswari, P. S., & Kottaisamy, U. (2019). An empirical study on consumer awareness on digital footprints. *International Journal of Advanced Science and Technology, 28*(17), 759–768.

Syam, N., & Sharma, A. (2018). Waiting for a sales renaissance in the fourth industrial revolution: Machine learning and artificial intelligence in sales research and practice. *Industrial Marketing Management, 69*, 135–146. doi:10.1016/j.indmarman.2017.12.019

Tabrizchi, H., & Kuchaki Rafsanjani, M. (2020). A survey on security challenges in cloud computing: Issues, threats, and solutions. *The Journal of Supercomputing, 76*(12), 9493–9532. doi:10.100711227-020-03213-1

Taecharungroj, V., & Mathayomchan, B. (2019). Analysing TripAdvisor reviews of tourist attractions in Phuket, Thailand. *Tourism Management, 75*, 550–568. doi:10.1016/j.tourman.2019.06.020

Taheam, K., Sharma, R., & Goswami, S. (2016). Drivers of digital wallet usage: Implications for leveraging digital marketing. *International Journal of Economic Research, 13*(1), 175–186.

Taherdoost, H., & Madanchian, M. (2023). Blockchain-Based E-Commerce: A Review on Applications and Challenges. *Electronics (Basel), 12*(8), 1889. doi:10.3390/electronics12081889

Tan, T. M., Makkonen, H., Kaur, P., & Salo, J. (2022). How do ethical consumers utilize sharing economy platforms as part of their sustainable resale behavior? The role of consumers' green consumption values. *Technological Forecasting and Social Change, 176*. doi:10.1016/j.techfore.2021.121432

Tangari, G., Ikram, M., Ijaz, K., Kaafar, M. A., & Berkovsky, S. (2021). Mobile health and privacy: cross sectional study. *BMJ, 373*.

Tang, Y., & Ning, X. (2023). Understanding user misrepresentation behavior on social apps: The perspective of privacy calculus theory. *Decision Support Systems, 165*, 113881. doi:10.1016/j.dss.2022.113881

Tapscott, D., & Tapscott, A. (2017). How blockchain will change organizations. *MIT Sloan Management Review, 58*(2), 10.

Tarhini, A., Alalwan, A. A., Shammout, A. B., & Al-Badi, A. (2019). An analysis of the factors affecting mobile commerce adoption in developing countries: Towards an integrated model. *Review of International Business and Strategy,* 29(3), 157-179. doi:10.1108/RIBS-10-2018-0092.

Tariq, B., Taimoor, S., Najam, H., Law, R., Hassan, W., & Han, H. (2020). Generating Marketing Outcomes through Internet of Things (IoT) Technologies. *Sustainability (Basel), 12*(22), 9670. doi:10.3390u12229670

Tavani, H. T., & Moor, J. H. (2001). Privacy protection, control of information, and privacy-enhancing technologies. *Computers & Society*, *31*(1), 6–11. doi:10.1145/572277.572278

Tayal, S., Rajagopal, K., & Mahajan, V. (2022, March). Virtual Reality based Metaverse of Gamification. In *2022 6th International Conference on Computing Methodologies and Communication (ICCMC)* (pp. 1597-1604). IEEE. 10.1109/ICCMC53470.2022.9753727

Tertulino, R., Antunes, N., & Morais, H. (2023). Privacy in electronic health records: A systematic mapping study. *Journal of Public Health (Berlin)*, 1–20. doi:10.100710389-022-01795-z

Tezinde, T., Smith, B., & Murphy, J. (2002). Getting permission: Exploring factors affecting permission marketing. *Journal of Interactive Marketing*, *16*(4), 28–36. doi:10.1002/dir.10041

Thakur, R., & Srivastava, M. (2015). A study on the impact of consumer risk perception and innovativeness on online shopping in India. *International Journal of Retail & Distribution Management*, *43*(2), 148–166. doi:10.1108/IJRDM-06-2013-0128

Tham, A., & Sigala, M. (2020). Road block(chain): Bit(coin)s for tourism sustainable development goals? *Journal of Hospitality and Tourism Technology*, *11*(1), 203–222. doi:10.1108/JHTT-05-2019-0069

Thananjeyan, B., Garg, A., Krishnan, S., Chen, C., Miller, L., & Goldberg, K. (2017). Multilateral surgical pattern cutting in 2D orthotropic gauze with deep reinforcement learning policies for tensioning. *Proc. IEEE Int. Conf. Robot. Autom.*, 2371–2378. 10.1109/ICRA.2017.7989275

Thejas, G. S., Dheeshjith, S., Iyengar, S. S., Sunitha, N. R., & Badrinath, P. (2021). A hybrid and effective learning approach for Click Fraud detection. *Machine Learning with Applications*, *3*, 100016. doi:10.1016/j.mlwa.2020.100016

Thirumuruganathan, S., Emadi, N. A., Jung, S., Salminen, J., Robillos, D. R., & Jansen, B. J. (2023). Will they take this offer? A machine learning price elasticity model for predicting upselling acceptance of premium airline seating. *Information & Management*, *60*(3), 103759. doi:10.1016/j.im.2023.103759

Thomaz, F., Salge, C., Karahanna, E., & Hulland, J. (2020). Learning from the Dark Web: Leveraging conversational agents in the era of hyper-privacy to enhance marketing. *Journal of the Academy of Marketing Science*, *48*(1), 43–63. doi:10.100711747-019-00704-3

Thomé, K. M., Cappellesso, G., Ramos, E. L. A., & Duarte, S. C. de L. (2021). Food Supply Chains and Short Food Supply Chains: Coexistence conceptual framework. *Journal of Cleaner Production*, *278*, 123207. doi:10.1016/j.jclepro.2020.123207

Thykier, C. (2022). Immersive technologies are shaping the future of e-commerce right now. *The Drum.* https://www.thedrum.com/opinion/2022/09/20/immersive-technologies-are-shaping-the-future-e-commerce-right-now?utm_campaign=Social%20Media:%20Thought%20leadership&utm_content=240335635&utm_medium=social&utm_source=linkedin&hss_channel=lcp-3290097

Tian, F. (2016). An agri-food supply chain traceability system for China based on RFID & blockchain technology. *2016 13th International Conference on Service Systems and Service Management (ICSSSM)*, 1–6. 10.1109/ICSSSM.2016.7538424

Tirunillai, S., & Tellis, G. J. (2014). Mining marketing meaning from online chatter: Strategic brand analysis of big data using latent dirichlet allocation. *JMR, Journal of Marketing Research*, *51*(4), 463–479. doi:10.1509/jmr.12.0106

Toader, D.-C., Boca, G., Toader, R., Măcelaru, M., Toader, C., Ighian, D., & Rădulescu, A.T. (2020). The effect of social presence and chatbot errors on trust. *Sustainability (Switzerland), 12*(1). doi:10.3390/su12010256

Todor, R. D. (2016). Blending traditional and digital marketing. *Bulletin of the Transilvania University of Brasov*, *9*(1), 51–56.

Toorajipour, R., Sohrabpour, V., Nazarpour, A., Oghazi, P., & Fischl, M. (2021). Artificial intelligence in supply chain management: A systematic literature review. *Journal of Business Research*, *122*, 502–517. doi:10.1016/j.jbusres.2020.09.009

Topsakal, O., & Topsakal, E. (2023). Framework for A Foreign Language Teaching Software for Children Utilizing AR, Voicebots and ChatGPT (Large Language Models). *The Journal of Cognitive Systems*, *7*(2), 33–38.

Torres, A., & Delgado, C. (2023). Assessing Customer Interactions with Chatbots in Online Shopping Experience: An Empirical Study. In J. Santos & B. Sousa (Eds.), *Promoting Organizational Performance Through 5G and Agile Marketing*. IGI Global., doi:10.4018/978-1-6684-5523-4

Torres, M. R., González, A. A., & Mendívil, B. C. (2017). Conceptual Model of Organizational Management as A Reference in The Development of An Integral Marketing Information System. *3c. Tic*, *6*(4), 54–69. doi:10.17993/3ctic.2017.58.54-69

Tran, A. D., Pallant, J. I., & Johnson, L. W. (2021). Exploring the impact of chatbots on consumer sentiment and expectations in retail. *Journal of Retailing and Consumer Services*, *63*, 102718. doi:10.1016/j.jretconser.2021.102718

Trappey, A. J. C., Trappey, C. V., & Lin, E. (2022). Intelligent trademark recognition and similarity analysis using a two-stage transfer learning approach. *Advanced Engineering Informatics*, *52*, 101567. doi:10.1016/j.aei.2022.101567

Trappey, A., Trappey, C. V., & Hsieh, A. (2021). An intelligent patent recommender adopting machine learning approach for natural language processing: A case study for smart machinery technology mining. *Technological Forecasting and Social Change*, *164*, 120511. doi:10.1016/j.techfore.2020.120511

Trappey, C. V., Trappey, A. J. C., & Lin, S. C. C. (2020). Intelligent trademark similarity analysis of image, spelling, and phonetic features using machine learning methodologies. *Advanced Engineering Informatics*, *45*, 101120. doi:10.1016/j.aei.2020.101120

Trappey, C. V., Trappey, A. J. C., & Liu, B.-H. (2020). Identify trademark legal case precedents - Using machine learning to enable semantic analysis of judgments. *World Patent Information*, *62*, 101980. doi:10.1016/j.wpi.2020.101980

Treiblmaier, H., & Petrozhitskaya, E. (2023). Is it time for marketing to reappraise B2C relationship management? The emergence of a new loyalty paradigm through blockchain technology. *Journal of Business Research*, *159*, 159. doi:10.1016/j.jbusres.2023.113725

Treiblmaier, H., & Sillaber, C. (2020). A case study of blockchain-induced digital transformation in the public sector. In *Blockchain and Distributed Ledger Technology Use Cases* (pp. 227–244). Springer. doi:10.1007/978-3-030-44337-5_11

Treiblmaier, H., & Sillaber, C. (2021). The impact of blockchain on e-commerce: A framework for salient research topics. *Electronic Commerce Research and Applications*, *48*, 101054. doi:10.1016/j.elerap.2021.101054

Trepte, S., & Masur, P. K. (2020). Need for privacy. Encyclopedia of personality and individual differences, 3132-3135.

Trepte, S. (2021). The social media privacy model: Privacy and communication in the light of social media affordances. *Communication Theory*, *31*(4), 549–570. doi:10.1093/ct/qtz035

Trunfio, M., Jung, T., & Campana, S. (2022). Mixed reality experiences in museums: Exploring the impact of functional elements of the devices on visitors' immersive experiences and post-experience behaviours. *Information & Management*, *59*(8), 103698. doi:10.1016/j.im.2022.103698

Tsai, J. Y., Egelman, S., Cranor, L., & Acquisti, A. (2011). The effect of online privacy information on purchasing behavior: An experimental study. *Information Systems Research*, *22*(2), 254–268. doi:10.1287/isre.1090.0260

Tucker, C. (2018). Privacy, Algorithms, and Artificial Intelligence. University of Chicago Press.

Tucker, C. E. (2014). Social networks, personalized advertising, and privacy controls. *JMR, Journal of Marketing Research*, *51*(5), 546–562. doi:10.1509/jmr.10.0355

Turner, F., & Welch, I. (2019). The Mixed Reality Toolkit as the Next Step in the Mass Customization Co-Design Experience. *International Journal of Industrial Engineering and Management*, *10*(2), 191–199. doi:10.24867/IJIEM-2019-2-239

Um, T., Kim, H., Kim, H., Lee, J., Koo, C., & Chung, N. (2022). Travel Incheon as a Metaverse: Smart Tourism Cities Development Case in Korea. In Information and Communication Technologies in Tourism 2022. Springer. doi:10.1007/978-3-030-94751-4_20

Uusitalo, O., & Oksanen, R. (2004). Ethical consumerism: A view from Finland. *International Journal of Consumer Studies*, *28*(3), 214–221. doi:10.1111/j.1470-6431.2003.00339.x

Valaskova, K., Machova, V., & Lewis, E. (2022). Virtual Marketplace Dynamics Data, Spatial Analytics, and Customer Engagement Tools in a Real-Time Interoperable Decentralized Metaverse. *Linguistic and Philosophical Investigations*, *21*(0), 105–120. doi:10.22381/lpi2120227

Van den Broeck, E., Zarouali, B., & Poels, K. (2019). Chatbot advertising effectiveness: When does the message get through? *Computers in Human Behavior*, *98*, 150–157. doi:10.1016/j.chb.2019.04.009

Van der Heijden, H. (2004). User acceptance of hedonic information systems. *Management Information Systems Quarterly*, *28*(4), 695–704. doi:10.2307/25148660

Van Eck, N. J., & Waltman, L. (2010). Software survey: VOSviewer, a computer program for bibliometric mapping. *Scientometrics*, *84*(2), 523–538. doi:10.100711192-009-0146-3 PMID:20585380

van Esch, P., Black, J. S., & Ferolie, J. (2019). Marketing AI recruitment: The next phase in job application and selection. *Computers in Human Behavior*, *90*, 215–222. doi:10.1016/j.chb.2018.09.009

van Esch, P., & Stewart Black, J. (2021). Artificial Intelligence (AI): Revolutionizing Digital Marketing. *Australasian Marketing Journal*, *29*(3), 199–203. doi:10.1177/18393349211037684

Van Rijmenam, M. (2022). *Step into the metaverse: How the immersive Internet will unlock a trillion-dollar social economy*. John Wiley & Sons.

Vargo, S. L., & Lusch, R. F. (2008). Service-dominant logic: Continuing the evolution. *Journal of the Academy of Marketing Science*, *36*(1), 1–10. doi:10.100711747-007-0069-6

Vatsa, M., Rastogi, S., Tiwari, A., & Jain, S. (2021). Impacts of cloud computing in digital marketing. *Proceedings of the 5th International Conference on Electronics, Communication and Aerospace Technology, ICECA 2021*, 1170-1174. 10.1109/ICECA52323.2021.9676043

Velinov, E., Leroy, I., & Cetlova, H. (2022, April). Marketing Process in Information Security Context: Comparison Between Czech Republic and Belgium. In *Proceedings of the International Conference Engineering Innovations and Sustainable Development* (pp. 567-577). Cham: Springer International Publishing. 10.1007/978-3-030-90843-0_64

Venkatesh, V., Morris, M. G., Davis, G. B., & Davis, F. D. (2003). User acceptance of information technology: Toward a unified view. *Management Information Systems Quarterly*, *47*(3), 425–478. doi:10.2307/30036540

Venkatesh, V., Thong, J. Y. L., & Xu, X. (2012). Consumer acceptance and use of information technology: Extending the unified theory of acceptance and use of technology. *Management Information Systems Quarterly*, *36*(1), 157–178. doi:10.2307/41410412

Verma, N., & Kulkarni, P. (2023). Impact of Blockchain Technology on E-Commerce. In *2023 International Conference on Innovative Data Communication Technologies and Application (ICIDCA)* (pp. 668-672). IEEE. 10.1109/ICIDCA56705.2023.10100222

Verma, S., Sharma, R., Deb, S., & Maitra, D. (2021). Artificial intelligence in marketing: Systematic review and future research direction. *International Journal of Information Management Data Insights*, *1*(1), 100002. doi:10.1016/j.jjimei.2020.100002

Vimalkumar, M., Sharma, S. K., Singh, J. B., & Dwivedi, Y. K. (2021). 'Okay google, what about my privacy?': User's privacy perceptions and acceptance of voice based digital assistants. *Computers in Human Behavior*, *120*, 106763. Advance online publication. doi:10.1016/j.chb.2021.106763

Vinaykarthik, B. C. (2022, October). Design of Artificial Intelligence (AI) based User Experience Websites for E-commerce Application and Future of Digital Marketing. In *2022 3rd International Conference on Smart Electronics and Communication (ICOSEC)* (pp. 1023-1029). IEEE.

Vlačić, B., Corbo, L., Costa e Silva, S., & Dabić, M. (2021). The evolving role of artificial intelligence in marketing: A review and research agenda. *Journal of Business Research*, *128*, 187–203. doi:10.1016/j.jbusres.2021.01.055

Volkmar, G., Fischer, P. M., & Reinecke, S. (2022). Artificial Intelligence and Machine Learning: Exploring drivers, barriers, and future developments in marketing management. *Journal of Business Research*, *149*, 599–614. doi:10.1016/j.jbusres.2022.04.007

Vrontis, D., Makrides, A., Christofi, M., & Thrassou, A. (2021). Social media influencer marketing: A systematic review, integrative framework and future research agenda. *International Journal of Consumer Studies*, *45*(4), 617–644. doi:10.1111/ijcs.12647

Wamba, S. F., & Queiroz, M. M. (2019). The Role of Social Influence in Blockchain Adoption: The Brazilian Supply Chain Case. *IFAC-PapersOnLine*, *52*(13), 1715–1720. doi:10.1016/j.ifacol.2019.11.448

Wang, W., Wang, F., Song, W., & Su, S. (2020). Application of augmented reality (AR) technologies in inhouse logistics. In E3S Web of Conferences (Vol. 145, p. 02018). EDP Sciences. doi:10.1051/e3sconf/202014502018

Wang, Y., & Wang, H. (2022). Reinventing the Wheel of Marketing: Assessing the Impact of Artificial Intelligence (AI) on Digital Marketing and Consumer Buying Behavior. In J. C. Hung, J.-W. Chang, Y. P., W.-C. Wu (Eds.), *Innovative Computing: Proceedings of the 4th International Conference on Innovative Computing (IC 2021)* (pp. 827-834). Springer.

Wang, D., & Wang, P. (2016). Two birds with one stone: Two-factor authentication with security beyond conventional bound. *IEEE Transactions on Dependable and Secure Computing*, *15*(4), 708–722. doi:10.1109/TDSC.2016.2605087

Wang, F. (2020). Digital marketing capabilities in international firms: A relational perspective. *International Marketing Review*, *37*(3), 559–577. doi:10.1108/IMR-04-2018-0128

Wang, X., Lin, X., & Shao, B. (2022). How does artificial intelligence create business agility? Evidence from chatbots. *International Journal of Information Management*, *66*, 102535. doi:10.1016/j.ijinfomgt.2022.102535

Wang, Y. (2008). Web-based Destination Marketing for Management and Implementation. *International Journal of Tourism Research*, *10*(1), 55–70. doi:10.1002/jtr.633

Wang, Y., Liu, S., Li, S., Duan, J., Hou, Z., Yu, J., & Ma, K. (2019). Stacking-based ensemble learning of self-media data for marketing intention detection. *Future Internet*, *11*(7), 155. doi:10.3390/fi11070155

Wang, Y., Ma, K., Garcia-Hernandez, L., Chen, J., Hou, Z., Ji, K., Chen, Z., & Abraham, A. (2020). A CLSTM-TMN for marketing intention detection. *Engineering Applications of Artificial Intelligence*, *91*, 103595. doi:10.1016/j.engappai.2020.103595

Watanuki, S., & Akama, H. (2022). Neural substrates of brand equity: Applying a quantitative meta-analytical method for neuroimage studies. *Heliyon*, *8*(6), e09702. doi:10.1016/j.heliyon.2022.e09702 PMID:35734557

Watson, A., Syrdal, H., Osborn, J., McGrath, R., Ringleb, A., Botten, T., . . . Waller, M. (2022). *Special session: The University of Google? A panel discussion about the disruptive changes in marketing education and what programs may look like in the not-so-distant future: An abstract.* . doi:10.1007/978-3-030-95346-1_54

Weber, I., Xu, X., Riveret, R., Governatori, G., Ponomarev, A., & Mendling, J. (2016). Untrusted Business Process Monitoring and Execution. *Proceedings of International Conference on Business Process Management*, 329-347.

Wedel, M., Bigné, E., & Zhang, J. (2020). Virtual and augmented reality: Advancing research in consumer marketing. *International Journal of Research in Marketing*, *37*(3), 443–465. doi:10.1016/j.ijresmar.2020.04.004

Weissman, J. (2021). *The Crowdsourced Panopticon: Conformity and Control on Social Media.* Rowman & Littlefield Publishers.

Wei, Y. Z., Moreau, L., & Jennings, N. R. (2005). Learning users' interests by quality classification in market-based recommender systems. *IEEE Transactions on Knowledge and Data Engineering*, *17*(12), 1678–1688. doi:10.1109/TKDE.2005.200

Weng, W. W.-H. (2021). Effect of Internet of Things on Marketing Intelligence and Business Strategy: An Organizational Capability Perspective. *International Journal of Electronic Commerce Studies*, *12*(2), 209. doi:10.7903/ijecs.1906

Westin, A. F. (1968). Privacy and freedom. *Washington and Lee Law Review, 25.*

Westin, A. F. (1967). Special report: Legal safeguards to insure privacy in a computer society. *Communications of the ACM*, *10*(9), 533–537. doi:10.1145/363566.363579

White, G. R. T. (2017). Future applications of blockchain in business and management: A Delphi study. *Strategic Change*, *26*(5), 439–451. doi:10.1002/jsc.2144

Wickramasinghe, C. S., Marino, D. L., Grandio, J., & Manic, M. (2020). Trustworthy AI development guidelines for human system interaction. *International Conference on Human System Interaction, HSI,* 130–136. 10.1109/HSI49210.2020.9142644

Wilk, V., Lambert, C., & Meek, S. (2022). Online brand detraction in an online opinion platform. *International Journal of Hospitality Management*, *107*, 103345. doi:10.1016/j.ijhm.2022.103345

Wirtz, J., Patterson, P. G., Kunz, W. H., Gruber, T., Lu, V. N., Paluch, S., Martins, A., & Lu, N. (2018). Brave new world: Service robots in the frontline. *Journal of Service Management*, *29*(5), 1757–5818. doi:10.1108/JOSM-04-2018-0119

Wolkenfelt, M. R. J., & Situmeang, F. B. I. (2020). Effects of app pricing structures on product evaluations. *Journal of Research in Interactive Marketing*, *14*(1), 89–110. doi:10.1108/JRIM-11-2018-0141

Wolpe, P (2019) Neuromarketing and AI—Powerful Together, but Needing Scrutiny, A JOB. *Neuroscience, 10*(2), 69-70. doi:10.1080/21507740.2019.1618414

Xu, Z., Alrabaee, S., Loyola-González, O., Zhang, X., Cahyani, N. D. W., & Rahman, N. H. A. (2022). *Cyber Security Intelligence and Analytics: The 4th International Conference on Cyber Security Intelligence and Analytics (CSIA 2022)* (vol. 1). Springer International Publishing.

Xu, F., Wang, L., & Gao, J. (2020). Thoughts on Application of Artificial Intelligence in Teaching of Different Disciplines. *2020 15th International Conference on Computer Science & Education (ICCSE)*. doi:10.1109/ACCESS.2018.2861429

Yakubu, A. M., & Chen, Y. P. P. (2020). Ensuring privacy and security of genomic data and functionalities. *Briefings in Bioinformatics*, *21*(2), 511–526. doi:10.1093/bib/bbz013 PMID:30759195

Yang, Q., Zhao, Y., Huang, H., Xiong, Z., Kang, J., & Zheng, Z. (2022). Fusing blockchain and AI with metaverse: A survey. *IEEE Open Journal of the Computer Society*, *3*, 122–136. doi:10.1109/OJCS.2022.3188249

Yang, Y., Xu, B., Shen, S., Shen, F., & Zhao, J. (2020). Operation-aware neural networks for user response prediction. *Neural Networks*, *121*, 161–168. doi:10.1016/j.neunet.2019.09.020 PMID:31563699

Yap, K. W., & Selvaratnam, D. P. (2018). Empirical analysis of factors influencing the public health expenditure in Malaysia. *Journal of Emerging Economies and Islamic Research*, *6*(3), 1–14. doi:10.24191/jeeir.v6i3.8783

Yasmin, A., Tasneem, S., & Fatema, K. (2015). Effectiveness of Digital Marketing in the Challenging Age: An Empirical Study. *The International Journal of Management Science and Business Administration*, *1*(5), 69–80. doi:10.18775/ijmsba.1849-5664-5419.2014.15.1006

Yi, Y., Zhu, N., He, J., Jurcut, A. D., Ma, X., & Luo, Y. (2023). A privacy-dependent condition-based privacy-preserving information sharing scheme in online social networks. *Computer Communications*, *200*, 149–160. Advance online publication. doi:10.1016/j.comcom.2023.01.010

Yontar, E. (2023). Critical success factor analysis of blockchain technology in agri-food supply chain management: A circular economy perspective. *Journal of Environmental Management, 330*(October 2022), 117173. doi:10.1016/j.jenvman.2022.117173

Yoo, K., Welden, R., Hewett, K., & Haenlein, M. (2023). The merchants of meta: A research agenda to understand the future of retailing in the metaverse. *Journal of Retailing*, *99*(2), 173–192. doi:10.1016/j.jretai.2023.02.002

Zadeh, L. A. (2008). Toward human level machine intelligence - Is it achievable? The need for a paradigm shift. *IEEE Computational Intelligence Magazine*, *3*(3), 11–22. doi:10.1109/MCI.2008.926583

Zamani, E. D., & Giaglis, G. M. (2018). With a little help from the miners: Distributed ledger technology and market disintermediation. *Industrial Management & Data Systems*, *118*(3), 637–652. doi:10.1108/IMDS-05-2017-0231

Zappin, A., Malik, H., Shakshuki, E. M., & Dampier, D. A. (2022). YouTube Monetization and Censorship by Proxy: A Machine Learning Prospective. *Procedia Computer Science*, *198*, 23–32. doi:10.1016/j.procs.2021.12.207

Zarouali, B., Van den Broeck, E., Walrave, M., & Poels, K. (2018). Predicting consumer responses to a chatbot on Facebook. *Cyberpsychology, Behavior, and Social Networking*, *21*(8), 491–497. doi:10.1089/cyber.2017.0518 PMID:30036074

Zarrin, J., Phang, H. W., Saheer, L. B., & Zarrin, B. (2021). Blockchain for decentralization of internet: Prospects, trends, and challenges. *Cluster Computing*, *24*(4), 2841–2866. [REMOVED HYPERLINK FIELD] doi:10.100710586-021-03301-8 PMID:34025209

Zhang, J., & Tao, D. (2021). Empowering Things With Intelligence: A Survey of the Progress, Challenges, and Opportunities in Artificial Intelligence of Things. IEEE Internet of Things Journal, 8(10).

Zhang, C., & Lu, Y. (2021). Study on artificial intelligence: The state of the art and future prospects. *Journal of Industrial Information Integration*, *23*, 100224. doi:10.1016/j.jii.2021.100224

Zhang, D., Zhou, L., Kehoe, J. L., & Kilic, I. Y. (2016). What online reviewer behaviors really matter? Effects of verbal and nonverbal behaviors on detection of fake online reviews. *Journal of Management Information Systems*, *33*(2), 456–481. doi:10.1080/07421222.2016.1205907

Zhang, J., & Letaief, K. B. (2019). Mobile edge intelligence and computing for the internet of vehicles. *Proceedings of the IEEE*, *108*(2), 246–261. doi:10.1109/JPROC.2019.2947490

Zhang, J., & Tao, D. (2021). Empowering Things with Intelligence: A Survey of the Progress, Challenges, and Opportunities in Artificial Intelligence of Things. *IEEE Internet of Things Journal*, *8*(10), 7789–7817. doi:10.1109/JIOT.2020.3039359

Zhang, X., & Ling, L. (2023). A Review of blockchain solutions in supply chain traceability. *Tsinghua Science and Technology*, *28*(3), 500–510. doi:10.26599/TST.2022.9010030

Zhang, X., Li, S., Burke, R. R., & Leykin, A. (2014). An examination of social influence on shopper behavior using video tracking data. *Journal of Marketing*, *78*(5), 24–41. doi:10.1509/jm.12.0106

Zhang, Y., & Wen, J. (2017). The IoT electric business model: Using blockchain technology for the internet of things. *Peer-to-Peer Networking and Applications*, *10*(4), 983–994. doi:10.100712083-016-0456-1

Zheng, X. R., & Lu, Y. (2022). Blockchain technology–recent research and future trend. *Enterprise Information Systems*, *16*(12), 1939895. doi:10.1080/17517575.2021.1939895

Zhuang, H., Leszczyc, P. T. L. P., & Lin, Y. (2018). Why is price dispersion higher online than offline? The impact of retailer type and shopping risk on price dispersion. *Journal of Retailing*, *94*(2), 136–153. doi:10.1016/j.jretai.2018.01.003

Zhu, S., Li, J., Wang, S., Xia, Y., & Wang, Y. (2023). The role of blockchain technology in the dual-channel supply chain dominated by a brand owner. *International Journal of Production Economics*, *258*(January), 108791. doi:10.1016/j.ijpe.2023.108791

Zhu, Y.-Q., & Kanjanamekanant, K. (2021). No trespassing: Exploring privacy boundaries in personalized advertisement and its effects on ad attitude and purchase intentions on social media. *Information & Management*, *58*(2), 103314. doi:10.1016/j.im.2020.103314

Zott, C., & Amit, R. (2008). The fit between product market strategy and business model: Implications for firm performance. *Strategic Management Journal*, *29*(1), 1–26. doi:10.1002mj.642

Zuboff, S. (2020). *A Era do Capitalismo da Vigilância. A Disputa por Um Futuro Humano na Nova Fronteira do Poder.* Relógio D'Água Editores.

Zuiderwijk, A., Chen, Y.-C., & Salem, F. (2021). Implications of the use of artificial intelligence in public governance: A systematic literature review and a research agenda. *Government Information Quarterly*, *38*(3), 101577. doi:10.1016/j.giq.2021.101577

About the Contributors

Paulo Alexandre Botelho Rodrigues Pires received his PhD in Management and has a master's degree in marketing.

José Duarte da Rocha Santos received his PhD in Management from Vigo University. He also holds MSc in Marketing and a bachelor's degree in Business Sciences. Between 1987 and 2002, he played various roles in sales, marketing, and management of companies in the information technology sector. From 2003 to 2018, he performed the functions of a management and marketing consultant. Since 1999, he has been a professor in higher education in Portugal in the fields of management and marketing. He is currently a marketing professor at the Accounting and Business School of the Polytechnic of Porto (ISCAP/P.PORTO). He is also a senior researcher at the CEOS.PP - Centre for Organizational and Social Studies of the Polytechnic of Porto, Portugal. His main research areas are Strategic Marketing and Digital Marketing Strategies.

Inês Pereira is a Marketing and Brand manager professor at ISCAP, from Polytechnic of Porto, with expertise in branding, social marketing and corporate social responsibility. Inês has edited books, published chapters and papers in journals and international congresses with referee. She has also organized 2 international congresses on social and non profit marketing. She is the director of Business Communication Degree and Post-graduation on Management and direction of Health care institutions.

Ana Isabel Torres holds a PhD in Management Science and MSc in Marketing and Strategy, both from University of Porto, Faculty of Economics. She has been teaching in higher education since 2004. Currently, she is a Professor at the Accounting and Business Administration Institute, University of Aveiro and a researcher at the Laboratory of Artificial Intelligence and Decision Support, Institute for Systems and Computer Engineering, Technology and Science - INESC TEC. Her teaching areas include Marketing Strategy, Digital Economy, Services Management and Digital Consumer Behaviour. She engages in multidisciplinary research that bridges managerial and design-related fields such as digital services management with technology-oriented fields. Her academic work has been published in several leading international scientific publications, such as the British Journal of Educational Technology, Journal of Intellectual Capital, Journal of Revenue and Pricing Management, Management Research, IGI Global, Exploring Service Science (Springer), and in proceedings of international conferences. She has business experience in Marketing Management consultancy across different industries and service sectors, for more than ten years.

***

Bráulio Alturas is Associate Professor of Department of Information Science and Technology of Iscte-Instituto Universitário de Lisboa (University Institute of Lisbon), Lisbon, and researcher of the Information Systems Group of ISTAR_Iscte (Information Sciences, Technologies and Architecture Research Center). He holds a PhD in Management with specialization in Marketing, a MSc in Management Information Systems, and a BSc in Business Organization and Management, all from ISCTE-IUL. His scientific research interests and publications are in acceptance and use of technology, digital marketing, social media, e-commerce, information management, information systems, direct selling and consumer behavior.

Dušan Barać is a professor and the Vice dean for digital development at University of Belgrade Faculty of Organizational Sciences. He is a member of the IEEE and the IEEE Computer Society. His research interests include: e-business, e-commerce, digital transformation, blockchain.

Gabriela Beirão (B.S. from University of Aveiro, Master and PhD from University of Porto) is Assistant Professor at Faculty of Engineering, University of Porto. Her research focuses on services, particularly on service ecosystems, value co-creation, innovation and sustainability. She has been involved in several research projects. Her research has been published in Journal of Service Management, Transport Policy, and others.

Alicia Blanco-González is Professor of Marketing on Rey Juan Carlos University. She is Director of Organizational Legitimacy Observatory (Blanquerna-Ramón Llull University). Her papers have been published in journals that occupy top positions or prominent positions in various categories of the JCR / SJR: Technological Forecasting and Social Change, Journal of Business Research, American Behavioral Scientist, International Entrepreneurship and Management Journal or Management Decision. Her research lines of research are organizational legitimacy, institutional theory social responsibility, sustainability.

Zorica Bogdanović is a professor and the head of the IoT center at University of Belgrade Faculty of Organizational Sciences. She is a member of the IEEE and the IEEE Computer Society. She is a secretary of IEEE Computer chapter CO 16 and the head of the seminar of IEEE Computer chapter CO 16. Her research interests include: e-business, internet of things, blockchain, cloud computing.

Kyle Coble is a graduate of St. Louis University with a PhD in International Business and Marketing, Dr. Coble enjoys teaching a wide variety of topics in marketing including social media, international and consumer behavior. His research often centers on creativity, subcultures and group to group relations.

Arokiaraj David working as an Associate Professor and Academic Coordinator of PGDM at SFIMAR, Mumbai. He passed the UGC's National Eligibility Test for Lectureship (NET) and he is the recipient of Junior and Senior Research Fellow. He had more than 10+ years of experience in teaching and research. His major area of research is Business Analytics, Data Analytics, consumer behaviour, Green Marketing, Environmental Responsibility, Sustainable Practice, and Environmental Management Systems. He has published more than 50+ research articles among that 11 published in Scopus, 08 in ABDC, 05 in Web of Science, 07 book chapters, 04 books, 05 patents, 01 copyright and 01 consultant project. He had comprehensive knowledge of research tools and techniques (such as SPSS, AMOS, E-Views, STATA, and PLS-SEM) as well as practical knowledge in both primary and secondary data analyses. Recently he has received a Best Research Award, Young Academician Award, and Young Scientist Award.

Marijana Despotović-Zrakić is a professor and Head od Department for e-business at the University of Belgrade Faculty of Organizational Sciences. She is a member of the IEEE and the IEEE Computer Society. She is a vice-president of IEEE Computer chapter CO 16 and the head of the seminar of IEEE Computer chapter CO 16. Her research interests include: internet technologies, blockchain, e-business, and computer simulation.

Raquel Maria do Espírito Santo Faria is currently doing her Master's degree in Services Engineering and Management at the Faculty of Engineering of the University of Porto. In 2019, she finished her bachelor's degree in Management from the University of Madeira. She works as an accounting technician and counts on a wide amount of experience while concluding her studies.

Mercy Dube is a lecturer in the Department of Information and Marketing Science at Midlands State University Faculty of Business Sciences, Gweru, Zimbabwe, Her research interests are in Digital Marketing, Social Marketing, Consumer buying behaviour and Relationship Marketing. She has published some articles on the mentioned areas of interest. She is involved in lecturing courses in digital marketing, e-commerce, consumer behaviour and neuro-marketing aspects of branding. ORCID ID 0000-0003-0429-8441

Marija Duranović is MSc student at University of Belgrade Faculty of organizational sciences, Serbia. Her areas of interest are: e-commerce, e-business, blockchain.

Sara El-Deeb is a Marketing scholar in the Faculty of Management Technology at the German University in Cairo (GUC), Egypt. She teaches a wide range of topics in Digital Marketing and Media Psychology in GUC Egypt and in GIU Berlin. She is particularly interested in cross-cultural studies, digital marketing, artificial intelligence, consumer behavior and media psychology. She is a researcher, practitioner and advisor in which she delivered corporate training and audits for startups and for multinational firms. She is also an expert in quantitative techniques including structural equation modelling and in various use of quantitative software programs. She is a reviewer for several journals including International Journal of Sociology and Social Policy and International Journal of Internet Marketing and Advertising.

Anna Fernandes is an Assistant Professor at Lusíada University of Lisbon, Catholic Portuguese University, and IADE.

Jeganathan Gomathi Sankar is an accomplished faculty member with over a decade of experience in research and teaching of marketing. With expertise in marketing technology and big data in marketing, Dr. Sankar's research has made significant contributions to the field. Dr. Sankar's research has been widely recognized and published in top-tier journals including Scopus and ABDC. He has authored numerous peer-reviewed articles and book chapters, demonstrating their expertise in marketing information technology and big data in marketing. Dr. Sankar has also presented their research at various national and international conferences, further demonstrating their commitment to advancing knowledge in their field. As an educator, Dr. Sankar is dedicated to providing a high-quality learning experience for their students. They have taught a range of courses in marketing, both at the undergraduate and graduate levels, and have supervised several thesis projects. Dr. Sankar's teaching is highly rated by students, with many praising their ability to explain complex concepts in a clear and concise manner. Dr. Sankar is an active member of the academic community, serving as a reviewer for several high-impact journals and as a program committee member for various conferences in their field. Their commitment to academic excellence and dedication to teaching has earned them a reputation as a highly respected and valued member of the faculty at BSSS Institute of Advanced Studies, India. With a focus on marketing technology, Dr. Sankar's research interests include exploring the impact of technology on consumer behavior and how marketers can effectively utilize big data to make informed marketing decisions. Dr. Sankar's research has practical implications for businesses seeking to enhance their marketing strategies in the digital age.

James Hutson is an administrator and researcher in higher education specializing in neurodiversity, immersive realities, digital humanities, and gamification of education. He received his BA in Art from the University of Tulsa, MA in Art History from Southern Methodist University, and his PhD in Art History from the University of Maryland, College Park. He has also received his MA in Leadership from Lindenwood University and is completing his MA in Game Design. Dr. Hutson has taught at five universities across the country since 2006 and came to Lindenwood University in 2010. He has served as chair of Art History and program manager of Pre-Art Therapy and Pre-Art Conservation, Assistant Dean of Graduate and Online Programs for the School of Arts, Media, and Communication, and now serves as Lead XR Disruptor and Department Head of Art History and Visual Culture for the College of Arts and Humanities. His scholarship focuses on digital cultural heritage and neurodiversity in the metaverse.

Amaresh Jha is a media professional, educator, and researcher with over two decades of experience in Television, New Media, and Media Advocacy. As a television journalist, he has been one of the pioneering transmedia producers to use the practice of data-driven storytelling.

Aleksandra Labus is a professor and the Chief of Blockchain Lab at University of Belgrade Faculty of Organizational Sciences. She is a member of the IEEE and the IEEE Computer Society. She is a treasurer of IEEE Computer chapter CO 16. Her research interests include: e-business, blockchain, internet of things.

Samuel Musungwini has research interests in Digital Marketing, Inclusive Digital Transformation and Cyber-security. ORCID ID 0000-0002-9315-6252

Michael Martins was born in Switzerland and raised in Lisbon, Michael Nobre Martins holds a Bachelor's degree in Business Management from Universidade Lusíada de Lisboa and is currently pursuing a Master's degree in Management with a major in Finance at the same institution. Michael currently works as a supply chain manager. He is a driven individual who is constantly seeking new challenges to further develop his expertise.

Inês Messias has a PhD in Education, with focus on eLearning, more specifically in the creation of hybrid environments and methods of social network analysis and educational network analysis (2017).

Had a scholarship at the special project for distance learning at Universidade de Coimbra (2017). Has a Master in Multimedia Education and Communication (2009) and a degree in Education (2003). She is currently an invited assistant professor at ISCTE-IUL, at the Science and Information Technology Department. She is a member for the consultant specialists' team of the European Comission for 2 projects: "Vocational education and training in e-skills and certification and accreditation (for the QUALITY project)" and "Projeto the Development of an e-skills vision and a scenario-based forecasting of s-skills demand and supply in European countries from 2012 - 2020 (for the VISION project)."

Giorgia Miotto has a PhD in Advanced Communication from the Ramon Lull University. Giorgia focuses her research in the relationship between ethics and organizational legitimacy in the new communicative environment. Giorgia has a Master Degree in Classical Literature from the Universitá degli Studi di Padova (Italy), is Executive MBA and Master in Communication Management from EADA Business School. At present, she is CEO and Associate Professor of Blanquerna - Ramon Lull University . Giorgia is visiting professor of the Marketing Communication Department of the Emerson College in Boston. Giorgia served as a member of the "Comité Ejecutivo de la Red Española del Pacto Mundial de Naciones Unidas" (UN Global Compact) and as member of the Academic Board of the PRME (Principle for Responsible Management Educations - United Nations).

Edward Mudzimba is a seasoned researcher with interests in digital marketing, relationship marketing and consumer behavior. He is responsible for lecturing Neuropreneurship, International Finance and Brand management at Midlands State University in the Faculty of Business Sciences.

Rana Nasr is an accomplished academic with a background in artificial intelligence and digital marketing. She received her Master's degree in Marketing from The German University in Cairo (GUC) and earned a Grade A* for her research in Voice Shopping. She is deeply committed to creating creative content in addition to her academic achievements. Thus, producing engaging, authoritative, and error-free work with minimal input. Her creative content strategies have reshaped concepts and positioned several businesses as industry leaders. She is widely regarded as a brilliant and innovative author, and is constantly pushing the boundaries of artificial intelligence and digital marketing research.

Pedro Pincho has a degree in Management from the European University, a Postgraduate Degree in Informatics Applied to Organizations and a Master's in Management of Information Systems from ISCTE-IUL. His professional career is based on project management.

Albérico Travassos Rosário, Ph.D. Marketing and Strategy of the Universities of Aveiro (UA), Minho (UM) and Beira Interior (UBI). With affiliation to the GOVCOPP research center of the University of Aveiro. Master in Marketing and Degree in Marketing, Advertising and Public Relations, degree from ISLA Campus Lisbon-European University | Laureate International Universities. Has the title of Marketing Specialist and teaches with the category of Assistant Professor at IADE-Faculty of Design, Technology and Communication of the European University and as a visiting Associate Professor at the Santarém Higher School of Management and Technology (ESGTS) of the Polytechnic Institute of Santarém. He taught at IPAM-School of Marketing | Laureate International Universities, ISLA- Higher Institute of Management and Administration of Santarém (ISLA-Santarém), was Director of the Commercial Management Course, Director of the Professional Technical Course (TeSP) of Sales and Commercial Management, Chairman of the Pedagogical Council and Member of the Technical Council and ISLA-Santarém Scientific Researcher. He is also a marketing and strategy consultant for SMEs.

Peter Valan is a multifaceted educator and researcher with a penchant for integrating technology and marketing. With an MBA in Marketing & Hospital Administration, he began his career as a Marketing Executive and transitioned into academia as an Assistant Professor at Don Bosco College. Currently, Mr Valan holds the position of Researcher in AI-driven Marketing at the Vellore Institute of Technology. His interests encompass AI in marketing, innovative pedagogy, and digital learning environments. He has played a pivotal role in guiding students' careers, upskilling initiatives, and establishing academic collaborations. As a Resource Person for faculty development programs, Mr Valan shares his expertise on digital trends and citizenship. Mr Valan's research focuses on the intersection of AI and marketing, exploring how artificial intelligence can revolutionize marketing strategies. With a commitment to lifelong learning and a passion for sharing knowledge, he actively contributes to the academic and professional community.

Nuno Valente holds a BSc in Management from ISCAL – Instituto Politécnico de Lisboa and a MSc in Information Systems Management from Instituto Universitário de Lisboa (ISCTE-IUL) (University Institute of Lisbon), Lisbon. Her scientific research interests encompass digital marketing, marketing information systems, customer experience, scrum and agile delivery methodologies, marketing cloud and CRM/C4C knowledge. He is currently working as Senior Business Processes Consultant, specialized in Customer Experience solutions (Marketing and Sales) at SAP.

Index

A

B

C

D

E

R

S

T

U

V

W

www.ingramcontent.com/pod-product-compliance
Lightning Source LLC
LaVergne TN
LVHW082301150926
848178LV00051B/1331

* 9 7 8 1 6 6 8 4 8 9 5 9 8 *